# WEBSTER'S NEW POCKET THESAURUS

# WEBSTER'S NEW POCKET THESAURUS

Charlton Laird

Project Editor
DONALD STEWART

Published by Wiley Publishing, Inc., Cleveland, Ohio
Published simultaneously in Canada



For general information on our other products and services please contact our Customer Care Department within the U.S. at 800-762-2974, outside the U.S. at 317-572-3993 or fax 317-572-4002.

Wiley also publishes its books in a variety of electronic formats. Some content that appears in print may not be available in electronic books. For more information about Wiley products, visit our web site at www.wiley.com.

ISBN 978-0-470-17767-9

Manufactured in the United States of America

10 9 8 7 6 5 4 3 2 1

# HOW TO USE THIS BOOK

This pocket thesaurus offers easy access to a broader vocabulary and will assist you in writing more effectively. Here in detail are the features you will find.

## THE ENTRIES IN THIS BOOK

### Order of Entries

All headwords in this book are set in boldface type and listed in strict alphabetical order. A word having more than one part of speech is given a separate entry block for each.

**calendar** *n.*
**call** *n.*
**call** *v.*
**call off** *v.*
**callous** *a.*

### Parts of Speech and Other Labels

Labels are given for all headwords. Parts of speech identified in this book are

*a.* adjective or adverb
*conj.* conjunction
*interj.* interjection
*n.* noun
*prep.* preposition
*pron.* pronoun
*v.* verb

Other labels are

*abbrev.* abbreviation
*pl.n.* plural noun

**A.M.** *abbrev.* after midnight, morning, early hours, ...
**archives** *pl.n.* **1** [Place to store documents] repository, ...

An asterisk (*) indicates an informal, slang, archaic, dialectal, or other level of usage that may not be appropriate in formal writing.

**beat*** *a.* weary, fatigued, tired.
**get** *v.* ... **9** [*To understand] comprehend, perceive, know. ...
**money** *n.* **1** [A medium of exchange] ... cash, currency, ... bucks*, hard cash*, bread*. ... **—in the money*** wealthy, flush*, loaded*.

### Synonyms

At least three synonyms (words that are similar in meaning) or spelling variants are given for each headword. In general, the most commonly used headwords will provide a larger number of synonyms.

**highway** *n.* roadway, parkway, superhighway, freeway, turnpike, ...
**hijack** *v.* highjack, privateer, capture.
**hill** *n.* mound, knoll, butte, bluff, promontory, precipice, cliff, ...
**historical** *a.* factual, traditional, chronicled.

## Antonyms

Antonyms (words that are opposite or nearly opposite in meaning) are listed after synonyms and are labeled "*Ant.*"

**advise** *v.* recommend, prescribe, ... straighten out.—*Ant.* deceive, misdirect, lead astray.

## Numbered Senses and Idiomatic Phrases

If a headword has more than one commonly used meaning, its synonyms will be grouped accordingly, following a brief definition or explanatory note. Each definition or note appears in brackets after a sense number.

**mild** *a.* **1** [Gentle; *said especially of persons*] meek, easygoing, patient. **2** [Temperate; *said especially of weather*] bland, untroubled, tropical, peaceful, summery, ... **3** [Easy; *said especially of burdens or punishment*] soft, light, tempered. **4** [Not irritating] bland, soothing, ...

Idiomatic phrases associated with a headword are listed alphabetically, with their own synonyms, after the headword's synonyms.

**order** *n.* **1** [A command] direction, demand, ... **6** [Kind] hierarchy, rank, degree. **—in order** working, efficient, operative. **—in order to** for the purpose of, as a means to, so that. **—in short order** rapidly, without delay, soon. **—on order** requested, on the way, sent for.

An asterisk beside a definition indicates that this *particular sense* of the headword is in some way unusual in usage or register. An asterisk beside a synonym or antonym indicates that this *particular* synonym or antonym, when used with this meaning, is in some way unusual in usage or register. In such cases, you may wish to consult a dictionary such as *Webster's New World™ College Dictionary, Fourth Edition*, for more extensive usage information.

## HOW TO LOOK FOR SYNONYMS

1. Look up a general word for which you want to substitute either a more precise term or a synonym with a different shade of meaning.
2. Unless you have thought of a word likely to be found only in a larger thesaurus, you should find in the Pocket Thesaurus a boldface headword with a number of synonyms and, perhaps, some antonyms.
3. Check to see whether more than one numbered definition is given. A headword's synonyms will be grouped according to these definitions.
4. Think your way through the list of synonyms, looking for the term that best fits your needs.
5. If you find a word or phrase you like, but you are unsure of its exact meaning, look it up in a dictionary. A college edition will provide finer shades of meaning as well as fuller information about the word's usage and register.

## WEBSTER'S NEW WORLD™ STAFF

**Editor in Chief**
Michael Agnes

**Project Editor**
Donald Stewart

**Editorial Staff**
Jonathan L. Goldman, Senior Editor
James E. Naso
Katherine Soltis
Andrew N. Sparks, Senior Editor
Stephen P. Teresi
Laura Borovac Walker

**Administrative, Data Processing, and Clerical Staff**
Cynthia M. Sadonick
Betty Dziedzic Thompson

**Citation Readers**
Batya Jundef
Joan Komic

**Production Coordinator**
Barbara Apanites

# A

**abandon** *n.* unrestraint, spontaneity, freedom, exuberance, spirit, enthusiasm, vigor.

**abandon** *v.* **1** [To give up] leave, quit, withdraw, discontinue, break off, go off from, cast away, cast aside, let go, cease, cast off, discard, vacate, give away, part with, evacuate, surrender, yield, desist, concede, renounce, abdicate, lose hope of, go back on, secede, waive, forgo, back down from, lay aside, dispose of, have done with, throw in the towel*, break the habit. **2** [To leave someone or something in trouble] desert, forsake, ostracize, back out on, break with, break up with, run away, defect, reject, disown, cast off, maroon, depart from, throw overboard, jettison, leave behind, slip away from, stand up*, leave in the lurch, turn one's back on, run out on*, walk out on*, doublecross*, let down, drop.

**abbreviation** *n.* contraction, abridgment, sketch, brief, abstract, synopsis, reduction, abstraction, condensation, digest, résumé, outline, summary, short form.

**abdicate** *v.* relinquish, give up, withdraw.

**ability** *n.* aptitude, intelligence, innate qualities, powers, potency, worth, talent, gift, genius, capability, competence, proficiency, adeptness, qualifications, knowledge, self-sufficiency, technique, craft, skill, artistry, cunning, skillfulness, dexterity, facility, finesse, mastery, cleverness, deftness, experience, ingenuity, strength, understanding, faculty, comprehension, makings, sense, what it takes*, brains, knack, hang of, know-how*.—*Ant.* ignorance, incompetence, inexperience.

**able** *a.* intelligent, ingenious, worthy, talented, gifted, fitted, capable, effective, efficient, qualified, masterful, adequate, competent, expert, experienced, skilled, learned, clever, suitable, smart, crafty, cunning, bright, knowing, dexterous, endowed, deft, apt, agile, adept, alert, adaptable, smooth, ready, versatile, equal to, suited, suited to, well-rounded, mighty, powerful, strong, robust, sturdy, brawny, vigorous, courageous, fit for, sharp, cut out for*, having an ear for.—*Ant.* stupid, bungling, unadaptable.

**abnormal** *a.* strange, irregular, unnatural.

**aboard** *a.* on board, on ship, shipped, loaded, on board ship, freight on board, being shipped, en route, consigned, in transit, being transported, embarked, afloat, at sea, on deck, traveling.

**abolish** *v.* suppress, eradicate, terminate, exterminate, obliterate, annul, remove, revoke, end, finish, nullify, set aside, annihilate, repeal, subvert, reverse, rescind, prohibit, extinguish, cancel, erase, root out, pull up, uproot, demolish, invalidate, overturn, overthrow, declare null and void, do away with, stamp out, undo, throw out, put an end to, inhibit, dispense with, cut out, raze, squelch*, ravage.

**about** *a. & prep.* **1** [Approximately] roughly, nearly, in general. **2** [Concerning] regarding, respecting, touching, of, on, in relation to, relative to, relating to, as regards, in regard to, in which, with respect to, in the matter of, with reference to, referring to, so far as something is concerned, in connection with, concerned with, as for, dealing with. **3** [Around] surrounding, round about, on all sides.

**above** *a. & prep.* **1** [High in position] over, high, higher, superior, beyond, raised, above one's head, in a higher place, aloft, overhead, toward the sky.—*Ant.* below, low, beneath. **2** [Referring to something earlier] before, foregoing, earlier.

**abrupt** *a.* **1** [*Said of things, usually landscape*] uneven, rough, jagged. **2** [*Said of people or acts of people*] blunt, hasty, gruff.

**absent** *a.* away, missing, elsewhere, vanished, gone, gone out, not at home, not present, out, wanting, lacking, abroad, lost, astray, nowhere to be found, on vacation, AWOL*, playing hooky*.

**absent-minded** *a.* preoccupied, dreamy, listless, lost, absent, thoughtless, oblivious, inattentive, daydreaming, unconscious, unaware, withdrawn, removed, faraway, distracted, remote, forgetful, in the clouds*.—*Ant.* observant, attentive, alert.

**absolute** *a.* **1** [Without limitation] total, complete, entire, infinite, unqualified, supreme, full, unrestricted, unlimited, unconditional, unbounded, independent, wholehearted, sheer, pure, unmitigated, utter, unabridged, thorough, clean, outright, downright, ideal, simple, perfect, full, blanket, all-out, out-and-out.—*Ant.* restricted, limited, qualified. **2** [Without limit in authority] authoritarian, domineering, supreme, arbitrary, official, autocratic, tyrannical, fascist, haughty, overbearing, czarist, nazi, totalitarian, oppressive, antidemocratic, imperative, dogmatic, commanding, controlling, compelling, despotic, intimidating, fanatic, dictatorial, arrogant, with an iron hand, high and mighty*.—*Ant.* lenient, tolerant, temperate. **3** [Certain] positive, unquestionable, undeniable.

**absolve** *v.* pardon, set free, clear.

**absorb** *v.* digest, take in, ingest, use up, assimilate, blot, imbibe, swallow, consume, incorporate, sop up, soak up, sponge up.—*Ant.* eject, expel, discharge.

**abstain** *v.* refrain, refrain from, renounce, desist, withhold, avoid, stop, deny oneself, refuse, decline, hold back, shun, evade, cease, dispense with, do without, fast, starve, have nothing to do with, let alone, do nothing, keep from, keep one's hands off, swear off, lay off*, turn over a new leaf, have no hand in, take the pledge.—*Ant.* join, indulge, gorge.

**absurd** *a.* preposterous, ridiculous, ludicrous.

**abuse** *v.* insult, injure, hurt, harm, damage, impair, offend, overwork, ill-treat, misuse, maltreat, mistreat, wrong, persecute, molest, victimize, oppress, ruin, mar, spoil, do wrong to, mishandle, pervert, profane, prostitute, desecrate, pollute, harass, manhandle, do an injustice to, violate, defile, impose upon, deprave, taint, debase, corrupt.—*Ant.* defend, protect, befriend.

**accent** *n.* stress, beat, stroke, emphasis, pitch, accentuation, inflection, intonation, rhythm, meter, cadence.

**accept** *v.* receive, get, admit, be resigned, give in to, believe, trust, surrender, suffer, endure, allow, tolerate, take in one's stride, consent, acquiesce.

**accessories** *pl.n.* frills, ornaments, adornments, decorations, additions, attachments, gimmicks*, doodads*.

**accidental** *a.* adventitious, chance, coincidental.

**accommodate** *v.* **1** [To render a service] help, aid, comfort, make comfortable, oblige, suit, serve, gratify, please, arrange, settle, provide, benefit, tender, supply, furnish, assist, support, sustain, do a favor, indulge, humor, pamper, accept, put oneself out for, do a service for. **2** [To suit one thing to another] fit, adapt, correspond. **3** [To provide lodging] house, rent, give lodging to.

**accompany** *v.* escort, attend, tend, be with, follow, keep company with, guard, guide, usher, show in, show around, show the way, conduct, go along, go along with, chaperon, associate with, consort with, look after, go hand in hand with, go side by side with, hang around with*.

**account** *n.* bulletin, annual, report. **—give a good account of oneself** acquit oneself creditably, do well, do oneself proud*, behave courageously. **—on account** charged, in layaway, on layaway, on call. **—on account of** because of, by virtue of, since. **—on no account** for no reason, no way, under no circumstances. **—on someone's account** because of someone, for someone's sake, in someone's behalf. **—take account of** judge, evaluate, investigate. **—take into account** judge, allow for, weigh.

**accumulate** *v.* hoard, get together, gather, gather into a mass, collect, heap, store, assemble, concentrate, compile, provide, pile up, accrue, scrape up, stockpile, store up, acquire, gain, load up, rake up, unite, add to, build up, gain control of, roll in*, bank.

**accurate** *a.* **1** [Free from error] exact, correct, perfect. **2** [Characterized by precision] deft, reliable, trustworthy, true, correct, exact, specific, dependable, skillful, methodical, systematic, distinct, particular, realistic, authentic, genuine, careful, close, critical, detailed, factual, severe, rigorous, rigid, strict, meticulous, sharp, faithful, punctual, scientific, objective, matter-of-fact, rational, unmistakable, reasonable, right, explicit, definite, defined, on the button*, on the dot*, on the nose*, solid.—*Ant.* incompetent, faulty, slipshod.

**accuse** *v.* denounce, charge, prosecute.

**accustomed to** *a.* in the habit of, used to, inclined to.

**achieve** *v.* complete, end, terminate, conclude, finish, finish up, finish off, do, perform, execute, fulfill, carry out, carry through, bring about, settle, effect, bring to a conclusion, close, stop, produce, realize, actualize, discharge, wind up, work out, adjust, resolve, solve, accomplish, make an end of, enact, manage, contrive, negotiate, sign, seal, bring to pass, see it through, get done, close up, carry to completion, follow through, take measures, lose oneself in, deliver, knock off*, fill the bill*, round out*, come through, polish off*, clean up*, mop up*, put across*, pull off*, make short work of, put through, go all the way*, go the limit*, call it a day*, put the finishing touch on*, dispose of.—*Ant.* abandon, fail, give up.

**achievement** *n.* fulfillment, feat, exploit, accomplishment, triumph, hit, success, realization, creation, completion, execution, actualization, masterpiece, performance, deed, act, enactment, victory, conquest, attainment, feather in one's cap.—*Ant.* failure, blunder, collapse.

**acknowledge** *v.* **1** [To admit] concede, confess, declare. **2** [To recognize the authority of] endorse, certify, confirm, uphold, support, recognize, ratify, approve, defend, subscribe to, accede to, attest to, take an oath by, defer to.

**acquaintance** *n.* **1** [A person one knows] colleague, associate, neighbor. **2** [Acquired knowledge] familiarity, awareness, experience.

**acquire** *v.* take, earn, procure.

**acquit** *v.* clear, absolve, vindicate.

**act** *n.* **1** [An action] deed, performance, exploit. **2** [An official or legal statement] law, proposal, judgment, commitment, verdict, amendment, order, announcement, edict, ordinance, decree, statute, writ, bull, warrant, summons, subpoena, document, bill, code, clause, law of the land*. **3** [A division of a play] scene, prologue, epilogue, introduction; first act, second act, third act, etc. **4** [A pose] falsification, feigning, affectation.

**act** *v.* **1** [To perform an action] do, execute, carry out, carry on, operate, transact, accomplish, achieve, consummate, carry into effect, perpetrate, persist, labor, work, officiate, function, preside, serve, go ahead, step into, take steps, play a part, begin, move, enforce, maneuver, create, practice, develop, make progress, be active, commit, fight, combat, respond, keep going, answer, pursue, put forth energy, hustle*, get going*.—*Ant.* wait, await, rest. **2** [To conduct oneself] behave, seem, appear, carry oneself, give the appearance of, represent oneself as, take on, play one's part, impress one as, put on airs. **3** [To take part in a play] perform, impersonate, represent, act out, simulate, pretend, mimic, burlesque, parody, feign, portray, rehearse, take a part, dramatize, star, play the part of, debut.

**action** *n.* **1** [Any state opposed to rest and quiet] activity, conflict, business, occupation, work, response, reaction, movement, industry, bustle, turmoil, stir, flurry, animation, vivacity, enterprise, energy, liveliness, alertness, vigor, life, commotion, rush, motion, mobility, haste, speed, go*, doings*. **2** [An individual deed] feat, exploit, performance, performing, execution, blow, stroke, maneuver, step, stunt, achievement, act, deed, thing, stratagem, something done, accomplishment, commission, effort, enterprise, move, movement, doing, effect, transaction, exertion, operation, handiwork, dealings, procedure. **—bring action** accuse, start a lawsuit, take to court. **—see action** do battle, engage in combat, fight. **—take action** become active, do, initiate activity.

**activate** *v.* stimulate, initiate, arouse.

**active** *a.* busy, eventful, lively, dynamic, energetic, alive, mobile, hasty, going, rapid, progressive, speedy, walking, traveling, movable, bustling, humming, efficient, functioning, working, moving, restless, swarming, rustling, flowing, in process, in effect, in force, simmering, overflowing, streaming, stirring, effective, at work, operating, operative, agitated, brisk, industrious, enthusiastic, agile, quick, nimble, rapid, dexterous, spry, fresh, sprightly, frisky, wiry, alert, ready, sharp, keen, wide-awake, animated, enlivened, ardent, purposeful, persevering, resolute, aggressive, forceful, intense, determined, diligent, hard-working, assiduous, enterprising, inventive, vigorous, strenuous, eager, zealous, bold, daring, dashing, high-spirited, hopping*, going full blast*, in high gear*, snappy*, on the ball*, peppy*, turned on to*.

**actor** *n.* player, performer, character, star, comedian, impersonator, leading man, leading woman, entertainer, artist, television star, villain, motion picture actor, stage player, supporting actor, mimic, mime, clown, ventriloquist, pantomimist, understudy, Thespian, protagonist, headliner, bit player*, ham*, extra, movie idol.

**acute** *a.* **1** [Crucial] decisive, important, vital. **2** [Sharp] severe, keen, cutting. **3** [Shrewd] clever, bright, perceptive.

**adapt** *v.* modify, revise, readjust.

**addicted (to)** *a.* disposed to, inclined, in the habit of, prone, accustomed, attached, abandoned, wedded, devoted, predisposed, used to, imbued with, fanatic about, obsessed with, hooked on*.

**address** *v.* **1** [To provide directions for delivery] label, mark, prepare for mailing. **2** [To speak formally to an assemblage] lecture, lecture to, discuss, give a talk, give an address, give a speech, take the floor, harangue, rant, sermonize, spout off*, spiel*.

**adequately** *a.* sufficiently, appropriately, suitably, fittingly, satisfactorily, abundantly, copiously, acceptably, tolerably, decently, modestly, fairly well, well enough, capably, good enough, to an acceptable degree, competently.—*Ant.* inadequately, badly, insufficiently.

**adjacent** *a.* beside, alongside, bordering.

**adjourn** *v.* leave, postpone, discontinue.

**adjust** *v.* **1** [To bring to agreement] settle, arrange, conclude, complete, accord, reconcile, clarify, conform, allocate, regulate, organize, systematize, coordinate, straighten, standardize, clean up. **2** [To place or regulate parts] fix, connect, square, balance, regulate, tighten, fit, repair, focus, fine-tune, readjust, rectify, correct, set, mend, improve, overhaul, grind, sharpen, renovate, polish, bring into line, align, calibrate, put in working order, temper, service.

**administer** *v.* **1** [To manage] conduct, direct, control. **2** [To furnish] extend, dispense, give.

**administration** *n.* **1** [The direction of affairs] government, supervision, command. **2** [Those who direct affairs] directors, administrators, officers, supervisors, superintendents, advisers, command, executives, strategists, officials, committee, board, board of directors, executive, executive branch, legislature, president, presidency, chief executive, cabinet, ministry, commander, chairman, general, admiral, commander in chief, central office, headquarters, the management, bureau, consulate, embassy, legation, department, Washington, party in power, brass*, front office, the powers that be, the Man*. **3** [The period in which a political administration is operative] term of office, regime, reign.

**admire** *v.* esteem, honor, applaud, praise, extol, respect, approve, revere, venerate, laud, boost, glorify, reverence, hold dear, appreciate, credit, commend, value, treasure, prize, look up to, rate highly, pay homage to, idolize, adore, hail, put a high price on, have a high opinion of, think highly of, show deference to, think well of, take stock in, put stock in, put on a pedestal.—*Ant.* blame, censure, deride.

**admit** *v.* **1** [To grant entrance] bring in, give access to, allow entrance to. **2** [To confess] acknowledge, indicate, disclose, bare, unveil, uncover, expose, proclaim, declare, open up, bring to light, go over, go into details, confide to, tell, relate, narrate, enumerate, divulge, reveal, communicate, make known, tell the whole story, plead guilty, own up to, talk, sing*, cough up*, come clean*, spill the beans*.—*Ant.* hide, cover up, obscure.

**adopt** *v.* **1** [To take as a son or daughter] pick, choose, select, transfer, father, mother, take in, raise, make one's heir, take as one's own, naturalize, foster. **2** [To take as one's own] embrace, appropriate, seize, take up, take over, choose, assume, use, utilize, imitate, borrow, mimic.—*Ant.* deny, repudiate, reject.

**adore** *v.* **1** [To worship] venerate, revere, glorify. **2** [To love] cherish, treasure, prize.

**adorn** *v.* beautify, embellish, ornament.

**adulterate** *v.* dilute, lessen, taint.

**advance** *n.* **1** [The act of moving forward] impetus, progression, motion. **2** [Promotion] enrichment, betterment, increase.

**advance** *v.* **1** [To move forward physically] progress, proceed, move on, forge ahead, press on, push ahead, go on, go forth, gain ground, make headway, step forward, come to the front, conquer territory, march on, move onward, continue ahead, push on, press on.—*Ant.* stop, halt, stand still. **2** [To propose] set forth, introduce, suggest. **3** [To promote] further, encourage, urge. **4** [To lend] loan, provide with, furnish. **5** [To improve] develop, make progress, get better.

**advantage** *n.* luck, favor, approval, help, aid, sanction, good, patronage, support, preference, odds, protection, start, leg up*, helping hand, upper hand, leverage, hold, opportunity, dominance, superiority, supremacy, lead, influence, power, mastery, authority, prestige, sway, pull*, edge*, ace in the hole*.—*Ant.* weakness, handicap, disadvantage. **—have the advantage of** be superior, have the opportunity, be privileged. **—take advantage of** exploit, profit by, utilize.

**adverse** *a.* untimely, improper, unfortunate.

**advertise** *v.* publicize, proclaim, herald, announce, declare, notify, warn, display, exhibit, show, reveal, expose, disclose, unmask, divulge, uncover, communicate, publish abroad, issue, broadcast, print, circulate, show off, parade, propagate, disseminate, inform, celebrate, spread, call public attention to, promulgate, give out, plug*, play up*.

**advise** *v.* recommend, prescribe, guide, exhort, direct, admonish, warn, point out, instruct, counsel, advocate, suggest, urge, prompt, show, tell, inform, move, caution, charge, encourage, preach, teach, persuade, offer an opinion to, forewarn, prepare, straighten out.—*Ant.* deceive, misdirect, lead astray.

**advocate** *v.* bolster, push, further, advance.

**affair** *n.* **1** [Business; *often plural*] concern, responsibility, matter, duty, topic, subject, case, circumstance, thing, question, function, private concern, personal business, calling, employment, occupation, profession, pursuit, avocation, obligation, job, province, realm, interest, mission, assignment, task. **2** [An illicit love affair] liaison, rendezvous, intimacy, romance, relationship.

**affect** *v.* impress, sway, induce.

**affected** *a.* **1** [Being subject to influence] moved, touched, melted, influenced, awakened, sympathetic, stimulated, stirred, grieved, overwhelmed, moved to tears, hurt, injured, excited, struck, impressed, overwrought, devoured by, concerned, reached, compassionate, tender, sorry, troubled, distressed.—*Ant.* indifferent, unmoved, untouched. **2** [Insincere or artificial] pretentious, melodramatic, unnatural, stilted, superficial, theatrical, stiff, strained, overdone, ostentatious, hollow, shallow, showy, fake, stuck-up*, put-on*.—*Ant.* simple, natural, genuine.

**affection** *n.* love, friendship, liking, attachment, goodwill, partiality, passion, ardor, zealous attachment, friendliness, concern, regard, desire, closeness, kindness, devotion, tenderness, fondness.—*Ant.* hatred, dislike, enmity.

**affliction** *n.* trouble, hardship, plight.

**afford** *v.* have enough for, make both ends meet, bear, manage, be able to, have the means for, be financially able, stand, be in the market for.

**afraid** *a.* hesitant, anxious, apprehensive, disturbed, frightened, fearful, nervous, uneasy, fidgety, alarmed, intimidated, discouraged, disheartened, perplexed, worried, perturbed, upset, panic-stricken, cowardly, scared, terrified, terrorized, shocked, frozen, aghast, alarmed, startled, aroused, horrified, petrified, stunned, rattled, struck dumb, trembling, distressed, jittery*, jumpy*, leery, shaky*.—*Ant.* confident, self-assured, poised.

**age** *n.* **1** [The period of one's existence] span, lifetime, duration. **2** [A particular point or time in one's life] infancy, childhood, girlhood, boyhood, adolescence, adulthood, youth, middle age, old age, senility. **3** [A period of time] epoch, era, period, time, century, decade, generation, millennium, interval, term, in the time of something. **—of age** adult, twenty-one, having attained majority.

**agent** *n.* broker, promoter, operator, representative, salesman, assistant, emissary, intermediary, appointee, servant, executor, attorney, lawyer, go-between, surrogate, mediary, deputy, minister, envoy, middleman, commissioner, delegate, proxy, substitute, steward, functionary, ambassador, proctor, negotiator, advocate, press agent, booking agent, bookie*.

**aggravate** *v.* exasperate, annoy, provoke.

**aggressive** *a.* warlike, attacking, combative, threatening, advancing, offensive, firm, strong, disruptive, disturbing, hostile, intrusive, contentious, destructive, intruding, invading, assailing, barbaric, up in arms, on the warpath.—*Ant.* serene, peace-loving, peaceful.

**agile** *a.* nimble, quick, spry, deft, vigorous, athletic, sure-footed, light-footed, frisky, spirited, lithe, sprightly, supple, dexterous, easy-moving, rapid, active, ready, alive, buoyant, energetic, stirring, brisk, lively, swift, alert, bustling.—*Ant.* awkward, slow, clumsy.

**agitate** *v.* stir, arouse, excite.

**agony** *n.* suffering, torture, anguish.

**agree** *v.* coincide, get along, side with, harmonize with, match up, concur, stand together, parallel, go along with, fit in, suit, say yes to, conform, go hand in hand with, equal, correspond, go together, synchronize, measure up to, square with, click*, hit it off with, see eye to eye.—*Ant.* differ, disagree, debate.

**ahead** *a.* before, earlier, in advance, ahead of, advanced, preceding, foremost, leading, in the lead, at the head of, in the foreground, to the fore, first, in front of, preliminary.—*Ant.* behind, back, toward the end. **—get ahead** advance, prosper, progress.

**aimless** *a.* purposeless, pointless, erratic, thoughtless, careless, heedless, rambling, wandering, blind, random, unsettled, flighty, capricious, wayward, without aim, chance, haphazard, to no purpose, drifting, stray, accidental, undirected, casual, indecisive, irresolute, fitful, fanciful, fickle, eccentric, unplanned, helpless, unpredictable, shiftless.—*Ant.* careful, purposeful, planned.

**airy** *a.* windy, breezy, drafty, exposed, ventilated, open, spacious, lofty, atmospheric, well-ventilated, aerial, out-of-doors, outdoors, in the open.

**alien** *a.* exotic, strange, unknown.

**alien** *n.* foreigner, stranger, refugee, displaced person, outsider, migrant, colonist, immigrant, guest, visitor, newcomer, barbarian, Ishmael, settler, stateless person, intruder, squatter, interloper, invader, noncitizen, man without a country.—*Ant.* inhabitant, native, citizen.

**align** *v.* arrange, straighten, regulate.

**alike** *a.* like, same, equal, identical, matching, selfsame, akin, similar, comparable, parallel, resembling, related, approximate, equivalent, allied, of a kind, twin, one, indistinguishable, facsimile, duplicate, matched, mated, one and the same, all one, in the same boat, on all fours with.

**all** *a.* **1** [Completely] totally, wholly, entirely. **2** [Each] every, any, each and every, any and every, every member of, for everybody, for anybody, for anyone, for anything, for everything, barring no one, bar none, beginning and end, from A to Z.—*Ant.* no, not any, none. **3** [Exclusively] alone, nothing but, solely.

**allegiance** *n.* fidelity, homage, fealty.

**alliance** *n.* **1** [The state of being allied] connection, membership, affinity, participation, cooperation, support, union, agreement, common understanding, marriage, kinship, relation, collaboration, federation, friendship, partnership, coalition, association, affiliation, confederation, implication, bond, tie. **2** [The act of joining] fusion, combination, coupling. **3** [A union] league, federation, company.

**allot** *v.* earmark, allocate, dole.

**allow** *v.* permit, let, sanction, grant, consent to, tolerate, favor, yield, bear, approve of, give leave, endorse, certify, have no objection to, release, pass, authorize, license, warrant, put up with, give the green light to*, give the go-ahead to.—*Ant.* deny, forbid, prohibit.

**almighty** *a.* **1** [Omnipotent] invincible, all-powerful, mighty. **2** [Omnipresent] infinite, eternal, godlike, all-knowing, all-seeing, deathless, immortal, celestial, divine, godly, pervading.

**almost** *a.* all but, nearly, approximately, roughly, to all intents, as good as, near to, substantially, essentially, in effect, on the verge of, relatively, for all practical purposes, to that effect, not quite, about to, with some exceptions, in the vicinity of, bordering on, within sight of, with little tolerance, close upon, in the neighborhood of, about, just about*, not quite, most*, around*, within a hair of, by a narrow squeak*.

**alone** *a.* lone, lonely, solitary, deserted, abandoned, individual, forsaken, desolate, detached, friendless, unaccompanied, isolated, lonesome, apart, by oneself, single, widowed, unattached, unconnected.—*Ant.* accompanied, attended, escorted. **—let alone** **1** [Besides] not to mention, also, in addition to. **2** [Neglect] ignore, isolate, refrain from disturbing. **—let well enough alone** forget, ignore, let alone.

**along** *a.* **1** [Near] by, at, adjacent. **2** [Ahead] on, onward, forward. **3** [Together with] with, accompanying, in addition to, in company with, along with, side by side, coupled with, at the same time, simultaneously. **—all along** all the time, from the beginning, constantly. **—get along** **1** [To succeed] prosper, get by, make ends meet. **2** [To advance] progress, move on, push ahead. **3** [To agree] accord, stand together, equal.

**also** *a.* too, likewise, besides, as well, in addition, additionally, along with, more than that, over and above, in conjunction with, thereto, together with, ditto, more, moreover, further, furthermore, including, plus, to boot.—*Ant.* without, excluding, otherwise.

**alter** *v.* **1** [To change for a purpose] vary, turn, diminish, replace, mutate, warp, alternate, remodel, renovate, evolve, translate, disguise, restyle, revolutionize, reduce, substitute, reorganize, increase, intensify, shape, shift, modify, transform, remake, convert, reform, tailor, adjust, adapt, invert, reverse, reconstruct. **2** [To become different] convert, develop, decay.

**alternate** *v.* **1** [To take or do by turns] substitute, follow in turn, happen by turns, follow one another, do by turns, do one then the other, relieve, fill in for, exchange. **2** [To fluctuate] vary, rise and fall, shift.

**A.M.** *abbrev.* after midnight, morning, early hours, before noon, forenoon, dawn, sunup.

**amateur** *n.* beginner, novice, learner, nonprofessional, dabbler, recruit, dilettante, hopeful, neophyte, initiate, apprentice, freshman, tenderfoot, rookie*, greenhorn, cub.—*Ant.* veteran, professional, expert.

**amaze** *v.* astonish, perplex, astound.

**amazing** *a.* astonishing, astounding, marvelous.

**ambiguous** *a.* equivocal, enigmatic, vague.

**ambition** *n.* hope, earnestness, aspiration, yearning, eagerness, longing, craving, passion, lust, itch, hunger, thirst, appetite, energy, ardor, zeal, enthusiasm, spirit, vigor, enterprise, get-up-and-go*, what it takes*.—*Ant.* indifference, apathy, laziness.

**ambitious** *a.* aspiring, longing, hopeful, zealous, hungry, thirsty, inspired, industrious, goal-oriented, enthusiastic, energetic, avid, sharp, climbing, ardent, designing, earnest, enterprising, aggressive, resourceful, pushy*.

**ambush** *v.* waylay, ensnare, lay for, set a trap, keep out of sight, decoy, entrap, hook in, lurk, lie in wait for, surround, hem in.

**amiable** *a.* pleasant, genial, charming.

**amuse** *v.* divert, cheer, enliven.

**analyze** *v.* dissect, examine, investigate, separate, break down, disintegrate, resolve into elements, determine the essential features of, decentralize.

**anchor** *n.* stay, tie, grapnel, mooring, grappling iron, support, mainstay, ballast, safeguard, security, protection, hold, fastener, grip, defense, protection, foothold.

**anger** *n.* wrath, rage, fury, passion, temper, bad temper, animosity, indignation, hatred, resentment, ire, hot temper, impatience, vexation, annoyance, provocation, violence, turbulence, excitement, frenzy, tantrum, exasperation, huff, irritation, dander*.—*Ant.* patience, mildness, calm.

**anger** *v.* infuriate, annoy, irritate.

**angry** *a.* enraged, fierce, fiery, irate, raging, fuming, infuriated, furious, wrathful, stormy, indignant, cross, vexed, resentful, irritated, bitter, ferocious, offended, sullen, hateful, annoyed, provoked, displeased, riled, affronted, huffy, hostile, rabid, having flown off the handle*, mad, up in the air*, hot under the collar*, boiling, steamed up*, at the boiling point, with one's back up*, all worked up, up in arms.—*Ant.* calm, quiet, restrained.

**anguish** *n.* wretchedness, pain, agony.

**animate** *v.* activate, vitalize, inform, make alive, arouse, give life to, energize, put life into, breathe new life into.

**anniversary** *n.* holiday, saint's day, birth date, birthday, yearly observance of an event, feast day, ceremony, annual meeting, biennial, triennial, quadrennial, silver anniversary, golden anniversary, diamond jubilee, jubilee, festival, fiesta, centennial, red-letter day.

**announcement** *n.* declaration, notification, prediction, proclamation, communication, publication, report, statement, advertisement, decision, news, tidings, returns, brief, bulletin, edict, white paper, message, notice, interim report, survey, advice, item, detail, communiqué, speech, release, handbill, poster, pamphlet, circular, billboard, brochure, form letter, telegram, cablegram, letter, leaflet.—*Ant.* secret, ban, silence.

**annoy** *v.* pester, irritate, trouble.

**anonymous** *a.* unsigned, nameless, unknown, unacknowledged, unnamed, unclaimed, unidentified, secret, of unknown authorship, without a name, bearing no name, incognito, pseudonymous.—*Ant.* named, signed, acknowledged.

**answer** *n.* **1** [A reply] response, return, statement, retort, echo, repartee, password, rebuttal, approval, acknowledgment, sign, rejoinder, comeback.—*Ant.* question, query, request. **2** [A solution] discovery, find, disclosure, revelation, explanation, interpretation, clue, resolution, key, the why and the wherefore.

**answer** *v.* **1** [To reply] reply, respond, rejoin, retort, acknowledge, give answer, say, echo, return, refute, react, rebut, argue, plead, claim, remark, talk back, come back*.—*Ant.* question, inquire, ask. **2** [To provide a solution] solve, elucidate, clarify.

**anticipate** *v.* expect, forecast, prophesy, predict, hope for, look forward to, wait for, count on, plan on, have a hunch, bargain for, hold in view, have in prospect, assume, suppose, divine, conjecture, promise oneself, lean upon, entertain the hope, await, reckon on, count on, have a funny feeling*, look into the future, feel it in one's bones.—*Ant.* fear, be surprised, be caught unawares.

**antiseptic** *n.* detergent, prophylactic, preservative, preventive, preventative, counterirritant, sterilizer, immunizing agent, germicide, insecticide, disinfectant, deodorant.

**anxious** *a.* **1** [Disturbed in mind] apprehensive, concerned, dreading. **2** [Eager] desirous, eager, fervent.

**apart** *a.* **1** [Separated] disconnected, distant, disassociated. **2** [Distinct] separate, special, isolated. **3** [Separately] freely, exclusively, alone. **—take apart** dismember, dissect, reduce. **—tell apart** characterize, discriminate, differentiate.

**apathy** *n.* dullness, insensitivity, unconcern.

**apologetic** *a.* regretful, self-incriminating, explanatory, atoning, rueful, contrite, remorseful, sorry, penitent, down on one's knees*.—*Ant.* stubborn, obstinate, unregenerate.

**appalling** *a.* horrifying, shocking, dreadful.

**apparatus** *n.* appliances, machinery, outfit.

**apparent** *a.* **1** [Open to view] visible, clear, manifest. **2** [Seeming, but not actual] probable, possible, plausible.

**appeal** *n.* **1** [A plea] request, bid, claim, suit, petition, question, entreaty, prayer, invocation, supplication, address, demand, call, requisition, application, proposition, proposal.—*Ant.* denial, refusal, renunciation. **2** [Attractiveness] charm, glamour, interest, seductiveness, sex appeal, class*.

**appeal** *v.* **1** [To ask another seriously] urge, request, petition. **2** [To attract] interest, engage, tempt.

**appearance** *n.* **1** [Looks] bearing, mien, features. **2** [That which only seems to be real] impression, idea, image, reflection, sound, mirage, vision, façade, dream, illusion, semblance, seeming.—*Ant.* fact, being, substance. **—keep up appearances** be outwardly proper, hide one's faults, keep up with the Joneses*. **—make** (or **put in**) **an appearance** appear publicly, be present, come.

**application** *n.* **1** [Putting to use] employment, appliance, utilization. **2** [The ability to apply oneself] devotion, zeal, diligence. **3** [A request] petition, entreaty, demand. **4** [The instrument by which a request is made] petition, form, blank, paper, letter, credentials, certificate, statement, requisition, draft, check, bill.

**apply** *v.* **1** [To make a request] petition, demand, appeal. **2** [To make use of] utilize, employ, practice, exploit. **3** [To be relevant] be pertinent, pertain, bear on, bear upon, have a bearing on, relate to, allude to, concern, touch on, touch upon, involve, affect, regard, have reference to, connect, refer, suit, be in relationship, hold true, come into play*.

**appointment** *n.* **1** [The act of appointing] designation, election, selection, nomination, approval, choice, promotion, assignment, authorization, installation, delegation, certification, empowering. **2** [An engagement] interview, meeting, rendezvous, assignment, invitation, errand, something to do, date.

**appraisal** *n.* examination, evaluation, assessment.

**appreciate** *v.* **1** [To be grateful] welcome, enjoy, be obliged, be indebted, acknowledge, never forget, give thanks, overflow with gratitude.—*Ant.* complain, find fault with, minimize, object. **2** [To recognize worth] esteem, honor, praise.

**appreciative** *a.* grateful, obliged, satisfied.

**apprehension** *n.* **1** [Foreboding] trepidation, dread, misgiving. **2** [Understanding] comprehension, grasp, perspicacity. **3** [Arrest] capture, seizure, detention.

**approach** *v.* **1** [To approach personally] appeal to, address, speak to, talk to, propose, request, make advances to, make overtures to, take aside, talk to in private, buttonhole, corner, descend on.—*Ant.* avoid, shun, turn away. **2** [To come near in space] drift toward, loom up, creep up, drive up, near, go near, draw near, close in, surround, come near to, come up to, bear down on, edge up to, ease up to, head into*.—*Ant.* leave, recede, depart. **3** [To come near in time] be imminent, threaten, near, draw near, impend, stare one in the face*.—*Ant.* increase, extend, stretch out. **4** [To approximate] come near, take after, come close to.

**approaching** *a.* nearing, advancing, impending, oncoming, touching, approximating, coming, drawing near, next to come, threatening, rising, moving closer, gaining.

**approve** *v.* ratify, affirm, encourage, support, endorse, seal, confirm, license, favor, consent to, agree to, sanction, empower, charter, validate, legalize, recognize, accredit, recommend, authorize, second, subscribe to, allow, go along with, maintain, vote for, advocate, establish, pass, OK*, give the green light to*, hold with.—*Ant.* oppose, reject, veto.

**approximate** *a.* rough, inexact, uncertain, guessed, imprecise, imperfect, close, surmised, unscientific, by means of trial and error, almost, more or less, not quite, coming close, fair, nearly correct.

**apt** *a.* **1** [Quick to learn] adept, clever, bright. **2** [Inclined] prone, tending, liable.

**aptitude** *n.* capability, competence, capacity.

**arbitrary** *a.* willful, tyrannical, temporary, unpremeditated, irrational, generalized, deceptive, superficial, unscientific, unreasonable, whimsical, fanciful, determined by no principle, optional, uncertain, inconsistent, discretionary, subject to individual will.

**archives** *pl.n.* **1** [Place to store documents] repository, vault, treasury. **2** [Documents] chronicles, annals, records.

**ardent** *a.* fervent, impassioned, zealous.

**arduous** *a.* hard, severe, laborious.

**area** *n.* section, lot, neighborhood, plot, zone, sector, patch, square, quarter, block, precinct, ward, field, territory, district, ghetto, township, region, tract, enclosure, parcel, division, city, parish, diocese, principality, dominion, kingdom, empire, state.

**argue** *v.* plead, appeal, explain, justify, show, reason with, dispute, contend, wrangle, oppose, battle, demonstrate, establish, have it out, put up an argument, bicker, have a brush with.—*Ant.* neglect, ignore, scorn.

**argument** *n.* **1** [An effort to convince] discussion, exchange, contention. **2** [Verbal disagreement] debate, quarrel, row.

**army** *n.* **1** [Military land forces] armed force, standing army, regulars, soldiery, troops, men, cavalry, infantry, artillery, air corps, reserves. **2** [A unit of an army] division, regiment, armored division, airborne division, infantry division, battalion, company, corps, brigade, flight, wing, amphibious force, task force, detail, detachment, squad, troop, blocking force, patrol, unit, command, formation, point, column, legion, platoon, outfit.

**arrange** *v.* **1** [To put in order] order, regulate, systematize. **2** [To make arrangements] determine, plan, devise, contrive, prepare for, get ready, make ready, draft, scheme, design, provide, make preparations, set the stage, prepare, put into shape, make plans for, line up, organize, adjust, manage, direct, establish, decide, resolve.—*Ant.* bother, disorganize, disturb.

**arrest** *v.* apprehend, hold, place under arrest, take into custody, capture, imprison, jail, incarcerate, detain, secure, seize, get, catch, take prisoner, nab*, pick up, bust*.—*Ant.* free, liberate, parole.

**arrive** *v.* enter, land, disembark, alight, dismount, halt, roll up, reach, get in, visit, make shore, drop anchor, reach home, appear, get to, hit*, touch*, blow into*, breeze in*, check in*, pull in, hit town*.—*Ant.* leave, go, depart.

**art** *n.* representation, illustration, abstraction, imitation, modeling, description, portrayal, design, performance, personification, sketching, molding, shaping, painting, characterization, creating, sculpting, carving.

**articulate** *v.* **1** [To speak clearly] enunciate, pronounce, verbalize. **2** [To join] fit together, combine, connect, link.

**artificial** *a.* unreal, synthetic, counterfeit.

**artist** *n.* master, creator, painter, composer, virtuoso, musician, poet, novelist, dramatist, essayist, actress, actor, playwright, writer, performing artist, cartoonist, opera singer, dancer, ballet performer, ballerina, sculptor, etcher, engraver, designer, architect, photographer.

**artistic** *a.* inventive, skillful, imaginative, discriminating, creative, graceful, talented, accomplished, well-executed, well-wrought, pleasing, sublime, ideal, cultured, tasteful, exquisite, sensitive, fine, elegant, harmonious, grand, stimulating, elevated, noble, beautiful.

**ashamed** *a.* embarrassed, shamed, regretful, meek, repentant, penitent, apologetic, debased, abashed, conscience-stricken, mortified, uncomfortable, hesitant, perplexed, bewildered, shamefaced, bowed down, disconcerted, sputtering, stammering, stuttering, gasping, floundering, rattled, muddled, confused, blushing, flustered, distraught, submissive, feeling like a jackass, off balance, in a hole*, taken down a peg, red in the face*, looking silly, at a loss.

**ask** *v.* request, query, question, interrogate, examine, cross-examine, demand, raise a question, inquire, frame a question, order, command, put questions to, requisition, bid, charge, petition, call upon, invite, urge to, challenge, pry into, scour, investigate, hunt for, quiz, grill, needle*, sound out, pump*, put through the third degree*.—*Ant.* answer, refute, rejoin.

**asleep** *a.* sleeping, dreaming, quiet, resting, snoring, in a sound sleep, fast asleep, sound asleep, slumbering, reposing, taking a siesta, hibernating, dozing, wakeless, napping, unconscious, dead to the world*, in the land of Nod, snoozing*, conked out*, out like a light*.—*Ant.* awake, waking, alert.

**aspire** *v.* strive, struggle, try.

**assemble** *v.* **1** [To bring together] rally, call, convoke, muster, round up, group, convene, summon, mobilize, call together, accumulate, amass, invite guests, gather, collect, hold a meeting, unite, pack them in, throw a party*, herd together*, rally round, gather around, gang around*.—*Ant.* scatter, break up, send away. **2** [To put together] piece together, set up, erect, construct, join, unite, solder, mold, weld, glue, model.—*Ant.* break, disassemble, break down.

**assert** *v.* state, say, affirm.

**assign** *v.* commit, commission, authorize, hand over, earmark, allocate, detail, appoint, allot, prescribe, nominate, name, select, hold responsible, empower, entrust, allow, cast, deputize, attach, charge, accredit, hire, elect, ordain, enroll, relegate, draft.—*Ant.* maintain, reserve, keep back.

**assimilate** *v.* **1** [To absorb] take up, digest, osmose. **2** [To understand] grasp, learn, sense.

**assist** *v.* support, aid, serve.

**associate** *n.* comrade, brother-in-arms, peer, colleague, partner, copartner, friend, ally, buddy*, accomplice, assistant, aid, aide, attendant, henchman, confederate, auxiliary, co-worker, helper, collaborator, fellow-worker, helping hand, right-hand man, man Friday, girl Friday, teammate.—*Ant.* enemy, foe, antagonist.

**associate** *v.* **1** [To keep company with] work with, join with, get along with, be friendly with. **2** [To relate] correlate, link, connect, join.

**association** *n.* **1** [The act of associating] frequenting, fraternization, friendship, acquaintanceship, cooperation, assistance, relationship, affiliation, agreement, participation, companionship, fellowship, familiarity, friendliness, camaraderie, membership, acquaintance, mingling, union, community.—*Ant.* disagreement, severance, rupture. **2** [The process of intellectual comparison] connection, relation, mental connection, train of thought, connection of ideas in thought, recollection, impression, remembrance, suggestibility, combination. **3** [An organization] union, federation, corporation.

**assume** *v.* suppose, presume, posit, understand, gather, find, collect, theorize, presuppose, ascertain, draw the inference, judge at random, divine, get the idea, have an idea that, suspect, postulate, regard, consider, infer, hypothesize, guess, conjecture, suppose as fact, deem, imagine, surmise, opine, judge, estimate, speculate, fancy, take the liberty, be of the opinion, dare say, deduce, conclude, put two and two together, be inclined to think, hold the opinion, think, calculate, hope, feel, be afraid, believe, have faith, take it, expect, allow, reckon*.—*Ant.* doubt, be surprised, be unaware that.

**assumption** *n.* **1** [The act of taking for granted] supposition, presupposition, presumption, conjecture, assuming, accepting, suspicion, surmise, theorization, hypothesization.—*Ant.* proof, demonstrating, establishing. **2** [Something assumed] hypothesis, theory, postulate.

**assured** *a.* **1** [Certain] sure, undoubted, guaranteed. **2** [Confident] self-possessed, bold, unhesitating.

**astonishing** *a.* surprising, startling, extraordinary.

**astound** *v.* amaze, shock, startle.

**atheism** *n.* heresy, agnosticism, godlessness, ungodliness, impiety, positivism, denial of God, iconoclasm, disbelief in God, irreverence, rationalism, infidelity, materialism, skepticism, freethinking, disbelief.

**athletic** *a.* muscular, husky, heavyset, wiry, springy, slim, fast, solid, strapping, hardy, robust, strong, vigorous, powerful, brawny, sinewy, sturdy, well-proportioned, well-built, manly, Herculean, Amazonian, built like an ox*.—*Ant.* sick, weak, fat.

**attach** *v.* **1** [To join] connect, append, add. **2** [To attribute] associate, impute, ascribe.

**attack** *n.* **1** [Offensive tactical action] assault, raid, onslaught, advance, charge, thrust, offense, drive, aggression, onset, outbreak, skirmish, encounter, volley, shooting, barrage, siege, firing, trespass, blockade, crossfire, invasion, offensive, intrusion, intervention, onrush, inroad, encroachment, incursion.—*Ant.* withdrawal, retreat, retirement. **2** [Verbal attack] libel, slander, denunciation. **3** [Illness] seizure, breakdown, relapse. **4** [Rape] assault, violation, defilement.

**attack** *v.* **1** [To fight offensively; *used of an army*] assault, beset, besiege, invade, storm, advance, infiltrate, raid, assail, march against, shell, board, take by surprise, make a push, bombard, bomb, go over the top, lay siege to, open fire, lay into, launch an attack, ambush, strafe, waylay, engage, tilt against, set upon, torpedo, stone, push, combat, attempt violence against, charge, strike the first blow, bayonet, saber, stab, close with, rake, have at.—*Ant.* retreat, fall back, recoil. **2** [To assault; *used of an individual*] molest, beat, overwhelm. **3** [To assail with words] revile, refute, reprove. **4** [To proceed vigorously] take up, deal with, start on.

**attain** *v.* win, achieve, accomplish.

**attempt** *v.* endeavor, strive, try.

**attend** *v.* be present at, frequent, sit in on, be a guest, revisit, haunt, be a member, be an habitué, make an appearance.—*Ant.* leave, be missing, absent oneself.

**attention** *n.* observation, observance, regard, vigilance, mindfulness, inspection, heed, heedfulness, watching, listening, consideration, intentness, study, alertness, thought, application, diligence, caution, preoccupation, thoroughness, recognition.

**attitude** *n.* mood, opinion, idea about, belief, air, demeanor, condition of mind, state of feeling, position, reaction, bias, set, leaning, bent, inclination, propensity, cast, emotion, temper, temperament, sensibility, disposition, mental state, notion, philosophy, view, orientation to, nature, makeup, frame of mind, character.

**attract** *v.* **1** [To draw] pull, drag, bring. **2** [To allure] entice, lure, charm.

**attribute** *n.* quality, trait, characteristic.

**audible** *a.* perceptible, discernible, distinct, actually heard, loud enough to be heard, capable of being heard, within earshot, within hearing distance, hearable, sounding, resounding, loud, deafening, roaring, aloud, clear, plain, emphatic.

**audit** *v.* examine, check, inspect.

**augment** *v.* enlarge, expand, magnify.

**austere** *a.* harsh, hard, ascetic.

**authentic** *a.* **1** [Reliable] trustworthy, authoritative, factual. **2** [Genuine] real, true, actual.

**authorize** *v.* **1** [To allow] permit, tolerate, suffer. **2** [To approve] sanction, ratify, endorse.

**autobiography** *n.* memoirs, personal history, self-portrayal, confession, life, experiences, diary, adventures, biography, life story, journal, letters, log.

**automatic** *a.* self-starting, motorized, self-regulating, automated, mechanized, under its own power, electric, cybernetic, computerized, self-moving, self-propelled, programmed, electronic, self-activating, push-button, involuntary, unthinking, mechanical, instinctive, spontaneous, reflex, intuitive, unintentional, unforced, unconscious, unwilling.

**available** *a.* accessible, usable, ready, convenient, serviceable, prepared, handy, on call, ready for use, open to, derivable from, obtainable, attainable, practicable, achievable, feasible, possible, procurable, realizable, reachable, within reach, at one's disposal, at one's beck and call, at hand, at one's elbow, on tap*, on deck*.—*Ant.* occupied, unavailable, unobtainable.

**average** *n.* midpoint, standard, center, median, norm, middle, normal individual, standard performance, typical kind, rule, average person.—*Ant.* extreme, highest, lowest. **—on the average** usually, commonly, ordinarily.

**average** *v.* **1** [To compute an average] split the difference, find the mean, find the arithmetic average. **2** [To do, on an average] complete, make, receive. **—average out** stabilize, balance, make even.

**avoid** *v.* keep away from, flee from, abstain from, shrink from, escape from, evade, shun, fall back, elude, dodge, give one the slip, draw back, hold off, turn aside, recoil from, keep at arm's length, withdraw, back out of, shirk, let alone, keep out of the way, keep clear of, keep at a respectful distance, let well enough alone, keep in the background, keep one's distance, keep away from, refrain from, steer clear of, lay off*, pass up*, shake off.—*Ant.* face, meet, undertake.

**awaken** *v.* awake, call, play reveille, arouse, rouse, wake up, excite, stir up, stimulate.

**aware** *a.* knowledgeable, cognizant, informed.

**away** *a.* absent, not present, distant, at a distance, not here, far afield, at arm's length, remote, out, far off, apart, beyond, off.—*Ant.* here, present, at hand. **—do away with** eliminate, get rid of, reject.

**awe** *n.* fright, wonder, admiration.

**awkward** *a.* clumsy, bungling, ungraceful, gawky, floundering, stumbling, ungainly, unwieldy, unable, fumbling, bumbling, lacking dexterity, without skill, unskilled, inept, unfit, inexperienced, shuffling, uncouth, incompetent, rusty, green, amateurish, butterfingered*, all thumbs, with two left feet*.—*Ant.* able, dexterous, smooth.

# B

**babble** *v.* talk incoherently, talk foolishly, rant, rave, gush, run on, go on*, gossip, murmur, chat, chatter, prattle, tattle, jabber, blurt, run off at the mouth*, talk off the top of one's head*, rattle on, gab*, cackle, blab, sputter, gibber, blabber*, clatter.

**baby** *v.* pamper, coddle, pet, spoil, fondle, caress, nurse, cherish, foster, cuddle, make much of, humor, indulge.

**back** *v.* **1** [To push backward] drive back, repel, repulse. **2** [To further] uphold, stand behind, encourage. **3** [To equip with a back] stiffen, reinforce, line.

**backed** *a.* **1** [Propelled backward] driven back, shoved, repelled, repulsed, pushed, retracted.—*Ant.* ahead, moved forward, impelled. **2** [Supported] upheld, encouraged, approved, heartened, aided, assisted, advanced, promoted, sustained, fostered, favored, championed, advocated, supplied, maintained, asserted, established, helped, bolstered, propped, furthered, seconded, prompted, served, pushed, boosted, primed.—*Ant.* opposed, discouraged, obstructed. **3** [Supplied with a back, or backing] stiffened, built up, strengthened.

**backer** *n.* benefactor, supporter, follower.

**backfire** *v.* **1** [To explode] burst, erupt, detonate. **2** [To go awry] boomerang, ricochet, have an unwanted result.

**background** *n.* **1** [Setting] backdrop, framework, environment. **2** [The total of one's experiences] education, qualifications, preparation, grounding, rearing, credentials, capacities, accomplishments, achievements, attainments, deeds, actions.

**backhanded** *a.* obscure, sarcastic, unfavorable.

**backward** *a.* **1** [To the rear] rearward, astern, behind, retrograde, regressive.—*Ant.* forward, progressive, onward. **2** [Reversed] turned around, counterclockwise, inverted. **3** [Behind in development] underdeveloped, slow, slow to develop, retarded, delayed, arrested, checked, late, undeveloped, underprivileged. —**bend over backward** try hard to please, conciliate, be fair.

**bad** *a.* **1** [Wicked] evil, sinful, immoral, wrong, corrupt, base, foul, gross, profane, naughty, degenerate, decadent, depraved, heartless, degraded, debauched, indecent, mean, scandalous, nasty, vicious, fiendish, devilish, criminal, murderous, sinister, monstrous, dangerous, vile, rotten*, dirty, crooked.—*Ant.* good, honest, pure. **2** [Spoiled] rancid, decayed, putrid. **3** [Below standard] defective, inferior, imperfect. **4** [In poor health] ill, diseased, ailing. **5** [Injurious] hurtful, damaging, detrimental. —**not bad*** all right, pretty good, passable.

**badge** *n.* **1** [Outward evidence] marker, symbol, identification. **2** [A device worn as evidence] pin, emblem, seal, medal, insignia, shield, epaulet, ribbon, medallion, marker, feather, rosette, clasp, button, signet, crest, star, chevron, stripe.

**badger** *v.* harass, annoy, pester.

**baffle** *v.* perplex, puzzle, bewilder.

**bail** *n.* bond, surety, recognizance, pledge, warrant, guaranty, collateral.

**bait** *n.* lure, inducement, bribe.

**bait** *v.* **1** [To torment] anger, nag, tease. **2** [To lure] entice, attract, draw.

**baked** *a.* parched, scorched, dried, toasted, warmed, heated, cooked, grilled, burned, charred, roasted, incinerated.

**balance** *n.* **1** [Whatever remains] excess, surplus, residue. **2** [An equilibrium] poise, counterpoise, symmetry, offset, equivalence, counterbalance, tension, equalization, equality of weight, parity.—*Ant.* inconsistency, topheaviness, imbalance. **3** [An excess of credits over debits] surplus, dividend, credit balance. —**in the balance** undetermined, undecided, critical.

**balance** *v.* **1** [To offset] counterbalance, compensate for, allow for. **2** [To place in balance] place in equilibrium, steady, stabilize, neutralize, set, level, equalize, support, poise, oppose, even, weigh, counteract, make equal, compensate, tie, adjust, square, parallel, coordinate, readjust, pair off, equate, match, level off, attune, harmonize, tune, accord, correspond.—*Ant.* upset, turn over, topple. **3** [To demonstrate that debits and credits are in balance] estimate, compare, audit.

**balk** *v.* turn down, demur, desist.

**balm** *n.* **1** [Anything healing and soothing] solace, consolation, comfort, relief, refreshment, remedy, cure. **2** [An ointment] salve, lotion, dressing.

**banal** *a.* dull, trite, hackneyed.

**band** *n.* **1** [A beltlike strip] circuit, meridian, latitude, circle, ring, orbit, zodiac, circumference, zone, ribbon, belt, line, strip, stripe, tape, sash, twine, scarf, bandage, girdle, thong, wristband, bond, tie, binding, stay, truss, belt, cord, harness, brace, strap, binding, waistband, collar, hatband, cable, rope, link, chain, line, string, guy wire. **2** [A company of people] group, collection, association. **3** [A group of musicians] orchestra, company, troupe, ensemble, string quartet, group, combo.

**banish** *v.* exile, deport, cast out, expel, expatriate, ostracize, sequester, excommunicate, transport, outlaw, extradite, isolate, dismiss.—*Ant.* receive, welcome, accept.

**baptize** *v.* immerse, purify, regenerate, sprinkle, dip, christen, name, administer baptism to.

**bar** *v.* **1** [To raise a physical obstruction] barricade, dam, dike, fence, wall, erect a barrier, brick up, blockade, clog, exclude, shut out, lock out, keep out, bolt, cork, plug, seal, stop, impede, roadblock.—*Ant.* open, free, clear. **2** [To obstruct by refusal] ban, forbid, deny, refuse, prevent, stop, boycott, ostracize, preclude, shut out, keep out, exclude, exile, reject, outlaw, condemn, discourage, interfere with, restrain, frustrate, circumvent, override, segregate, interdict, freeze out*.—*Ant.* allow, admit, welcome. **3** [To close] shut, lock, seal.

**barbarian** *n.* savage, brute, cannibal, rascal, ruffian, monster, yahoo, Philistine, troglodyte, clod.

**bare** *a.* **1** [Without covering] uncovered, bald, stripped. **2** [Plain] unadorned, simple, unornamented. **3** [Without content] barren, void, unfurnished.

**barren** *a.* **1** [Incapable of producing young] impotent, infertile, childless. **2** [Incapable of producing vegetation] fallow, unproductive, fruitless.

**barricade** *n.* obstacle, bar, obstruction.

**barrier** *n.* bar, obstruction, difficulty, hindrance, obstacle, hurdle, stumbling block, fence, sound barrier, restriction, restraint, impediment, drawback, check, stop, stay, bulwark, barricade, rampart, wall, earthwork, embankment, blockade, barbed wire, bamboo curtain, iron curtain.—*Ant.* way, path, trail.

**barter** *v.* trade, bargain, swap*.

**base** *a.* low, foul, sordid.

**base** *n.* **1** [A point from which the action is initiated] camp, field, landing field, airport, airfield, airstrip, port, headquarters, terminal, base camp, home base, firebase, base of operations, center, depot, supply base, dock, harbor, station. **2** [The bottom, thought of as a support] root, foot, footing. **3** [Foundation of a belief or statement] principle, authority, evidence. **4** [A goal, especially in baseball] mark, bound, station, plate, post, goal; first base, second base, third base, home plate. **—off base*** erring, mistaken, incorrect.

**basic** *a.* essential, central, primary.

**basis** *n.* support, foundation, justification, reason, explanation, background, source, authority, principle, groundwork, assumption, premise, backing, sanction, proof, evidence, nucleus, center.

**battle** *n.* strife, contention, struggle, combat, bombing, fighting, bloodshed, clash, onslaught, onset, barrage, conflict, warfare, fray, assault, crusade, military campaign, hostilities, havoc, carnage. **—give** (or **do**) **battle** fight back, struggle, engage in battle.

**beacon** *n.* flare, lantern, guide, signal fire, lighthouse, lamp, beam, radar, sonar, airline beacon, radio beacon, air control beacon.

**beam** *v.* **1** [To emit] transmit, broadcast, give out. **2** [To shine] radiate, glitter, glare. **3** [To smile] grin, laugh, smirk.

**bear** *v.* **1** [To suffer] tolerate, support, undergo. **2** [To support weight] sustain, hold up, shoulder. **3** [To give birth to] be delivered of, bring to birth, bring forth.

**bearing** *n.* **1** [A point of support] frame, ball bearing, roller bearing. **2** [Manner of carriage] mien, deportment, manner.

**beastly** *a.* brutal, savage, coarse, repulsive, gluttonous, obscene, unclean, piggish, hoggish, irrational, boorish, brutish, depraved, abominable, loathsome, vile, low, degraded, sensual, foul, base, disgusting, inhuman, gross, vulgar.—*Ant.* refined, sweet, nice.

**beat*** *a.* weary, fatigued, tired.

**beat** *n.* **1** [A throb] thump, pound, quake, flutter, pulse, pulsation, cadence, flow, vibration, turn, ripple, pressure, impulse, quiver, shake, surge, swell, palpitation, undulation, rhythm. **2** [A unit of music] accent, vibration, division, stress, measure, rhythm.

**beat** *v.* **1** [To thrash] hit, punish, whip, pistol-whip, flog, trounce, spank, scourge, switch, lash, slap, cuff, box, strap, birch, cane, horsewhip, buffet, pommel, tap, rap, strike, bump, pat, knock, pound, club, punch, bat, flail, batter, maul, whack, hammer, clout, smack, bang, swat, slug*, beat black and blue*, whale*, belt*, whack, beat the tar out of*, beat the daylights out of*, beat the hell out of*, knock the stuffing out of*, wallop*, lick*, paste*, bash*, work over*, thwack. **2** [To pulsate] pound, thump, pulse. **3** [To worst] overcome, surpass, conquer. **4** [To mix] stir, whip, knead.

**beaten** *a.* **1** [Defeated] worsted, humbled, thwarted, bested, disappointed, frustrated, baffled, conquered, overthrown, subjugated, ruined, mastered, trounced, undone, vanquished, crushed, overwhelmed, overpowered, licked*, done in*, done for*, kayoed*, mugged, skinned*, trimmed*, had it*, washed up*, sunk*.—*Ant.* successful, victorious, triumphant. **2** [Made firm and hard] hammered, tramped, stamped, rolled, milled, forged, trod, pounded, tramped down, tamped.—*Ant.* soft, spongy, loose. **3** [Made light by beating] whipped, frothy, foamy, mixed, churned, creamy, bubbly, meringued.

**beautiful** *a.* lovely, attractive, appealing, comely, pleasing, pretty, fair, fine, nice, dainty, good-looking, delightful, charming, enticing, fascinating, admirable, rich, graceful, ideal, delicate, refined, elegant, symmetrical, well-formed, shapely, well-made, splendid, gorgeous, brilliant, radiant, exquisite, dazzling, resplendent, magnificent, superb, marvelous, wonderful, grand, awe-inspiring, imposing, majestic, excellent, impressive, handsome, divine, blooming, rosy, beauteous, statuesque, well-favored, bewitching, personable, taking, alluring, slender, svelte, lissome, lithe, bright-eyed, classy*, easy on the eyes*, long on looks*, built*.—*Ant.* ugly, deformed, hideous.

**become** *v.* develop into, change into, turn into, grow into, eventually be, emerge as, turn out to be, come to be, shift, assume the form of, be reformed, be converted to, convert, mature, shift toward, incline to, melt into.

**becoming** *a.* attractive, beautiful, neat, agreeable, handsome, seemly, comely, tasteful, well-chosen, fair, trim, graceful, flattering, effective, excellent, acceptable, welcome, nice.

**bedlam** *n.* confusion, pandemonium, clamor.

**before** *a.* previously, earlier, in the past, since, gone by, in old days, heretofore, former, formerly, back, sooner, up to now, ahead, in front, in advance, facing.—*Ant.* afterward, in the future, to come.

**beg** *v.* entreat, implore, beseech, supplicate, crave, solicit, pray for, urge, plead, sue, importune, petition, apply to, request, press, appeal to, requisition, conjure, adjure, apostrophize, canvass.—*Ant.* admit, concede, accede.

**begin** *v.* **1** [To initiate] start, cause, inaugurate, make, occasion, impel, produce, effect, set in motion, launch, mount, start in, start on, start up, start off, induce, do, create, bring about, get going, set about, institute, lead up to, undertake, enter upon, open, animate, motivate, go ahead, lead the way, bring on, bring to pass, act on, generate, drive, actualize, introduce, originate, found, establish, set up, trigger, give birth to, take the lead, plunge into, lay the foundation for, break ground.—*Ant.* end, finish, terminate. **2** [To come into being, or start functioning] commence, get under way, set out, start in, start out, come out, arise, rise, dawn, sprout, originate, crop up, come to birth, come into the world, be born, emanate, come into existence, occur, burst forth, issue forth, come forth, bud, grow, flower, blossom, break out, set to work, kick off, jump off*, go to it*, dig in*, take off*.—*Ant.* stop, cease, subside.

**behalf** *n.* interest, benefit, sake.

**behave** *v.* act with decorum, follow the golden rule, do unto others as you would have others do unto you, be nice, be good, be civil, mind one's p's and q's, be orderly, play one's part, live up to, observe the law, reform, mind one's manners, comport oneself, deport oneself, behave oneself, be on one's best behavior, act one's age, avoid offense, toe the line, play fair.

**behind** *a. & prep.* **1** [To the rear in space] back of, following, after. **2** [Late in time] tardy, dilatory, behind time. **3** [Slow in progress] sluggish, slow-moving, delayed, backward, underdeveloped, retarded, behind schedule, belated.—*Ant.* fast, rapid, on time.

**belated** *a.* remiss, tardy, overdue.

**belief** *n.* idea, opinion, faith, feeling, hope, intuition, view, expectation, acceptance, trust, notion, persuasion, position, understanding, conviction, confidence, suspicion, knowledge, conclusion, presumption, surmise, hypothesis, thinking, judgment, certainty, impression, assumption, conjecture, fancy, theory, guess, conception, inference.

**believable** *a.* trustworthy, creditable, acceptable.

**believe** *v.* accept, hold, think, understand, consider, swear by, conceive, affirm, conclude, be of the opinion, have faith, have no doubt, take at one's word, take someone's word for, be convinced, be certain of, give credence to, rest assured.—*Ant.* deny, doubt, suspect.

**believer** *n.* convert, devotee, adherent, apostle, disciple, prophet, confirmed believer.

**belittle** *v.* lower, disparage, decry.

**belligerent** *a.* warlike, pugnacious, hostile.

**beloved** *a.* loved, adored, worshiped, cherished, dear, favorite, idolized, precious, prized, dearest, yearned for, revered, treasured, favored, doted on, nearest to someone's heart, dearly beloved, after someone's own heart, darling, admired, popular, well-liked, cared for, respected, pleasing.—*Ant.* hated, abhorred, disliked.

**below** *a. & prep.* **1** [Lower in position] beneath, underneath, down from. **2** [Lower in rank or importance] inferior, subject, under. **3** [Farther along in written material] later, on a following page, in a statement to be made, hereafter, subsequently.—*Ant.* above, earlier, on a former page. **4** [On earth] existing, in this world, here below, under the sun, on the face of the earth, in this our life, here. **5** [In hell] in the underworld, damned, condemned.

**bend** *v.* twist, contort, deform, round, crimp, flex, spiral, coil, crinkle, detour, curl, buckle, crook, bow, incline, deflect, double, loop, twine, curve, arch, wind, stoop, lean, waver, zigzag, reel, crumple, meander, circle, swerve, diverge, droop.—*Ant.* straighten, extend, stretch.

**beneficiary** *n.* recipient, inheritor, heir.

**bent** *a.* curved, warped, hooked, beaked, looped, twined, crooked, bowed, contorted, stooped, doubled over, wilted, drooping, humped, slumped, hunched, humpbacked, bowlegged, inclined.—*Ant.* straight, rigid, erect.

**beside** *a. & prep.* at the side of, at the edge of, adjacent to, next to, adjoining, alongside, near, close at hand, by, with, abreast, side by side, bordering on, neighboring, overlooking, next door to, to one side, nearby, connected with.

**besides** *a.* in addition to, additionally, moreover, over and above, added to, likewise, further, furthermore, beyond, exceeding, secondly, more than, apart from, extra, in excess of, plus, also, in other respects, exclusive of, with the exception of, as well as, not counting, other than, too, to boot, on top of that, aside from, else.

**bestow** *v.* bequeath, present, give.

**bet** *v.* wager, gamble, stake, bet on, bet against, venture, hazard, trust, play against, speculate, play for, put money down, put money on, risk, chance, make a bet, take a chance, lay down, buy in on*, lay odds, lay even money*. —**you bet*** certainly, by all means, yes indeed.

**betray** *v.* **1** [To deliver into the hands of an enemy] delude, trick, double-cross*. **2** [To reveal] divulge, disclose, make known.

**bewildered** *a.* confused, amazed, misguided, lost, astonished, thunderstruck, shocked, muddled, upset, dazed, giddy, dizzy, reeling, puzzled, misled, uncertain, surprised, baffled, disconcerted, appalled, aghast, adrift, at sea, off the track, awed, stupefied, astounded, struck speechless, breathless, befuddled, startled, struck dumb, dumbfounded, dazzled, stunned, electrified, confounded, staggered, petrified, awestruck, flabbergasted, flustered, all balled up*, rattled, up in the air*, stumped*, goofy*.

**beyond** *a. & prep.* on the other side, on the far side, over there, in advance of, away, out of range, a long way off, yonder, past, free of, clear of, farther off, ahead, behind, more remote.—*Ant.* here, on this side, nearer.

**big** *a.* **1** [Of great size] huge, great, swollen, fat, obese, bloated, overgrown, gross, mammoth, wide, grand, vast, immense, considerable, substantial, massive, extensive, spacious, colossal, gigantic, titanic, monstrous, towering, mighty, magnificent, enormous, giant, tremendous, whopping*.—*Ant.* little, tiny, small. **2** [Grown, or partially grown] grown-up, full-grown, adult. **3** [Important] prominent, significant, influential. **4** [Pompous] presumptuous, pretentious, imperious. **5** [Generous] magnanimous, liberal, unselfish.

**bigoted** *a.* biased, dogmatic, prejudiced.

**bind** *v.* **1** [To constrain with bonds] truss up, tie up, shackle, fetter, cinch, clamp, chain, leash, constrict, manacle, enchain, lace, pin, restrict, hamper, handcuff, muzzle, hitch, secure, yoke, pin down, fix, strap, tether, bind up, lash down, clamp down on, hogtie*. **2** [To hold together or in place] secure, attach, adhere. **3** [To obligate] oblige, necessitate, compel. **4** [To dress] treat, dress, bandage. **5** [To join] unite, put together, connect.

**biography** *n.* life story, saga, memoir, journal, experiences, autobiography, life, adventures, life history, confessions, personal anecdote, profile, sketch, biographical account.

**bit** *n.* **1** [A small quantity] piece, fragment, crumb, dot, particle, jot, trifle, mite, iota, whit, splinter, parcel, portion, droplet, trickle, driblet, morsel, pinch, snip, shred, atom, speck, molecule, shard, chip, fraction, sliver, segment, section, lump, slice, shaving, sample, specimen, scale, flake, excerpt, scrap, part, division, share, trace, item, chunk, paring, taste, mouthful, stub, butt, stump, a drop in the bucket*, peanuts*, chicken feed*, hunk*. **2** [A small degree] jot, minimum, inch, hairbreadth, trifle, iota, mite, fraction, tolerance, margin, whisker, hair, skin of one's teeth. **—do one's bit** participate, share, do one's share. **—every bit** wholly, altogether, entirely.

**bite** *v.* **1** [To seize or sever with the teeth] snap, gnaw, sink one's teeth in, nip, nibble, chew, mouth, gulp, worry, taste, masticate, clamp, champ, munch, bite into, crunch, mangle, chaw*. **2** [To be given to biting] snap, be vicious, attack. **3** [To cut or corrode] rot, decay, decompose.

**bitter** *a.* **1** [Acrid] astringent, acid, tart. **2** [Intense] sharp, harsh, severe. **3** [Sarcastic] acrimonious, caustic, biting.

**bizarre** *a.* odd, fantastic, unusual.

**blame** *n.* disapproval, condemnation, denunciation, disparagement, depreciation, opposition, abuse, disfavor, objection, reproach, criticism, repudiation, reprimand, invective, slur, accusation, reproof, attack, chiding, rebuke, impeachment, complaint, diatribe, tirade, charge, indictment, recrimination, arraignment, implication, calumny, frowning upon.—*Ant.* praise, commendation, appreciation. **—be to blame** guilty, at fault, culpable.

**blame** *v.* charge, condemn, criticize, arraign, challenge, involve, attack, brand, implicate, arrest, sue, prosecute, slander, impeach, bring to trial, connect with, indict, impute, put the finger on*, smear, point the finger at*, bring home to.

**blank** *a.* white, clear, virgin, fresh, plain, empty, untouched, pale, new, spotless, vacant, hollow, meaningless.

**blank** *n.* **1** [An empty space] void, hollow, hole, cavity, vacancy, womb, gulf, nothingness, hollowness, abyss, opening, vacuum, gap, interval. **2** [A form] questionnaire, data sheet, information blank. **—draw a blank** be unable to remember, lose one's memory, disremember*.

**blaze** *n.* conflagration, burning, fire.

**blaze** *v.* flame, flash, flare up.

**bleak** *a.* dreary, desolate, bare, cheerless, wild, exposed, barren, blank, disheartening, weary, melancholy, lonely, flat, somber, distressing, depressing, comfortless, joyless, uninviting, dull, sad, mournful, monotonous, waste, gloomy, dismal, unsheltered, unpopulated, desert, deserted, scorched, stony, burned over, bulldozed, cleared, frozen.—*Ant.* green, verdant, fruitful.

**blemish** *n.* flaw, defect, stain, spot, smudge, imperfection, disfigurement, defacement, blot, blur, chip, taint, tarnish, smirch, stigma, brand, deformity, dent, discoloration, mole, pockmark, blister, birthmark, wart, scar, impurity, speckle, bruise, freckle, pimple, patch, lump.—*Ant.* perfection, flawlessness, purity.

**blend** *n.* combination, amalgam, mixture.

**bless** *v.* baptize, canonize, glorify, honor, dedicate, make holy, pronounce holy, exalt, give benediction to, absolve, anoint, ordain, hallow, consecrate, beatify, sanctify, enshrine, offer, render acceptable to, sacrifice, commend.

**blight** *v.* decay, spoil, ruin.

**blindly** *a.* at random, wildly, in all directions, frantically, heedlessly, carelessly, recklessly, passionately, thoughtlessly, impulsively, inconsiderately, willfully, unreasonably, without rhyme or reason, senselessly, instinctively, madly, pell-mell, purposelessly, aimlessly, indiscriminately.—*Ant.* carefully, directly, considerately.

**bliss** *n.* joy, rapture, ecstasy.

**block** *n.* **1** [A mass, usually with flat surfaces] slab, chunk, piece, square, cake, cube, slice, segment, loaf, clod, bar, hunk. **2** [The area between streets] vicinity, square, lots. **3** [The distance of the side of a city block] street, city block, intersection. **4** [An obstruction] hindrance, bar, obstacle. **—knock someone's block off*** thrash, hit, beat up*.

**bloom** *v.* flower, burst into bloom, open, bud, prosper, grow, wax, bear fruit, thrive, germinate, flourish, be in health, blossom, come out in flower, be in flower.

**blow** *n.* hit, strike, swing, bump, wallop, rap, bang, whack, thwack, cuff, box, uppercut, knock, clout, slam, bruise, swipe, kick, stroke, punch, jab, gouge, lunge, thrust, swat, poke, prod, slap, the old one-two*, belt*, lick*, crack, kayo*, K.O.*.

**blow** *v.* **1** [To send forth air rapidly] puff, blast, pant, fan, whiff, whisk, whisper, puff away, exhale, waft, breathe, whistle. **2** [To carry on the wind] waft, flutter, bear, whisk, drive, fling, whirl, flap, flip, wave, buffet, sweep. **3** [To play a wind instrument] pipe, toot, mouth. **4** [To sound when blown] trumpet, vibrate, blare. **5** [To give form by inflation] inflate, swell, puff up, pump up. **6** [*To fail] miss, flounder, miscarry. **7** [*To spend] lay out, pay out, waste, squander.

**bluff** *v.* fool, mislead, trick.

**blunder** *n.* mistake, lapse, error.

**blunt** *a.* **1** [Dull] unsharpened, unpointed, round. **2** [Abrupt] brusque, curt, bluff.

**blush** *v.* change color, flush, redden, turn red, glow, have rosy cheeks.

**bluster** *v.* brag, swagger, strut.

**boast** *n.* brag, vaunt, source of pride, pretension, self-satisfaction, bravado.

**boast** *v.* gloat, triumph, swagger, bully, exult, show off, vaunt, swell, brag, strut, bluff, flaunt, bluster, flourish, blow*, sound off*, crow, pat oneself on the back, blow one's own horn*, attract attention.—*Ant.* apologize, humble oneself, admit defeat.

**bodily** *a.* carnal, fleshly, gross, somatic, solid, physical, unspiritual, tangible, material, substantial, human, natural, normal, organic.

**body** *n.* **1** [The human organism] frame, physique, form, figure, shape, make, carcass*, build, makeup. **2** [A corpse] cadaver, *corpus delecti* (Latin), dust, clay, carcass*, dead body, relics, the dead, the deceased, mummy, skeleton, ashes, carrion, bones, remains, stiff*, goner*. **3** [The central portion of an object] chassis, basis, groundwork, frame, fuselage, assembly, trunk, hull, bed, box, skeleton, scaffold, anatomy, bones, guts*. **4** [Individuals having an organization] society, group, party. **5** [A unified or organized mass] reservoir, supply, variety. —**keep body and soul together** stay alive, endure, earn a living.

**boil** *v.* steep, seethe, stew, bubble, simmer, steam, parboil, boil over, evaporate.

**bold** *a.* **1** [Courageous] intrepid, fearless, daring. **2** [Impertinent] brazen, audacious, presumptuous. **3** [Prominent] strong, clear, plain.

**boldly** *a.* **1** [*Said of animate beings*] impetuously, headlong, intrepidly, fearlessly, recklessly, courageously, dauntlessly, daringly, valiantly, stoutly, resolutely, brazenly, firmly.—*Ant.* cowardly, fearfully, cravenly. **2** [*Said of inanimate objects*] prominently, conspicuously, saliently, sharply, clearly, plainly, openly, abruptly, steeply, eminently, vividly, strongly, palpably, commandingly, compellingly, showily.—*Ant.* vaguely, inconspicuously, unobtrusively.

**bolster** *v.* prop, hold up, reinforce, sustain.

**bolt** *n.* staple, brad, nut, skewer, peg, rivet, pin, spike, stud, coupling, key, pin, pipe.

**bombing** *n.* bombardment, shelling, attack.

**bond** *n.* **1** [A link] attachment, union, obligation, connection, relation, affinity, affiliation, bond of union, restraint. **2** [A secured debenture] security, warranty, debenture, certificate, registered bond, government bond, municipal bond, long-term bond, short-term bond. **3** [Bail] surety, guaranty, warrant.

**bonus** *n.* gratuity, reward, additional compensation.

**boorish** *a.* awkward, clumsy, churlish.

**booth** *n.* stall, counter, nook, corner, pew, berth, compartment, shed, manger, cubbyhole, coop, pen, hut, enclosure, stand, cubicle, box.

**border** *n.* **1** [Edge] hem, end, trim. **2** [Boundary] frontier, outpost, perimeter.

**border** *v.* be adjacent to, adjoin, abut on.

**bored** *a.* wearied, fatigued, jaded, dull, irked, annoyed, bored to death*, in a rut, sick and tired, bored stiff*, bored silly*, fed up*.—*Ant.* excited, thrilled, exhilarated.

**boredom** *n.* lack of interest, tiresomeness, apathy, doldrums, listlessness, monotony, tedium, indifference.

**borrowed** *a.* appropriated, taken, acquired, assumed, adopted, hired, plagiarized, imported, cultivated, imitated.—*Ant.* owned, possessed, titular.

**botch** *v.* bungle, spoil, mar, ruin, wreck, mutilate, fumble, distort, blunder, mishandle, do clumsily, muddle, make a mess of, trip, flounder, err, fall down, be mistaken, misjudge, mismanage, miscalculate, misconstrue, misestimate, execute clumsily, do unskillfully, stumble, put one's foot in it*, goof up*, butcher, screw up*, mess up, put out of whack*.—*Ant.* succeed, fix, do well.

**bother** *v.* **1** [To take trouble] put oneself out, fret, go out of one's way, make a fuss about, fuss over, take pains, make an effort, exert oneself, concern oneself, be concerned about, worry about. **2** [To give trouble] plague, vex, annoy, perplex, pester, molest, irritate, irk, provoke, insult, harass, heckle, aggravate, badger, discommode, discompose, mortify, goad, intrude upon, disquiet, pursue, hinder, impede, carp at, scare, exasperate, bore, afflict, taunt, torment, torture, bedevil, browbeat, tease, tantalize, ride, rub the wrong way, pick on, nag, needle*, bug*, get under someone's skin*.—*Ant.* help, please, delight.

**bothersome** *a.* vexing, troublesome, disturbing.

**bounce** *v.* ricochet, recoil, glance off, spring back, leap, hop, bolt, vault, skip, bob, buck, jump, bound, jerk up and down, snap back, boomerang, backlash.

**bound** *a.* **1** [Literally confined in bonds] fettered, shackled, trussed up, manacled, enchained, handcuffed, hobbled, captive, pinioned, muzzled, in leash, tied up, harnessed, bound hand and foot, lashed fast, pinned down, tethered, picketed, secured, roped, gagged.—*Ant.* free, unrestrained, loose. **2** [Figuratively constrained] impelled, compelled, obliged, obligated, restrained, under compulsion, constrained, forced, coerced, driven, pressed, urged, necessitated, under necessity, made, having no alternative, required.

**bound** *v.* **1** [To move in leaps] leap, spring, vault. **2** [To rebound] bounce, ricochet, recoil. **3** [To set limits] restrict, confine, circumscribe. **—out of bounds** off limits, not permitted, restricted.

**boundary** *n.* outline, border, verge, rim, beginning, end, confine, bounds, radius, terminus, landmark, march, extremity, fence, compass, side, hem, frame, skirt, termination, margin, line, barrier, frontier, outpost, perimeter, parameter, extent, circumference, horizon, periphery, fringe, mark, confines, limit, borderland.

**bounty** *n.* prize, premium, bonus.

**brace** *n.* prop, bolster, stay, support, lever, beam, girder, block, rib, buttress, reinforcement, bearing, upholder, bracket, strengthener, band, bracer, stirrup, arm, splint, boom, bar, staff, rafter, jack, crutch.

**brag** *v.* swagger, exult, gloat.

**brake** *n.* check, hamper, curb, deterrent, obstacle, damper, hindrance, retarding device, governor.

**branch** *n.* **1** [A part, usually of secondary importance] office, bureau, division. **2** [A secondary shoot] bough, limb, offshoot, sprig, twig, bud, arm, fork, growth.

**brandish** *v.* flourish, gesture, warn.

**brave** *a.* fearless, daring, dauntless, valiant, intrepid, undaunted, undismayed, confident, unabashed, chivalrous, valorous, heroic, bold, imprudent, adventurous, reckless, foolhardy, dashing, venturesome, forward, audacious, gallant, resolute, militant, defiant, hardy, unafraid, stout, stouthearted, lionhearted, manly, firm, plucky, high-spirited, unshrinking, strong, stalwart, unflinching, game, unyielding, indomitable, unconquerable, spunky*, nervy, gutsy*.—*Ant.* cowardly, timid, craven.

**breach** *n.* violation, infringement, transgression.

**breadth** *n.* largeness, extent, vastness, compass, magnitude, greatness, extensiveness, scope, broadness, width, comprehensiveness, amplitude.

**break** *n.* **1** [The act of breaking] fracture, rift, split, schism, cleavage, breach, rupture, eruption, bursting, failure, division, parting, collapse.—*Ant.* repair, mending, maintenance. **2** [A pause] intermission, interim, lapse. **3** [*Fortunate change or event; *often plural*] good luck, advantage, favorable circumstances.

**break** *v.* **1** [To start a rupture] burst, split, crack, rend, sunder, sever, fracture, tear, cleave, break into, break through, force open, puncture, split, snap, slash, gash, dissect, slice, disjoin, separate. **2** [To shatter] smash, shiver, crash, break up, crush, splinter, pull to pieces, burst, break into pieces, break into smithereens*, fall apart, fall to pieces, collapse, break down, come apart, come unglued, go to wrack and ruin, get wrecked, bust*, split up. **3** [To bring to ruin or to an end] demolish, annihilate, eradicate. **4** [To happen] come to pass, occur, develop.

**break down** *v.* **1** [To analyze] examine, investigate, dissect. **2** [To malfunction] fail, stop, falter, misfire, give out, go down, crack up*, cease, backfire, conk out*, peter out*, fizzle out*, collapse, go kaput*, come unglued*, run out of gas*.

**break up** *v.* **1** [To scatter] disperse, disband, separate. **2** [To stop] put an end to, halt, terminate. **3** [*To distress] hurt, sadden, wound. **4** [*To end relations] discontinue, break off, stop.

**breast** *n.* **1** [The forepart of the body above the abdomen] thorax, heart, bosom. **2** [An enlarged mammary gland or glands] bosom, chest, teat, nipple, bust, udder. **—beat one's breast** repent, humble oneself, be sorry. **—make a clean breast of** confess, reveal, expose.

**breathe** *v.* respire, use one's lungs, inhale, exhale, draw in, breathe in, breathe out, gasp, pant, wheeze, snort, sigh, take air into one's nostrils, scent, sniff.

**breathless** *a.* out of breath, winded, spent, exhausted, used up, gasping, choking, windless, wheezing, short-winded, puffing, panting, asthmatic, short of breath, out of wind.

**breed** *n.* strain, variety, kind.

**breed** *v.* **1** [To produce] give birth to, deliver, bring forth. **2** [To cause] bring about, effect, produce.

**brief** *a.* **1** [Abrupt] hasty, curt, blunt. **2** [Short in time] short-term, fleeting, concise.

**bright** *a.* **1** [Shining or vivid] gleaming, shiny, glittering, luminous, lustrous, burnished, polished, sparkling, mirrorlike, glowing, flashing, scintillating, shimmering, incandescent, twinkling, illumined, light, golden, silvery, illuminated, shining, irradiated, glistening, radiant, burning, glaring, beaming, glimmering, splendid, resplendent, brilliant, dazzling, alight, aglow, lighted up, full of light, ablaze, flamelike, moonlit, sunlit, on fire, phosphorescent, blazing, glossy, colored, colorful, tinted, intense, deep, sharp, rich, tinged, hued, touched with color, fresh, clear, ruddy, psychedelic.—*Ant.* dull, clouded, dark. **2** [Intelligent] clever, quick, alert. **3** [Not rainy] clear, sunny, mild. **4** [Cheerful] lively, vivacious, happy.

**brilliant** *a.* **1** [Shining] dazzling, gleaming, sparkling. **2** [Showing remarkable ability] ingenious, profound, smart.

**bring** *v.* **1** [To transport] convey, take along, bear. **2** [To be worth in sale] sell for, earn, bring in. **3** [To cause] produce, effect, make.

**bring up** *v.* **1** [To rear] educate, teach, train. **2** [To discuss] tender, submit, propose.

**brisk** *a.* lively, refreshing, invigorating.

**broad** *a.* **1** [Physically wide] extended, large, extensive, ample, spacious, deep, expansive, immense, wide, roomy, outstretched, thick, widespread, full, stocky.—*Ant.* narrow, thin, slender. **2** [Wide in range] cultivated, experienced, cosmopolitan. **3** [Tolerant] progressive, open-minded, unbiased.

**broadcast** *v.* announce, relay, telephone, send out, telegraph, radio, transmit, televise, telecast, air, put on the air, go on the air, be on the air.

**broad-minded** *a.* tolerant, progressive, unprejudiced.

**broken** *a.* **1** [Fractured] shattered, hurt, ruptured, burst, splintered, smashed, in pieces, collapsed, destroyed, pulverized, crumbled, mutilated, bruised, injured, damaged, rent, split, cracked, mangled, dismembered, fragmentary, disintegrated, crippled, shredded, crushed, gashed, defective.—*Ant.* whole, intact, sound. **2** [Not functioning properly] defective, inoperable, in need of repair, in disrepair, out of order, busted*, gone to pot*, screwed up*, shot*, gone haywire*, on the fritz*, on the blink*, gone to pieces, out of whack*, out of commission. **3** [Discontinuous] spasmodic, erratic, intermittent. **4** [Incoherent; *said of speech*] muttered, unintelligible, mumbled.

**brokenhearted** *a.* despondent, crushed, grieved.

**brood** *v.* **1** [To hatch] set, cover, incubate, warm, sit. **2** [To nurse one's troubles] think, meditate, grieve, fret, sulk, mope, ponder, consider, muse, deliberate, dwell upon, speculate, daydream, reflect, dream, chafe inwardly, give oneself over to reflections, mull over, eat one's heart out.

**brotherhood** *n.* fellowship, equality, kinship, intimacy, relationship, affiliation, association, society, fraternity, family, race, comradeship, camaraderie, friendship, amity.

**browbeat** *v.* bully, intimidate, frighten.

**browse** *v.* skim, peruse, scan, glance at, look through, run through, flip through, look over, survey, inspect loosely, examine cursorily, glance over, check over, run over, go through carelessly, dip into, wander here and there.

**brutal** *a.* pitiless, harsh, unmerciful.

**bubble** *v.* froth, gurgle, gush, well, trickle, effervesce, boil, percolate, simmer, seep, eddy, ferment, erupt, issue, fester.

**build** *v.* create, form, erect, frame, raise, make, manufacture, put together, fit together, fabricate, contrive, assemble, put up, model, hammer together, set up, reconstruct, pile stone on stone, sculpture, fashion, compose, evolve, compile, cast, produce, forge, bring about, devise, carve, weave.—*Ant.* destroy, demolish, wreck.

**building** *n.* edifice, erection, construction, fabrication, house, framework, superstructure, frame, structure, apartment house, barn, castle, church, factory, home, hotel, motel, skyscraper, temple, office building, mosque, mall, store, school.

**bulk** *n.* greater part, main part, predominant part, better part, most, majority, plurality, biggest share, greater number, nearly all, body, more than half, best, gross, lion's share.—*Ant.* bit, remnant, fraction.

**bulky** *a.* massive, big, huge.

**bump** *n.* **1** [A jarring collision] knock, bang, bounce, jar, box, smash, pat, crack, jolt, crash, sideswipe, punch, hit, clap, push, shove, thrust, boost, shock, clash, impact, stroke, rap, tap, slap, clout, jab, jerk, prod, slam, nudge, buffet, swat, bash*, wallop*, belt*, bat*, swipe*, thump, whack*, poke*, clump*, clunk*, sock*, whop*, lick*, smack*, cuff, slug*. **2** [A swelling] projection, protuberance, knob.

**bundle** *n.* packet, parcel, pack.

**bungle** *v.* blunder, fumble, mishandle.

**burden** *v.* weigh down, force, hinder, encumber, overwhelm, hamper, strain, load with, saddle with, handicap, obligate, tax, afflict, vex, try, trouble, pile, bog down, crush, depress, impede, overload, oppress, make heavy, press down.—*Ant.* lighten, relieve, unload.

**burn** *n.* scorch, wound, impairment.

**burn** *v.* ignite, kindle, incinerate, burn up, burn down, blaze, flame, flare, burst into flame, rage, consume, enkindle, cremate, consume with flames, set a match to, set on fire, set ablaze, set afire, sear, singe, scorch, brand, fire, light, torch, char, roast, toast, heat, bake.—*Ant.* extinguish, put out, quench.

**burning** *a.* fiery, blazing, glowing, ablaze, afire, on fire, smoking, in flames, aflame, inflamed, kindled, enkindled, ignited, scorching, turning to ashes, searing, in a blaze, blistering, red-hot, white-hot.—*Ant.* cold, frozen, out.

**burst** *v.* **1** [To explode] blow up, erupt, rupture. **2** [To break] crack, split, fracture.

**bury** *v.* **1** [To inter] lay in the grave, entomb, enshrine, deposit in the earth, give burial to, embalm, hold funeral services for, hold last rites for, lay out. **2** [To cover] conceal, mask, stow away. **3** [To defeat] overcome, win over, conquer.

**bush** *n.* bramble, thicket, hedge, shrubbery, briar bush, rose bush. —**beat around the bush** speak evasively, avoid the subject, be deceptive.

**bushy** *a.* fuzzy, disordered, thick, shaggy, rough, full, tufted, fringed, woolly, nappy, fluffy, furry, crinkly, stiff, wiry, rumpled, prickly, feathery, leafy, bristly, heavy.—*Ant.* thin, sleek, smooth.

**business** *n.* **1** [Industry and trade] commerce, exchange, trade, traffic, barter, commercial enterprise, gainful occupation, buying and selling, negotiation, production and distribution, dealings, affairs, sales, contracts, bargaining, trading, transaction, banking, marketing, undertaking, speculation, market, mercantilism, wholesale and retail, capital and labor, free enterprise, game*, racket*. **2** [Occupation] trade, profession, vocation. **3** [A person's proper concerns] affair, concern, interest. **4** [A commercial enterprise] firm, factory, mill, store, company, shop, corporation, concern, combine, conglomerate, cooperative, establishment, enterprise, partnership, institution, house, market, syndicate, cartel, trust, monopoly, holding company. —**do business with** deal with, trade with, patronize. —**get the business*** be mistreated, be abused, endure. —**give the business*** mistreat, bother, victimize. —**mean business*** be serious, stress, impress.

**busy** *a.* **1** [Engaged] occupied, diligent, employed, working, in conference, in a meeting, in the field, in the laboratory, on an assignment, on duty, on the job, at work, busy with, on the run, on the road, hardworking, busy as a bee*, hustling*, up to one's ears*, hard at it*, having other fish to fry.—*Ant.* idle, unemployed, unoccupied. **2** [In use] employed, occupied, taken.

**busybody** *n.* meddler, tattletale, gossip.

**butt** *v.* hit, ram, push headfirst, bump, batter, knock, collide with, run into, smack, strike, gore, buck, toss, crash into.

**buy** *v.* purchase, get, bargain for, procure, gain, contract for, sign for, get in exchange, go marketing, buy and sell, order, invest in, make an investment, shop for, acquire ownership of, procure title to, pay for, redeem, pay a price for, buy into, score*.

**buzz** *v.* drone, hum, whir.

# C

**cackle** *v.* chuckle, snicker, giggle.

**cad** *n.* rogue, scoundrel, rake.

**calamity** *n.* cataclysm, distress, trial.

**calculate** *v.* count, measure, reckon, enumerate, determine, rate, forecast, weigh, gauge, number, figure, figure up, account, compute, sum up, divide, multiply, subtract, add, work out, cipher, tally, dope out*.

**calendar** *n.* list, program, record, timetable, schedule, annals, journal, diary, daybook, chronology, log, logbook, table, register, almanac, agenda, docket.

**call** *n.* **1** [A shout] yell, whoop, hail. **2** [Characteristic sound] twitter, tweet, shriek. **3** [A visit] visiting, a few words, afternoon call. **4** [Word of command] summons, battle cry, reveille. **5** [An invitation] bidding, solicitation, proposal. **—on call** usable, ready, prepared. **—within call** close by, approximate, not far away.

**call** *v.* **1** [To raise the voice] shout, call out, exclaim. **2** [To bring a body of people together] collect, convene, muster. **3** [To address] denominate, designate, term. **4** [To invite] summon, request, ask.

**call off** *v.* cancel, postpone, cease.

**callous** *a.* unfeeling, hardened, insensitive.

**calm** *a.* **1** [*Said especially of persons*] dignified, reserved, cool, composed, collected, unmoved, levelheaded, coolheaded, impassive, detached, aloof, unconcerned, disinterested, unhurried, neutral, gentle, sedate, serene, unanxious, unexcited, contented, meek, satisfied, pleased, amiable, temperate, placid, civil, kind, moderate, confident, poised, tranquil, self-possessed, restful, relaxed, dispassionate, mild, still, patient, self-controlled, untroubled, cool as a cucumber*, unflappable*.—*Ant.* violent, excited, furious. **2** [*Said often of things*] quiet, undisturbed, unruffled, comfortable, moderate, in order, soothing, at peace, placid, smooth, still, restful, harmonious, peaceful, pacific, balmy, waveless, windless, serene, motionless, slow.—*Ant.* rough, agitated, aroused.

**calm** *n.* **1** [Peace] stillness, peacefulness, quiet. **2** [Composure] serenity, tranquillity, peace of mind.

**calm** *v.* tranquilize, soothe, pacify.

**calm down** *v.* compose oneself, control oneself, calm oneself, keep oneself under control, keep cool, take it easy*, get organized, rest, get hold of oneself, cool it*, cool off, cool down, simmer down, keep one's shirt on*.

**campaign** *v.* crusade, electioneer, run, agitate, contend for, contest, canvass for, solicit votes, lobby, barnstorm, mend fences, go to the grass roots*, stump, beat the bushes*, whistle-stop.

**cancel** *v.* repudiate, nullify, ignore, invalidate, suppress, countermand, call off, set aside, rule out, refute, rescind, remove, repeal, counteract, recall, retract, abrogate, discharge, void, make void, put an end to, abort, offset, revoke, overthrow, scratch, drop.—*Ant.* sustain, approve, uphold.

**cancer** *n.* growth, tumor, malignancy.

**candid** *a.* straightforward, sincere, open.

**candidate** *n.* aspirant, possible choice, nominee, applicant, political contestant, office-seeker, successor, competitor, bidder, solicitor, petitioner.

**capacity** *n.* contents, limit, space, room, size, volume, holding power, extent, compass, magnitude, spread, expanse, scope, latitude, bulk, dimensions, measure, range, quantity, size, reach, holding ability, sweep, proportions, mass, sufficiency.

**cape** *n.* **1** [Land jutting into the water] headland, peninsula, foreland, point, promontory, jetty, head, tongue, neck of land, ness, mole, finger, arm. **2** [An overgarment] cloak, wrapper, mantilla, mantle, shawl, wrap, overdress, poncho.

**capital** *n.* **1** [A seat of government] metropolis, principal city, capitol. **2** [Money and property] cash, assets, interests. **3** [A letter usually used initially] initial, uppercase, majuscule.

**capitulate** *v.* surrender, submit, give up.

**captivity** *n.* imprisonment, jail, restraint, slavery, bondage, subjection, servitude, duress, detention, incarceration, enslavement, constraint, the guardhouse, custody.—*Ant.* freedom, liberty, independence.

**capture** *v.* seize, take, apprehend.

**captured** *a.* taken, seized, arrested, apprehended, detained, grasped, overtaken, grabbed, snatched, kidnapped, abducted, netted, hooked, secured, collared*, nabbed*, bagged.—*Ant.* released, unbound, loosed.

**care** *n.* **1** [Careful conduct] heed, concern, caution, consideration, regard, thoughtfulness, forethought, attention, precaution, wariness, vigilance, watchfulness, watching, diligence, nicety, pains, application, conscientiousness, thought, discrimination, exactness, exactitude, watch, concentration.—*Ant.* carelessness, neglect, negligence. **2** [Worry] concern, anxiety, distress. **3** [Custody] supervision, administration, keeping. **4** [A cause of worry] problem, care, concern. **—take care** be careful, be cautious, beware, heed. **—take care of** protect, attend to, be responsible for.

**care** *v.* **1** [To be concerned] attend, take pains, regard. **2** [To be careful] look out for, be on guard, watch out.

**career** *n.* occupation, vocation, work.

**careful** *a.* thorough, concerned, deliberate, conservative, prudent, meticulous, particular, rigorous, fussy, finicky, prim, exacting, wary, sober, vigilant, watchful, suspicious, alert, wide-awake, scrupulous, religious, hard to please, discriminating, sure-footed, precise, painstaking, exact, on one's guard, on the alert, conscientious, attentive, calculating, mindful, cautious, guarded, considerate, shy, circumspect, discreet, noncommittal, self-possessed, cool, calm, self-disciplined, solid, farsighted, frugal, thrifty, stealthy, observant, on guard, apprehensive, leery, choosy*, picky*, feeling one's way, seeing how the land lies, going to great lengths.—*Ant.* careless, heedless, haphazard.

**careless** *a.* loose, lax, remiss, unguarded, incautious, forgetful, unthinking, unobservant, reckless, unheeding, indiscreet, inadvertent, unconcerned, wasteful, regardless, imprudent, unconsidered, hasty, inconsiderate, heedless, mindless, untroubled, negligent, neglectful, thoughtless, indifferent, casual, oblivious, absent-minded, listless, abstracted, nonchalant, undiscerning, offhand, slack, blundering.—*Ant.* thoughtful, attentive, careful.

**caress** *n.* embrace, stroke, feel*.

**caress** *v.* embrace, cuddle, pat.

**carriage** *n.* **1** [The manner of carrying the body] walk, pace, step, attitude, aspect, presence, look, cast, gait, bearing, posture, pose, demeanor, poise, air. **2** [A horse-drawn passenger vehicle] buggy, surrey, coach, coach-and-four, buckboard, cart, dogcart, two-wheeler, trap, gig, sulky, hansom, coupe, four-wheeler, stagecoach, chariot, hack, hackney coach.

**carry** *v.* **1** [To transport] convey, move, transplant, transfer, cart, import, transmit, freight, remove, conduct, bear, take, bring, shift, haul, change, convoy, relocate, relay, lug, tote, fetch. **2** [To transmit] pass on, transfer, relay. **3** [To support weight] bear, sustain, shoulder. **4** [To give support] corroborate, back up, confirm. **—carried away** zealous, aroused, exuberant.

**cart** *n.* truck, wheelbarrow, little wagon, tip cart, handcart, gig, dray, two-wheeler, pushcart, go-cart, two-wheeled cart. **—put the cart before the horse** reverse, be illogical, err.

**carve** *v.* create, form, hew, chisel, engrave, etch, sculpture, incise, mold, fashion, cut, shape, model, tool, block out, scrape, pattern, trim.

**case** *n.* **1** [An example] instance, illustration, sample. **2** [Actual conditions] incident, occurrence, fact. **3** [A legal action] suit, litigation, lawsuit. **4** [An organized argument] argument, petition, evidence. **5** [A container or its contents] carton, canister, crate, crating, box, baggage, trunk, casing, chest, drawer, holder, tray, receptacle, coffer, crib, chamber, bin, bag, grip, cabinet, sheath, scabbard, wallet, safe, basket, casket. **—in any case** in any event, anyway, however. **—in case (of)** in the event that, provided that, supposing.

**cash** *n.* money in hand, ready money, liquid assets, currency, legal tender, principal, available means, working assets, funds, payment, capital, finances, stock, resources, wherewithal, investments, savings, riches, reserve, treasure, moneys, security.

**cast** *n.* **1** [A plaster reproduction] facsimile, duplicate, replica. **2** [Those in a play] persons in the play, list of characters, players, roles, parts, dramatis personae, company, troupe, producers, dramatic artists. **3** [Aspect] complexion, face, appearance. **4** [A surgical dressing] plaster-of-Paris dressing, plaster cast, arm cast, leg cast, knee cast, body cast, splints. **5** [A tinge] hue, shade, tint.

**castrate** *v.* emasculate, sterilize, asexualize, mutilate, cut, spay, geld, unman, steer, caponize, effeminize, deprive of manhood.

**catalog** *n.* register, file, directory, schedule, inventory, index, bulletin, syllabus, brief, slate, table, calendar, list, docket, classification, record, draft, roll, timetable, table of contents, prospectus, program, rent roll.

**catch** *n.* **1** [A likely mate] boyfriend, sweetheart, fiancé. **2** [Something stolen] capture, grab, haul*. **3** [*A trick] puzzle, trick, trap. **4** [A hook] clasp, clamp, snap.

**catch** *v.* **1** [To seize hold of] snatch, take, take hold of, snag, grab, pick, pounce on, fasten upon, snare, pluck, hook, claw, clench, clasp, grasp, clutch, grip, nab, net, bag*. **2** [To bring into captivity] trap, apprehend, capture. **3** [To come to from behind] overtake, reach, come upon. **4** [To contract a disease] get, fall ill with, become infected with, incur, become subject to, be liable to, fall victim to, take, succumb to, break out with, receive, come down with.—*Ant.* escape, ward off, get over.

**cattle** *n.* stock, cows, steers, calves, herd, beef cattle, dairy cattle.

**cause** *n.* **1** [Purpose] motive, causation, object, purpose, explanation, inducement, incitement, prime mover, motive power, mainspring, ultimate cause, ground, matter, element, stimulation, instigation, foundation, the why and wherefore.—*Ant.* result, effect, outcome. **2** [Moving force] agent, case, condition. **3** [A belief] principles, conviction, creed.

**cause** *v.* originate, provoke, generate, occasion, let, kindle, give rise to, lie at the root of, be at the bottom of, bring to pass, bring to effect, sow the seeds of.

**caution** *n.* care, heed, discretion.

**cease** *v.* desist, terminate, discontinue.

**celebrate** *v.* **1** [To recognize an occasion] keep, observe, consecrate, hallow, dedicate, commemorate, honor, proclaim, ritualize.—*Ant.* forget, overlook, neglect. **2** [To indulge in celebration] feast, give a party, carouse, rejoice, kill the fatted calf, revel, go on a spree, make whoopee*, blow off steam*, let off steam*, have a party, have a ball*, kick up one's heels*, let loose*, let go, live it up*, whoop it up*, make merry, kick up a row*, beat the drum*.

**celebrated** *a.* well-known, renowned, noted.

**cemetery** *n.* burial ground, memorial park, funerary grounds, churchyard, necropolis, potter's field, catacomb, city of the dead, tomb, vault, crypt, charnel house, sepulcher, graveyard, mortuary, last resting place, Golgotha, boneyard*.

**censor** *v.* control, restrict, strike out, forbid, suppress, ban, withhold, enforce censorship, control the flow of news, inspect, oversee, abridge, expurgate, review, criticize, exert pressure, conceal, prevent publication, blacklist, blue-pencil, cut, black out.

**censure** *n.* criticism, reproof, admonition.

**center** *n.* **1** [A central point] point, middle, focus, nucleus, core, place, heart, hub, navel, point of convergence, point of concentration, focal point, midst, middle point, centrality, marrow, kernel, bull's-eye, pivot, axis, pith, dead center. **2** [A point that attracts people] city, town, metropolis, plaza, capital, shopping center, trading center, station, hub, mart, market, crossroads, mall, social center, meeting place, club, market place. **3** [Essence] core, gist, kernel.

**central** *a.* middle, midway, equidistant, medial, focal, nuclear, midmost, mean, inner, median, inmost, middlemost, intermediate, interior, in the center of.—*Ant.* outer, peripheral, verging on.

**ceremony** *n.* **1** [A public event] function, commemoration, services. **2** [A rite] observance, ritual, rite, service, solemnity, formality, custom, tradition, liturgy, ordinance, sacrament, liturgical practice, conformity, etiquette, politeness, decorum, propriety, preciseness, strictness, nicety, formalism, conventionality.

**certain** *a.* **1** [Confident] calm, assured, sure, positive, satisfied, self-confident, undoubting, believing, secure, untroubled, unconcerned, undisturbed, unperturbed, fully convinced, assertive, cocksure. **2** [Beyond doubt] indisputable, unquestionable, assured, positive, real, true, genuine, plain, clear, undoubted, guaranteed, unmistakable, sure, incontrovertible, undeniable, definite, supreme, unqualified, infallible, undisputed, unerring, sound, reliable, trustworthy, evident, conclusive, authoritative, irrefutable, unconditional, incontestable, unquestioned, absolute, unequivocal, inescapable, conclusive, in the bag*, on ice*, done up*, salted away*. **3** [Fixed] settled, concluded, set. **4** [Specific but not named] special, definite, individual, marked, specified, defined, one, some, a few, a couple, several, upwards of, regular, particular, singular, precise, specific, express. **—for certain** without doubt, absolutely, certainly.

**certificate** *n.* declaration, warrant, voucher, testimonial, credentials, license, testament, endorsement, affidavit, certification, coupon, document, pass, ticket, warranty, guarantee, testimony, receipt, affirmation, docket, record.

**certify** *v.* swear, attest, state.

**chairman** *n.* chairperson, chairwoman, chair, president, administrator, director, toastmaster, speaker, moderator, monitor, leader, principal, captain, master of ceremonies, MC, emcee.

**chance** *a.* accidental, unplanned, unintentional.

**change** *n.* **1** [An alteration] modification, correction, remodeling, switch, reformation, reconstruction, shift, reform, conversion, transformation, revolution, rearrangement, adjustment, readjustment, reorganization, reshaping, renovation, realignment, redirection, reprogramming, variation, addition, refinement, advance, development, diversification, turn, turnover, enlargement, revision, qualification, distortion, compression, contraction, widening, narrowing, lengthening, flattening, shortening, fitting, setting, adjusting, rounding, gone every which way*, ups and downs. **2** [Substitution] switch, replacement, exchange. **3** [Variety] diversity, novelty, variance. **4** [Small coins] silver, coins, chicken feed*.

**change** *v.* **1** [To make different] vary, turn, alternate. **2** [To become different] alter, vary, modify, evolve, be converted, turn into, resolve into, grow, ripen, mellow, mature, transform, reform, moderate, adapt, adjust. **3** [To put in place of another] displace, supplant, transpose. **4** [To change clothing] undress, disrobe, make one's toilet.

**changeable** *a.* **1** [*Said of persons*] fickle, flighty, unreliable. **2** [*Said of conditions*] variable, unsteady, unsettled.

**channel** *n.* conduit, tube, canal, duct, course, gutter, furrow, trough, runway, tunnel, strait, sound, race, sewer, main, artery, vein, ditch, aqueduct, canyon.

**chaos** *n.* turmoil, anarchy, discord.

**chaotic** *a.* disorganized, disordered, uncontrolled.

**character** *n.* **1** [The dominant quality] temper, temperament, attitude, nature, sense, complex, mood, streak, attribute, badge, tone, style, aspect, complexion, spirit, genius, humor, frame, grain, vein. **2** [The sum of a person's characteristics] personality, reputation, constitution, repute, individuality, estimation, record, caliber, standing, type, shape, quality, habit, appearance. **3** [A symbol, especially in writing] sign, figure, emblem. **4** [A queer or striking person] personality, figure, personage, original, eccentric, crank*, nut*, oddball*, weirdo*, freak*, psycho*. —**in character** consistent, usual, predictable. —**out of character** inconsistent, unpredictable, unusual.

**characteristic** *a.* innate, fixed, essential, distinctive, distinguishing, marked, discriminative, symbolic, individualizing, representative, specific, personal, original, peculiar, individualistic, individual, idiosyncratic, unique, special, particular, symptomatic, private, exclusive, inherent, inborn, inbred, ingrained, native, indicative, inseparable, in the blood.—*Ant.* irregular, erratic, aberrant.

**characteristic** *n.* flavor, attribute, quality, faculty, peculiarity, individuality, style, aspect, tone, tinge, feature, distinction, manner, bearing, inclination, nature, personality, temperament, frame, originality, singularity, qualification, virtue, mark, essence, caliber, complexion, particularity, idiosyncrasy, trick, earmark, mannerism, trademark, badge, symptom, disposition, specialty, mood, character, bent, tendency, component, thing.

**charge** *v.* **1** [To ask a price] require, sell for, fix the price at. **2** [To enter on a charge account] debit, put to account, charge to, run up an account, take on account, put on one's account, incur a debt, put down, credit, encumber, sell on credit, buy on credit, chalk up, put on the books, carry, put on the cuff*. **3** [To attack] assail, assault, invade. **4** [To accuse] indict, censure, impute.

**charming** *a.* enchanting, bewitching, entrancing, captivating, cute, fascinating, delightful, lovable, sweet, winning, irresistible, attractive, amiable, appealing, alluring, charismatic, pleasing, nice, graceful, winsome, seducing, seductive, desirable, enticing, tempting, inviting, ravishing, enrapturing, glamorous, elegant, infatuating, dainty, delicate, absorbing, tantalizing, engrossing, titillating, engaging, enthralling, rapturous, electrifying, lovely, intriguing, thrilling, fair, exquisite, likable, diverting, fetching, provocative, delectable, sexy*, sharp*, smooth*.—*Ant.* offensive, disgusting, unpleasant.

**chart** *n.* graph, outline, diagram.

**chaste** *a.* immaculate, unstained, clean, innocent, virginal, unblemished, unsullied, moral, modest, proper, decent, uncontaminated, virgin, celibate, platonic, controlled, unmarried, unwed, spotless, infallible, strong.—*Ant.* weak, corruptible, frail.

**chastise** *v.* scold, discipline, spank.

**cheap** *a.* **1** [Low in relative price] inexpensive, low-priced, moderate, family-size, economy-size, budget, depreciated, slashed, cut-rate, on sale, competitive, lowered, thrifty, bargain, irregular, reduced, cut-priced, low-cost, at a bargain, reasonable, marked down, half-priced, popular-priced, worth the money, dime-a-dozen*, dirt-cheap*, for peanuts*, for a song*, second, bargain-basement*.—*Ant.* expensive, dear, costly. **2** [Low in quality] inferior, ordinary, shoddy. **3** [Dishonest or base] dirty, tawdry, low.

**cheat** *n.* rogue, cheater, confidence man, quack, charlatan, conniver, fraud, swindler, chiseler*, beguiler, fake, bluff, deceiver, inveigler, hypocrite, trickster, pretender, dodger, humbug, crook, wolf in sheep's clothing, con man*, shark*, fourflusher*, shill*.

**cheat** *v.* defraud, swindle, beguile.

**check** *v.* **1** [To bring under control] bridle, repress, inhibit, control, checkmate, counteract, discourage, repulse, neutralize, squelch.—*Ant.* free, liberate, loose. **2** [To determine accuracy] review, monitor, balance accounts, balance the books, keep account of, correct, compare, find out, investigate, vet*, count, tell, call the roll, take account of, take stock, go through, go over with a fine-toothed comb*, keep tabs on*, keep track of. **3** [To halt] hold, terminate, cut short.

**cheerful** *a.* **1** [*Said especially of persons*] gay, merry, joyful. **2** [*Said especially of things*] bright, sunny, sparkling.

**cheer up** *v.* enliven, inspirit, exhilarate, inspire, brighten, rally, restore, perk up, boost, buck up*, pat on the back.

**cherish** *v.* treasure, value, adore.

**chief** *a.* leading, first, foremost.

**chief** *n.* principal, manager, overseer, governor, president, foreman, proprietor, supervisor, director, chairman, ringleader, general, master, dictator, superintendent, head, prince, emperor, duke, majesty, monarch, overlord, lord, potentate, sovereign, chieftain, ruler, captain, commander, bigwig*, prima donna*, boss, it*.

**child** *n.* newborn, infant, youth, adolescent, youngster, daughter, son, grandchild, stepchild, offspring, innocent, minor, juvenile, tot, cherub, papoose, moppet*, kid*, kiddie*, whelp*, brat*, imp, small fry.—*Ant.* parent, forefather, adult. **—with child** carrying a child, going to have a baby, fertile.

**childhood** *n.* infancy, youth, minority, school days, adolescence, nursery days, babyhood, boyhood, girlhood, teens, puberty, immaturity, tender age.—*Ant.* age, maturity, senility.

**childish** *a.* childlike, foolish, stupid, baby, infantile, juvenile, youthful, babyish, boyish, girlish, adolescent, green, soft, immature.—*Ant.* mature, adult, grown.

**chivalrous** *a.* courteous, heroic, valiant.

**choice** *a.* superior, fine, exceptional.

**choice** *n.* selection, preference, alternative, election, substitute, favorite, pick, a good bet.

**choke** *v.* asphyxiate, strangle, strangulate, stifle, throttle, garrote, drown, noose, smother, grab by the throat, wring the neck of, stop the breath of, gag, gasp, suffocate, choke off, be choked, die out, die by asphyxiation.

**choose** *v.* decide, take, pick out, draw lots, cull, prefer, make a choice of, accept, weigh, judge, sort, appoint, embrace, will, call for, fancy, take up, separate, favor, determine, resolve, discriminate, make a decision, adopt, collect, mark out for, cut out, arrange, keep, take up, make one's choice, pick and choose, settle on, use one's discretion, determine upon, fix on, place one's trust in, glean, single out, espouse, exercise one's option, make up one's mind, set aside, set apart, commit oneself, separate the wheat from the chaff, incline toward, opt for, burn one's bridges.—*Ant.* discard, reject, refuse.

**chore** *n.* task, errand, job.

**Christmas** *n.* Xmas*, Noel, Yule.

**chronic** *a.* inveterate, confirmed, settled, rooted, deep-seated, continuing, persistent, stubborn, incurable, lasting, lingering, deep-rooted, perennial, fixed, continual, incessant, long-standing, recurring, continuous, of long duration, long-lived, protracted, ceaseless, sustained, lifelong, prolonged, recurrent, obstinate, inborn, inbred, ingrained, ever-present.—*Ant.* temporary, acute, casual.

**chronological** *a.* temporal, historical, tabulated, classified according to chronology, in the order of time, sequential, consecutive, properly dated, measured in time, in sequence, progressive in time, ordered, in order, in due course.

**chubby** *a.* plump, round, pudgy.

**chunk** *n.* piece, mass, lump.

**church** *n.* **1** [A building consecrated to worship] cathedral, house of God, Lord's house, temple, synagogue, mosque, house of worship, meetinghouse, chapel, basilica, tabernacle, abbey, sanctuary, house of prayer, mission, shrine, pagoda. **2** [A divine service] rite, prayers, prayer meeting, Sunday school, worship, Mass, Lord's Supper, sacrament, the holy sacrament, rosary, ritual, religious rite, morning service, evening service, congregational worship, fellowship, devotion, office, revival meeting, chapel service, sermon, communion. **3** [An organized religious body] congregation, gathering, denomination, sect, chapter, body, order, communion, faith, religion, religious order, affiliation, persuasion, belief, faction, doctrine, creed, cult.

**circle** *n.* **1** [A round closed plane figure] ring, loop, wheel, sphere, globe, orb, orbit, zodiac, bowl, vortex, hoop, horizon, perimeter, periphery, circumference, full turn, circuit, disk, meridian, equator, ecliptic, cycle, bracelet, belt, wreath. **2** [An endless sequence of events] cycle, course, succession. **—come full circle** go through a cycle, come back, revert.

**circle** *v.* round, encircle, loop, tour, circumnavigate, ring, belt, embrace, encompass, wind about, revolve around, circumscribe, curve around, circuit, enclose, spiral, coil, circulate, detour, wind, roll, wheel, swing past, go round about, evade.—*Ant.* divide, bisect, cut across.

**circumference** *n.* perimeter, periphery, border.

**circumstance** *n.* **1** [An attendant condition] situation, condition, contingency, phase, factor, detail, item, fact, case, place, time, cause, status, element, feature, point, incident, article, stipulation, concern, matter, event, occurrence, crisis, coincidence, happenstance*. **2** [An occurrence] episode, happening, incident.

**circumstances** *pl.n.* **1** [Condition in life] worldly goods, outlook, prospects, chances, means, assets, prosperity, financial condition, resources, standing, property, net worth, financial standing, credit rating, terms, way of life, rank, class, degree, capital, position, financial responsibility, footing, income, sphere, substance, stock in trade, lot, prestige, what one is worth, place on the ladder. **2** [Attendant conditions] situation, environment, surroundings, facts, particulars, factors, features, motives, controlling factors, governing factors, the times, occasion, basis, grounds, setting, background, needs, requirements, necessities, course of events, legal status, change, life, fluctuation, phase, case, condition, state of affairs, surrounding facts, the score*, the scene*, the story*, where it's at*, how the land lies, the lay of the land, current regime, ups and downs. **—under no circumstances** under no conditions, by no means, absolutely not. **—under the circumstances** conditions being what they are, for this reason, because of this.

**citizen** *n.* inhabitant, denizen, national, subject, cosmopolite, commoner, civilian, urbanite, taxpayer, member of the community, householder, native, occupant, settler, voter, dweller, immigrant, naturalized person, townsman, the man on the street, villager, John Q. Public.

**civic** *a.* civil, urban, municipal.

**civil** *a.* **1** [Civic] local, civic, public. **2** [Polite] formal, courteous, refined.

**civilization** *n.* cultivation, polish, enlightenment, refinement, civility, illumination, advancement of knowledge, elevation, edification, culture, advancement, social well-being, degree of cultivation, material well-being, education, breeding.—*Ant.* barbarism, savagery, degeneration.

**civilize** *v.* enlighten, cultivate, enrich, reclaim, refine, acculturate, spiritualize, humanize, edify, uplift, tame, foster, instruct, promote, indoctrinate, idealize, elevate, educate, advance, ennoble.

**claim** *n.* demand, declaration, profession, entreaty, petition, suit, ultimatum, call, request, requirement, application, case, assertion, plea, right, interest, title, part. **—lay claim to** demand, challenge, stake out a claim to.

**clamp** *n.* fastener, clasp, catch.

**clarify** *v.* interpret, define, elucidate.

**clash** *v.* be dissimilar, mismatch, not go with.

**clasp** *n.* buckle, pin, clamp.

**class** *n.* **1** [A classification] degree, order, rank, grade, standing, genus, division, distinction, breed, type, kingdom, subdivision, phylum, subphylum, superorder, family, sect, category, rate, collection, denomination, department, sort, species, variety, branch, group, genre, range, brand, set, kind, section, domain, nature, color, origin, character, temperament, school, designation, sphere, spirit, vein, persuasion, province, make, grain, source, name, habit, form, selection, stamp, status, range, property, aspect, disposition, tone. **2** [A group organized for study] lecture, seminar, study session. **3** [A division of society] set, caste, social level. **—in a class by itself** unusual, different, one of a kind.

**classify** *v.* arrange, order, pigeonhole, tabulate, organize, distribute, categorize, systematize, coordinate, correlate, incorporate, label, alphabetize, place in a category, range, form into classes, divide, allocate, number, rate, class, rank, catalog, segregate, distinguish, allot, analyze, regiment, name, group, tag, type, put in order, break down, assort, sort, index, grade, match, size, reduce to order.—*Ant.* disorganize, disorder, disarrange.

**clean** *a.* **1** [Not soiled] spotless, washed, stainless, laundered, untarnished, unstained, neat, tidy, clear, blank, white, unblemished, unspotted, snowy, well-kept, dustless, cleansed, immaculate, unsoiled, unpolluted, spick-and-span*, clean as a whistle*.—*Ant.* dirty, soiled, stained. **2** [Not contaminated] unadulterated, wholesome, sanitary. **3** [Having sharp outlines] clear-cut, sharp, distinct. **4** [Thorough] complete, entire, total. **5** [Fair] reliable, decent, lawful. —**come clean*** confess, reveal, expose.

**clean** *v.* cleanse, clean up, clear up, clear out, purify, soak, shake out, wash down, scrub off, disinfect, tidy up, deodorize, swab, polish, sterilize, scrape, sweep out, scour, launder, vacuum, scald, dust, mop, cauterize, rinse, sponge, brush, dress, comb, whisk, scrub, sweep, wipe up, clarify, rake, clean away, make clear, bathe, soap, erase, neaten, shampoo, refine, flush, blot, do up*, spruce up, slick up*.—*Ant.* dirty, soil, smear.

**clear** *a.* **1** [Open to the sight or understanding] explicit, plain, manifest. **2** [Offering little impediment to the vision] lucid, pure, transparent, apparent, limpid, translucent, crystal, crystalline, thin, crystal clear.—*Ant.* opaque, dark, muddy. **3** [Unclouded] sunny, bright, rainless. **4** [Freed from legal charges] free, guiltless, cleared, exonerated, blameless, innocent, sinless, dismissed, discharged, absolved.—*Ant.* guilty, accused, blamed. **5** [Audible] loud enough to be heard, distinct, definite. —**in the clear** guiltless, not suspected, cleared.

**clear** *v.* **1** [To free from uncertainty] clear up, relieve, clarify. **2** [To free from obstacles] disentangle, rid, unloose. **3** [To profit] realize, net, make.

**clench** *v.* grip, grasp, double up.

**clerical** *a.* **1** [Concerning clerks] stenographic, accounting, bookkeeping, secretarial, typing, written, assistant, subordinate. **2** [Concerning the clergy] ministerial, priestly, apostolic, monastic, monkish, churchly, papal, episcopal, canonical, pontifical, ecclesiastic, sacred, holy, ecclesiastical, in God's service, devoted to the Lord, in the Lord's work.

**clerk** *n.* salesgirl, saleswoman, saleslady, shopgirl, shop assistant, salesclerk, salesman, salesperson, counterman, seller, auditor, bookkeeper, recorder, registrar, stenographer, office girl, office boy, timekeeper, cashier, teller, office worker, notary, controller, copyist, law clerk, switchboard operator.

**clever** *a.* **1** [Apt, particularly with one's hands] skillful, expert, adroit. **2** [Mentally quick] smart, bright, shrewd.

**cliché** *n.* commonplace, platitude, stereotype, proverb, saying, slogan, trite phrase, stereotyped saying, vapid expression, triteness, banality, triviality, staleness, hackneyed phrase, trite idea.

**client** *n.* customer, patient, patron.

**climate** *n.* characteristic weather, atmospheric conditions, meteorologic conditions, aridity, humidity, weather conditions.

**climax** *n.* peak, apex, highest point, culmination, acme, pinnacle, crest, zenith, summit, apogee, extremity, limit, utmost extent, highest degree, turning point, crowning point.—*Ant.* depression, anticlimax, nadir.

**climb** *v.* scale, work one's way up, ascend gradually, scramble up, clamber up, swarm up, start up, go up, ascend, struggle up, get on, climb on, progress upward, rise, lift, rise hand over hand, come up, creep up, escalate, surmount, shinny up, shoot up.

**cling** *v.* adhere, clasp, hold fast.

**close** *a.* **1** [Nearby] neighboring, across the street, around the corner. **2** [Intimate] confidential, intimate, familiar. **3** [Compact] dense, solid, compressed. **4** [Stingy] narrow, parsimonious, niggardly. **5** [Stifling] sticky, stuffy, unventilated, moldy, heavy, motionless, uncomfortable, choky, stale-smelling, musty, stagnant, confined, suffocating, sweltering, tight, stale, oppressive, breathless.—*Ant.* fresh, refreshing, brisk. **6** [Similar] resembling, having common qualities, much the same.

**close** *n.* termination, adjournment, ending.

**close** *v.* **1** [To put a stop to] conclude, finish, terminate. **2** [To put a stopper into] shut, stop down, choke off, stuff, clog, prevent passage, shut off, turn off, lock, block, bar, dam, cork, seal, button.—*Ant.* open, uncork, unseal. **3** [To come together] meet, unite, agree. **4** [To shut] slam, close down, shut down, shut up, seal, fasten, bolt, clench, bar, shutter, clap, lock, bring to.

**clothes** *pl.n.* wearing apparel, raiment, clothing, garments, garb, vesture, vestments, attire, array, casual wear, informal wear, evening clothes, work clothes, suit of clothes, costume, wardrobe, trappings, gear, underclothes, outfit, get-up*, rags, togs*, duds*, threads*, things.

**clue** *n.* evidence, trace, mark.

**clumsy** *a.* ungainly, awkward, inexpert.

**coarse** *a.* **1** [Not fine] rough, rude, unrefined. **2** [Vulgar] low, common, base.

**coat** *n.* **1** [An outer garment] topcoat, overcoat, cloak, suit coat, tuxedo, dinner jacket, sport coat, dress coat, mink coat, fur coat, ski jacket, mackintosh, raincoat, jacket, windbreaker, peacoat, three-quarter-length coat, wrap, leather jacket, southwester, slicker. **2** [The covering of an animal] protective covering, shell, scale, fleece, epidermis, ectoderm, pelt, membrane. **3** [An applied covering] coating, layer, wash, primer, finish, glaze, crust, painting, overlay, whitewashing, varnish, lacquer, gloss, tinge, prime coat, plaster.

**coax** *v.* persuade, cajole, inveigle.

**coerce** *v.* impel, compel, constrain.

**coil** *n.* curl, turn, ring, wind, convolution, twine, twist, twirl, lap, loop, curlicue, corkscrew, roll, spiral, helix, scroll.

**cold** *a.* **1** [*Said of the weather*] crisp, cool, icy, freezing, frosty, frigid, wintry, bleak, nippy, brisk, keen, penetrating, snowy, frozen, cutting, snappy, piercing, chill, bitter, numbing, severe, stinging, glacial, intense, Siberian, chilly, sharp, raw, nipping, arctic, polar, below zero, biting.—*Ant.* hot, warm, heated. **2** [*Said of persons, animals, etc.*] cold-blooded, frozen, clammy, stiff, chilled, frostbitten, shivering, blue from cold.—*Ant.* hot, perspiring, thawed. **3** [*Said of temperament*] unconcerned, apathetic, distant. **—have** (or **get**) **cold feet** go back on one's word, hold back, back down. **—throw cold water on** dishearten, squelch, dampen.

**cold** *n.* **1** [Conditions having a cold temperature] coldness, frozenness, chilliness, frostiness, draft, frostbite, absence of warmth, want of heat, chill, shivers, coolness, shivering, goose flesh, numbness, iciness, frigidity, freeze, glaciation, refrigeration.—*Ant.* heat, warmth, heat wave. **2** [Head or respiratory congestion] cough, sore throat, sickness, cold in the head, sinus trouble, cold in one's chest, bronchial irritation, common cold, laryngitis, hay fever, whooping cough, influenza, flu, asthma, bronchitis, strep throat*, strep*, sniffles*, frog in one's throat. **—catch cold** come down with a cold, become ill, get a cold. **—(out) in the cold** forgotten, ignored, rejected.

**collapse** *n.* breakdown, downfall, destruction.

**collect** *v.* **1** [To bring into one place] amass, consolidate, convoke. **2** [To come together] congregate, assemble, flock. **3** [To obtain funds] solicit, raise, secure.

**collection** *n.* specimens, samples, examples, extracts, gems, models, assortment, medley, accumulation, pile, stack, group, assemblage, compilation, mass, quantity, selection, treasury, anthology, miscellany, aggregation, combination, number, store, stock, digest, arrangement, concentration, discoveries, finds, batch, mess, lot, heap, bunch.

**college** *n.* institute, institution, community college, liberal arts college, teachers college, junior college, state college, denominational college, nondenominational college, private college, business school, technical school, higher education, graduate school, medical school, law school, seminary.

**collision** *n.* impact, contact, shock, accident, encounter, crash, colliding, bump, jar, jolt, sideswipe, strike, hit, slam, blow, thud, thump, knock, smash, butt, rap, head-on crash, fender bender*.

**colony** *n.* settlement, dependency, subject state, colonial state, dominion, offshoot, political possession, province, group, new land, protectorate, hive, daughter country, satellite state, community, group migration.

**color** *n.* hue, tone, tint, shade, tinge, dye, complexion, brilliance, undertone, value, iridescence, intensity, coloration, discoloration, pigmentation, coloring, cast, glow, blush, wash, tincture. **—change color** flush, redden, become red in the face. **—lose color** become pale, blanch, faint.

**color** *v.* chalk, daub, gild, enamel, lacquer, suffuse, stipple, pigment, glaze, tinge, tint, stain, tone, shade, dye, wash, crayon, chrome, enliven, embellish, give color to, adorn, imbue, emblazon, illuminate, rouge.

**column** *n.* **1** [A pillar] support, prop, shaft, monument, totem, pylon, obelisk, tower, minaret, cylinder, mast, monolith, upright, pedestal. **2** [Journalistic commentary] comment, article, editorial.

**combination** *n.* **1** [The act of combining] uniting, joining, unification. **2** [An association] union, alliance, federation. **3** [Something formed by combining] compound, aggregate, blend.

**come** *v.* **1** [To move toward] close in, advance, draw near. **2** [To arrive] appear at, reach, attain. **3** [To be available] appear, be at one's disposal, be ready, be obtainable, be handy, be accessible, be able to be reached, show up, turn up. **4** [*To have an orgasm] to reach sexual fulfillment, ejaculate, climax. **—as good as they come** excellent, superior, fine. **—how come?*** for what reason?, how so?, what is the cause of that?

**come about** *v.* occur, take place, result.

**comedy** *n.* comic drama, tragicomedy, stand-up comedy, situation comedy, sitcom, musical comedy, farce, satire, burlesque, slapstick, light entertainment.

**come through** *v.* **1** [To be successful] accomplish, score, triumph. **2** [To survive] live through, persist, withstand. **3** [To do] accomplish, achieve, carry out.

**comfort** *n.* rest, quiet, relaxation, repose, relief, poise, well-being, cheer, abundance, sufficiency, gratification, luxury, warmth, plenty, pleasure, happiness, contentment, restfulness, peacefulness, cheerfulness, coziness, exhilaration, complacency, bed of roses*.—*Ant.* weakness, discomfort, uneasiness.

**comfort** *v.* **1** [To console] share with, commiserate, solace, grieve with, cheer, gladden, uphold, hearten, pat on the back, put someone in a good humor, sustain, support, help, aid, confirm, reassure, refresh.—*Ant.* discourage, be indifferent, depress. **2** [To make easy physically] alleviate, relieve, make comfortable, assuage, soothe, mitigate, gladden, quiet one's fears, help one in need, lighten one's burden, encourage, calm, revive, sustain, aid, assist, nourish, support, compose oneself, delight, divert, bolster up, invigorate, refresh, put at ease, reassure, warm, lighten, soften, remedy, release, restore, free, make well, revitalize.—*Ant.* weaken, make uneasy, worsen.

**comfortable** *a.* **1** [In physical ease] contented, cheerful, easy, at rest, relaxed, at ease, untroubled, healthy, rested, pleased, complacent, soothed, relieved, strengthened, restored, in comfort, at home with, without care, snug as a bug in a rug*.—*Ant.* uneasy, ill, disturbed. **2** [Conducive to physical ease] satisfactory, snug, cozy, warm, sheltered, convenient, protected, cared for, appropriate, useful, roomy, spacious, luxurious, rich, satisfying, restful, in comfort, well-off, well-to-do.—*Ant.* shabby, run-down, uncomfortable.

**comforting** *a.* sympathetic, cheering, encouraging, invigorating, health-giving, warming, consoling, sustaining, reassuring, inspiring, refreshing, upholding, relieving, soothing, lightening, mitigating, alleviating, softening, curing, restoring, releasing, freeing, revitalizing, tranquilizing.—*Ant.* disturbing, distressing, upsetting.

**coming** *a.* **1** [Approaching] advancing, drawing near, progressing, nearing, in the offing, arriving, gaining upon, pursuing, getting near, converging, subsequent, coming in, close at hand, coming on, near at hand, almost upon, immediate, future, in view, preparing to come, eventual, fated, written, hereafter, at hand, in store, due, about to happen, hoped for, deserved, close, imminent, prospective, anticipated, forthcoming, certain, ordained, impending, to be, expected, near, pending, foreseen, in the cards, in the wind.—*Ant.* distant, going, leaving. **2** [Having a promising future] promising, advancing, probable. **3** [Future] lying ahead, pending, impending.

**command** *n.* order, injunction, direction, dictation, demand, decree, prohibition, interdiction, canon, rule, call, summons, imposition, precept, mandate, charge, behest, edict, proclamation, instruction, proscription, ban, requirement, dictate, subpoena, commandment, dictum, word of command, writ, citation, notification, will, regulation, ordinance, act, fiat, bidding, word, requisition, ultimatum, exaction, enactment, caveat, prescript, warrant.

**command** *v.* **1** [To issue an order] charge, tell, demand. **2** [To have control] rule, dominate, master.

**commandeer** *v.* appropriate, take, confiscate.

**commemorate** *v.* solemnize, honor, memorialize.

**commemoration** *n.* recognition, remembrance, observance.

**commend** *v.* laud, support, acclaim.

**comment** *v.* observe, remark, criticize, notice, state, express, pronounce, assert, affirm, mention, interject, say, note, touch upon, disclose, bring out, point out, conclude.

**commercial** *a.* trading, business, financial, economic, materialistic, practical, profitable, mercantile, merchandising, bartering, exchange, fiscal, monetary, trade, market, retail, wholesale, marketable, in the market, for sale, profit-making, money-making, across the counter.

**commission** *v.* send, delegate, appoint, authorize, charge, empower, constitute, ordain, commit, entrust, send out, dispatch, deputize, assign, engage, employ, inaugurate, invest, name, nominate, hire, enable, license, command, elect, select.

**commit** *v.* **1** [To perpetrate] do something wrong, be guilty of, execute. **2** [To entrust] confide, delegate, relegate to, leave to, give to do, promise, assign, turn over to, put in the hands of, charge, invest, rely upon, depend upon, confer a trust, bind over, make responsible for, put an obligation upon, employ, dispatch, send, vest in, engage, commission.—*Ant.* dismiss, relieve of, discharge.

**commitment** *n.* pledge, responsibility, agreement.

**committee** *n.* consultants, board, bureau, council, cabinet, investigators, trustees, appointed group, board of inquiry, representatives, investigating committee, executive committee, standing committee, planning board, ad hoc committee, special committee, grand jury, referees, task force, study group, subcommittee.

**commodity** *n.* goods, articles, stocks, merchandise, wares, materials, possessions, property, assets, belongings, things, stock in trade, consumers' goods, line, what one handles, what one is showing.

**common** *a.* **1** [Ordinary] universal, familiar, natural, normal, everyday, accepted, commonplace, characteristic, customary, bourgeois, conventional, passable, general, informal, wearisome, unassuming, pedestrian, lower-level, habitual, prevalent, probable, typical, prosaic, simple, current, prevailing, trite, household, second-rate, banal, unvaried, homely, colloquial, trivial, stock, oft-repeated, indiscriminate, tedious, worn-out, hackneyed, monotonous, stale, casual, undistinguished, uneducated, artless, workaday, provincial, unsophisticated, unrefined, untutored, plain, uncultured, vulgar, unadorned, ugly, obvious, average, orthodox, mediocre, humdrum, well-known, insipid, stereotyped, patent, moderate, middling, abiding, indifferent, tolerable, temperate, innocuous, undistinguished, run-of-the-mill, not too bad*, garden-variety, fair-to-middling*, so-so, nothing to write home about*.—*Ant.* unique, extraordinary, unnatural. **2** [Of frequent occurrence] customary, constant, usual. **3** [Generally known] general, prevalent, well-known. **4** [Low] cheap, inferior, shoddy. **5** [Held or enjoyed in common] shared, joint, mutual. **—in common** shared, communal, mutually held.

**commotion** *n.* violence, tumult, uproar.

**communal** *a.* shared, cooperative, mutual.

**communicate** *v.* **1** [To impart information] convey, inform, advise. **2** [To be in communication] correspond, be in touch, have access to, contact, reach, hear from, be within reach, be in correspondence with, be near, be close to, have the confidence of, associate with, establish contact with, be in agreement with, be in agreement about, confer, talk, converse, chat, speak together, deal with, write to, telephone, wire, cable, fax, network, reply, answer, have a meeting of minds, find a common denominator.—*Ant.* avoid, withdraw, elude.

**communication** *n.* talk, utterance, announcing, extrasensory perception, telepathy, ESP, publication, writing, drawing, painting, broadcasting, televising, correspondence, disclosure, speaking, disclosing, conference, faxing, telephoning, wiring, cabling, networking, description, mention, announcement, presentation, interchange, expression, narration, relation, declaration, assertion, elucidation, transmission, reception, reading, translating, interpreting, news, ideas, statement, speech, language, warning, communiqué, briefing, bulletin, summary, information, report, account, publicity, translation, printed work, advice, tidings, conversation.

**company** *n.* **1** [A group of people] assembly, throng, band. **2** [People organized for business] partnership, firm, corporation. **3** [A guest or guests] visitors, callers, overnight guests. **—keep (a person) company** stay with, visit, amuse. **—part company** separate, part, stop associating with.

**compare** *v.* **1** [To liken] relate, connect, make like, notice the similarities, associate, link, distinguish between, bring near, put alongside, reduce to a common denominator, declare similar, equate, match, express by metaphor, correlate, parallel, show to be analogous, identify with, bring into meaningful relation with, collate, balance, parallel, bring into comparison, estimate relatively, set over against, compare notes, exchange observations, weigh one thing against another, set side by side, correlate, measure, place in juxtaposition, note the similarities and differences of, juxtapose, draw a parallel between, tie up, come up to, stack up with. **2** [To examine on a comparative basis] contrast, set against, weigh. **3** [To stand in relationship to another] match, vie, rival. **—beyond** (or **past** or **without**) **compare** incomparable, without equal, distinctive.

**compensation** *n.* remuneration, recompense, indemnity, satisfaction, remittal, return for services, commission, gratuity, reimbursement, allowance, deserts, remittance, salary, stipend, wages, hire, earnings, settlement, honorarium, coverage, consideration, damages, repayment, fee, reckoning, bonus, premium, amends, reward, advantage, profit, benefit, gain, kickback*.—*Ant.* loss, deprivation, confiscation.

**compete** *v.* enter competition, take part, strive, struggle, vie with, be in the running, become a competitor, enter the lists, run for, participate in, engage in a contest, oppose, wrestle, be rivals, battle, bid, spar, fence, collide, face, clash, encounter, match wits, play, grapple, take on all comers, go in for*, lock horns, go out for.

**competition** *n.* race, match, contest, meet, fight, bout, boxing match, game of skill, trial, sport, athletic event, wrestling.

**compile** *v.* collect, arrange, assemble.

**complacent** *a.* self-satisfied, contented, self-righteous.

**complain** *v.* disapprove, accuse, deplore, criticize, denounce, differ, disagree, dissent, charge, report adversely, reproach, oppose, grumble, whine, whimper, remonstrate, fret, protest, fuss, moan, make a fuss, take exception to, object to, deprecate, enter a demurrer, demur, defy, carp, impute, indict, attack, refute, grouse*, kick*, bitch*, grouch, gripe*, grunt, beef*, bellyache*, kick up a fuss*.—*Ant.* approve, sanction, countenance.

**complementary** *a.* paired, mated, corresponding.

**complete** *a.* **1** [Not lacking in any part] total, replete, entire. **2** [Finished] concluded, terminated, ended. **3** [Perfect] flawless, unblemished, impeccable.

**complete** *v.* execute, consummate, perfect, accomplish, realize, perform, achieve, fill out, fulfill, equip, actualize, furnish, make up, elaborate, make good, make complete, develop, fill in, refine, effect, carry out, crown, get through, round out.—*Ant.* begin, start, commence.

**complex** *a.* **1** [Composed of several parts] composite, heterogeneous, conglomerate, multiple, mosaic, manifold, multiform, compound, complicated, aggregated, involved, combined, compact, compounded, miscellaneous, multiplex, multifarious, variegated. **2** [Difficult to understand] entangled, tangled, circuitous, convoluted, puzzling, mixed, mingled, muddled, jumbled, impenetrable, inscrutable, unfathomable, undecipherable, bewildering, intricate, perplexing, complicated, involved, enigmatic, hidden, knotted, meandering, winding, tortuous, snarled, rambling, twisted, disordered, devious, discursive, cryptic, inextricable, knotty, roundabout.—*Ant.* understandable, plain, apparent.

**complex** *n.* **1** [An obsession] phobia, mania, repressed emotions, repressed desires. **2** [A composite] conglomerate, syndrome, ecosystem, aggregation, association, totality.

**complicate** *v.* combine, fold, multiply, twist, snarl up, associate with, involve, obscure, confound, muddle, clog, jumble, interrelate, elaborate, embarrass, implicate, tangle, conceal, mix up, impede, perplex, hinder, hamper, handicap, tie up with, ball up*.—*Ant.* simplify, clear up, unfold.

**compliment** *n.* felicitation, tribute, approval, commendation, endorsement, confirmation, sanction, applause, flattery, acclaim, adulation, notice, puff, regards, honor, appreciation, respects, blessing, ovation, veneration, admiration, congratulation, homage, good word, sentiment.—*Ant.* abuse, censure, disapproval.

**compliment** *v.* wish joy to, remember, commemorate, pay one's respects, honor, cheer, salute, hail, toast, applaud, extol, celebrate, felicitate, pay tribute to, be in favor of, commend, endorse, sanction, confirm, acclaim, pay a compliment to, sing the praises of, speak highly of, exalt, applaud, worship, eulogize, glorify, magnify, fawn upon, butter up*, puff, hand it to*.—*Ant.* denounce, disapprove of, censure.

**complimentary** *a.* flattering, laudatory, approving, celebrating, honoring, respectful, congratulatory, well-wishing, highly favorable, praising, singing the praises of, with highest recommendations, with high praise.

**compose** *v.* **1** [To be the parts or the ingredients] constitute, comprise*, go into the making of, make up, merge into, be a component, be an element of, belong to, consist of, be made of. **2** [To create] fabricate, produce, write music, score, orchestrate, forge, discover, design, conceive, imagine, make up, turn out, draw up.

**composure** *n.* serenity, peace of mind, calm, calmness, self-possession, nonchalance, cool-headedness, control, self-control, balance, contentment, tranquillity, stability, harmony, assurance, self-assurance, poise, composed state of mind, even temper, equanimity, coolness, level-headedness, fortitude, moderation, gravity, sobriety, a cool head, presence of mind, equilibrium, aplomb, self-restraint, ease, evenness, complacence, tolerance, content, quiet, command of one's faculties, forbearance, cool*.—*Ant.* exuberance, passion, wildness.

**compress** *v.* condense, compact, press together, consolidate, squeeze together, tighten, cramp, contract, crowd, constrict, abbreviate, shrivel, make brief, reduce, dehydrate, pack, shorten, shrink, narrow, abridge, bind tightly, wrap closely, wedge, boil down, cram.—*Ant.* spread, stretch, expand.

**compromise** *v.* agree, conciliate, find a middle ground.

**concede** *v.* yield, grant, acknowledge.

**concentrate** *v.* **1** [To bring or come together] amass, mass, assemble, combine, consolidate, compact, condense, reduce, hoard, garner, centralize, store, bring into a small compass, bring toward a central point, embody, localize, strengthen, direct toward one object, constrict, fix, cramp, focus, reduce, intensify, crowd together, flock together, contract, muster, bunch, heap up, swarm, conglomerate, stow away, congest, narrow, compress, converge, center, collect, cluster, congregate, huddle. **2** [To employ all one's mental powers] think intensely, give attention to, meditate upon, ponder, focus attention on, direct attention to one object, weigh, consider closely, scrutinize, regard carefully, contemplate, study deeply, examine closely, brood over, put one's mind to, be engrossed in, be absorbed in, attend, give exclusive attention to, occupy the thoughts with, fix one's attention, apply the mind, give heed, focus one's thought, give the mind to, direct the mind upon, center, think hard, rack one's brains, be on the beam*, keep one's eye on the ball*, knuckle down, buckle down.—*Ant.* drift, be inattentive, ignore.

**concept** *n.* idea, theory, notion.

**conception** *n.* **1** [The act of conceiving mentally] perception, apprehension, comprehension, imagining, speculating, meditation, dreaming, cogitating, deliberating, concentrating, meditating, realization, consideration, speculation, understanding, cognition, mental grasp, apperception, forming an idea, formulation of a principle. **2** [The act of conceiving physically] inception, impregnation, insemination.

**concern** *v.* **1** [To have reference to] refer to, pertain to, relate to, be related to, have significance for, bear on, regard, be connected with, be about, have to do with, be a matter of concern to, have a bearing on, have connections with, be applicable to, depend upon, be dependent upon, answer to, deal with, belong to, touch upon, figure in. **2** [Concern oneself] be concerned, become involved, take pains.

**concise** *a.* succinct, brief, condensed.

**conclusion** *n.* **1** [An end] finish, termination, completion. **2** [A decision] determination, resolve, resolution. —**in conclusion** lastly, in closing, in the end.

**concrete** *a.* **1** [Specific] particular, solid, precise. **2** [Made of concrete] cement, poured, prefabricated, precast, concrete and steel, compact, unyielding.

**concurrent** *a.* synchronal, parallel, coexisting.

**condition** *n.* **1** [A state] situation, position, status. **2** [A requisite] stipulation, contingency, provision. **3** [A limitation] restriction, qualification, prohibition. **4** [State of health] fitness, tone, trim, shape*. **5** [*Illness] ailment, infirmity, temper.

**conduct** *n.* **1** [Behavior] deportment, demeanor, manner. **2** [Management] supervision, plan, organization.

**conduct** *v.* **1** [To guide] escort, convoy, attend. **2** [To manage] administer, handle, carry on.

**confession** *n.* **1** [The act of confessing] concession, allowance, owning to, owning up, revelation, disclosure, publication, affirmation, assertion, admission, declaration, telling, exposure, narration, exposé, proclamation, making public.—*Ant.* denial, concealment, disclaimer. **2** [A sacrament] absolution, contrition, repentance.

**confidence** *n.* self-confidence, self-reliance, morale, fearlessness, boldness, resolution, firmness, sureness, faith in oneself, tenacity, fortitude, certainty, daring, spirit, reliance, grit, cool*, heart, backbone, nerve, spunk*.

**confidential** *a.* classified, intimate, privy.

**confined** *a.* **1** [Restricted] limited, hampered, compassed. **2** [Bedridden] on one's back, ill, laid up. **3** [In prison] behind bars, locked up, in bonds, in irons, in chains, in jail, imprisoned, jailed, immured, incarcerated, detained, under lock and key.—*Ant.* free, released, at liberty.

**confirm** *v.* **1** [To ratify] sanction, affirm, settle. **2** [To prove] verify, authenticate, validate.

**confirmation** *n.* ratification, proving, authentication, corroboration, support, endorsement, sanction, authorization, verification, affirmation, acceptance, passage, validation, approval, attestation, assent, admission, recognition, witness, consent, testimony, agreement, evidence.—*Ant.* cancellation, annulment, disapproval.

**conflict** *n.* struggle, strife, engagement.

**conflict** *v.* clash, contrast, contend.

**conform** *v.* comply, accord, submit, accommodate, live up to, fit, suit, acclimate, accustom, be regular, harmonize, adapt, be guided by, fit the pattern, be in fashion, reconcile, obey, grow used to, do as others do, get in line, fall in with, go by, adhere to, adjust to, keep to, keep up, get one's bearings, keep up with the Joneses*, chime in with, join the parade, play the game*, go according to Hoyle, follow the beaten path, toe the line, follow suit, run with the pack, follow the crowd, when in Rome do as the Romans do*.—*Ant.* differ, conflict, disagree.

**confuse** *v.* upset, befuddle, mislead, misinform, puzzle, perplex, confound, fluster, bewilder, embarrass, daze, astonish, disarrange, disorder, jumble, blend, mix, mingle, cloud, fog, stir up, disconcert, abash, agitate, amaze, worry, trouble, snarl, unsettle, muddle, clutter, complicate, involve, rattle, derange, baffle, frustrate, perturb, dismay, distract, entangle, encumber, befog, obscure, mystify, make a mess of, throw off the scent, cross up, foul up, mix up, ball up*, lead astray, stump, rattle, make one's head swim.—*Ant.* clear up, clarify, untangle.

**confusion** *n.* complication, intricacy, muss, untidiness, complexity, difficulty, mistake, bewilderment, turmoil, tumult, pandemonium, commotion, stir, ferment, disarray, jumble, convulsion, bustle, trouble, row, riot, uproar, fracas, distraction, agitation, emotional upset, daze, astonishment, surprise, fog, haze, consternation, racket, excitement, chaos, turbulence, dismay, uncertainty, irregularity, maze, interruption, stoppage, clutter, entanglement, backlash, clog, break, breakdown, knot, obstruction, trauma, congestion, interference, nervousness, disorganization, muddle, mass, lump, snarl, to-do*, hubbub, tie-up, botch, rumpus, scramble, shuffle, mess, hodgepodge, stew, going round and round*, jam*, fix*, bull in a china shop.—*Ant.* order, quiet, calm.

**congestion** *n.* profusion, crowdedness, overpopulation, press, traffic jam, overcrowding, overdevelopment, too many, too much, concentration, surplus.

**connect** *v.* **1** [To join] combine, unite, attach. **2** [To associate] relate, equate, correlate.

**connection** *n.* **1** [Relationship] kinship, association, reciprocity. **2** [A junction] combination, juncture, consolidation. **3** [A link] attachment, fastening, bond. **—in connection with** in conjunction with, associated with, together with.

**conquer** *v.* subdue, overcome, crush.

**conscious** *a.* cognizant, informed, sure, certain, assured, discerning, knowing, sensible, sensitive, acquainted, attentive, watchful, mindful, vigilant, understanding, keen, alert, alert to, alive to, sensitive to, conscious of, mindful of, cognizant of, hip to*, on to*, with it*.—*Ant.* unaware, insensitive, inattentive.

**consecutive** *a.* continuous, chronological, serial, in turn, progressive, connected, in order, in sequence, sequential, going on, continuing, one after another, one after the other, serialized, numerical.

**consent** *n.* assent, approval, acquiescence.

**consent** *v.* accede, assent, acquiesce.

**conservative** *a.* conserving, preserving, unchanging, unchangeable, stable, constant, steady, traditional, reactionary, conventional, moderate, unprogressive, firm, obstinate, inflexible, opposed to change, cautious, sober, Tory, taking no chances, timid, fearful, unimaginative, right-wing, in a rut*, in a groove*.—*Ant.* radical, risky, changing.

**consider** *v.* allow for, provide for, grant, take up, concede, acknowledge, recognize, favor, value, take under advisement, deal with, regard, make allowance for, take into consideration, keep in mind, reckon with, play around with*, toss around, see about.—*Ant.* refuse, deny, reject.

**conspicuous** *a.* outstanding, eminent, distinguished, celebrated, noted, renowned, famed, notorious, important, influential, notable, illustrious, striking, prominent, well-known, arresting, remarkable, noticeable, flagrant, glaring, standing out like a sore thumb*.—*Ant.* unknown, inconspicuous, unsung.

**constant** *a.* steady, uniform, perpetual, unchanging, continual, uninterrupted, unvarying, connected, even, incessant, unbroken, nonstop, monotonous, standardized, regularized.

**constitute** *v.* **1** [To found] establish, develop, create. **2** [To make up] frame, compound, aggregate.

**construction** *n.* **1** [The act of constructing] formation, manufacture, building. **2** [A method of constructing] structure, arrangement, organization, system, plan, development, steel and concrete, contour, format, mold, cast, outline, type, shape, build, cut, fabric, formation, turn, framework, configuration, brick and mortar, prefab.

**consult** *v.* take counsel, deliberate, confer, parley, conspire with, be closeted with, compare notes about, put heads together, commune, treat, negotiate, debate, argue, talk over, call in, ask advice of, turn to, seek advice.

**consume** *v.* **1** [To use] use, use up, wear out. **2** [To eat or drink] absorb, feed, devour.

**contagious** *a.* communicable, infectious, transmittable, spreading, poisonous, epidemic, deadly, endemic, tending to spread.

**contain** *v.* **1** [Include] comprehend, embrace, be composed of. **2** [Restrict] hold, keep back, stop.

**container** *n.* receptacle, basket, bin, bowl, dish, tub, holder, cauldron, vessel, capsule, package, packet, chest, purse, pod, pouch, cask, sack, pot, pottery, jug, bucket, canteen, pit, box, carton, canister, crate, pail, kettle.

**contaminate** *v.* pollute, infect, defile.

**contemporary** *a.* present, fashionable, current.

**continual** *a.* uninterrupted, unbroken, connected.

**continue** *interj.* keep on, carry on; keep going, keep talking, keep reading, etc.; keep it up.

**continue** *v.* **1** [To persist] persevere, carry forward, maintain, carry on, keep on, go on, run on, live on, never stop, sustain, promote, progress, uphold, forge ahead, remain, press onward, make headway, move ahead, keep the ball rolling, leave no stone unturned*, chip away at*.—*Ant.* end, cease, give up. **2** [To resume] begin again, renew, begin over, return to, take up again, begin where one left off, be reestablished, be restored.—*Ant.* halt, discontinue, postpone.

**contract** *n.* agreement, compact, stipulation, contractual statement, contractual obligation, understanding, promise, pledge, covenant, obligation, guarantee, settlement, gentlemen's agreement, commitment, bargain, pact, arrangement, the papers, deal.

**contract** *v.* **1** [To diminish] draw in, draw back, shrivel, weaken, shrink, become smaller, decline, fall away, subside, grow less, ebb, wane, lessen, lose, dwindle, recede, fall off, wither, waste, condense, constrict, deflate, evaporate.—*Ant.* stretch, expand, strengthen. **2** [To cause to diminish] abbreviate, narrow, condense. **3** [To enter into an agreement by contract] pledge, undertake, come to terms, make terms, adjust, dicker, make a bargain, agree on, limit, bound, establish by agreement, engage, stipulate, consent, enter into a contractual obligation, sign the papers, negotiate a contract, accept an offer, obligate oneself, put something in writing, swear to, sign for, give one's word, shake hands on it, initial, close. **4** [To catch; *said of diseases*] get, incur, become infected with.

**contradict** *v.* differ, call in question, confront.

**contrary** *a.* **1** [Opposed] antagonistic to, hostile, counter. **2** [Unfavorable] untimely, bad, unpropitious. **3** [Obstinate] willful, contradictory, headstrong.

**contrast** *n.* divergence, incompatibility, variation, variance, dissimilarity, inequality, distinction, oppositeness, contradiction, diversity, disagreement, opposition.—*Ant.* agreement, similarity, uniformity.

**contribute** *v.* add, share, endow, supply, furnish, bestow, present, confer, commit, dispense, settle upon, grant, afford, donate, dispense, assign, give away, subscribe, devote, will, bequeath, subsidize, hand out, ante up*, chip in*, kick in*, have a hand in, get in the act*, go Dutch*.—*Ant.* receive, accept, take.

**contribution** *n.* donation, present, bestowal.

**contrive** *v.* make, improvise, devise.

**control** *v.* **1** [To hold in check] constrain, master, repress. **2** [To direct] lead, rule, dominate, direct, determine, master, conquer, conduct, administer, supervise, run, coach, head, dictate, manage, influence, prevail, domineer, constrain, charge, subdue, push, coerce, oblige, train, limit, officiate, drive, move, regulate, take over, rule the roost*, crack the whip*, call the shots*.

**controversial** *a.* disputable, debatable, suspect.

**convenient** *a.* **1** [Serving one's convenience] ready, favorable, suitable, adapted, available, fitted, suited, adaptable, roomy, well-arranged, appropriate, well-planned, decent, agreeable, acceptable, useful, serviceable, assisting, aiding, beneficial, accommodating, advantageous, conducive, comfortable, opportune, timesaving, labor-saving.—*Ant.*

disturbing, unserviceable, disadvantageous. **2** [Near] handy, close by, easy to reach.

**convention** *n.* **1** [An occasion for which delegates assemble] assembly, convocation, meeting. **2** [Custom] practice, habit, fashion.

**conventional** *a.* **1** [Established by convention] accustomed, prevailing, accepted, customary, regular, standard, orthodox, normal, typical, expected, usual, routine, general, everyday, commonplace, ordinary, plain, current, popular, prevalent, predominant, expected, well-known, stereotyped, in established usage.—*Ant.* unusual, atypical, unpopular. **2** [In accordance with convention] established, sanctioned, correct. **3** [Devoted to or bound by convention] formal, stereotyped, orthodox, narrow, narrow-minded, dogmatic, parochial, strict, rigid, puritanical, inflexible, hidebound, conservative, conforming, believing, not heretical, literal, bigoted, obstinate, straight*, straight-laced.—*Ant.* liberal, broad-minded, unconventional.

**conversation** *n.* talk, discussion, communion, consultation, hearing, conference, gossip, chat, rap*, dialogue, discourse, expression of views, mutual exchange, questions and answers, traffic in ideas, getting to know one another, general conversation, question, talking it out, heart-to-heart talk, powwow*, bull session*, chitchat.

**convey** *v.* pass on, communicate, conduct.

**cook** *v.* prepare, fix, warm up, warm over, stew, simmer, sear, braise, scald, broil, parch, scorch, poach, dry, chafe, fricasee, percolate, steam, bake, griddle, brew, boil down, seethe, barbecue, grill, roast, pan-fry, panbroil, deep-fry, French fry, brown.

**cool** *a.* **1** [Having a low temperature] cooling, frigid, frosty, wintry, somewhat cold, chilly, shivery, chill, chilling, refrigerated, air-conditioned, snappy, nippy, biting.—*Ant.* warm, tepid, heated. **2** [Calm] unruffled, imperturbable, composed. **3** [Somewhat angry or disapproving] disapproving, annoyed, offended. **4** [*Excellent] neat*, keen*, groovy*. **—play it cool** hold back, underplay, exercise restraint.

**cool** *v.* lose heat, lessen, freeze, reduce, calm, chill, cool off, become cold, be chilled to the bone, become chilly, moderate, refrigerate, air-cool, air-condition, pre-cool, frost, freeze, quick-freeze.—*Ant.* burn, warm, defrost.

**cooperate** *v.* unite, combine, concur, conspire, pool, join forces, act in concert, hold together, stick together, comply with, join in, go along with, make common cause, unite efforts, share in, second, take part, work in unison, participate, work side by side with, side with, take sides with, join hands with, play along with, play fair, throw in with, fall in with, be in cahoots*, chip in*, stand shoulder to shoulder, pull together.—*Ant.* differ, act independently, diverge.

**cooperative** *a.* cooperating, agreeing, joining, combining, collaborating, coactive, uniting, concurring, participating, in joint operation.

**coordinate** *v.* harmonize, regulate, organize.

**copy** *n.* imitation, facsimile, photostat, likeness, print, similarity, mimeograph sheet, simulation, mirror, impersonation, offprint, Xerox (trademark), semblance, imitation of an original, forgery, counterfeit, reprint, rubbing, transcript, carbon, replica, typescript, cast, tracing, counterpart, likeness, portrait, model, reflection, representation, study, photograph, carbon copy, certified copy, office copy, typed copy, pencil copy, fair copy, ditto.

**copy** *v.* **1** [To imitate] follow, mimic, ape. **2** [To reproduce] represent, duplicate, counterfeit, forge, cartoon, depict, portray, picture, draw, sketch, paint, sculpture, mold, engrave.

**corner** *n.* **1** [A projecting edge] ridge, sharp edge, projection. **2** [A recess] niche, nook, indentation. **3** [A sharp turn] bend, veer, shift. **4** [The angle made where ways intersect] V, Y, intersection. **5** [*Difficulty] impediment, distress, knot. **—around the corner** immediate, imminent, next. **—cut corners** cut down, shorten, reduce.

**correct** *a.* **1** [Accurate] exact, true, right. **2** [Proper] suitable, becoming, fitting.

**correct** *v.* better, help, remove the errors of, remove the faults of, remedy, alter, rectify, accommodate for, make right, mend, amend, fix up, do over, reform, remodel, review, reconstruct, reorganize, edit, revise, make corrections, put to rights, put in order, doctor*, touch up, polish.

**correspond** *v.* **1** [To be alike] compare, match, be identical. **2** [To communicate with, usually by letter] write to, reply to, drop a line to.

**corrode** *v.* rot, degenerate, deteriorate.

**corrupt** *v.* pervert, degrade, demean, lower, pull down, reduce, adulterate, depreciate, deprave, debauch, defile, demoralize, pollute, taint, contaminate, infect, stain, spoil, blight, blemish, undermine, impair, mar, injure, harm, hurt, damage, deface, disfigure, deform, abuse, maltreat, ill-treat, outrage, mistreat, misuse, dishonor, disgrace, violate, waste, ravage, cause to degenerate.—*Ant.* clean, purify, restore.

**corruption** *n.* **1** [Vice] baseness, depravity, degradation. **2** [Conduct involving graft] extortion, exploitation, fraudulence, misrepresentation, dishonesty, bribery, racket.

**costly** *a.* high-priced, dear, precious.

**council** *n.* advisory board, cabinet, directorate.

**counsel** *n.* **1** [Advice] guidance, instruction, information. **2** [A lawyer] attorney, legal adviser, barrister. **—keep one's own counsel** be secretive, conceal oneself, keep quiet.

**counselor** *n.* guide, instructor, mentor.

**count** *v.* compute, reckon, enumerate, number, add up, figure, count off, count up, foot up, count noses.

**country** *a.* **1** [*Said of people*] rural, homey, unpolished. **2** [*Said of areas*] rustic, agrarian, rural.

**country** *n.* **1** [Rural areas] farms, farmland, farming district, rural region, rural area, range, country district, back country, bush, forests, woodlands, backwoods, sparsely settled areas, sticks*, the boondocks*, boonies*.—*Ant.* city, borough, municipality. **2** [A nation] government, a people, a sovereign state. **3** [Land and all that is associated with it] homeland, native land, fatherland.

**courage** *n.* bravery, valor, boldness, fearlessness, spirit, audacity, audaciousness, temerity, manliness, pluck, mettle, enterprise, stoutheartedness, firmness, self-reliance, hardihood, heroism, gallantry, daring, prowess, power, resolution, dash, recklessness, defiance, the courage of one's convictions, spunk*, grit, backbone, guts*, what it takes*, nerve.—*Ant.* fear, cowardice, timidity.

**course** *n.* **1** [A route] passage, path, way. **2** [A prepared way, especially for racing] lap, cinder path, cinder track. **3** [A plan of study] subject, studies, curriculum. **4** [A series of lessons] classes, lectures, seminar. **—in due course** in due time, properly, conveniently. **—in the course of** during, in the process of, when. **—of course** certainly, by all means, indeed. **—off course** misdirected, erratic, going the wrong way. **—on course** on target, correct, going in the right direction.

**court** *n.* **1** [An enclosed, roofless area] square, courtyard, patio. **2** [An instrument for administering justice] tribunal, bench, magistrate, bar, session. **3** [A ruler and his surroundings] lords and ladies, attendants, royal household. **4** [An area for playing certain games] arena, rink, ring.

**courtesy** *n.* **1** [Courteous conduct] kindness, friendliness, affability, courteousness, gentleness, consideration, thoughtfulness, sympathy, geniality, cordiality, graciousness, tact, good manners, politeness, refinement, chivalry, gallantry, respect, deference, polished manners, good breeding. **2** [Courteous act] compassion, generosity, charity.

**cove** *n.* inlet, sound, lagoon.

**cover** *n.* **1** [A covering object] covering, ceiling, canopy, hood, sheath, sheet, awning, tent, umbrella, dome, stopper, lid, canvas, tarpaulin, book cover, folder, wrapper, wrapping paper, jacket, case, spread, tarp*. **2** [A covering substance] paint, varnish, polish. **3** [Shelter] harbor, asylum, refuge. **—take cover** conceal oneself, take shelter, go indoors. **—under cover** secretive, hiding, concealed.

**cover** *v.* **1** [To place as a covering] carpet, put on, overlay, surface, board up, superimpose, black in, black out. **2** [To wrap] envelop, enshroud, encase. **3** [To protect] shield, screen, house. **4** [To hide] screen, camouflage, mask. **5** [To include] embrace, comprise, incorporate. **6** [To travel] traverse, journey over, cross. **7** [To send down in plenty] drench, engulf, overcome. **8** [To report upon, especially for a newspaper] recount, narrate, relate.

**coward** *n.* sneak, milksop, shirker, deserter, weakling, alarmist, quitter*, chicken*, lily-liver*, scaredy-cat*, chicken-heart*, fraidy-cat*, yellow-belly*.

**cowardly** *a.* timid, frightened, afraid, fearful, shy, backward, cowering, apprehensive, nervous, anxious, dismayed, fainthearted, panicky, scared, scary*, jittery*, craven, mean-spirited, weak, soft, chicken-livered*, lily-livered*, yellow*, skulking, sneaking, cringing, trembling, shaken, crouching, running, quaking, shaking like a leaf, shaking in one's boots*.—*Ant.* brave, fearless, open.

**cozy** *a.* secure, sheltered, snug.

**crack** *n.* **1** [An incomplete break] chink, split, cut. **2** [A crevice] cleft, fissure, rift. **3** [A blow] hit, thwack, stroke. **4** [*A witty or brazen comment] return, witticism, jest.

**craft** *n.* **1** [Skill] proficiency, competence, aptitude. **2** [Trade] occupation, career, work. **3** [Ship] vessel, aircraft, spacecraft.

**crafty** *a.* clever, sharp, shrewd.

**cranky** *a.* disagreeable, cross, perverse.

**crash** *n.* **1** [A crashing sound] clatter, clash, din. **2** [A collision] wreck, accident, shock.

**craving** *n.* need, longing, yearning.

**crawl** *v.* creep, worm along, wriggle, squirm, slither, move on hands and knees, writhe, go on all fours, worm one's way, go on one's belly.

**crazy** *a.* demented, mad, insane.

**create** *v.* make, produce, form, perform, cause to exist, bring into being, bring into existence, build, fashion, constitute, originate, generate, construct, discover, shape, forge, design, plan, fabricate, cause to be, conceive, give birth to.

**creative** *a.* inventive, productive, artistic.

**credit** *n.* **1** [Belief] credence, reliance, confidence. **2** [Unencumbered funds] assets, stocks, bonds, paper credit, bank account, mortgages, liens, securities, debentures, cash. **3** [Permission to defer payment] extension, respite, continuance, trust. **—do credit to** bring approval to, please, do honor to. **—give credit to** believe in, rely on, have confidence in. **—give one credit for** believe in, rely on, have confidence in. **—on credit** on loan, delayed, postponed. **—to one's credit** good, honorable, beneficial.

**creep** *v.* slither, writhe, worm along.

**crime** *n.* transgression, misdemeanor, vice, outrage, wickedness, immorality, infringement, depravity, evil behavior, wrongdoing, misconduct, corruption, delinquency, wrong, trespass, malefaction, dereliction, lawlessness, atrocity, felony, capital crime, offense, white-collar crime, scandal, infraction, violation, coldblooded crime, mortal sin, homicide, voluntary manslaughter, involuntary manslaughter, simple assault, aggravated assault, battery, larceny, robbery, burglary, holdup, kidnapping, swindling, fraud, defrauding, embezzlement, smuggling, extortion, bribery, mugging, rape, statutory rape, attack, sexual molestation, breach of promise, malicious mischief, breach of the peace, libel, perjury, fornication, sodomy, conspiracy, counterfeiting, inciting to revolt, sedition.

**criminal** *n.* lawbreaker, felon, crook.

**crisis** *n.* straits, urgency, necessity, dilemma, puzzle, pressure, embarrassment, pinch, juncture, pass, change, contingency, situation, condition, plight, impasse, deadlock, predicament, corner, trauma, quandary, extremity, trial, crux, moment of truth, turning point, critical situation, pickle*, stew*, fix*, mess, big trouble*, hot water*.—*Ant.* stability, normality, regularity.

**criterion** *n.* basis, foundation, test, standard, rule, proof, scale, prototype, pattern, example, standard of judgment, standard of criticism, archetype, norm, original, precedent, fact, law, principle.

**critical** *a.* **1** [Disapproving] faultfinding, trenchant, derogatory, disapproving, hypercritical, demanding, satirical, cynical, nagging, scolding, condemning, censuring, reproachful, disapproving, disparaging, exacting, sharp, cutting, biting. **2** [Capable of observing and judging] penetrating, perceptive, discerning. **3** [Crucial] decisive, significant, deciding.

**criticize** *v.* **1** [To make a considered criticism] study, probe, scrutinize. **2** [To make adverse comments] chastise, reprove, reprimand.

**crooked** *a.* **1** [Having a crook] curved, curving, hooked, devious, winding, bowed, spiral, serpentine, not straight, zigzag, twisted, meandering, tortuous, sinuous.—*Ant.* straight, unbent, direct. **2** [Dishonest] iniquitous, corrupt, nefarious.

**crowd** *n.* host, horde, flock, mob, company, swarm, press, crush, surge, legion, rout, group, body, pack, army, drove, party, flood, throng, troupe, deluge, multitude, congregation, cluster, assembly, crew, herd, bunch, gang, batch.

**crowd** *v.* stuff, jam, squeeze.

**cruel** *a.* malevolent, spiteful, depraved, wicked, vengeful, evil, sinful, degenerate, brutish, demonic, rampant, outrageous, tyrannical, gross, demoralized, evil-minded, vicious, brutal, rough, wild, bestial, ferocious, monstrous, demoniac, debased, destructive, harmful, mischievous, callous, unnatural, merciless, sadistic, unpitying, unmerciful, unyielding, remorseless, pitiless, unfeeling, inflexible, bloodthirsty, unrelenting, relentless, grim, inhuman, atrocious, harsh, heartless, stony, unconcerned, knowing no mercy*, turning a deaf ear*, hard as nails*.—*Ant.* merciful, kindly, compassionate.

**cruelty** *n.* brutality, barbarity, sadism, inhumanity, barbarism, mercilessness, wickedness, coarseness, ruthlessness, severity, malice, rancor, venom, coldness, unfeelingness, insensibility, indifference, fierceness, bestiality, ferocity, savagery, grimness, monstrousness, inflexibility, fiendishness, hardness of heart, bloodthirstiness, torture, relentlessness, persecution, harshness, heartlessness, atrocity.—*Ant.* kindness, benevolence, humanity.

**cry** *n.* **1** [A loud utterance] outcry, exclamation, clamor, shout, call, battle cry, halloo, hurrah, cheer, scream, shriek, yell, whoop, squall, groan, bellow, howl, bawl, holler, uproar, acclamation, roar.—*Ant.* whisper, murmur, silence. **2** [A characteristic call] howl, hoot, wail, bawl, screech, bark, squawk, squeak, yelp, meow, whinny, moo, chatter, bay, cluck, crow, whine, pipe, trill, quack, clack, cackle, caw, bellow, coo, whistle, gobble, hiss, growl. **3** [A fit of weeping] sobbing, wailing, shedding tears, sorrowing, mourning, whimpering. **—a far cry (from)** unlike, dissimilar, opposed to.

**cry** *v.* **1** [To weep] weep, sob, wail, shed tears, snivel, squall, lament, bewail, bemoan, moan, howl, keen, whimper, whine, weep over, complain, deplore, sorrow, grieve, fret, groan, burst into tears, choke up, cry one's eyes out, break down, break up*, blubber, bawl.—*Ant.* laugh, rejoice, exult. **2** [To call; *said of other than human creatures*] howl, bark, hoot, scream, screech, squawk, squeak, yelp, grunt, roar, shriek, meow, whinny, moo, bawl, snarl, chatter, bay, cluck, crow, whine, pipe, trill, coo, whistle, caw, bellow, quack, gabble, hiss, growl, croak, cackle, twitter, tweet.

**cultivate** *v.* **1** [Plant] till, garden, seed. **2** [Educate] nurture, refine, improve.

**culture** *n.* **1** [Civilizing tradition] folklore, folkways, instruction, education, study, law, society, family, convention, habit, inheritance, learning, arts, sciences, custom, mores, knowledge, letters, literature, poetry, painting, music, lore, architecture, history, religion, humanism, the arts and sciences.—*Ant.* disorder, barbarism, chaos. **2** [Refinement and education] breeding, gentility, enlightenment, learning, capacity, ability, skill, science, lore, education, training, art, perception, discrimination, finish, taste, grace, dignity, politeness, savoir-faire, manners, urbanity, dress, fashion, address, tact, nobility, kindness, polish.—*Ant.* ignorance, crudeness, vulgarity.

**cup** *n.* vessel, bowl, goblet, mug, tumbler, beaker, stein, bumper, teacup, coffee cup, measuring cup, chalice.

**cure** *n.* restorative, healing agent, antidote.

**cure** *v.* make healthy, restore, make whole.

**curious** *a.* **1** [Strange or odd] rare, queer, unique. **2** [Interested] inquiring, inquisitive, questioning.

**curl** *v.* curve, coil, bend, spiral, crinkle, wind, twine, loop, crimp, scallop, lap, fold, roll, contort, form into a spiral, form into a curved shape, meander, ripple, buckle, zigzag, wrinkle, twirl.—*Ant.* straighten, uncurl, unbend.

**curly** *a.* curled, kinky, wavy, waving, coiled, crinkly, looped, winding, wound.

**current** *a.* prevailing, contemporary, in fashion.

**current** *n.* drift, tidal motion, ebb and flow.

**curse** *n.* oath, blasphemy, obscenity, sacrilege, anathema, ban, cursing, profanity, denunciation, damning, cuss word*, cussing*, swearword*, four-letter word*.

**curse** *v.* blaspheme, profane, swear, use foul language, be foulmouthed, be obscene, take the Lord's name in vain, damn, turn the air blue*, abuse, revile, swear at, insult, call down curses on the head of, blast, doom, fulminate, denounce, call names, cuss*, cuss out*.

**curve** *n.* sweep, bow, arch, circuit, curvature, crook.

**curve** *v.* bow, crook, twist.

**custodian** *n.* superintendent, janitor, porter, cleaner, cleaning man, cleaning woman, attendant, caretaker, building superintendent, keeper, gatekeeper, night watchman.

**custody** *n.* care, guardianship, supervision, keeping, safekeeping, watch, superintendence, safeguard. **—take into custody** capture, apprehend, seize.

**custom** *n.* habit, practice, usage, wont, fashion, routine, precedent, use, addiction, rule, procedure, observance, characteristic, second nature, matter of course, beaten path, rut, manner, way, mode, method, system, style, vogue, convention, habit, rule, practice, formality, form, mold, pattern, design, type, taste, character, ritual, rite, attitude, mores, dictate of society, unwritten law, etiquette, conventionality.—*Ant.* departure, deviation, shift.

**customer** *n.* clientele, patron, consumer.

**cut** *n.* **1** [The using of a sharp instrument] slash, thrust, dig, prick, gouge, penetrating, dividing, separation, severance, slitting, hack, slice, carve, chop, stroke, incision, cleavage, penetration, gash, cleft, mark, nick, notch, opening, passage, groove, furrow, slit, wound, fissure. **2** [A reduction] decrease, diminution, lessening. **3** [The shape] fashion, figure, construction. **4** [A section] segment, slice, portion. **5** [A piece of butchered meat] piece, slice, chunk. **6** [*An insult] indignity, offense, abuse. **—a cut above*** superior, higher; more capable or competent or efficient, etc.

**cut** *v.* **1** [To sever] separate, slice through, slice, cut into, cleave, mow, prune, reap, shear, dice, chop down, chop, slit, split, cut apart, hew, fell, rip, saw through, chisel, cut away, snip, chip, quarter, clip, behead, scissor, bite, shave, dissect, bisect, amputate, gash, incise, truncate, lacerate, slash, notch, nick, indent, score, mark, scratch, rake, furrow, wound, gouge. **2** [To cross] intersect, pass, move across. **3** [To shorten] curtail, delete, lessen. **4** [To divide] split, break apart, separate. **5** [*To absent oneself] shirk, avoid, stay away. **6** [To record electronically] make a record, film, tape.

**cynic** *n.* misanthrope, misogynist, mocker, satirist, scoffer, pessimist, sarcastic person, sneerer, unbeliever, egotist, man-hater, skeptic, doubter, questioner, detractor, doubting Thomas.—*Ant.* believer, optimist, idealist.

**cynical** *a.* scornful, sneering, sarcastic.

# D

**dab** *n.* small quantity, fragment, lump.

**daily** *a.* diurnal, per diem, every day, occurring every day, issued every day, periodic, cyclic, day after day, once daily, by day, once a day, during the day, day by day, from day to day.

**dainty** *a.* delicate, fragile, petite, frail, thin, light, pretty, beautiful, lovely, attractive, trim, graceful, fine, neat, elegant, exquisite, precious, rare, soft, tender, airy, lacy, nice, darling*, cute*, sweet.—*Ant.* rough, coarse, gross.

**dam** *n.* dike, ditch, wall, bank, embankment, gate, levee, irrigation dam, beaver dam, cofferdam.

**damage** *n.* **1** [Injury] harm, hurt, wound, bruise, wrong, casualty, suffering, illness, stroke, affliction, accident, catastrophe, adversity, outrage, hardship, disturbance, mutilation, impairment, mishap, evil, blow, devastation, mischief, reverse.—*Ant.* blessing, benefit, boon. **2** [Loss occasioned by injury] ruin, breakage, ruined goods, wreckage, deprivation, waste, shrinkage, depreciation, pollution, corruption, blemish, contamination, defacement, degeneration, deterioration, ravage, havoc, erosion, disrepair, debasement, corrosion, wear and tear, foul play.—*Ant.* improvement, betterment, growth.

**damage** *v.* ruin, wreck, tarnish, burn, scorch, dirty, rot, smash, bleach, drench, batter, discolor, mutilate, scratch, smudge, crack, bang up, abuse, maltreat, mar, deface, disfigure, mangle, contaminate, crumple, dismantle, cheapen, blight, disintegrate, pollute, ravage, sap, stain, tear, undermine, gnaw, corrode, break, split, stab, crack, pierce, lacerate, cripple, rust, warp, maim, wound, taint, despoil, incapacitate, pervert, bruise, spoil, wear away, abuse, defile, wrong, corrupt, infect.

**danger** *n.* uncertainty, risk, peril, jeopardy, threat, hazard, insecurity, instability, exposure, venture, menace, vulnerability.—*Ant.* safety, security, certainty.

**dangerous** *a.* perilous, critical, serious, pressing, vital, vulnerable, exposed, full of risk, threatening, alarming, urgent, hazardous, risky, menacing, serious, ugly, nasty, formidable, terrible, deadly, insecure, precarious, ticklish, delicate, unstable, touchy, treacherous, bad, thorny, breakneck, shaky*, on a collision course*, hairy*, under fire*, unhealthy, hot*.—*Ant.* certain, sure, secure.

**dare** *v.* **1** [To be courageous] take a chance, venture, adventure, undertake, try, attempt, endeavor, try one's hand, hazard, take the bull by the horns*, go ahead, go for it*.—*Ant.* avoid, dread, fear. **2** [To defy] meet, confront, oppose, disregard, brave, scorn, insult, resist, threaten, spurn, denounce, bully, mock, laugh at, challenge, have the nerve, have the courage of one's convictions, face the music*, face up to, call someone's bluff.—*Ant.* avoid, shun, evade.

**dark** *a.* **1** [Lacking illumination] unlighted, unlit, dim, shadowy, somber, cloudy, foggy, sunless, lightless, indistinct, dull, faint, vague, dusky, murky, gloomy, misty, obscure, nebulous, shady, shaded, clouded, darkened, overcast, opaque, without light, inky.—*Ant.* bright, lighted, illuminated. **2** [Dark in complexion] tan, swarthy, dark-complexioned. **3** [Evil] wicked, immoral, corrupt.

**dark** *n.* gloom, evening, dusk. **—in the dark** uninformed, unaware, naive.

**dash** *n.* **1** [A short, swift movement] spurt, charge, rush. **2** [Punctuation marking a break in thought] em, em dash, en dash, hyphen. **3** [A little of something] a few drops, hint, sprinkle, scattering, seasoning, touch, grain, trace, suspicion, suggestion, squirt, taste.—*Ant.* too much, quantity, excess.

**dash** *v.* **1** [To discourage] dampen, dismay, dispirit. **2** [To sprint] race, speed, hurry.

**data** *n.* evidence, reports, details, results, notes, documents, abstracts, testimony, facts, raw data, memorandums, statistics, figures, measurements, conclusions, information, circumstances, experiments, info*, dope*.

**dazed** *a.* confused, bewildered, perplexed.

**dead** *a.* **1** [Without life] not existing, expired, deceased, perished, lifeless, inanimate, late, defunct, breathless, no longer living, devoid of life, departed, brain-dead, clinically dead, gone, no more*, done for*, gone the way of all flesh*, gone to one's reward*, gone to meet one's Maker*, at rest with God*, out of one's misery*, snuffed out*, pushing up daisies*, rubbed out*, wasted*, liquidated*, erased*, gone by the board*, resting in peace*.—*Ant.* alive, animate, enduring. **2** [Without the appearance of life] inert, still, stagnant. **3** [Numb] insensible, deadened, anesthetized. **4** [*Exhausted] wearied, worn, spent.

**deadlock** *n.* standstill, stalemate, cessation.

**deadly** *a.* fatal, lethal, murderous, mortal, homicidal, virulent, poisonous, bloody, destructive, venomous, malignant, injurious, carcinogenic, suicidal, bloodthirsty, cannibalistic, harmful, violent.

**deal** *n.* **1** [An agreement] pledge, compromise, pact. **2** [A secret or dishonest agreement] swindle, robbery, graft. **3** [A lot] much, abundance, superabundance. **—a good** (or **great**) **deal** a lot, quite a bit, a considerable amount. **—make a big deal out of*** expand, magnify, blow up.

**dealer** *n.* retailer, vendor, merchant.

**death** *n.* decease, dying, demise, passing, loss of life, departure, release, parting, end of life, afterlife, other world, grave, tomb, paradise, heaven, hell, extinction, mortality, exit*, end, finish*, the way of all flesh*, the Grim Reaper*, eternal rest, last rest*.—*Ant.* life, birth, beginning. **—at death's door** failing, wasting away, nearly dead. **—to death** very much, extremely, to the extreme. **—to the death** to the end, constantly, faithfully.

**debate** *v.* refute, oppose, question, contend, contest, reason with, wrangle, answer, ponder, weigh, differ, dispute, quarrel, bandy words with, argue the pros and cons of.—*Ant.* agree, concur, concede.

**decay** *n.* decline, decrease, consumption, decomposition, collapse, downfall, decadence, depreciation, corruption, spoilage, wasting away, degeneration, dry rot, putrefaction, dissolution, rottenness, spoiling, breakup, breakdown, mold, rust, atrophy, emaciation, blight, mildew, deterioration, ruination, extinction, disintegration, ruin, crumbling, waste, corrosion, wear and tear, crack-up*.

**decay** *v.* corrode, rot, wither.

**deceive** *v.* mislead, swindle, outwit, fool, delude, rob, defraud, not play fair, play a practical joke on, victimize, betray, beguile, take advantage of, entrap, ensnare, hoodwink, dupe, fleece, con*, skin*, sucker*, string along*, screw out of*, do in*, lead astray*, bamboozle*, cross up*, bilk*, gouge*, clip*, fake, gyp*, put on*, burn*, sell out*, chisel*, double-cross*, shake down*, make a sucker out of*, take to the cleaners*, take for a ride*, snow*, put one over on*, take in*, pull the wool over someone's eyes*, flimflam*, give someone the runaround*, do a snow job on*, play upon*, make a monkey of*, stack the cards*.

**decent** *a.* **1** [In accordance with common standards] accepted, standard, approved. **2** [In accordance with the moral code] nice, proper, moral, honest, honorable, chaste, modest, pure, ethical, reserved, spotless, respectable, prudent, mannerly, virtuous, immaculate, delicate, stainless, clean, trustworthy, upright, worthy, untarnished, unblemished, straight.

**deception** *n.* trickery, double-dealing, untruth, insincerity, craftiness, juggling, treachery, treason, betrayal, mendacity, disinformation, falsehood, trickiness, lying, deceitfulness, deceit, duplicity, cunning, fast one*, snow job*, hokum*.—*Ant.* honesty, frankness, sincerity.

**deceptive** *a.* misleading, ambiguous, deceitful.

**decide** *v.* settle, determine, judge, conclude, compromise, choose, terminate, vote, poll, make a decision, come to a conclusion, form an opinion, form a judgment, make up one's mind, make a selection, select, pick, make one's choice, commit oneself, come to an agreement, have the final word.—*Ant.* delay, hesitate, hedge.

**declaration** *n.* statement, assertion, utterance, information, affirmation, profession, manifesto, announcement, document, bulletin, denunciation, proclamation, confirmation, ultimatum, notice, notification, resolution, affidavit, testimony, charge, indictment, allegation, canon, bill of rights, constitution, creed, article of faith, presentation, exposition, communication, disclosure, explanation, revelation, publication, answer, advertisement, saying, report, oath, admission, acknowledgment.

**declare** *v.* assert, announce, pronounce, claim, tell, state, point out, affirm, maintain, attest to, testify to, confess, reveal, swear, disclose, impart, represent, indicate, notify, repeat, insist, contend, advance, allege, argue, demonstrate, propound, bring forward, put forward, set forth, stress, cite, advocate, pass, proclaim, acknowledge, profess, give out, certify, swear.—*Ant.* hide, equivocate, withhold.

**decline** *n.* deterioration, dissolution, lessening.

**decline** *v.* **1** [To refuse] desist, beg to be excused, send regrets. **2** [To decrease] degenerate, deteriorate, backslide.

**decompose** *v.* rot, crumble, disintegrate.

**decorate** *v.* adorn, beautify, ornament, deck, paint, color, renovate, enrich, brighten, enhance, festoon, embellish, illuminate, spangle, elaborate, enamel, bead, polish, varnish, grace, garnish, finish, tile, redecorate, add the finishing touches, perfect, dress up, fix up, deck out, pretty up.

**decrease** *n.* shrinkage, lessening, reduction.

**decrease** *v.* **1** [To grow less] lessen, diminish, decline, wane, deteriorate, degenerate, dwindle, sink, settle, lighten, slacken, ebb, melt, lower, moderate, subside, shrink, shrivel up, depreciate, soften, quiet, narrow down, waste, fade away, run low, weaken, crumble, let up, dry up, slow down, calm down, burn away, burn down, die away, die down, decay, evaporate, slack off, wear off, wear away, wear out, wear down, slump.—*Ant.* grow, increase, multiply. **2** [To make less] cut, reduce, check, curb, restrain, quell, tame, compose, hush, still, sober, pacify, blunt, lessen, lower, subtract, abridge, abbreviate, condense, shorten, minimize, diminish, slash, dilute, shave, pare, prune, modify, digest, limit, level, deflate, compress, strip, thin, make smaller, curtail, clip, lighten, trim, level off, take from, take off, roll back, hold down, step down, scale down, boil down, let up, cut off, cut down, cut short, cut back, chisel*, wind down, knock off*.—*Ant.* increase, expand, augment.

**deep** *a.* **1** [Situated or extending far down] low, below, beneath, bottomless, submerged, subterranean, submarine, inmost, deep-seated, immersed, dark, dim, impenetrable, buried, inward, underground, down-reaching, of great depth, depthless, immeasurable, yawning.—*Ant.* shallow, near the surface, surface. **2** [Extending laterally or vertically] extensive, far, wide, yawning, penetrating, distant, thick, fat, spread out, to the bone*, to the hilt.—*Ant.* narrow, thin, shallow. **3** [Showing evidence of thought and understanding] penetrating, acute, incisive. **—go off the deep end*** **1** [To act rashly] go to extremes, go too far, rant. **2** [To break down] collapse, lose control of oneself, become insane.

**defeat** *n.* repulse, reverse, rebuff, conquest, rout, overthrow, subjugation, destruction, breakdown, collapse, extermination, annihilation, check, trap, ambush, breakthrough, withdrawal, setback, stalemate, ruin, blow, loss, butchery, massacre, Waterloo, beating, whipping, thrashing, fall, comedown, upset, battering*, pasting*, walloping*, whaling*, slaughter*, massacre*, KO*, the old one-two*.—*Ant.* victory, triumph, conquest.

**defeat** *v.* **1** [To get the better of another] master, subjugate, overwhelm. **2** [To worst in war] overcome, vanquish, conquer, rout, entrap, subdue, overrun, best, overthrow, crush, smash, drive off, annihilate, overwhelm, scatter, repulse, halt, reduce, outflank, finish off, encircle, slaughter, butcher, outmaneuver, ambush, demolish, sack, torpedo, sink, swamp, wipe out, decimate, obliterate, roll back, mop up*, chew up*, mow down*.—*Ant.* yield, give up, relinquish. **3** [To worst in sport or in personal combat] beat, overpower, outplay, trounce, knock out, throw, floor, pommel, pound, flog, outhit, outrun, outjump, thrash, edge*, shade*, lay low*, skin*, lick*, wallop*, clean up on*, beat up*, take*, KO*, put down*, beat the pants off of*, pulverize*, steamroll*, plow under*, smear*, cream*.—*Ant.* fail, suffer, be defeated.

**defect** *n.* imperfection, flaw, drawback.

**defect** *v.* run away, forsake, desert.

**defend** *v.* **1** [To keep off an enemy; *often used figuratively*] shield, shelter, protect. **2** [To support an accused person or thing] plead for, justify, uphold, second, exonerate, back, vindicate, aid, espouse the cause of, befriend, say in defense of, guarantee, endorse, warrant, maintain, recommend, rationalize, plead someone's cause, say a good word for, speak for, stand up for, put in a good word for, apologize for, go to bat for*, cover for*, back up, stick up for*.—*Ant.* convict, accuse, charge.

**defense** *n.* **1** [The act of defending] resistance, protection, safeguard, preservation, security, custody, stand, front, backing, guardianship, the defensive, precaution, inoculation, excusing, apologizing, explaining, justifying, exoneration, explanation.—*Ant.* offense, retaliation, aggression. **2** [A means or system for defending] trench, bulwark, dike, stockade, machine-gun nest, bastion, fortification, fort, chemical and biological warfare, barricade, garrison, rampart, fence, wall, embankment, citadel, fortress, armor, antiaircraft, camouflage, gas mask, shield, screen, stronghold, parapet, buttress, guard.—*Ant.* attack, siege, blitzkrieg. **3** [In law, the reply of the accused] denial, plea, answer.

**defiant** *a.* resistant, disobedient, rebellious.

**define** *v.* **1** [To set limits] bound, confine, limit, outline, fix, settle, circumscribe, mark, set, distinguish, establish, encompass, mark the limits of, determine the boundaries of, fix the limits of, curb, edge, border, enclose, set bounds to, fence in, rim, encircle, hedge in, wall in, envelop, flank, stake out.—*Ant.* confuse, distort, mix. **2** [To provide a name or description] determine, entitle, label, designate, characterize, elucidate, interpret, illustrate, represent, individuate, find out, popularize, spell out, translate, exemplify, specify, prescribe, nickname, dub.—*Ant.* misunderstand, misconceive, mistitle.

**definite** *a.* **1** [Determined with exactness] fixed, exact, precise, positive, accurate, correct, decisive, absolute, clearly defined, well-defined, limited, strict, explicit, specific, settled, decided, prescribed, restricted, assigned, unequivocal, special, conclusive, categorical, particular, unerring, to the point, beyond doubt.—*Ant.* obscure, indefinite, inexact. **2** [Clear in detail] sharp, visible, audible, tangible, distinct, vivid, unmistakable in meaning, straightforward, obvious, marked, plain, not vague, well-drawn, clearly defined, well-marked, well-defined, clear-cut, explicit, unmistakable, distinguishable, undistorted, crisp, bold, graphic, downright, undisguised, in plain sight, clear as day, standing out like a sore thumb*.—*Ant.* confused, vague, hazy. **3** [Positive] sure, beyond doubt, convinced.

**deform** *v.* disfigure, deface, injure.

**deformed** *a.* damaged, distorted, misshapen, disfigured, crippled, misproportioned, malformed, cramped, badly made, disjointed, unseemly, ill-favored, dwarfed, hunchbacked, warped, mangled, crushed, unshapely, clubfooted, curved, contorted, gnarled, crooked, grotesque, lame, irregular.—*Ant.* regular, shapely, well-formed.

**degrade** *v.* demote, discredit, diminish.

**degree** *n.* **1** [One in a series used for measurement] measure, grade, step, mark, interval, space, measurement, gradation, size, dimension, shade, point, line, plane, step in a series, gauge, rung, term, tier, stair, ratio, period, level. **2** [An expression of relative excellence, attainment, or the like] extent, station, order, quality, development, height, expanse, length, potency, range, proportion, compass, quantity, standing, strength, reach, intensity, scope, caliber, pitch, stage, sort, status, rate. **3** [Recognition of academic achievement] distinction, testimonial, honor, qualification, dignity, eminence, credit, credentials, baccalaureate, doctorate, sheepskin*. **—by degrees** step by step, slowly but surely, inch by inch. **—to a degree** somewhat, partially, to an extent.

**delay** *n.* deferment, adjournment, putting off, procrastination, suspension, moratorium, reprieve, setback, stay, stop, discontinuation, cooling-off period*, holdup*.

**delay** *v.* postpone, defer, retard, hold up, deter, clog, choke, slacken, keep, hold, keep back, impede, discourage, interfere with, detain, stay, stop, withhold, arrest, check, prevent, repress, curb, obstruct, inhibit, restrict, prolong, encumber, procrastinate, adjourn, block, bar, suspend, table, slow, put aside, hold back, hold off, hold everything*, bide one's time, slow up, stall, put off, restrain, put on ice*, shelve*, pigeonhole.—*Ant.* speed, accelerate, encourage.

**deliberate** *a.* thought out, predetermined, conscious, advised, prearranged, fixed, with forethought, well-considered, cautious, studied, intentional, planned in advance, done on purpose, willful, considered, thoughtful, purposed, planned, reasoned, calculated, intended, purposeful, premeditated, voluntary, designed, coldblooded, resolved, cut-and-dried.

**delicate** *a.* **1** [Sickly] susceptible, in delicate health, feeble. **2** [Dainty] fragile, frail, fine.

**delicious** *a.* tasty, savory, good, appetizing, choice, well-seasoned, well-done, spicy, sweet, rich, delectable, exquisite, dainty, luscious, tempting, yummy*, fit for a king*.—*Ant.* rotten, flat, stale.

**delightful** *a.* charming, amusing, clever.

**delinquent** *a.* **1** [Lax in duty] slack, behindhand, tardy, procrastinating, criminal, neglectful, faulty, blamable, negligent, derelict, remiss.—*Ant.* punctual, punctilious, scrupulous. **2** [Not paid on time; *said especially of taxes*] owed, back, overdue.

**deliver** *v.* **1** [To free] set free, liberate, save. **2** [To transfer] pass, remit, hand over. **3** [To speak formally] present, read, give. **4** [To bring to birth] bring forth, be delivered of, provide obstetrical attention. **5** [To distribute] allot, dispense, give out.

**delusion** *n.* hallucination, fancy, illusion.

**deluxe** *a.* elegant, luxurious, grand.

**demand** *n.* **1** [A peremptory communication] order, call, charge. **2** [Willingness to purchase] trade, request, sale, bid, need, requirement, interest, call, rush, search, inquiry, desire to buy.—*Ant.* indifference, lack of interest, sales resistance. **—in demand** sought, needed, requested. **—on demand** ready, prepared, usable.

**demand** *v.* charge, direct, command.

**democracy** *n.* justice, the greatest good for the greatest number, equality, popular suffrage, individual enterprise, capitalism, laissez faire, rugged individualism, freedom of religion, freedom of speech, freedom of the press, the right to work, private ownership, emancipation, political equality, democratic spirit, the American Way*.—*Ant.* dictatorship, feudalism, tyranny.

**democratic** *a.* popular, constitutional, representative, free, equal, common, bourgeois, individualistic, communal, laissez-faire.

**demolish** *v.* wreck, devastate, obliterate.

**demonstrate** *v.* **1** [To prove] show, make evident, confirm. **2** [To present for effect] exhibit, manifest, parade.

**dense** *a.* **1** [Close together] solid, compact, impenetrable. **2** [Slow-witted] stupid, imbecilic, dull.

**deny** *v.* contradict, disagree with, disprove, disallow, gainsay, disavow, disclaim, negate, repudiate, controvert, revoke, rebuff, reject, renounce, discard, not admit, take exception to, disbelieve, spurn, doubt, veto, discredit, nullify, say "no" to.—*Ant.* admit, accept, affirm.

**department** *n.* **1** [The field of one's activity] jurisdiction, activity, interest, occupation, province, bureau, business, capacity, dominion, administration, station, function, office, walk of life, vocation, specialty, field, duty, assignment, bailiwick. **2** [An organized subdivision] section, office, bureau, precinct, tract, range, quarter, area, arena, corps, agency, board, administration, circuit, territory, ward, state office, district office, force, staff, beat.

**depend on** *v.* **1** [To be contingent] be determined by, rest with, rest on, be subordinate to, be dependent on, be based on, be subject to, hinge on, turn on, turn upon, be in the power of, be conditioned by, revolve on, trust to, be at the mercy of. **2** [To rely on] put faith in, confide in, trust.

**deposit** *v.* **1** [To lay down] drop, place, put. **2** [To present money for safekeeping] invest, amass, store, keep, stock up, bank, hoard, collect, treasure, lay away, put in the bank, entrust, transfer, put for safekeeping, put aside for a rainy day*, salt away*.—*Ant.* spend, withdraw, put out. **—on deposit** hoarded, stored, saved.

**depress** *v.* **1** [To bring to a lower level] press down, squash, settle. **2** [To bring to a lower state] reduce, dampen, dishearten, debase, degrade, abase, dismay, sadden, mock, darken, scorn, reduce to tears, deject, weigh down, keep down, cast down, beat down, chill, dull, oppress, lower in spirits, throw cold water on*.—*Ant.* urge, animate, stimulate.

**deride** *v.* scorn, jeer, mock.

**derive** *v.* draw a conclusion, work out, conclude.

**descend** *v.* slide, settle, gravitate, slip, dismount, topple, plunge, sink, dip, pass downward, pitch, light, deplane, tumble, move downward, come down upon, slump, trip, stumble, flutter down, plummet, submerge, step down, climb down, go down, swoop down, get off.—*Ant.* climb, ascend, mount.

**description** *n.* narration, story, portrayal, word picture, account, report, delineation, sketch, specifications, characterization, declaration, rehearsal, information, definition, record, brief, summary, depiction, explanation, write-up*.

**desert** *n.* waste, sand, wastelands, barren plains, arid region, deserted region, sand dunes, lava beds, infertile region, salt flats, abandoned land.

**desert** *v.* defect, be absent without leave, abandon one's post, sneak off, run away from duty, violate one's oath, leave unlawfully, go AWOL*, go over the hill*.—*Ant.* obey, stay, do one's duty.

**deserve** *v.* merit, be worthy of, earn, be deserving, lay claim to, have the right to, be given one's due, be entitled to, warrant, rate*, have it coming*.—*Ant.* fail, be unworthy, usurp.

**deserving** *a.* needy, rightful, worthy.

**designate** *v.* indicate, point out, name.

**desire** *n.* **1** [The wish to enjoy] aspiration, wish, motive, will, urge, eagerness, propensity, fancy, frenzy, craze, mania, hunger, thirst, attraction, longing, yearning, fondness, liking, inclination, proclivity, craving, relish, hankering*, itch*, yen*.—*Ant.* indifference, unconcern, apathy. **2** [Erotic wish to possess] lust, passion, hunger, appetite, fascination, infatuation, fervor, excitement, nymphomania, sexual love, libido, sensual appetite, carnal passion, eroticism, biological urge, rut*, heat*.—*Ant.* abstinence, coldness, frigidity.

**desire** *v.* **1** [To wish for] covet, crave, wish for. **2** [To request] ask for, seek, solicit. **3** [To want sexually] lust after, hunger for, have the hots for*, be turned on by*.

**desolate** *a.* deserted, forsaken, uninhabited.

**despair** *n.* hopelessness, depression, discouragement.
**despair** *v.* lose hope, lose faith, lose heart, give up hope, abandon hope, have no hope, have a heavy heart, abandon oneself to fate.
**despise** *v.* scorn, disdain, hate.
**dessert** *n.* sweet, tart, cobbler, jelly, custard, ice, sundae, compote, fruit salad, pudding, ice cream.
**destined** *a.* fated, compulsory, foreordained, menacing, near, forthcoming, threatening, in prospect, predestined, predetermined, compelled, condemned, at hand, impending, inexorable, that is to be, in store, to come, directed, ordained, settled, sealed, closed, predesigned, in the wind, in the cards.—*Ant.* involuntary, at will, by chance.
**destiny** *n.* fate, future, fortune.
**destitute** *a.* impoverished, poverty-stricken, penniless.
**destroy** *v.* ruin, demolish, exterminate, raze, tear down, plunder, ransack, eradicate, overthrow, root up, root out, devastate, butcher, consume, liquidate, break up, dissolve, blot out, quash, quell, level, abort, stamp out, suppress, squelch, scuttle, undo, annihilate, lay waste, overturn, impair, damage, ravish, deface, shatter, split up, crush, obliterate, knock to pieces, abolish, crash, extinguish, wreck, dismantle, upset, bomb, mutilate, smash, trample, overturn, maim, mar, end, nullify, blast, neutralize, gut, snuff out, erase, sabotage, repeal, pull down, terminate, conclude, finish, bring to ruin, stop, put a stop to, wipe out, do in*, do away with, finish off, make short work of, total*, cream*, destruct, self-destruct, put an end to.—*Ant.* build, construct, establish.
**detach** *v.* separate, withdraw, disengage.
**detail** *n.* item, portion, particular, trait, specialty, feature, aspect, article, peculiarity, fraction, specification, technicality.—*Ant.* whole, entirety, synthesis. —**in detail** item by item, in all details, with particulars, comprehensively, minutely.
**detail** *v.* itemize, exhibit, show, report, relate, narrate, tell, designate, catalogue, recite, specialize, depict, enumerate, mention, uncover, reveal, recount, recapitulate, analyze, set forth, produce, go into the particulars.—*Ant.* dabble, summarize, epitomize.
**detective** *n.* policeman, agent, plainclothesman, private eye*, narcotics agent, police sergeant, police officer, FBI agent, wiretapper, investigator, criminologist, prosecutor, patrolman, sleuth, shadow, eavesdropper, spy, shamus*, flatfoot*, dick*, G-man*, copper*, cop*, fed*, narc*.
**determine** *v.* **1** [To define] limit, circumscribe, delimit. **2** [To find out the facts] ascertain, find out, learn. **3** [To resolve] fix upon, settle, conclude.
**detract** *v.* decrease, take away a part, subtract, draw away, diminish, lessen, withdraw, derogate, depreciate, discredit.
**develop** *v.* **1** [To improve] enlarge, expand, extend, promote, advance, magnify, build up, refine, enrich, cultivate, elaborate, polish, finish, perfect, deepen, lengthen, heighten, widen, intensify, fix up, shape up*.—*Ant.* damage, disfigure, spoil. **2** [To grow] mature, evolve, advance. **3** [To reveal slowly] unfold, disclose, exhibit, unravel, disentangle, uncover, make known, explain, unroll, explicate, produce,

detail, tell, state, recount, account for, give an account of.—*Ant.* hide, conceal, blurt out. **4** [To work out] enlarge upon, elaborate upon, go into detail.

**deviate** *v.* deflect, digress, swerve, vary, wander, stray, turn aside, keep aside, stay aside, go out of control, shy away, depart, break the pattern, not conform, go out of the way, veer, go off on a tangent, go haywire*, swim against the stream*.—*Ant.* conform, keep on, keep in line.

**device** *n.* **1** [An instrument] invention, contrivance, mechanism, gear, equipment, appliance, contraption, means, agent, material, implement, utensil, construction, apparatus, outfit, article, accessory, gadget, thing, whatnot, whatsit*, whatchamacallit*. **2** [A shrewd method] artifice, scheme, design, trap, dodge, trick, pattern, loophole, wile, craft, ruse, expedient, subterfuge, plan, project, plot, racket*, game, finesse, catch*.

**devil** *n.* Satan, fiend, adversary, error, sin, imp, mischiefmaker, Beelzebub, fallen angel, hellhound, Mammon, Molech, Hades, Lucifer, Mephistopheles, diabolical force, the Tempter, Prince of Darkness, Evil One.—*Ant.* God, angel, Christ. **—give the devil his due** give one credit, give credit where credit is due, recognize. **—go to the devil 1** [To decay] degenerate, fall into bad habits, go to pot. **2** [A curse] go to hell, damn you, be damned. **—raise the devil*** cause trouble, riot, be unruly.

**devote** *v.* apply, consecrate, give.

**devout** *a.* devoted, pious, reverent.

**diagnosis** *n.* analysis, determination, investigation.

**dialect** *n.* idiom, accent, local speech, regional speech, broken English, pidgin English, brogue, lingo, trade language, lingua franca, usage level, pig Latin, jargon, cant, vernacular, patois.

**dialogue** *n.* talk, exchange, conversation.

**dictate** *v.* speak, deliver, give forth, interview, compose, formulate, verbalize, record, orate, give an account.

**dictator** *n.* autocrat, despot, tyrant, czar, fascist, absolute ruler, oppressor, terrorist, master, leader, ringleader, magnate, lord, commander, chief, advisor, overlord, taskmaster, disciplinarian, headman, cock of the walk*, man at the wheel*, slave driver*.

**dictatorial** *a.* despotic, authoritarian, arbitrary.

**die** *v.* **1** [To cease living] expire, pass away, pass on, depart, perish, succumb, go, commit suicide, suffocate, lose one's life, cease to exist, drown, hang, fall, meet one's death, be no more, drop dead, be done for*, rest in peace*, go to one's final resting place*, pass over to the great beyond*, give up the ghost*, go the way of all flesh*, return to dust*, cash in one's chips*, push up daisies*, buy the farm*, kick the bucket*, bite the dust*, lay down one's life*, breathe one's last, croak*, check out*, kick off*, go by the board*.—*Ant.* live, thrive, exist. **2** [To cease existing] disappear, vanish, become extinct. **3** [To decline as though death were inevitable] fade, ebb, wither.

**differ** *v.* **1** [To be unlike] vary, modify, not conform, digress, take exception, turn, reverse, qualify, alter, change, diverge from, contrast with, bear no resemblance, not look like, jar with, clash with, conflict with, be distinguished from, diversify, stand apart, depart from, go off on a tangent.—*Ant.* resemble, parallel, take after. **2** [To oppose] disagree, object, fight.

**different** *a.* **1** [Unlike in nature] distinct, separate, not the same. **2** [Composed of unlike things] diverse, miscellaneous, assorted. **3** [Unusual] unconventional, strange, startling.

**difficult** *a.* **1** [Hard to achieve] laborious, hard, unyielding, strenuous, exacting, stiff, heavy, arduous, painful, labored, trying, bothersome, troublesome, demanding, burdensome, backbreaking, not easy, wearisome, onerous, rigid, crucial, uphill, challenging, exacting, formidable, ambitious, immense, tough, heavy*, no picnic*, stiff.—*Ant.* easy, wieldy, light. **2** [Hard to understand] intricate, involved, perplexing, abstruse, abstract, delicate, hard, knotty, thorny, troublesome, ticklish, obstinate, puzzling, mysterious, mystifying, subtle, confusing, bewildering, confounding, esoteric, unclear, mystical, tangled, hard to explain, hard to solve, profound, rambling, loose, meandering, inexplicable, awkward, complex, complicated, deep, stubborn, hidden, formidable, enigmatic, paradoxical, incomprehensible, unintelligible, inscrutable, inexplicable, unanswerable, not understandable, unsolvable, unfathomable, concealed, unaccountable, ambiguous, equivocal, metaphysical, inconceivable, unknown, deep, over one's head*, too deep for, not making sense, Greek to*.—*Ant.* clear, obvious, simple.

**difficulty** *n.* **1** [Something in one's way] obstacle, obstruction, stumbling block, impediment, complication, hardship, adversity, misfortune, distress, deadlock, dilemma, hard job, maze, stone wall, barricade, impasse, knot, opposition, quandary, struggle, crisis, trouble, embarrassment, entanglement, thwart, mess, paradox, muddle, emergency, matter, standstill, hindrance, perplexity, bar, trial, check, predicament, hot water*, pickle*, fix*, stew*, scrape, hard nut to crack*, hitch*, dead end*, snag, monkey wrench in the works*, pinch, deep water*, jam*, the devil to pay*, hangup*.—*Ant.* help, aid, assistance. **2** [Something mentally disturbing] trouble, annoyance, to-do, ado, worry, weight, complication, distress, oppression, depression, aggravation, anxiety, discouragement, touchy situation, embarrassment, burden, grievance, irritation, strife, puzzle, responsibility, frustration, harassment, misery, predicament, setback, pressure, stress, strain, charge, struggle, maze, jam*, hangup*, mess*, pickle*, pinch, scrape.—*Ant.* ease, comfort, happiness.

**dig** *v.* **1** [To stir the earth] delve, spade, mine, excavate, channel, deepen, till, drive a shaft, clean, undermine, burrow, dig out, gouge, dredge, scoop out, tunnel out, hollow out, clean out, stope, grub, bulldoze.—*Ant.* bury, embed, fill. **2** [To remove by digging] dig up, uncover, turn up.

**dignified** *a.* stately, somber, solemn, courtly, reserved, ornate, elegant, classic, lordly, aristocratic, majestic, formal, noble, regal, superior, magnificent, grand, eminent, sublime, august, grave, distinguished, magisterial, imposing, portly, haughty, honorable, decorous, lofty, proud, classy*, snazzy*, sober as a judge*, highbrow*.—*Ant.* rude, undignified, boorish.

**dignity** *n.* nobility, self-respect, lofty bearing, grand air, quality, culture, distinction, stateliness, elevation, worth, character, importance, renown, splendor, majesty, class*.—*Ant.* humility, lowness, meekness.

**dilemma** *n.* quandary, perplexity, predicament.

**diligence** *n.* alertness, earnestness, quickness, perseverance, industry, vigor, carefulness, intent, intensity.—*Ant.* carelessness, sloth, laziness.

**dim** *a.* faint, dusky, shadowy.

**diminish** *v.* lessen, depreciate, decrease.

**dip** *n.* **1** [The action of dipping] plunge, immersion, soaking, ducking, drenching, sinking. **2** [Material into which something is dipped] preparation, solution, suspension, dilution, concoction, saturation, mixture. **3** [A low place] depression, slope, inclination. **4** [A swim] plunge, bath, dive.

**dip** *v.* **1** [To put into a liquid] plunge, lower, wet, slosh, submerge, irrigate, steep, drench, douse, souse, moisten, splash, slop, water, duck, bathe, rinse, baptize, dunk. **2** [To transfer by means of a vessel] scoop, shovel, ladle, bale, spoon, dredge, lift, draw, dish, dip up, dip out, offer.—*Ant.* empty, pour, let stand. **3** [To fall] slope, decline, recede, tilt, swoop, slip, spiral, sink, plunge, bend, verge, veer, slant, settle, slump, slide, go down.

**diplomatic** *a.* tactful, suave, gracious, calculating, shrewd, opportunistic, smooth, capable, conciliatory, conniving, sly, artful, wily, subtle, crafty, sharp, cunning, contriving, scheming, discreet, deft, intriguing, politic, strategic, astute, clever.

**direct** *a.* **1** [Without divergence] in a straight line, straight ahead, undeviating, uninterrupted, unswerving, shortest, nonstop, as the crow flies, straight as an arrow*, in a beeline, point-blank.—*Ant.* zigzag, roundabout, crooked. **2** [Frank] straightforward, outspoken, candid. **3** [Immediate] prompt, succeeding, resultant.

**direct** *v.* **1** [To show the way] conduct, show, guide. **2** [To decide the course of affairs] regulate, govern, influence. **3** [To aim a weapon] sight, train, level. **4** [To command] command, bid, charge.

**dirty** *a.* **1** [Containing dirt] soiled, unclean, unsanitary, unhygienic, filthy, polluted, nasty, slovenly, dusty, messy, squalid, sloppy, disheveled, uncombed, unsightly, untidy, straggly, unwashed, stained, tarnished, spotted, smudged, foul, fouled, grimy, greasy, muddy, mucky, sooty, smoked, slimy, rusty, unlaundered, unswept, crummy*, grubby, scuzzy*, scummy.—*Ant.* pure, unspotted, sanitary. **2** [Obscene] pornographic, smutty, lewd. **3** [Nasty] mean, contemptible, disagreeable.

**dirty** *v.* soil, sully, defile, pollute, foul, tarnish, spot, smear, blot, blur, smudge, smoke, spoil, sweat up, blotch, spatter, splash, stain, debase, corrupt, taint, contaminate.—*Ant.* clean, cleanse, rinse.

**disadvantage** *n.* **1** [Loss] damage, harm, deprivation. **2** [A position involving difficulties] bar, obstacle, handicap. **3** [Unfavorable details or prospects; *often plural*] inconvenience, obstacle, drawbacks.

**disagreement** *n.* **1** [Discord] contention, strife, conflict, controversy, wrangle, dissension, animosity, ill feeling, ill will, misunderstanding, division, opposition, hostility, breach, discord, feud, clashing, antagonism, bickering, squabble, tension, split, quarreling, falling-out, break, rupture, quarrel, clash, opposition, contest, friction. **2** [Inconsistency] discrepancy, dissimilarity, disparity. **3** [A quarrel] fight, argument, feud.

**disappointment** *n.* **1** [The state of being disappointed] dissatisfaction, frustration, chagrin, lack of success, despondency, displeasure, distress, discouragement, disillusionment, check, disillusion, setback, adversity, hard fortune.—*Ant.* success, fulfillment, realization. **2** [A person or thing that disappoints] miscarriage, misfortune, calamity, blunder, bad luck, setback, downfall, slip, defeat, mishap, error, mistake, discouragement, obstacle, miscalculation, fiasco, no go*, blind alley, washout*, lemon*, dud*, letdown, bust*, false alarm*.—*Ant.* achievement, successful venture, success.

**disapproval** *n.* criticism, censure, disparagement.

**disaster** *n.* accident, calamity, mishap, debacle, casualty, emergency, adversity, harm, misadventure, collapse, slip, fall, collision, crash, hazard, setback, defeat, failure, woe, trouble, scourge, grief, undoing, cure, tragedy, blight, cataclysm, downfall, rainy day, bankruptcy, upset, blast, blow, wreck, bad luck, comedown, crackup, pileup*, smashup, washout*, flop*, bust*.

**discard** *v.* reject, expel, repudiate, protest, cast aside, cast away, cast out, cast off, throw away, throw aside, throw overboard, throw out, get rid of, give up, renounce, have done with, dump, make away with, dismantle, discharge, write off, banish, eject, divorce, dispossess, dispense with, shake off, pass up, free oneself from, free of, give away, part with, dispose of, do away with, dispense with, shed, relinquish, thrust aside, sweep away, cancel, abandon, forsake, desert, cut, have nothing to do with, brush away, scotch, chuck*, drop, wash one's hands of*, junk*.—*Ant.* save, retain, preserve.

**discern** *v.* find out, determine, discover.

**discipline** *n.* **1** [Mental self-training] preparation, development, exercise, drilling, training, regulation, self-disciplining. **2** [A system of obedience] conduct, regulation, drill, orderliness, restraint, limitation, curb, indoctrination, brainwashing*.

**disclosure** *n.* acknowledgment, confession, admission.

**discolor** *v.* stain, rust, tarnish.

**disconnect** *v.* separate, detach, disengage.

**discord** *n.* **1** [Conflict] strife, contention, dissension. **2** [Noise] din, tumult, racket.

**discount** *n.* deduction, allowance, rebate, decrease, markdown, concession, percentage, premium, subtraction, commission, exemption, modification, qualification, drawback, depreciation, cut rate.—*Ant.* increase, markup, surcharge. **—at a discount** discounted, cheap, below face value.

**discouraged** *a.* downcast, pessimistic, depressed.

**discover** *v.* invent, find out, ascertain, detect, discern, recognize, distinguish, determine, observe, explore, hear of, hear about, awake to, bring to light, uncover, ferret out, root out, trace out, unearth, look up, stumble on, stumble upon, come on, come upon, run across, fall upon, strike upon, think of, perceive, glimpse, identify, devise, catch, spot, create, make out, sense, feel, sight, smell, hear, spy, bring out, find a clue, put one's finger on, get wise to*, dig out, dig up, turn up, sniff out, come up with, happen upon, get wind of, hit upon, lay one's hands on.—*Ant.* miss, pass by, omit.

**discreet** *a.* cautious, prudent, discerning, discriminating, not rash, strategic, noncommittal, heedful, vigilant, civil, sensible, reserved, alert, awake, wary, watchful, wise, circumspect, attentive, considerate, intelligent, guarded, politic, diplomatic, tight-lipped, cagey*.—*Ant.* rash, indiscreet, imprudent.

**discriminate** *v.* **1** [To differentiate] specify, separate, tell apart. **2** [To be (racially) prejudiced] be a bigot, show prejudice, set apart, segregate.

**discuss** *v.* argue, debate, dispute, talk of, talk about, explain, contest, confer, deal with, reason with, take up, look over, consider, talk over, talk out, take up in conference, engage in conversation, go into, think over, telephone about, have a conference on, discourse about, argue for and against, canvass, consider, handle, present, review, recite, treat of, speak of, converse, discourse, take under advisement, comment upon, have out, speak on, kick around*, toss around*, chew the fat*, jaw*, air out*, knock around*, compare notes*, chew the rag*.—*Ant.* delay, table, postpone.

**disease** *n.* **1** [A bodily infirmity] sickness, malady, ailment. **2** [Loosely used term for any ailment] condition, defect, infirmity.

**disgrace** *n.* scandal, shame, stain, slur, slight, stigma, brand, spot, slander, dishonor, infamy, reproach, disrepute, humiliation, degradation, taint, tarnish, mark of Cain*, scarlet letter.—*Ant.* pride, praise, credit.

**disgrace** *v.* debase, shame, degrade, abase, dishonor, disparage, discredit, deride, disregard, strip of honors, dismiss from favor, disrespect, mock, humble, reduce, put to shame, tarnish, stain, blot, sully, taint, defile, stigmatize, brand, tar and feather, put down, snub, derogate, belittle, take down a peg*.—*Ant.* praise, honor, exalt.

**disguise** *n.* mask, deceptive covering, makeup, faking, false front, deception, smoke screen, blind, concealment, counterfeit, pseudonym, costume, masquerade, veil, cover, facade, put-on*.

**disgust** *n.* loathing, abhorrence, aversion.

**disgust** *v.* repel, revolt, offend, displease, nauseate, sicken, make one sick, fill with loathing, cause aversion, be repulsive, irk, scandalize, shock, upset, turn one's stomach*.

**dishonest** *a.* deceiving, fraudulent, double-dealing, backbiting, treacherous, deceitful, cunning, sneaky, tricky, wily, crooked, deceptive, misleading, elusive, slippery, shady, swindling, cheating, sneaking, traitorous, villainous, sinister, lying, underhanded, two-timing*, two-faced, double-crossing*, unprincipled, shiftless, unscrupulous, undependable, disreputable, questionable, dishonorable, counterfeit, infamous, corrupt, immoral, discredited, unworthy, shabby, mean, low, venial, self-serving, contemptible, rotten, fishy*, crooked.—*Ant.* honest, irreproachable, scrupulous.

**disintegrate** *v.* break down, separate, divide, dismantle, break into pieces, disunite, disperse, crumble, disband, take apart, disorganize, detach, break apart, come apart, fall apart, sever, disconnect, fall to pieces, fade away, reduce to ashes.—*Ant.* unite, put together, combine.

**disjointed** *a.* disconnected, divided, unattached.

**dislike** *v.* detest, condemn, deplore, regret, lose interest in, speak down to, have hard feelings toward, not take kindly to, not be able to say much for, not have the stomach for, not speak well of, not have any part of, not care for, bear a grudge, have nothing to do with, keep one's distance from, care nothing for, resent, not appreciate, not endure, be averse to, abhor, hate, abominate, disapprove, loathe, despise, object to, shun, shrink from, mind, shudder at, scorn, avoid, be displeased by, turn up the nose at, look on with aversion, not be able to stomach, regard with displeasure, not like, take a dim view of, have it in for*, be down on*, look down one's nose at*, have a bone to pick with*.

**dismal** *a.* gloomy, monotonous, dim, melancholy, desolate, dreary, sorrowful, morbid, troublesome, horrid, shadowy, overcast, cloudy, unhappy, discouraging, hopeless, black, unfortunate, ghastly, horrible, boring, gruesome, tedious, mournful, dull, disheartening, regrettable, cheerless, dusky, dingy, sepulchral, joyless, funereal, comfortless, murky, wan, bleak, somber, disagreeable, creepy, spooky*, blue.—*Ant.* happy, joyful, cheerful.

**dismay** *n.* terror, dread, anxiety.

**dismiss** *v.* discard, reject, decline, repel, let out, repudiate, disband, detach, lay off, pack off, cast off, cast out, relinquish, dispense with, disperse, remove, expel, abolish, relegate, push aside, shed, do without, have done with, dispose of, sweep away, clear, rid, chase, dispossess, boycott, exile, expatriate, banish, outlaw, deport, excommunicate, get rid of, send packing, drop, brush off*, kick out*, blackball, write off.—*Ant.* maintain, retain, keep.

**disobedience** *n.* insubordination, defiance, insurgence, disregard, violation, neglect, mutiny, revolt, nonobservance, strike, stubbornness, noncompliance, infraction of the rules, unruliness, sedition, rebellion, sabotage, riot.

**disobey** *v.* balk, decline, neglect, desert, be remiss, ignore the commands of, refuse submission to, disagree, differ, evade, disregard the authority of, break rules, object, defy, resist, revolt, strike, violate, infringe, transgress, shirk, misbehave, withstand, counteract, take the law into one's own hands, not mind, pay no attention to, go counter to, not listen to.—*Ant.* obey, follow, fulfill.

**disorderly** *a.* **1** [Lacking orderly arrangement] confused, jumbled, undisciplined, unrestrained, scattered, dislocated, unsystematic, messy, slovenly, untidy, cluttered, unkempt, scrambled, badly managed, in confusion, disorganized, untrained, out of control, topsy-turvy, all over the place*, mixed-up.—*Ant.* regular, neat, trim. **2** [Creating a disturbance] intemperate, drunk, rowdy.

**disorganize** *v.* break up, disperse, destroy, scatter, litter, clutter, break down, put out of order, disarrange, disorder, upset, disrupt, derange, dislocate, disband, jumble, muddle, unsettle, disturb, perturb, shuffle, toss, turn topsy-turvy, complicate, confound, overthrow, overturn, scramble.—*Ant.* systematize, order, distribute.

**dispense** *v.* apportion, assign, allocate.

**display** *n.* exhibition, exhibit, presentation, representation, exposition, arrangement, demonstration, performance, revelation, procession, parade, pageant, example, appearance, waxworks, fireworks, carnival, fair, pomp, splendor, unfolding.

**display** *v.* show, show off, exhibit, uncover, open up, unfold, spread, parade, unmask, present, represent, perform, flaunt, lay out, put out, set out, disclose, unveil, arrange, make known.—*Ant.* hide, conceal, veil.

**displease** *v.* vex, provoke, enrage.

**disposition** *n.* **1** [Arrangement] decision, method, distribution. **2** [Temperament] character, nature, temper.

**disprove** *v.* prove false, throw out, set aside, find fault in, invalidate, weaken, overthrow, tear down, confound, expose, cut the ground from under, poke holes in*.

**dispute** *n.* argument, quarrel, debate, misunderstanding, conflict, strife, discussion, polemic, bickering, squabble, disturbance, feud, commotion, tiff, fracas, controversy, altercation, dissension, squall, difference of opinion, rumpus*, row, flare-up, fuss, fire-works*.

**disregard** *v.* ignore, pass over, let pass, make light of, have no use for, laugh off, take no account of, brush aside, turn a deaf ear to, be blind to, shut one's eyes to.

**disrespectful** *a.* discourteous, impolite, rude.

**dissent** *n.* nonconformity, difference, heresy.

**distance** *n.* **1** [A degree or quantity of space] reach, span, range. **2** [A place or places far away] background, horizon, as far as the eye can see, sky, heavens, outskirts, foreign countries, different worlds, strange places, distant terrain, objective, the country, beyond the horizon.—*Ant.* neighborhood, surroundings, neighbors. **3** [A measure of space] statute mile, rod, yard, foot, kilometer, meter, centimeter, millimeter, league, fathom, span, hand, cubit, furlong, a stone's throw. **—go the distance** finish, bring to an end, see through. **—keep at a distance** ignore, reject, shun. **—keep one's distance** be aloof, ignore, shun.

**distant** *a.* afar, far off, abroad, faraway, yonder, backwoods, removed, abstracted, inaccessible, unapproachable, out-of-the-way, at arm's length, stretching to, out of range, out of reach, out of earshot, out of sight, in the background, in the distance, separate, farther, further, far away, at a distance, different.—*Ant.* close, near, next.

**distinguish** *v.* **1** [To make distinctions] discriminate, differentiate, classify, specify, identify, individualize, characterize, separate, divide, collate, sort out, sort into, set apart, mark off, criticize, select, draw the line, tell from, pick and choose, separate the wheat from the chaff, separate the men from the boys. **2** [To discern] detect, discriminate, notice. **3** [To bestow honor upon] pay tribute to, honor, celebrate.

**distinguished** *a.* **1** [Made recognizable by markings] characterized, labeled, marked, stamped, signed, signified, identified, made certain, obvious, set apart, branded, earmarked, separate, unique, differentiated, observed, distinct, conspicuous.—*Ant.* typical, unidentified, indistinct. **2** [Notable for excellence] eminent, illustrious, venerable, renowned, honored, memorable, celebrated, well-known, noted, noteworthy, highly regarded, well-thought-of, esteemed, prominent, reputable, superior, outstanding, brilliant, glorious, extraordinary, singular, great, special, striking, unforgettable, shining, foremost, dignified, famed, talked of, first-rate, big-name*, headline*.—*Ant.* obscure, insignificant, unimportant.

**distract** *v.* detract, occupy, amuse, entertain, draw away, call away, draw one's attention from, lead astray, attract from.

**distress** *n.* worry, anxiety, misery, sorrow, wretchedness, pain, dejection, irritation, suffering, ache, heartache, ordeal, desolation, anguish, affliction, woe, torment, shame, embarrassment, disappointment, tribulation, pang.—*Ant.* joy, happiness, jollity.

**distress** *v.* irritate, disturb, upset.

**distribute** *v.* dispense, divide, share, deal, bestow, issue, dispose, disperse, mete out, pass out, parcel out, dole out, hand out, give away, assign, allocate, ration, appropriate, pay dividends, dish out, divvy up*.—*Ant.* hold, keep, preserve.

**district** *n.* neighborhood, community, vicinity.

**disturb** *v.* trouble, worry, agitate, perplex, rattle, startle, shake, amaze, astound, alarm, excite, arouse, badger, plague, fuss, perturb, vex, upset, outrage, molest, grieve, depress, distress, irk, ail, tire, provoke, afflict, irritate, pain, make uneasy, harass, exasperate, pique, gall, displease, complicate, involve, astonish, fluster, ruffle, burn up*.—*Ant.* quiet, calm, soothe.

**disturbing** *a.* disquieting, upsetting, tiresome, perturbing, bothersome, unpleasant, provoking, annoying, alarming, painful, discomforting, inauspicious, foreboding, aggravating, disagreeable, troublesome, worrisome, burdensome, trying, frightening, startling, perplexing, threatening, distressing, galling, difficult, severe, hard, inconvenient, discouraging, pessimistic, gloomy, depressing, irritating, harassing, unpropitious, unlikely, embarrassing, ruffling, agitating.

**ditch** *n.* canal, furrow, trench.

**dive** *v.* plunge, spring, jump, vault, leap, go headfirst, plummet, sink, dip, duck, submerge, nose-dive.

**diverse** *a.* different, assorted, distinct.

**divert** *v.* **1** [To deflect] turn aside, redirect, avert. **2** [To distract] attract the attention of, lead away from, disturb.

**divide** *v.* part, cut up, fence off, detach, disengage, dissolve, sever, rupture, dismember, sunder, split, unravel, carve, cleave, intersect, cross, bisect, rend, tear, segment, halve, quarter, third, break down, divorce, dissociate, isolate, count off, pull away, chop, slash, gash, carve, splinter, pull to pieces, tear apart, break apart, segregate, fork, branch, tear limb from limb*, split off, split up.—*Ant.* unite, combine, connect.

**divine** *a.* sacred, hallowed, spiritual, sacramental, ceremonial, ritualistic, consecrated, dedicated, devoted, venerable, pious, religious, anointed, sanctified, ordained, sanctioned, set apart, sacrosanct, scriptural, blessed, worshiped, revered, venerated, mystical, adored, solemn, faithful.

**division** *n.* **1** [The act or result of dividing] separation, detachment, apportionment, partition, parting, distribution, severance, cutting, subdivision, dismemberment, distinction, distinguishing, selection, analysis, diagnosis, reduction, splitting, breakdown, fracture, disjuncture.—*Ant.* union, joining, gluing. **2** [A part produced by dividing] section, kind, sort, portion, compartment, share, split, member, subdivision, parcel, segment, fragment, department, category, branch, fraction, dividend, degree, piece, slice, lump, wedge, cut, book, chapter, verse, class, race, clan, tribe, caste. **3** [Discord or disunion] trouble, words, difficulty. **4** [A military unit] armored division, airborne division, infantry division. **5** [An organized area] state, government, range.

**divorce** *n.* separation, partition, divorcement, bill of divorcement, annulment, separate maintenance, parting of the ways, dissolution, split-up*.—*Ant.* marriage, betrothal, wedding.

**divulge** *v.* disclose, impart, confess.

**dizzy** *a.* confused, lightheaded, giddy, bemused, staggering, upset, dazzled, dazed, dumb, faint, with spots before one's eyes, out of control, weak-kneed, wobbly.

**docile** *a.* meek, mild, tractable, pliant, submissive, accommodating, adaptable, resigned, agreeable, willing, obliging, well-behaved, manageable, tame, yielding, teachable, easily influenced, easygoing, usable, soft, childlike.

**doctrine** *n.* principle, proposition, precept, article, concept, conviction, opinion, convention, attitude, tradition, unwritten law, natural law, common law, teachings, accepted belief, article of faith, canon, regulation, rule, pronouncement, declaration.

**document** *n.* paper, diary, report.

**dodge** *v.* duck, elude, evade.

**domestic** *a.* **1** [Home-loving] house-loving, domesticated, stay-at-home, household, family, quiet, sedentary, indoor, tame, settled.—*Ant.* unruly, roving, restless. **2** [Homegrown] indigenous, handcrafted, native.

**dominant** *a.* commanding, authoritative, assertive.

**dominate** *v.* rule, manage, control, dictate to, subject, subjugate, tyrannize, have one's own way, have influence over, domineer, lead by the nose, boss*, keep under one's thumb.

**domineering** *a.* despotic, imperious, oppressive.

**donate** *v.* grant, bestow, bequeath.

**donor** *n.* benefactor, contributor, patron, philanthropist, giver, subscriber, altruist, Good Samaritan, fairy godmother*.

**doom** *n.* fate, lot, destination, predestination, future, fortune, ruin, goal.

**doomed** *a.* ruined, cursed, sentenced, lost, condemned, unfortunate, ill-fated, foreordained, predestined, threatened, menaced, suppressed, wrecked.

**door** *n.* entry, portal, hatchway, doorway, gateway, opening. **—out of doors** outside, in the air, out. **—show someone the door** show out, ask to leave, eject.

**doubt** *n.* distrust, mistrust, disbelief, suspicion, misgiving, skepticism, apprehension, agnosticism, incredulity, lack of faith, lack of confidence, jealousy, rejection, scruple, misgiving, indecision, lack of conviction, ambiguity, dilemma, reluctance, quandary, feeling of inferiority.—*Ant.* belief, conviction, certainty. **—beyond** (or **without**) **doubt** doubtless, certainly, without a doubt. **—no doubt** doubtless, in all likelihood, certainly.

**doubt** *v.* wonder, question, query, ponder, dispute, be dubious, be uncertain, be doubtful, refuse to believe, demur, have doubts about, have one's doubts, stop to consider, have qualms, call in question, give no credit to, throw doubt upon, have no conception, not know which way to turn, not know what to make of, close one's mind, not admit, not believe, refuse to believe, not buy*.—*Ant.* trust, believe, confide.

**doubtful** *a.* **1** [Uncertain in mind] dubious, doubting, questioning, undecided, unsure, wavering, hesitating, undetermined, uncertain, unsettled, confused, disturbed, lost, puzzled, perplexed, flustered, baffled, distracted, unresolved, in a quandary, of two minds, unable to make up one's mind, troubled with doubt, having little faith, of little faith, in question, not knowing what's what, not following, up a tree*, not able to make head or tail of, going around in circles*, out of focus, up in the air, wishy-washy*, iffy*. **2** [Improbable] probably wrong, questionable, unconvincing.

**douse** *v.* submerge, splash, drench.

**downright** *a.* total, complete, utter.

**downstairs** *n.* first floor, ground floor, basement.

**down-to-earth** *a.* sensible, mundane, practical.

**doze** *v.* nap, drowse, slumber.

**drain** *v.* **1** [To withdraw fluid] tap, draw off, remove. **2** [To withdraw strength] exhaust, weary, tire out. **3** [To seep away] run off, run out, flow away, seep out, exude, trickle out, filter off, ooze, find an opening, decline, diminish, leave dry.

**drama** *n.* play, theatrical piece, theatrical production, dramatization, stage show, theatre.

**draw** *v.* **1** [To move an object] pull, drag, attract, move, bring, tug, lug, tow, carry, jerk, wrench, yank, haul, extract.—*Ant.* repel, repulse, reject. **2** [To make a likeness by drawing] sketch, describe, etch, pencil, outline, trace, make a picture of, depict, model, portray, engrave, chart, map. **—beat to the draw*** be quicker than another, forestall, stop.

**drawback** *n.* detriment, hindrance, check.

**dream** *n.* nightmare, apparition, hallucination, image, trance, idea, impression, emotion, reverie, daydream, castle in the air, castle in Spain, chimera.—*Ant.* reality, verity, truth.

**dream** *v.* **1** [To have visions, usually during sleep or fever] hallucinate, fancy, visualize. **2** [To entertain or delude oneself with imagined things] fancy, imagine, conceive, have notions, conjure up, create, picture, idealize, daydream, fantasize, be in the clouds, pipedream*.

**dreamy** *a.* whimsical, fanciful, daydreaming, visionary, given to reverie, illusory, introspective, otherworldly, idealistic, mythical, utopian, romantic.—*Ant.* practical, active, real.

**dreary** *a.* damp, raw, windy.

**drench** *v.* wet, saturate, flood.

**dress** *n.* **1** [Clothing] ensemble, attire, garments, outfit, garb, apparel, array, costume, wardrobe, uniform, habit, livery, formal dress, evening clothes, trappings, things, get-up*, threads*, rags*, duds*. **2** [A woman's outer garment] frock, gown, wedding dress, evening gown, formal, cocktail dress, suit, skirt, robe, shift, sundress, wraparound, housedress, smock.

**dress** *v.* **1** [To put on clothes] don, wear, garb, clothe, robe, attire, drape, array, cover, spruce up, dress up, bundle up, get into*, doll up*, put on the dog*, dress to the nines*. **2** [To provide with clothes] costume, outfit, clothe. **3** [To give medical treatment] treat, bandage, give first aid.

**drift** *n.* **1** [The tendency in movement] bent, trend, tendency, end, inclination, impulse, propulsion, aim, scope, goal, push, bias, set, leaning, progress, disposition, bearing, line, set.—*Ant.* indifference, aimlessness, inertia. **2** [The measure or character of movement] current, diversion, sweep.

**drift** *v.* float, ride, sail, wander, sweep, move with the current, gravitate, tend, be carried along by the current, move toward, go with the tide, be caught in the current, move without effort, move slowly.—*Ant.* lead, steer, pull.

**drill** *n.* **1** [Practice] preparation, repetition, learning by doing. **2** [A tool for boring holes] borer, wood bit, steel drill, steam drill, diamond drill, compressed-air drill, boring tool, tap-borer, auger, corkscrew, awl, riveter, jackhammer. **3** [Exercise, especially in military formation] training, maneuvers, marching, close-order drill, open-order drill, conditioning, survival training, guerrilla training. **4** [Device for planting seed in holes] planter, seeder, implement.

**drink** *n.* **1** [A draft] gulp, sip, potion, drop, bottle, glass, refreshment, tall drink, shot, stiff one*, slug*, belt*, nip, swig*, spot*, short one*, nightcap*, hair of the dog*, one for the road*. **2** [Something drunk] rye, bourbon, Scotch, Irish whiskey, ale, stout, rum, liqueur, tequila, vodka, distilled water, mineral water, carbonated water, mixer, tonic, seltzer, cocoa, hot chocolate, chocolate milk, milkshake, frappé, lemonade, punch, soft drink, soda water, ginger ale, ice-cream soda; orange juice, tomato juice, grapefruit juice, etc.; pop, soda, soda pop.

**drink** *v.* **1** [To swallow liquid] gulp down, take in, sip, suck in, guzzle, imbibe, wash down, gargle. **2** [To consume alcoholic liquor] tipple, swill, swig, guzzle, belt*, take a drop*, take a nip, wet one's whistle*, down*, booze*, hit the bottle*, go on a binge*.

**drive** *n.* **1** [A ride in a vehicle] ride, trip, outing, airing, tour, excursion, jaunt, spin, Sunday drive*. **2** [A road] approach, avenue, boulevard, entrance, street, roadway, parkway, lane, track, path, pavement. **3** [Impelling force] energy, effort, impulse.

**drive** *v.* **1** [To urge on] impel, propel, instigate, incite, animate, hasten, egg on, urge on, compel, coerce, induce, force, press, stimulate, hurry, provoke, arouse, make, put up to, inspire, prompt, rouse, work on, act upon.—*Ant.* stop, hinder, drag. **2** [To manage a propelled vehicle] direct, manage, handle, run, wheel, bicycle, bike*, cycle, transport, float, drift, dash, put in motion, start, set going, speed, roll, coast, get under way, keep going, back up, burn up the road*, go like hell*, step on it*, floor it*, gun it*, burn rubber*, give it the gas*.—*Ant.* walk, crawl, stay.

**drone** *v.* hum, buzz, vibrate.

**drool** *v.* drivel, drip, salivate, spit, dribble, trickle, ooze, run.

**drop** *n.* **1** [Enough fluid to fall] drip, trickle, droplet, bead, teardrop, dewdrop, raindrop. **2** [A lowering or falling] fall, tumble, reduction, decrease, slide, descent, slump, lapse, slip, decline, downfall, upset. **3** [A small quantity] speck, dash, dab. **—at the drop of a hat*** without warning, at the slightest provocation, quickly.

**drop** *v.* **1** [To fall in drops] drip, fall, dribble, trickle, descend, leak, ooze, seep, drain, filter, sink, bleed, bead, splash, hail.—*Ant.* rise, spurt, squirt. **2** [To cause or to permit to fall] let go, give up, release, shed, relinquish, abandon, loosen, lower, floor, ground, shoot, knock down, fell, topple.—*Ant.* raise, elevate, send up. **3** [To discontinue] give up, quit, leave. **4** [To break off an acquaintance] break with, part from, cast off.

**drudge** *n.* slave, menial, hard worker.

**drunk** *a.* intoxicated, inebriated, befuddled, tipsy, overcome, sottish, drunken, stoned*, feeling no pain*, out of it*, seeing double*, smashed*, blotto*, gassed*, plowed*, under the table*, tanked*, wiped out*, soused*, high*, pickled*, stewed*, boozed up*, tight*, higher than a kite*.—*Ant.* sober, steady, temperate.

**dry** *a.* **1** [Having little or no moisture] arid, parched, waterless, hard, dried up, evaporated, desiccated, barren, dehydrated, drained, rainless, not irrigated, bare, thirsty, waterproof, rainproof, baked, shriveled, desert, dusty, depleted, dry as a bone*.—*Ant.* wet, moist, damp. **2** [Thirsty] parched, dehydrated, athirst. **3** [Lacking in interest] boring, uninteresting, tedious. **4** [Possessed of intellectual humor] sarcastic, cynical, biting.

**dry** *v.* **1** [To become dry] dry up, shrivel, wilt. **2** [To cause to become dry] air-dry, condense, concentrate, dehydrate, freeze-dry, blot, sponge, parch, scorch, dry up, exhaust.

**dubious** *a.* **1** [Doubtful] indecisive, perplexed, hesitant. **2** [Vague] ambiguous, indefinite, unclear.

**duct** *n.* tube, canal, channel.

**due** *a.* payable, owed, owing, overdue, collectible, unsatisfied, unsettled, not met, receivable, to be paid, chargeable, outstanding, in arrears. **—become** (or **fall**) **due** be owed, payable, remain unsatisfied, mature.

**due to** *a. & conj.* because of, resulting from, accordingly.

**dull** *a.* **1** [Without point or edge] blunt, blunted, unsharpened, pointless, unpointed, round, square, flat, nicked, broken, toothless.—*Ant.* sharp, sharpened, keen. **2** [Lacking brightness or color] gloomy, sober, somber, drab, dismal, dark, dingy, dim, dusky, colorless, plain, obscure, tarnished, opaque, leaden, grave, grimy, pitchy, sooty, inky, dead, black, coal-black, unlighted, sordid, dirty, muddy, gray, lifeless, rusty, flat.—*Ant.* bright, colorful, gleaming. **3** [Lacking intelligence; *said usually of living beings*] slow, retarded, witless. **4** [Lacking interest; *said usually of writing, speaking, or inanimate things*] heavy, prosaic, trite, hackneyed, monotonous, humdrum, tedious, dreary, dismal, dry, arid, colorless, insipid, boring, vapid, flat, senseless, long-winded, stupid, commonplace, ordinary, common, usual, old, ancient, stale, moth-eaten, out-of-date, archaic, worn-out, tiring, banal, tired, uninteresting, driveling, pointless, uninspiring, piddling, senile, proverbial, tame, routine, familiar, known, well-known, conventional, depressing, sluggish, repetitious, repetitive, soporific, tiresome, lifeless, wearying, unexciting, flat, stereotyped, stock, the usual thing, the same old thing, the same thing day after day, slow, dry as a bone*, cut and dried, dead as a doornail*.—*Ant.* exciting, fascinating, exhilarating. **5** [Not loud or distinct] low, soft, softened. **6** [Showing little activity] still, routine, regular. **7** [Gloomy] cloudy, dim, unlit.

**dump** *v.* empty, unload, deposit, unpack, discharge, evacuate, drain, eject, exude, expel, throw out, throw over, throw overboard.—*Ant.* load, fill, pack.

**duplicate** *n.* double, second, mate, facsimile, replica, carbon copy, likeness, counterpart, analogue, parallel, correlate, repetition, duplication, recurrence, match, twin, Xerox (trademark), chip off the old block. **—in duplicate** duplicated, doubled, copied.

**durable** *a.* strong, firm, enduring.

**dusk** *n.* gloom, twilight, dawn.

**dust** *n.* dirt, lint, soil, sand, flakes, ashes, cinders, grime, soot, grit, filings, sawdust. **—bite the dust*** be killed, fall in battle, succumb. **—make the dust fly** move swiftly, work hard, be active.

**duty** *n.* **1** [A personal sense of what one should do] moral obligation, conscience, liability, charge, accountability, faithfulness, pledge, burden, good faith, honesty, integrity, sense of duty, call of duty.—*Ant.* dishonesty, irresponsibility, disloyalty. **2** [Whatever one has to do] work, task, occupation, function, business, province, part, calling, charge, office, service, mission, obligation, contract, station, trust, burden, undertaking, commission, engagement, assignment, routine, chore, pains, responsibility.—*Ant.* entertainment, amusement, sport. **3** [A levy, especially on goods] revenue, custom, tax. **—off duty** not engaged, free, inactive. **—on duty** employed, engaged, at work.

**dwell** *v.* live, inhabit, stay, lodge, stop, settle, remain, live in, live at, continue, go on living, rent, tenant, have a lease on, make one's home at, have one's address at, keep house, be at home, room, bunk*.

**dwelling** *n.* house, establishment, lodging.

**dying** *a.* **1** [Losing life] sinking, passing away, fated, going, perishing, failing, expiring, moribund, withering away, at death's door*, done for*, cashing in one's chips*, with one foot in the grave*. **2** [Becoming worse or less] declining, going down, receding, retarding, decreasing, disappearing, dissolving, disintegrating, vanishing, failing, fading, ebbing, decaying, overripe, decadent, passé, doomed, neglected.

**dynamic** *a.* energetic, potent, compelling, forceful, changing, progressive, productive, vigorous, magnetic, electric, effective, influential, charismatic, high-powered, peppy*, hopped up*.

# E

**each** *a.* **1** [Every] all, any, one by one, separate, particular, specific, private, several, respective, various, piece by piece, individual, personal, without exception. **2** [For each time, person, or the like] individually, proportionately, respectively, for one, per unit, singly, per capita, apiece, separately, every, without exception, by the, per, a whack*, a throw*, a shot*.

**eager** *a.* anxious, keen, fervent.

**early** *a.* **1** [Near the beginning] recent, primitive, prime, new, brand-new, fresh, budding.—*Ant.* late, old, superannuated. **2** [Sooner than might have been expected] quick, premature, in advance, far ahead, in the bud, preceding, advanced, immediate, unexpected, speedy, ahead of time, direct, prompt, punctual, briefly, shortly, presently, beforehand, on short notice, on the dot*, with time to spare.—*Ant.* slow, late, tardy.

**earth** *n.* **1** [The world] globe, sphere, planet, *terra*, mundane world, creation, terrestrial sphere, orb, cosmos, universe, star. **2** [The earthly crust] dirt, clean dirt, loam, humus, clay, gravel, sand, land, dry land, terrain, mud, muck, soil, ground, fill, compost, topsoil, alluvium, terrane, surface, shore, coast, deposit. **—come back** (or **down**) **to earth** be practical, be sensible, return to one's senses, quit dreaming. **—down to earth** earthly, realistic, mundane. **—on earth** of all things, of everything, what.

**earthen** *a.* clay, stone, mud, dirt, rock, fictile, made of earth, made of baked clay.

**earthly** *a.* human, mortal, global, mundane, worldly, under the sun, in all creation.—*Ant.* unnatural, unearthly, superhuman.

**ease** *n.* **1** [Freedom from pain] comfort, rest, quietness, peace, prosperity, leisure, repose, satisfaction, calm, calmness, restfulness, tranquility, solace, consolation.—*Ant.* pain, discomfort, unrest. **2** [Freedom from difficulty] expertness, facility, efficiency, knack, readiness, quickness, skillfulness, dexterity, cleverness, smoothness; child's play, clear sailing*, snap*, breeze*, cinch*, pushover*.—*Ant.* difficulty, trouble, clumsiness. **—at ease** relaxed, collected, resting.

**ease** *v.* **1** [To relieve of pain] alleviate, allay, drug, keep under sedation, tranquilize, sedate, anesthetize, give relief, comfort, relieve pressure, cure, attend to, doctor, nurse, relieve, soothe, set at ease, cheer.—*Ant.* hurt, injure, pain. **2** [To lessen pressure or tension] prop up, lift, bear, hold up, make comfortable, raise, unburden, release, soften, relieve one's mind, lighten, let up on, give rest to, relax, quiet, calm, pacify. **3** [To move carefully] induce, remove, extricate, set right, right, insert, join, slide, maneuver, handle.—*Ant.* hurry, rush, blunder.

**easy** *a.* **1** [Free from constraint] secure, at ease, prosperous, leisurely, unembarrassed, spontaneous, calm, peaceful, tranquil, careless, contented, carefree, untroubled, moderate, hospitable, soft*.—*Ant.* difficult, impoverished, hard. **2** [Providing no difficulty] simple, facile, obvious, apparent, yielding, easily done, smooth, manageable, accessible, wieldy, slight, little, paltry, inconsiderable, nothing to it*, simple as ABC*, pushover*, easy as pie*, like taking candy from a baby*.—*Ant.* hard, difficult, complicated. **3** [Lax] lenient, indulgent, easygoing. **—take it easy** relax, rest, slow down.

**easygoing** *a.* tranquil, carefree, patient.

**eat** *v.* **1** [To take as food] consume, bite, chew, devour, swallow, feast on, dine out, peck at, gorge, gobble up, eat up, digest, masticate, feed on, breakfast, dine, eat out, sup, lunch, feed, feast, banquet, fall to, live on, feed on, take in, enjoy a meal, have a bite, put away*, make a pig of oneself*, eat out of house and home*.—*Ant.* fast, starve, vomit. **2** [To reduce gradually] eat up, eat away, liquefy, melt, disappear, vanish, waste, rust away, spill, dissipate, squander, drain, spill, fool away, run through.—*Ant.* increase, swell, build. **3** [To bother] worry, vex, disturb.

**eavesdrop** *v.* overhear, wiretap, listen, listen in on, try to overhear, bend an ear*, bug*, tap.

**ebb** *v.* recede, subside, retire, flow back, sink, decline, decrease, drop off, melt, fall away, peter out*, wane, fall off, decay.—*Ant.* increase, flow, rise.

**eccentric** *a.* odd, queer, strange.

**economical** *a.* **1** [Careful of expenditures] saving, sparing, careful, economizing, thrifty, prudent, frugal, miserly, stingy, mean, close, watchful, tight*, closefisted, penny-pinching*.—*Ant.* generous, liberal, wasteful. **2** [Advantageously priced] cheap, sound, low, reasonable, fair, moderate, inexpensive, marked down, on sale. **3** [Making good use of materials] practical, efficient, methodical.

**economize** *v.* husband, manage, stint, conserve, scrimp, skimp, be frugal, be prudent, pinch, cut costs, cut corners, meet expenses, keep within one's means, cut down, meet a budget, make both ends meet, tighten one's belt*, save for a rainy day*, pinch pennies.—*Ant.* spend, waste, splurge.

**ecstasy** *n.* joy, rapture, delight.

**edge** *n.* **1** [The outer portion] border, frontier, extremity, threshold, brink, boundary, end, limit, brim, rim, margin, ring, frame, side, corner, point, bend, peak, turn, crust, verge, bound, ledge, skirt, outskirt, lip, limb, hem, seam, fringe, frill, mouth, shore, strand, bank, beach, curb, periphery, circumference.—*Ant.* center, surface, interior. **2** [Anything linear and sharp] blade, cutting edge, razor edge. **—on edge** nervous, tense, uptight*. **—set one's teeth on edge** irritate, annoy, provoke. **—take the edge off** weaken, subdue, dull.

**edible** *a.* palatable, good, delicious, satisfying, fit to eat, savory, tasty, culinary, yummy*, nutritious, digestible.

**edit** *v.* revise, alter, rewrite, arrange materials for publication, prepare for the press, compose, compile, select, arrange, set up, censor, polish, finish, analyze, revise and correct, delete, condense, discard, strike out, write, proofread, cut, trim, blue-pencil, doctor up*.

**educate** *v.* tutor, instruct, teach.

**educated** *a.* trained, accomplished, skilled, well-taught, scientific, scholarly, intelligent, learned, well-informed, well-read, well-versed, well-grounded, disciplined, prepared, instructed, developed, civilized, fitted, versed in, informed in, acquainted with, professional, expert, polished, cultured, finished, initiated, enlightened, literate, lettered, tutored, schooled.—*Ant.* ignorant, illiterate, unlettered.

**education** *n.* **1** [The process of directing learning] schooling, study, training, direction, instruction, guidance, apprenticeship, teaching, tutelage, learning, reading, discipline, preparation, adult education, book learning, information, indoctrination, brainwashing, cultivation, background, rearing. **2** [Knowledge acquired through education] learning, wisdom, scholarship. **3** [The teaching profession] teaching, tutoring, pedagogy, instruction, training, the field of education, the educational profession, progressive education, lecturing.

**eerie** *a.* strange, ghostly, weird.

**effect** *n.* conclusion, consequence, outcome. **—in effect** as a result, in fact, actually. **—take effect** work, produce results, become operative. **—to the effect** (**that**) as a result, so that, therefore.

**effect** *v.* produce, cause, make.

**effective** *a.* efficient, serviceable, useful, operative, effectual, sufficient, adequate, productive, capable, competent, yielding, practical, valid, resultant.—*Ant.* useless, inoperative, inefficient.

**efficient** *a.* **1** [*Said of persons*] competent, businesslike, good at, apt, adequate, fitted, able, capable, qualified, skillful, clever, talented, energetic, skilled, adapted, familiar with, deft, adept, expert, experienced, equal to, practiced, practical, proficient, accomplished, active, productive, dynamic, decisive, tough, shrewd.—*Ant.* incompetent, inefficient, incapable. **2** [*Said of things*] economical, fitting, suitable, suited, effectual, effective, adequate, serviceable, useful, saving, profitable, valuable, expedient, handy, conducive, well-designed, streamlined, good for.—*Ant.* inadequate, unsuitable, ineffectual.

**effort** *n.* attempt, enterprise, undertaking, struggle, battle, try, trial, work, venture, aim, aspiration, purpose, intention, resolution, exercise, discipline, crack*, go*, whirl*.

**egg** *n.* ovum, seed, germ, spawn, bud, embryo, nucleus, cell. **—lay an egg*** be unsuccessful, err, make a mistake. **—put** (or **have**) **all one's eggs in one basket** chance, gamble, bet.

**ego** *n.* personality, individuality, self.

**egotistic** *a.* conceited, vain, boastful, inflated, pompous, arrogant, insolent, puffed up, affected, self-centered, self-glorifying, presumptuous, blustering, showy, boisterous, haughty, snobbish, contemptuous, proud, bullying, sneering, aloof, pretentious, assuming, cocky*, brazen, impertinent, selfish, bragging, insulting, theatrical, garish, gaudy, spectacular, reckless, impudent, inflated, stiff, overbearing, domineering, bold, rash, overconfident, self-satisfied, stuck up*, looking down one's nose*, snooty*, uppity*, wrapped up in oneself*, on one's high horse*, high and mighty*, too big for one's breeches*, big as you please*.—*Ant.* humble, meek, modest.

**eject** *v.* dislodge, discard, reject, run out, kick out, throw out, put out, force out, spit out, turn out, squeeze out, oust, do away with, evict, banish, throw off, vomit, excrete, dump, get rid of, send packing, give the boot*, ditch*, bounce*.

**elaborate** *a.* **1** [Ornamented] gaudy, decorated, garnished, showy, fussy, dressy, refined, flowery, flashy.—*Ant.* common, ordinary, unpolished. **2** [Detailed] complicated, extensive, laborious, minute, intricate, involved, many-faceted, complex, a great many, painstaking, studied.—*Ant.* general, usual, unified.

**elastic** *a.* plastic, tempered, pliant.

**elderly** *a.* declining, retired, venerable.

**elegant** *a.* ornate, polished, perfected, elaborate, finished, ornamented, adorned, embellished, embroidered, flowing, artistic, fancy, rich, pure, fluent, neat.—*Ant.* dull, ill-chosen, inarticulate.

**element** *n.* portion, particle, detail, component, constituent, ingredient, factor.

**elementary** *a.* **1** [Suited to beginners] primary, introductory, rudimentary. **2** [Fundamental] foundational, essential, basic.

**elevate** *v.* **1** [To lift bodily] hoist, heave, tilt. **2** [To promote] advance, appoint, further.

**eligible** *a.* qualified, fit, suitable, suited, equal to, worthy of being chosen, capable of, fitted for, satisfactory, trained, employable, usable, becoming, likely, in the running, in line for, up to*.—*Ant.* unfit, ineligible, disqualified.

**eliminate** *v.* take out, wipe out, clean out, throw out, stamp out, blot out, cut out, phase out, drive out, dispose of, get rid of, do away with, put aside, set aside, exclude, eject, cast off, disqualify, oust, depose, evict, cancel, eradicate, erase, expel, discharge, dislodge, reduce, invalidate, abolish, repeal, exterminate, annihilate, kill, murder, throw overboard, be done with, discard, dismiss, obliterate, discount, exile, banish, deport, expatriate, maroon, blackball, ostracize, fire, dump*, can*, ditch*, scrap, bounce*, sack*, downsize*, drop.—*Ant.* include, accept, welcome.

**eloquence** *n.* fluency, wit, wittiness, expression, expressiveness, appeal, ability, diction, articulation, delivery, power, force, vigor, facility, style, poise, expressiveness, flow, command of language, gift of gab*.

**emaciated** *a.* gaunt, famished, wasted.

**emanate** *v.* exude, radiate, emit.

**emancipate** *v.* release, liberate, deliver.

**embalm** *v.* preserve, process, freeze, anoint, wrap, mummify, prepare for burial, lay out.

**embarrass** *v.* perplex, annoy, puzzle, vex, distress, disconcert, agitate, bewilder, confuse, chagrin, confound, upset, bother, plague, tease, worry, trouble, distract, discomfort, disturb, let down, perturb, fluster, irk, shame, stun, rattle, put on the spot*, make a monkey out of*.—*Ant.* encourage, cheer, please.

**emblem** *n.* symbol, figure, image, design, token, sign, insignia, banner, seal, colors, crest, coat of arms, representation, effigy, reminder, mark, badge, souvenir, keepsake, memento, medal, character, motto, hallmark, flag, pennant, banner, standard.

**emergency** *n.* accident, unforeseen occurrence, misadventure, strait, urgency, necessity, pressure, tension, distress, turn of events, obligation, pass, crisis, predicament, turning point, impasse, dilemma, quandary, pinch, fix*, hole*.

**emigration** *n.* reestablishing, departure, removal, leaving, expatriation, displacement, moving away, crossing, migrating, exodus, exile, trek, journey, movement, trend, march, travel, voyage, wayfaring, wandering, migration, shift, settling, homesteading.—*Ant.* immigration, arriving, remaining.

**emotion** *n.* agitation, tremor, commotion, excitement, disturbance, sentiment, feeling, tumult, turmoil, sensation.

**emphatic** *a.* assured, strong, determined, forceful, forcible, earnest, positive, energetic, potent, powerful, dynamic, stressed, pointed, flat, definitive, categorical, dogmatic, explicit.

**employee** *n.* worker, laborer, servant, domestic, agent, representative, hired hand, salesman, salesperson, assistant, associate, attendant, apprentice, operator, workman, laboring man, workingman, breadwinner, craftsman, wage earner, hireling, lackey, underling, flunky.

**employer** *n.* owner, manager, proprietor, management, head, director, executive, superintendent, supervisor, president, chief, businessman, manufacturer, corporation, company, boss, front office.

**employment** *n.* job, profession, vocation.

**empty** *a.* hollow, bare, clear, blank, unfilled, unfurnished, unoccupied, vacated, vacant, void, vacuous, void of, devoid, lacking, wanting, barren, emptied, abandoned, exhausted, depleted, deserted, stark, deprived of, dry, destitute, negative, deflated, evacuated.—*Ant.* full, filled, occupied.

**empty** *v.* **1** [To become empty] discharge, leave, pour, flow out, ebb, run out, open into, be discharged, void, release, exhaust, leak, drain off, drain, rush out, escape.—*Ant.* absorb, flow in, enter. **2** [To cause to become empty] dump, dip, ladle, tap, void, pour, spill out, let out, deplete, exhaust, deflate, drain, bail out, clean out, clear out, evacuate, eject, expel, draw off, draw out, disgorge, suck dry, drink.—*Ant.* fill, pack, stuff.

**emulate** *v.* challenge, contend, imitate.

**enchant** *v.* entrance, allure, fascinate.

**enclose** *v.* insert, jail, corral, impound, confine, blockade, imprison, block off, fence off, set apart, lock up, lock in, keep in, box in, close in, shut in, wall in, box off, box up.—*Ant.* free, liberate, open.

**encourage** *v.* cheer, refresh, enliven, exhilarate, inspire, cheer up, praise, restore, revitalize, gladden, fortify, console, ease, relieve, help, aid, comfort, approve, reassure, assist, befriend, uphold, reinforce, back, bolster, brace, further, favor, strengthen, side with, cheer on, back up, egg on, root for*, pat on the back.—*Ant.* restrain, discourage, caution.

**end** *v.* **1** [To bring to a halt] stop, finish, quit, close, halt, shut down, settle, bring to an end, make an end of, break off, break up, put an end to, discontinue, postpone, delay, conclude, interrupt, dispose of, drop, call it a day*, cut short, wind up, get done, call off, give up, wrap up*.—*Ant.* begin, initiate, start. **2** [To bring to a conclusion] settle, conclude, terminate. **3** [To come to an end] desist, cease, die. **4** [To die] expire, depart, pass away. —**keep one's end up*** do one's share, join, participate. —**make ends meet** manage, get by, survive. —**no end*** very much, extremely, greatly. —**on end** **1** [Endless] ceaseless, without interruption, constant. **2** [Upright] erect, vertical, standing up. —**put an end to** stop, finish, cease.

**endanger** *v.* imperil, jeopardize, expose to danger, expose to hazard, expose to peril, be careless with, lay open, put on the spot*, leave in the middle.—*Ant.* save, protect, preserve.

**endeavor** *v.* attempt, aim, essay.

**endless** *a.* infinite, interminable, untold, without end, unbounded, unlimited, immeasurable, limitless, boundless, incalculable, unfathomable.

**endorse** *v.* **1** [To inscribe one's name] sign, put one's signature to, put one's signature on, countersign, underwrite, sign one's name on, subscribe, notarize, add one's name to, put one's John Hancock on*, sign on the dotted line*. **2** [To indicate one's active support of] approve, confirm, sanction, ratify, guarantee, underwrite, support, stand up for, stand behind, be behind, vouch for, uphold, recommend, praise, give one's word for, OK*, back up, go to bat for*.—*Ant.* blame, censure, condemn.

**endow** *v.* enrich, provide, supply.

**endurance** *n.* sufferance, fortitude, capacity to endure, long-suffering, resignation, patience, tolerance, courage, perseverance, stamina, restraint, resistance, will, backbone, guts*, spunk*.—*Ant.* weakness, feebleness, infirmity.

**enemy** *n.* foe, rival, assailant, competitor, attacker, antagonist, opponent, adversary, public enemy, criminal, opposition, guerrillas, guerrilla force, fifth column, saboteur, spy, foreign agent, assassin, murderer, betrayer, traitor, terrorist, revolutionary, rebel, invader.—*Ant.* friend, ally, supporter.

**enforced** *a.* compelled, established, exacted, required, executed, pressed, sanctioned, forced upon, kept, dictated, admonished, advocated, charged, meted out, cracked down.

**engaged** *a.* **1** [Promised in marriage] bound, pledged, betrothed, matched, hooked*.—*Ant.* free, unpledged, unbetrothed. **2** [Not at liberty] working, occupied, employed. **3** [In a profession, business, or the like] employed, practicing, performing, dealing in, doing, interested, absorbed in, pursuing, at work, involved with, engaged with, involved in, engaged in, working at, connected with.—*Ant.* unemployed, out of a job, without connection.

**engraved** *a.* carved, decorated, etched, scratched, bitten into, embossed, furrowed, incised, deepened, marked deeply, lithographed.

**enhance** *v.* heighten, magnify, amplify.

**enjoyment** *n.* satisfaction, gratification, triumph, loving, enjoying, rejoicing, having, using, occupation, use, diversion, entertainment, luxury, sensuality, indulgence, self-indulgence, hedonism.—*Ant.* abuse, dislike, displeasure.

**enlarged** *a.* increased, augmented, expanded, developed, exaggerated, extended, amplified, spread, added to, lengthened, broadened, widened, thickened, magnified, filled-out, inflated, stretched, heightened, intensified, blown up*.

**enmity** *n.* animosity, malice, rancor.

**enormous** *a.* monstrous, immense, huge.

**enough** *a.* **1** [Sufficient] plenty, abundant, adequate, acceptable, ample, satisfactory, complete, copious, plentiful, satisfying, unlimited, suitable.—*Ant.* inadequate, deficient, insufficient. **2** [Sufficiently] satisfactorily, amply, abundantly. **3** [Fully] quite, rather, just. **4** [Just adequately] tolerably, fairly, barely.

**enroll** *v.* **1** [To obtain for service] recruit, obtain, employ. **2** [To register oneself] enter, sign up, enlist.

**enslave** *v.* bind, imprison, incarcerate, shut in, enclose, confine, hold under, hold, subjugate, restrain, oppress, restrict, fetter, coerce, check, subdue, capture, suppress, make a slave of, hold in bondage, compel, chain, jail, deprive, tie, shackle.

**entangle** *v.* ensnare, entrap, trap, implicate, complicate, involve, snarl, corner, catch, embroil, tangle, ravel, unsettle, foul up*.—*Ant.* free, liberate, disentangle.

**enter** *v.* invade, set foot in, pass into, come in, drive in, burst in, rush in, go in, break into, get in, barge in, penetrate, intrude, reenter, slip, sneak, infiltrate, insert, move in, fall into*, crowd in, worm oneself into.—*Ant.* leave, depart, exit.

**entertain** *v.* **1** [To keep others amused] amuse, cheer, please, interest, enliven, delight, divert, beguile, charm, captivate, inspire, stimulate, satisfy, humor, enthrall, elate, tickle, distract, indulge, flatter, relax, make merry, comfort.—*Ant.* tire, bore, weary. **2** [To act as host or hostess] receive, host, invite, treat, charm, feed, dine, wine, give a party, do the honors, welcome, give a warm reception to, receive with open arms.—*Ant.* neglect, ignore, bore.

**entertaining** *a.* diverting, amusing, engaging, enchanting, sprightly, lively, witty, clever, interesting, gay, charming, enjoyable, delightful, funny, pleasing, edifying, engrossing, compelling, rousing, cheerful, relaxing, moving, inspiring, captivating, thrilling, entrancing, stirring, poignant, impressive, soul-stirring, stimulating, absorbing, exciting, provocative, fascinating, ravishing, satisfying, seductive.—*Ant.* boring, irritating, dull.

**entertainment** *n.* amusement, enjoyment, merriment, fun, pleasure, sport, recreation, pastime, diversion, relaxation, distraction, play, feast, banquet, picnic, show, television, the movies, treat, game, party, reception, spree.

**enthusiastic** *a.* interested, fascinated, willing, thrilled, feverish, concerned, passionate, raging, pleased, excited, attracted, exhilarated, anxious, eager, yearning, dying to*, inflamed, absorbed, devoted, diligent, ardent, fiery, longing, desiring, spirited, zestful, fervent, ecstatic, impatient, delighted, enraptured, avid, wild about*, crazy about*, mad about*, hot for*, gung-ho*, aching to*.—*Ant.* opposed, reluctant, apathetic.

**entice** *v.* lure, allure, attract.

**entrance** *n.* **1** [The act of coming in] arrival, entry, passage, approach, induction, initiation, admission, admittance, appearance, introduction, penetration, trespass, debut, enrollment, baptism, invasion, immigration.—*Ant.* escape, exit, issue. **2** [The opening that permits entry] gate, door, doorway, vestibule, entry, gateway, portal, port, inlet, opening, passage, staircase, porch, hall, hallway, path, way, passageway, threshold, lobby, corridor, approach.

**enumerate** *v.* list, mention, identify.

**envious** *a.* covetous, desirous, resentful, desiring, wishful, longing for, aspiring, greedy, grasping, craving, begrudging, green-eyed, hankering, green with envy.—*Ant.* generous, trustful, charitable.

**environment** *n.* conditions, living conditions, circumstances, surroundings, scene, external conditions, background, milieu, setting, habitat, situation.

**envy** *n.* jealousy, ill will, spite, rivalry, opposition, grudge, malice, prejudice, malevolence, covetousness, enviousness, backbiting, maliciousness, the green-eyed monster*.

**envy** *v.* begrudge, covet, lust after, crave, be envious of, feel ill toward, have hard feelings toward, feel resentful toward, have a grudge against, object to.

**equal** *a.* even, regular, like, same, identical, similar, uniform, invariable, fair, unvarying, commensurate, just, impartial, unbiased, to the same degree, on a footing with, without distinction, equitable, one and the same, level, parallel, corresponding, equivalent, proportionate, comparable, tantamount.—*Ant.* irregular, unequal, uneven.

**equipment** *n.* material, materiel, tools, facilities, implements, utensils, apparatus, furnishings, appliances, paraphernalia, belongings, devices, outfit, accessories, attachments, extras, conveniences, articles, tackle, rig, machinery, fittings, trappings, fixtures, contraptions, supplies, accompaniments, gear, fixings, stuff, gadgets, things.

**eradicate** *v.* eliminate, exterminate, annihilate.

**erase** *v.* delete, expunge, omit, obliterate, cut, clean, nullify, eradicate.

**erode** *v.* decay, corrode, disintegrate.

**erratic** *a.* **1** [Wandering] nomadic, rambling, roving. **2** [Strange] eccentric, irregular, unusual. **3** [Variable] inconsistent, unpredictable, variable.

**error** *n.* blunder, mistake, fault, oversight, inaccuracy, omission, deviation, misdoing, faux pas, fall, slip, wrong, lapse, miss, failure, slight, misunderstanding, flaw, boner*, bad job, blooper*, muff, boo-boo*, botch.

**escape** *v.* flee, fly, leave, depart, elude, avoid, evade, shun, run off, run away, make off, disappear, vanish, steal off, steal away, flow out, get away, break out, wriggle out, break away, desert, slip away, elope, run out*, go scot-free, take flight, duck out*, get clear of, break loose, cut and run, worm out of, clear out*, bail out*, crawl out of, save one's neck, scram*, make a break*.—*Ant.* return, come back, remain.

**escort** *n.* guide, guard, companion.

**essential** *a.* **1** [Necessary] imperative, required, indispensable. **2** [Rooted in the basis or essence] basic, primary, quintessential.

**established** *a.* **1** [Set up to endure] endowed, founded, organized, instituted, set up, originated, chartered, incorporated, settled, begun, initiated, realized, codified, produced, completed, finished.—*Ant.* temporary, unsound, insolvent. **2** [Conclusively proved] approved, verified, guaranteed, endorsed, demonstrated, determined, confirmed, substantiated, assured, concluded, authenticated, ascertained, achieved, upheld, certain, validated, identified, proved, undeniable.—*Ant.* false, invalidated, untrue.

**esteem** *n.* regard, respect, appreciation.

**estimate** *n.* evaluation, assessment, valuation, guess, appraisal, estimation, calculation, gauging, rating, survey, measure, reckoning.

**estimate** *v.* rate, value, measure, calculate, appraise, assess, account, compute, evaluate, count, number, reckon, guess, expect, judge, figure, plan, outline, run over, rank, furnish an estimate, set a value on, set a figure, appraise, assay, consider, predict, suppose, suspect, reason, think through, surmise, determine, decide, budget.

**eternal** *a.* endless, interminable, continual, unbroken, continuous, continued, unceasing, ceaseless, constant, unending, incessant, relentless, undying, enduring, persistent, always, uninterrupted, everlasting, perpetual, indestructible, unconquerable, never-ending, indefinite, permanent, ageless, boundless, timeless, immortal, forever, indeterminable, immeasurable, having no limit, imperishable, to one's dying day, for ever and ever*.—*Ant.* temporary, finite, ending.

**eternity** *n.* endlessness, forever, infinite, duration, timelessness, world without end, the future, infinity, all eternity, other world, afterlife, life after death, for ever and ever*.—*Ant.* instant, moment, second.

**ethics** *pl.n.* conduct, morality, mores, decency, integrity, moral conduct, social values, moral code, principles, right and wrong, natural law, honesty, goodness, honor, social laws, human nature, the Golden Rule.

**evade** *v.* lie, prevaricate, dodge, shun, put off, avoid, elude, trick, baffle, quibble, shift, mystify, cloak, cover, conceal, deceive, screen, veil, hide, drop the subject, pretend, confuse, dodge the issue, beat around the bush, give someone the runaround*, throw off the scent*, lead on a merry chase, pass up, put off, get around, lie out of.—*Ant.* explain, make clear, elucidate.

**evaluate** *v.* appraise, judge, assess.

**evangelical** *a.* pious, fervent, spiritual.

**evaporate** *v.* diffuse, vanish, fade, dissolve, dissipate, steam, steam away, boil away, fume, distill, turn to steam, rise in a mist.

**evaporation** *n.* drying, dehydration, vanishing, steaming away, boiling away, vaporization, distillation, dissipation, disappearance, vanishing into thin air.

**evasive** *a.* elusory, fugitive, shifty.

**even** *a.* **1** [Lying in a smooth plane] smooth, level, surfaced. **2** [Similar] uniform, unbroken, homogeneous. **3** [Equal] commensurate, coterminous, equivalent. **4** [In addition] also, too, as well. **—break even** make nothing, tie, neither win nor lose.

**evening** *n.* twilight, dusk, late afternoon.

**event** *n.* occurrence, happening, episode, incident, circumstance, affair, phenomenon, development, function, transaction, experience, appearance, turn, tide, shift, phase, accident, chance, pass, situation, story, case, matter, occasion, catastrophe, mishap, mistake, experience, parade, triumph, coincidence, miracle, adventure, holiday, wonder, marvel, celebration, crisis, predicament, misfortune, situation, calamity, emergency, something to write home about*. **—in any event** anyway, no matter what happens, however. **—in the event of** (or **that**) in case of, if it should happen that, if there should happen to be.

**eventual** *a.* inevitable, ultimate, consequent.

**everything** *pron.* all, all things, the universe, the whole complex, the whole, many things, all that, every little thing, the whole kit and caboodle*; lock, stock, and barrel*; the works*, the lot*.

**evident** *a.* apparent, visible, manifest.

**evil** *n.* **1** [The quality of being evil] sin, wickedness, depravity, crime, sinfulness, corruption, vice, immorality, iniquity, perversity, badness, vileness, baseness, meanness, malevolence, indecency, hatred, viciousness, wrong, debauchery, lewdness, wantonness, grossness, foulness, degradation, obscenity.—*Ant.* virtue, good, goodness. **2** [A harmful or malicious action] ill, harm, mischief, misfortune, scandal, calamity, pollution, contamination, catastrophe, blow, disaster, plague, outrage, foul play, ill wind*, crying shame*, double cross*, raw deal*.

**exact** *a.* **1** [Accurate] precise, correct, perfect. **2** [Clear] sharp, distinct, clear-cut.

**exactly** *a.* precisely, specifically, correctly.

**exaggerate** *v.* overestimate, overstate, misrepresent, falsify, magnify, expand, amplify, pile up, heighten, intensify, distort, enlarge on, stretch, overdo, misquote, go to extremes, give color to, misjudge, elaborate, romance, embroider, color, make too much of, lie, fabricate, corrupt, paint in glowing colors*, carry too far*, lay it on thick*, make a mountain out of a molehill, cook up*, build up, make much of, make the most of.—*Ant.* underestimate, tell the truth, minimize.

**examine** *v.* **1** [To inspect with care] inspect, analyze, criticize, scrutinize, investigate, go into, inquire into, scan, probe, sift, explore, reconnoiter, audit, take stock of, take note of, make an inventory of, consider, canvass, find out, search out, review, assay, check, check out, check up on, reexamine, go back over, concentrate on, give one's attention to, look at, look into, look over, conduct research on, run checks on, put to the test, sound out, feel out, subject to scrutiny, peer into, look into, pry into, hold up to the light, finger, pick over, sample, experiment with, give the once-over*, size up*, smell around, see about, see into, poke into, nose around, look up and down, go over with a fine-toothed comb*, dig into*. **2** [To test] question, interrogate, cross-examine.

**example** *n.* **1** [A representative] illustration, representation, warning, sample, citation, case in point, concrete example, case, prototype, archetype, stereotype, original, copy, instance, quotation. **2** [Something to be imitated] standard, pattern, sample. **—set an example** instruct, behave as a model, set a pattern.

**exceed** *v.* excel, outdo, overdo, outdistance, pass, outrun, beat, get the better of, go beyond, surpass, transcend, eclipse, rise above, pass over, run circles around*, get the edge on*, excel in, have it all over someone*, get the drop on*, beat to the draw*, break the record*, have the best of, have the jump on*, be ahead of the game, have the advantage, gain the upper hand.

**excel** *v.* surpass, transcend, exceed.

**excellent** *a.* first-class, premium, choice, first, choicest, prime, high, picked, the best obtainable, select, exquisite, high-grade, very fine, finest, good, desirable, admirable, distinctive, attractive, great, highest, superior, exceptional, superb, striking, supreme, unique, custom-made, incomparable, surprising, transcendent, priceless, rare, invaluable, highest priced, magnificent, wonderful, skillfull, above par, superlative, worthy, refined, well-done, cultivated, to be desired, competent, skilled, notable, first-rate, terrific*, sensational*, sharp*, all right, A-1*, grade A*, classy*, top-notch*, cream*, tops*.—*Ant.* poor, inferior, imperfect.

**exception** *n.* exclusion, omission, making an exception of, rejection, barring, reservation, leaving out, segregation, limitation, exemption, elimination, expulsion, excusing. **—take exception (to)** **1** [To differ] object, disagree, demur. **2** [To dislike] resent, be offended, take offense.

**excerpt** *n.* selection, extract, quotation.

**excessive** *a.* immoderate, extravagant, exorbitant.

**exchange** *v.* **1** [To replace one thing with another] substitute, transfer, replace, go over to, give in exchange, remove, pass to, reverse, provide a replacement, shuffle, shift, revise, rearrange, change, interchange, transact, reset, change hands, borrow from Peter to pay Paul, swap*. **2** [To give and receive reciprocally] reciprocate, barter, trade with, buy and sell, deal with, do business with, correspond, swap*.

**excited** *a.* aroused, stimulated, inflamed, agitated, hot, annoyed, seething, wrought up, frantic, flushed, overwrought, restless, feverish, apprehensive, roused, disturbed, perturbed, flustered, upset, angry, tense, discomposed, embarrassed, hurt, angered, distracted, distraught, edgy, furious, beside oneself, delighted, eager, enthusiastic, frenzied, troubled, ruffled, moved, avid, hysterical, passionate, provoked, quickened, inspired, wild, nervous, animated, ill at ease, jumpy, jittery*, turned on*, hyped up*, hopped up*, worked up*, in a tizzy*, uptight*, all nerves*, blue in the face*, on fire*.—*Ant.* calm, reserved, self-confident.

**excitement** *n.* confusion, disturbance, tumult, enthusiasm, rage, turmoil, stir, excitation, agitation, movement, feeling, exhilaration, emotion, stimulation, drama, melodrama, activity, commotion, fuss, hullabaloo, bother, dither, hubbub, bustle, to-do*.—*Ant.* peace, calm, quiet.

**exciting** *a.* stimulating, moving, animating, provocative, arousing, arresting, stirring, thrilling, dangerous, breathtaking, overwhelming, interesting, new, mysterious, overpowering, inspiring, impressive, soul-stirring, sensational, astonishing, bracing, appealing, bloodcurdling, racy, hair-raising, mindblowing*.—*Ant.* dull, pacifying, tranquilizing.

**exclude** *v.* shut out, reject, ban.

**exclusive** *a.* restricted, restrictive, fashionable, aristocratic, preferential, privileged, particular, licensed, select, private, segregated, prohibitive, clannish, independent, swank*.—*Ant.* free, inclusive, unrestricted.

**excrete** *v.* remove, eliminate, eject, defecate, urinate, discharge, secrete, go to the bathroom, go to the toilet, answer a call of nature, pass, expel, exude, perspire, sweat, squeeze out, give off, poop*.

**excuse** *v.* pardon, forgive, justify, discharge, vindicate, apologize for, release from, dispense with, free, set free, overlook, purge, exempt from, rationalize, acquit, condone, appease, reprieve, absolve, exonerate, clear of, give absolution to, pass over, give as an excuse, make excuses for, make allowances for, make apologies for, grant amnesty to, provide with an alibi, plead ignorance of, whitewash, let off easy, let go scot-free, wink at*, wipe the slate clean, shrug off, take the rap for*.

**executive** *n.* businessman, businesswoman, president, vice-president, secretary, treasurer, supervisor, chairman, chairwoman, chairperson, chair, dean, head, chief, superintendent, bureaucrat, leader, governor, controller, organizer, commander, director, boss, big shot*, official, manager.

**exempt** *a.* freed, cleared, liberated, privileged, excused, absolved, not subject to, released from, not responsible to, not responsible for, set apart, excluded, released, not liable, unrestrained, unbound, uncontrolled, unrestricted, freed from, not restricted by, not restricted to, outside.—*Ant.* responsible, liable, subject.

**exemption** *n.* exception, immunity, privilege.

**exercise** *v.* **1** [To move the body] stretch, bend, pull, tug, hike, work, promote muscle tone, labor, strain, loosen up, discipline, drill, execute, perform exercises, practice, take a walk, work out, limber up, warm up. **2** [To use] employ, practice, exert, apply, operate, execute, handle, utilize, devote, put in practice. **3** [To train] drill, discipline, give training to.

**exhausted** *a.* **1** [Without further physical resources] debilitated, wearied, worn. **2** [Having nothing remaining] all gone, consumed, used.

**exorbitant** *a.* excessive, extravagant, too much.

**exotic** *a.* **1** [Foreign] imported, not native, extrinsic. **2** [Peculiar] strange, fascinating, different.

**expand** *v.* extend, augment, dilate.

**expect** *v.* **1** [To anticipate] await, look for, look forward to, count on, plan on, assume, suppose, lean on, feel it in one's bones*, wait for, hope for. **2** [To require] demand, insist upon, exact. **3** [To assume] presume, suppose, suspect.

**expedition** *n.* **1** [Travel undertaken] excursion, voyage, campaign. **2** [That which undertakes travel] party, hunters, explorers, pioneers, traders, soldiers, scouts, archaeologists, tourists, sightseers, caravan, posse.

**expense** *n.* expenditure, responsibility, obligation, loan, mortgage, lien, debt, liability, investment, insurance, upkeep, alimony, debit, account, cost, price, outlay, charge, payment, outgo, value, worth, sum, amount, risk, capital, rate, tax, carrying charges, budgeted items, cost of materials, overhead, time, payroll, investment.—*Ant.* profit, income, receipts. **—at the expense of** paid by, at the cost of, charged to.

**expensive** *a.* dear, precious, valuable, invaluable, rare, high-priced, costly, prized, choice, rich, priceless, high, too high, unreasonable, exorbitant, extravagant, at a premium, out of sight*, at great cost, sky-high, steep*, stiff*.—*Ant.* cheap, inexpensive, low.

**experienced** *a.* skilled, practiced, instructed, accomplished, versed, qualified, able, skillful, knowing, trained, wise, expert, veteran, mature, with a good background, rounded, knowing the score*, knowing the ropes*, having all the answers, having been around*, having been through the mill*, broken in*.—*Ant.* new, apprentice, beginning.

**experiment** *n.* analysis, essay, examination, trial, inspection, search, organized observation, research, scrutiny, speculation, check, proof, operation, test, exercise, quiz, investigation.

**explain** *v.* interpret, explicate, account for, elucidate, illustrate, clarify, illuminate, make clear, describe, expound, teach, reveal, point out, demonstrate, tell, read, translate, paraphrase, put in other words, define, justify, untangle, unravel, make plain, come to the point, put across, throw light upon, comment on, remark upon, remark on, offer an explanation of, resolve, clear up, get right, set right, put someone on the right track, spell out, go into detail, get to the bottom of, figure out, cast light upon, get across, get through, bring out, work out, solve, put in plain English*.—*Ant.* confuse, puzzle, confound.

**explicit** *a.* express, sure, plain.

**exploit** *v.* utilize, take advantage of, employ.

**explosive** *a.* stormy, fiery, forceful, raging, wild, violent, uncontrollable, vehement, sharp, hysterical, frenzied, savage.—*Ant.* mild, gentle, uneventful.

**expose** *v.* **1** [To uncover] disclose, smoke out, show up, present, prove, reveal, air, exhibit, unmask, lay open, lay bare, bring to light, open, dig up, give away, bring into view, unfold, let the cat out of the bag, drag through the mud, put the finger on*. **2** [To endeavor to attract attention] show, show off, bare. **3** [To open to danger] lay open to, subject to, imperil.

**expression** *n.* **1** [Significant appearance] look, cast, character. **2** [Putting into understandable form] representation, art product, utterance, narration, interpretation, invention, creation, declaration, commentary, diagnosis, definition, explanation, illustration. **3** [A traditional form of speech] locution, idiom, speech pattern. **4** [Facial cast] grimace, smile, smirk, mug*, sneer, pout, grin.

**expressive** *a.* eloquent, demonstrative, revealing, indicative, representative, dramatic, stirring, sympathetic, articulate, touching, significant, meaningful, spirited, emphatic, strong, forcible, energetic, lively, tender, passionate, warm, colorful, vivid, picturesque, brilliant, stimulating.—*Ant.* indifferent, impassive, dead.

**extend** *v.* **1** [To make larger] lengthen, enlarge, prolong. **2** [To occupy space to a given point] continue, go as far as, spread.

**extent** *n.* degree, limit, span, space, area, measure, size, bulk, length, compass, scope, reach, wideness, width, range, amount, expanse, magnitude, intensity.

**exterior** *a.* outer, outlying, outermost.

**exterminate** *v.* annihilate, eradicate, abolish.

**extinct** *a.* dead, ended, terminated, exterminated, deceased, lost, unknown, no longer known.

**extra** *a.* additional, in addition, other, one more, spare, reserve, supplemental, increased, another, new, auxiliary, added, adjunct, besides, also, further, more, beyond, over and above, plus, supplementary, accessory, unused.—*Ant.* less, short, subtracted.

**extract** *n.* distillation, infusion, concentration.

**extract** *v.* evoke, derive, secure.

**extreme** *a.* radical, intemperate, immoderate, imprudent, excessive, inordinate, extravagant, flagrant, outrageous, unreasonable, irrational, improper, preposterous, thorough, far, fanatical, desperate, severe, intense, drastic, sheer, total, advanced, violent, sharp, acute, unseemly, beyond control, fantastic, to the extreme, absurd, foolish, monstrous, exaggerated.—*Ant.* restrained, cautious, moderate.

**exuberant** *a.* ardent, vivacious, passionate.

**eye** *n.* **1** [The organ of sight] eyeball, instrument of vision, compound eye, simple eye, naked eye, optic, orb, peeper*, lamp*. **2** [Appreciation] perception, taste, discrimination. **3** [A center] focus, core, heart. —**private eye*** detective, investigator, gumshoe*. —**all eyes*** attentive, aware, perceptive. —**an eye for an eye** punishment, retaliation, vengeance. —**catch one's eye** attract one's attention, cause notice, stand out. —**easy on the eyes*** attractive, appealing, pleasant to look at. —**give a person the eye*** attract, charm, invite. —**have an eye for** appreciate, be interested in, desire. —**have an eye to** watch out for, be mindful of, attend to. —**have eyes for*** appreciate, be interested in, desire. —**in a pig's eye*** under no circumstances, impossible, no way. —**in the public eye** well-known, renowned, celebrated. —**keep an eye on** look after, watch over, protect. —**keep an eye out for** watch for, be mindful of, attend to. —**keep one's eyes open** (or **peeled**) be aware, be watchful, look out. —**lay eyes on** look at, stare, survey. —**make eyes at** attract, charm, invite. —**open someone's eyes** make aware, inform, apprise. —**shut one's eyes to** refuse, reject, ignore. —**with an eye to** considering, mindful of, aware of.

# F

**fabulous** *a.* remarkable, amazing, immense.

**face** *n.* **1** [The front of the head] visage, countenance, appearance, features, silhouette, profile, front, mug*. **2** [A plane surface] front, surface, finish. **3** [Prestige] status, standing, social position. —**make a face** distort one's face, grimace, scowl. —**on the face of it** to all appearances, seemingly, according to the evidence. —**pull** (or **wear**) **a long face*** look sad, scowl, pout. —**show one's face** be seen, show up, come. —**to one's face** candidly, openly, frankly.

**face** *v.* **1** [To confront conflict or trouble] confront, oppose, defy, meet, dare, brave, challenge, withstand, encounter, risk, tolerate, endure, sustain, suffer, bear, tell to one's face, make a stand, meet face to face, cope with, allow, stand, submit, abide, go up against, swallow, stomach, take, take it.—*Ant.* evade, elude, shun. **2** [To put a face on a building] refinish, front, redecorate. **3** [To look out on] front, border, be turned toward.

**facile** *a.* simple, obvious, apparent.

**fact** *n.* **1** [A reliable generality] certainty, truth, appearance, experience, matter, the very thing, not an illusion, what has really happened, something concrete, what is the case, matter of fact, hard evidence, actuality, naked truth, gospel, reality, law, basis, state of being, hard facts*.—*Ant.* fancy, fiction, imagination. **2** [An individual reality] circumstance, detail, factor, case, evidence, event, action, deed, happening, occurrence, creation, conception, manifestation, being, entity, experience, affair, episode, performance, proceeding, phenomenon, incident, thing done, act, plain fact, accomplishment, accomplished fact, *fait accompli* (French).—*Ant.* error, illusion, untruth. —**as a matter of fact** in reality, in fact, actually.

**faction** *n.* cabal, combine, party, conspiracy, plot, gang, crew, wing, block, junta, clique, splinter group, set, clan, club, lobby, camp, inner circle, sect, coterie, partnership, cell, unit, mob, side, machine, band, team, knot, circle, concern, guild, schism, outfit, crowd*, bunch*.

**factory** *n.* manufactory, plant, shop, industry, workshop, machine shop, mill, laboratory, assembly plant, foundry, forge, loom, mint, carpenter shop, brewery, sawmill, supply house, processing plant, works, workroom, firm, packing plant.

**faculty** *n.* **1** [A peculiar aptitude] peculiarity, strength, forte. **2** [A group of specialists, usually engaged in instruction or research] staff, teachers, research workers, personnel, instructors, university, college, institute, teaching staff, research staff, teaching assistants, professorate, society, body, organization, mentors, professors, assistant professors, associate professors, docents, tutors, foundation, department, pedagogues, lecturers, advisors, masters, scholars, fellows, profs*.

**fad** *n.* fancy, style, craze, fashion, humor, fit, prank, quirk, kink, eccentricity, popular innovation, vogue, fantasy, whimsy, passing fancy, latest word, all the rage, the latest thing, the last word*.—*Ant.* custom, convention, practice.

**fade** *v.* **1** [To lose color or light] bleach, tone down, wash out, blanch, tarnish, dim, discolor, pale, grow dim, neutralize, become dull, lose brightness, lose luster, lose color.—*Ant.* color, brighten, glow. **2** [To diminish in sound] hush, quiet, sink.

**fail** *v.* **1** [To be unsuccessful] fall short, miss, back out, abandon, desert, neglect, slip, lose ground, come to naught, come to nothing, falter, flounder, blunder, break down, get into trouble, abort, fault*, come down, fall flat, go amiss, go astray, fall down, get left, be found lacking, go down, go under, not hold a candle to, fold up, go on the rocks, not have it in one, miss the boat*, not measure up, lose out, give out, fall short of, not make the grade*, miss the mark, lose control, fall down on the job*, go wrong, be out of it, blow it*, fizzle out*, hit rock bottom, go up in smoke, bomb*, not get to first base*, get hung up*, get bogged down*, flunk out*, flop*, conk out*, peter out*.—*Ant.* win, succeed, triumph. **2** [To prove unsatisfactory] lose out, come short of, displease. **3** [To grow less] lessen, worsen, sink. **4** [To become insolvent] go bankrupt, go out of business, go broke*. **—without fail** constantly, dependably, reliably.

**faint** *a.* **1** [Having little physical strength] shaky, faltering, dizzy. **2** [Having little light or color] vague, thin, hazy. **3** [Having little volume of sound] whispered, breathless, murmuring, inaudible, indistinct, low, stifled, dull, hoarse, soft, heard in the distance, quiet, low-pitched, muffled, hushed, distant, subdued, gentle, softened, from afar, deep, rumbling, far-off, out of earshot.—*Ant.* loud, audible, raucous.

**fainthearted** *a.* irresolute, halfhearted, weak.

**fair** *a.* **1** [Just] forthright, impartial, plain, scrupulous, upright, candid, generous, frank, open, sincere, straightforward, honest, lawful, clean, legitimate, decent, honorable, virtuous, righteous, temperate, unbiased, reasonable, civil, courteous, blameless, uncorrupted, square, equitable, fair-minded, dispassionate, uncolored, objective, unprejudiced, evenhanded, good, principled, moderate, praiseworthy, aboveboard, trustworthy, due, fit, appropriate, on the level*, on the up-and-up*, fair and square*, straight*.—*Ant.* unfair, unjust, biased. **2** [Moderately satisfactory] average, pretty good, not bad, up to standard, ordinary, mediocre, usual, common, all right, commonplace, fair to middling*, so-so, OK*.—*Ant.* poor, bad, unsatisfactory. **3** [Not stormy or likely to storm] clear, pleasant, sunny, bright, calm, placid, tranquil, favorable, balmy, mild.—*Ant.* stormy, threatening, overcast. **4** [Of light complexion] blond, blonde, light-colored, light-complexioned, pale, white, bleached, white-skinned, flaxen, fair-haired, snow-white, snowy, whitish, light, lily-white, faded, neutral, platinum blonde, peroxide blonde, bleached blond*, pale-faced, white as a sheet, white as a ghost.—*Ant.* dark, brunet, black.

**fair** *n.* exposition, county fair, state fair, world's fair, carnival, bazaar, exhibition, display, festival, market, exchange, centennial, observance, celebration.

**fairy** *n.* spirit, sprite, good fairy, evil spirit, elf, goblin, hobgoblin, nymph, pixie, mermaid, siren, bogy, genie, jinni, imp, enchantress, enchanter, sorceress, sorcerer, witch, warlock, banshee, werewolf, ogre, demon, succubus, incubus, devil, ghoul, Harpy, poltergeist, troll, dwarf, giant, gremlin, gnome, leprechaun, satyr, fiend, Fate, Weird Sister, Puck.

**faith** *n.* **1** [Complete trust] confidence, trust, credence, credit, assurance, acceptance, troth, dependence, conviction, sureness, fidelity, loyalty, certainty, allegiance, reliance.—*Ant.* doubt, suspicion, distrust. **2** [A formal system of beliefs] creed, doctrine, dogma, tenet, revelation, credo, gospel, profession, conviction, canon, principle, church, worship, teaching, theology, denomination, cult, sect. **—bad faith** insincerity, duplicity, infidelity. **—break faith** be disloyal, abandon, fail. **—good faith** sincerity, honor, trustworthiness. **—in faith** indeed, in fact, in reality. **—keep faith** be loyal, adhere, follow.

**faithful** *a.* reliable, genuine, dependable, incorruptible, straight, honest, upright, honorable, scrupulous, firm, sure, unswerving, conscientious, enduring, unchanging, steady, staunch, attached, obedient, steadfast, sincere, resolute, on the level*, devoted, true, dutiful.—*Ant.* false, fickle, faithless.

**fake** *a.* pretended, fraudulent, bogus.

**fake** *v.* feign, simulate, disguise.

**fall** *v.* **1** [To pass quickly downward] sink, topple, drop, settle, droop, stumble, trip, plunge, tumble, descend, totter, break down, cave in, make a forced landing, decline, subside, collapse, drop down, pitch, be precipitated, fall down, fall flat, fall in, fold up, keel over, tip over, slip, recede, ebb, diminish, flop.—*Ant.* rise, ascend, climb. **2** [To be overthrown] submit, yield, surrender, succumb, be destroyed, be taken, bend, defer to, obey, resign, capitulate, back down, fall to pieces, break up.—*Ant.* endure, prevail, resist. **—fall in love (with)** lose one's heart, become enamored, take a fancy to, take a liking to, become attached to, become fond of, have eyes for*.

**fallacy** *n.* inconsistency, quibbling, evasion, fallacious reasoning, illogical reasoning, mistake, deceit, deception, subterfuge, inexactness, perversion, bias, prejudice, preconception, ambiguity, paradox, miscalculation, quirk, flaw, irrelevancy, erratum, heresy.—*Ant.* law, theory, reason.

**fallible** *a.* deceptive, frail, imperfect, ignorant, uncertain, erring, unpredictable, unreliable, in question, prone to error, untrustworthy, questionable.

**fallow** *a.* unplowed, unplanted, unproductive.

**false** *a.* **1** [*Said of persons*] faithless, treacherous, unfaithful, disloyal, dishonest, lying, foul, hypocritical, double-dealing, malevolent, mean, malicious, deceitful, underhanded, corrupt, wicked, unscrupulous, untrustworthy, dishonorable, two-faced.—*Ant.* faithful, true, honorable. **2** [*Said of statements or supposed facts*] untrue, spurious, fanciful, lying, untruthful, fictitious, deceptive, fallacious, incorrect, misleading, delusive, imaginary, illusive, erroneous, invalid, inaccurate, deceiving, fraudulent, trumped-up.—*Ant.* accurate, correct, established. **3** [*Said of things*] sham, counterfeit, fabricated, manufactured, synthetic, bogus, spurious, make-believe, assumed, unreal, copied, forged, pretended, faked, made-up, simulated, pseudo, hollow, mock, feigned, bastard, alloyed, artificial, contrived, colored, disguised, deceptive, adulterated, so-called, fake, phony*, shoddy, not what it's cracked up to be*.—*Ant.* real, genuine, authentic.

**falsehood** *n.* deception, prevarication, story*.

**familiar** *a.* everyday, well-known, customary, frequent, homely, humble, usual, intimate, habitual, accustomed, common, ordinary, informal, unceremonious, plain, simple, matter-of-fact, workaday, prosaic, commonplace, homespun, natural, native, unsophisticated, old hat*, garden-variety.—*Ant.* unusual, exotic, strange.

**family** *n.* kin, folk, clan, relationship, relations, tribe, dynasty, breed, house, kith and kin, blood, blood tie, progeny, offspring, descendants, forebears, heirs, race, ancestry, pedigree, genealogy, descent, parentage, extraction, paternity, inheritance, kinship, lineage, line, one's own flesh and blood, strain, siblings, in-laws, people.

**famous** *a.* eminent, foremost, famed, preeminent, acclaimed, illustrious, celebrated, noted, conspicuous, prominent, honored, reputable, renowned, recognized, notable, important, well-known, of note, notorious, exalted, remarkable, extraordinary, great, powerful, noble, grand, mighty, imposing, towering, influential, leading, noteworthy, talked of, outstanding, distinguished, excellent, memorable, elevated, in the spotlight, in the limelight.—*Ant.* unknown, obscure, humble.

**fanaticism** *n.* bigotry, intolerance, obsession, prejudice, hatred, superstition, narrow-mindedness, injustice, obstinacy, stubbornness, bias, unfairness, partiality, devotion, violence, immoderation, zeal, willfulness, single-mindedness, infatuation, dogma, arbitrariness, unruliness, enthusiasm, frenzy, passion, rage.—*Ant.* indifference, tolerance, moderation.

**fancy** *a.* elegant, embellished, rich, adorned, ostentatious, gaudy, showy, intricate, baroque, lavish.

**fantastic** *a.* whimsical, capricious, extravagant, freakish, strange, odd, queer, quaint, peculiar, outlandish, farfetched, wonderful, comical, humorous, foreign, exotic, extreme, ludicrous, ridiculous, preposterous, grotesque, frenzied, absurd, vague, hallucinatory, high-flown, affected, artificial, out of sight*.—*Ant.* common, conventional, routine.

**far** *a.* **1** [Distant from the speaker] removed, faraway, remote. **2** [To a considerable degree] extremely, incomparably, notably. **—by far** very much, considerably, to a great degree. **—few and far between** scarce, sparse, in short supply. **—(in) so far as** to the extent that, in spite of, within limits. **—so far** thus far, until now, up to this point. **—so far, so good** all right, favorable, going well.

**farmer** *n.* planter, grower, livestock breeder, stockman, agriculturist, rancher, dirt farmer, lessee, homesteader, producer, tiller of the soil, peasant, peon, herdsman, plowman, sharecropper, hired man, cropper, grazer, cattleman, sheepman, harvester, truck gardener, gardener, nurseryman, horticulturist, settler, sodbuster*, farm hand, hired hand.

**farsighted** *a.* aware, perceptive, sagacious.

**fascinated** *a.* enchanted, bewitched, dazzled, captivated, attracted, seduced, enraptured, charmed, hypnotized, delighted, infatuated, thrilled, spellbound.—*Ant.* disgusted, repelled, disenchanted.

**fascism** *n.* dictatorship, totalitarianism, Nazism.—*Ant.* democracy, self-government, socialism.

**fashion** *n.* **1** [The manner of behavior] way, custom, convention, style, vogue, mode, tendency, trend, formality, formula, procedure, practice, device, usage, observance, new look. **2** [Whatever is temporarily in vogue] craze, sport, caprice, whim, hobby, innovation, custom, amusement, eccentricity, rage. **—after** (or **in**) **a fashion** somewhat, to some extent, in a way.

**fast** *a.* **1** [Rapid] swift, fleet, quick, speedy, brisk, accelerated, hasty, nimble, active, electric, agile, ready, quick as lightning, like a flash, racing, like a bat out of hell*, like a house afire*.—*Ant.* slow, sluggish, tardy. **2** [Firmly fixed] adherent, attached, immovable.

**fast** *n.* abstinence, day of fasting, Lent.

**fast** *v.* not eat, go hungry, observe a fast.

**fastener** *n.* buckle, hook, hasp, lock, clamp, tie, stud, vise, grip, grappling iron, clasp, snap, bolt, bar, lace, cinch, pin, safety pin, nail, rivet, tack, thumbtack, screw, dowel, brake, binder, binding, button, padlock, catch, bond, band, mooring, rope, cable, anchor, chain, harness, strap, thong, girdle, latch, staple, zipper.

**fat** *a.* portly, stout, obese, corpulent, fleshy, potbellied, beefy, brawny, solid, plumpish, plump, burly, bulky, unwieldy, heavy, husky, puffy, on the heavy side, in need of reducing, swollen, inflated, ponderous, lumpish, fat as a pig, tubby*.—*Ant.* thin, lean, skinny.

**fatal** *a.* inevitable, mortal, lethal.

**fate** *n.* fortune, destination, luck.

**fatherly** *a.* paternal, patriarchal, benevolent.

**fatigue** *n.* weariness, lassitude, exhaustion, weakness, feebleness, faintness, battle fatigue, nervous exhaustion, dullness, heaviness, listlessness, tiredness.

**fault** *n.* **1** [A moral delinquency] misdemeanor, weakness, offense, wrongdoing, transgression, crime, sin, impropriety, juvenile delinquency, misconduct, malpractice, failing. **2** [An error] blunder, mistake, misdeed. **3** [Responsibility] liability, accountability, blame. **—at fault** culpable, blamable, in the wrong. **—find fault** (**with**) complain about, carp at, criticize.

**favor** *v.* prefer, like, approve, sanction, praise, regard favorably, be in favor of, pick, choose, lean toward, incline toward, value, prize, esteem, think well of, set great store by, look up to, think the world of*, be partial to, grant favors to, promote, play favorites, show consideration for, spare, make an exception for, pull strings for.—*Ant.* hate, dislike, disesteem.

**favorable** *a.* **1** [Friendly] well-disposed, kind, well-intentioned. **2** [Displaying suitable or promising qualities] propitious, convenient, beneficial. **3** [Commendatory] approving, commending, assenting, complimentary, well-disposed toward, in favor of, agreeable, in one's favor.

**faze** *v.* bother, intimidate, worry.

**fear** *n.* fright, terror, horror, panic, dread, dismay, awe, scare, revulsion, aversion, tremor, mortal terror, cowardice, timidity, misgiving, trembling, anxiety, phobia, foreboding, despair, agitation, hesitation, worry, concern, suspicion, doubt, qualm, funk*, cold feet*, cold sweat.—*Ant.* courage, intrepidity, dash. **—for fear of** avoiding, lest, in order to prevent, out of apprehension concerning.

**fear** *v.* be afraid, shun, avoid, falter, lose courage, be alarmed, be frightened, be scared, live in terror, dare not, have qualms about, cower, flinch, shrink, quail, cringe, turn pale, tremble, break out in a sweat*.—*Ant.* dare, outface, withstand.

**feasible** *a.* **1** [Suitable] fit, expedient, worthwhile. **2** [Likely] probable, practicable, attainable.

**feed** *v.* feast, give food to, satisfy the hunger of, nourish, supply, support, satisfy, fill, stuff, cram, gorge, banquet, dine, nurse, maintain, fatten, provide food for, cater to, stock, furnish, nurture, sustain, encourage, serve.—*Ant.* starve, deprive, quench.

**feeling** *n.* **1** [The sense of touch] tactile sensation, tactility, power of perceiving by touch. **2** [State of the body, or of a part of it] sense, sensation, sensibility, feel, sensitiveness, sensory response, perception, perceptivity, susceptibility, activity, consciousness, receptivity, responsiveness, excitability, excitement, awareness, enjoyment, sensuality, pain, pleasure, reaction, motor response, reflex, excitation.—*Ant.* indifference, apathy, numbness. **3** [A personal reaction] opinion, thought, outlook. **4** [Sensitivity] taste, emotion, passion, tenderness, discrimination, delicacy, discernment, sentiment, sentimentality, refinement, culture, cultivation, capacity, faculty, judgment, affection, sympathy, imagination, intelligence, intuition, spirit, soul, appreciation, response.—*Ant.* rudeness, crudeness, coldness.

**feign** *v.* simulate, imagine, fabricate.

**female** *a.* reproductive, fertile, childbearing, of the female gender.—*Ant.* male, masculine, virile.

**fence** *n.* **1** [That which surrounds an enclosure] picket fence, wire fence, board fence, barbed-wire fence, rail fence, chain fence, iron fence, hedge, backstop, rail, railing, barricade, net, barrier, wall, dike. **2** [A receiver of stolen goods] accomplice, front*, uncle*. **—mend one's fences** renew contacts, look after one's political interests, solicit votes. **—on the fence** undecided, uncommitted, indifferent.

**ferment** *v.* effervesce, sour, foam, froth, bubble, seethe, fizz, sparkle, boil, work, ripen, dissolve, evaporate, rise.

**ferocious** *a.* fierce, savage, wild.—*Ant.* gentle, meek, mild.

**fertile** *a.* fruitful, rich, productive, fat, teeming, yielding, arable, flowering.—*Ant.* sterile, barren, desert.

**fervent** *a.* zealous, eager, ardent.

**fester** *v.* rankle, putrefy, rot.

**fetch** *v.* bring, get, retrieve.

**few** *a.* not many, scarcely any, less, sparse, scanty, thin, widely spaced, inconsiderable, negligible, infrequent, not too many, some, any, scarce, rare, seldom, few and far between.—*Ant.* many, numerous, innumerable.

**few** *pron.* not many, a small number, a handful, scarcely any, not too many, several, a scattering, three or four, a sprinkling.—*Ant.* many, a multitude, a great many. **—quite a few** several, some, a large number.

**fictitious** *a.* made-up, untrue, counterfeit.

**fidelity** *n.* fealty, loyalty, devotion.

**field** *n.* **1** [Open land] grainfield, hayfield, meadow, pasture, range, acreage, plot, patch, garden, cultivated ground, grassland, green, ranchland, arable land, plowed land, cleared land, cropland, tract, vineyard. **2** [An area devoted to sport] diamond, gridiron, track, rink, court, course, racecourse, golf course, racetrack, arena, stadium, theater, amphitheater, playground, park, turf, green, fairground. **3** [An area devoted to a specialized activity] airfield, airport, flying field, terminal, battlefield, battleground, sector, field of fire, terrain, no man's land, theater of war, field of battle, field of honor, parade ground, range. **—play the field** experiment, explore, look elsewhere.

**fiend** *n.* **1** [A wicked or cruel person] monster, barbarian, brute. **2** [*An addict] fan, aficionado, monomaniac.

**fierce** *a.* ferocious, wild, furious, enraged, raging, impetuous, untamed, angry, passionate, savage, primitive, brutish, animal, raving, outrageous, terrible, vehement, frightening, awful, horrible, venomous, bold, malevolent, malign, brutal, monstrous, severe, rough, rude, vicious, dangerous, frenzied, mad, insane, desperate, ravening, frantic, wrathful, irate, fanatical, bestial, boisterous, violent, threatening, stormy, thunderous, howling, tumultuous, turbulent, uncontrolled, storming, blustering, cyclonic, torrential, frightful, fearful, devastating, hellish, rip-roaring*.—*Ant.* mild, moderate, calm.

**fight** *n.* **1** [A violent physical struggle] strife, contention, feud, quarrel, contest, encounter, row, dispute, disagreement, battle, confrontation, controversy, brawl, bout, match, fisticuffs, round, fracas, difficulty, altercation, bickering, wrangling, riot, argument, debate, competition, rivalry, conflict, skirmish, clash, scuffle, collision, brush, action, engagement, combat, blow, exchange of blows, wrestling match, squabble, game, discord, estrangement, fuss, tussle, scrap*, free-for-all, ruckus*, run-in*, tiff, flare-up, go*, set-to*, difference of opinion. **2** [Willingness or eagerness to fight] mettle, hardihood, boldness.

**fight** *v.* strive, war, struggle, resist, assert oneself, challenge, meet, contend, attack, carry on war, withstand, give blow for blow, do battle, war against, persevere, force, go to war, exchange blows, encounter, oppose, tussle, grapple, flare up, engage with, combat, wrestle, box, spar, skirmish, quarrel, bicker, dispute, have it out, squabble, come to grips with, row, light into*, tear into*, mix it up with*.—*Ant.* retreat, submit, yield.

**fighting** *a.* combative, battling, brawling, unbeatable, resolute, argumentative, angry, ferocious, quarrelsome, ready to fight, belligerent, boxing, wrestling, warlike, contending, up in arms.

**file** *n.* **1** [An orderly collection of papers] card index, card file, portfolio, record, classified index, list, register, dossier, notebook. **2** [Steel abrasive] rasp, steel, sharpener. **3** [A line] rank, row, column. **—on file** filed, cataloged, registered.

**file** *v.* **1** [To arrange in order] classify, index, deposit, categorize, catalog, record, register, list, arrange. **2** [To use an abrasive] abrade, rasp, scrape, smooth, rub down, level off, finish, sharpen.

**fill** *v.* **1** [To pour to the capacity of the container] pack, stuff, replenish, furnish, supply, satisfy, blow up, fill up, pump up, fill to capacity, fill to overflowing, brim over, swell, charge, inflate.—*Ant.* empty, exhaust, drain. **2** [To occupy available space] take up, pervade, overflow, stretch, bulge out, distend, brim over, stretch, swell, blow up, run over at the top, permeate, take over.

**filter** *v.* **1** [To soak slowly] seep, penetrate, percolate. **2** [To clean by filtering] strain, purify, sift, sieve, refine, clarify, clean, separate.

**filth** *n.* dirt, dung, feces, contamination, corruption, pollution, foul matter, sewage, muck, manure, slop, squalor, trash, grime, mud, smudge, silt, garbage, carrion, slush, slime, sludge, foulness, filthiness, excrement, dregs, lees, sediment, rottenness, impurity.—*Ant.* cleanliness, purity, spotlessness.

**final** *a.* terminal, concluding, ultimate.

**finally** *a.* **1** [As though a matter were settled] with finality, with conviction, settled, in a final manner, certainly, officially, irrevocably, decisively, definitely, beyond recall, permanently, for all time, conclusively, assuredly, done with, once and for all, for good, beyond the shadow of a doubt.—*Ant.* temporarily, momentarily, for the time being. **2** [After a long period] at length, at last, in the end, subsequently, in conclusion, lastly, after all, after a while, eventually, ultimately, at long last, at the final point, at the last moment, at the end, tardily, belatedly, when all is said and done, in spite of all.

**financial** *a.* economic, business, monetary.

**find** *v.* discover, detect, notice, observe, perceive, arrive at, discern, hit upon, encounter, uncover, recover, expose, stumble on, happen upon, come across, track down, dig up, turn up, scare up*, run across, run into, lay one's hands on, bring to light, spot.—*Ant.* lose, mislay, miss.

**fine** *a.* **1** [Not coarse] light, powdery, granular. **2** [Of superior quality] well-made, supreme, fashionable. **3** [Exact] precise, distinct, strict.

**finish** *n.* **1** [The end] close, termination, ending. **2** [An applied surface] shine, polish, glaze, surface.

**finish** *v.* **1** [To bring to an end] complete, end, perfect. **2** [To develop a surface] polish, wax, stain. **3** [To come to an end] cease, close, end.

**finished** *a.* **1** [Completed] done, accomplished, perfected, achieved, ended, performed, executed, dispatched, concluded, complete, through, fulfilled, closed, over, decided, brought about, ceased, stopped, resolved, settled, made, worked out, rounded out, discharged, satisfied, disposed of, realized, finalized, effected, put into effect, all over with, attained, done with, made an end of, brought to a close, said and done, sewed up*, wound up.—*Ant.* unfinished, imperfect, incomplete. **2** [Given a finish] polished, coated, varnished.

**fire** *n.* **1** [Burning] flame, conflagration, blaze, campfire, coals, flame and smoke, blazing fire, hearth, burning coals, tinder, bonfire, bed of coals, embers, source of heat, sparks, heat, glow, warmth, luminosity, combustion. **2** [The discharge of ordnance] artillery attack, bombardment, rounds, barrage, explosions, bombings, curtain of fire, volley, sniping, mortar attack, salvos, shells, pattern of fire, fire superiority, crossfire, machine-gun fire, rifle fire, small-arms fire, antiaircraft fire. **—catch** (**on**) **fire** begin burning, ignite, flare up. **—on fire** **1** [Burning] flaming, fiery, hot. **2** [Excited] full of ardor, enthusiastic, zealous. **—open fire** start shooting, shoot, attack. **—play with fire** gamble, endanger one's interests, do something dangerous. **—set fire to** ignite, oxidize, make burn. **—set the world on fire** achieve, become famous, excel. **—under fire** criticized, censured, under attack.

**firm** *a.* **1** [Stable] fixed, solid, rooted, immovable, fastened, motionless, secured, steady, substantial, durable, rigid, bolted, welded, riveted, soldered, embedded, nailed, tightened, fast, secure, sound, immobile, unmovable, mounted, stationary, set, settled.—*Ant.* loose, movable, mobile. **2** [Firm in texture] solid, dense, compact, hard, stiff, impenetrable, impervious, rigid, hardened, inflexible, unyielding, thick, compressed, substantial, heavy, close, condensed, impermeable.—*Ant.* soft, porous, flabby. **3** [Settled in purpose] determined, steadfast, resolute. **—stand** (or **hold**) **firm** be steadfast, endure, maintain one's resolution.

**firmly** *a.* **1** [Not easily moved] immovably, solidly, rigidly, stably, durably, enduringly, substantially, securely, heavily, stiffly, inflexibly, soundly, strongly, thoroughly.—*Ant.* lightly, tenuously, insecurely. **2** [Showing determination] resolutely, steadfastly, doggedly, stolidly, tenaciously, determinedly, staunchly, constantly, intently, purposefully, persistently, obstinately, stubbornly, unwaveringly, unchangeably, through thick and thin.

**first** *a.* beginning, original, primary, prime, primal, antecedent, initial, virgin, earliest, opening, introductory, primeval, leading, in the beginning, front, head, rudimentary.—*Ant.* last, ultimate, final. **—in the first place** firstly, initially, to begin with.

**first-rate** *a.* prime, very good, choice.

**fit** *a.* **1** [Appropriate by nature] suitable, proper, fitting, likely, expedient, appropriate, convenient, timely, opportune, feasible, practicable, wise, advantageous, favorable, preferable, beneficial, desirable, adequate, tasteful, becoming, agreeable, seasonable, due, rightful, equitable, legitimate, decent, harmonious, pertinent, according, relevant, in keeping, consistent, applicable, compatible, admissible, concurrent, to the point, adapted to, fitted, suited, calculated, prepared, qualified, competent, matched, ready-made, accommodated, right, happy, lucky, cut out for*.—*Ant.* unfit, unseemly, inappropriate. **2** [In good physical condition] trim, robust, healthy.

**fit** *n.* **1** [Sudden attack of disease] muscular convulsion, spasm, seizure, stroke, epileptic attack, paroxysm, spell*. **2** [Transitory spell of action or feeling] impulsive action, burst, rush, outbreak, torrent, tantrum, mood, outburst, whimsy, huff, rage, spell. **—have** (or **throw**) **a fit*** become angry, lose one's temper, give vent to emotion.

**fit** *v.* **1** [To be suitable in character] agree, suit, accord, harmonize, apply, belong, conform, consist, fit right in, be in keeping, parallel, relate, concur, match, correspond, be comfortable, respond, have its place, answer the purpose, meet, click*.—*Ant.* oppose, disagree, clash. **2** [To make suitable] arrange, alter, adapt.

**fix** *v.* **1** [To make firm] plant, implant, secure. **2** [To prepare a meal] prepare, heat, get ready. **3** [To put in order] correct, improve, settle, put into shape, reform, patch, rejuvenate, touch up, revive, refresh, renew, renovate, rebuild, make compatible, clean, align, adapt, mend, adjust.

**fixed** *a.* **1** [Firm] solid, rigid, immovable. **2** [Repaired] rebuilt, in order, timed, synchronized, adjusted, settled, mended, rearranged, adapted, corrected, restored, renewed, improved, patched up, put together, in working order. **3** [*Prearranged] predesigned, put-up*, set up*.

**flag** *n.* banner, standard, colors.

**flagrant** *a.* notorious, disgraceful, infamous.

**flash** *n.* glimmer, sparkle, glitter, glisten, gleam, beam, blaze, flicker, flame, glare, burst, impulse, vision, dazzle, shimmer, shine, glow, twinkle, twinkling, phosphorescence, reflection, radiation, ray, luster, spark, streak, stream, illumination, incandescence.

**flash** *v.* glimmer, sparkle, glitter, glisten, gleam, beam, blaze, flame, glare, dazzle, shimmer, shine, glow, twinkle, reflect, radiate, shoot out beams, flicker.

**flat** *a.* **1** [Lying in a smooth plane] level, even, smooth, spread out, extended, prostrate, horizontal, low, on a level, fallen, level with the ground, prone.—*Ant.* rough, raised, uneven. **2** [Lacking savor] unseasoned, insipid, flavorless.

**flatter** *v.* overpraise, adulate, glorify.

**flavor** *n.* taste, savor, tang, relish, smack, twang, gusto, tartness, sweetness, acidity, saltiness, spiciness, pungency, piquancy, bitterness, sourness.

**flesh** *n.* meat, fat, muscle, brawn, tissue, cells, flesh and blood, protoplasm, plasm, plasma, body parts, heart, insides*. **—one's** (**own**) **flesh and blood** family, kindred, kin.

**flexible** *a.* limber, lithe, supple, plastic, elastic, bending, malleable, pliable, soft, spongy, tractable, moldable, yielding, formable, bendable, impressionable, like putty, like wax, adjustable, stretchable.—*Ant.* stiff, hard, rigid.

**flippant** *a.* impudent, saucy, smart.

**float** *v.* waft, stay afloat, swim.

**floor** *n.* **1** [The lower limit of a room] floorboards, deck, flagstones, tiles, planking, ground, carpet, rug, linoleum. **2** [The space in a building between two floors] story, stage, landing, level, basement, cellar, ground floor, ground story, lower story, first floor, mezzanine, upper story, downstairs, upstairs, loft, attic, garret, penthouse.

**flounder** *v.* struggle, wallow, blunder.

**flourish** *v.* thrive, increase, wax.

**flow** *n.* current, movement, progress, stream, tide, run, river, flood, ebb, gush, spurt, spout, leakage, dribble, oozing, flux, overflow, issue, discharge, drift, course, draft, downdraft, up-current, wind, breeze.

**flow** *v.* stream, course, slide, slip, glide, move, progress, run, pass, float, sweep, rush, whirl, surge, roll, swell, ebb, pour out, spurt, squirt, flood, jet, spout, rush, gush, well up, drop, drip, seep, trickle, overflow, spill, run, spew, stream, brim, surge, leak, run out, ooze, splash, pour forth, bubble.

**fluctuate** *v.* vacillate, waver, falter.

**fluent** *a.* eloquent, voluble, glib, wordy, smooth, talkative, smooth-spoken, garrulous, verbose, chatty, argumentative, articulate, vocal, cogent, persuasive, silver-tongued*, having the gift of gab*.—*Ant.* dumb, tongue-tied, stammering.

**fly** *v.* **1** [To pass through the air] wing, soar, float, glide, remain aloft, take flight, take wing, hover, sail, swoop, dart, drift, flutter, circle. **2** [To move swiftly] rush, dart, flee. **3** [To flee from danger] retreat, hide, withdraw. **4** [To manage a plane in the air] pilot, navigate, control, jet, take off, operate, glide, climb, dive, manipulate, maneuver.

**focus** *v.* **1** [To draw toward a center] attract, converge, convene. **2** [To make an image clear] adjust, bring out, get detail.

**fog** *n.* mist, haze, cloud, film, steam, wisp, smoke, smog, soup*, pea soup*.

**follow** *v.* **1** [To be later in time] come next, ensue, postdate. **2** [To regulate one's action] conform, observe, imitate, copy, take after, match, mirror, reflect, follow the example of, do as, mimic, follow suit, do like, tag along, obey, abide by, adhere to, comply, be in keeping, be consistent with.—*Ant.* neglect, disregard, depart from. **3** [To observe] heed, regard, keep an eye on. **4** [To understand] comprehend, catch, realize. **5** [To result] proceed from, happen, ensue. **—as follows** the following, next, succeeding.

**follower** *n.* henchman, attendant, hanger-on, companion, lackey, helper, partisan, recruit, disciple, pupil, protégé, imitator, apostle, adherent, supporter, zealot, backer, participant, sponsor, witness, devotee, believer, advocate, member, admirer, patron, promoter, upholder, copycat*, yes man*.—*Ant.* opponent, deserter, heretic.

**food** *n.* victuals, foodstuffs, meat and drink, meat, nutriment, refreshment, edibles, table, comestibles, provisions, stores, sustenance, subsistence, rations, board, cooking, cookery, cuisine, nourishment, fare, grub*, vittles*, eats*, chow*.

**fool** *n.* nitwit, simpleton, dunce, oaf, ninny, cretin, nincompoop, dolt, idiot, jackass, ass, buffoon, blockhead, numskull, boob*, goose, ignoramus, imbecile, moron, clown, loon, dullard, fathead*, half-wit, bonehead*, dope*, sap*, birdbrain*, jerk*, dum-dum*.—*Ant.* philosopher, sage, scholar. **—no** (or **nobody's**) **fool** shrewd, calculating, capable. —**play the fool** be silly, show off, clown.

**foolish** *a.* silly, simple, half-witted.

**foot** *n.* **1** [A unit of measurement] twelve inches, running foot, front foot, board foot, square foot, cubic foot. **2** [End of the leg] pedal extremity, hoof, paw, pad, dog*, tootsy*. **3** [A foundation] footing, base, pier. **4** [A metrical unit in verse] measure, accent, interval, meter, duple meter, triple meter. **—on foot** running, hiking, moving. **—on one's feet** **1** [Upright] standing, erect, vertical. **2** [Established] sound, settled, secure. **—on the wrong foot** unfavorably, ineptly, incapably. **—put one's best foot forward*** do one's best, appear at one's best, try hard. **—put one's foot down*** be firm, act decisively, determine. **—under foot** on the ground, at one's feet, in the way.

**for** *prep.* toward, to, in favor of, intended to be given to, in order to get, under the authority of, in the interest of, during, in order to, in the direction of, to go to, to the amount of, in place of, in exchange for, as, in spite of, supposing, concerning, with respect to, with regard to, notwithstanding, with a view to, for the sake of, in consideration of, in the name of, on the part of.

**forbid** *v.* prohibit, debar, embargo, restrain, inhibit, preclude, oppose, cancel, hinder, obstruct, bar, prevent, censor, outlaw, declare illegal, withhold, restrict, deny, block, check, disallow, deprive, exclude, ban, taboo, say no to, put under an injunction.—*Ant.* approve, recommend, authorize.

**force** *n.* **1** [Force conceived as a physical property] power, might, energy. **2** [Force conceived as part of one's personality] forcefulness, dominance, competence, energy, persistence, willpower, drive, determination, effectiveness, efficiency, authority, impressiveness, ability, capability, potency, sapience, guts*.—*Ant.* indifference, impotence, incompetence. **3** [An organization] group, band, unit. **—in force** **1** [Powerfully] in full strength, totally, all together. **2** [In operation] operative, valid, in effect.

**force** *v.* compel, coerce, press, drive, make, impel, constrain, oblige, obligate, necessitate, require, enforce, demand, order, command, inflict, burden, impose, insist, exact, put under obligation, contract, charge, restrict, limit, pin down, bring pressure to bear upon, bear down, ram down someone's throat*, high-pressure*, strong-arm*, put the squeeze on*.

**forecast** *v.* predetermine, predict, guess.

**foreign** *a.* remote, exotic, strange, far, distant, inaccessible, unaccustomed, different, unknown, alien, imported, borrowed, immigrant, outside, expatriate, exiled, from abroad, coming from another land, not native, not domestic, nonresident, alienated, faraway, far-off, outlandish.—*Ant.* local, national, indigenous.

**foreshadow** *v.* imply, presage, suggest.

**forest** *n.* wood, jungle, timber, growth, stand of trees, grove, woodland, park, greenwood, cover, clump, forested area, shelter, brake, backwoods, tall timber.

**forestall** *v.* thwart, prevent, preclude.

**foretell** *v.* predict, prophesy, divine, foresee, announce in advance, prognosticate, augur, portend, foreshadow.—*Ant.* record, confirm, recount.

**forever** *a.* everlastingly, permanently, immortally, on and on, ever, perpetually, always, in perpetuity, world without end, eternally, interminably, infinitely, enduringly, unchangingly, durably, ever and again, indestructibly, endlessly, forevermore, for good, till hell freezes over*, for keeps*, for always, now and forever, for life, till death do us part.—*Ant.* temporarily, for a time, at present.

**for example** *a.* for instance, as a model, as an example, to illustrate, to cite an instance, to give an illustration, a case in point, like.

**forget** *v.* lose consciousness of, put out of one's head, fail to remember, be forgetful, have a short memory, overlook, ignore, omit, neglect, slight, disregard, lose sight of, pass over, skip, think no more of, close one's eyes to, not give another thought, draw a blank*, dismiss from the mind, kiss off*, laugh off*.—*Ant.* remember, recall, recollect.

**forgive** *v.* pardon, forgive and forget, let pass, excuse, condone, remit, forget, relent, bear no malice, exonerate, exculpate, let bygones be bygones, laugh it off, let up on, let it go, kiss and make up*, bury the hatchet*, turn the other cheek, make allowance, write off.—*Ant.* hate, resent, retaliate.

**forgotten** *a.* not remembered, not recalled, not recollected, lost, out of one's mind, erased from one's consciousness, beyond recollection, past recall, not recoverable, blanked out, lapsed.

**form** *n.* **1** [Shape] figure, appearance, plan, arrangement, design, outline, configuration, formation, structure, style, construction, fashion, mode, scheme, framework, contour, stance, profile, silhouette, skeleton, anatomy. **2** [The human form] body, frame, torso. **3** [The approved procedure] manner, mode, custom. **4** [Anything intended to give form] pattern, model, die. **5** [A standard letter or blank] mimeographed letter, duplicate, form letter, data sheet, information blank, chart, card, reference form, order form, questionnaire, application.

**form** *v.* **1** [To give shape to a thing] mold, pattern, model, arrange, make, block out, fashion, construct, devise, plan, design, contrive, produce, invent, frame, scheme, plot, compose, erect, build, cast, cut, carve, chisel, hammer out, put together, whittle, assemble, conceive, create, outline, trace, develop, cultivate, work, complete, finish, perfect, fix, regulate, establish, sculpture, bend, twist, knead, set, determine, arrive at, reach.—*Ant.* destroy, demolish, shatter. **2** [To give character to a person] instruct, rear, breed. **3** [To comprise] constitute, figure in, act as. **4** [To take form] accumulate, condense, harden, set, settle, rise, appear, take shape, grow, develop, unfold, mature, materialize, become a reality, take on character, become visible, shape up*, fall into place*, get into shape*.—*Ant.* disappear, dissolve, waste away.

**formal** *a.* **1** [Notable for arrangement] orderly, precise, set. **2** [Concerned with etiquette and behavior] reserved, distant, stiff. **3** [Official] confirmed, directed, lawful. **4** [In evening clothes] full dress, black-tie, dressed up.

**formerly** *a.* before now, some time ago, once, once upon a time, already, in former times, previously, earlier, in the early days, eons ago, centuries ago, in the past, in the olden days, used to be, long ago, before this, in time past, heretofore, a while back*.—*Ant.* recently, subsequently, immediately.

**formula** *n.* specifications, description, recipe.

**forthcoming** *a.* expected, inevitable, anticipated, future, impending, pending, resulting, awaited, destined, fated, predestined, approaching, in store, at hand, inescapable, imminent, in prospect, prospective, in the wind, in preparation, in the cards*.

**fortification** *n.* fort, fortress, defense, dugout, trench, entrenchment, gun emplacement, barricade, battlement, stockade, outpost, citadel, support, wall, barrier, earthwork, castle, pillbox, bastion, bulwark, breastwork, blockhouse.

**fortitude** *n.* firmness, resolution, persistence.

**fortunate** *a.* lucky, blessed, prosperous, successful, having a charmed life, in luck, favored, well-to-do, happy, triumphant, victorious, overcoming, affluent, thriving, flourishing, healthy, wealthy, well-fixed*, well-heeled*, born with a silver spoon in one's mouth*.—*Ant.* unfortunate, unlucky, cursed.

**forward** *a.* **1** [Going forward] advancing, progressing, ahead, leading, progressive, onward, propulsive, in advance.—*Ant.* backward, retreating, regressive. **2** [Bold] presumptuous, impertinent, fresh.

**foster** *v.* cherish, nurse, nourish.

**foundation** *n.* **1** [An intellectual basis] reason, justification, authority. **2** [A physical basis] footing, base, foot, basement, pier, groundwork, bed, ground, bottom, substructure, wall, underpinning, solid rock, infrastructure, pile, roadbed, support, prop, stand, shore, post, pillar, skeleton, column, shaft, pedestal, buttress, framework, scaffold, beam. **3** [That which has been founded] institution, organization, endowment, institute, society, establishment, company, guild, corporation, association, charity, scholarship fund, trust.

**fountain** *n.* jet, stream, gush, spout, geyser, spurt, spring, pond, basin, pool.

**fragile** *a.* brittle, frail, delicate.

**frank** *a.* candid, sincere, free, easy, familiar, open, direct, unreserved, uninhibited, downright, ingenuous, unsophisticated, unaffected, plain, aboveboard, forthright, outspoken, tactless, guileless, straightforward, plain-spoken, natural, blunt, matter-of-fact.—*Ant.* dishonest, insincere, secretive.

**frantic** *a.* distracted, mad, wild, frenetic, furious, raging, raving, frenzied, violent, agitated, deranged, crazy, delirious, insane, angry.—*Ant.* calm, composed, subdued.

**fraudulent** *a.* deceitful, tricky, swindling.

**free** *a.* **1** [Not restricted politically] sovereign, independent, released, autonomous, self-ruling, freed, liberated, self-governing, democratic, at liberty, unconstrained.—*Ant.* restricted, enslaved, subject. **2** [Not restricted in space; *said of persons*] unconfined, at large, cast loose, escaped, let out, scot-free, free as air, free to come and go, unfettered, footloose and fancy-free, freewheeling*, on the loose*.—*Ant.* confined, imprisoned, restrained. **3** [Not restricted in space; *said of things*] unimpeded, unobstructed, unhampered, unattached, loose, not attached, clear from, unentangled, unengaged, disengaged, unfastened.—*Ant.* fixed, fastened, rooted. **4** [Given without charge] gratuitous, gratis, for nothing, without charge, free of cost, complimentary, for free*, on the house.—*Ant.* paid, charged, costly. **—for free*** without cost, gratis, for nothing. **—set free** release, liberate, emancipate.

**free** *v.* release, discharge, deliver, save, emancipate, rescue, extricate, loosen, unbind, disengage, undo, set free, let out, let loose, bail out, cut loose, relieve, absolve, acquit, dismiss, pardon, clear, ransom, redeem, unbind, unchain, disentangle, untie, let go, unlock, unhand, let out of prison, open the cage, turn loose, unfetter, unshackle.—*Ant.* seize, capture, incarcerate.

**freedom** *n.* **1** [Political liberty] independence, sovereignty, autonomy, democracy, self-government, citizenship, representative government, self-determination.—*Ant.* slavery, bondage, regimentation. **2** [Exemption from necessity] privilege, immunity, license, indulgence, facility, range, latitude, scope, play, own accord, free rein, leeway.—*Ant.* restraint, constraint, hindrance. **3** [Natural ease and facility] readiness, forthrightness, spontaneity.

**freely** *a.* **1** [Without physical restriction] loosely, without encumbrance, unhindered, without restraint, as one pleases, easily, smoothly.—*Ant.* with difficulty, uneasily, stressfully. **2** [Without mental restriction] voluntarily, willingly, fancy-free, of one's own accord, at will, at pleasure, of one's own free will, purposely, deliberately, intentionally, advisedly, spontaneously, frankly, openly.—*Ant.* unwillingly, under compulsion, hesitantly.

**free will** *n.* willingness, volition, intention, purpose, choice, free choice, power of choice, freedom, pleasure, discretion, inclination, desire, wish, intent, option, determination, mind, consent, assent.—*Ant.* restraint, predestination, unwillingness.

**freight** *n.* burden, load, contents, weight, bulk, encumbrance, bales, shipment, cargo, shipping, consignment, goods, tonnage, packages, ware.

**frequent** *a.* **1** [Happening often] many, repeated, numerous, common, habitual, monotonous, profuse, incessant, continual, customary, intermittent, familiar, commonplace, expected, various, a good many.—*Ant.* rare, infrequent, occasional. **2** [Happening regularly] recurrent, usual, periodic.

**fresh** *a.* **1** [Newly produced] new, green, crisp, raw, recent, current, late, this season's, factory-fresh, garden-fresh, farm-fresh, brand-new, newborn, immature, young, beginning, hot off the press*, just out, newfangled.—*Ant.* old, stale, musty. **2** [Not preserved] unsalted, uncured, unsmoked. **3** [Unspoiled] uncontaminated, green, not stale, good, undecayed, well-preserved, odor-free, in good condition, unblemished, unspotted, preserved, new, virgin, unimpaired.—*Ant.* decayed, spoiled, contaminated. **4** [Not faded] colorful, vivid, sharp. **5** [Not salt; *said of water*] potable, drinkable, cool, clear, pure, clean, sweet, fit to drink, safe.—*Ant.* dirty, brackish, briny. **6** [Refreshed] rested, restored, rehabilitated, like new, unused, new, relaxed, stimulated, relieved, freshened, revived.—*Ant.* tired, exhausted, worn-out. **7** [Inexperienced] untrained, untried, unskilled.

**friend** *n.* familiar, schoolmate, playmate, best friend, roommate, companion, intimate, confidant, comrade, mate, amigo, fellow, pal*, chum*, crony*, buddy*, side-kick*.—*Ant.* enemy, foe, stranger. —**make** (or **be**) **friends with** befriend, stand by, become familiar with.

**friendly** *a.* kind, kindly, helpful, sympathetic, amiable, well-disposed, neighborly, well-intentioned, sociable, civil, peaceful, loving, affectionate, fond, warmhearted, attentive, brotherly, agreeable, genial, affable, benevolent, accommodating, unoffensive, pleasant, tender, companionable, with open arms, cordial, familiar, intimate, close, devoted, dear, attached, loyal, faithful, steadfast, true, responsive, understanding, congenial, approachable, cheerful, convivial, good-humored, good-natured, generous, gracious, cooperative, wholehearted, bighearted*, chummy*, folksy*, thick*, arm in arm.—*Ant.* unfriendly, antagonistic, spiteful.

**frighten** *v.* scare, scare away, scare off, dismay, terrify, cow, shock, intimidate, threaten, badger, petrify, panic, demoralize, disrupt, give cause for alarm, terrorize, horrify, astound, awe, perturb, disturb, startle, frighten out of one's wits, take someone's breath away, chill to the bone, make someone's hair stand on end, make someone's blood run cold, make someone's flesh creep*, scare one stiff*, curdle the blood.

**frivolous** *a.* superficial, petty, trifling.

**front** *n.* **1** [The forward part or surface] exterior, forepart, anterior, bow, foreground, face, head, breast, frontal area.—*Ant.* rear, posterior, back. **2** [The fighting line] front line, no man's land, advance position, line of battle, vanguard, outpost, field of fire, advance guard. **3** [The appearance one presents before others] mien, demeanor, aspect, countenance, face, presence, expression, figure, exterior. —**in front of** before, preceding, leading.

**frugal** *a.* thrifty, prudent, parsimonious.

**fruitless** *a.* vain, unprofitable, futile.

**frustrate** *v.* defeat, foil, balk.

**fry** *v.* sauté, sear, singe, brown, grill, pan-fry, deep-fry, French fry, sizzle. —**small fry** children, infants, toddlers.

**fulfilled** *a.* accomplished, completed, achieved, realized, effected, finished, obtained, perfected, attained, reached, actualized, executed, concluded, brought about, performed, carried out, put into effect, made good, brought to a close.—*Ant.* disappointed, unfulfilled, unrealized.

**full** *a.* **1** [Filled] running over, abundant, weighted, satisfied, saturated, crammed, packed, stuffed, jammed, glutted, gorged, loaded, chock-full, stocked, satiated, crowded, stuffed to the gills*, jam-packed*, crawling with*, up to the brim, packed like sardines*.—*Ant.* empty, exhausted, void. **2** [Well-supplied] abundant, complete, copious, ample, plentiful, sufficient, adequate, competent, lavish, extravagant, profuse.—*Ant.* inadequate, scanty, insufficient. **3** [Not limited] broad, unlimited, extensive. —**in full** for the entire amount, fully, thoroughly.

**fun** *n.* play, game, sport, jest, amusement, relaxation, pastime, diversion, frolic, mirth, entertainment, solace, merriment, pleasure, caper, foolery, romping, joke, absurdity, playfulness, laughter, festivity, carnival, tomfoolery, ball*, escapade, antic, romp, prank, comedy, teasing, celebration, holiday, rejoicing, good humor, joking, enjoyment, gladness, good cheer, delight, glee, treat, lark, recreation, joy, time of one's life, blast*, big time*, picnic*, riot*.—*Ant.* unhappiness, tedium, sorrow. —**for** (or **in**) **fun** for amusement, not seriously, playfully. —**make fun of** mock, satirize, poke fun at.

**function** *n.* employment, capacity, use.

**function** *v.* perform, run, work.

**fundamental** *a.* basic, underlying, primary, first, rudimentary, elemental, supporting, elementary, cardinal, organic, theoretical, structural, sustaining, central, original.—*Ant.* superficial, incidental, consequent.

**funeral** *n.* interment, last rites, burial, burial ceremony, entombment, requiem, cremation.

**funny** *a.* **1** [Stirring to laughter] laughable, comic, comical, whimsical, amusing, entertaining, diverting, humorous, witty, jesting, jocular, waggish, droll, facetious, clever, mirthful, ludicrous, jolly, absurd, ridiculous, sly, sportive, playful, merry, joyful, joyous, good-humored, glad, gleeful, hilarious, jovial, farcical, joking, sidesplitting.—*Ant.* sad, serious, melancholy. **2** [*Likely to arouse suspicion] curious, unusual, odd.

**fur** *n.* pelt, hide, hair, coat, brush. —**make the fur fly*** fight, bicker, stir up trouble.

**furnish** *v.* fit out, equip, stock.

**furthest** *a.* most remote, most distant, remotest, farthest, uttermost, outermost, ultimate, extreme, outmost.

**fussy** *a.* fastidious, particular, meticulous.

**futile** *a.* vain, useless, in vain, fruitless, hopeless, impractical, worthless, unprofitable, to no effect, not successful, to no purpose, unneeded, unsatisfactory, unsatisfying, ineffective, ineffectual, unproductive, idle, empty, hollow, unreal.—*Ant.* hopeful, practical, effective.

**future** *n.* infinity, eternity, world to come, subsequent time, coming time, events to come, prospect, tomorrow, the hereafter, by and by.—*Ant.* past, historic ages, recorded time.

# G

**gag** *v.* **1** [To stop the mouth] choke, muzzle, muffle, obstruct, stifle, throttle, tape up, deaden. **2** [To retch] be nauseated, sicken, choke.

**gallant** *a.* bold, courageous, intrepid.

**gamble** *v.* game, wager, bet, play, plunge, play at dice, cut the cards*, bet against, speculate, back, lay money on, lay odds on, try one's luck, go for broke*, shoot craps.

**gap** *n.* **1** [A breach] cleft, break, rift. **2** [A break in continuity] hiatus, recess, lull. **3** [A mountain pass] way, chasm, hollow, cleft, ravine, gorge, arroyo, canyon, passageway, notch, gully, gulch.

**garbage** *n.* refuse, waste, trash.

**gargantuan** *a.* enormous, huge, immense.

**garment** *n.* dress, attire, apparel.

**gather** *v.* **1** [To come together] assemble, meet, gather around, congregate, flock in, pour in, rally, crowd, throng, come together, convene, collect, unite, reunite, associate, hold a meeting, hold a reunion, swarm, huddle, draw in, group, converge, concentrate.—*Ant.* scatter, disperse, part. **2** [To bring together] collect, aggregate, amass. **3** [To conclude] infer, deduce, find.

**gathering** *n.* assembly, meeeting, conclave, caucus, parley, council, conference, band, congregation, company, rally, crowd, throng, bunch, collection, union, association, society, committee, legislature, house, senate, parliament, swarm, huddle, group, body, mass, herd, turnout, flock, combination, convention, discussion, panel, reunion, meet, congress, attendance, multitude, audience, horde, mob, crush, party, social gathering, crew, gang, school, bevy, troop, drove, concentration, convocation, get-together, bull session*.

**gaudy** *a.* showy, flashy, ornate.

**gawk** *v.* stare, ogle, gaze.

**gem** *n.* **1** [A jewel] precious stone, bauble, ornament. **2** [Anything excellent, especially if small and beautiful] jewel, pearl of great price, paragon, ace*, nonpareil, perfection, ideal.

**generally** *a.* usually, commonly, ordinarily.

**generic** *a.* universal, general, nonexclusive.

**generosity** *n.* hospitality, benevolence, charity, liberality, philanthropy, altruism, unselfishness.—*Ant.* greed, miserliness, stinginess.

**generous** *a.* **1** [Openhanded] bountiful, liberal, charitable, altruistic, freehanded, beneficient, lavish, profuse, unselfish, hospitable, philanthropic, prodigal, unsparing, unstinting.—*Ant.* stingy, close, tight-fisted. **2** [Considerate] kindly, magnanimous, reasonable.

**genial** *a.* cordial, kind, warmhearted.

**genius** *n.* **1** [The highest degree of intellectual capacity] ability, talent, intellect, brains, intelligence, inspiration, imagination, gift, aptitude, wisdom, astuteness, penetration, grasp, discernment, acumen, acuteness, power, capability, accomplishment, sagacity, understanding, reach, enthusiasm, creative gift, knack, bent, turn. **2** [One having genius] gifted person, prodigy, adept.

**gentle** *a.* **1** [Soft] tender, smooth, sensitive. **2** [Kind] tender, considerate, benign. **3** [Tamed] domesticated, housebroken, disciplined, educated, trained, civilized, tractable, pliable, taught, cultivated, tame.—*Ant.* wild, savage, untamed.

**genuine** *a.* **1** [Authentic; *said of things*] real, true, actual, original, veritable, unadulterated, official, whole, accurate, proved, tested, good, natural, unimpeachable, pure, unquestionable, authenticated, existent, essential, substantial, factual, palpable, exact, precise, positive, valid, literal, sound, plain, certain, legitimate, legit*, for real*, honest-to-goodness*, in the flesh*.—*Ant.* vulgar, spurious, sham. **2**

[Sincere] real, actual, unaffected, unquestionable, certain, absolute, unimpeachable, definite, incontrovertible, well-established, known, reliable, bona fide, staunch, trustworthy, certain, valid, positive, frank.

**germ** *n.* microbe, antibody, bacteria, disease germ, microorganism, virus, parasite, bug*.

**gesture** *n.* gesticulation, indication, intimation.

**gesture** *v.* make a sign, motion, signal, pantomime, act out, use sign language, use one's hands, indicate, signalize, point, nod.

**get** *v.* **1** [To obtain] gain, procure, occupy, reach, capture, recover, take, grab, accomplish, attain, win, secure, achieve, collect, purchase, earn, receive, realize, possess, get possession of, take title to, acquire. **2** [To become] grow, develop into, go. **3** [To receive] be given, take, accept. **4** [To induce] persuade, talk into, compel. **5** [*To overcome] beat, vanquish, overpower. **6** [To prepare] make, arrange, dress. **7** [To contract; *said of bodily disorders*] catch, succumb to, get sick. **8** [To learn] acquire, gain, receive. **9** [*To understand] comprehend, perceive, know. **10** [*To irritate] annoy, provoke, vex. **11** [To arrive] come to, reach, land.

**get in touch (with)** *v.* call, telephone, write to, contact, wire, telegraph, e-mail*, correspond with, communicate with, reach, keep in contact with, make overtures.

**get together** *v.* **1** [To gather] collect, accumulate, congregate. **2** [To reach an agreement] come to terms, settle, make a bargain.

**ghastly** *a.* **1** [Terrifying] hideous, horrible, frightening. **2** [*Unpleasant] repulsive, disgusting, abhorrent.

**ghost** *n.* vision, specter, apparition, spirit, demon, shade, phantom, appearance, spook*.

**giant** *a.* monstrous, colossal, enormous.

**giant** *n.* ogre, Cyclops, Titan, colossus, Goliath, Hercules, Atlas, mammoth, behemoth, monster, whale, elephant, leviathan, mountain, hulk, lump, bulk.

**gift** *n.* **1** [A present] presentation, donation, grant, gratuity, alms, endowment, bequest, bounty, charity, favor, legacy, award, reward, offering, souvenir, token, remembrance, courtesy, bonus, subsidy, tribute, subvention, contribution, subscription, relief, ration, benefit, tip, allowance, handout, hand-me-down. **2** [An aptitude] faculty, capacity, capability. **—look a gift horse in the mouth** carp, criticize, be ungrateful.

**gifted** *a.* smart, skilled, talented.

**gigantic** *a.* massive, huge, immense.

**gist** *n.* substance, essence, significance.

**give** *v.* **1** [To transfer] grant, bestow, confer, impart, present, endow, bequeath, award, dispense, subsidize, contribute, hand out, dole out, hand in, hand over, deliver, let have, tip, pass down, convey, deed, sell, will, make over to, put into the hands of, contribute to, consign, relinquish, cede, lease, invest, dispose of, part with, lay upon, turn over, come through with*, come across with*, shell out*, fork over*, kick in*, palm off*.—*Ant.* maintain, withhold, take. **2** [To yield under pressure] give way, retreat, collapse, fall, contract, shrink, recede, open, relax, sag, bend, flex, crumble, yield.—*Ant.* resist, remain rigid, stand firm. **3** [To allot] assign, dispense, deal. **4** [To pass on] communicate, transmit, transfer. **5** [To administer] minister, provide with, dispense.

**give back** *v.* return, refund, reimburse.

**give up** *v.* **1** [To surrender] stop fighting, cede, hand over. **2** [To stop] quit, halt, cease.

**gladly** *a.* joyously, happily, gaily, blithely, cheerfully, ecstatically, blissfully, contendedly, readily, gratefully, enthusiastically, merrily, heartily, willingly, zealously, pleasantly, pleasurably, zestfully, complacently, delightfully, gleefully, cheerily, warmly, passionately, ardently, lovingly, cordially, genially, sweetly, joyfully, with relish, with satisfaction, with full agreement, with full approval, with delight.—*Ant.* sadly, unwillingly, gloomily.

**glamorous** *a.* fascinating, alluring, captivating, bewitching, dazzling.

**glaring** *a.* **1** [Shining] blinding, dazzling, blazing. **2** [Obvious] evident, conspicuous, obtrusive.

**glasses** *pl.n.* spectacles, eyeglasses, bifocals, trifocals, goggles, field glasses, opera glasses, contact lenses, specs*.

**glassy** *a.* vitreous, lustrous, polished.

**glide** *n.* floating, continuous motion, smooth movement, flowing, slide, drift, swoop, skimming, flight, soaring, slither.

**glide** *v.* float, slide, drift, waft, skim, skip, trip, fly, coast, flit, wing, soar, coast along, slide along, skim along.—*Ant.* hit, rattle, lurch.

**gloomy** *a.* dreary, depressing, discouraging.

**glorious** *a.* famous, renowned, famed, well-known, distinguished, splendid, excellent, noble, exalted, grand, illustrious, notable, celebrated, esteemed, honored, eminent, remarkable, brilliant, great, heroic, memorable, immortal, time-honored, admirable, praiseworthy, remarkable.—*Ant.* unimportant, inglorious, ignominious.

**glossy** *a.* shining, reflecting, lustrous.

**glow** *v.* gleam, radiate, shine.

**glut** *n.* oversupply, overabundance, excess.

**go** *v.* **1** [To leave] quit, withdraw, take leave, depart, move, set out, go away, take off, start, leave, vanish, retire, vacate, flee, get out, fly, run along, say goodby, escape, run away, clear out*, pull out, push off*, scram*, split*, blow*, beat it*, take a powder*, get along*, fade away. **2** [To proceed] travel, progress, proceed. **3** [To function] work, run, perform. **4** [To fit or suit] conform, accord, harmonize. **5** [To extend] stretch, cover, spread. **6** [To elapse] be spent, waste away, transpire. **7** [To continue] maintain, carry on, persist. **8** [To die] pass on, depart, succumb. **9** [To end] terminate, finish, conclude. **10** [To endure] persevere, go on, persist. **—as people** (or **things**) **go** in comparison with others, by all standards, according to certain criteria. **—from the word "go"** from the outset, at the start, beginning with. **—have a go at*** attempt, endeavor, try one's hand at. **—let go** let free, give up, release. **—let oneself go** be unrestrained, free oneself, have fun. **—no**

**go*** impossible, worthless, without value. **—on the go*** in constant motion, moving, busy.

**goad** *v.* prod, urge, prick, prompt, spur, drive, whip, press, push, impel, force, stimulate, provoke, tease, excite, needle*, instigate, arouse, animate, encourage, bully, coerce.—*Ant.* restrain, curb, rein in.

**goal** *n.* object, aim, intent.

**go-between** *n.* middleman, referee, mediator.

**god** *n.* deity, divinity, divine being, spirit, numen, power, demigod, oversoul, prime mover, godhead, omnipotence, world soul, universal life force, infinite spirit.

**go down** *v.* **1** [To sink] descend, decline, submerge. **2** [To lose] be defeated, submit, succumb. **3** [To decrease] fall, decline, lessen.

**go for** *v.* **1** [To reach for] try to get, aim at, clutch at. **2** [*To attack] rush upon, run at, spring at. **3** [*To like] be fond of, fancy, care for.

**good** *a.* **1** [Moral] upright, just, honest, worthy, respectable, noble, ethical, fair, guiltless, blameless, pure, truthful, decent, kind, conscientious, honorable, charitable. **2** [Kind] considerate, tolerant, generous. **3** [Proper] suitable, becoming, desirable. **4** [Reliable] trustworthy, dependable, loyal. **5** [Sound] safe, solid, stable. **6** [Pleasant] agreeable, satisfying, enjoyable. **7** [Qualified] suited, competent, suitable. **8** [Of approved quality] choice, select, high-grade. **9** [Healthy] sound, normal, vigorous. **10** [Obedient] dutiful, tractable, well-behaved. **11** [Genuine] valid, real, sound. **12** [Delicious] tasty, flavorful, tasteful. **13** [Considerable] great, big, immeasurable. **14** [Favorable] approving, commendatory, commending. **—as good as** in effect, virtually, nearly. **—come to no good** come to a bad end, get into trouble, have difficulty. **—make good** fulfill, satisfy the requirements, accomplish. **—no good** useless, valueless, unserviceable. **—to the good** favorable, advantageous, beneficial.

**good** *n.* **1** [A benefit] welfare, gain, asset. **2** [That which is morally approved] ethic, merit, virtue.

**goodbye** *interj.* farewell, fare you well, God bless you and keep you, God be with you, adieu, adios, ciao, so long*, bye*, bye-bye*, see you later, take it easy, have a nice day.

**good-natured** *a.* cordial, kindly, amiable.

**goodness** *n.* decency, morality, honesty.

**goodwill** *n.* benevolence, charity, kindness, cordiality, sympathy, tolerance, helpfulness, altruism.—*Ant.* hatred, malevolence, animosity.

**goof*** *v.* err, make a mistake, flub*.

**gorge** *n.* chasm, abyss, crevasse.

**gossip** *n.* **1** [Local, petty talk] babble, chatter, meddling, small talk, malicious talk, hearsay, rumor, scandal, news, slander, defamation, injury, blackening, skinny*, the grapevine*. **2** [One who indulges in gossip] snoop, busybody, meddler, tattler, newsmonger, scandalmonger, muckraker, backbiter, chatterbox, talkative person, babbler.

**gossip** *v.* tattle, prattle, tell tales, talk idly, chat, chatter, rumor, report, tell secrets, blab, babble, repeat.

**go together** *v.* **1** [To harmonize] be suitable, match, fit. **2** [To keep company] go steady*, go with, date.

**govern** *v.* command, administer, reign, rule, legislate, oversee, assume command, hold office, administer the laws, exercise authority, be in power, supervise, direct, dictate, tyrannize.

**government** *n.* **1** [The process of governing] rule, control, command, regulation, bureaucracy, direction, dominion, sway, authority, jurisdiction, sovereignty, direction, power, management, authorization, mastery, supervision, superintendence, supremacy, domination, influence, politics, state, political practice. **2** [The instrument of governing] administration, assembly, legislature, congress, cabinet, excutive power, authority, party, council, parliament, senate, department of justice, synod, convocation, convention, court, house.

**grab** *v.* clutch, grasp, seize.

**grace** *n.* **1** [The quality of being graceful] suppleness, ease of movement, nimbleness, agility, pliancy, smoothness, form, poise, dexterity, symmetry, balance, style, harmony.—*Ant.* awkwardness, stiffness, maladroitness. **2** [Mercy] forgiveness, love, charity. **—in the bad graces of** in disfavor, rejected, disapproved. **—in the good graces of** favored, accepted, admired.

**graceful** *a.* **1** [*Said of movement*] supple, agile, lithe, pliant, nimble, elastic, springy, easy, dexterous, adroit, smooth, controlled, athletic, light-footed, willowy, poised, practiced, skilled, rhythmic, sprightly, elegant.—*Ant.* awkward, fumbling, stiff. **2** [*Said of objects*] elegant, neat, well-proportioned, trim, balanced, symmetrical, dainty, pretty, harmonious, beautiful, comely, seemly, handsome, fair, delicate, tasteful, slender, decorative, artistic, exquisite, statuesque.—*Ant.* ugly, shapeless, cumbersome. **3** [*Said of conduct*] cultured, seemly, becoming.

**gracious** *a.* **1** [Genial] amiable, courteous, polite. **2** [Merciful] tender, loving, charitable.

**grade** *n.* **1** [An incline] slope, inclined plane, gradient, slant, inclination, pitch, ascent, descent, ramp, upgrade, downgrade, climb, elevation, height. **2** [An embankment] fill, causeway, dike. **3** [Rank or degree] class, category, classification. **4** [A division of a school] standard, form, rank. **—make the grade** win, prosper, achieve.

**grade** *v.* rate, give a grade to, rank.

**gradual** *a.* creeping, regular, continuous.

**gradually** *a.* step by step, by degrees, steadily, increasingly, slowly, regularly, a little at a time, little by little, bit by bit, inch by inch, by installments, in small doses, continually, continuously, progressively, successively, sequentially, constantly, unceasingly, imperceptibly, deliberately.—*Ant.* quickly, haphazardly, by leaps and bounds.

**graduated** *a.* **1** [Granted a degree] certified, ordained, passed. **2** [Arranged or marked according to a scale] graded, sequential, progressive.

**grand** *a.* lofty, stately, dignified, elevated, high, regal, noble, illustrious, sublime, great, ambitious, august, majestic, solemn, grave, preeminent, extraordinary, monumental, stupendous, huge, chief, commanding, towering, overwhelming, impressive, imposing, awe-inspiring, mighty, terrific*.—*Ant.* poor, low, mediocre.

**grandeur** *n.* splendor, magnificence, pomp, circumstance, impressiveness, eminence, distinction, fame, glory, brilliancy, richness, luxury, stateliness, beauty, ceremony, importance, celebrity, solemnity, fineness, majesty, sublimity, nobility, scope, dignity, elevation, preeminence, height, greatness, might, breadth, immensity, amplitude, vastness.

**grant** *n.* gift, boon, reward, present, allowance, stipend, donation, matching grant, benefaction, gratuity, endowment, concession, bequest, privilege, federal grant.—*Ant.* discount, deprivation, deduction.

**grant** *v.* **1** [To permit] yield, cede, impart. **2** [To accept as true] concede, accede, acquiesce.

**graphic** *a.* **1** [Pictorial] visible, illustrated, descriptive, photographic, visual, depicted, seen, drawn, portrayed, traced, sketched, outlined, pictured, painted, engraved, etched, chiseled, penciled, printed.—*Ant.* unreal, imagined, chimerical. **2** [Vivid] forcible, telling, picturesque, intelligible, comprehensible, clear, explicit, striking, definite, distinct, precise, expressive, eloquent, moving, stirring, concrete, energetic, colorful, strong, figurative, poetic.—*Ant.* obscure, ambiguous, abstract.

**grasp** *n.* hold, clutch, grip.

**grateful** *a.* appreciative, pleased, thankful.

**gratitude** *n.* thankfulness, appreciation, acknowledgment, response, sense of indebtedness, feeling of obligation, responsiveness, thanks, praise, recognition, honor, thanksgiving, grace.—*Ant.* indifference, ingratitude, thanklessness.

**grave** *a.* **1** [Important] momentous, weighty, consequential. **2** [Dangerous] critical, serious, ominous. **3** [Solemn] serious, sober, earnest.

**grave** *n.* vault, sepulcher, tomb, pit, crypt, mausoleum, catacomb, long home*, six feet of earth, final resting place, place of interment, mound, burial place, charnel house, last home*. **—make one turn (over) in one's grave** do something shocking, sin, err. **—one foot in the grave** old, infirm, near death.

**gravity** *n.* **1** [Weight] heaviness, pressure, force. **2** [Importance] seriousness, concern, significance.

**graze** *v.* **1** [To touch or score lightly] brush, scrape, rub. **2** [To pasture] browse, feed, crop, gnaw, nibble, bite, uproot, pull grass, forage, eat, munch, ruminate.

**grease** *n.* oil, wax, fat, lubricant, salve, petrolatum, petroleum jelly, Vaseline (trademark), olive oil, axle grease.

**great** *a.* **1** [Eminent] noble, grand, majestic, dignified, exalted, commanding, famous, renowned, widely acclaimed, famed, celebrated, distinguished, noted, conspicuous, elevated, prominent, high, stately, honorable, magnificent, glorious, regal, royal, kingly, imposing, preeminent, unrivaled, fabulous, fabled, storied.—*Ant.* obscure, retired, anonymous. **2** [Large] numerous, big, vast. **3** [*Excellent] exceptional, surpassing, transcendent.

**greedy** *a.* avid, grasping, rapacious, selfish, miserly, parsimonious, close, closefisted, tight, tightfisted, niggardly, exploitative, grudging, devouring, ravenous, omnivorous, carnivorous, intemperate, gobbling, indulging one's appetites, mercenary, stingy, covetous, penny-pinching.—*Ant.* generous, munificent, bountiful.

**greet** *v.* welcome, speak to, salute, address, hail, recognize, embrace, shake hands, nod, receive, call to, stop, acknowledge, bow to, approach, give one's love, hold out one's hand, herald, bid good day, bid hello, bid welcome, exchange greetings, usher in, attend, pay one's respects.—*Ant.* ignore, snub, slight.

**grief** *n.* sorrow, sadness, regret, melancholy, mourning, misery, trouble, anguish, despondency, pain, worry, harassment, anxiety, woe, heartache, malaise, disquiet, discomfort, affliction, gloom, unhappiness, desolation, despair, agony, torture, purgatory.—*Ant.* happiness, exhilaration, pleasure.

**grieve** *v.* lament, bewail, sorrow for.

**grind** *v.* crush, powder, mill, grate, granulate, disintegrate, rasp, scrape, file, abrade, pound, reduce to fine particles, crunch, roll out, pound out, chop up, crumble.—*Ant.* organize, mold, solidify.

**groan** *n.* moan, sob, grunt.

**groove** *n.* channel, trench, gouge, depression, scratch, canal, valley, notch, furrow, rut, incision, slit, gutter, ditch, crease. **—in the groove*** efficient, skillful, operative.

**gross** *a.* **1** [Fat] corpulent, obese, huge. **2** [Obscene] foul, indecent, lewd. **3** [Without deduction] in sum, total, entire.

**group** *n.* **1** [A gathering of persons] assembly, assemblage, crowd. **2** [Collected things] accumulation, assortment, combination. **3** [An organized body of people] association, club, society.

**grovel** *v.* crawl, beg, sneak, stoop, kneel, crouch before, kowtow to, sponge, cower, snivel, beseech, wheedle, flatter, cater to, humor, pamper, curry favor with, court, act up to, play up to, beg for mercy, prostrate oneself, soft-soap*, butter up*, make up to, lick another's boots*, knuckle under, polish the apple*, eat dirt*, brown-nose*.—*Ant.* hate, spurn, scorn.

**grow** *v.* **1** [To become larger] increase, expand in size, swell, wax, thrive, gain, enlarge, advance, dilate, stretch, mount, build, burst forth, spread, multiply, develop, mature, flourish, grow up, rise, sprout, shoot up, jump up, start up, spring up, spread like wildfire*.—*Ant.* wither, lessen, shrink. **2** [To change slowly] become, develop, alter, tend, pass, evolve, flower, shift, flow, progress, advance; get bigger, larger, etc.; wax, turn into, improve, mellow, age, better, ripen into, blossom, open out, resolve itself into, mature. **3** [To cultivate] raise, nurture, tend, nurse, foster, produce, plant, breed.—*Ant.* harm, impede, neglect.

**growl** *n.* snarl, gnarl, moan, bark, bellow, rumble, roar, howl, grumble, grunt.

**grueling** *a.* exhausting, tiring, fatiguing.

**gruesome** *a.* grim, grisly, fearful.

**guarantee** *v.* attest, testify, vouch for, declare, assure, answer for, be responsible for, pledge, give bond, go bail, wager, stake, give a guarantee, stand good for, back, sign for, become surety for, endorse, secure, make certain, warrant, insure, witness, prove, reassure, support, affirm, confirm, cross one's heart*.

**guard** *v.* watch, observe, superintend, patrol, picket, police, look out, look after, see after, supervise, tend, keep in view, keep an eye on, attend, overlook, hold in custody, stand over, babysit, care for, see to, chaperone, oversee, ride herd on*, keep tabs on*.—*Ant.* neglect, disregard, forsake.

**guess** *n.* conjecture, surmise, supposition, theory, hypothesis, presumption, opinion, postulate, estimate, suspicion, guesswork, view, belief, assumption, speculation, fancy, inference, conclusion, deduction, induction, shot in the dark.

**guess** *v.* conjecture, presume, infer, suspect, speculate, imagine, surmise, theorize, hazard a guess, suggest, figure, venture, suppose, presume, imagine, think likely, reckon*, calculate.

**guide** *n.* pilot, captain, pathfinder, scout, escort, courier, director, explorer, lead, guru, conductor, pioneer, leader, superintendent.

**guide** *v.* conduct, escort, lead.

**guilt** *n.* culpability, blame, error, fault, crime, sin, offense, liability, criminality, sinfulness, misconduct, misbehavior, malpractice, delinquency, transgression, indiscretion, weakness, failing, felonious conduct.—*Ant.* innocence, blamelessness, honor.

**guilty** *a.* found guilty, guilty as charged, condemned, sentenced, criminal, censured, impeached, incriminated, indicted, liable, convictable, judged, damned, doomed, at fault, sinful, to blame, in the wrong, in error, wrong, blameable, reproachable, chargeable.—*Ant.* innocent, blameless, right.

**gullible** *a.* innocent, trustful, naive.

# H

**habit** *n.* **1** [A customary action] mode, wont, routine, rule, characteristic, practice, disposition, way, fashion, manner, propensity, bent, turn, proclivity, addiction, predisposition, susceptibility, weakness, bias, persuasion, second nature. **2** [An obsession] addiction, fixation, hang-up*.

**habitual** *a.* ingrained, confirmed, frequent, periodic, continual, routine, mechanical, automatic, seasoned, permanent, perpetual, fixed, rooted, systematic, recurrent, periodical, methodical, repeated, disciplined, practiced, accustomed, established, set, repetitious, cyclic, reiterated, settled, trite, stereotyped, in a groove, in a rut.—*Ant.* different, exceptional, departing.

**hack** *v.* chop, whack, mangle.

**hag** *n.* crone, virago, withered old woman, shrew, ogress, hellcat, fishwife, harridan, old witch, battle-ax*.

**hairy** *a.* bristly, shaggy, woolly, unshorn, downy, fleecy, whiskered, tufted, unshaven, bearded, bewhiskered, furry, fuzzy, hirsute, fluffy.—*Ant.* bald, hairless, smooth.

**half** *a.* partial, divided by two, equally distributed in halves, mixed, divided, halved, bisected.—*Ant.* full, all, whole. **—by half** considerably, many, very much. **—in half** into halves, split, divided. **—not the half of it** not all of it, partial, incomplete.

**halfhearted** *a.* lukewarm, indecisive, irresolute.

**halfway** *a.* midway, half the distance, in the middle, incomplete, unsatisfactory, partially, fairly, imperfectly, in part, partly, nearly, insufficiently, to a degree, to some extent, comparatively, moderately, at half the distance, in some measure, middling*.—*Ant.* completely, wholly, entirely.

**hall** *n.* **1** [A large public or semipublic building or room] legislative chamber, assembly room, meeting place, banquet hall, town hall, concert hall, dance hall, music hall, arena, ballroom, clubroom, church, salon, lounge, chamber, stateroom, gymnasium, dining hall, armory, amphitheater, council chamber, reception room, waiting room, lecture room, gallery, gym*, mess hall. **2** [An entranceway] foyer, corridor, hallway.

**hallway** *n.* foyer, entranceway, entrance.

**halt** *v.* pull up, check, terminate, suspend, put an end to, interrupt, break into, block, cut short, adjourn, hold off, cause to halt, stem, deter, bring to a standstill, stall, bring to an end, curb, stop, restrict, arrest, hold in check, defeat, thwart, hamper, frustrate, suppress, clog, intercept, extinguish, blockade, obstruct, repress, inhibit, hinder, barricade, impede, overthrow, vanquish, override, dam, upset, stand in the way of, baffle, contravene, overturn, reduce, counteract, quell, prohibit, outdo, put down, finish, forbid, oppose, crush, nip in the bud*, break it up, put on the brakes*, hold on*, throw a wet blanket on*, throw a monkey wrench in the works*, clip one's wings*, tie one's hands*, take the wind out of one's sails, squelch*.—*Ant.* begin, start, instigate.

**halve** *v.* split, bisect, cut in two.

**hand** *n.* **1** [The termination of the arm] fingers, palm, grip, grasp, hold, knuckles. **2** [A workman] helper, worker, hired hand. **3** [Handwriting] chirography, script, penmanship. **4** [Aid] help, guidance, instruction. **5** [Applause] standing ovation, thunderous reception, handclapping. **6** [Round of cards] single hand, deal, round. **—at hand** immediate, approximate, close by. **—by hand** handcrafted, handmade, manual. **—change hands** transfer, pass on, shift. **—from hand to hand** shifted, given over, changed. **—from hand to mouth** from day to day, by necessity, in poverty. **—hold hands** touch, press, squeeze. **—in hand** under control, in order, all right. **—join hands** unite, associate, agree. **—keep one's hand in** carry on, continue, make a practice of. **—not lift a hand** do nothing, be lazy, not try. **—off one's hands** out of one's responsibility, no longer one's concern, not accountable for. **—on hand** ready, close by, usable. **—on one's hands** in one's care or responsibility, chargeable to one, accountable to. **—on the other hand** otherwise, conversely, from the opposite position. **—out of hand** out of control, wild, unmanageable. **—take in hand** take responsibility for, take over, handle. **—throw up one's hands** give up, resign, quit. **—wash one's hands of** deny, reject, refuse.

**hand** *v.* deliver, give to, return.

**handle** *n.* **1** [A holder] handhold, hilt, grasp, crank, knob, stem, grip, arm. **2** [*A title] nickname, designation, moniker*. **—fly off the handle** become angry, lose one's temper, blow off steam*.

**handle** *v.* **1** [To deal in] retail, market, offer for sale. **2** [To touch] finger, check, examine. **3** [To do whatever is necessary] manipulate, operate, work.

**handsome** *a.* smart, impressive, stately, good-looking, attractive, athletic, personable, strong, muscular, robust, well-dressed, slick*.—*Ant.* ugly, homely, unsightly.

**hang** *v.* **1** [To suspend] dangle, attach, drape, hook up, hang up, nail on the wall, put on a clothesline, fix, pin up, tack up, drape on the wall, fasten up.—*Ant.* drop, throw down, let fall. **2** [To be suspended] overhang, wave, flap, be loose, droop, flop, be in midair, swing, dangle, be fastened, hover, stay up.—*Ant.* fall, come down, drop. **3** [To kill by hanging] execute, lynch, hang by the neck until dead. **—get** (or **have**) **the hang of** have the knack of, comprehend, learn. **—not care** (or **give**) **a hang about** be indifferent toward, not care about, ignore.

**haphazard** *a.* offhand, casual, random, careless, slipshod, incidental, unthinking, unconscious, uncoordinated, reckless, unconcerned, unpremeditated, loose, indiscriminate, unrestricted, irregular, blind, purposeless, unplanned, hit-or-miss, willy-nilly.—*Ant.* careful, studied, planned.

**happen** *v.* **1** [To be by chance] come up, come about, turn up, crop up, chance, occur unexpectedly, come face to face with, befall, hit one like a ton of bricks*, be just one's luck. **2** [To occur] take place, come to pass, arrive, ensue, befall, come after, arise, take effect, come into existence, recur, come into being, spring, proceed, follow, come about, fall, repeat, appear, go on, become a fact, turn out, become known, be found, come to mind, transpire, come off.

**happening** *n.* incident, affair, accident.

**happy** *a.* joyous, joyful, merry, mirthful, glad, gleeful, delighted, cheerful, gay, laughing, contented, genial, satisfied, enraptured, congenial, cheery, jolly, hilarious, sparkling, enchanted, transported, rejoicing, blissful, jovial, delightful, delirious, exhilarated, pleased, gratified, peaceful, comfortable, intoxicated, debonair, light, bright, ecstatic, charmed, pleasant, hearty, overjoyed, lighthearted, radiant, vivacious, sunny, smiling, content, animated, lively, spirited, exuberant, good-humored, elated, jubilant, rollicking, playful, thrilled, fun-loving, carefree, at peace, in good spirits, in high spirits, happy as a lark, in ecstasy, beside oneself, bubbling over, tickled pink*, tickled to death*, tickled silly*, happy-go-lucky, in seventh heaven.—*Ant.* sad, sorrowful, melancholy.

**harass** *v.* tease, vex, irritate.

**hard** *a.* **1** [Compact] unyielding, thick, solid, heavy, strong, impermeable, tough, tempered, hardened, dense. **2** [Difficult] arduous, tricky, impossible, trying, tedious, complex, abstract, puzzling, troublesome, laborious. **3** [Cruel] perverse, unrelenting, vengeful. **4** [Severe] harsh, exacting, grim. **5** [Alcoholic] intoxicating, inebriating, stimulating. **6** [With difficulty] strenuously, laboriously, with great effort. **—be hard on** treat severely, be harsh toward, be painful to.

**harden** *v.* steel, temper, solidify, precipitate, crystallize, freeze, coagulate, clot, granulate, make firm, make compact, make tight, make hard, petrify, starch, cure, bake, dry, flatten, cement, compact, concentrate, sun, fire, fossilize, vulcanize, toughen, concrete, encrust.—*Ant.* soften, unloose, melt.

**hardheaded** *a.* willful, stubborn, headstrong.

**hardhearted** *a.* cold, unfeeling, heartless.

**hardly** *a.* scarcely, barely, just, merely, imperceptibly, not noticeably, gradually, not markedly, no more than, not likely, not a bit, almost not, only just, with difficulty, with trouble, by a narrow margin, not by a great deal, seldom, almost not at all, but just, in no manner, by no means, little, infrequently, somewhat, not quite, here and there, simply, not much, rarely, slightly, sparsely, not often, once in a blue moon*, by the skin of one's teeth*.—*Ant.* easily, without difficulty, readily.

**hardy** *a.* tough, toughened, in good shape, in good condition, hardened, resistant, solid, staunch, seasoned, capable of endurance, able-bodied, physically fit, well-equipped, acclimatized, rugged, mighty, well, fit, robust, hearty, sound, fresh, hale, brawny, able, vigorous, powerful, firm, sturdy, solid, substantial.—*Ant.* weak, unaccustomed, unhabituated.

**harmful** *a.* injurious, detrimental, hurtful, noxious, evil, mischievous, ruinous, adverse, sinister, subversive, incendiary, virulent, cataclysmic, corroding, toxic, baleful, painful, wounding, crippling, bad, malicious, malignant, sinful, pernicious, unwholesome, corrupting, menacing, dire, prejudicial, damaging, corrupt, vicious, insidious, treacherous, catastrophic, disastrous, wild, murderous, destructive, unhealthy, killing, fatal, mortal, serious, dangerous, fraught with evil, doing harm, doing evil, sore, distressing, diabolic, brutal, unhealthful, satanic, grievous, lethal, venomous, cruel, unfortunate, disadvantageous, felonious, objectionable, fiendish, unlucky, malign, devilish, corrosive.

**harmless** *a.* pure, innocent, painless, powerless, controllable, manageable, safe, sure, reliable, trustworthy, sanitary, germproof, sound, sterile, disarmed.—*Ant.* harmful, injurious, poisonous.

**harmonious** *a.* **1** [Harmonic] melodious, tuneful, musical, rhythmical, melodic, symphonic, in tune, in unison. **2** [Congruous] agreeable to, corresponding, suitable, adapted, similar, like, peaceful, cooperative, in step, in accordance with, in concord with, in favor with, in harmony with, on a footing with, friendly, conforming, well-matched, evenly balanced, symmetrical, congruent.—*Ant.* opposed, incongruous, incompatible.

**harmony** *n.* **1** [Musical concord] chord, consonance, accord, symphony, harmonics, counterpoint, concert, music, chorus, blending, unity, accordance, chime, unison, overtone, musical pattern, musical blend. **2** [Social concord] compatibility, equanimity, unanimity. **3** [Musical composition] melody, piece, arrangement.

**harsh** *a.* discordant, jangling, cacophonous, grating, rusty, dissonant, assonant, strident, creaking, clashing, sharp, jarring, jangled, clamorous, cracked, hoarse, out of tune, unmelodious, rasping, screeching, earsplitting, disturbing, noisy, flat, sour, out of key, tuneless, unmusical, off-key.

**harvest** *n.* reaping, yield, crop.

**harvest** *v.* gather, accumulate, pile up, collect, garner, crop, cut, pluck, pick, cull, take in, draw in, glean, gather in the harvest, hoard, mow.—*Ant.* sow, plant, seed.

**haste** *n.* hurry, scramble, bustle, scurry, precipitation, flurry, hurly-burly, impetuosity, rashness, dispatch, impetuousness, foolhardiness, want of caution, hustling, press, recklessness, rush, hastiness, carelessness, irrationality, rashness, giddiness, impatience, heedlessness, plunge, testiness, excitation, outburst, abruptness, anticipation.—*Ant.* prudence, caution, attention. **—in haste** hastening, in a hurry, moving fast. **—make haste** hurry, act quickly, speed up.

**hasten** *v.* **1** [To make haste] rush, fly, sprint. **2** [To expedite] accelerate, speed up, advance, move up, quicken, stimulate, hurry up, push, make short work of, urge, goad, press, agitate, push ahead, put into action, get started, give a start, drive on, set in motion, take in hand, blast off, gear up.—*Ant.* delay, defer, put off.

**hasty** *a.* **1** [Hurried] quick, speedy, swift. **2** [Careless] ill-advised, precipitate, foolhardy.

**hate** *n.* ill will, animosity, enmity.

**hate** *v.* **1** [To detest] abhor, abominate, loathe, scorn, despise, have an aversion toward, look at with loathing, spit upon, curse, dislike intensely, shudder at, not care for, have enough of, be repelled by, feel repulsion for, have no use for, object to, bear a grudge against, shun, denounce, resent, curse, be sick of, be tired of, reject, revolt against, deride, have no stomach for, disfavor, look down upon, hold in contempt, be disgusted with, view with horror, be down on*, have it in for*.—*Ant.* love, adore, worship. **2** [To dislike; *often used with infinitive or participle*] object to, shudder at, not like.

**hateful** *a.* odious, detestable, repugnant.

**hatred** *n.* abhorrence, loathing, rancor, detestation, antipathy, repugnance, repulsion, disgust, contempt, intense dislike, scorn, abomination, distaste, disapproval, horror, hard feelings, displeasure, ill will, bitterness, antagonism, animosity, pique, grudge, malice, malevolence, revulsion, prejudice, spite, revenge, hate, venom, envy, spleen, coldness, hostility, alienation, bad blood, chip on one's shoulder*, grudge.—*Ant.* devotion, friendship, affection.

**haul** *n.* **1** [A pull] tug, lift, wrench. **2** [The distance something is hauled] trip, voyage, yards. **3** [*Something obtained, especially loot] find, spoils, take.

**haul** *v.* pull, drag, bring.

**hazardous** *a.* perilous, uncertain, precarious.

**hazy** *a.* cloudy, foggy, murky, misty, unclear, overcast, steaming, screened, filmy, gauzy, vaporous, smoky, dim, dull, indistinct, nebulous, shadowy, dusky, obscure, thick, opaque, frosty, veiled, blurred, semitransparent, blurry, faint.—*Ant.* clear, bright, cloudless.

**head** *n.* **1** [The skull] brainpan, scalp, crown, headpiece, bean*, noggin*, noodle*. **2** [A leader or supervisor] commander, commanding officer, ruler. **3** [The top] summit, peak, crest. **4** [The beginning] front, start, source. **5** [An attachment] cap, bottle top, cork. **6** [*Intelligence] brains, foresight, ingenuity. **—come to a head** culminate, reach a crisis, come to a climax. **—get it through one's head** learn, comprehend, see. **—go to one's head** stir mentally, stimulate, intoxicate. **—hang** (or **hide**) **one's head** repent, be sorry, grieve. **—keep one's head** remain calm, keep one's self-control, hold one's emotions in check. **—lose one's head** become excited, become angry, rave. **—make head or tail of** comprehend, apprehend, see. **—one's head off** greatly, extremely, considerably. **—on** (or **upon**) **one's head** burdensome, taxing, strenuous. **—out of** (or **off**) **one's head*** crazy, delirious, raving. **—over one's head** incomprehensible, not understandable, hard.

**heading** *n.* headline, subtitle, address, caption, legend, head, banner head, subject, capital, superscription, ticket, headnote, display line, preface, prologue, streamer, preamble, topic, designation, specification.

**headquarters** *n.* main office, home office, chief office, central station, central place, distributing center, police station, meeting place, meeting house, manager's office, quarters, base, military station, military town, post, center of operations, base of operations, HQ.

**heal** *v.* restore, renew, treat, attend, make healthy, return to health, fix, repair, regenerate, bring around, remedy, purify, rejuvenate, medicate, make clean, dress a wound, rebuild, revive, rehabilitate, work a cure, cause to heal, resuscitate, salve, help to get well, ameliorate, doctor*, put one on his feet again, breathe new life into*.—*Ant.* expose, make ill, infect.

**health** *n.* vigor, wholeness, good condition, healthfulness, good health, fitness, bloom, soundness of body, physical fitness, tone, hardiness, well-being, stamina, energy, full bloom, rosy cheeks*, good shape*, clean bill of health*.

**healthy** *a.* sound, trim, all right, normal, robust, hale, vigorous, well, hearty, athletic, rosy-cheeked, hardy, able-bodied, virile, muscular, blooming, sturdy, safe and sound, in good condition, in full possession of one's faculties, in good health, full of pep*, never feeling better, fresh, whole, firm, lively, undecayed, flourishing, good, physically fit, clear-eyed, in fine fettle, youthful, free from disease, fine, fine and dandy*, hunky-dory*, in the pink*, rugged, fit as a fiddle, feeling one's oats*.—*Ant.* unhealthy, ill, diseased.

**heap** *n.* pile, mass, stack.

**heap** *v.* pile, add, lump.

**hear** *v.* **1** [To perceive by ear] listen to, give attention, attend to, make out, become aware of, catch, apprehend, take in, eavesdrop, detect, perceive by the ear, overhear, take cognizance of, keep one's ears open, have the sense of hearing, read loud and clear, strain one's ears, listen in, get an earful*. **2** [To receive information aurally] overhear, eavesdrop, find out. **3** [To hold a hearing] preside over, put on trial, summon to court. **—not hear of** not allow, refuse to consider, reject.

**heart** *n.* **1** [The pump in the circulatory system] vital organ, vascular organ, blood pump, cardiac organ, ventricle, ticker*. **2** [Feeling] response, sympathy, sensitivity. **3** [The center] core, middle, pith. **4** [The most important portion] gist, essence, root. **5** [Courage] fortitude, gallantry, spirit. **—after one's own heart** suitable, pleasing, lovable. **—break one's heart** grieve, disappoint, pain. **—by heart** from memory, memorized, learned. **—change of heart** change of mind, reversal, alteration. **—do one's heart good** please, make content, delight. **—eat one's heart out** worry, regret, nurse one's troubles. **—from (the bottom of) one's heart** deeply, honestly, frankly. **—have a heart** be kind, empathize, take pity. **—lose one's heart (to)** love, cherish, adore. **—set one's heart at rest** calm, placate, soothe. **—set one's heart on** long for, need, desire. **—take to heart** think about, take into account, believe. **—wear one's heart on one's sleeve** disclose, divulge, confess. **—with all one's heart** honestly, deeply, frankly.

**heartbreaking** *a.* cheerless, deplorable, joyless.

**heartless** *a.* unkind, unthinking, insensitive.

**hearty** *a.* warm, zealous, sincere, cheery, cheerful, jovial, wholehearted, neighborly, well-meant, animated, jolly, ardent, genial, glowing, enthusiastic, genuine, avid, deepest, passionate, deep, intense, exuberant, profuse, eager, devout, deep-felt, unfeigned, fervent, warmhearted, authentic, impassioned, heartfelt, responsive.—*Ant.* false, mock, sham.

**heat** *n.* **1** [Warmth] torridity, high temperature, hot wind, heat wave, fever, hot weather, temperature, hotness, warmness, sultriness, white heat, torridness, tropical heat, dog days.—*Ant.* cold, frost, frigidity. **2** [Fervor] ardor, passion, excitement. **3** [Sources of heat] flame, radiation, solar energy.

**heat** *v.* **1** [To make hot] warm, fire, heat up, inflame, kindle, enkindle, subject to heat, put on the fire, make hot, make warm, scald, thaw, boil, char, roast, chafe, seethe, toast, oxidize, set fire to, melt, cauterize, reheat, steam, incinerate, sear, singe, scorch, fry, turn on the heat.—*Ant.* cool, freeze, chill. **2** [To become hot] glow, warm up, rise in temperature, grow hot, blaze, flame, seethe, burst into flame, kindle, ignite, thaw, swelter, perspire.

**heave** *v.* rock, bob, pitch, go up and down, lurch, roll, reel, sway, swell, dilate, expand, be raised, swirl, throb, waft, ebb and flow, wax and wane, puff, slosh, wash.—*Ant.* rest, lie still, quiet.

**heavy** *a.* **1** [Weighty] bulky, massive, unwieldy, ponderous, huge, overweight, top-heavy, of great weight, burdensome, weighty, stout, big, hard to carry, dense, fat, substantial, ample, hefty*, chunky.—*Ant.* light, buoyant, feather-light. **2** [Burdensome] troublesome, oppressive, vexatious. **3** [Dull] listless, slow, apathetic. **4** [Gloomy] dejected, cloudy, overcast.

**heed** *v.* pay attention to, notice, be aware.

**hefty*** *a.* sturdy, husky, stout, beefy, strapping, substantial, massive.

**height** *n.* elevation, extent upward, prominence, loftiness, highness, perpendicular distance, upright distance, tallness, stature.—*Ant.* depth, breadth, width.

**heir** *n.* future possessor, legal heir, heir apparent, successor, descendent, one who inherits, heiress, beneficiary, inheritor, crown prince.

**help** *n.* **1** [Assistance] advice, comfort, aid, favor, support, gift, reward, charity, encouragement, advancement, advice, subsidy, service, relief, care, endowment, cooperation, guidance. **2** [Employees] aides, representatives, hired help. **3** [Physical relief] maintenance, sustenance, nourishment.

**help** *v.* assist, uphold, advise, encourage, stand by, cooperate, intercede for, befriend, accommodate, work for, back up, maintain, sustain, benefit, bolster, lend a hand, do a service, see through, do one's part, give a hand, be of use, come to the aid of, be of some help, help along, do a favor, promote, back, advocate, abet, stimulate, further, stick up for*, take under one's wing, go to bat for*, side with, give a lift, boost, pitch in*.—*Ant.* oppose, rival, combat. **—cannot help but** be obliged to, cannot fail to, have to. **—cannot help oneself** be compelled to, have a need to, be the victim of habit. **—so help me** (**God**) as God is my witness, by God, I swear.

**helpful** *a.* **1** [Useful] valuable, important, significant, crucial, essential, cooperative, symbiotic, serviceable, profitable, advantageous, favorable, convenient, suitable, practical, operative, usable, applicable, conducive, improving, bettering, of service, all-purpose, desirable, instrumental, contributive, good for, to one's advantage, at one's command.—*Ant.* useless, ineffective, impractical. **2** [Curative] healthy, salutary, restorative. **3** [Obliging] accommodating, considerate, neighborly.

**helping** *n.* serving, plateful, portion.

**helpless** *a.* **1** [Dependent] feeble, unable, invalid. **2** [Incompetent] incapable, unfit, inexpert.

**here** *a.* in this place, hereabout, in this direction, on this spot, over here, up here, down here, right here, on hand, on board, on deck*, in the face of, within reach.

**here and there** *a.* often, patchily, sometimes.

**heritage** *n.* **1** [Inheritance] legacy, birthright, heirship, ancestry, right, dowry. **2** [Tradition] convention, endowment, cultural inheritance.

**hermit** *n.* holy man, ascetic, anchorite, solitary, recluse, anchoress, anchoret.

**hero** *n.* **1** [One distinguished for action] brave man, model, conqueror, victorious general, god, martyr, champion, prize athlete, master, brave, warrior, saint, man of courage, star, popular figure, great man, knight-errant, a man among men, man of the hour. **2** [Principal male character in a literary composition] protagonist, male lead, leading man.

**heroic** *a.* valiant, valorous, fearless.

**heroine** *n.* **1** [A female hero] courageous woman, champion, goddess, ideal, intrepid woman, resourceful woman, supremely courageous woman, woman of heroic character, woman of the hour. **2** [Leading female character in a literary composition] protagonist, leading lady, prima donna.

**heroism** *n.* rare fortitude, valor, bravery.

**hesitate** *v.* falter, fluctuate, vacillate, pause, stop, hold off, hold back, be dubious, be uncertain, flounder, alternate, ponder, think about, defer, delay, think it over, change one's mind, recoil, not know what to do, pull back, catch one's breath, weigh, consider, hang back, swerve, debate, shift, wait, deliberate, linger, balance, think twice, drag one's feet, hem and haw, blow hot and cold, dillydally, straddle the fence, leave up in the air.—*Ant.* resolve, decide, conclude.

**hidden** *a.* secluded, out of sight, private, covert, concealed, undercover, occult, in the dark, in a haze, in a fog, in darkness, masked, screened, veiled, cloaked, obscured, disguised, invisible, clouded, sealed, unobserved, blotted, impenetrable, unseen, eclipsed, camouflaged, shrouded, shadowy, unknown, buried, undetected, deep, unsuspected, inscrutable, illegible, puzzling, unobserved, out of view, dim, clandestine, subterranean, cloistered, suppressed, dark, inward, underground, unrevealed, withheld, surreptitious, underhand, kept in the dark, under wraps.—*Ant.* obvious, open, apparent.

**hide** *n.* pelt, rawhide, pigskin, chamois, bearskin, goatskin, jacket, sheepskin, sealskin, snakeskin, alligator skin, calfskin. **—neither hide nor hair** nothing whatsoever, no indication, not at all.

**hide** *v.* **1** [To conceal] shroud, curtain, veil, camouflage, cover, mask, cloak, not give away, screen, blot out, bury, suppress, withhold, keep underground, stifle, keep secret, hush up, shield, eclipse, not tell, lock up, confuse, put out of sight, put out of the way, hold back, keep from, secrete, smuggle, shadow, conceal from sight, keep out of sight, stow away, protect, hoard, store, seclude, closet, conceal, hush, obscure, wrap, shelter, throw a veil over, keep in the dark, keep under one's hat*, seal one's lips*, put the lid on*, salt away*.—*Ant.* expose, lay bare, uncover. **2** [To keep oneself concealed] disguise oneself, change one's identity, cover one's traces, keep out of sight, go underground, lie in ambush, sneak, prowl, burrow, skulk, avoid notice, lie in wait, hibernate, lie concealed, lie low, conceal oneself, lurk, shut oneself up, seclude oneself, lie hidden, keep out of the way, stay in hiding, hide out, cover up, duck*, keep in the background.

**hideous** *a.* ghastly, grisly, frightful.

**high** *a.* **1** [Tall] towering, gigantic, big, colossal, tremendous, great, giant, huge, formidable, immense, long, sky-scraping, steep, sky-high.—*Ant.* short, diminutive, undersized. **2** [Elevated] lofty, uplifted, soaring, aerial, high-reaching, flying, hovering, overtopping, jutting.—*Ant.* low, depressed, underground. **3** [Exalted] eminent, leading, powerful. **4** [Expensive] high-priced, costly, precious. **5** [To an unusual degree] great, extraordinary, special. **6** [Shrill] piercing, sharp, penetrating. **7** [*Drunk] intoxicated, tipsy, inebriated. **8** [*Under the influence of drugs] stoned*, freaked-out*, wasted*, turned-on*, on a trip*, tripping*, hyped-up*, spaced-out*, zonked out*.

**highway** *n.* roadway, parkway, superhighway, freeway, turnpike, toll road, state highway, national highway.

**hijack** *v.* highjack, privateer, capture.

**hill** *n.* mound, knoll, butte, bluff, promontory, precipice, cliff, range, rising ground, headland, upland, downgrade, inclination, descent, slope, ascent, slant, grade, incline, height, highland, rise, foothill, dune, climb, elevation, ridge, heap, hillside, upgrade, hilltop, vantage point, gradient, summit.

**hinder** *v.* impede, obstruct, interfere with, check, retard, fetter, block, thwart, bar, clog, encumber, burden, cripple, handicap, cramp, preclude, inhibit, shackle, interrupt, arrest, curb, resist, oppose, baffle, deter, hamper, frustrate, outwit, stop, counteract, offset, neutralize, tie up, hold up, embarrass, delay, postpone, keep back, set back, dam, close, box in, end, terminate, shut out, choke, intercept, bottleneck, defeat, trap, control, conflict with, deadlock, hold back, clash with, be an obstacle to, cross, exclude, limit, shorten, go against, prohibit, withhold, slow down, stall, bring to a standstill, smother, disappoint, spoil, gag, annul, silence, invalidate, detain, stalemate, taboo, suspend, set against, clip one's wings*, tie one's hands, get in the way of, throw a monkey wrench into the works*, knock the props from under*.—*Ant.* help, assist, aid.

**hint** *n.* allusion, inkling, insinuation, implication, reference, advice, observation, reminder, communication, notice, information, announcement, inside information, tip, clue, token, idea, omen, scent, cue, trace, notion, whisper, taste, suspicion, evidence, reminder, innuendo, symptom, sign, bare suggestion, impression, supposition, inference, premonition, broad hint, gentle hint, word to the wise, indication, tip-off, pointer*.

**hire** *v.* engage, sign up, draft, obtain, secure, enlist, give a job to, take on, put to work, bring in, occupy, use, fill a position, appoint, delegate, authorize, retain, commission, empower, book, utilize, select, pick, contract, procure, fill an opening, find help, find a place for, exploit, make use of, use another's services, add to the payroll.—*Ant.* dismiss, discharge, fire.

**hiss** *v.* sibilate, fizz, seethe.

**historical** *a.* factual, traditional, chronicled.

**history** *n.* annals, records, archives, recorded history, chronicle, historical knowledge, historical writings, historical evidence, historical development. —**make history** accomplish, do something important, achieve.

**hit** *n.* **1** [A blow] slap, rap, punch. **2** [A popular success] favorite, sell-out*, smash. **3** [In baseball, a batted ball that cannot be fielded] base hit or single, two-base hit or double, three base-hit or triple, home run, Texas leaguer, two-bagger*, three-bagger*, homer*.

**hit** *v.* **1** [To strike] knock, beat, sock*, slap, jostle, butt, knock against, scrape, bump, run against, thump, collide with, bump into, punch, punish, hammer, strike down, bang, whack, thwack, jab, tap, smack, kick at, pelt, flail, thrash, cuff, kick, rap, clout*, club, bat around, lash out at, hit at, hit out at, let have it, crack, pop*, bash*. **2** [To fire in time; *said of an internal combustion motor*] catch, go, run. **3** [In baseball, to hit safely] make a hit, get on, get on base.

**hit or miss** *a.* at random, uncertainly, sometimes.

**hoard** *v.* store up, acquire, keep.

**hoarse** *a.* grating, rough, uneven, harsh, raucous, discordant, gruff, husky, thick, growling, croaking, cracked, guttural, dry, piercing, scratching, indistinct, squawking, jarring, rasping.—*Ant.* pure, sweet, mellifluous.

**hoax** *n.* falsification, fabrication, deceit.

**hobby** *n.* avocation, pastime, diversion, side interest, leisure-time activity, specialty, whim, fancy, whimsy, labor of love, play, craze, sport, amusement, craft, fun, art, game, sideline.

**hold** *v.* **1** [To have in one's grasp] grasp, grip, clutch, carry, embrace, cling to, detain, enclose, restrain, confine, check, take hold of, contain, hold down, hold onto, not let go, hang on, squeeze, press, hug, handle, fondle, have in hand, keep in hand, get a grip on, retain, keep, clasp, hold fast, hold tight, keep a firm hold on, tie, take, catch.—*Ant.* drop, let fall, release. **2** [To have in one's possession] keep, retain, possess. **3** [To remain firm] resist, persevere, keep staunch. **4** [To adhere] attach, cling, take hold. **5** [To be valid] exist, continue, operate.—*Ant.* stop, expire, be out of date. **6** [To contain] have capacity for, carry, be equipped for. **7** [To support; *often used with "up"*] sustain, brace, buttress, prop, lock, stay, shoulder, uphold, bear up.

**holdup** *n.* robbery, burglary, stickup*.

**hole** *n.* **1** [A perforation or cavity] notch, puncture, slot, eyelet, keyhole, porthole, buttonhole, peephole, loophole, air hole, window, crack, rent, split, tear, cleft, opening, fissure, gap, gash, rift, rupture, fracture, break, leak, aperture, space, chasm, breach, slit, nick, cut, chink, incision, orifice, eye, acupuncture, crater, mouth, gorge, throat, gullet, cranny, dent, opening, depression, indentation, impression, corner, pockmark, pocket, dimple, dip, drop, gulf, depth, pit, abyss, hollow, crevasse, mine, shaft, chamber, valley, ravine, burrow, cell, niche. **2** [A cave] burrow, den, lair. **3** [*Serious difficulty] impasse, tangle, mess. **—in the hole*** broke, without money, in debt.

**holiday** *n.* feast day, fiesta, legal holiday, holy day, festival, centennial, carnival, jubilee, red-letter day.

**hollow** *a.* **1** [Concave] curving inward, bell-shaped, curved, carved out, sunken, depressed, arched, vaulted, cup-shaped, excavated, hollowed-out, indented, cupped.—*Ant.* raised, convex, elevated. **2** [Sounding as though from a cave] cavernous, echoing deep, resonant, booming, roaring, rumbling, reverberating, muffled, dull, resounding, sepulchral, vibrating, low, ringing, deep-toned, thunderous.—*Ant.* dead, mute, silent.

**holy** *a.* **1** [Sinless] devout, pious, blessed, righteous, moral, just, good, angelic, godly, reverent, venerable, immaculate, pure, spotless, clean, humble, saintly, innocent, godlike, saintlike, perfect, faultless, undefiled, untainted, chaste, upright, virtuous, revered, sainted, heaven-sent, believing, profoundly good, sanctified, devotional, spiritual, unstained, pure in heart, dedicated, unspotted.—*Ant.* bad, wicked, sinful. **2** [Concerned with worship] devotional, religious, ceremonial.

**homage** *n.* respect, adoration, deference.

**home** *a.* in one's home, at ease, at rest, homely, domestic, familiar, being oneself, homey, in the bosom of one's family, down home, in one's element.

**home** *n.* **1** [A dwelling place] house, dwelling, residence, habitation, tenement, abode, lodging, quarters, homestead, domicile, dormitory, apartment house, flat*, living quarters, chalet, shelter, asylum, hut, cabin, cottage, mansion, castle, summer home, rooming house, place, address, hovel, lodge, hotel, inn, farmhouse, tent, pad*, hangout*, digs*, nest. **2** [An asylum] orphanage, sanatorium, mental hospital. —**at home** relaxed, at ease, familiar. —**come home** come back, return home, regress.

**homesick** *a.* nostalgic, pining, yearning for home, ill with longing, unhappy, alienated, rootless.

**honest** *a.* **1** [Truthful] true, trustworthy, correct, exact, verifiable, undisguised, candid, straightforward, aboveboard, just, frank, impartial, respectful, factual, sound, unimpeachable, legitimate, unquestionable, realistic, true-to-life, reasonable, naked, plain, square, honest as the day is long*, on the level*, kosher*, fair and square*, straight.—*Ant.* deceptive, false, misleading. **2** [Frank] candid, straightforward, aboveboard. **3** [Fair] just, equitable, impartial.

**honesty** *n.* honor, fidelity, scrupulousness, self-respect, straightforwardness, trustworthiness, confidence, soundness, right, principle, truthfulness, candor, frankness, openness, morality, goodness, responsibility, loyalty, faithfulness, good faith, probity, courage, moral strength, virtue, reliability, character, conscience, worth, conscientiousness, trustiness, faith, justice, respectability.—*Ant.* dishonesty, deception, deceit.

**honor** *n.* **1** [Respect] reverence, esteem, worship, adoration, veneration, high regard, trust, faith, confidence, righteousness, recognition, praise, attention, deference, notice, consideration, renown, reputation, elevation, credit, tribute, popularity.—*Ant.* disgrace, opprobrium, disrepute. **2** [Integrity] courage, character, truthfulness. —**do the honors** act as host or hostess, present, host. —**on** (or **upon**) **one's honor** by one's faith, on one's word, staking one's good name.

**honor** *v.* **1** [To treat with respect] worship, sanctify, venerate. **2** [To recognize worth] esteem, value, look up to. **3** [To recognize as valid] clear, pass, accept.

**honorary** *a.* titular, nominal, privileged.

**hook** *n.* lock, catch, clasp.

**hook** *v.* **1** [To curve in the shape of a hook] angle, crook, curve. **2** [To catch on a hook] pin, catch, secure.

**hope** *n.* **1** [Reliance upon the future] faith, expectation, confidence. **2** [The object of hope] wish, goal, dream.

**hope** *v.* be hopeful, lean on, wish, desire, live in hope, rely, depend, count on, aspire to, doubt not, keep one's fingers crossed, hope for the best, be of good cheer, pray, cherish the hope, look forward to, await, dream, presume, watch for, bank on, foresee, think to, promise oneself, suppose, deem likely, believe, suspect, surmise, hold, be assured, feel confident, anticipate, be prepared for, make plans for, have faith, rest assured, be sure of, be reassured, take heart, hope to hell*, knock on wood*.

**hopeful** *a.* **1** [Optimistic] expectant, assured, sanguine, buoyant, enthusiastic, trustful, reassured, emboldened, full of hope, cheerful, anticipating, trusting, expecting, in hopes of, forward-looking, light-hearted, serene, calm, poised, comfortable, eager, elated, looking through rose-colored glasses. **2** [Encouraging] promising, reassuring, favorable, bright, cheering, flattering, gracious, opportune, timely, fortunate, propitious, auspicious, well-timed, fit, suitable, convenient, beneficial, fair, uplifting, heartening, inspiring, exciting, pleasing, fine, lucky, stirring, making glad, helpful, rose-colored, rosy, animating, attractive, satisfactory, refreshing, probable, good, conducive, advantageous, pleasant, of promise, happy, cheerful.—*Ant.* unfortunate, discouraging, unfavorable.

**hopefully** *a.* **1** [Optimistically] confidently, expectantly, with confidence, with hope, trustingly, naively, with some reassurance, trustfully.—*Ant.* hopelessly, doubtfully, gloomily. **2** [Probably] expectedly, conceivably, feasibly.

**hopeless** *a.* unfortunate, threatening, bad, sinister, unyielding, incurable, past hope, past cure, vain, irreversible, irreparable, without hope, with no hope, impracticable, ill-fated, disastrous, menacing, foreboding, unfavorable, dying, worsening, past saving, tragic, fatal, desperate, helpless, lost, to no avail, gone, empty, idle, useless, pointless, worthless.—*Ant.* favorable, heartening, cheering.

**horde** *n.* pack, throng, swarm.

**horrible** *a.* **1** [Offensive] repulsive, dreadful, disgusting. **2** [Frightful] shameful, shocking, awful.

**host** *n.* **1** [A person who entertains] man of the house, woman of the house, entertainer, toastmaster, master of ceremonies. **2** [A large group] throng, multitude, army. **3** [Organism on which a parasite subsists] host mother, host body, animal.

**hostile** *a.* antagonistic, hateful, unfriendly.

**hot** *a.* **1** [Having a high temperature] torrid, burning, fiery, flaming, blazing, very warm, baking, roasting, smoking, scorching, blistering, searing, sizzling, tropical, warm, broiling, red-hot, grilling, piping hot, white-hot, scalding, parching, sultry, on fire, at high temperature, incandescent, smoldering, thermal, toasting, simmering, blazing hot*, boiling hot*, like an oven*, hotter than blazes*.—*Ant.* cold, frigid, chilly. **2** [Aroused] furious, ill-tempered, indignant. **3** [*Erotic] spicy, salacious, carnal. **—get hot*** become excited, become enthusiastic, burn with fervor, get angry, rave. **—make it hot for*** create discomfort for, cause trouble for, vex.

**hotel** *n.* stopping place, inn, lodging house, halfway house, boarding house, hostel, motel, motor hotel, resort, tavern, spa, rooming house, flophouse*.

**house** *n.* **1** [A habitation] dwelling, apartment house, residence. **2** [A family] line, family tradition, ancestry. **3** [A legislative body] congress, council, parliament. **—bring down the house*** receive applause, create enthusiasm, please. **—clean house** arrange, put in order, tidy up. —**keep house** manage a home, run a house, be a housekeeper. —**like a house on fire** (or **afire**) actively, vigorously, energetically. —**on the house** without expense, gratis, complimentary.

**housing** *n.* habitation, home construction, housing development, low-cost housing, house-building program, sheltering, installation, abode, domicile, house, accommodations, quarters, roof, dwelling, lodging, pad*, residence, headquarters.

**howl** *n.* wail, lament, shriek.

**howl** *v.* bawl, wail, lament.

**hub** *n.* core, heart, middle.

**hug** *v.* embrace, squeeze, clasp, press, love, hold, be near to, cling, fold in the arms, clutch, seize, envelop, enfold, nestle, welcome, cuddle, lock, press to the bosom, snuggle.

**huge** *a.* tremendous, enormous, immense.

**humane** *a.* benevolent, sympathetic, understanding, pitying, compassionate, kindhearted, human, tenderhearted, forgiving, gracious, charitable, gentle, tender, friendly, generous, lenient, tolerant, democratic, good-natured, liberal, open-minded, broad-minded, altruistic, philanthropic, helpful, magnanimous, amiable, genial, cordial, unselfish, warmhearted, bighearted, softhearted, good, soft, easy.—*Ant.* cruel, barbaric, inhuman.

**humble** *a.* **1** [Meek] lowly, submissive, gentle, quiet, unassuming, diffident, simple, retiring, bashful, shy, timid, reserved, deferential, self-conscious, soft-spoken, sheepish, mild, withdrawn, unpretentious, hesitant, fearful, tentative, poor in spirit, sedate, unpresuming, manageable, ordinary, unambitious, commonplace, free from pride, without arrogance, peaceable, obedient, passive, tame, restrained, unostentatious, unimportant, gentle as a lamb, resigned, subdued, tolerant, content, eating humble pie.—*Ant.* proud, haughty, conceited. **2** [Lowly] unpretentious, unassuming, modest, seemly, becoming, homespun, natural, low, proletarian, servile, undistinguished, pitiful, sordid, shabby, underprivileged, meager, beggarly, commonplace, unimportant, insignificant, small, poor, rough, hard, base, meek, little, of low birth, obscure, inferior, plain, common, homely, simple, uncouth, miserable, scrubby, ordinary, humdrum, trivial, vulgar.—*Ant.* noble, upper-class, privileged.

**humble** *v.* shame, mortify, chasten, demean, demote, lower, crush, bring low, put to shame, silence, reduce, humiliate, degrade, overcome, strike dumb, put down, pull down, bring down, snub, discredit, deflate, upset, make ashamed, take down a peg, pull rank on*, squelch*, squash*.—*Ant.* praise, exalt, glorify.

**humid** *a.* stuffy, sticky, muggy.

**humiliate** *v.* debase, chasten, mortify, make a fool of, put to shame, humble, degrade, crush, shame, confuse, snub, confound, lower, dishonor, depress, fill with shame, break, demean, bring low, conquer, make ashamed, vanquish, take down a peg.

**hunch** *n.* idea, notion, feeling, premonition, forecast, presentiment, instinct, expectation, anticipation, precognition, prescience, forewarning, clue, foreboding, hint, portent, apprehension, misgiving, qualm, suspicion, inkling, glimmer.

**hungry** *a.* starved, famished, ravenous, desirous, hankering, unsatisfied, unfilled, starving, insatiate, voracious, half-starved, omnivorous, piggish, hoggish, on an empty stomach*, hungry as a wolf*, empty*.—*Ant.* full, satisfied, fed.

**hunt** *v.* **1** [To pursue with intent to kill] follow, give chase, stalk, hound, trail, dog, seek, capture, kill, shoot, track, heel, shadow, chase, hunt out, snare, look for, fish, fish for, poach, gun for*, go gunning for*. **2** [To try to find] investigate, probe, look for.

**hunter** *n.* huntsman, stalker, chaser, sportsman, pursuer, big-game hunter, gunner, poacher, horsewoman, huntress, horseman, archer, deerstalker, angler, fisherman, bowman, shooter.

**hurdle** *n.* barricade, obstacle, barrier.

**hurry** *n.* dispatch, haste, rush.

**hurry** *v.* **1** [To act hastily] hasten, be quick, make haste, scurry, scuttle, fly, tear, dash, sprint, be in a hurry, lose no time, move quickly, move rapidly, bolt, bustle, rush, make short work of, scoot*, work at high speed, dash on, hurry about, hurry off, hurry up, run off, waste no time, plunge, skip, gallop, zoom, dart, spring, make good time, whip, go by forced marches, speed, work under pressure, run like mad*, go at full tilt, make strides, act on a moment's notice, step on the gas*, floor it*, get cracking*, step on it*, shake a leg*.—*Ant.* delay, lose time, procrastinate. **2** [To move rapidly] fly, bustle, dash off. **3** [To urge others] push, spur, goad on.

**hurt** *a.* injured, damaged, harmed, marred, wounded, in critical condition, impaired, shot, struck, bruised, stricken, battered, mauled, hit, stabbed, mutilated, disfigured, in pain, suffering, distressed, tortured, unhappy, grazed, scratched, nicked, winged.

**hurt** *n.* **1** [A wound] blow, gash, ache. **2** [Damage] ill-treatment, harm, persecution.

**hurt** *v.* **1** [To cause pain] cramp, squeeze, cut, bruise, tear, torment, afflict, kick, puncture, do violence to, slap, abuse, flog, whip, torture, gnaw, stab, pierce, maul, cut up, harm, injure, wound, lacerate, sting, bite, inflict pain, burn, crucify, tweak, thrash, punch, pinch, spank, punish, trounce, scourge, lash, cane, switch, work over*, wallop*, slug*.—*Ant.* ease, comfort, soothe. **2** [To harm] maltreat, injure, spoil. **3** [To give a feeling of pain] ache, throb, sting.

**hush** *n.* peace, stillness, quiet.

**hush** *v.* silence, gag, stifle.

**hypocrite** *n.* pretender, fraud, faker, fake, deceiver, charlatan, bigot, quack, pharisee, sham, actor, cheat, informer, trickster, confidence man, malingerer, humbug, imposter, swindler, informer, rascal, traitor, wolf in sheep's clothing, masquerader, four-flusher*, two-timer*, two-face*.

**hypothesis** *n.* supposition, theory, assumption.

**hysterical** *a.* convulsed, uncontrolled, raving, delirious, wildly emotional, unnerved, neurotic, spasmodic, emotional, rabid, emotionally disordered, distracted, fuming, distraught, unrestrained, possessed, fanatical, irrepressible, convulsive, carried away, seething, beside oneself, rampant, out of one's wits, mad, uncontrollable, agitated, raging, frenzied, confused, tempestuous, maddened, crazy, impetuous, crazed, furious, violent, impassioned, panic-stricken, nervous, vehement, overwrought, fiery, passionate, jittery*, wild-eyed, on a crying jag*.

# I

**ice** *n.* crystal, hail, floe, glacier, icicle, ice cube, cube ice, dry ice, black ice, white ice, chunk ice, iceberg, permafrost. —**break the ice** make a start, initiate, commence. —**on ice*** in reserve, held, in abeyance. —**on thin ice*** in a dangerous situation, imperiled, insecure.

**idea** *n.* **1** [A concept] conception, plans, view, fancy, impression, image, understanding, observation, belief, feeling, opinion, guess, inference, theory, hypothesis, supposition, assumption, intuition, conjecture, design, approach, mental impression, notion. **2** [Fancy] whimsy, whim, fantasy. **3** [Meaning] sense, import, purport.

**ideal** *a.* **1** [Typical] prototypical, model, archetypical. **2** [Perfect] supreme, fitting, exemplary.

**identical** *a.* like, twin, indistinguishable.

**identify** *v.* classify, catalog, analyze.

**idle** *a.* unoccupied, fallow, vacant, deserted, not in use, barren, void, empty, abandoned, still, quiet, motionless, inert, dead, rusty, dusty, out of action, out of a job, out of work, resting.—*Ant.* active, busy, engaged.

**idol** *n.* icon, graven image, god, false god, figurine, fetish, totem, golden calf, pagan deity.

**ignorant** *a.* **1** [Unaware] unconscious of, uninformed about, unknowing, uninitiated, inexperienced, unwitting, unmindful, disregardful, misinformed, unsuspecting, unaware of, unmindful of, unconscious of, mindless, witless, not conversant with, unintelligent, obtuse, thick, dense, unscientific, birdbrained*, lowbrow*, green.—*Ant.* intelligent, alert, aware. **2** [Untrained] illiterate, uneducated, unlettered, untaught, uninstructed, uncultivated, unenlightened, untutored, unschooled, unread, benighted, shallow, superficial, gross, coarse, vulgar, crude, green, knowing nothing, misinformed, misguided, just beginning, apprenticed, unbriefed.—*Ant.* learned, cognizant, tutored.

**ignore** *v.* disregard, overlook, neglect.

**illegal** *a.* illicit, unlawful, contraband, unwarranted, banned, unconstitutional, outside the law, extralegal, outlawed, not legal, unauthorized, unlicensed, lawless, actionable, illegitimate, prohibited, forbidden, criminal, against the law, not approved, uncertified, unlicensed, smuggled, bootlegged, hot*.—*Ant.* legal, lawful, authorized.

**illiterate** *a.* uneducated, unenlightened, ignorant.

**illness** *n.* **1** [Poor health] sickness, failing health, seizure, ailing, infirmity, disorder, relapse, attack, fit, convalescence, complaint, delicate health, collapse, breakdown, confinement, disturbance, ill health. **2** [A particular disease] sickness, ailment, malady, ache, infection, stroke, allergy.

**illuminate** *v.* **1** [To make light(er)] lighten, irradiate, illume. **2** [To explain] interpret, elucidate, clarify.

**illusion** *n.* fancy, hallucination, mirage, apparition, ghost, delusion, figment of the imagination, image, trick of vision, myth, make-believe.

**ill will** *n.* malevolence, dislike, hostility.

**imagine** *v.* conceive, picture, conjure up, envisage, envision, see in one's mind, invent, fabricate, formulate, devise, think of, make up, conceptualize, dream, dream up*, perceive, dramatize, create.

**imitate** *v.* **1** [To mimic] impersonate, mirror, copy, mime, ape, simulate, duplicate, act, repeat, echo, parody, emulate, do like, reflect, pretend, play a part, take off*. **2** [To copy] duplicate, counterfeit, falsify. **3** [To resemble] be like, simulate, parallel.

**immaculate** *a.* unsullied, spotless, stainless.

**immediately** *a.* at once, without delay, instantly, directly, right away, at the first opportunity, at short notice, now, this instant, speedily, quickly, promptly, on the spot, rapidly, instantaneously, shortly, on the double*, in a jiffy*.—*Ant.* later, in the future, in a while.

**immense** *a.* gigantic, tremendous, enormous.

**immerse** *v.* submerge, dip, douse, plunge, duck, cover with water, drown, bathe, steep, soak, drench, dunk, souse.

**immortal** *a.* **1** [Deathless] undying, permanent, imperishable, endless, timeless, everlasting, death-defying, unfading, never-ending, perennial, constant, ceaseless, indestructible, enduring.—*Ant.* mortal, perishable, corrupt. **2** [Illustrious] celebrated, eminent, glorious.

**immune** *a.* free, unaffected by, hardened to, unsusceptible, privileged, not liable, excused.

**impertinent** *a.* saucy, insolent, impudent.

**implement** *n.* utensil, instrument, tool.

**imply** *v.* **1** [To indicate] intimate, hint at, suggest. **2** [To mean] import, indicate, signify.

**importance** *n.* import, force, sense, consequence, bearing, denotation, gist, effect, distinction, influence, usefulness, moment, weightiness, momentousness, emphasis, standing, stress, accent, weight, concern, attention, interest, seriousness, point, substance, relevance, sum and substance.—*Ant.* insignificance, triviality, emptiness.

**important** *a.* **1** [Weighty; *said usually of things*] significant, considerable, momentous, essential, great, decisive, critical, determining, chief, paramount, primary, foremost, principal, influential, marked, of great consequence, ponderous, of importance, never to be overlooked, of note, valuable, crucial, substantial, vital, serious, grave, relevant, pressing, far-reaching, extensive, conspicuous, heavy, big-league*, big*.—*Ant.* trivial, inconsequential, unimportant. **2** [Eminent; *said usually of persons*] illustrious, well-known, influential. **3** [Relevant] material, influential, significant.

**impose on** or **upon** *v.* intrude, interrupt, presume.

**impossible** *a.* inconceivable, vain, unachievable, unattainable, out of the question, too much, insurmountable, useless, inaccessible, unworkable, preposterous, unimaginable, unobtainable, not to be thought of, hardly possible, like finding a needle in a haystack*, a hundred to one*.—*Ant.* reasonable, possible, likely.

**impostor** *n.* pretender, charlatan, quack.

**impractical** *a.* unreal, unrealistic, unworkable, improbable, illogical, unreasonable, absurd, wild, abstract, impossible, idealistic, unfeasible, out of the question.—*Ant.* practical, logical, reasonable.

**impress** *v.* **1** [To make an impression] indent, emboss, imprint. **2** [To attract attention] stand out, be conspicuous, cause a stir, create an impression, make an impression on, direct attention to, make an impact upon, engage the thoughts of, engage the attention of, be listened to, find favor with, make a hit*, make a dent in.

**impression** *n.* **1** [An imprint] print, footprint, fingerprint, dent, mold, indentation, depression, cast, form, track, pattern. **2** [An effect] response, consequence, reaction. **3** [A notion based on scanty evidence] theory, conjecture, supposition.

**impressive** *a.* stirring, moving, inspiring, effective, affecting, eloquent, impassioned, thrilling, exciting, intense, well-done, dramatic, absorbing, deep, profound, penetrating, remarkable, extraordinary, notable, important, momentous, vital.—*Ant.* dull, uninteresting, common.

**imprison** *v.* jail, lock up, confine, incarcerate, immure, impound, detain, keep in, hold, intern, shut in, lock in, box in, fence in, cage, send to prison, keep as captive, hold captive, hold as hostage, enclose, keep in custody, put behind bars, put away*, send up*.—*Ant.* free, liberate, release.

**improbable** *a.* doubtful, not to be expected, unlikely.

**improper** *a.* at odds, ill-advised, unsuited, incongruous, out of place, ludicrous, incorrect, preposterous, unwarranted, undue, imprudent, abnormal, irregular, inexpedient, unseasonable, inadvisable, untimely, inopportune, unfit, malapropos, unfitting, inappropriate, unbefitting, ill-timed, awkward, inharmonious, inapplicable, odd.

**improve** *v.* **1** [To make better] mend, update, refine. **2** [To become better] regenerate, advance, progress, renew, enrich, enhance, augment, gain strength, develop, get better, grow better, grow, make progress, widen, increase, mellow, mature, come along, get on, look up, shape up*, pick up, perk up, come around, make headway, snap out of*.—*Ant.* weaken, worsen, grow worse.

**improvement** *n.* **1** [The process of becoming better] amelioration, betterment, rectification, change, alteration, reformation, progression, advance, advancement, development, growth, rise, civilization, gain, cultivation, increase, enrichment, promotion, elevation, recovery, regeneration, renovation, reorganization, amendment, reform, revision, elaboration, refinement, modernization, enhancement, remodeling.—*Ant.* decay, deterioration, retrogression. **2** [That which has been improved] addition, supplement, repair, extra, attachment, correction, reform, remodeling, repairing, refinement, luxury, advance, latest thing, last word.

**impulse** *n.* **1** [A throb] surge, pulse, pulsation. **2** [A sudden urge] fancy, whim, caprice, motive, motivation, spontaneity, drive, appeal, notion, inclination, disposition, wish, whimsy, inspiration, hunch, flash, thought.

**impure** *a.* **1** [Adulterated] not pure, loaded, weighted, salted, diluted, debased, contaminated, mixed, watered down, polluted, corrupted, raw, tainted, cut, adulterated, doctored*, tampered with. **2** [Not chaste] unclean, unchaste, corrupt.

**inaccurate** *a.* fallacious, in error, incorrect.

**inadequate** *a.* lacking, scanty, short, meager, failing, unequal, not enough, sparing, stinted, stunted, feeble, sparse, too little, small, thin, deficient, incomplete, inconsiderable, spare, bare, niggardly, miserly, scarce, barren, depleted, low, weak, impotent, unproductive, dry, sterile, imperfect, defective, lame, skimpy*.—*Ant.* enough, adequate, sufficient.

**inaugurate** *v.* introduce, initiate, originate.

**incentive** *n.* spur, inducement, motive, stimulus, stimulation, impetus, provocation, enticement, temptation, bait, consideration, excuse, rationale, urge, influence, lure, persuasion, inspiration, encouragement, insistence, instigation, incitement, reason why.

**incident** *n.* episode, happening, occurrence.

**incinerate** *v.* cremate, parch, burn up.

**incite** *v.* arouse, rouse, impel, stimulate, instigate, provoke, excite, spur, goad, persuade, influence, induce, taunt, activate, animate, inspirit, coax, stir up, motivate, prompt, urge on, inspire, force, work up*, talk into*, egg on, fan the flame*.—*Ant.* discourage, dissuade, check.

**inclination** *n.* **1** [A tendency] bias, bent, propensity, predilection, penchant, attachment, capability, capacity, aptness, leaning, fondness, disposition, liking, preference, movement, susceptibility, weakness, drift, trend, turn, slant, impulse, attraction, affection, desire, temperament, whim, idiosyncrasy, urge, persuasion. **2** [A slant] pitch, slope, incline, angle, ramp, bank, lean, list.

**incline** *v.* **1** [To lean] bow, nod, cock. **2** [To tend toward] prefer, be disposed, favor.

**include** *v.* **1** [To contain] hold, admit, cover, embrace, involve, consist of, take in, entail, incorporate, constitute, accommodate, be comprised of, be composed of, embody, be made up of, number among, carry, bear.—*Ant.* bar, omit, exclude. **2** [To place into or among] enter, introduce, take in, incorporate, make room for, build, work in, inject, interject, add on, insert, combine, make a part of, make allowance for, give consideration to, count in.—*Ant.* discard, exclude, reject.

**incoherent** *a.* mumbling, stammering, confused, speechless, puzzling, indistinct, faltering, stuttering, unintelligible, muttered, mumbled, jumbled, gasping, breathless, disconnected, tongue-tied, muffled, indistinguishable, incomprehensible, muddled.—*Ant.* clear, eloquent, distinct.

**income** *n.* earnings, salary, wages, returns, profit, dividends, assets, proceeds, benefits, receipts, gains, commission, drawings, rent, royalty, honorarium, net income, gross income, taxable income, cash, take.—*Ant.* expense, expenditures, outgo.

**incompatible** *a.* inconsistent, contrary, clashing, inappropriate, contradictory, disagreeing, inconstant, unadapted, opposite, jarring, discordant, incoherent, inadmissible.

**incompetent** *a.* incapable, inefficient, unskillful, not qualified, inadequate, unfit, unskilled, bungling, inexpert, ineffectual, unsuitable, untrained, clumsy, awkward, uninitiated, raw, inexperienced, unadapted, not equal to, amateurish.—*Ant.* able, fit, qualified.

**incomplete** *a.* rough, half-done, unfinished.

**inconsiderate** *a.* boorish, impolite, discourteous.

**inconsistent** *a.* contradictory, illogical, incoherent.

**inconspicuous** *a.* concealed, indistinct, retiring.

**incorrect** *a.* inaccurate, false, mistaken.

**increase** *n.* development, spread, enlargement, expansion, escalation, elaboration, swelling, addition, incorporation, merger, inflation, heightening, extension, dilation, multiplication, rise, broadening, advance, intensification, deepening, swell, amplification, progression, improvement, boost, hike*, jump, boom.—*Ant.* reduction, decline, decrease. **—on the increase** growing, developing, spreading.

**increase** *v.* extend, enlarge, expand, dilate, broaden, widen, thicken, deepen, heighten, build, lengthen, magnify, add on, augment, escalate, let out, branch out, further, mark up, sharpen, build up, raise, enhance, amplify, reinforce, supplement, annex, double, triple, stretch, multiply, intensify, exaggerate, prolong, redouble, boost, step up, rev up*.—*Ant.* decrease, reduce, abridge.

**indecent** *a.* immoral, shocking, shameless.

**indeed** *a.* **1** [Surely] naturally, of course, certainly. **2** [Really] For sure?, Honestly?, So?

**independence** *n.* sovereignty, autonomy, freedom.

**indicate** *v.* **1** [To signify] symbolize, betoken, intimate. **2** [To designate] show, point to, register.

**indifferent** *a.* listless, cold, cool, unemotional, unsympathetic, heartless, unresponsive, unfeeling, uncommunicative, nonchalant, impassive, detached, callous, uninterested, stony, reticent, remote, reserved, distant, unsocial, scornful, apathetic, heedless, unmoved, not inclined toward, neutral, uncaring, aloof, silent, disdainful, haughty, superior, condescending, snobbish, arrogant, not caring about.—*Ant.* excited, aroused, warm.

**indignant** *a.* upset, displeased, angry.

**indirect** *a.* roundabout, out-of-the-way, tortuous, twisting, long, complicated, devious, erratic, sidelong, zigzag, crooked, backhanded, obscure, sinister, rambling, long-winded, secondary, implied, oblique.—*Ant.* direct, straight, immediate.

**indiscreet** *a.* naive, inopportune, tactless.

**individual** *a.* specific, personal, special, proper, own, particular, definite, lone, alone, solitary, secluded, original, distinct, distinctive, personalized, individualized, exclusive, select, single, only, reserved, separate, sole.—*Ant.* public, collective, social.

**individual** *n.* human being, self, somebody.

**individuality** *n.* personality, distinctiveness, particularity, separateness, dissimilarity, singularity, idiosyncrasy, air, manner, habit, eccentricity, oddity, rarity, way of doing things.

**induce** *v.* produce, effect, make.

**indulgence** *n.* **1** [Humoring] coddling, pampering, petting, fondling, babying, spoiling, placating, pleasing, toadying, favoring, kowtowing, gratifying. **2** [Revelry] intemperance, overindulgence, self-indulgence.

**industrial** *a.* manufacturing, manufactured, mechanized, automated, industrialized, in industry, factory-made, machine-made, modern, streamlined, technical.—*Ant.* homemade, handmade, domestic.

**industry** *n.* **1** [Attention to work] activity, persistence, application, patience, intentness, perseverance, enterprise, hard work, zeal, energy, dynamism, pains, inventiveness.—*Ant.* laziness, lethargy, idleness. **2** [Business as a division of society] big business, management, corporation officers, shareholders, high finance, entrepreneurs, capital, private enterprise, monied interests, stockholders.

**inefficient** *a.* extravagant, prodigal, improvident.

**inept** *a.* clumsy, gauche, awkward.

**inequality** *n.* disparity, dissimilarity, irregularity.

**inevitable** *a.* fated, sure, unavoidable, impending, inescapable, necessary, unpreventable, irresistible, destined, assured, unalterable, compulsory, obligatory, binding, irrevocable, inexorable, without fail, undeniable, fateful, doomed, determined, decreed, fixed, ordained, foreordained, decided, in the cards, come rain or shine*.—*Ant.* doubtful, contingent, indeterminate.

**inexperienced** *a.* unused, unaccustomed, unadapted, unskilled, common, ordinary, unlicensed, untried, youthful, undeveloped, naive, amateur, untrained, untutored, inefficient, fresh, ignorant, innocent, uninformed, unacquainted, undisciplined, new, immature, tender, not dry behind the ears*, soft, raw, green.—*Ant.* experienced, seasoned, hardened.

**infant** *n.* small child, tot, baby.

**infectious** *a.* communicable, catching, contagious.

**infer** *v.* deduce, gather, reach the conclusion that.

**infinite** *a.* unlimited, incalculable, unbounded, boundless, unconfined, countless, interminable, measureless, inexhaustible, bottomless, without end, limitless, tremendous, immense, having no limit, never-ending, immeasurable.—*Ant.* restricted, limited, bounded.

**inflate** *v.* **1** [To fill with air or gas] pump up, expand, swell. **2** [To swell] exaggerate, bloat, cram, expand, balloon, distend, swell up, widen, augment, spread out, enlarge, magnify, exalt, build up, raise, maximize, overestimate.

**inflexible** *a.* rigid, hardened, stiff.

**influence** *n.* control, weight, authority, supremacy, command, domination, esteem, political influence, monopoly, rule, fame, prominence, prestige, character, reputation, force, importance, money, power behind the throne*, pull*, clout*.

**influence** *v.* sway, affect, impress, carry weight, be influential, determine, make oneself felt, have influence over, lead to believe, bring pressure to bear, bribe, seduce, talk one into, alter, change, act upon, act on, lead, brainwash, direct, modify, regulate, rule, compel, urge, incite, bias, prejudice, train, channel, mold, form, shape, carry weight, exert influence, get at, be recognized, induce, convince, cajole, persuade, motivate, have an in*, pull strings, lead by the nose*, fix*.

**informal** *a.* intimate, relaxed, frank, open, straightforward, ordinary, everyday, inconspicuous, habitual, free, extemporaneous, spontaneous, congenial, easygoing, unrestrained, unconventional, without ceremony.—*Ant.* restrained, ceremonial, ritualistic.

**information** *n.* **1** [Derived knowledge] acquired facts, evidence, knowledge, reports, details, results, notes, documents, testimony, facts, figures, statistics, measurements, conclusions, deductions, plans, field notes, lab notes, learning, erudition. **2** [News] report, notice, message.

**ingredients** *pl.n.* parts, elements, additives, constituents, pieces, components, makings, fixings*.

**inhabit** *v.* occupy, live in, dwell.

**inhabitant** *n.* occupant, dweller, settler, denizen, lodger, permanent resident, roomer, boarder, occupier, householder, addressee, inmate, tenant, settler, colonist, squatter, native.—*Ant.* alien, transient, nonresident.

**inherit** *v.* succeed to, acquire, receive, obtain, get one's inheritance, fall heir to, come into, come in for*, take over, receive an endowment.—*Ant.* lose, be disowned, miss.

**injure** *v.* harm, damage, wound.

**injury** *n.* harm, sprain, damage, mutilation, blemish, cut, gash, scratch, stab, impairment, bite, fracture, hemorrhage, sting, bruise, sore, cramp, trauma, abrasion, burn, lesion, swelling, wound, scar, laceration, affliction, deformation.

**injustice** *n.* wrongdoing, malpractice, offense, crime, villainy, injury, unfairness, miscarriage, infringement, violation, abuse, criminal negligence, transgression, grievance, breach, damage, infraction, a crying shame*.—*Ant.* right, just decision, honest verdict.

**inner** *a.* innate, inherent, essential, inward, internal, interior, inside, nuclear, central, spiritual, private, subconscious, intrinsic, deep-seated, deep-rooted, intuitive.—*Ant.* outer, surface, external.

**innocent** *a.* **1** [Guiltless] not guilty, blameless, impeccable, faultless, safe, upright, free of, uninvolved, above suspicion, clean*.—*Ant.* guilty, culpable, blameworthy. **2** [Without guile] open, fresh, guileless. **3** [Morally pure] sinless, unblemished, pure, unsullied, undefiled, spotless, unspotted, wholesome, upright, unimpeachable, clean, virtuous, virginal, immaculate, impeccable, righteous, uncorrupted, irreproachable, unstained, stainless, moral, angelic.—*Ant.* dishonest, sinful, corrupt. **4** [Harmless] innocuous, powerless, inoffensive.

**inoculation** *n.* vaccination, injection, shot.

**input** *n.* information, facts, data.

**inquisitive** *a.* curious, inquiring, speculative, questioning, meddling, searching, intrusive, challenging, analytical, scrutinizing, prying, forward, presumptuous, impertinent, snoopy*, nosy*.—*Ant.* indifferent, unconcerned, aloof.

**insanity** *n.* mental derangement, delusions, hysteria, anxiety, obsession, compulsion, madness, dementia, lunacy, psychosis, alienation, neurosis, phobia, mania.—*Ant.* sanity, reason, normality.

**inside** *a.* **1** [Within] inner, in, within the boundaries of, bounded, surrounded by.—*Ant.* beyond, after, outside. **2** [Within doors] indoors, under a roof, in a house, out of the open, behind closed doors, under a shelter, in the interior.—*Ant.* outside, out-of-doors, in the open.

**insignificance** *n.* unimportance, worthlessness, indifference, triviality, nothingness, smallness, pettiness, matter of no consequence, nothing to speak of, nothing particular, trifling matter, drop in the bucket*, molehill*.

**insignificant** *a.* irrelevant, petty, trifling.

**insinuate** *v.* imply, suggest, purport.

**inspector** *n.* police inspector, chief detective, investigating officer, customs officer, immigration inspector, government inspector, checker, FBI agent, narc*, postal inspector.

**inspire** *v.* fire, be the cause of, start off, urge, stimulate, cause, put one in the mood, give one the idea for, motivate, give an impetus.

**instability** *n.* inconstancy, changeability, immaturity, variability, inconsistency, irregularity, imbalance, unsteadiness, restlessness, anxiety, fluctuation, alternation, disquiet, fitfulness, impermanence, transience, vacillation, hesitation, oscillation, flightiness, capriciousness, wavering, fickleness.

**install** *v.* set up, establish, build in, put in, place, invest, introduce, inaugurate, furnish with, fix up.

**instance** *n.* case, occurrence, example. **—for instance** as an example, by way of illustration, for example.

**instant** *n.* short while, second, flash, split second, wink of the eye, jiffy*. **—on the instant** instantly, without delay, simultaneously.

**instead** *a.* in place of, as a substitute, alternative, on second thought, in lieu of, on behalf of, alternatively, rather.

**instill** *v.* inject, infiltrate, inoculate, impregnate, inseminate, implant, inspire, impress, brainwash*, introduce, inculcate, indoctrinate, impart, insert, force in, imbue, put into someone's head*.—*Ant.* remove, draw out, extract.

**instruction** *n.* guidance, preparation, education.

**insulate** *v.* protect, coat, treat, apply insulation, tape up, glass in, pad, caulk, weatherstrip, paint.

**insult** *n.* indignity, offense, affront, abuse, outrage, impudence, insolence, blasphemy, mockery, derision, impertinence, discourtesy, invective, disrespect, slight, slander, libel, slap in the face, black eye*.—*Ant.* praise, tribute, homage.

**insult** *v.* revile, libel, offend, outrage, vilify, humiliate, mock, vex, tease, irritate, annoy, aggravate, provoke, taunt, ridicule, abuse, deride, jeer, step on someone's toes*.

**intellectual** *n.* genius, philosopher, academician, highbrow, member of the intelligentsia, egghead*, brain*, Einstein*.

**intelligent** *a.* clever, bright, exceptional, astute, smart, gifted, brilliant, perceptive, well-informed, resourceful, profound, penetrating, original, keen, imaginative, inventive, reasonable, capable, able, ingenious, knowledgeable, creative, responsible, understanding, alert, quick-witted, clearheaded, quick, sharp, witty, ready, calculating, comprehending, discerning, discriminating, knowing, intellectual, studious, contemplative, having a head on one's shoulders*, talented, apt, wise, shrewd, smart as a whip*, on the ball*, on the beam*, not born yesterday*.—*Ant.* dull, slow-minded, shallow.

**intend** *v.* **1** [To propose] plan, purpose, aim, expect, be resolved, be determined to, aspire to, have in mind, hope to, contemplate, think, aim at, take into one's head. **2** [To destine for] design, mean, devote to, reserve, appoint, set apart, aim at, aim for. **3** [To mean] indicate, signify, denote.

**intense** *a.* intensified, deep, profound, extraordinary, exceptional, heightened, marked, vivid, ardent, powerful, passionate, impassioned, diligent, hard, full, great, exaggerated, violent, excessive, acute, keen, piercing, cutting, bitter, severe, concentrated, intensive, forceful, sharp, biting, stinging, shrill, high-pitched, strenuous, fervent, earnest, zealous, vehement, harsh, strong, brilliant.

**intensify** *v.* heighten, sharpen, strengthen.

**intention** *n.* aim, end, purpose.

**intercept** *v.* cut off, stop, ambush, block, catch, take away, appropriate, hijack, head off.

**interested** *a.* **1** [Having one's interest aroused] stimulated, attentive, curious, drawn, touched, moved, affected, inspired, sympathetic to, responsive, struck, impressed, roused, awakened, stirred, open to suggestion, all for, all wrapped up in.—*Ant.* bored, tired, annoyed. **2** [Concerned with or engaged in] occupied, engrossed, partial, prejudiced, biased, taken, obsessed with, absorbed in.—*Ant.* indifferent, impartial, disinterested.

**interesting** *a.* pleasing, pleasurable, fine, satisfying, fascinating, arresting, engaging, readable, absorbing, stirring, affecting, exotic, unusual, lovely, gracious, impressive, attractive, captivating, enchanting, beautiful, inviting, winning, magnetic, delightful, amusing, genial, refreshing.—*Ant.* dull, shallow, boring.

**interfere** *v.* intervene, interpose, meddle.

**intermittent** *a.* periodic, coming and going, recurrent.

**international** *a.* worldwide, worldly, world, intercontinental, between nations, all over the world, universal, all-embracing, foreign, cosmopolitan.—*Ant.* domestic, national, internal.

**interpret** *v.* give one's impression of, render, play, perform, depict, delineate, enact, portray, make sense of, read into, improvise on, reenact, mimic, gather from, view as, give one an idea about.

**interrogate** *v.* cross-examine, ask, give the third degree*, examine, question.

**interrupt** *v.* intrude, intervene, cut in on, break into, interfere, infringe, cut off, break someone's train of thought, come between, butt in*, burst in, crash*.

**interruption** *n.* check, break, suspension, intrusion, obstruction, holding over.

**intervene** *v.* step in, intercede, mediate.
**interview** *n.* meeting, audience, conference.
**intimate** *a.* close, trusted, private.
**intricate** *a.* involved, tricky, abstruse.
**introduce** *v.* **1** [To bring in] freight, carry in, transport. **2** [To present] set forth, submit, advance. **3** [To make strangers acquainted] present, give an introduction, make known, put on speaking terms with, do the honors, break the ice. **4** [To insert] put in, add, enter.
**introduction** *n.* **1** [The act of bringing in] admittance, initiation, installation. **2** [The act of making strangers acquainted] presentation, debut, meeting, formal acquaintance, preliminary encounter. **3** [Introductory knowledge] first acquaintance, elementary statement, first contact, start, awakening, first taste, baptism, preliminary training, basic principles. **4** [An introductory explanation] preface, preamble, foreword, prologue, prelude, overture. **5** [A work supplying introductory knowledge] primer, manual, handbook.
**intrude** *v.* interfere, interrupt, meddle.
**intruder** *n.* prowler, thief, unwelcome guest, meddler, invader, snooper, unwanted person, interferer, interrupter, interloper, trespasser.
**invade** *v.* **1** [To enter with armed force] force a landing, penetrate, attack. **2** [To encroach upon] infringe on, trespass, interfere with.
**invent** *v.* **1** [To create or discover] originate, devise, fashion, form, project, design, find, improvise, contrive, execute, come upon, conceive, author, plan, think up, make up, bear, turn out, forge, make, hatch, dream up*, cook up*. **2** [To fabricate] misrepresent, fake, make believe.
**investigate** *v.* look into, review, examine.
**invite** *v.* bid, request, beg, suggest, encourage, entice, solicit, pray, petition, persuade, insist, press, ply, propose, appeal to, implore, call upon, ask, have over, have in, formally invite, send an invitation to.
**iron** *a.* ferrous, ironclad, hard, robust, strong, unyielding, dense, inflexible, heavy.
**iron** *v.* use a steam iron on, press, mangle, roll, finish, smooth out.
**ironic** *a.* contradictory, twisted, ridiculous, mocking, satiric, paradoxical, critical, derisive, exaggerated, caustic, biting, incisive, scathing, satirical, sardonic, bitter.
**irrational** *a.* **1** [Illogical] unreasonable, specious, fallacious. **2** [Stupid] senseless, silly, ridiculous.
**irregular** *a.* **1** [Not even] uneven, spasmodic, fitful, uncertain, random, unsettled, inconstant, unsteady, fragmentary, unsystematic, occasional, infrequent, fluctuating, wavering, intermittent, sporadic, changeable, capricious, variable, shifting, unmethodical, jerky, up and down.—*Ant.* regular, even, punctual. **2** [Not customary] unique, extraordinary, abnormal. **3** [Questionable] strange, overt, debatable. **4** [Not regular in form or in outline] not uniform, unsymmetrical, uneven, unequal, craggy, hilly, broken, jagged, notched, eccentric, bumpy, meandering, variable, wobbly, lumpy, off balance, off center, lopsided, pock-marked, scarred, bumpy, sprawling, out of proportion.
**irregularity** *n.* peculiarity, singularity, abnormality, strangeness,

uniqueness, exception, excess, malformation, deviation, allowance, exemption, privilege, nonconformity, innovation, oddity, eccentricity, rarity.—*Ant.* custom, regularity, rule.

**irrelevant** *a.* inapplicable, impertinent, off the topic, inappropriate, unrelated, extraneous, unconnected, off the point, foreign, beside the question, out of order, out of place, pointless, beside the point, not pertaining to, without reference to, out of the way, remote, neither here nor there.

**irresponsible** *a.* untrustworthy, capricious, flighty, fickle, thoughtless, rash, undependable, unstable, loose, lax, immoral, shiftless, unpredictable, wild, devil-may-care.—*Ant.* responsible, trustworthy, dependable.

**irrigation** *n.* watering, flooding, inundation.

**irritable** *a.* sensitive, touchy, testy, peevish, ill-tempered, huffy, petulant, tense, resentful, fretting, carping, crabbed, hypercritical, quick-tempered, easily offended, glum, complaining, brooding, dissatisfied, snarling, grumbling, surly, gloomy, ill-natured, morose, moody, snappish, waspish, in bad humor, cantankerous, fretful, hypersensitive, annoyed, cross, churlish, grouchy, sulky, sullen, high-strung, thin-skinned, grumpy.—*Ant.* pleasant, agreeable, good-natured.

**irritate** *v.* **1** [To bother] provoke, exasperate, pester. **2** [To inflame] redden, chafe, swell, erupt, pain, sting.

**isolate** *v.* confine, detach, seclude.

**issue** *n.* **1** [Question] point, matter, problem, concern, point in question, argument. **2** [Result] upshot, culmination, effect. **3** [Edition] number, copy, impression. **—at issue** in dispute, unsettled, controversial. **—take issue** differ, disagree, take a stand against.

**itch** *n.* tingling, prickling, crawling, creeping sensation, rawness, psoriasis, scabbiness.

**item** *n.* piece, article, matter.

**itinerant** *a.* roving, nomadic, peripatetic.

**itinerant** *n.* nomad, wanderer, vagrant.

# J

**jail** *n.* penitentiary, cage, cell, dungeon, bastille, pound, reformatory, stockade, detention camp, gaol, concentration camp, penal institution, house of detention, prison, lockup, death house, pen*, stir*, clink*, can*.

**jam** *v.* **1** [To force one's way] jostle, squeeze, crowd, throng, press, thrust, pack. **2** [To compress] bind, squeeze, push.

**jar** *n.* **1** [A glass or earthen container] crock, pot, fruit jar, can, vessel, basin, beaker, jug, cruet, vat, decanter, pitcher, bottle, flagon, flask, vial, vase, chalice, urn. **2** [A jolt] jounce, thud, thump.

**jargon** *n.* **1** [Trite speech] banality, patter, hackneyed terms, overused words, commonplace phrases, shopworn language, trite vocabulary, hocus-pocus. **2** [Specialized vocabulary or pronunciation, etc.] argot, patois, lingo, broken English, idiom, pidgin English, vernacular, colloquialism, coined words, pig Latin, localism, rhyming slang, double-talk, officialese, newspeak, journalese.

**jealous** *a.* possessive, demanding, monopolizing, envious, watchful, resentful, mistrustful, doubting, apprehensive.—*Ant.* trusting, confiding, believing.

**jeopardy** *n.* risk, peril, exposure.

**jerk** *n.* **1** [A twitch] tic, shrug, wiggle, shake, quiver, flick, jiggle. **2** [*A contemptible person] scoundrel, rat*, twerp*.

**jewelry** *n.* gems, jewels, baubles, trinkets, adornments, frippery, ornaments, costume jewelry, bangles.

**job** *n.* **1** [Gainful employment] situation, place, position, appointment, operation, task, line, calling, vocation, handicraft, career, craft, pursuit, office, function, means of livelihood. **2** [Something to be done] task, business, action, act, mission, assignment, affair, concern, obligation, enterprise, undertaking, project, chore, errand, care, matter in hand, commission, function, responsibility, office, tour of duty, operation. **3** [The amount of work done] assignment, day's work, output. —**odd jobs** miscellaneous duties, chores, occasional labor. —**on the job** busy, engaged, occupied.

**jog** *n.* **1** [A slow run] trot, amble, pace. **2** [A bump] nudge, poke, shake.

**join** *v.* **1** [To unite] put together, blend, combine, bring in contact with, touch, connect, couple, mix, assemble, bind together, fasten, attach, annex, pair with, link, yoke, marry, wed, copulate, cement, weld, clasp, fuse, lock, grapple, clamp, entwine.—*Ant.* separate, sunder, sever. **2** [To enter the company of] go to, seek, associate with, join forces, go to the aid of, place by the side of, follow, register, team up with, take up with, be in, sign on, sign up, go in with, fall in with, consort, enlist, fraternize, throw in with*, pair with, affiliate, side with, make one of, take part in, seek a place among, advance toward, seek reception, go to meet.—*Ant.* desert, leave, abandon. **3** [*To adjoin] lie next to, neighbor, border, fringe, verge upon, be adjacent to, open into, be close to, bound, lie beside, be at hand, touch, skirt, parallel, rim, hem.

**joint** *n.* **1** [A juncture] union, coupling, hinge, tie, swivel, link, connection, point of union, bond, splice, bend, hyphen, junction, bridge. **2** [A section] piece, unit, portion. **3** [*An establishment, particularly one providing entertainment] hangout*, dive*, hole in the wall*. **4** [*A marijuana cigarette] roach*, doobie*, reefer*, stick*. —**out of joint** dislocated, disjointed, wrong.

**joke** *n.* prank, put-on*, game, sport, frolic, practical joke, jest, pun, witticism, play on words, quip, pleasantry, banter, drollery, retort, repartee, crack*, wisecrack*, clowning, caper, mischief, escapade, tomfoolery, play, antic, spree, farce, monkeyshine*, shenanigan*, horseplay, stunt, gag*.

**joke** *v.* jest, quip, banter, laugh, raise laughter, poke fun, play, frolic, play tricks, pun, twit, trick, fool, make merry, play the fool, wisecrack*, pull someone's leg*.

**jolly** *a.* gay, merry, joyful.

**jolt** *n.* **1** [A bump] jar, punch, bounce. **2** [A surprise] jar, start, shock.

**journey** *n.* trip, visit, run, passage, tour, excursion, jaunt, pilgrimage, voyage, crossing, expedition, patrol, beat, venture, adventure, drive, flight, cruise, course, route, sojourn, traveling, travels, trek, migration, caravan, roaming, quest, safari, exploration, hike, airing, outing, march, picnic, survey, mission, ride.

**joy** *n.* mirth, cheerfulness, delight, pleasure, gratification, treat, diversion, sport, refreshment, revelry, frolic, playfulness, gaiety, geniality, good humor, merriment, merrymaking, levity, rejoicing, liveliness, high spirits, good spirits, jubilation, celebration.—*Ant.* complaining, weeping, wailing.

**judge** *n.* **1** [A legal official] justice, executive judge, magistrate, justice of the peace, chief justice, associate justice, judiciary, circuit judge, county judge, judge of the district court, appellate judge. **2** [A connoisseur] expert, person of taste, professional.

**judge** *v.* adjudge, adjudicate, rule on, pass on, sit in judgment, sentence, give a hearing to, hold the scales.

**judgment** *n.* **1** [Discernment] discrimination, taste, shrewdness, sapience, understanding, knowledge, wit, keenness, sharpness, critical faculty, rational faculty, reason, rationality, intuition, mentality, acuteness, intelligence, awareness, experience, profundity, depth, brilliance, sanity, intellectual power, capacity, comprehension, mother wit, quickness, readiness, grasp, apprehension, perspicacity, soundness, genius, good sense, common sense, astuteness, prudence, wisdom, gray matter*, brains, savvy*, horse sense*.—*Ant.* stupidity, simplicity, naiveté. **2** [The act of judging] decision, consideration, appraisal, examination, weighing, sifting the evidence, determination, inspection, assessment, estimate, estimation, probing, appreciation, evaluation, review, contemplation, analysis, inquiry, inquisition, inquest, search, quest, pursuit, scrutiny, exploration, close study, observation, exhaustive inquiry. **3** [A pronouncement] conclusion, appraisal, estimate, opinion, report, view, summary, belief, idea, conviction, inference, resolution, deduction, induction, determination, decree, supposition, commentary, finding, recommendation.

**judicial** *a.* legalistic, authoritative, administrative.

**juicy** *a.* **1** [Succulent] moist, wet, watery, humid, dewy, sappy, dank, dripping, sodden, soaked, liquid, oily, sirupy.—*Ant.* dry, dehydrated, bone-dry. **2** [*Full of interest] spicy, piquant, intriguing, racy, risqué, fascinating, colorful. **3** [*Profitable] lucrative, remunerative, fruitful.

**jump** *n.* **1** [A leap up or across] skip, hop, rise, pounce, lunge, jumping, broad jump, high jump, vault, bounce, hurdle, spring, bound, caper. **2** [A leap down] plunge, plummet, fall. **3** [Distance jumped] leap, stretch, vault. **4** [*An advantage] upper hand, handicap, head start. **5** [A sudden rise] ascent, spurt, inflation.

**jump** *v.* **1** [To leap across or up] vault, leap over, spring, lurch, lunge, pop up, bound, hop, skip, high-jump, broad-jump, hurdle, top. **2** [To leap down] drop, plummet, plunge. **3** [To pass over] skip, traverse, remove, nullify. **4** [To vibrate] jiggle, wobble, rattle. **5** [*To accost belligerently] attack suddenly, assault, mug*.

**junk** *n.* waste, garbage, filth.

**justice** *n.* **1** [Fairness] right, truth, equity. **2** [Lawfulness] legality, equity, prescriptive right, statutory right, established right, legitimacy, sanction, legalization, constitutionality, authority, code, charter, decree, rule, legal process, authorization.—*Ant.* wrong, illegality, illegitimacy. **3** [The administration of law] adjudication, settlement, arbitration, hearing, legal process, due process, judicial procedure, jury trial, trial by jury, regulation, decision, pronouncement, review, appeal, sentence, consideration, taking evidence, litigation, prosecution.—*Ant.* disorder, lawlessness, despotism. **4** [A judge] magistrate, umpire, chancellor. **—do justice to** treat fairly, do right by, help. **—do oneself justice** be fair to oneself, give oneself credit, behave in a worthy way.

**justly** *a.* **1** [Honorably] impartially, honestly, frankly, candidly, straightforwardly, reasonably, fairly, moderately, temperately, evenhandedly, rightly, equitably, equably, tolerantly, charitably, respectably, lawfully, legally, legitimately, rightfully, properly, duly, in justice, as it ought to be. **2** [Exactly] properly, precisely, rationally.

# K

**keen** *a.* **1** [Sharp] pointed, edged, acute. **2** [Astute] bright, clever, shrewd. **3** [Eager] ardent, interested, intent.

**keep** *v.* **1** [To hold] retain, grip, own, possess, have, take, seize, save, grasp. **2** [To maintain] preserve, conserve, care for. **3** [To continue] keep going, carry on, sustain. **4** [To operate] administer, run, direct. **5** [To tend] care for, minister to, attend. **6** [To remain] stay, continue, abide. **7** [To store] deposit, hoard, retain, store, preserve, reserve, put away, conserve, warehouse, stash away*, put away, cache. **8** [To prevent; *used with "from"*] stop, block, avert. **9** [To retain] not spoil, season, put up. **—for keeps*** permanently, changelessly, perpetually.

**keep on** *v.* finish, repeat, pursue.

**key** *n.* **1** [Instrument to open a lock] latchkey, opener, master key, passkey, skeleton key. **2** [A means of solution] clue, code, indicator.

**kick** *n.* **1** [A blow with the foot] boot, swift kick, jolt, jar, hit. **2** [In sports, a kicked ball] punt, drop kick, place kick. **3** [*Pleasant reaction] joy, pleasant sensation, refreshment.

**kick** *v.* **1** [To give a blow with the foot] boot, jolt, punt, drop-kick, placekick, kick off. **2** [*To object] make a complaint, criticize, carp.

**kidnap** *v.* abduct, ravish, capture, steal, rape, carry away, hold for ransom, shanghai, carry off, make off with, make away with, grab, spirit away, pirate, snatch*, bundle off.—*Ant.* rescue, ransom, release.

**kill** *v.* **1** [To deprive of life] slay, slaughter, murder, assassinate, massacre, butcher, hang, lynch, electrocute, dispatch, execute, knife, sacrifice, shoot, strangle, poison, choke, smother, suffocate, asphyxiate, drown, behead, guillotine, crucify, dismember, decapitate, disembowel, quarter, tear limb from limb, destroy, give the death blow, give the *coup de grâce*, put to death, deprive of life, put an end to, exterminate, stab, cut the throat of, shoot down, mangle, cut down, bring down, mow down, machine-gun, pick off, liquidate, put someone out of his or her misery, starve, do away with, commit murder, bump off*, rub out*, wipe out*, do in*, knock off*, finish off*, blow someone's brains out*, put to sleep*, brain*, zap*.—*Ant.* rescue, resuscitate, animate. **2** [To cancel] annul, nullify, counteract. **3** [To turn off] turn out, shut off, stop. **4** [To veto] cancel, prohibit, refuse.

**kin** *n.* blood relation, member of the family, sibling.

**kind** *a.* tender, well-meaning, considerate, charitable, loving, pleasant, amiable, soft, softhearted, compassionate, sympathetic, understanding, solicitous, sweet, generous, helpful, obliging, neighborly, accommodating, indulgent, delicate, tactful, gentle, tenderhearted, kindhearted, good-natured, inoffensive, benevolent, altruistic, lenient, easygoing, patient, tolerant, mellow, genial, sensitive, courteous, agreeable, thoughtful, well-disposed.—*Ant.* rough, brutal, harsh.

**kind** *n.* **1** [Class] classification, species, genus. **2** [Type] sort, variety, description, stamp, character, tendency, gender, habit, breed, set, tribe, denomination, persuasion, manner, connection, designation.

**kindhearted** *a.* amiable, generous, good.

**kindly** *a.* generous, helpful, good.

**kindness** *n.* **1** [The quality of being kind] tenderness, good intention, consideration, sympathy, sweetness, helpfulness, tact, benignity, mildness, courtesy, thoughtfulness, humanity, courteousness, understanding, compassion, unselfishness, altruism, warmheartedness, softheartedness, politeness, kindliness, clemency, benevolence, goodness, philanthropy, charity, friendliness, affection, lovingkindness, cordiality, mercy, amiability, forbearance, graciousness, kindheartedness, virtue.—*Ant.* cruelty, brutality, selfishness. **2** [A kindly act] good service, relief, charity, benevolence, philanthropy, favor, good deed, good turn, self-sacrifice, mercy, lift, boost.—*Ant.* injury, transgression, wrong.

**kind of*** *a.* somewhat, having the nature of, sort of*.

**king** *n.* **1** [A male sovereign] monarch, tyrant, prince, autocrat, czar, caesar, lord, emperor, overlord, crowned head, imperator, majesty, regal personage, sultan, caliph, shah, rajah, maharajah.—*Ant.* servant, slave, subordinate. **2** [A very superior being] lord, chief, head.

**kit** *n.* **1** [Equipment] material, tools, outfit. **2** [A pack] poke*, knapsack, satchel.

**knack** *n.* trick, skill, faculty.

**kneel** *v.* bend the knee, rest on the knees, genuflect, bend, stoop, bow down, curtsey.

**knife** *n.* blade, cutter, sword, bayonet, cutting edge, dagger, stiletto, lance, machete, poniard, scalpel, edge, dirk, sickle, scythe, saber, scimitar, broadsword, point, pigsticker*, toad-stabber*, shiv*.

**knob** *n.* **1** [A projection] hump, bulge, knot, node, bump, protuberance. **2** [A door handle] doorknob, latch, door latch.

**knot** *n.* **1** [An arrangement of strands] tie, clinch, hitch, splice, ligature, bond. **2** [A hard or twisted portion] snarl, gnarl, snag, bunch, coil, entanglement, tangle, twist, twirl, whirl.

**knot** *v.* bind, tie, cord.

**know** *v.* **1** [To possess information] be cognizant, be acquainted, be informed, be in possession of the facts, have knowledge of, be schooled in, be versed in, be conversant with, recognize, know full well, have at one's fingertips, be master of, know by heart, know inside out*, be instructed, awaken to, keep up on, have information about, know what's what*, know all the answers, have someone's number*, have the jump on*, have down cold*, know one's stuff*, know the score*, know the ropes*.—*Ant.* neglect, be oblivious of (or to), overlook. **2** [To understand] comprehend, apprehend, see into. **3** [To recognize] perceive, discern, be familiar with, have the friendship of, acknowledge, be accustomed to, associate with, get acquainted.

**knowledge** *n.* **1** [Information] learning, lore, scholarship, facts, wisdom, instruction, book learning, enlightenment, expertise, intelligence, light, theory, science, principles, philosophy, awareness, insight, education, substance, store of learning, know-how*.—*Ant.* ignorance, emptiness, pretension. **2** [Culture] dexterity, cultivation, learning.

# L

**label** *n.* tag, marker, mark, stamp, hallmark, insignia, design, number, identification, description, classification.

**labor** *n.* **1** [The act of doing work] activity, toil, operation. **2** [Work to be done] task, employment, undertaking. **3** [Exertion required in work] exertion, energy, industry, diligence, strain, stress, drudgery. **4** [The body of workers] laborers, workers, workingmen, workingwomen, proletariat, work force, labor force, working people, employees.—*Ant.* employer, capitalist, businessman. **5** [Childbirth] parturition, giving birth, labor pains.

**labor** *v.* toil, strive, get cracking*.

**laborer** *n.* day laborer, unskilled worker, hand, manual laborer, ranch hand, farm hand, apprentice, hired man, transient worker, toiler, seasonal laborer, ditch digger, pick-and-shovel man, roustabout, stevedore, miner, street cleaner, peon, flunky, lackey, hireling, hack, beast of burden*, doormat*.

**lack** *n.* **1** [The state of being lacking] destitution, absence, need, shortage, paucity, deprivation, deficiency, scarcity, insufficiency, inadequacy, privation, poverty, distress, scantiness.—*Ant.* plenty, sufficiency, abundance. **2** [That which is lacking] need, decrease, want, loss, depletion, shrinkage, shortage, defect, inferiority, paucity, stint, curtailment, reduction.—*Ant.* wealth, overflow, satisfaction.

**lack** *v.* want, require, have need of.

**lady** *n.* **1** [A woman] female, matron, woman. **2** [A woman of gentle breeding] gentlewoman, well-bred woman, woman of quality, cultured woman, high-born lady, mistress of an estate, noblewoman, titled lady.

**lag** *v.* dawdle, linger, fall back, loiter, tarry, straggle, get behind, slacken, slow up, fall behind, procrastinate, plod, trudge, lounge, shuffle, falter, stagger, limp, get no place fast*.—*Ant.* hurry, hasten, keep pace with.

**lair** *n.* cave, home, den.

**lame** *a.* **1** [Forced to limp] crippled, unable to walk, halt, weak, paralyzed, impaired, handicapped, disabled, limping. **2** [Weak; *usually used figuratively*] inefficient, ineffective, faltering.

**land** *n.* **1** [The solid surface of the earth] ground, soil, dirt, clay, loam, gravel, subsoil, clod, sand, rock, mineral, pebble, stone, dry land, valley, desert, hill, bank, seaside, shore, beach, crag, cliff, boulder, ledge, peninsula, delta, promontory.—*Ant.* sea, stream, ocean. **2** [Land as property] estate, tract, ranch, farm, home, lot, real estate. **3** [A country] nation, continent, province, region.

**land** *v.* **1** [To come into port; *said of a ship*] dock, berth, make port, tie up, come to land, drop anchor, put in.—*Ant.* leave, weigh anchor, cast off. **2** [To go ashore] disembark, come ashore, arrive, alight, leave the boat or ship, go down the gangplank, hit the beach*. **3** [To bring an airplane to earth] touch down, ground, take down, alight, come in, settle, level off, come down, descend upon, make a forced landing, crash-land, nose over, overshoot, splash down, check in, undershoot, pancake, settle her down hot*, fishtail down.

**landmark** *n.* **1** [A notable relic] remnant, vestige, souvenir. **2** [A point from which a course may be taken] vantage point, mark, blaze, guide, marker, stone, tree, hill, mountain, bend, promontory.

**landscape** *n.* scene, scenery, panorama.

**language** *n.* **1** [A means of communication] voice, utterance, expression, vocalization, sound, phonation, tongue, mother tongue, articulation, metalanguage, physical language; language of diplomacy, language of chemistry, language of flowers, etc.; accent, word, sign, signal, pantomime, gesture, vocabulary, diction, dialect, idiom, local speech, broken English, pidgin English, polyglot, patois, vernacular, lingua franca, gibberish, pig Latin. **2** [The study of language] linguistics, grammar, semantics, psycholinguistics, morphology, phonology, phonemics, morphemics, morphophonemics, phonics, phonetics, criticism, letters, linguistic studies, history of language, etymology, dialectology, linguistic geography. —**speak the same language** understand one another, communicate, get along.

**lap** *n.* **1** [That portion of the body that is formed when one sits down] knees, legs, thighs, front. **2** [The portion that overlaps] extension, projection, fold. **3** [Part of a race] circuit, round, course. —**drop into someone's lap** transfer responsibility, shift blame, pass the buck*. —**in the lap of luxury** surrounded by luxury, living elegantly, prospering.

**lapse** *n.* slip, mistake, failure.

**lapse** *v.* slip, deteriorate, decline.

**large** *a.* **1** [Of great size] huge, big, wide, grand, great, considerable, substantial, vast, massive, immense, spacious, bulky, colossal, gigantic, mountainous, immeasurable, extensive, plentiful, copious, populous, ample, abundant, liberal, comprehensive, lavish, swollen, bloated, puffy, obese, monstrous, towering, mighty, magnificent, enormous, giant, tremendous, monumental, stupendous, voluminous, cumbersome, ponderous, gross, immoderate, extravagant, super*, booming, bumper, whopping*.—*Ant.* little, small, tiny. **2** [Involving great plans] extensive, extended, considerable.

**largely** *a.* **1** [In large measure] mostly, mainly, chiefly. **2** [In a large way] extensively, abundantly, comprehensively.

**last** *a.* **1** [Final] untimate, utmost, lowest, meanest, least, end, extreme, remotest, furthest, outermost, farthest, uttermost, concluding, hindmost, far, far-off, ulterior, once and for all, definitive, after all others, ending, at the end, terminal, eventual, settling, resolving, decisive, crowning, climactic, closing, ending, finishing, irrefutable.—*Ant.* first, foremost, beginning. **2** [Most recent] latest, newest, current, freshest, immediate, in the fashion, modish, the last word*, trendy*.—*Ant.* old, stale, outmoded.

**last** *v.* **1** [To endure] remain, carry on, survive, hold out, suffer, stay, overcome, persist, stick it out*, stick with it*, go on. **2** [To be sufficient] hold out, be adequate, be enough, serve, do, accomplish the purpose, answer.

**late** *a.* **1** [Tardy] too late, held up, overdue, stayed, postponed, put off, not on time, belated, behind time, lagging, delayed, backward, not in time.—*Ant.* early, punctual, on time. **2** [Recently dead] defunct, deceased, departed. **3** [Recent] new, just out, recently published. **4** [Far into the night] nocturnal, night-loving, advanced, tardy, toward morning, after midnight. **—of late** lately, in recent times, a short time ago.

**latent** *a.* underdeveloped, potential, dormant, inactive.

**laugh** *n.* mirth, merriment, amusement, rejoicing, shout, chuckle, chortle, cackle, peal of laughter, horselaugh, guffaw, titter, snicker, giggle, roar, snort.—*Ant.* cry, sob, whimper. **—have the last laugh** defeat finally, beat in the end, overcome all obstacles.

**laugh** *v.* chuckle, chortle, guffaw, laugh off, snicker, titter, giggle, burst out laughing, shriek, roar, beam, grin, smile, smirk, shout, die laughing*, break up*, crack up*, howl, roll in the aisles*, be in stitches.—*Ant.* cry, sob, weep. **—no laughing matter** serious, grave, significant.

**launch** *v.* **1** [To initiate] originate, start, set going. **2** [To send off] set in motion, propel, drive, thrust, fire off, send forth, eject.

**lavish** *a.* generous, unstinted, unsparing.

**law** *n.* **1** [The judicial system] judicial procedure, legal process, the legal authorities, the police, due process, precept, summons, notice, warrant, search warrant, warrant of arrest, subpoena. **2** [Bodies of law] code, constitution, criminal law, statute law, civil law, martial law, military law, private law, public law, commercial law, probate law, statutory law, statutes, civil code, ordinances, equity, cases, common law, canon law, decisions, unwritten law, natural law. **3** [An enactment] statute, edict, decree, order, ordinance, judicial decision, ruling, injunction, summons, act, enactment, requirement, demand, canon, regulation, commandment, mandate, dictate, instruction, legislation. **4** [A principle] foundation, fundamental, origin, source, ultimate cause, truth, axiom, maxim, ground, base, reason, rule, theorem, guide, precept, usage, postulate, proposition, generalization, assumption, hard and fast rule. **5** [Officers appointed to enforce the law] sheriff, state police, city police. **—lay down the law** establish rules, order, prohibit.

**lawful** *a.* legal, legalized, legitimate, statutory, passed, decreed, judged, judicial, juridical, commanded, ruled, ordered, constitutional, legislated, enacted, official, enforced, protected, vested, within the law, legitimized, established.—*Ant.* illegal, unlawful, illegitimate.

**lawless** *a.* **1** [Without law] wild, untamed, uncivilized, savage, uncultivated, barbarous, fierce, violent, tempestuous, disordered, agitated, disturbed, warlike.—*Ant.* cultured, cultivated, controlled. **2** [Not restrained by law] riotous, insubordinate, disobedient.

**lawyer** *n.* professional man, legal adviser, jurist, defender, prosecuting attorney, prosecutor, attorney, solicitor, counsel, counselor, counselor-at-law, barrister, advocate, professor of law, attorney at law, public attorney, private attorney, attorney general, district attorney, Philadelphia lawyer*, legal eagle*, shyster*, mouthpiece*.

**layer** *n.* thickness, fold, band, overlay, lap, overlap, seam, floor, story, tier, zone, stripe, coating, flap, panel.

**layout** *n.* arrangement, design, draft.

**lazy** *a.* **1** [Indolent] indolent, idle, remiss, sluggish, lagging, apathetic, loafing, dallying, passive, asleep on the job, procrastinating, neglectful, indifferent, dilatory, tardy, slack, inattentive, careless, flagging, weary, tired.—*Ant.* active, businesslike, indefatigable. **2** [Slow] slothful, inactive, lethargic.

**lead** *n.* **1** [The position at the front] head, advance, first place, point, edge, front rank, first line, scout, outpost, scouting party, patrol, advance position, forerunner.—*Ant.* end, rear, last place. **2** [Leadership] direction, guidance, headship. **3** [A clue] evidence, trace, hint. **4** [A leading role] principal part, important role, chief character.

**lead** *n.* metallic lead, galena, blue lead.

**lead** *v.* **1** [To conduct] guide, steer, pilot, show the way, point the way, show in, point out, escort, accompany, protect, guard, safeguard, watch over, drive, discover the way, find a way through, be responsible for.—*Ant.* follow, be conveyed, be piloted. **2** [To exercise leadership] direct, manage, supervise. **3** [To extend] traverse, pass along, span.

**leader** *n.* **1** [A guide] conductor, lead, pilot. **2** [One who provides leadership] general, commander, director, manager, head, officer, captain, master, chieftain, governor, ruler, executor, boss, brains*.

**leadership** *n.* authority, control, administration, effectiveness, superiority, supremacy, skill, initiative, foresight, energy, capacity.

**leak** *n.* **1** [Loss through leakage] leakage, loss, flow, seepage, escape, falling off, expenditure, decrease. **2** [An aperture through which a leak may take place] puncture, chink, crevice. **3** [Surreptitious news] news leak, exposé, slip.

**leak** *v.* **1** [To escape by leaking] drip, ooze, drool. **2** [To permit leakage] be cracked, be split, have a fissure, be out of order, have a slow leak.

**leap** *v.* spring, vault, bound.

**learn** *v.* acquire, receive, get, take in, drink in, pick up, read, master, ground oneself in, pore over, gain information, ascertain, determine, unearth, hear, find out, learn by heart, memorize, be taught a lesson, improve one's mind.

**learned** *a.* **1** [Having great learning; *said of people*] scholarly, erudite, academic, accomplished, conversant with, lettered, instructed, collegiate, well-informed, bookish, pedantic, professorial.—*Ant.* ignorant, incapable, illiterate. **2** [Showing evidence of learning; *said of productions*] deep, sound, solemn.

**lease** *n.* document of use, permission to rent, charter.

**lease** *v.* let, charter, rent out.

**least** *a.* **1** [Smallest] tiniest, infinitesimal, microscopic. **2** [Least important] slightest, piddling, next to nothing. **3** [In the lowest degree] minimal, most inferior, bottom. **—at (the) least** in any event, with no less than, at any rate. **—not in the least** not at all, in no way, not in the slightest degree.

**leather** *n.* tanned hide, parchment, calfskin, horsehide, buckskin, deerskin, elk hide, goatskin, sheepskin, rawhide, cowhide, snakeskin, sharkskin, lizard, shoe leather, glove leather, chamois skin, alligator hide.

**leave** *v.* **1** [To go away] go, depart, take leave, withdraw, move, set out, come away, go forth, take off, start, step down, quit a place, part company, defect, vanish, walk out, walk away, get out, get away, slip out, slip away, break away, break out, ride off, ride away, go off, go out, go away, move out, move away, vacate, abscond, flee, flit, migrate, fly, run along, embark, say goodbye, emigrate, clear out*, cut out, pull out, push off*, cast off, scram*, split*, sign out, check out, beat it*, take a powder*, pull up stakes*.—*Ant.* arrive, get to, reach. **2** [To abandon] back out, forsake, desert. **3** [To allow to remain] let stay, leave behind, let continue, let go, drop, lay down, omit, forget.—*Ant.* seize, take away, keep. **4** [To allow to fall to another] bequeath, hand down, transmit.

**left** *a.* **1** [Opposite to right] leftward, left-hand, near, sinister, larboard, port, portside.—*Ant.* right, right-hand, starboard. **2** [Remaining] staying, continuing, over. **3** [Radical] left-wing, liberal, progressive. **4** [Departed] gone out, absent, lacking.

**legal** *a.* lawful, constitutional, permissible, allowable, allowed, proper, legalized, sanctioned, legitimate, right, just, justifiable, justified, fair, authorized, accustomed, due, rightful, warranted, admitted, sound, granted, acknowledged, equitable, within the law, protected, enforced, judged, decreed, statutory, contractual, customary, chartered, clean*, legit*, straight*, on the up and up*.—*Ant.* illegal, unlawful, prohibited.

**legendary** *a.* fabulous, mythical, mythological, fanciful, imaginative, created, invented, allegorical, apocryphal, improbable, imaginary, dubious, not historical, doubtful, romantic, storied, unverifiable.

**legible** *a.* distinct, plain, sharp.

**legislator** *n.* lawmaker, lawgiver, assemblyman, representative, congressman, congresswoman, senator, member of parliament, floor leader, councilman, councilwoman, alderman.

**leisure** *n.* freedom, free time, spare time, spare moments, relaxation, recreation, ease, recess, holiday, vacation, hiatus, leave of absence, convenience, idle hours, opportunity.—*Ant.* work, toil, travail. **—at leisure** idle, resting, not busy. **—at one's leisure** when one has time, at one's convenience, at an early opportunity.

**lend** *v.* advance, provide with, let out, furnish, permit to borrow, allow, trust with, lend on security, extend credit, entrust, accommodate.—*Ant.* borrow, repay, pay back.

**length** *n.* **1** [Linear distance] space, measure, span, reach, range, remoteness, magnitude, compass, portion, dimension, unit, radius, diameter, longness, mileage, stretch, extensiveness, spaciousness, height, expansion.—*Ant.* nearness, shortness, closeness. **2** [Duration] period, interval, season, year, month, week, day, minute, limit.

**lenient** *a.* soft, mild, tolerant.

**let** *v.* **1** [To permit] suffer, give permission, allow, condone, approve, authorize, consent, permit, tolerate. **2** [To rent] lease, hire, sublet.

**letter** *n.* **1** [A unit of the alphabet] capital, uppercase letter, lowercase letter, small letter, vowel, consonant, digraph, rune. **2** [A written communication] note, epistle, missive, message, memorandum, report, line. **—to the letter** just as directed, perfectly, precisely.

**level** *a.* **1** [Smooth] polished, rolled, planed. **2** [Of an even height] regular, equal, uniform, flush, of the same height, same, constant, straight, balanced, steady, stable, trim, precise, exact, matched, unbroken, on a line, lined up, aligned, uninterrupted, continuous.—*Ant.* irregular, uneven, crooked. **3** [Horizontal] plane, leveled, lying prone, in the same plane, on one plane. **—one's level best*** one's best, the best one can do, all one's effort. **—on the level*** fair, sincere, truthful.

**level** *v.* **1** [To straighten] surface, bulldoze, equalize. **2** [To demolish] ruin, waste, wreck. **3** [*To be honest with] be frank with, come to terms, be open and aboveboard.

**levy** *n.* toll, duty, customs.

**liable** *a.* **1** [Responsible] answerable, subject, accountable. **2** [Likely] tending, apt, inclined.

**liar** *n.* prevaricator, false witness, deceiver, perjurer, trickster, cheat, misleader, falsifier, storyteller*, equivocator, fibber, fabricator.

**liberal** *a.* tolerant, receptive, nonconformist, progressive, advanced, left, radical, interested, wide-awake, broad-minded, understanding, permissive, indulgent, impartial, unprejudiced, reasonable, rational, unbiased, detached, dispassionate, unconventional, avant-garde, left-wing, objective, magnanimous.—*Ant.* prejudiced, intolerant, biased.

**liberal** *n.* individualist, insurgent, rebel, radical, progressive, leftist, revolutionary, nonconformist, independent, reformer, socialist, eccentric, freethinker, left-winger.

**liberty** *n.* **1** [Freedom from bondage] deliverance, emancipation, enfranchisement. **2** [Freedom from occupation] rest, leave, relaxation. **3** [Freedom to choose] permission, alternative, decision. **4** [The rights supposedly natural to human beings] freedom, independence, power of choice. **—at liberty** unrestricted, unlimited, not confined. **—take liberties** be too impertinent, act too freely, use carelessly.

**lick** *v.* **1** [To pass the tongue over] stroke, rub, touch, pass over, pass across, caress, wash, graze, brush, glance, tongue, fondle. **2** [To play over; *said of flames*] rise and fall, fluctuate, leap. **3** [*To beat] whip, trim*, thrash. **4** [*To defeat] overcome, vanquish, frustrate.

**lid** *n.* cap, top, roof.

**lie** *n.* falsehood, untruth, fiction, inaccuracy, misstatement, myth, fable, deceptiveness, misrepresentation, lying, prevarication, falsification, falseness, defamation, tall story*, fabrication, deception, slander, aspersion, tale, perjury, libel, forgery, distortion, fib, white lie, fish story*, whopper*.—*Ant.* truth, veracity, truthfulness.

**lie** *v.* **1** [To utter an untruth] falsify, prevaricate, tell a lie, deceive, mislead, misinform, exaggerate, distort, concoct, equivocate, be untruthful, be a liar, break one's word, bear false witness, go back on, say one thing and mean another, misrepresent, dissemble, perjure oneself, delude, invent.—*Ant.* declare, tell the truth, be honest. **2** [To be situated] extend, be on, be beside, be located, be fixed, be established, be placed, be seated, be set, be level, be smooth, be even, exist in space, stretch along, reach along, spread along. **3** [To be prostrate] be flat, be prone, sprawl, loll, be stretched out.—*Ant.* stand, be upright, sit. **4** [To assume a prostrate position] lie down, recline, stretch out, go to bed, turn in, retire, take a nap, take a siesta, hit the sack*, hit the hay*.—*Ant.* rise, get up, arise. **—take lying down** submit, surrender, be passive.

**life** *n.* **1** [The fact or act of living] being, entity, growth, animation, endurance, survival, presence, living, consciousness, breath, continuance, flesh and blood, viability, metabolism, vitality, vital spark.—*Ant.* death, discontinuance, nonexistence. **2** [The sum of one's experiences] life experience, conduct, behavior, way of life, reaction, response, participation, enjoyment, joy, suffering, happiness, tide of events, circumstances, realization, knowledge, enlightenment, attainment, development, growth, personality. **3** [A biography] life story, memoir, memorial. **4** [Duration] lifetime, one's natural life, period of existence, duration of life, endurance, continuance, span, history, career, course, era, epoch, century, decade, days, generation, time, period, life span, season, cycle, record. **5** [One who promotes gaiety] animator, entertainer, life of the party*. **6** [Vital spirit] vital force, vital principle, *élan vital* (French). **—as large** (or **big**) **as life** actually, truly, in actual fact. **—for dear life** intensely, desperately, for all one is worth. **—for life** for the duration of one's life, for a long time, as long as one lives. **—for the life of me*** by any means, as if one's life were at stake, whatever happens. **—matter of life and death** crisis, grave concern, something vitally important. **—not on your life*** by no means, certainly not, never. **—take one's own life** kill oneself, die by one's own hand, commit suicide. **—true to life** true to reality, realistic, representational.

**lifetime** *n.* existence, endurance, continuance.

**lift** *n.* **1** [The work of lifting] pull, lifting, ascension, raising, weight, foot pounds, elevation, escalation, ascent, mounting. **2** [A ride] transportation, drive, passage. **3** [Aid] help, assistance, support.

**lift** *v.* hoist, elevate, upheave.

**light** *a.* **1** [Having illumination] illuminated, radiant, luminous. **2** [Having color] vivid, rich, clear. **3** [Having little content] superficial, slight, frivolous. **4** [Having gaiety and spirit] lively, merry, animated. **5** [Having little weight] airy, fluffy, feathery, slender, downy, floating, lighter than air, light as air, floatable, light as a feather, frothy, buoyant, dainty, thin, sheer, insubstantial, ethereal, graceful, weightless.—*Ant.* heavy, ponderous, weighty. **6** [Digestible] slight, edible, moderate. **7** [Small in quantity or number] wee, small, tiny, minute, thin, inadequate, insufficient, hardly enough, not much, hardly any, not many, slender, scanty, slight, sparse, fragmentary, fractional.—*Ant.* large, great, immense.

**light** *n.* **1** [The condition opposed to darkness] radiance, brilliance, splendor, glare, brightness, clearness, lightness, incandescence, shine, luster, sheen, sparkle, glitter, glimmer, flood of light, blare, radiation, gleam.—*Ant.* darkness, blackness, blankness. **2** [Emanations from a source of light] radiation, stream, blaze. **3** [A source of light] match, candle, sun, planet, star, moon, lightning, torch, flashlight, chandelier, spotlight, light bulb, halo, corona. **4** [Day] daylight, sun, sunrise. **5** [Aspect] point of view, condition, standing. **—in (the) light of** with knowledge of, because of, in view of. **—see the light (of day)** **1** come into being, exist, begin. **2** comprehend, realize, be aware.

**light** *v.* **1** [To provide light] illuminate, illumine, lighten, brighten, give light to, shine upon, furnish with light, light up, turn on the electricity, make visible, provide adequate illumination, switch on a light, floodlight, make bright, flood with light, fill with light.—*Ant.* shade, put out, darken. **2** [To cause to ignite] inflame, spark, kindle. **3** [To become ignited] take fire, become inflamed, flame. **4** [To come to rest from flight or travel] rest, come down, arrive. **—make light of** make fun of, mock, belittle.

**lighthearted** *a.* gay, joyous, cheerful.

**like** *a.* similar, same, alike, near, close, matching, equaling, not unlike, akin, related, analogous, twin, corresponding, allied, much the same, of the same form, comparable, identical, parallel, homologous, consistent.—*Ant.* unlike, different, unrelated.

**like** *prep.* similar to, same as, near to.

**like** *v.* **1** [To enjoy] take delight in, relish, derive pleasure from, be keen on, be pleased by, revel in, indulge in, rejoice in, find agreeable, find appealing, be gratified by, take satisfaction in, savor, fancy, dote on, take an interest in, develop interest for, delight in, regard with favor, have a liking for, love, have a taste for, care to, get a kick out of*, be tickled by, eat up*, go in for*.—*Ant.* endure, detest, dislike. **2** [To be fond of] have a fondness for, admire, take a fancy to, love, adore, feel affectionately toward, prize, esteem, hold dear, care about, care for, approve of, be pleased with, take to, have a soft spot in one's heart for, hanker for, dote on, have a yen for*, become attached to, be sweet on*, have eyes for*.—*Ant.* hate, disapprove, dislike. **3** [To be inclined] choose, feel disposed, wish, desire, have a preference for, prefer, fancy, feel like, incline toward, want.

**likely** *a.* **1** [Probable] apparent, probable, seeming, credible, possible, feasible, presumable, conceivable, reasonable, workable, attainable, achievable, believable, rational, thinkable, imaginable, ostensible, plausible, anticipated, expected, imminent.—*Ant.* impossible, doubtful, questionable. **2** [Promising] suitable, apt, assuring. **3** [Believable] plausible, true, acceptable. **4** [Apt] inclined, tending, disposed, predisposed, prone, liable, subject to, on the verge of, in the habit of, given to, in favor of, having a weakness for.

**likeness** *n.* **1** [Similarity] resemblance, correspondence, affinity. **2** [A representation] image, effigy, portrait.

**likewise** *a.* in like manner, furthermore, moreover.

**limit** *n.* **1** [The boundary] end, frontier, border. **2** [The ultimate] utmost, farthest point, farthest reach, destination, goal, conclusion, extremity, eventuality, termination, absolute, the bitter end, deadline, cut-off point.—*Ant.* origin, start.

**limit** *v.* bound, confine, curb.

**line** *n.* **1** [A straight, narrow formation] array, list, rank, file, catalog, order, group, arrangement, ridge, range, seam, series, sequence, succession, procession, chain, train, string, column, formation, division, queue, channel, furrow, scar, trench, groove, mark, thread, fissure, crack, straight line. **2** [A mark] outline, tracing, stroke. **3** [A rope] string, cable, towline. **4** [Lineal descent] ancestry, pedigree, lineage. **5** [A borderline] border, mark, limit. **6** [Matter printed in a row of type] row, words, letters. **7** [A military front] disposition, formation, position. **8** [A transportation system] trunk line, bus line, steamship line, railroad line, airline. **9** [Goods handled by a given company] wares, merchandise, produce. **10** [*Talk intended to influence another] rhetoric, lecture, propaganda, advertising. —**all along the line** at every turn, completely, constantly. —**bring** (or **come** or **get**) **into line** align, make uniform, regulate. —**draw the** (or **a**) **line** set a limit, prohibit, restrain. —**get a line on*** find out about, investigate, expose. —**in line** agreeing, conforming, uniform. —**in line for** being considered for, ready, thought about. —**lay** (or **put**) **it on the line** speak frankly, define, clarify. —**on a line** straight, even, level. —**out of line** misdirected, not uniform, not even. —**read between the lines** read meaning into, discover a hidden meaning, expose.

**line** *v.* **1** [To provide a lining] interline, stuff, wad, panel, pad, quilt, fill. **2** [To provide lines] trace, delineate, outline. **3** [To be in a line] border, edge, outline, rim, bound, fall in, fall into line, fringe, follow. **4** [To arrange in a line] align, queue, marshal, arrange, range, array, group, set out, bring into a line with, fix, place, draw up.—*Ant.* scatter, disarrange, disperse.

**linger** *v.* tarry, saunter, lag, hesitate, trail, vacillate, delay, plod, trudge, falter, dawdle, procrastinate, slouch, shuffle, crawl, loll, take one's time, wait, putter, be tardy, be long, sit around, hang around*.—*Ant.* hurry, hasten, speed.

**lining** *a.* edging, outlining, rimming.

**link** *n.* ring, loop, coupling, coupler, section, seam, weld, hitch, intersection, copula, connective, connection, fastening, splice, interconnection, junction, joining, ligature, articulation.

**link** *v.* connect, associate, combine.

**liquid** *a.* **1** [In a state neither solid nor gaseous] watery, molten, damp, moist, aqueous, liquefied, dissolved, melted, thawed. **2** [Having qualities suggestive of fluids] flowing, running, splashing, thin, moving, viscous, diluting.

**list** *n.* roll, record, schedule, agenda, arrangement, enrollment, slate, draft, panel, brief, invoice, register, memorandum, inventory, account, outline, tally, bulletin, directory, roster, subscribers, subscription list, muster, poll, ballot, table of contents, menu, dictionary, thesaurus, glossary, lexicon, vocabulary, docket.

**list** *v.* **1** [To enter in a list] set down, arrange, bill, catalogue, schedule, enter, note, add, place, file, record, insert, enroll, register, tally, inventory, index, draft, enumerate, tabulate, book, take a census, poll, slate, keep count of, run down, call the roll.—*Ant.* remove, wipe out, obliterate. **2** [To lean] pitch, slant, incline.

**listless** *a.* passive, sluggish, lifeless.

**literal** *a.* true, verbatim, accurate.

**literary** *a.* scholarly, bookish, literate.

**literature** *n.* **1** [Artistic production in language] letters, lore, belles-lettres, literary works, literary productions, the humanities, classics, books, writings. **2** [Written matter treating a given subject] discourse, composition, treatise, dissertation, thesis, paper, treatment, essay, discussion, research, observation, comment, critique, findings, abstract, report, summary.

**little** *a.* **1** [Small in size] diminutive, small, tiny, wee, undersized, stubby, truncated, stunted, limited, cramped, imperceptible, light, slight, microscopic, short, runty, shriveled, toy, miniature, puny, pygmy, dwarfed, bantam, half-pint*, pocket-size*, pint-size*.—*Ant.* large, big, huge. **2** [Inadequate] wanting, deficient, insufficient. **3** [Few in number] scarce, not many, hardly any. **4** [Brief] concise, succinct, abrupt. **5** [Small in importance] trifling, shallow, petty, superficial, frivolous, irrelevant, meaningless, slight, paltry, insignificant, inconsiderable. **6** [Small in character] base, weak, shallow, small-minded, prejudiced, bigoted, low, sneaky, mean, petty. **7** [Weak] stunted, runty, undersized. **—make little of** make fun of, mock, abuse.

**live** *v.* **1** [To have life] exist, continue, subsist, prevail, survive, breathe, be alive. **2** [To enjoy life] relish, savor, experience, love, delight in, make every moment count, experience life to the fullest, live it up*, make the most of life, take pleasure in, get a great deal from life.—*Ant.* suffer, endure pain, be discouraged. **3** [To dwell] live in, inhabit, settle. **4** [To gain subsistence] earn a living, support oneself, earn money, get ahead, provide for one's needs, make ends meet, subsist, maintain oneself. **5** [To persist in human memory] remain, last, be remembered. **—where one lives*** personally, in a vulnerable area, at one's heart.

**lively** *a.* vigorous, brisk, active.

**living** *a.* **1** [Alive] existing, breathing, having being. **2** [Vigorous] awake, brisk, alert.

**living** *n.* **1** [A means of survival] existence, sustenance, subsistence. **2** [Those not dead; *usually used with "the"*] the world, everyone, people.

**loaf** *v.* idle, trifle, lounge, kill time, be inactive, be slothful, be lazy, take it easy, not lift a finger, putter, rest, dally, let down, slack off, vegetate, loll, malinger, drift, relax, slack, shirk, waste time, slow down, evade, dillydally, stand around, dream, goof off*, bum*, stall, piddle.

**loafer** *n.* idler, lounger, lazy person, ne'er-do-well, good-for-nothing, lazybones*, malingerer, waster, slacker, shirker, wanderer, bum*, goldbrick*.

**locale** *n.* vicinity, territory, district.

**locate** *v.* **1** [To determine a location] discover, search out, find, come across, position, ferret out, stumble on, discover the location of, get at, hit upon, come upon, lay one's hands on, track down, unearth, establish, determine, station, place. **2** [To take up residence] settle down, establish oneself, inhabit.

**lofty** *a.* tall, elevated, towering.

**logical** *a.* coherent, consistent, probable, sound, pertinent, germane, legitimate, cogent, relevant, congruent with, reasonable.

**loiter** *v.* saunter, stroll, dawdle, delay, lag, shuffle, waste time, procrastinate, tarry, fritter away time, loll, loaf, dabble, wait, pause, dillydally, hang back, trail, drag, ramble, idle.—*Ant.* hurry, hasten, stride along.

**loneliness** *n.* detachment, separation, solitude, desolation, isolation, aloneness, lonesomeness, forlornness.

**lonely** *a.* abandoned, homesick, forlorn, forsaken, friendless, deserted, desolate, homeless, left, lone, lonesome, solitary, empty, companionless, renounced, withdrawn, secluded, unattended, by oneself, apart, reclusive, single, rejected, unaccompanied.—*Ant.* accompanied, joined, associated.

**long** *a.* **1** [Extended in space] lengthy, extended, outstretched, elongated, interminable, boundless, endless, unending, limitless, stretching, great, high, deep, drawn out, enlarged, expanded, spread, tall, lofty, towering, lengthened, stringy, rangy, lanky, gangling, far-reaching, distant, running, faraway, far-off, remote.—*Ant.* short, small, stubby. **2** [Extended in time] protracted, prolonged, enduring, unending, meandering, long-winded, spun out, lengthy, for ages, without end, perpetual, forever and a day, lasting, continued, long-lived, sustained, lingering; day after day, hour after hour, etc.—*Ant.* short, brief, uncontinued. **3** [Tedious] hard, boring, long-drawn-out. **4** [Having (a certain commodity) in excess] rich, profuse, abundant. **—as** (or **so**) **long as** seeing that, provided, since. **—before long** in the near future, immediately, shortly.

**long** *v.* desire, yearn for, wish.

**long-lived** *a.* long-lasting, perpetual, enduring.

**look** *v.* **1** [To appear] seem to be, look like, resemble. **2** [To endeavor to see] view, gaze, glance at, scan, stare, behold, contemplate, watch, survey, scrutinize, regard, inspect, discern, spy, observe, attend, examine, mark, gape, give attention, peer, ogle, have an eye on, study, peep, look at, take a gander at*, get a load of*. **—it looks like** probably, it seems that there will be, it seems as if.

**looks*** *pl.n.* appearance, countenance, aspect, manner, demeanor, face, expression, features, form, shape, posture, bearing, presence.

**loose** *a.* **1** [Unbound] unfastened, undone, untied, insecure, relaxed, unattached, unconnected, disconnected, untethered, unbuttoned, unclasped, unhooked, unsewed, unstuck, slack, loosened, baggy, unconfined, unlatched, unlocked, unbolted, unscrewed, unhinged, worked free.—*Ant.* tight, confined, bound. **2** [Movable] unattached, free, wobbly. **3** [Vague] disconnected, random, detached. **4** [Wanton] dissolute, licentious, disreputable. **—on the loose*** unconfined, unrestrained, wild. **—set** (or **turn**) **loose** set free, release, untie.

**loot** *n.* spoils, plunder, booty.

**loot** *v.* plunder, thieve, rifle.

**lopsided** *a.* uneven, unbalanced, crooked.

**lose** *v.* **1** [To bring about a loss] mislay, misfile, disturb, disorder, confuse, mix, scatter, mess, muss, disorganize, forget, be careless with. **2** [To incur loss] suffer, miss, be deprived of, fail to keep, suffer loss, be impoverished from, become poorer by, let slip through the fingers*.—*Ant.* profit, gain, improve. **3** [To fail to win] be defeated, suffer defeat, go down in defeat, succumb, fall, be the loser, miss, have the worst of it, be humbled, take defeat at the hands of, go down for the count*, be sunk*.—*Ant.* win, triumph, be victorious. **4** [To suffer financially] squander, expend, dissipate.

**loss** *n.* **1** [The act or fact of losing] ruin, destruction, mishap, misfortune, giving up, ill fortune, accident, calamity, trouble, disaster, sacrifice, catastrophe, trial, failure. **2** [Damage caused by losing something] hurt, injury, wound. **3** [The result of unprofitable activity] privation, want, bereavement, deprivation, need, destitution, being without, lack, waste, deterioration, impairment, degeneration, decline, disadvantage, wreck, wreckage, undoing, annihilation, bane, end, undoing, disorganization, breaking up, suppression, relapse.—*Ant.* advantage, advancement, supply. **—at a loss** confused, puzzled, unsure.

**lost** *a.* **1** [Not to be found] misplaced, mislaid, missing, hidden, obscured, gone astray, nowhere to be found, strayed, lacking, wandered off, absent, forfeited, vanished, wandering, without, gone out of one's possession.—*Ant.* found, come back, returned. **2** [Ignorant of the way] perplexed, bewildered, ignorant. **3** [Destroyed] demolished, devastated, wasted. **4** [No longer to be gained] gone, passed, costly. **5** [Helpless] feeble, sickly, disabled. **—get lost*** go away!, leave!, begone!

**lot** *n.* **1** [A small parcel of land] parcel, part, division, patch, clearing, piece of ground, plat, plot, field, tract, block, portion, parking lot, piece, property, acreage. **2** [A number of individual items, usually alike] batch, consignment, requisition. **3** [Destiny] doom, portion, fate. **4** [*A great quantity] large amount, abundance, plenty, considerable amount, great numbers, bundle, bunch, cluster, group, pack, large numbers, very much, very many, quite a lot, quite a bit, a good deal, a whole bunch*, loads*, oodles*.

**loud** *a.* **1** [Having volume of sound] deafening, ringing, ear-piercing, earsplitting, booming, intense, resounding, piercing, blaring, sonorous, resonant, crashing, deep, full, powerful, emphatic, thundering, heavy, big, deep-toned, full-tongued, roaring, enough to wake the dead*.—*Ant.* soft, faint, feeble. **2** [Producing loud sounds] clamorous, noisy, uproarious, blatant, vociferous, turbulent, tumultuous, blustering, lusty, loud-voiced, boisterous, cacophonous, raucous.—*Ant.* quiet, soft-voiced, calm. **3** [*Lacking manners and refinement] loud-mouthed, brash, offensive. **4** [*Lacking good taste, especially in colors] garish, flashy, tawdry.

**lovable** *a.* winning, winsome, friendly.

**love** *n.* **1** [Passionate and tender devotion] attachment, devotedness, passion, infatuation, yearning, flame, rapture, enchantment, ardor, emotion, sentiment, fondness, tenderness, adoration, crush*.—*Ant.* hate, aversion, antipathy. **2** [Affection based on esteem] respect, regard, appreciation. **3** [A lively and enduring interest] involvement, concern, enjoyment. **4** [A beloved] dear one, loved one, cherished one. **—for the love of** for the sake of, with fond concern for, because of. **—in love** enamored, infatuated, charmed. **—not for love or money** under no conditions, by no means, no.

**love** *v.* **1** [To be passionately devoted] adore, be in love with, care for, hold dear, choose, fancy, be enchanted by, be passionately attached to, have affection for, dote on, glorify, idolize, prize, be fascinated by, hold high, think the world of, treasure, prefer, yearn for, be fond of, admire, long for, flip over*, fall for*, be nuts about*, be crazy about*, go for*.—*Ant.* hate, detest, loathe. **2** [To express love by caresses] cherish, fondle, kiss, make love to, embrace, cling to, clasp, hug, take into one's arms, hold, pet, stroke, draw close, bring to one's side.—*Ant.* refuse, exclude, spurn. **3** [To possess a deep and abiding interest] enjoy, delight in, relish.

**loveliness** *n.* appeal, charm, beauty.

**loving** *a.* admiring, respecting, valuing, liking, fond, tender, kind, enamored, attached, devoted, appreciative, attentive, thoughtful, passionate, ardent, amiable, warm, amorous, affectionate, anxious, concerned, sentimental, earnest, benevolent, cordial, caring, considerate, loyal, generous.

**low** *a.* **1** [Close to the earth] squat, flat, level, low-lying, prostrate, crouched, below, not far above the horizon, low-hanging, knee-high, beneath, under, depressed, sunken, nether, inferior, lying under.—*Ant.* high, lofty, elevated. **2** [Far down on a scale] muffled, hushed, quiet. **3** [Low in spirits] dejected, moody, blue. **4** [Vulgar] base, mean, coarse. **5** [Faint] ill, dizzy, feeble. **6** [Simple] economical, moderate, inexpensive. **—lay low** bring to ruin, overcome, kill. **—lie low** wait, conceal oneself, take cover.

**loyalty** *n.* allegiance, faithfulness, fidelity, trustworthiness, constancy, integrity, attachment, sincerity, adherence, bond, tie, honor, reliability, good faith, conscientiousness, dependability, devotedness, support, zeal, ardor, earnestness, resolution, obedience, duty, honesty, truthfulness.—*Ant.* dishonesty, disloyalty, faithlessness.

**lucky** *a.* **1** [Enjoying good luck] blessed, wealthy, victorious, happy, favored, winning, in luck, successful, prosperous. **2** [Supposed to bring good luck] providential, propitious, auspicious.

**lucrative** *a.* fruitful, productive, profitable.

**ludicrous** *a.* comical, odd, farcical.

**lukewarm** *a.* cool, tepid, room-temperature.

**lump** *n.* handful, protuberance, bunch, bump, hump, block, bulk, chunk, piece, portion, section.

**lure** *n.* bait, decoy, fake.

**lure** *v.* enchant, bewitch, allure.

**lush** *a.* **1** [Green] verdant, dense, grassy. **2** [Delicious] rich, juicy, succulent. **3** [Elaborate] extensive, luxurious, ornamental.

**luxury** *n.* **1** [Indulgence of the senses, regardless of the cost] gratification, costliness, expensiveness, richness, idleness, leisure, high living, lavishness.—*Ant.* poverty, poorness, lack. **2** [An indulgence beyond one's means] extravagance, exorbitance, wastefulness.

**lyrical** *a.* melodious, sweet, musical.

# M

**mad** *a.* **1** [Insane] demented, deranged, psychotic. **2** [Angry] provoked, enraged, exasperated.

**magazine** *n.* publication, broadside, pamphlet, booklet, manual, circular, journal, periodical, weekly, monthly, quarterly, annual, bulletin, transactions, review, supplement, gazette, report, brochure, pulp, zine, glossy*, slick*.

**magic** *a.* magical, mystic, diabolic, Satanic, necromantic, fiendish, demoniac, malevolent, shamanist, voodooistic, conjuring, spellbinding, enchanting, fascinating, cryptic, transcendental, supernatural, alchemistic, spooky, ghostly, haunted, weird, uncanny, eerie, disembodied, immaterial, astral, spiritualistic, psychic, supersensory, otherworldly, fairylike, mythical, mythic, charmed, enchanted, bewitched, entranced, spellbound, under a spell, cursed, prophetic, telepathic, clairvoyant, telekinetic, parapsychological.

**magic** *n.* **1** [The controlling of supernatural powers] occultism, legerdemain, necromancy, incantation, spell, wizardry, alchemy, superstition, enchantment, sorcery, prophecy, divination, astrology, taboo, witchcraft, black magic, voodooism, fire worship. **2** [An example of magic] incantation, prediction, soothsaying, fortunetelling, foreboding, exorcism, ghost dance.

**magician** *n.* enchanter, necromancer, conjurer, seer, soothsayer, diviner, sorcerer, sorceress, witch, wizard, warlock, medicine man, shaman, exorcist.

**magnificence** *n.* grandeur, majesty, stateliness, nobleness, glory, radiance, grace, beauty, style, flourish, luxuriousness, glitter, nobility, greatness, lavishness, brilliance, splendor, richness, pomp, swank*.—*Ant.* dullness, simplicity, unostentatiousness.

**magnitude** *n.* **1** [Size] extent, breadth, dimension. **2** [Importance] greatness, consequence, significance.

**maim** *v.* mutilate, disable, disfigure.

**main** *a.* **1** [Principal] chief, dominant, first, authoritative, significant, most important, superior, foremost, leading. **2** [Only] utter, pure, simple.

**maintain** *v.* **1** [To uphold] hold up, advance, keep. **2** [To assert] state, affirm, attest. **3** [To keep ready for use] preserve, keep, conserve, repair, withhold, renew, reserve, defer, hold back, have in store, care for, save, put away, set aside, store up, keep for, lay aside, lay away, set by, keep on hand, keep in reserve, set apart, keep up, keep aside, control, hold over, manage, direct, have, own, sustain, secure, stick to, stand by.—*Ant.* waste, neglect, consume. **4** [To continue] carry on, persevere, keep on. **5** [To support] provide for, take care of, keep.

**majesty** *n.* **1** [Grandeur] nobility, illustriousness, greatness. **2** [A form of address; *usually capital*] Lord, King, Emperor, Prince, Royal Highness, Highness, Sire, Eminence, Queen.

**major** *a.* **1** [Greater] higher, larger, dominant, primary, upper, exceeding, extreme, ultra, over, above. **2** [Important] significant, main, influential.

**majority** *n.* **1** [The larger part] more than half, preponderance, most, best, gross, lion's share, greater number. **2** [Legal maturity] legal age, adulthood, voting age.

**make** *v.* **1** [To manufacture] construct, fabricate, assemble, fashion, compose, compile, create, effect, produce. **2** [To total] add up to, come to, equal. **3** [To create] originate, actualize, effect, generate, compose, plan, devise, construct, cause, conceive. **4** [To acquire] gain, get, secure. **5** [To force] constrain, compel, coerce. **6** [To cause] start, effect, initiate. **7** [To wage] carry on, conduct, engage in. **8** [To prepare] get ready, arrange, cook.

**make out** *v.* **1** [To understand] perceive, recognize, see. **2** [To succeed] accomplish, achieve, prosper. **3** [To see] discern, perceive, detect.

**make sense** *v.* be reasonable, be intelligible, be clear, be understandable, be logical, be coherent, articulate, add up, follow, infer, deduce, hang together*, hold water*, put two and two together, straighten out, stand to reason.

**make up** *v.* **1** [To compose] compound, combine, mingle. **2** [To constitute] comprise, belong to, go into the making of, be contained in, be an element of, be a portion of, include, consist of. **3** [To invent] fabricate, devise, fashion. **4** [To reconcile] conciliate, pacify, accommodate. **5** [To apply cosmetics] powder; apply face powder, apply lipstick, apply eye shadow, etc.; beautify, do up*, put one's face on.

**male** *a.* manlike, virile, powerful.

**male** *n.* male sex, man, he.

**malice** *n.* spite, animosity, resentment.

**malignant** *a.* **1** [Diseased] cancerous, lethal, poisonous. **2** [Harmful] deleterious, corrupt, sapping.

**manage** *v.* **1** [To direct] lead, oversee, indicate, designate, instruct, mastermind, engineer, show, disburse, distribute, execute, handle, watch, guide, supervise, conduct, engage in, officiate, pilot, steer, run, minister, regulate, administer, manipulate, superintend, preside, suggest, advocate, counsel, request, call upon, maintain, care for, take over, take care of, carry on, watch over, have in one's charge, look after, see to, run the show*, call the shots*, run a tight ship*.—*Ant.* obey, follow, take orders. **2** [To contrive] accomplish, bring about, effect. **3** [To get along] bear up, survive, get by.

**management** *n.* **1** [Direction] supervision, superintendence, government, command, guidance, conduct, organization, handling, policy, order, power, control. **2** [Those who undertake management; *usually preceded by "the"*] directors, administrators, executives.

**mandatory** *a.* compulsory, forced, obligatory.

**mangle** *v.* **1** [To mutilate] tear, lacerate, wound, injure, cripple, maim, rend, disfigure, cut, slit, butcher, slash, slice, carve, bruise. **2** [To iron with a power roller] steam press, smooth, iron.

**mania** *n.* craze, lunacy, madness.

**man-made** *a.* manufactured, artificial, synthetic, unnatural, counterfeit, not organic, ersatz, false, faux, not genuine.

**mannerism** *n.* idiosyncrasy, pretension, peculiarity.

**manual** *a.* hand-operated, not automatic, standard.

**manufacturing** *n.* fabrication, building, construction, assembling, preparing for market, putting in production, continuing production, keeping in production, forging, formation, erection, composition, accomplishment, completion, finishing, doing, turning out.—*Ant.* destruction, wreck, demolition.

**many** *a.* numerous, multiplied, manifold, multitudinous, multifarious, diverse, sundry, profuse, innumerable, not a few, numberless, a world of, countless, uncounted, alive with, teeming, in heaps, several, of every description, prevalent, no end of, no end to, everywhere, crowded, common, usual, plentiful, abundant, galore.—*Ant.* few, meager, scanty.

**many** *n.* a great number, abundance, thousands*. —**a good** (or **great**) **many** a great number, abundance, thousands*. —**as many** (**as**) as much as, an equal number, a similar amount.

**march** *n.* **1** [The act of marching] progression, movement, advancing, advancement, countermarch, goose step, military parade. **2** [The distance or route marched] walk, trek, hike. **3** [Music for marching] martial music, wedding march, processional. —**on the march** proceeding, advancing, tramping.

**march** *v.* move, advance, step out, go on, proceed, step, tread, tramp, patrol, prowl, parade, goose-step, file, range, strut, progress, go ahead, forge ahead.—*Ant.* pause, halt, retreat.

**marital** *a.* conjugal, connubial, nuptial.

**maritime** *a.* naval, marine, oceanic, seagoing, hydrographic, seafaring, aquatic, natatorial, Neptunian, nautical.

**mark** *n.* **1** [The physical result of marking] brand, stamp, blaze, imprint, impression, line, trace, check, stroke, streak, dot, point, nick.

**2** [A target] butt, prey, bull's-eye. **3** [Effect] manifestation, consequence, value. **—hit the mark** achieve, accomplish, do well. **—make one's mark** accomplish, prosper, become famous. **—miss the mark** be unsuccessful, err, fail.

**mark** *v.* **1** [To make a mark] brand, stamp, imprint, blaze, print, check, chalk, label, sign, identify, check off, trace, stroke, streak, dot, point, nick, x, underline. **2** [To designate] earmark, point out, stake out, indicate, check off, mark off, signify, denote. **3** [To distinguish] characterize, signalize, qualify. **4** [To put prices upon] ticket, label, tag.

**market** *n.* **1** [A place devoted to sale] trading post, mart, shopping mall, mall, shopping center, emporium, exchange, city market, public market, supermarket, meat market, fish market, stock market, stock exchange, fair, dime store, drug store, discount store, department store, variety store, bazaar, warehouse, business, delicatessen. **2** [The state of trade] supply and demand, sale, run. **—be in the market (for)** want to buy, be willing to purchase, need. **—on the market** salable, ready for purchase, available.

**marriage** *n.* wedding, espousal, spousal, nuptials, pledging, mating, matrimony, conjugality, union, match, wedlock, wedded state, wedded bliss, holy matrimony.

**marry** *v.* **1** [To take a spouse] wed, espouse, enter the matrimonial state, take wedding vows, pledge in marriage, mate, lead to the altar, tie the knot*, get hitched*, get hooked*.—*Ant.* divorce, separate, reject. **2** [To join in wedlock] unite, give, join in matrimony, pronounce man and wife.—*Ant.* divorce, annul, separate.

**martial** *a.* warlike, soldierly, combative.

**mash** *v.* crush, bruise, squash, chew, masticate, smash, pound, reduce, squeeze, brew, pulverize.

**mass** *n.* **1** [A body of matter] lump, bulk, piece, portion, section, batch, block, body, core, clot, coagulation, wad*, gob*. **2** [A considerable quantity] heap, volume, crowd. **3** [Size] magnitude, volume, span.

**master** *n.* **1** [One who directs others] chief, director, boss. **2** [A teacher] instructor, preceptor, mentor. **3** [One who possesses great skill] genius, maestro, sage, scientist, past master, champion, prima donna, connoisseur, fellow, doctor.—*Ant.* disciple, beginner, undergraduate.

**masterful** *a.* commanding, expert, skillful.

**match** *n.* **1** [An instrument to produce fire] safety match, sulphur match, matchstick, fuse. **2** [An article that is like another] peer, equivalent, mate, analogue, counterpart, approximation. **3** [A formal contest] race, event, rivalry.

**match** *v.* **1** [To find or make equals] equalize, liken, equate, make equal, pair, coordinate, level, even, match up, balance, mate, marry, unite. **2** [To be alike] harmonize, suit, be twins, be counterparts, be doubles, check with, go together, go with, rhyme with, take after.—*Ant.* differ, be unlike, bear no resemblance. **3** [To meet in contest] equal, meet, compete with.

**material** *a.* palpable, sensible, corporeal.

**material** *n.* **1** [Matter] body, corporeality, substance. **2** [Unfinished matter; *often plural*] raw material, stuff, stock, staple, ore, stockpile, crop, supply, accumulation.

**materialistic** *a.* possessive, acquisitive, opportunistic.

**materialize** *v.* be realized, take on form, become real, actualize, become concrete, metamorphose, reintegrate.—*Ant.* dissolve, disintegrate, disperse.

**matter** *n.* **1** [Substance] body, material, substantiality, corporeality, constituents, stuff, object, thing, physical world.—*Ant.* nothing, nothingness, immateriality. **2** [Subject] interest, focus, resolution. **3** [An affair] undertaking, circumstance, concern. **—as a matter of fact** in fact, in actuality, truly. **—for that matter** in regard to that, as far as that is concerned, concerning that. **—no matter** it does not matter, it is of no concern, regardless of.

**matter-of-fact** *a.* objective, prosaic, feasible.

**mature** *a.* full-grown, middle-aged, grown, grown-up, of age, in full bloom, womanly, manly, matronly, developed, prepared, settled, cultivated, cultured, sophisticated.—*Ant.* young, adolescent, immature.

**maxim** *n.* aphorism, adage, saying.

**maximum** *n.* supremacy, height, pinnacle, preeminence, culmination, matchlessness, preponderance, apex, peak, greatest number, highest degree, summit.—*Ant.* minimum, foot, bottom.

**meadow** *n.* grass, pasture, mountain meadow, upland pasture, meadow land, bottom land, bottoms, pasturage; hay meadow, clover meadow, bluegrass meadow, etc.; salt marsh, steppe, heath, pampa, savanna.

**meager** *a.* lank, lanky, gaunt, starved, emaciated, lean, bony, slender, slim, spare, little, bare, scant, stinted, lacking, wanting, scrawny, withered, lithe, narrow, tenuous, slightly-made, skinny.—*Ant.* fat, plump, stout.

**mean** *a.* **1** [Small-minded] base, low, debased. **2** [Of low estate] servile, pitiful, shabby. **3** [Vicious] shameless, dishonorable, degraded, contemptible, evil, infamous, treacherous, crooked, fraudulent, faithless, unfaithful, ill-tempered, dangerous, despicable, degenerate, knavish, unscrupulous, hard as nails. **4** [Average] mediocre, middling, halfway.

**mean** *n.* middle, median, midpoint.

**mean** *v.* **1** [To have as meaning] indicate, spell, denote, signify, add up, determine, symbolize, imply, involve, speak of, touch on, stand for, drive at, point to, connote, suggest, express, designate, intimate, tell the meaning of, purport. **2** [To have in mind] anticipate, propose, expect. **3** [To design for] destine for, aim at, set apart.

**meander** *v.* twist and turn, roam, flow.

**meaningful** *a.* significant, essential, important.

**meaningless** *a.* vague, insignificant, trivial.

**means** *pl.n.* **1** [An instrumentality or instrumentalities] machinery, mechanism, agency, organ, channel, medium, factor, agent, power, organization. **2** [Wealth] resources, substance, property. **—by all means** of course, certainly, yes indeed. **—by any means** in any way, at all, somehow. —**by means of** with the aid of, somehow, through. —**by no (manner of) means** in no way, not possible, definitely not.

**meanwhile** *a.* meantime, during the interval, in the interim, ad interim, for the time being, until, till, up to, in the meantime, when.

**measure** *n.* **1** [A unit of measurement] dimension, capacity, weight, volume, distance, degree, quantity, area, mass, frequency, density, intensity, rapidity, speed, caliber, bulk, sum, duration, magnitude, amplitude, size, pitch, ratio, depth, scope, height, strength, breadth, amplification. **2** [Anything used as a standard] rule, test, trial, example, standard, yardstick, norm, pattern, type, model. **3** [A beat] rhythm, tempo, time, step, throb, stroke, accent, meter, cadence, tune, melody, stress, vibration, division. —**for good measure** added, as a bonus, additionally. —**take measures** take action, do things to accomplish a purpose, employ.

**measure** *v.* **1** [To apply a standard of measurement] rule, weigh, mark, lay out, grade, graduate, gauge, sound, pitch, beat, stroke, time, mark off, scale, rank, even, level, gradate, line, align, line out, regulate, portion, set a standard, average, equate, square, calibrate, block in, survey, map. **2** [To contain by measurement] hold, cover, contain.

**mechanical** *a.* **1** [Concerning machinery] engineering, production, manufacturing, tooling, tuning, implementing, fabricating, forging, machining, building, construction, constructing. **2** [Like a machine] made to a pattern, machinelike, stereotyped, standardized, without variation, unchanging, monotonous.—*Ant.* original, varied, changing. **3** [Operated by the use of machinery] power-driven, involuntary, programmed.

**meddlesome** *a.* obtrusive, interfering, officious, meddling, intrusive, impertinent, interposing, interrupting, obstructive, impeding, hindering, encumbering, curious, tampering, prying, snooping, troublesome, snoopy*, nosy*, kibitzing*, chiseling*.

**medical** *a.* healing, medicinal, curative, therapeutic, restorative, prophylactic, preventive, alleviating, medicating, pharmaceutical, sedative, narcotic, tonic, disinfectant, corrective, pathological, cathartic, health-bringing, demulcent, balsamic, emollient.—*Ant.* harmful, destructive, disease-giving.

**mediocre** *a.* average, ordinary, standard.

**meet** *v.* **1** [To come together] converge, assemble, crowd, rally, convene, collect, associate, unite, swarm, get together, enter in. **2** [To go to a place of meeting] resort, be present at, gather together, convene, congregate, muster, appear, go to the meeting.—*Ant.* leave, disperse, scatter. **3** [To touch] reach, coincide, adhere. **4** [To become acquainted] make the acquaintance of, be presented to, be introduced, present oneself, make oneself known, get next to*, get to know. **5** [To fulfill] answer, fit, suffice. **6** [To encounter] fall in with, come upon, meet by accident, come across, meet face to face, face up to, bump into, touch shoulders with, meet at every turn, engage, join issue with, battle, match, push, brush against, shove.—*Ant.* abandon, turn one's back on, leave.

**mellow** *a.* **1** [Ripe] sweet, soft, perfected. **2** [Culturally mature] cultured, fully developed, broad-minded.

**melody** *n.* **1** [The quality of being melodious] concord, unison, chime. **2** [A melodious arrangement] air, lyric, strain.

**melt** *v.* **1** [To liquefy] thaw, fuse, blend, merge, soften, flow, run, disintegrate, waste away.—*Ant.* freeze, harden, coagulate. **2** [To relent] forgive, show mercy, become lenient. **3** [To decrease] vanish, pass away, go.

**member** *n.* **1** [A person or group] constituent, charter member, active member, member in good standing, honorary member, affiliate, brother, sister, comrade, chapter, post, branch, lodge, district, county, town, township, state, country, countries, company, battalion, regiment, division. **2** [A part] portion, segment, fragment. **3** [A part of the body] organ, arm, leg.

**memorize** *v.* fix in the memory, make memorable, record, commemorate, memorialize, retain, commit to memory, imprint in one's mind, bear in mind, give word for word, get down pat*, have in one's head*, have at one's fingertips*, learn by heart.—*Ant.* neglect, forget, fail to remember.

**menacing** *a.* imminent, impending, threatening.

**mend** *v.* **1** [To repair] heal, patch, fix. **2** [To improve] aid, remedy, cure.

**menial** *a.* common, servile, abject.

**mention** *v.* notice, specify, cite, introduce, state, declare, quote, refer to, discuss, touch on, instance, intimate, notify, communicate, suggest, make known, point out, speak of, throw out, toss off.—*Ant.* overlook, take no notice of, disregard.

**merchandise** *n.* wares, commodities, stock.

**merchandise** *v.* market, distribute, sell.

**merchant** *n.* trader, storekeeper, retailer, shopkeeper, wholesaler, exporter, shipper, dealer, jobber, tradesman.

**mercy** *n.* leniency, soft-heartedness, mildness, clemency, tenderness, gentleness, compassion.—*Ant.* indifference, intolerance, selfishness. **—at the mercy of** in the power of, vulnerable to, controlled by.

**merit** *n.* **1** [Worth] credit, benefit, advantage. **2** [A creditable quality] worthiness, excellence, honor.

**mess** *n.* **1** [A mixture] combination, compound, blend. **2** [A confusion] jumble, muss, chaos, clutter, clog, congestion, snag, scramble, complexity, mayhem, hodgepodge.

**metallic** *a.* **1** [Made of metal] hard, rocklike, iron, leaden, silvery, golden, metallurgic, mineral, geologic. **2** [Suggestive of metal; *said especially of sound*] ringing, resounding, resonant, bell-like, clanging.

**metaphorical** *a.* symbolical, allegorical, figurative.

**method** *n.* mode, style, standard procedure, fashion, way, means, process, proceeding, adjustment, disposition, practice, routine, technique, attack, mode of operation, manner of working, ways and means, habit, custom, manner, formula, course, rule.

**methodical** *a.* well-regulated, systematic, exact.

**microphone** *n.* sound transmitter, receiver, pickup instrument, mike*, bug*, wire*, walkie-talkie.

**middle** *a.* mean, midway, medial, average, equidistant.

**middle** *n.* mean, focus, core, nucleus, heart, navel, midst, marrow, pivot, axis, medium, midpoint.

**midnight** *n.* dead of night, stroke of midnight, twelve midnight, noon of night, witching hour. —**burn the midnight oil** stay up late, work late, keep late hours.

**mighty** *a.* **1** [Strong] powerful, stalwart, muscular. **2** [Powerful through influence] great, all-powerful, omnipotent. **3** [Imposing] great, extensive, impressive, gigantic, magnificent, towering, dynamic, notable, extraordinary, grand, considerable, monumental, tremendous.—*Ant.* plain, unimpressive, ordinary. **4** [*To a high degree] exceedingly, greatly, extremely.

**migrate** *v.* move, emigrate, immigrate.

**mild** *a.* **1** [Gentle; *said especially of persons*] meek, easygoing, patient. **2** [Temperate; *said especially of weather*] bland, untroubled, tropical, peaceful, summery, tepid, cool, balmy, breezy, gentle, soft, lukewarm, clear, moderate, mellow, fine, uncloudy, sunny, warm.—*Ant.* rough, cold, stormy. **3** [Easy; *said especially of burdens or punishment*] soft, light, tempered. **4** [Not irritating] bland, soothing, soft, smooth, gentle, moderate, easy, mellow, delicate, temperate.

**militant** *a.* combative, belligerent, aggressive.

**milky** *a.* opaque, pearly, cloudy.

**mind** *n.* **1** [Intellectual potentiality] soul, spirit, intellect, brain, consciousness, thought, mentality, intuition, perception, conception, intelligence, intellectuality, capacity, judgment, understanding, wisdom, genius, talent, reasoning, instinct, wit, mental faculties, intellectual faculties, creativity, ingenuity, intellectual powers, gray matter*, brainpower. **2** [Purpose] intention, inclination, determination. —**bear** (or **keep**) **in mind** heed, recollect, recall. —**be in one's right mind** be mentally well, be rational, be sane. —**be of one mind** have the same opinion, concur, be in accord. —**call to mind** recall, recollect, bring to mind. —**change one's mind** alter one's opinion, change one's views, decide against, modify one's ideas. —**give someone a piece of one's mind** rebuke, confute, criticize. —**have a good mind to** be inclined to, propose, tend to. —**have half a mind to** be inclined to, propose, tend to. —**have in mind** **1** recall, recollect, think of. **2** purpose, propose, be inclined to. —**know one's own mind** know oneself, be deliberate, have a plan. —**make up one's mind** form a definite opinion, choose, finalize. —**meeting of the minds** concurrence, unity, harmony. —**on one's mind** occupying one's thoughts, causing concern, worrying one. —**out of one's mind** mentally ill, raving, mad. —**take one's mind off** turn one's attention from, divert, change.

**mind** *v.* **1** [To obey] be under the authority of, heed, do as told. **2** [To give one's attention] heed, regard, be attentive to. **3** [To be careful] tend, watch out for, take care, be wary, be concerned for, mind one's *p's* and *q's**.—*Ant.* neglect, ignore, be careless. **4** [*To remember] recollect, recall, bring to mind. **5** [To object to] complain, deplore, be opposed to.

**mindful** *a.* attentive, heedful, watchful.

**mindless** *a.* **1** [Careless] inattentive, oblivious, neglectful. **2** [Stupid] foolish, senseless, unintelligent.

**mingle** *v.* combine, blend, merge.

**miniature** *a.* diminutive, small, tiny.

**minimum** *n.* smallest, least, lowest, narrowest, atom, molecule, particle, dot, jot, iota, spark, shadow, gleam, grain, scruple.

**minor** *a.* secondary, lesser, insignificant.

**miraculous** *a.* **1** [Caused by divine intervention] supernatural, marvelous, superhuman, beyond understanding, phenomenal, unimaginable, stupendous, awesome.—*Ant.* natural, familiar, imaginable. **2** [So unusual as to suggest a miracle] extraordinary, freakish, wondrous.

**mirage** *n.* phantasm, delusion, hallucination.

**misbehave** *v.* do wrong, sin, fail, trip, blunder, offend, trespass, behave badly, misdo, err, lapse, be delinquent, be at fault, be culpable, be guilty, be bad, forget oneself, be dissolute, be indecorous, carry on*, be naughty, go astray, sow one's wild oats*, cut up*.—*Ant.* behave, be good, do well.

**miscellaneous** *a.* **1** [Lacking unity] diverse, disparate, unmatched. **2** [Lacking order] mixed, muddled, scattered.

**mischief** *n.* troublesomeness, harmfulness, prankishness, playfulness, acting like a brat, impishness, misbehavior, misconduct, fault, transgression, wrongdoing, misdoing, naughtiness, mischiefmaking, friskiness.—*Ant.* dignity, demureness, sedateness.

**miser** *n.* extortioner, usurer, misanthropist, stingy person, skinflint, Scrooge, money-grubber.—*Ant.* beggar, spendthrift, waster.

**miserly** *a.* covetous, parsimonious, closefisted.

**mislead** *v.* delude, cheat, defraud, bilk, take in, outwit, trick, entangle, advice badly, victimize, lure, beguile, hoax, dupe, bait, misrepresent, bluff, give a bum steer*, throw off the scent*, bamboozle, hoodwink, put on*.

**misplace** *v.* mislay, displace, shuffle, disarrange, remove, disturb, take out of its place, disorder, tumble, confuse, mix, scatter, unsettle, muss, disorganize.—*Ant.* find, locate, place.

**miss** *v.* **1** [To feel a want] desire, crave, yearn. **2** [To fail to catch] snatch at, drop, fumble, have butterfingers*, muff*, boot*.—*Ant.* catch, grab, hold. **3** [To fail to hit] miss one's aim, miss the mark, be wide of the mark, overshoot, undershoot, fan the air*.—*Ant.* hit, shoot, get.

**mist** *n.* rain, haze, fog.

**mistake** *n.* **1** [A blunder] false step, blunder, slip, error, omission, failure, confusion, wrongdoing, sin, crime, goof*. **2** [A misunderstanding] misapprehension, confusion, muddle, misconception, delusion, illusion, overestimation, underestimation, impression, confounding, misinterpretation, perversion, perplexity, bewilderment, misjudgment.—*Ant.* knowledge, certainty, interpretation.

**mistake** *v.* err, blunder, slip, lapse, miss, overlook, omit, underestimate, overestimate, substitute, misjudge, misapprehend, misconceive, misunderstand, confound, misinterpret, confuse, botch, bungle, have the wrong impression, tangle, snarl, slip up, make a mess of*, miss the boat*.—*Ant.* succeed, be accurate, explain.

**mistreat** *v.* harm, injure, wrong.

**misunderstand** *v.* err, misconceive, misinterpret, miscomprehend, misjudge, miscalculate, misconstrue, be perplexed, be bewildered, confuse, confound, have the wrong impression, fail to understand, misapprehend, overestimate, underestimate, be misled, be unfamiliar with, have the wrong slant on*, not register.—*Ant.* understand, grasp, apprehend.

**mix** *v.* **1** [To blend] fuse, merge, coalesce, brew, unite, combine, cross, interbreed, amalgamate, incorporate, alloy, mingle, compound, intermingle, weave, interweave, throw together, adulterate, infiltrate, twine, knead, stir, suffuse, instill, transfuse, synthesize, stir around, infuse, saturate, dye, season. **2** [To confuse] mix up, jumble, tangle. **3** [To associate] fraternize, get along, consort with.

**mixture** *n.* **1** [A combination] blend, compound, composite, amalgam, miscellany, mishmash, mingling, medley, mix, potpourri, alloy, fusion, jumble, brew, merger, hybrid, crossing, infiltration, transfusion, infusion, mélange, saturation, assimilation, incorporation, hodgepodge. **2** [A mess] mix-up, muddle, disorder.

**mob** *n.* **1** [A disorderly crowd of people] swarm, rabble, throng, press, multitude, populace, horde, riot, host, lawless element. **2** [The lower classes] bourgeoisie, plebeians, proletariat.

**mobilize** *v.* assemble, prepare, gather.

**model** *n.* **1** [A person worthy of imitation] archetype, prototype, exemplar, paradigm, ideal, good man, good woman, good example, role model, hero, demigod, saint. **2** [Anything that serves as a copy] original, text, guide, copy, tracing, facsimile, duplicate, pattern, design, gauge, ideal, shape, form, specimen, mold, principle, basis, standard, sketch, painting, precedent, archetype, prototype. **3** [A duplicate on a small scale] miniature, image, illustration, representation, reduction, statue, figure, figurine, effigy, mock-up, skeleton, portrait, photograph, relief, print, engraving. **4** [One who poses professionally] poser, sitter, mannequin.

**model** *v.* **1** [To form] shape, mold, fashion. **2** [To imitate a model] trace, duplicate, sketch, reduce, represent, print, counterfeit, caricature, parody. **3** [To serve as a model] sit, act as model, set an example. **4** [To demonstrate] show off, wear, parade in.

**moderate** *a.* **1** [Not expensive] inexpensive, low-priced, reasonable. **2** [Not violent] modest, cool, tranquil. **3** [Not radical] tolerant, judicious, nonpartisan, liberal, middle-of-the-road, unopinionated, not given to extremes, measured, low-key, evenly balanced, neutral, impartial, straight, midway, in the mean, average, restrained, sound, cautious, considered, considerate, respectable, middle-class, compromising.—*Ant.* radical, unbalanced, partial. **4** [Not intemperate] pleasant, gentle, soft, balmy, inexcessive, tepid, easy, not rigorous, not severe, temperate, favorable, tolerable, bearable, tame, untroubled, unruffled, monotonous, even.—*Ant.* severe, rigorous, bitter. **5** [Not indulgent] sparing, frugal, regulated, self-denying, abstinent, non-indulgent, self-controlled, disciplined, careful, on the wagon*, sworn off*, teetotalling.—*Ant.* wasteful, excessive, self-indulgent.

**moderate** *v.* abate, modify, decline.

**modern** *a.* **1** [Up-to-date] stylish, modish, chic, smart, up-to-the-minute, late, current, recent, of the present, prevailing, prevalent, avant-garde, present-day, latest, most recent, advanced, streamlined, breaking with tradition, new, newest, untraditional, contemporary, in vogue, in use, common, newfangled, cool*, sharp*, smooth*, just out, mod*.—*Ant.* old-fashioned, out-of-date, out-of-style. **2** [Having the comforts of modern life] modernistic, modernized, renovated, functional, with modern conveniences, done over, having modern improvements, high-tech. **3** [Concerning recent times] contemporary, contemporaneous, recent, concurrent, present-day, coincident, twentieth-century, twenty-first-century, latter-day, mechanical, of the Machine Age, of the Computer Age, automated, of modern times, modernist.—*Ant.* old, medieval, primordial.

**modest** *a.* **1** [Humble] unassuming, meek, diffident. **2** [Not showy] unpretentious, plain, unostentatious, unobtrusive, demure, quiet, seemly, proper, decorous, simple, natural, unassuming, humble, tasteful, unadorned, unaffected, homely. **3** [Moderate] reasonable, inexpensive, average. **4** [Proper] pure, chaste, seemly. **5** [Lowly] plain, simple, unaffected.

**modesty** *n.* **1** [The attitude that leads one to make a modest self-estimate] humility, delicacy, reticence, constraint, unobtrusiveness, meekness.—*Ant.* vanity, conceit, egotism. **2** [Shyness] inhibition, timidity, diffidence. **3** [Chastity] decency, innocence, celibacy.

**modification** *n.* alteration, correction, adjustment.

**modify** *v.* **1** [To change] alter, modify, vary. **2** [To moderate] mitigate, restrain, curb.

**moisten** *v.* sprinkle, dampen, saturate, drench, waterlog, steep, sog, sop, dip, rinse, wash over, wet down, water down, squirt, shower, rain on, splash, splatter, bathe, steam, spray, sponge.

**momentary** *a.* fleeting, quick, passing, flitting, flashing, transient, impermanent, shifting, ephemeral, vanishing, cursory, temporary, dreamlike, in the wink of an eye*.—*Ant.* eternal, continual, ceaseless.

**money** *n.* **1** [A medium of exchange] gold, silver, cash, currency, check, bills, notes, specie, legal tender, Almighty Dollar*, gravy*, dough*, long green*, coins*, lucre, folding money*, wad*, bucks*, hard cash*, bread*. **2** [Wealth] funds, capital, property. **3** [Pay] payment, salary, wages. **—for one's money*** for one's choice, in one's opinion, to one's mind. **—in the money*** wealthy, flush*, loaded*. **—make money** gain profits, become wealthy, earn. **—one's money's worth** full value, gain, benefit. **—put money into** invest in, support, underwrite.

**monk** *n.* hermit, religious, ascetic, solitary, recluse, abbot, prior.

**monopoly** *n.* trust, syndicate, cartel.

**monotony** *n.* invariability, likeness, tediousness, tedium, similarity, continuity, continuance, oneness, evenness, levelness, flatness, the same old thing.—*Ant.* variety, difference, variability.

**monument** *n.* **1** [Anything erected to preserve a memory] tomb, shaft, column, pillar, headstone, tombstone, gravestone, mausoleum, obelisk, shrine, statue, building, tower, monolith, tablet, slab, stone. **2** [A landmark in the history of creative work] work of art, magnum opus, permanent contribution.

**mood** *n.* **1** [A state of mind] state, condition, frame of mind, temper, humor, disposition, inclination, caprice, whim, fancy, pleasure, freak, wish, desire. **2** [A quality of mind] bent, propensity, tendency.

**moody** *a.* pensive, unhappy, low-spirited.

**moral** *a.* **1** [Characterized by conventional virtues] trustworthy, kindly, courteous, respectable, proper, scrupulous, conscientious, good, truthful, decent, just, honorable, honest, high-minded, saintly, pure, worthy, correct, seemly, aboveboard, dutiful, principled, conscientious, chaste, ethical.—*Ant.* lying, dishonest, unscrupulous. **2** [Having to do with approved relationships between the sexes] virtuous, immaculate, decent.

**morale** *n.* resolve, spirit, confidence.

**morbid** *a.* **1** [Diseased] sickly, unhealthy, ailing. **2** [Pathological] gloomy, melancholic, depressed.

**more** *a.* **1** [Additional] also, likewise, and, over and above, more than that, in addition, further, besides, added.—*Ant.* less, less than, subtracted from. **2** [Greater in quantity, amount, degree, or quality] numerous, many, exceeding, extra, expanded, increased, major, augmented, extended, enhanced, added to, larger, higher, wider, deeper, heavier, solider, stronger, above the mark.—*Ant.* weaker, lessened, decreased.

**morning** *n.* **1** [Dawn] the East, morn, daybreak, break of day, first blush of morning, daylight, cockcrow, sunup, the wee small hours*, crack of dawn*. **2** [The time before noon] forenoon, morningtide*, after midnight, before noon, breakfast time, before lunch.

**moronic** *a.* foolish, dumb*, stupid.

**mortal** *a.* **1** [Causing death] malignant, fatal, lethal. **2** [Subject to death] human, transient, temporal, passing, frail, impermanent, perishable, fading, passing away, momentary.—*Ant.* eternal, perpetual, everlasting.

**mortal** *n.* creature, being, human.

**mortality** *n.* dying, extinction, fatality.

**motel** *n.* motor inn, inn, cabins, stopping place, roadhouse, court, motor court.

**motherly** *a.* maternal, devoted, careful, watchful, kind, warm, gentle, tender, sympathetic, supporting, protective.

**motionless** *a.* **1** [Not moving] still, unmoving, dead, deathly still, inert, stock-still, stagnant, quiet.—*Ant.* moving, changing, shifting. **2** [Firm] unmovable, fixed, stationary.

**motive** *n.* cause, purpose, reason.

**motto** *n.* maxim, adage, saw, epigram, aphorism, sentiment, slogan, catchword, axiom.

**mountain** *n.* **1** [A lofty land mass] mount, elevation, peak, sierra, butte, hill, alp, range, ridge, pike, bluff, headland, volcano, crater, tableland, mesa, plateau, height, crag, precipice, cliff, earth mass.—*Ant.* valley, ravine, flatland. **2** [A pile] mass, mound, glob.

**mountainous** *a.* mountainlike, with mountains, steep, lofty, hilly, alpine, upland, elevated, volcanic, towering, craggy, cliffy, rugged.—*Ant.* low, small, flat.

**mourn** *v.* deplore, grieve, fret, sorrow, rue, regret, bemoan, sigh, long for, miss, droop, languish, yearn, pine, anguish, complain, agonize, weep, suffer, wring one's hands, be brokenhearted, be in distress, be sad.—*Ant.* celebrate, rejoice, be happy.

**mournful** *a.* sorrowful, unhappy, sad.

**move** *v.* **1** [To be in motion] go, walk, run, glide, travel, drift, budge, stir, shift, pass, cross, roll, flow, march, travel, progress, proceed, traverse, drive, ride, fly, hurry, head for, bustle, climb, crawl, scooch*, leap, hop to it*, get a move on*, get going, get cracking*.—*Ant.* stop, remain stationary, stay quiet. **2** [To set in motion] impel, actuate, propel. **3** [To arouse the emotions of] influence, stir, instigate, stimulate, touch, play on, sway, induce, rouse, prevail upon, work upon, strike a sympathetic chord.—*Ant.* quiet, lull, pacify. **4** [To take up another residence] pack up, move out, move in. **5** [To propose an action formally] suggest, introduce, submit.

**movement** *n.* **1** [The act of moving] move, transit, passage, progress, journey, advance, mobility, change, shift, alteration, ascension, descension, propulsion, flow, flux, action, flight, wandering, journeying, voyaging, migration, emigration, transplanting, evolving, shifting, changing, locomotion, drive, evolution, undertaking, regression.—*Ant.* quiet, rest, fixity. **2** [An example of movement] journey, trip, immigration, migration, march, crusade, patrol, sweep, emigration, evolution, unrest, transition, change, transfer, displacement, withdrawal, ascension, descension, progression, regression, transportation, removal, departure, shift, flight, slip, slide, step, footfall, stride, gesture, act, action, pilgrimage, expedition, locomotion. **3** [A trend] drift, tendency, bent.

**movie** *n.* moving picture, motion picture, photoplay, cinema, film, show, screenplay, feature film, cartoon, animated cartoon, serial, comedy, foreign film, travelogue, short, documentary, videotape, flick*.

**moving** *a.* **1** [In motion] going, changing, progressing, advancing, shifting, evolving, withdrawing, rising, going down, descending, ascending, getting up, traveling, journeying, on the march, moving up, starting, proceeding, flying, climbing. **2** [Going to another residence] migrating, emigrating, vacating, removing, departing, leaving, going away, changing residences. **3** [Exciting] affecting, emotional, touching.

**much** *a.* **1** [To a great degree or extent] important, weighty, notable, considerable, prominent, memorable, momentous, stirring, eventful, serious, urgent, pressing, critical, paramount, principal, leading, significant, telling, first-rate, in the front rank.—*Ant.* little, inconsiderable, trivial. **2** [In great quantity] full, many, very many, abundant, satisfying, enough, sufficient, adequate, considerable, substantial, ample, everywhere, copious, voluminous, plentiful, profuse, complete, lavish, generous, immeasurable, endless, countless, extravagant, no end*.—*Ant.* inadequate, insufficient, limited. **3** [Very] greatly, enormously, extremely.

**much** *n.* a great quantity, abundance, quantities, a great deal, riches, wealth, volume, very much, breadth, plentifulness, fullness, completeness, lavishness, lot*, lots*, quite a bit*, gobs*, thousands*, tons*, oodles*.—*Ant.* little, penury, scarcity. **—as much as** practically, virtually, in effect. **—make much of** treat with importance, expand, exaggerate. **—not much of a** inferior, mediocre, unsatisfactory.

**mud** *n.* dirt, muck, clay, mire, slush, silt, muddiness, stickiness, ooze, bog, marsh, swamp.

**muddled** *a.* uncertain, addled, confused.

**multiply** *v.* **1** [To increase] add, augment, double. **2** [To bring forth young] generate, populate, reproduce. **3** [To employ multiplication as an arithmetical process] square, cube, raise to a higher power.

**multitude** *n.* throng, drove, mob, crowd, gathering.

**mundane** *a.* normal, ordinary, everyday.

**murder** *n.* killing, homicide, death, destruction, annihilation, carnage, putting an end to, slaying, shooting, knifing, assassination, lynching, crime, felony, killing with malice aforethought, murder in the first degree, first-degree murder, contract killing, murder in the second degree, murder in the third degree, massacre, genocide, butchery, parricide, patricide, matricide, infanticide, fratricide, genocide, suicide, foul play. **—get away with murder*** escape punishment, take flight, avoid punishment.

**murderer** *n.* slayer, assassin, killer.

**murky** *a.* dim, dusky, dingy.

**murmur** *v.* **1** [To make a low, continuous sound] ripple, moan, trickle, burble, babble, tinkle, gurgle, meander, flow gently.—*Ant.* sound, peal, clang. **2** [To mutter] mumble, rumble, growl.

**muscular** *a.* brawny, powerful, husky.

**mushy** *a.* **1** [Soft] pulpy, mashy, muddy. **2** [*Sentimental] romantic, maudlin, effusive.

**musical** *a.* **1** [Having the qualities of music] tuneful, sweet, pleasing, agreeable, symphonic, lyric, mellow, vocal, choral, consonant, rhythmical.—*Ant.* harsh, tuneless, discordant. **2** [Having aptitude for music] gifted, talented, musically inclined.

**must** *v.* ought, should, have to, have got to, be compelled, be obliged, be required, be doomed, be destined, be ordered, be made, have no choice, be one's fate.

**mutiny** *n.* insurrection, revolt, revolution.

**mutter** *v.* **1** [To make a low, mumbling sound] rumble, growl, snarl. **2** [To speak as if to oneself] murmur, grunt, grumble, sputter, whisper, speak inarticulately, speak indistinctly, speak in an undertone, swallow one's words*, mumble. **3** [To complain] grumble, moan, groan.

**mutual** *a.* **1** [Reciprocal] interchangeable, two-sided, given and taken. **2** [Common] joint, shared, belonging equally to each.

**mysterious** *a.* **1** [Puzzling] enigmatic, enigmatical, strange. **2** [Concerning powers beyond those supposedly natural] mystic, occult, dark, mystifying, transcendental, spiritual, symbolic, subjective, mystical, magical, dark, veiled, strange, astrological, unknowable, unfathomable, esoteric, cryptic, oracular, unrevealed, incredible. **3** [Not generally known] obscure, hidden, ambiguous.

**mystery** *n.* **1** [The quality of being mysterious] inscrutability, occultism, cabalism. **2** [Something difficult to know] riddle, conundrum, enigma. **3** [A trick] sleight-of-hand, trick of magic, juggle.

**mystic** *a.* occult, transcendental, spiritual.

**mystify** *v.* perplex, trick, hoodwink.

**myth** *n.* fable, folk tale, legend, lore, saga, folk ballad, allegory, parable, tale.

# N

**naive** *a.* unaffected, childish, plain, artless, innocent, untrained, countrified, callow, natural, unschooled, ignorant, untaught, provincial, unsophisticated, unworldly, guileless, spontaneous, instinctive, impulsive, simple-minded, innocuous, unsuspecting, unsuspicious, harmless, gullible, credulous, trusting, original, fresh, unpolished, rude, primitive, ingenuous, sincere, open, candid, forthright, aboveboard, romantic, fanciful, unpretentious, transparent, straightforward, uncomplicated, easily imposed upon.—*Ant.* experienced, sophisticated, complicated.

**naiveté** *n.* simplicity, childishness, inexperience.

**naked** *a.* **1** [Nude] unclothed, undressed, stripped, unclad, unrobed, disrobed, leafless, hairless, bare, undraped, exposed, having nothing on, unappareled, denuded, unveiled, uncovered, uncloaked, stark naked, topless, bottomless, bald, in one's birthday suit*, in the buff, peeled*, without a stitch, in the raw. **2** [Unadorned] plain, simple, artless.

**name** *n.* **1** [A title] proper name, Christian name, given name, cognomen, appellation, designation, first name, family name, title, denomination, surname, sign, handle*. **2** [Reputation] renown, honor, repute. **3** [An epithet] nickname, pen name, pseudonym, sobriquet, stage name, nom de plume, nom de guerre, pet name, fictitious name, alias. **4** [A famous person] star, hero, celebrity. **—call names** swear at, insult, slander. **—in one's name** belonging to one, in one's possession, possessed by. **—in the name of** by authority of, in reference to, as representative of.

**name** *v.* **1** [To give a name] call, christen, baptize, style, term, label, identify, designate, classify, denominate, title, entitle, nickname, characterize, label, ticket, dub*. **2** [To indicate by name] refer to, specify, signify, denote, single out, mark, suggest, connote, point to, note, remark, index, list, cite, mention. **3** [To appoint] elect, nominate, select.

**narrow** *a.* **1** [Lacking breadth] close, cramped, tight, confined, shrunken, compressed, slender, thin, fine, linear, threadlike, tapering, tapered, slim, scant, scanty, lanky, small, meager.—*Ant.* broad, wide, extensive. **2** [Lacking tolerance] dogmatic, narrow-minded, parochial. **3** [Lacking a comfortable margin] close, near, precarious.

**narrow-minded** *a.* bigoted, biased, provincial.

**nation** *n.* **1** [An organized state] realm, country, commonwealth, republic, democracy, state, monarchy, dominion, body politic, land, domain, empire, kingdom, principality, sovereignty, colony. **2** [A people having some unity] populace, community, public.

**native** *a.* **1** [Natural] innate, inherent, inborn, implanted, inbred, ingrained, congenital, fundamental, hereditary, inherited, essential, constitutional.—*Ant.* unnatural, foreign, alien. **2** [Characteristic of a region] aboriginal, indigenous, original, primitive, primary, primeval, vernacular, domestic, local, found locally.—*Ant.* imported, brought in, transplanted.

**natural** *a.* **1** [Rooted in nature] intrinsic, original, essential, true, fundamental, inborn, ingrained, inherent, instinctive, implanted, innate, inbred, incarnate, subjective, inherited, congenital, genetic.—*Ant.* foreign, alien, acquired. **2** [To be expected] normal, typical, characteristic, usual, customary, habitual, accustomed, involuntary, spontaneous, uncontrolled, uncontrollable, familiar, common, universal, prevailing, prevalent, general, probable, uniform, constant, consistent, ordinary, logical, reasonable, anticipated, looked for, hoped for, counted on, relied on.—*Ant.* unknown, unexpected, unheard of. **3** [Not affected] ingenuous, simple, artless, innocent, unstudied, spontaneous, impulsive, childlike, unfeigned, open, frank, candid, unsophisticated, unpolished, homey, unpretentious, forthright, sincere, straightforward, being oneself, unsuspecting, credulous, trusting, plain, direct, rustic.—*Ant.* ornate, pretentious, sophisticated. **4** [Concerning the physical universe] actual, tangible, according to nature.

**naughty** *a.* wayward, disobedient, mischievous, impish, fiendish, badly behaved, roguish, bad, unmanageable, ungovernable, insubordinate, wanton, recalcitrant.

**nausea** *n.* motion sickness, queasiness, vomiting.

**nauseate** *v.* sicken, offend, disgust.

**nauseous** *a.* queasy, ill, squeamish.

**nautical** *a.* oceangoing, marine, naval, oceanic, deep-sea, aquatic, sailing, seafaring, seaworthy, seagoing, boating, yachting, cruising, whaling, oceanographic, rowing, navigating, maritime.

**navigate** *v.* pilot, steer, lie to, head out for, ride out, lay a course, operate.

**near** *a.* **1** [Not distant in space] proximate, adjacent, adjoining, neighboring, not remote, close at hand, contiguous, handy, near by, next door to, at close quarters, beside, side by side, in close proximity.—*Ant.* distant, removed, far off. **2** [Not distant in relationship] touching, close, akin. **3** [Not distant in time] at hand, approaching, next.

**nearly** *a.* all but, approximately, almost.

**neat** *a.* **1** [Clean and orderly] tidy, trim, prim, spruce, dapper, smart, correct, shipshape, methodical, regular, orderly, systematic, spotless, nice, meticulous, elegant, spick-and-span, immaculate, chic, well-groomed, exact, precise, proper, neat as a pin, in good order, spruced up.—*Ant.* disordered, messy, slovenly. **2** [Clever; *said of something done*] dexterous, deft, skillful, expert, proficient, handy, apt, ready, artful, nimble, quick, agile, adept, speedy, finished, practiced, easy, effortless.—*Ant.* awkward, clumsy, fumbling.

**necessary** *a.* important, needed, requisite, expedient, needful, indispensable, required, urgent, wanted, imperative, prerequisite, pressing, vital, fundamental, quintessential, cardinal, significant, momentous, compulsory, mandatory, basic, paramount, obligatory, essential, compelling, incumbent upon, all-important, binding, specified, unavoidable, decisive, crucial, elementary, chief, principal, prime, intrinsic, fixed, constant, permanent, inherent, ingrained, innate, without choice.

**necessity** *n.* **1** [The state of being required] need, essentiality, indispensability. **2** [That which is needed] need, want, requisite, vital part, essential, demand, imperative, fundamental, claim. **3** [The state of being forced by circumstances] exigency, pinch, stress, urgency, destitution, extremity, privation, obligation, case of life or death. **—of necessity** inevitably, importantly, surely.

**need** *n.* **1** [Poverty] want, destitution, indigence. **2** [Lack] insufficiency, shortage, inadequacy. **3** [A requirement] obligation, necessity, urgency. **—if need be** if it is required, if the occasion demands, if necessary.

**need** *v.* lack, require, feel the necessity for, be in need of, suffer privation, be in want, be destitute, be short, be inadequate, have occasion for, have use for, miss, be without, do without, be needy, be poor, be deficient, go hungry, live from hand to mouth, feel the pinch*, be down and out*, be hard up*.—*Ant.* own, have, hold.

**needless** *a.* unwanted, excessive, unnecessary.

**needy** *a.* destitute, indigent, poor.

**neglect** *n.* **1** [The act of showing indifference to a person] slight, disregard, thoughtlessness, disrespect, carelessness, scorn, oversight, heedlessness, inattention, unconcern, inconsideration, disdain, coolness. **2** [The act of neglecting duties or charges] negligence, slovenliness, neglectfulness.

**neglect** *v.* **1** [To treat with indifference] slight, scorn, overlook, disregard, disdain, detest, rebuff, affront, despise, ignore, depreciate, spurn, underestimate, undervalue, shake off, make light of, laugh off, keep one's distance, pass over, pass up, have nothing to do with, let alone, let go, not care for, pay no attention to, pay no heed, leave alone, leave well enough alone, play possum*, keep at arm's length.—*Ant.* consider, appreciate, value. **2** [To fail to attend to responsibilities] pass over, defer, procrastinate, suspend, dismiss, discard, let slip, miss, skip, omit, skimp, gloss over, be remiss, be derelict, let go, ignore, trifle, postpone, lose sight of, look the other way, let it go, not trouble oneself with, evade, be careless, be irresponsible.—*Ant.* watch, care for, attend.

**negligent** *a.* indifferent, inattentive, neglectful.

**negotiate** *v.* **1** [To make arrangements for] arrange, bargain, confer, consult, parley, transact, mediate, make peace, contract, settle, adjust, conciliate, accomodate, arbitrate, referee, umpire, compromise, bring to terms, make terms, make the best of, treat with, moderate, work out, dicker*, haggle, bury the hatchet*. **2** [To transfer] barter, allocate, transmit.

**neighbor** *n.* acquaintance, companion, associate, next-door neighbor, nearby resident.

**neighborly** *a.* sociable, hospitable, friendly.

**nervous** *a.* **1** [Excitable] sensitive, irritable, impatient, moody, peevish, restless, uneasy, impulsive, rash, hasty, reckless, touchy, readily upset, high-strung, neurotic. **2** [Excited] agitated, bothered, annoyed.

**network** *n.* **1** [System of channels] tracks, circuitry, channels, system, labyrinth, artery, arrangement. **2** [Netting] fiber, weave, mesh.

**neutral** *a.* **1** [Not fighting] noncombatant, nonpartisan, on the sidelines, nonparticipating, inactive, disengaged, uninvolved, bystanding, standing by, inert, on the fence.—*Ant.* engaged, involved, active. **2** [Without opinion] nonchalant, disinterested, impartial. **3** [Without distinctive color] drab, indeterminate, vague.

**never** *a.* not ever, at no time, not at any time, not in the least, not in any way, in no way, not at all, not under any condition, nevermore, never again, noway.

**new** *a.* **1** [Recent] current, brand-new, newborn, young, newfangled, latest, just out. **2** [Modern] modish, popular, faddish, up to the minute, contemporary, latest. **3** [Novel] unique, original, unusual. **4** [Different] unlike, dissimilar, distinct. **5** [Additional] further, increased, supplementary. **6** [Inexperienced] unseasoned, unskilled, untrained. **7** [Recently] newly, freshly, lately.

**news** *n.* **1** [Information] intelligence, tidings, advice, discovery, recognition, the scoop*, the goods*, headlines, front-page news. **2** [A specific report] telling, narration, recital, account, description, message, copy, communication, release, communiqué, telegram, cable, radiogram, broadcast, telecast, bulletin, dispatch, news story, scoop*, big news, eye opener*. **—make news** become famous, accomplish, create events.

**next** *a.* **1** [Following in order] succeeding, later, afterwards, presently, resulting, subsequent, ensuing. **2** [Adjacent] beside, close, alongside, on one side, on the side, adjoining, neighboring, meeting, touching, bordering on, cheek by jowl, side by side, attached, abutting, back to back, to the left, to the right.

**nice** *a.* **1** [Approved] likable, superior, admirable. **2** [Behaving in a becoming manner] pleasing, agreeable, winning, refined, cultured, amiable, delightful, charming, inviting, pleasant, cordial, courteous, considerate, kind, kindly, helpful, gracious, obliging, genial, gentle, becoming, unassuming, modest, demure.—*Ant.* rude, indecorous, crude.

**night** *n.* **1** [The diurnal dark period] after dark, evening, from dusk to dawn, nightfall, after nightfall, twilight, nighttime, bedtime, midnight, before dawn, the dark hours, dead of night. **2** [The dark] blackness, duskiness, gloom.

**nobility** *n.* [*Usually used with "the"*] ruling class, gentry, aristocracy.

**noble** *a.* **1** [Possessing an exalted mind and character] generous, princely, magnanimous, magnificent, courtly, lofty, elevated, splendid, excellent, supreme, eminent, lordly, dignified, great, good, superior, great-hearted, high-minded, honorable, distinguished, liberal, tolerant, gracious, humane, benevolent, charitable, sympathetic, bounteous, brilliant, extraordinary, remarkable, devoted, heroic, resolute, valorous.—*Ant.* corrupt, low, ignoble. **2** [Possessing excellent qualities or properties] meritorious, virtuous, worthy, valuable, useful, first-rate, refined, cultivated, chivalrous, trustworthy, candid, liberal, gracious, princely, magnanimous, generous, sincere, truthful, constant, faithful, upright, honest, warmhearted, true, incorruptible, distinctive, reputable, respectable, admirable, good, aboveboard, fair, just, estimable.—*Ant.* poor, inferior, second-rate. **3** [Belonging to the nobility] titled, aristocratic, patrician, highborn, wellborn, blue-blooded, of gentle birth, imperial, lordly, highbred, princely, of good breed, kingly.—*Ant.* common, plebeian, lowborn. **4** [Grand] stately, impressive, imposing.

**nod** *v.* **1** [To make a nodding movement] assent, sign, signal, greet, bend, curtsy, incline the head, bow, nod yes, acquiesce, consent, respond, fall in with, concur, acknowledge, recognize.—*Ant.* deny, dissent, disagree. **2** [To become sleepy or inattentive] drowse, nap, drift off.

**noise** *n.* **1** [A sound] sound, something heard, impact of sound waves. **2** [Clamor] racket, fracas, din.

**noiseless** *a.* **1** [Containing no noise] silent, still, soundless. **2** [Making no noise] voiceless, speechless, wordless.

**noisy** *a.* clamorous, vociferous, boisterous.

**nomad** *n.* wanderer, migrant, vagabond.

**nominal** *a.* professed, pretended, in name only.

**nonchalant** *a.* **1** [Cool and casual] uncaring, unconcerned, untroubled, apathetic, cold, frigid, unfeeling, impassive, imperturbable, easygoing, listless, lackadaisical, unruffled, lukewarm, composed, collected, aloof, detached, calm, serene, placid, disinterested, easy, effortless, light, smooth, neutral.—*Ant.* warm, ardent, enthusiastic. **2** [Careless] negligent, neglectful, trifling.

**nonconformist** *n.* rebel, eccentric, maverick, malcontent, dissenter, demonstrator, beatnik, hippie, protester, dissident.

**none** *pron.* **1** [No person] no one, not one, not anyone, no one at all, not a person, not a soul, neither one nor the other.—*Ant.* many, some, a few. **2** [No thing] not a thing, not anything, not any.

**nonpartisan** *a.* unprejudiced, unbiased, independent.

**nonsense** *n.* **1** [Matter that has no meaning] balderdash, rubbish, trash, scrawl, inanity, senselessness, buncombe, idle chatter, prattle, rant, bombast, claptrap, bull*, baloney*, hooey*, bunk*, poppycock*, guff*, hot air*. **2** [Frivolous behavior] unsteadiness, flightiness, stupidity, thoughtlessness, fickleness, foolishness, giddiness, rashness, infatuation, extravagance, imprudence, madness, irrationality, senselessness, inconsistency, shallowness.—*Ant.* consideration, steadiness, thoughtfulness. **3** [Pure fun] absurdity, jest, joke.

**no one** *pron.* not one, nobody, none.

**normal** *a.* **1** [Usual] ordinary, run-of-the-mill, typical. **2** [Regular] routine, orderly, methodical. **3** [Sane] lucid, right-minded, rational. **4** [Showing no abnormal bodily condition] whole, sound, healthy.

**normality** *n.* **1** [Mediocrity] ordinariness, uniformity, commonness. **2** [Sanity] normalcy, mental balance, reason.

**nose** *n.* **1** [The organ of smell] nasal organ, nasal cavity, nares, nasal passages, nostrils, olfactory nerves, snoot*, schnoz*, beak, bill. **2** [A projection] snout, nozzle, muzzle. **—by a nose** by a very small margin, too close for comfort, barely. **—look down one's nose at*** disdain, snub, be disgusted by. **—on the nose*** precisely, to the point, correctly. **—turn up one's nose at** sneer at, refuse, scorn. **—under one's very nose** in plain sight, visible, at one's fingertips.

**nostalgic** *a.* lonesome, sentimental, homesick.

**nosy** *a.* snooping*, curious, inquisitive.

**note** *n.* **1** [A representation] sign, figure, mark. **2** [A brief record] notation, jotting, scribble, reminder, scrawl, annotation, agenda, entry, memorandum, journal, inscription, calendar, diary. **3** [A brief communication] dispatch, epistle, letter. **4** [A musical tone, or its symbol] tone, key, scale, interval, degree, step, sharp, flat, natural.

**note** *v.* **1** [To notice] remark, heed, perceive. **2** [To record] write down, enter, transcribe.

**noted** *a.* well-known, celebrated, famous.

**notes** *pl.n.* commentary, interpretation, explanation, findings, recordings, field notes, observations. **—compare notes** exchange views, confer, go over. **—take notes** write down, keep a record, enter.

**nothing** *n.* not anything, no thing, trifle, blank, emptiness, nothingness, nonexistence, inexistence, nonbeing, nullity, zero, extinction, oblivion, obliteration, annihilation, nonentity, neither hide nor hair. **—for nothing** **1** gratis, without cost, unencumbered. **2** in vain, for naught, emptily. **—in nothing flat*** in almost no time at all, speedily, rapidly. **—think nothing of** minimize, underplay, disregard.

**notice** *v.* mark, remark, see.

**noticeable** *a.* observable, conspicuous, obvious.

**notify** *v.* declare, announce, inform.

**novelty** *n.* **1** [The quality of being novel] modernity, freshness, originality. **2** [Something popular because it is new] innovation, creation, fad.

**now** *a.* **1** [At the present] at this time, right now, at the moment, just now, momentarily, this day, these days, here and now. **2** [In the immediate future] promptly, in a moment, in a minute. **3** [Immediately] at once, forthwith, instantly.

**nucleus** *n.* **1** [Essence] core, gist, kernel. **2** [Center] hub, focus, pivot.

**nude** *a.* unclothed, bare, naked.

**nudity** *n.* bareness, undress, nakedness.

**nuisance** *n.* **1** [A bother] annoyance, vexation, bore. **2** [An offense against the public] breach, infraction, affront. **3** [An unpleasant or unwelcome person] problem child, frump, bother, holy terror*, bad egg*, insect*, louse*, pain in the neck*, poor excuse*, bum*.

**numb** *a.* **1** [Insensible] deadened, dead, unfeeling, numbed, asleep, senseless, anesthetized, comatose. **2** [Insensitive] apathetic, lethargic, phlegmatic.

**numbness** *n.* deadness, anesthesia, dullness, insensitivity, insensibility, paralysis, loss of sensation.

**numerical** *a.* arithmetical, statistical, fractional, exponential, logarithmic, differential, integral, digital, mathematical, binary.

# O

**oath** *n.* **1** [An attestation of the truth] affirmation, declaration, affidavit, vow, sworn statement, testimony, word, contract, pledge.—*Ant.* denial, disavowal, lie. **2** [The name of the Lord taken in vain] malediction, swearword, blasphemy.

**obedient** *a.* **1** [Dutiful] loyal, law-abiding, governable, resigned, devoted, respectful, controllable, attentive, obliging, willing, tractable, deferential, under control, at one's command, at one's beck and call, on a string*, wrapped around one's little finger*.—*Ant.* unruly, disobedient, undutiful. **2** [Docile] pliant, acquiescent, compliant.

**obey** *v.* submit, answer to, respond, act upon, act on, bow to, surrender, yield, perform, do, carry out, attend to orders, do what one is told, accept, consent, do what is expected of one, do one's duty, do as someone says, serve, concur, assent, conform, acquiesce, mind, take orders, do someone's bidding, comply, fulfill.—*Ant.* rebel, disobey, mutiny.

**object** *n.* **1** [A corporeal body] article, something, gadget. **2** [A purpose] objective, aim, wish. **3** [One who receives] recipient, target, victim.

**object** *v.* protest, take exception to, dispute.

**objectionable** *a.* **1** [Revolting] gross, repugnant, abhorrent. **2** [Undesirable] unacceptable, unsatisfactory, inexpedient.

**objective** *a.* **1** [Existing independently of the mind] actual, external, material, scientific, sure, extrinsic, measurable, extraneous, reified, tactile, corporeal, bodily, palpable, physical, sensible, outward, outside, determinable, unchangeable, invariable.—*Ant.* mental, subjective, introspective. **2** [Free from personal bias] detached, impersonal, unbiased.

**objective** *n.* goal, aim, aspiration.

**obligatory** *a.* required, essential, binding.

**obliging** *a.* amiable, accommodating, helpful.

**oblique** *a.* inclined, inclining, diverging, leaning, sloping, angled, askew, asymmetrical, turned, twisted, awry, strained, askance, distorted, off level, sideways, slanted, tipping, tipped, at an angle, on the bias.—*Ant.* straight, vertical, perpendicular.

**obscenity** *n.* vulgarity, impropriety, smut.

**obscure** *a.* **1** [Vague] indistinct, ambiguous, indefinite, indecisive, unintelligible, impenetrable, inscrutable, unfathomable, unclear, vague, involved, undefined, intricate, illegible, incomprehensible, hazy, dark, dim, inexplicable, inconceivable, unbelievable, incredible, complicated, illogical, unreasoned, mixed-up, doubtful, questionable, dubious, inexact, unreasoned, loose, ill-defined, unidentified, invisible, undisclosed, perplexing, cryptic, escaping notice, mystical, secret, enigmatic, concealed, mysterious, esoteric, puzzling, lacking clarity, unreadable, contradictory, out of focus, unrelated, clear as mud*, over one's head, deep, far out*, complex, confused, confusing, difficult.—*Ant.* clear, definite, distinct. **2** [Dark] cloudy, dense, hazy. **3** [Little known] unknown, rare, hidden, covered, remote, reticent, secretive, seldom seen, unseen, inconspicuous, humble, invisible, mysterious, deep, cryptic, enigmatic, esoteric, arcane, undisclosed, dark.

**obscure** *v.* **1** [To dim] shadow, cloud, screen. **2** [To conceal] cover, veil, wrap up.

**observant** *a.* keen, alert, penetrating, wide-awake, discerning, perceptive, sharp, eager, interested, discovering, detecting, discriminating, judicious, searching, understanding, questioning, deducing, surveying, considering, sensitive, clear-sighted, comprehending, bright, intelligent, on the ball*, on one's toes*.—*Ant.* thoughtless, unobservant, insensitive.

**observe** *v.* **1** [To watch] scrutinize, inspect, examine. **2** [To comment] note, remark, mention. **3** [To commemorate] dedicate, solemnize, keep. **4** [To abide by] conform to, comply, adopt.

**obsession** *n.* fixation, fascination, passion, fancy, phantom, craze, delusion, mania, infatuation, fixed idea, compulsion, bee in one's bonnet*, hang-up*.

**obsolete** *a.* antiquated, archaic, out-of-date.

**obstacle** *n.* restriction, obstruction, hindrance.

**obvious** *a.* **1** [Clearly apparent to the eye] clear, visible, apparent, public, transparent, observable, perceptible, exposed, noticeable, plain, conspicuous, overt, glaring, prominent, standing out, light, bright, open, unmistakable, evident, recognizable, discernible, in evidence, in view, in sight, perceivable, discoverable, distinguishable, palpable, distinct, clear as a bell*, clear as day*, hitting one in the face*.—*Ant.* obscure, hidden, indistinct. **2** [Clearly apparent to the mind] lucid, apparent, conclusive, explicit, understood, intelligible, comprehensible, self-evident, indisputable, unquestionable, undeniable, proverbial, aphoristic, reasonable, broad, unambiguous, on the surface, as plain as the nose on one's face*, going without saying*, staring one in the face*, open-and-shut*.—*Ant.* profound, ambiguous, equivocal.

**occasional** *a.* **1** [Occurring at odd times] sporadic, random, infrequent. **2** [Intended for special use] special, particular, specific.

**occupy** *v.* **1** [To take possession] conquer, take over, invade. **2** [To fill space] remain, tenant, reside, live in, hold, take up, pervade, keep, own, command, be in command, extend, control, maintain, permeate.—*Ant.* empty, remove, move. **3** [To absorb attention] engage, engross, monopolize, interest, immerse, arrest, absorb, take up, utilize, involve, keep busy, busy.

**occurrence** *n.* happening, incident, episode.

**odd** *a.* **1** [Unusual] queer, unique, strange. **2** [Miscellaneous] fragmentary, odd-lot, varied. **3** [Single] sole, unpaired, unmatched. **4** [Not even] remaining, over and above, leftover.

**odorous** *a.* **1** [Having an offensive odor] smelly, stinking, putrid. **2** [Having a pleasant odor] spicy, sweet-smelling, fragrant.

**off** *a. & prep.* **1** [Situated at a distance] ahead, behind, up front, to one side, divergent, beside, aside, below, beneath, above, far, absent, not here, removed, apart, in the distance, at a distance, gone, away.—*Ant.* here, at hand, present. **2** [Moving away] into the distance, away from, farther away, disappearing, vanishing, removing, turning aside.—*Ant.* approaching, returning, coming. **3** [Started] initiated, commenced, originated. **4** [Mistaken] erring, in error, confused. **5** [*Crazy] odd, peculiar, queer. **6** [*Not employed] not on duty, on vacation, gone.

**offend** *v.* annoy, affront, outrage.

**offense** *n.* **1** [A misdeed] misdemeanor, malfeasance, transgression. **2** [An attack] assault, aggression, battery. **3** [Resentment] umbrage, pique, indignation.

**offensive** *a.* **1** [Concerned with an attack] assaulting, attacking, invading. **2** [Revolting] disgusting, horrid, repulsive, shocking, gross, dreadful, detestable, repugnant, obnoxious, hideous, horrible, displeasing, disagreeable, repellent, nauseating, invidious, nauseous, revolting, distasteful, unspeakable, accursed, unutterable, terrible, grisly, ghastly, bloody, gory, hateful, low, foul, corrupt, bad, indecent, nasty, dirty, unclean, filthy, sickening, malignant, rancid, putrid, vile, impure, beastly, monstrous, coarse, loathsome, abominable, stinking, reeking, obscene, smutty, damnable, distressing, irritating, unpleasant, contaminated, frightful, unattractive, forbidding, repelling, incompatible, unsavory, intolerable, unpalatable, disatisfactory, unpleasing, unsuited, objectionable, to one's disgust, beneath contempt, icky*, lousy*.—*Ant.* pleasant, agreeable, likable. **3** [Insolent] impertinent, impudent, insulting.

**offer** *v.* **1** [To present] proffer, tender, administer, donate, put forth, advance, extend, submit, hold out, grant, allow, award, volunteer, accord, place at one's disposal, lay at one's feet, put up.—*Ant.* refuse, withhold, keep. **2** [To propose] suggest, submit, advise.

**offering** *n.* contribution, donation, present.

**officer** *n.* **1** [An executive] manager, director, president. **2** [One who enforces civil law] magistrate, military police, deputy. **3** [One holding a responsible post in the armed forces] General, Colonel, Major, Captain, Admiral, Commander, Lieutenant, Ensign, Sergeant, Corporal.

**official** *a.* **1** [Having to do with one's office] formal, fitting, suitable, precise, established, according to precedent, according to protocol, proper, correct, accepted, recognized, customary.—*Ant.* informal, ill-fitting, unceremonious. **2** [Authorized] ordered, endorsed, sanctioned. **3** [Reliable] authoritative, authentic, trustworthy.

**official** *n.* **1** [Administrator] comptroller, director, executive. **2** [A sports official] referee, umpire, linesman.

**offset** *v.* counterbalance, compensate, allow for.

**offspring** *n.* progeny, issue, descendants, children, kids, siblings, lineage, generation, brood, seed, family, heirs, offshoots, heredity, succession, successors, next generation.

**oil** *n.* **1** [Liquid, greasy substance] melted fat, unction, lubricant, grease, mineral oil, volatile oil, machine oil, crude oil, lubricating oil, olive oil, castor oil, corn oil, canola oil, whale oil, linseed oil, soybean oil, cod-liver oil, lard, tallow, margarine, Vaseline (trademark), lanolin, petroleum, turpentine. **2** [Liquid substance used for power or illumination] petroleum, kerosene, coal oil, crude oil, liquid coal, fossil oil.

**oily** *a.* **1** [Rich with oil] fatty, greasy, buttery, oil-soaked, rich, lardy, oleaginous, soapy, soothing, creamy, oil-bearing.—*Ant.* dry, dried, gritty. **2** [Having a surface suggestive of oil] oiled, waxy, sleek, slippery, smooth, polished, lustrous, bright, brilliant, gleaming, glistening, shining.—*Ant.* rough, dull, unpolished. **3** [Unctuous] fulsome, suave, flattering.

**OK*** *n.* approval, endorsement, affirmation.

**old** *a.* **1** [No longer vigorous] aged, elderly, patriarchal, gray, venerable, not young, of long life, past one's prime, far advanced in years, matured, having lived long, full of years, seasoned, infirm, inactive, enfeebled, decrepit, superannuated, exhausted, tired, impaired, broken down, wasted, doddering, senile, ancient, having one foot in the grave, gone to seed.—*Ant.* young, fresh, youthful. **2** [Worn] timeworn, worn-out, thin, patched, ragged, faded, used, in holes, rubbed off, mended, broken-down, fallen to pieces, fallen in, given way, out of use, rusted, crumbled, dilapidated, battered, shattered, shabby, cast-off, decayed, decaying, stale, useless, tattered, in rags, torn, moth-eaten.—*Ant.* fresh, new, unused. **3** [Ancient] archaic, time-honored, prehistoric, bygone, early, antique, forgotten, immemorial, antediluvian, olden, remote, past, distant, former, of old, gone by, classic, medieval, in the Middle Ages, out of the dim past, primordial, primeval, before history, dateless, unrecorded, handed down, of earliest time, of the old order, ancestral, traditional, time out of mind, in the dawn of history, old as the hills.—*Ant.* modern, recent, late.

**old-fashioned** *a.* antiquated, out-of-date, obsolete, obsolescent, outmoded, *démodé* (French), unfashionable, traditional, unstylish, passé, before the War, Victorian, not modern, old-time, time-honored, not current, antique, ancient, no longer prevailing, bygone, archaic, grown old, primitive, quaint, amusing, odd, neglected, of long standing, unused, past, behind the times, gone by, of the old school, extinct, out, gone out, out of it*.—*Ant.* modern, fashionable, stylish.

**ominous** *a.* threatening, forbidding, foreboding, menacing, dark, suggestive, fateful, premonitory, dire, grim, gloomy, haunting, perilous, ill-starred, ill-fated, impending, fearful, prophetic.—*Ant.* favorable, encouraging, auspicious.

**omission** *n.* **1** [The act of omitting] overlooking, missing, leaving out.—*Ant.* addition, mention, insertion. **2** [Something omitted] need, want, imperfection.

**on** *a. & prep.* **1** [Upon] above, in contact with, touching, supported by, situated upon, resting upon, on top of, about, held by, moving across, moving over, covering.—*Ant.* under, underneath, below. **2** [Against] in contact with, close to, leaning on. **3** [Toward] proceeding, at, moving. **4** [Forward] onward, ahead, advancing. **5** [Near] beside, close to, adjacent to. **—and so on** and so forth, also, in addition.

**once** *a.* **1** [One time] this time, but once, once only, one time before, already, one, just this once, not more than once, never again, a single time, one time previously, on one occasion, only one time.—*Ant.* frequently, twice, many times. **2** [Formerly] long ago, previously, earlier. **—all at once** simultaneously, all at the same time, unanimously. **—at once** now, quickly, this moment. **—for once** for at least one time, once only, just this once.

**oncoming** *a.* impending, expected, imminent.

**one** *a.* individual, peculiar, special, specific, separate, single, singular, odd, one and only, precise, definite, sole, uncommon.—*Ant.* common, several, imprecise.

**one-sided** *a.* **1** [Unilateral] single, uneven, partial. **2** [Prejudiced] biased, partial, narrow-minded.

**ongoing** *a.* open-ended, continuous, in process.

**only** *a.* **1** [Solely] exclusively, uniquely, wholly, entirely, particularly, and no other, and no more, and nothing else, nothing but, totally, utterly, first and last, one and only. **2** [Merely] just, simply, plainly, barely, solely. **3** [Sole] single, companionless, without another, by oneself, isolated, apart, unaccompained, exclusive, unique.

**onward** *a.* on ahead, beyond, forward.

**ooze** *v.* seep, exude, leak.

**opaque** *a.* not transparent, dim, dusky, darkened, murky, gloomy, smoky, thick, misty, cloudy, clouded, shady, muddy, dull, blurred, frosty, filmy, foggy, sooty, dirty, dusty, coated over, covered.—*Ant.* clear, transparent, translucent.

**open** *a.* **1** [Not closed] unclosed, accessible, clear, open to view, uncovered, disclosed, divulged, introduced, initiated, begun, full-blown, unfurled, susceptible, ajar, gaping, wide, rent, torn, spacious, unshut, expansive, extensive, spread out, revealed.—*Ant.* closed, tight, shut. **2** [Not obstructed] unlocked, unbarred, unbolted, unblocked, unfastened, cleared away, removed, made passable, unsealed, unobstructed, unoccupied, vacated, unburdened, emptied.—*Ant.* taken, barred, blocked. **3** [Not forbidden] free of entrance, unrestricted, permitted, allowable, free of access, public, welcoming.—*Ant.* refused, restricted, forbidden. **4** [Not protected] unguarded, unsecluded, liable, exposed, uncovered, apart, unshut, unroofed, insecure, unsafe, conspicuous, unhidden, unconcealed, subject, sensitive.—*Ant.* safe, secluded, secure. **5** [Not decided] in question, up for discussion, debatable. **6** [Frank] plain, candid, straightforward.

**open** *v.* **1** [To begin] start, inaugurate, initiate. **2** [To move aside a prepared obstruction] unbar, unlock, unclose, clear, admit, reopen, open the lock, lift the latch, free, loosen, disengage, unfasten, undo, unbolt, turn the key, turn the knob.—*Ant.* close, shut, lock. **3** [To make an opening] force an entrance, breach, cut in, tear down, push in, shatter, destroy, burst in, break open, cave in, burst out from, penetrate, pierce, force one's way into, smash, punch a hole into, slit, puncture, crack, muscle in*, jimmy*.—*Ant.* repair, seal, mend. **4** [To make available] make accessible, put on sale, put on view, open to the public, make public, put forward, free, make usable, prepare, present, make ready.—*Ant.* remove, put away, lock up. **5** [To expose to fuller view] unroll, unfold, uncover.

**openly** *a.* **1** [Frankly] naturally, simply, artlessly, naively, unsophisticatedly, out in the open, candidly, aboveboard, straightforwardly, honestly, unreservedly, fully, readily, willingly, without restraint, plainly, without reserve, to one's face, in public, face to face.—*Ant.* secretly, furtively, surreptitiously. **2** [Shamelessly] immodestly, brazenly, not caring, regardlessly, insensibly, unconcernedly, crassly, insolently, flagrantly, wantonly, unblushingly, notoriously, without pretense, in defiance of the law.—*Ant.* carefully, prudently, discreetly.

**open-minded** *a.* tolerant, fair-minded, just.

**operate** *v.* **1** [To keep in operation] manipulate, conduct, administer. **2** [To be in operation] function, work, serve, carry on, run, revolve, act, behave, fulfill, turn, roll, spin, pump, lift, burn, move, progress, advance, proceed, go, contact, engage, transport, convey, click*, tick*.—*Ant.* stop, stall, break down. **3** [To produce an effect] react, act on, influence, bring about, determine, turn, bend, contrive, work, accomplish, fulfill, finish, complete, benefit, compel, promote, concern, enforce, take effect, have effect, work on, succeed, get results, get across. **4** [To perform a surgical operation] remove diseased tissue, amputate, transplant.

**operation** *n.* **1** [The act of causing to function] execution, guidance, superintendence, carrying out, ordering, order, maintenance, handling, manipulating, manipulation, supervision, control, agency, enforcement, advancement, regulating, running, supervising, directing, transacting, conducting, management. **2** [An action] performance, act, employment, labor, service, carrying on, transaction, deed, doing, proceeding, handiwork, workmanship, enterprise, movement, progress, development, engagement, undertaking, work. **3** [A method] process, formula, procedure. **4** [Surgical treatment] surgery, transplant, amputation, dismemberment, vivisection, dissection, biopsy, emergency operation, acupuncture, exploratory operation, section, resection, excision, incision, removal, tonsillectomy, appendectomy, open-heart surgery, abortion, autopsy, the knife*.

**operator** *n.* **1** [One who operates a machine] engineer, skilled employee, laborer, worker. **2** [One who operates workable property] executive, supervisor, director. **3** [*Manipulator] speculator, scoundrel, fraud.

**opinion** *n.* **1** [A belief] notion, view, sentiment, conception, idea, surmise, impression, inference, conjecture, inclination, fancy, imagining, supposition, suspicion, assumption, guess, theory, thesis, theorem, postulate, hypothesis, point of view, presumption, presupposition, persuasion, mind. **2** [A considered judgment] estimation, estimate, view, summary, belief, idea, resolution, determination, recommendation, finding, conviction, conclusion, verdict.

**opinionated** *a.* bigoted, stubborn, unyielding.

**opponent** *n.* **1** [A rival] competitor, contender, challenger, candidate, equal, entrant, the opposition, aspirant, bidder.—*Ant.* supporter, defender, abettor. **2** [An opposing contestant] antagonist, contestant, litigant. **3** [An enemy] foe, adversary, assailant.

**opportunity** *n.* **1** [Favorable circumstances] chance, occasion, suitable circumstance, excuse, happening, event, probability, good fortune, luck, break. **2** [A suitable time] occasion, moment, time.

**oppose** *v.* **1** [To hold a contrary opinion] object, disapprove, debate, dispute, disagree, contradict, argue, deny, run counter to, protest, defy, cross, speak against, confront, thwart, neutralize, reverse, turn the tables, be opposed to, oppose change, not have any part of, face down, interfere with, disapprove of, cry out against, disagree with, not conform, run against, run counter to, come in conflict with, go contrary to, frown at, not accept, call into question, conflict with, grapple with, doubt, be against, be unwilling, reject, dislike, take exception, repudiate, question, probe, resist, confound, confute, refute, buck*, turn thumbs down*.—*Ant.* agree, approve, accept. **2** [To fight] resist, battle, encounter, assault, attack, assail, storm, protest, clash, meet, skirmish, engage, contest, face, restrain, go against, turn against, uphold, defend, rebel, revolt, mutiny, strike back, combat, run counter to, defy, snub, grapple with, fight off, withstand, repel, guard, counterattack, struggle, outflank, antagonize, retaliate, impede, overpower, take on all comers*, lock horns with.

**opposite** *a.* **1** [Contrary] antithetical, diametric, reversed. **2** [In conflict] adverse, inimical, antagonistic, rival, unfavorable, averse, argumentative, contradictory, hostile. **3** [So situated as to seem to oppose] facing, fronting, in front of, on di fferent sides of, on opposite sides, in opposition to, contrasting, on the other side of, contrary, over against, front to front, back to back, nose to nose, face to face, on the farther side, opposing, diametrical, eyeball to eyeball*.—*Ant.* matched, on the same side, side by side.

**opposite** *n.* contradiction, contrary, converse, direct opposite, opposition, vice versa, antithesis, antonym, counter term, counterpart, inverse, reverse, adverse, the opposite pole, the other extreme, the other side, the opposite idea.—*Ant.* equal, like, similar thing.

**oppression** *n.* tyranny, hardness, domination, coercion, dictatorship, fascism, persecution, severity, harshness, abuse, conquering, overthrowing, compulsion, force, torment, martial law.—*Ant.* freedom, liberalism, voluntary control.

**optimism** *n.* **1** [Belief in the essential goodness of the universe] philosophy of goodness, belief in progress, faith. **2** [An inclination to expect or to hope for the best] cheerfulness, hopefulness, hope, con fidence, assurance, encouragement, happiness, brightness, enthusiasm, good cheer, trust, calmness, elation, expectancy, expectation, anticipation, certainty.—*Ant.* gloom, despair, melancholy.

**optimistic** *a.* cheerful, sanguine, assured, confident, hopeful, trusting.

**option** *n.* **1** [A choice] selection, alternative, dilemma. **2** [A privilege to purchase] right, prerogative, grant, claim, license, lease, franchise, advantage, security, immunity, benefit, title, prior claim, dibs*.

**optional** *a.* discretionary, elective, noncompulsory, free, unrestricted, arbitrary, not required, with no strings attached*, take it or leave it*, voluntary.—*Ant.* necessary, compulsory, enforced.

**oral** *a.* vocal, verbal, uttered, voiced, unwritten, phonetic, sounded, not written, by word of mouth, spoken.—*Ant.* written, printed, unspoken.

**orbit** *n.* **1** [Path described by one body revolving around another] ellipse, circle, ring, circuit, apogee, course, perigee, lap, round, cycle, curve, flight path. **2** [Range of activity or influence] range, field, boundary.

**ordeal** *n.* tribulation, distress, calamity.

**order** *n.* **1** [A command] direction, demand, decree, rule, edict, charge, requirement, ordinance, act, warrant, mandate, injunction. **2** [Sequence] progression, succession, procession. **3** [Orderly arrangement] regulation, plan, disposition, management, establishment, method, distribution, placement, scale, rule, computation, adjustment, adaptation, ordering, ranging, standardizing, lining up, trimming, grouping, composition, assortment, disposal, scheme, form, routine, array, procedure, index, regularity, uniformity, symmetry, harmony, layout, lineup, setup, classification, system.—*Ant.* confusion, disarray, displacement. **4** [Organization] society, sect, company. **5** [A formal agreement to purchase] engagement, reserve, application, requisition, request, stipulation, booking, arrangement, reservation. **6** [Kind] hierarchy, rank, degree. **—in order** working, efficient, operative. **—in order to** for the purpose of, as a means to, so that. **—in short order** rapidly, without delay, soon. **—on order** requested, on the way, sent for.

**order** *v.* **1** [To give a command] direct, command, instruct, bid, tell, demand, impose, give directions, dictate, decree. **2** [To authorize a purchase] secure, reserve, request. **3** [To put in order] arrange, plan, furnish, regulate, establish, manage, systematize, space, file, put away, classify, distribute, alphabetize, regularize, pattern, formalize, settle, fix, locate, dress up, sort out, index, put to rights, set guidelines for, adjust, adapt, set in order, assign, place, align, standardize, group, organize.—*Ant.* confuse, disarrange, disarray.

**orderly** *a.* **1** [Ordered; *said of objects and places*] neat, tidy, arranged. **2** [Methodical; *said of persons*] systematic, correct, formal, businesslike, exact, tidy, neat, thorough, precise, careful.—*Ant.* irregular, inaccurate, unmethodical.

**ordinary** *a.* **1** [In accordance with a regular order or sequence] customary, normal, regular, constant, usual, habitual, routine, mundane, everyday, common. **2** [Lacking distinction] average, mediocre, familiar, natural, everyday, accepted, typical, commonplace, characteristic, prosaic, simple, banal, bland, trite, monotonous, stale, tedious, plain, normal, common, conventional, dull. **—out of the ordinary** extraordinary, uncommon, special.

**organ** *n.* **1** [An instrument] medium, means, way. **2** [A part of an organism having a specialized use] vital part, functional division, process, gland, brain, heart, eye, ear, nose, tongue, lung, kidney, stomach, intestine, pancreas, gall bladder, liver. **3** [A musical instrument] wind instrument, keyboard instrument, calliope, hurdy-gurdy, accordion, pipe organ, reed organ, electric organ.

**organic** *a.* basic, vital, essential.

**organization** *n.* **1** [The process or manner of organizing] establishment, plan, planning, ordering, creation, grouping, design, provision, working out, assembling, construction, regulation, systematization, system, method, coordination, adjustment, harmony, unity, correlation, standard, standardization, settlement, arrangement, disposition, classification, alignment, institution, foundation, preparation, rehearsal, direction, structure, situation, formation, association, uniformity.—*Ant.* confusion, bedlam, chance. **2** [An organized body] aggregation, association, federation, combine, corporation, union, institute, trust, cartel, confederation, monopoly, combination, machine, business, industry, company, society, league, club, fraternity, sorority, house, order, alliance, party, cooperative, guild, profession, trade, coalition, syndicate, fellowship, lodge, brotherhood, sisterhood, confederacy, affiliation, body, band, team, squad, crew, clique, circle, set, troupe, group.

**organized** *a.* established, methodized, coordinated, systematized, systematic, constituted, directed, adjusted, assigned, distributed, grouped, fixed up, standardized, in order, in succession, in good form, placed, put away, orderly, in sequence, arranged, prepared, made ready, constructed, settled, composed, framed, planned, ranked, put in order, ordered, regulated, ranged, disposed, formulated, formed, fashioned, shaped, made, projected, designed, harmonized, related, correlated, founded, associated.

**orientation** *n.* familiarization, bearings, introduction.

**origin** *n.* **1** [The act of beginning] rise, start, foundation. **2** [The place or time of beginning] source, spring, issue, fountain, inlet, derivation, root, stem, shoot, twig, sapling, portal, door, gate, gateway, fountainhead, wellspring, font, fount, birthplace, cradle, nest, womb, reservoir, infancy, babyhood, childhood, youth.—*Ant.* result, outcome, issue. **3** [Cause] seed, germ, stock, parentage, ancestry, parent, ancestor, egg, sperm, embryo, principle, element, nucleus, first cause, author, creator, prime mover, producer, causation, source, influence, generator, occasion, root, spring, antecedent, motive, inspiration.—*Ant.* result, consequence, conclusion.

**original** *a.* **1** [Pertaining to the source] primary, primeval, primordial, rudimentary, elementary, inceptive, in embryo, fundamental, primitive, initial, beginning, commencing, starting, opening, dawning, incipient.—*Ant.* late, recent, developed. **2** [Creative] originative, productive, causal, causative, generative, imaginative, inventive, formative, resourceful, ready, quick, seminal, envisioning, sensitive, archetypal, inspiring, devising, conceiving, fertile, fashioning, molding.—*Ant.* stupid, imitative, unproductive. **3** [Not copied] primary, principal, first, genuine, new, firsthand, uncopied, fresh, novel, independent, one, sole, lone, single, solitary, authentic, unique, pure, rare, unusual, not translated, not copied, not imitated, real, absolute, sheer.—*Ant.* imitated, copied, repeated.

**originality** *n.* creativeness, inventiveness, invention, ingenuity, conception, authenticity, novelty, freshness, newness, individuality, brilliance.

**originate** *v.* start, introduce, found.

**ornament** *n.* embellishment, adornment, beautification.

**ornamental** *a.* **1** [Intended for ornament] fancy, luxurious, showy. **2** [Beautiful] delicate, exquisite, spiritual.

**ornate** *a.* showy, gaudy, sumptuous, lavish, bright, colored, tinseled, jeweled, embroidered, glossy, burnished, polished, gorgeous, pompous, stylish, magnificent, adorned, trimmed, gilded, embellished, inlaid, garnished, flowered, glowing, vivid, radiant, fine, alluring, dazzling, sparkling, shining, flashing, glistening, glamorous, artificial, pretentious, baroque, rococo, tawdry, flashy.

**otherwise** *a.* **1** [In another way] in a different way, contrarily, in an opposed way, under other conditions, in different circumstances, on the other hand, in other respects, in other ways.—*Ant.* like, so, in like manner. **2** [Introducing an alternative threat] unless you do, with this exception, except on these conditions, barring this, in any other circumstances, except that, without this, unless...then, other than.—*Ant.* therefore, hence, as a result.

**ought (to)** *v.* should, have to, is necessary, is fitting, is becoming, is expedient, behooves, is reasonable, is logical, is natural, requires, is in need of, is responsible for, must.

**oust** *v.* eject, discharge, dispossess, evict, dislodge, remove, deprive, expel, drive out, force out, show the door, chase out, cast out, depose, dethrone, disinherit, banish, boot out*, bundle off*, send packing*, give the gate*, pack off*.

**out** *a. & prep.* **1** [In motion from within] out of, away from, from, from within, out from, out toward, outward, on the way.—*Ant.* in, in from, into. **2** [Not situated within] on the outer side, on the surface, external, extrinsic, outer, outdoors, out-of-doors, unconcealed, open, exposed, in the open.—*Ant.* within, inside, on the inner side. **3** [Beyond] distant, removed, removed from. **4** [Continued to the limit or near it] ended, accomplished, fulfilled. **5** [Not at home or at one's office] not in, away, busy, on vacation, at lunch, gone, left.—*Ant.* in, receiving, not busy. **6** [*Unconscious] insensible, out cold, blotto*. **7** [Wanting] lacking, missing, without. **—all out*** wholeheartedly, with great effort, entirely.

**outbreak** *n.* **1** [A sudden violent appearance] eruption, explosion, outburst, disruption, burst, bursting forth, detonation, thunder, commotion, rending, break, breaking out, breaking forth, gush, gushing forth, outpouring, pouring forth, tumult, discharge, blast, blowup, crash, roar, earthquake, squall, paroxysm, spasm, convulsion, fit, effervescence, boiling, flash, flare, crack.—*Ant.* peace, tranquillity, quiet. **2** [Sudden violence] fury, mutiny, brawl.

**outburst** *n.* discharge, upheaval, eruption.

**outer** *a.* outward, without, external, exterior, foreign, alien to, beyond, exposed.—*Ant.* inner, inward, inside.

**outline** *n.* **1** [A skeletonized plan] frame, skeleton, framework. **2** [The line surrounding an object; *often plural*] contour, side, boundary. **3** [A shape seen in outline] silhouette, profile, configuration, shape, figure, formation, aspect, appearance.

**outline** *v.* **1** [To draw] sketch, paint, describe. **2** [To plan] block out, draft, sketch.

**outlook** *n.* **1** [Point of view] scope, vision, standpoint. **2** [Apparent future] probability, prospects, likelihood, possibility, chances, opportunity, appearances, probable future, openings, normal course of events, probabilities, risk, law of averages.

**out of** *a.* **1** [Having none in stock] all out of stock, not in stock, gone. **2** [From] out from, away from, from within. **3** [Beyond] outside of, on the border of, in the outskirts.

**output** *n.* yield, amount, crop.

**outrage** *n.* indignity, abuse, affront.

**outrage** *v.* offend, wrong, affront.

**outrageous** *a.* wanton, notorious, shameless, disgraceful, brazen, barefaced, gross, scandalous, disorderly, insulting, affronting, abusive, oppressive, dishonorable, injurious, glaring, immoderate, extreme, flagrant, contemptible, ignoble, malevolent, odious, monstrous, atrocious, nefarious, vicious, iniquitous, wicked, shocking, violent, unbearable, villainous, infamous, corrupt, degenerate, criminal, sinful, abandoned, vile, abominable.—*Ant.* excellent, laudable, honorable.

**outside** *a.* extreme, outermost, farthest, apart from, external, away from, farther.—*Ant.* inner, inside, interior.

**outside** *n.* **1** [An outer surface] exterior, outer side, surface, skin, cover, covering, topside, upper side, front side, face, appearance, outer aspect, seeming.—*Ant.* inside, interior, inner side. **2** [The limit] outline, border, bounds. **—at the outside** at the most, at the absolute limit, not more than.

**outward** *a.* **1** [In an outward direction] out, toward the edge, from within. **2** [To outward appearance] on the surface, visible, to the eye.

**over** *a. & prep.* **1** [Situated above] aloft, overhead, up beyond, covering, roofing, protecting, upper, higher than, farther up, upstairs, in the sky, straight up, high up, up there, in the clouds, among the stars, in heaven, just over, up from, outer, on top of.—*Ant.* under, below, beneath. **2** [Passing above] overhead, aloft, up high. **3** [Again] once more, afresh, another time. **4** [Beyond] past, farther on, out of sight. **5** [Done] accomplished, ended, completed. **6** [*In addition] over and above, extra, additionally. **7** [Having authority] superior to, in authority, above.

**overbearing** *a.* despotic, tyrannical, dictatorial.

**overcast** *a.* cloudy, gloomy, not clear or fair.

**overcome** *v.* overwhelm, best, vanquish, conquer, outdo, surpass, overpower, overwhelm, beat, trounce, subdue, master.

**overconfident** *a.* reckless, imprudent, heedless.

**overdo** *v.* **1** [To do too much] magnify, amplify, overestimate, overreach, stretch, go too far, overrate, exaggerate, go to extremes, overstate, enlarge, enhance, exalt, bite off more than one can chew*, run into the ground*, do to death, go overboard*, burn the candle at both ends, lay it on*, have too many irons in the fire, have one's cake and eat it too*.—*Ant.* neglect, underdo, slack. **2** [To overtax oneself physically] tire, fatigue, exhaust.

**overdue** *a.* delayed, belated, tardy.

**overflow** *v.* **1** [To flow over the top, or out at a vent] spill over, run over, pour out, waste, shed, cascade, spout forth, jet, spurt, drain, leak, squirt, spray, shower, gush, shoot, issue, rush, wave, surge, brim over, bubble over. **2** [To flow out upon] inundate, water, wet.

**overgrowth** *n.* growth, abundance, luxuriance.

**overlook** *v.* **1** [To occupy a commanding height] look over, top, survey, inspect, watch over, look out, view, give upon, give on, front on, have a prospect of. **2** [To ignore deliberately] slight, make light of, disdain. **3** [To fail to see] miss, leave out, neglect.

**overpower** *v.* overwhelm, master, subjugate.

**override** *v.* **1** [To dismiss] pass over, not heed, take no account of. **2** [To thwart] make void, reverse, annul.

**overrule** *v.* **1** [To nullify] invalidate, rule against, override. **2** [To rule] direct, control, manage.

**overwhelm** *v.* **1** [To defeat] overcome, overthrow, conquer. **2** [To astonish] puzzle, bewilder, confound.

**overwhelming** *a.* overpowering, ruinous, overthrowing, crushing, smashing, extinguishing, invading, ravaging, overriding, upsetting, inundating, drowning, deluging, surging, obliterating, dissolving, blotting out, wrecking, erasing, effacing, expunging, burying, immersing, engulfing, engrossing, covering.

**owe** *v.* be under obligation, be indebted to, be obligated to, have an obligation, be bound, get on credit, feel bound, be bound to pay, be contracted to, be in debt for, have signed a note for, have borrowed, have lost.

**own** *v.* **1** [To possess] hold, have, enjoy, fall heir to, have title to, have rights to, be master of, occupy, control, dominate, have claim upon, reserve, retain, keep, have in hand, have a deed for.—*Ant.* lack, want, need. **2** [To acknowledge] assent to, grant, recognize. **—come into one's own** receive what one deserves, gain proper recognition, thrive. **—of one's own** personal, private, belonging to one. **—on one's own** by oneself, acting independently, singly.

**ownership** *n.* possession, having, holding, claim, deed, title, control, buying, purchasing, heirship, proprietorship, occupancy, use, residence, tenancy, dominion.

# P

**pacify** *v.* conciliate, appease, placate.

**pack** *v.* **1** [To prepare for transportation] prepare, gather, collect, ready, get ready, put in order, stow away, dispose, tie, bind, brace, fasten.—*Ant.* undo, untie, take out. **2** [To stow compactly] stuff, squeeze, bind, compress, condense, arrange, ram, cram, jam, insert, press, contract, put away.—*Ant.* scatter, loosen, fluff up.

**pagan** *a.* unchristian, idolatrous, heathenish.

**pagan** *n.* pantheist, heathen, doubter, scoffer, unbeliever, atheist, infidel.

**paid** *a.* rewarded, paid off, reimbursed, indemnified, remunerated, solvent, unindebted, unowed, recompensed, salaried, hired, out of debt, refunded.

**pail** *n.* pot, receptacle, jug.

**pain** *n.* **1** [Suffering, physical or mental] hurt, anguish, distress, discomfort, agony, misery, martyrdom, wretchedness, shock, torture, torment, passion.—*Ant.* health, well-being, ease. **2** [Suffering, usually physical] ache, twinge, catch, throe, spasm, cramp, torture, malady, sickness, laceration, soreness, fever, burning, torment, distress, agony, affliction, discomfort, hurt, wound, strain, sting, burn, crick. **3** [Suffering, usually mental] despondency, worry, anxiety, depression, grief, sadness. **—feeling no pain*** intoxicated, inebriated, stoned*.

**painful** *a.* **1** [Referring to physical anguish] raw, aching, throbbing, burning, torturing, hurtful, biting, piercing, sharp, severe, caustic, tormenting, smarting, extreme, grievous, stinging, bruised, sensitive, tender, irritated, distressing, inflamed, burned, unpleasant, ulcerated, abcessed, uncomfortable.—*Ant.* healthy, comfortable, well. **2** [Referring to mental anguish] worrying, depressing, saddening.

**paint** *n.* **1** [Pigment] coloring material, chroma, oil, acrylic, watercolor, tempera, house paint, enamel, varnish, latex, stain, whitewash, fresco, flat paint, high-gloss paint, metallic paint, barn paint, interior paint, exterior paint, white lead. **2** [Covering] overlay, varnish, finish.

**pair** *n.* couple, mates, two, two of a kind, twosome, twins, fellows, duality, brace.

**pair** *v.* combine, match, balance.

**pale** *a.* **1** [Wan] pallid, sickly, anemic, bloodless, ghastly, cadaverous, haggard, deathlike, ghostly. **2** [Lacking color] white, colorless, bleached.

**pale** *v.* grow pale, lose color, blanch.

**pamper** *v.* spoil, indulge, pet, cater to, humor, gratify, yield to, coddle, overindulge, please, spare the rod and spoil the child*.

**pan** *n.* vessel, kettle, container, pail, bucket, baking pan, stewpan, saucepan, double boiler, roaster, casserole, cake pan, bread pan, pie pan, cookie sheet, frying pan, skillet, dishpan.

**panic** *n.* dread, alarm, fright.

**panorama** *n.* spectacle, scenery, prospect.

**paper** *n.* **1** [A piece of legal or official writing] document, official document, legal paper. **2** [A newspaper] journal, daily, tabloid. **3** [A piece of writing] essay, article, theme. **4** [A manufactured product] writing paper, typing paper, stationery, bond, letterhead, second sheet, onionskin, carbon paper, ruled paper, notepad, notepaper, notecard, vellum, parchment, newsprint, rice paper, crepe paper, butcher's paper, wax paper, wrapping paper, tissue paper, brown paper, tar paper, tracing paper, graph paper, filter paper, toilet paper, wallpaper, paper towel, facial tissue, foolscap, computer paper, copier paper, kraft, cardboard, blotting paper, scrap paper, photographic paper. **—on paper** **1** recorded, signed, official. **2** in theory, assumed to be feasible, not yet in practice.

**paradox** *n.* mystery, enigma, ambiguity.

**paragon** *n.* ideal, perfection, best.

**parallel** *a.* **1** [Equidistant at all points] side by side, never meeting, running parallel, coordinate, coextending, lateral, laterally, in the same direction, extending equally. **2** [Similar in kind, position, or the like] identical, equal, conforming.

**pardon** *v.* **1** [To reduce punishment] exonerate, clear, absolve, reprieve, acquit, set free, liberate, discharge, rescue, justify, suspend charges, put on probation, grant amnesty to, free, release.—*Ant.* punish, chastise, sentence. **2** [To forgive] condone, overlook, exculpate, excuse, forgive.

**pardoned** *a.* forgiven, freed, excused, released, granted amnesty, given a pardon, reprieved, granted a reprieve, acquitted, let off, sprung*, back in circulation.—*Ant.* accused, convicted, condemned.

**pare** *v.* skin, strip, flay.

**park** *n.* **1** [A place designated for outdoor recreation] square, plaza, lawn, green, village green, promenade, tract, recreational area, pleasure ground, national park, national monument, enclosure, woodland, meadow. **2** [A place designed for outdoor storage] parking lot, parking space, lot.

**park** *v.* mass, collect, order, place in order, station, place in rows, leave, store, impound, deposit.

**parody** *v.* mimic, copy, caricature.

**part** *n.* **1** [A portion] piece, fragment, fraction, section, sector, member, segment, division, allotment, apportionment, ingredient, element, slab, subdivision, partition, particle, installment, component, constituent, bit, slice, scrap, chip, chunk, lump, sliver, splinter, shaving, molecule, atom, electron, proton, neutron.—*Ant.* whole, total, aggregate. **2** [A part of speech] noun, verb, modifier, preposition, conjunction. **3** [A machine part] molding, casting, fitting, lever, shaft, cam, spring, band, belt, chain, pulley, clutch, spare part, replacement, gear, wheel. **4** [A character in a drama] hero, heroine, character, role. **—for the most part** mainly, mostly, to the greatest extent. **—in part** to a certain extent, somewhat, slightly. **—on one's part** privately, as far as one is concerned, coming from one. **—play a part** join, take part, participate.

**part** *v.* **1** [To put apart] separate, break, sever. **2** [To depart] withdraw, leave, part company.

**participate** *v.* **1** [To take part in] share, partake, aid, cooperate, join in, come in, associate with, be a party to, have a hand in, concur, take an interest in, take part in, enter into, have to do with, get into the act*, go into, chip in*.—*Ant.* retire, withdraw, refuse. **2** [To engage in a contest] play, strive, engage.

**partisan** *n.* adherent, supporter, disciple.

**partly** *a.* in part, partially, to a degree, measurably, somewhat, noticeably, notably, in some part, incompletely, insufficiently, inadequately, up to a certain point, so far as possible, not entirely, as much as could be expected, to some extent, within limits, slightly, to a slight degree, in some ways, in certain particulars, only in details, in a general way, not strictly speaking, in bits and pieces, by fits and starts, short of the end, at best, at worst, at most, at least, at the outside.—*Ant.* completely, wholly, entirely.

**partner** *n.* co-worker, ally, comrade.

**partnership** *n.* alliance, union, cooperation, company, combination, corporation, connection, brotherhood, sisterhood, society, lodge, club, fellowship, fraternity, sorority, confederation, band, body, crew, clique, gang, ring, faction, party, community, conjunction, joining, companionship, friendship.

**party** *n.* **1** [A social affair] at-home, tea, luncheon, dinner party, dinner, cocktail hour, surprise party, house party, social, reception, banquet, feast, affair, gathering, function, fete, ball, recreation, amusement, performance, entertainment, festive occasion, carousal, diversion, high tea, binge*, spree*, blowout*, bash*. **2** [A group of people] multitude, mob, company. **3** [A political organization] organized group, body, electorate, combine, combination, bloc, ring, junta, partisans, cabal. **4** [A specified but unnamed individual] party of the first part, someone, individual, person.

**pass** *n.* **1** [An opening through mountains] gorge, ravine, crossing, track, way, path, passageway, gap. **2** [A document assuring permission to pass] ticket, permit, passport, visa, order, admission, furlough, permission, right, license. **3** [In sports, the passing of the ball from one player to another] toss, throw, fling. **4** [*An advance] approach, sexual overture, proposition.

**pass** *v.* **1** [To move past] go by, run by, run past, flit by, come by, shoot ahead of, catch, come to the front, go beyond, roll on, fly past, reach, roll by, cross, flow past, glide by, go in opposite directions. **2** [To elapse] transpire, slip away, slip by, pass away, pass by, fly, fly by, linger, glide by, run out, drag, crawl. **3** [To complete a course successfully] satisfy the requirements, be graduated, pass with honors. **4** [To hand to others] transfer, relinquish, hand over. **5** [To enact] legislate, establish, vote in. **6** [To become enacted] carry, become law, become valid, be ratified, be established, be ordained, be sanctioned. **7** [To exceed] excel, transcend, go beyond. **8** [To spend time] fill, occupy oneself, while away. **9** [To proceed] progress, get ahead, move on, go on, advance. **10** [To emit] give off, send forth, exude. **—bring to pass** bring about, initiate, start. **—come to pass** occur, develop, come about.

**passion** *n.* lust, craving, excitement.

**passionate** *a.* **1** [Excitable] vehement, hotheaded, tempestuous. **2** [Ardent] intense, impassioned, loving, fervent, moving, inspiring, dramatic, melodramatic, romantic, poignant, swelling, enthusiastic, tragic, stimulating, wistful, stirring, thrilling, warm, burning, glowing, vehement, deep, affecting, eloquent, spirited, fiery, expressive, forceful, heated, hot. **3** [Intense] strong, vehement, violent.

**past** *a.* **1** [Having occurred previously] former, preceding, gone by, foregoing, elapsed, anterior, antecedent, prior. **2** [No longer serving] ex-, retired, earlier.

**patch** *v.* darn, mend, repair.

**path** *n.* trail, way, track, shortcut, footpath, crosscut, footway, roadway, cinder track, byway, path.

**patience** *n.* **1** [Willingness to endure] forbearance, fortitude, composure, submission, endurance, nonresistance, self-control, passiveness, bearing, serenity, humility, yielding, poise, sufferance, long-suffering, moderation, leniency.—*Ant.* nervousness, fretfulness, restlessness. **2** [Ability to continue] perseverance, persistence, endurance.

**patient** *a.* **1** [Enduring without complaint] submissive, meek, forbearing, mild-tempered, composed, tranquil, serene, long-suffering, unruffled, imperturbable, passive, coldblooded, easygoing, tolerant, gentle, unresentful.—*Ant.* irritable, violent, resentful. **2** [Quietly persistent in an activity] steady, dependable, calm, reliable, stable, composed, unwavering, quiet, serene, unimpassioned, enduring.—*Ant.* restless, irrepressible, feverish.

**patient** *n.* case, inmate, victim, sufferer, sick individual, medical case, surgical case, inpatient, outpatient, bed patient, emergency patient, convalescent, hospital case, hospitalized person, subject.

**patriotic** *a.* devoted, zealous, public-spirited, dedicated, jingoistic, chauvinistic.

**patron** *n.* philanthropist, benefactor, helper, protector, encourager, champion, backer, advocate, defender, guide, leader, friend, ally, sympathizer, well-wisher, partisan, buyer, angel, sugar daddy*, booster.—*Ant.* enemy, obstructionist, adversary.

**pattern** *n.* original, guide, model.

**pause** *v.* delay, halt, rest, catch one's breath, cease, hold back, reflect, deliberate, suspend, think twice, discontinue, interrupt, hesitate.

**pause** *n.* lull, rest, stop, halt, truce, stay, respite, standstill, stand, deadlock, stillness, intermission, suspension, discontinuance, breathing room, hitch, hesitancy, interlude, hiatus, interim, lapse, cessation, stopover, interval, rest period, gap, stoppage.

**pay** *n.* **1** [Monetary return] profit, proceeds, interest, return, recompense, indemnity, reparation, rake-off*, reward, consideration, defrayment.—*Ant.* expense, disbursement, outlay. **2** [Wages] compensation, salary, payment, hire, remuneration, commission, redress, fee, stipend, earnings, settlement, consideration, reimbursement, satisfaction, reward, time, time and a half, double time, overtime.

**pay** *v.* **1** [To give payment] pay up, compensate, recompense, make payment, reward, remunerate, charge, discharge, pay a bill, foot the bill*, refund, settle, get even with, reckon with, put down, make restitution, make reparation, hand over, repay, liquidate, handle, take care of, give, confer, bequeath, defray, meet, disburse, clear, adjust, satisfy, reimburse, kick in*, plunk down*, put up*, pay as you go, fork out*, fork over*, ante up*, even the score*, chip in*.—*Ant.* deceive, swindle, victimize. **2** [To produce a profit] return, pay off, pay out, show profit, yield profit, yield excess, show gain, pay dividends.—*Ant.* fail, lose, become bankrupt. **3** [To retaliate] repay, punish, requite.

**payment** *n.* **1** [The act of paying] recompense, reimbursement, restitution, subsidy, return, redress, refund, remittance, reparation, disbursement, money down, amends, cash, salary, wage, sum, payoff, repayment, defrayment, retaliation. **2** [An installment] portion, part, amount.

**peace** *n.* **1** [The state of being without war] armistice, pacification, conciliation, order, concord, amity, union, unity, reconciliation, brotherhood, love, unanimity.—*Ant.* war, warfare, battle. **2** [State of being without disturbance] calm, repose, quiet, tranquillity, harmony, lull, hush, congeniality, equanimity, silence, stillness.—*Ant.* fight, noisiness, quarrel. **3** [Mental or emotional calm] calmness, repose, harmony, concord, contentment, sympathy.—*Ant.* distress, disturbance, agitation. **—at peace** peaceful, quiet, tranquil. **—hold** (or **keep**) **one's peace** be silent, keep quiet, not speak. **—make peace** end hostilities, settle, reconcile.

**peculiar** *a.* **1** [Unusual] wonderful, singular, outlandish. **2** [Characteristic of only one] uncommon, eccentric, unique.

**peddler** *n.* hawker, vender, seller.

**peer** *v.* gaze, inspect, scrutinize.

**penalty** *n.* fine, discipline, punishment.

**penetrate** *v.* bore, perforate, enter, insert, go through, make an entrance, stick into, jab, thrust, stab, force, make a hole, run into, run through, punch, puncture, drive into, stick, drill, eat through, spear, impale, wound, gore, sting, sink into, knife, go through, pass through.—*Ant.* leave, withdraw, turn aside.

**people** *pl.n.* **1** [Humankind] humanity, mankind, the human race. **2** [A body of persons having racial or social ties] nationality, tribe, community. **3** [The middle and lower classes of society] mass, folk, proletariat, rabble, masses, the multitude, the majority, democracy, crowd, common people, common herd, rank and file, the underprivileged, the public, the man in the street, bourgeoisie, riffraff, the herd*, the horde, the many, the great unwashed*, hoi polloi, John Q. Public, Jane Q. Public. **4** [Family] close relatives, kin, siblings. **5** [Society in general] they, anybody, the public.

**percentage** *n.* percent, rate, rate per cent, portion, section, allotment, duty, discount, commission, winnings, cut*, rake-off*, payoff, slice*.

**perceptible** *a.* perceivable, discernible, cognizable.

**perception** *n.* **1** [The act of perceiving] realizing, understanding, apprehending. **2** [The result of perceiving] insight, knowledge, observation.

**perfect** *a.* **1** [Having all necessary qualities] complete, sound, entire. **2** [Without defect] excelling, faultless, flawless, impeccable, immaculate, unblemished, foolproof, untainted, unspotted, absolute, classical, stainless, spotless, crowning, culminating, supreme, ideal, sublime, beyond all praise, beyond compare.—*Ant.* ruined, damaged, faulty. **3** [Exact] precise, sharp, distinct.

**perfect** *v.* fulfill, realize, develop.

**perform** *v.* **1** [To accomplish an action] do, make, achieve, rehearse, accomplish, fulfill, execute, transact, carry out, carry through, discharge, effect, enforce, administer, complete, consummate, operate, finish, realize, go about, go through with, put through, work out, devote oneself to, come through, be engrossed in, be engaged in, see to it, bring about, engage in, concern oneself with, have effect, fall to, do justice to, do one's part, make a move, follow through, apply oneself to, deal with, do something, look to, take measures, act on, lose oneself in, make it one's business, dispose of, bring to pass, do what is expected of one, put into effect, occupy oneself with, take action, address oneself to, put in action, lift a finger*, keep one's hand in*, pull off*. **2** [To present a performance] give, present, enact, play, offer, impersonate, show, exhibit, display, act out, dramatize, execute, put on the stage, produce, act the part of, put on an act, act one's part.

**perfume** *n.* scent, fragrance, aroma, odor, sweetness, bouquet, incense, smell.

**perhaps** *a.* conceivably, possibly, maybe.

**period** *n.* **1** [A measure of time] epoch, time, era. **2** [An end] limit, conclusion, close. **3** [A mark of punctuation] point, full stop, full pause, dot.

**permanent** *a.* durable, enduring, abiding, uninterrupted, stable, continuing, lasting, firm, hard, tough, strong, hardy, robust, sound, sturdy, steadfast, imperishable, surviving, living, long-lived, long-standing, invariable, persisting, tenacious, persevering, unyielding, persisting, resistant, impenetrable, recurring, wearing, constant, changeless, persistent, perennial.

**permission** *n.* leave, liberty, consent, assent, acceptance, letting, approbation, agreement, license, permit, allowance, authority, tolerance, toleration, authorization, approval, acknowledgment, admission, verification, recognition, concurrence, promise, avowal, support, corroboration, guarantee, guaranty, visa, encouragement, ratification, grace, authority, sanction, confirmation, endorsement, affirmation, assurance, empowering, legalization, grant, indulgence, trust, concession, adjustment, settlement, accord, nod*, OK*, rubber stamp*, the go-ahead*, high sign, green light*.—*Ant.* denial, injunction, interdiction.

**permit** *v.* sanction, tolerate, let.

**perpetual** *a.* **1** [Never stopping] continuous, unceasing, constant. **2** [Continually repeating] repetitious, repeating, recurrent.

**persecute** *v.* afflict, harass, victimize.

**person** *n.* **1** [An individual] human being, child, somebody, self, oneself, I, me, soul, spirit, character, individuality, personage, personality, identity. **2** [An individual enjoying distinction] distinguished person, personality, success. **3** [Bodily form] physique, frame, form. **—in person** personally, in the flesh, present.

**personal** *a.* **1** [Private] secluded, secret, retired. **2** [Individual] claimed, peculiar, particular. **3** [Pertaining to one's person] fleshly, corporeal, bodily.

**persuade** *v.* convince, move, induce, assure, cajole, incline, talk someone into something, win over, bring around, lead to believe, lead to do something, gain the confidence of, prevail upon, overcome another's resistance, wear down, bring a person to his or her senses, win an argument, make one's point, gain the confidence of, make someone see the light.—*Ant.* neglect, dissuade, dampen.

**persuasive** *a.* convincing, alluring, luring, seductive, influential, winning, enticing, impelling, moving, actuating, efficient, effective, effectual, compelling, touching, forceful, potent, powerful, swaying, pointed, strong, energetic, forcible, plausible, inveigling.

**pertaining to** *a.* belonging to, appropriate to, connected with, having to do with.

**pest** *n.* **1** [Anything destructive] virus, germ, insect pest, bug. **2** [A nuisance] bore, tease, annoyance.

**pet** *v.* **1** [To caress] fondle, cuddle, kiss. **2** [*To make love] embrace, hug, neck*.

**phase** *n.* condition, stage, appearance, point, aspect.

**philanthropic** *a.* kindhearted, benevolent, humanitarian.

**philosophy** *n.* **1** [The study of knowledge] theory, reasoned doctrine, explanation of phenomena, logical concept, systematic view, theory of knowledge, early science, natural philosophy. **2** [A fundamental principle] truth, axiom, conception. **3** [A personal attitude or belief] outlook, view, position.

**phobia** *n.* fear, aversion, hatred.

**phony*** *a.* counterfeit, imitation, artificial.

**photography** *n.* picture-taking, portrait photography, view photography, aerial photography, tactical photography, candid camera, microphotography, photomicrography, videotaping.

**phrase** *n.* group of words, expression, slogan, catchword, maxim, word-group.

**physical** *a.* **1** [Concerning matter] material, corporeal, visible, tangible, environmental, palpable, substantial, natural, sensible, concrete, materialistic. **2** [Concerning the body] corporal, corporeal, fleshly. **3** [Concerning physics] mechanical, motive, electrical, sonic, vibratory, vibrational, thermal, radioactive, atomic, relating to matter, dynamic.

**physician** *n.* practitioner, doctor of medicine, surgeon.

**pick** *n.* **1** [An implement for picking] pickax, mattock, ice pick. **2** [A blow with a pointed instrument] peck, nip, dent. **3** [A selection] choice, election, preference.

**pick** *v.* **1** [To choose] select, pick out, separate. **2** [To gather] pluck, pull, accumulate. **3** [To use a pointed instrument] dent, indent, strike.

**pick up** *v.* **1** [To acquire incidentally] happen upon, find, secure. **2** [To take up in the hand or arms] lift, elevate, hold up. **3** [To receive] get, take, acquire. **4** [To increase] improve, do better, grow. **5** [To improve physically] get better, get well, recover health. **6** [To call for] stop for, bring along, go to get, accompany, get, invite.

**picture** *n.* **1** [A scene before the eye or the imagination] spectacle, panorama, pageant. **2** [A human likeness] portrait, representation, photo, photograph, snapshot, cartoon, image, effigy, statue, statuette, figure, icon, figurine, close-up. **3** [A pictorial representation] illustration, engraving, etching, woodcut, cut, outline, cartoon, draft, hologram, fax, graph, halftone, still, ad*, crayon sketch, pastel, watercolor, poster, oil, chart, map, plot, mosaic, blueprint, advertisement, facsimile, animation, tracing, photograph, lithograph, print. **4** [A motion picture] cinema, film, movie. **5** [A description] depiction, delineation, portrayal.

**piece** *n.* **1** [Part] portion, share, section. **2** [Work of art] study, composition, creation. **3** [Musical, literary, or theatrical composition] suite, orchestration, production, opus, aria, song, study, arrangement, treatise, exposition, sketch, play, novel, thesis, dissertation, discourse, discussion, treatment, essay, article, paper, memoir, homily, poem, theme, monograph, commentary, review, paragraph, criticism, play, drama, melodrama, pageant, monologue, opera, overture, prelude, étude, ballet. **—go to pieces** **1** come apart, break up, fail. **2** quit, collapse, lose control. **—speak one's piece** air one's opinions, talk, reveal.

**pier** *n.* wharf, landing, quay.

**pierce** *v.* stab, intrude, penetrate.

**pile** *v.* heap, stack, gather.

**pin** *n.* **1** [A device to fasten goods by piercing or clasping] clip, catch, needle, bodkin, quill, clasp, nail. **2** [A piece of jewelry] tiepin, stickpin, brooch, badge, stud, sorority pin, fraternity pin, school pin.

**pin** *v.* close, clasp, bind.

**pinch** *v.* **1** [To squeeze] nip, grasp, compress, press, cramp, grab, contract, confine, limit, torment. **2** [*To steal] take, rob, pilfer. **3** [*To arrest] apprehend, detain, hold.

**pioneer** *n.* **1** [One who prepares the way] pathfinder, scout, explorer. **2** [One in the vanguard of civilization] early settler, colonist, pilgrim, immigrant, colonizer, homesteader, squatter.

**pious** *a.* divine, holy, devout.

**pipe** *n.* pipeline, drain pipe, sewer, conduit, culvert, waterpipe, aqueduct, trough, passage, duct, canal, vessel.

**pirate** *n.* thief, freebooter, plunderer, pillager, marauder, privateer, soldier of fortune, buccaneer, sea rover.

**pit** *n.* abyss, cavity, depression.

**pitiful** *a.* miserable, mournful, sorrowful, woeful, distressed, distressing, cheerless, comfortless, deplorable, joyless, dismal, touching, pathetic, affecting, stirring, arousing, lamentable, poignant, heartbreaking, human, dramatic, impressive, tearful, gratifying, heartrending, depressing, afflicted, suffering, moving, vile.—*Ant.* happy, cheerful, joyful.

**pitiless** *a.* unfeeling, heartless, cold.

**pity** *n.* sympathy, compassion, charity, softheartedness, tenderness, goodness, understanding, forbearance, mercy, kindness, warmheartedness, kindliness, brotherly love, unselfishness, benevolence, favor, condolence, commiseration, clemency, humanity.—*Ant.* hatred, severity, ferocity. **—have** (or **take**) **pity on** show pity to, spare, pardon.

**pity** *v.* **1** [To feel pity] feel for, sympathize with, commiserate, be sorry for, bleed for, be sympathetic to, show sympathy, express sympathy for, grieve with, weep for. **2** [To be merciful to] spare, take pity on, show pity to, show forgiveness to, be merciful to, give quarter, put out of one's misery, pardon, reprieve, grant amnesty to.—*Ant.* destroy, condemn, accuse.

**pivot** *v.* whirl, swivel, rotate.

**place** *n.* **1** [Position] station, point, spot. **2** [Space] room, compass, stead, void, distance, area, seat, volume, berth, reservation, accommodation. **3** [Locality] spot, locus, site, community, district, suburb, country, section, habitat, home, residence, abode, house, quarters. **4** [Rank] status, position, station. —**go places*** attain success, achieve, advance. —**in place** fitting, timely, appropriate. —**in place of** as a substitute for, instead of, taking the place of. —**out of place** inappropriate, unsuitable, not fitting. —**put someone in his place** humiliate, reprimand, shame. —**take place** occur, come into being, be. —**take the place of** replace, act in one's stead, serve as proxy for.

**plague** *n.* epidemic, pestilence, disease.

**plain** *a.* **1** [Obvious] open, manifest, clear. **2** [Simple] unadorned, unostentatious, unpretentious. **3** [Ordinary] everyday, average, commonplace. **4** [Homely] plain-featured, coarse-featured, unattractive. **5** [In blunt language] outspoken, candid, impolite.

**plain** *n.* prairie, steppe, pampas, expanse, open country, lowland, flat, level land, mesa, savanna, moorland, moor, heath, tundra, veldt, downs, the High Plains.

**plan** *n.* **1** [A preliminary sketch] draft, diagram, map, chart, timeline, design, outline, representation, form, drawing, view, projection, rough, rough draft, road map. **2** [A proposed sequence of action] plans, scheme, project, flowchart, scope, outline, idea, handling, manipulating, projection, undertaking, method, design, tactics, procedure, treatment, intention, policy, course of action, plot, conspiracy, expedient, strategy, stratagem, arrangement, way of doing things, angle*, the picture. **3** [Arrangement] layout, method, disposition.

**plan** *v.* **1** [To plot an action in advance] prepare, scheme, devise, invent, outline, project, contrive, shape, design, map, plot a course, form a plan, think out, concoct, engineer, figure on, intrigue, conspire, frame, steer one's course, establish guidelines, set parameters, work up, work out, line up, plan an attack, come through, calculate on, make arrangements, take measures, bargain for, cook up*, put on ice*. **2** [To arrange in a preliminary way] outline, draft, sketch, lay out, map out, preprint, organize, prepare a sketch, chart, map, draw, trace, design, illustrate, depict, delineate, represent, shape, chalk out, rough in, block out, block in. **3** [To have in mind] propose, think, contemplate.

**plane** *n.* **1** [A plane surface] level, extension, horizontal, flat, sphere, face, stratum. **2** [A tool for smoothing wood] electric planer, jointer, foreplane. **3** [An airplane] aircraft, airliner, aeroplane, airship, heavier-than-air craft, shuttle, jet, jet plane.

**planet** *n.* celestial body, heavenly body, luminous body, wandering star, planetoid, asteroid, star.

**plant** *n.* shrub, weed, bush, slip, bulb, shoot, cutting, sprout, seedling, plantlet, flower.

**plastic** *n.* synthetic, artificial product, substitute, plastic material, processed material, polymerized substance, thermoplastic, cellophane, melamine, vinyl, nylon, PVC.

**platform** *n.* **1** [A stage] dais, pulpit, speaker's platform, rostrum, stand, floor, staging, terrace. **2** [A program] principles, policies, the party planks*.

**plausible** *a.* probable, credible, likely.

**play** *v.* **1** [To amuse oneself] entertain oneself, revel, make merry, carouse, play games, rejoice, have a good time, idle away, horse around*.—*Ant.* mourn, grieve, sulk. **2** [To frolic] frisk, sport, cavort, joke, dance, play games, make jokes, be a practical joker, show off, jump about, skip, gambol, caper.—*Ant.* drag, mope, droop. **3** [To produce music] perform, execute, work, cause to sound, finger, pedal, bow, plunk, tinkle, pipe, toot, mouth, pump, fiddle, sound, strike, saw, scrape, twang, pound, thump, tickle. **4** [To engage in sport] participate, engage, practice. **5** [To pretend] imagine, suppose, think.

**plea** *n.* **1** [An appeal] overture, request, supplication. **2** [A form of legal defense] pleading, argument, case.

**pleasant** *a.* **1** [Affable] agreeable, attractive, obliging, charming, mild, amusing, kindly, mild-mannered, gracious, genial, amiable, polite, urbane, cheerful, sympathetic, civil, cordial, engaging, social, bland, diplomatic, civilized, good-humored, good-natured, soft, fun, delightful, jovial, jolly.—*Ant.* sullen, unsympathetic, unkind. **2** [Giving pleasure; *said of occasions, experiences, and the like*] gratifying, pleasurable, agreeable, cheering, amusing, welcome, refreshing, satisfying, all right, satisfactory, adequate, acceptable, comfortable, diverting, fascinating, adorable, enjoyable, delightful, sociable, lively, exciting, glad, festive, cheerful, entertaining, relaxing, joyous, joyful, merry, happy, pleasing, favorable, bright, sunny, brisk, catchy, sparkling, enlivening, colorful, light, humorous, laughable, comforting.—*Ant.* sad, unhappy, disagreeable.

**pleasure** *n.* **1** [Enjoyment] bliss, delight, ease. **2** [Will] want, preference, wish.

**pledge** *n.* guarantee, agreement, promise.

**pledge** *v.* swear, vow, vouch.

**plentiful** *a.* **1** [Bountiful] prolific, fruitful, profuse, lavish, liberal, unsparing, inexhaustible, replete, generous, abundant, extravagant, improvident, excessive, copious, superabundant, over-liberal, superfluous, overflowing, flowing.—*Ant.* stingy, niggardly, skimpy. **2** [Existing in plenty] sufficient, abundant, copious, ample, overflowing, large, chock-full, teeming, unlimited, well-provided, flowing, full, flush, lush with, pouring, fruitful, swarming, swimming, abounding.—*Ant.* poor, scant, scanty.

**plenty** *n.* abundance, fruitfulness, fullness, lavishness, deluge, torrent, sufficient, bounty, profusion, adequacy, flood, avalanche, good store, limit, capacity, adequate stock, enough and to spare, everything, all kinds of, all one wants, all one can eat and drink, more than one knows what to do with, too much of a good thing, a good bit, all one needs, all one can use, a great deal, a lot*, lots*, oodles*.

**pliable** *a.* limber, supple, plastic.

**plot** *n.* **1** [An intrigue] conspiracy, scheme, artifice. **2** [The action of a story] plan, scheme, outline, design, development, progress, unfolding, movement, climax, events, incidents, enactment, suspense, structure, buildup, scenario. **3** [A piece of ground] parcel, land, division.

**plot** *v.* **1** [To devise an intrigue] frame, contrive, scheme. **2** [To plan] sketch, outline, draft.

**plow** *v.* break, furrow, cultivate, turn, plow up, turn over, till, list, ridge, break ground, do the plowing.

**plug** *n.* **1** [An implement to stop an opening] cork, stopper, stopple, filling, stoppage, spigot, wedge. **2** [An electrical fitting] attachment plug, fitting, connection, wall plug, floor plug, plug fuse. **3** [A large pipe with a discharge valve] water plug, fire hydrant, fire plug.

**plug** *v.* stop, fill, obstruct, secure, ram, make tight, drive in.

**P.M.** *abbrev.* after noon, afternoon, evening, before midnight, shank of the evening, sunset.

**poem** *n.* poetry, lyric, sonnet, ballad, quatrain, verse, blank verse, free verse, song, composition, creation.

**poetic** *a.* poetical, lyric, lyrical, metrical, tuneful, elegiac, romantic, dramatic, iambic, dactylic, spondaic, trochaic, anapestic, imaginative.

**point** *n.* **1** [A position having no extent] location, spot, locality. **2** [A sharp, tapered end] end, pointed end, needle point, pinpoint, barb, prick, spur, spike, snag, spine, claw, tooth, calk, sticker. **3** [Anything having a point] sword, dagger, stiletto. **4** [Purpose] aim, object, intent. **5** [Meaning] force, drift, import. **6** [A detail] case, feature, point at issue. **—at** (or **on**) **the point of** on the verge of, close to, almost. **—beside the point** immaterial, not pertinent, not germane. **—make a point of** stress, emphasize, make an issue of. **—to the point** pertinent, apt, exact.

**point of view** *n.* outlook, position, approach.

**poise** *n.* balance, gravity, equilibrium, composure, dignity.

**poison** *n.* virus, bane, toxin, infection, germ, bacteria, oil, vapor, gas.

**police** *n.* arm of the law, law enforcement body, FBI, police officers, policemen, police force, detective force, military police, Royal Canadian Mounted Police, New York's Finest*.

**policy** *n.* course, procedure, method, system, strategy, tactics, administration, management, theory, doctrine, behavior, scheme, design, arrangement, organization, plan, order.

**polish** *n.* shine, burnish, glaze.

**polish** *v.* burnish, furbish, finish.

**polite** *a.* obliging, thoughtful, mannerly, attentive, pleasant, gentle, mild, nice, concerned, considerate, solicitous, bland, condescending, honey-tongued, amiable, gracious, cordial, considerate, good-natured, sympathetic, interested, smooth, diplomatic, kindly, kind, kindly disposed, affable, agreeable, civil, complacent, respectful, amenable, gallant, genteel, gentlemanly, mannered, sociable, ingratiating, neighborly, friendly, respectful.—*Ant.* egotistic, insolent, pompous.

**politics** *n.* practical government, functional government, systematic government, domestic affairs, internal affairs, foreign affairs, matters of state, campaigning, getting votes, seeking nomination, electioneering, being up for election, running for office.

**pollution** *n.* corruption, defilement, adulteration, blight, soiling, fouling, foulness, taint, tainting, polluting, decomposition, desecration, profanation, abuse, deterioration, rottenness, impairment, misuse, infection, besmearing, besmirching, smirching.

**ponder** *v.* meditate, deliberate, consider.

**poor** *a.* **1** [Lacking worldly goods] indigent, penniless, moneyless, impecunious, destitute, needy, poverty-stricken, underprivileged, fortuneless, starved, pinched, reduced, beggared, homeless, empty-handed, meager, scanty, insolvent, ill-provided, ill-furnished, in want, suffering privation, in need, poor as a church mouse*, broke*, hard up*, down and out.—*Ant.* wealthy, well-to-do, affluent. **2** [Lacking excellence] pitiful, paltry, contemptible, miserable, pitiable, dwarfed, insignificant, diminutive, ordinary, common, mediocre, trashy, shoddy, worthless, sorry, base, mean, coarse, vulgar, inferior, imperfect, smaller, lesser, below par, subnormal, under average; second-rate, third-rate, fourth-rate, etc.; reduced, defective, deficient, lower, subordinate, minor, secondary, humble, secondhand, pedestrian, beggarly, tawdry, petty, unimportant, bad, cheap, flimsy, threadbare, badly made, less than good, unwholesome, lacking in quality, dowdy, second-class, shabby, gaudy, mass-produced, squalid, trivial, sleazy, trifling, unsuccessful, second-best, tasteless, insipid, rustic, crude, odd, rock-bottom, garish, flashy, showy, loud, unsightly, affected, ramshackle, tumbledown, glaring, artificial, newfangled, out-of-date, crummy*, junky*, two-bit*, raunchy*, corny*, cheesy*. **3** [Lacking strength] puny, feeble, infirm. **4** [Lacking vigor or health] indisposed, impaired, sick. **5** [Lacking fertility] infertile, unproductive, barren.

**poor** *n.* needy, forgotten man, the unemployed, underdogs, the underprivileged, beggars, the homeless, the impoverished masses, second-class citizen, have-nots.

**popular** *a.* **1** [Generally liked] favorite, well-liked, approved, pleasing, suitable, well-received, sought, fashionable, stylish, beloved, likable, lovable, attractive, praised, promoted, recommended, in the public eye, celebrated, noted, admired, famous, run after*.—*Ant.* unknown, in disrepute, out of favor. **2** [Cheap] low-priced, popular-priced, marked down. **3** [Commonly accepted] general, familiar, demanded, in demand, prevalent, prevailing, current, in use, widespread, ordinary, adopted, embraced, having caught on, in the majority. **4** [Pertaining to the common people] proletarian, accessible, neighborly.

**population** *n.* inhabitants, dwellers, citizenry, natives, group, residents, culture, community, state, populace.

**pornographic** *a.* dirty, obscene, lewd.

**portion** *n.* section, piece, part, division, share.

**pose** *v.* **1** [To pretend] profess, feign, make believe. **2** [To assume a pose for a picture] model, adopt a position, sit.

**position** *n.* **1** [A physical position] location, locality, spot, seat, ground, environment, post, whereabouts, bearings, station, point, place, stand, space, surroundings, situation, site, geography, region, tract, district, scene, setting. **2** [An intellectual position] view, belief, attitude. **3** [An occupational position] office, employment, job. **4** [A social position] station, state, status. **5** [Posture] pose, carriage, bearing.

**positive** *a.* **1** [Definite] decisive, actual, concrete. **2** [Emphatic] peremptory, assertive, obstinate. **3** [Certain] sure, convinced, confident.

**possess** *v.* hold, occupy, own.

**possessions** *pl.n.* belongings, goods, effects, estate, property.

**possibility** *n.* **1** [The condition of being possible] plausibility, feasibility, workableness. **2** [A possible happening] hazard, chance, occasion, circumstance, hope, occurrence, hap, happening, outside chance, incident, instance.

**possible** *a.* **1** [Within the realm of possibility] conceivable, imaginable, thinkable. **2** [Acceptable] expedient, desirable, welcome. **3** [Contingent upon the future] indeterminate, fortuitous, adventitious.

**post** *n.* **1** [An upright in the ground] prop, support, pillar, pedestal, stake, stud, upright, doorpost. **2** [The mails] postal service, post office, PO.

**postponed** *a.* deferred, delayed, put off, set for a later time, to be done later, withheld, shelved, tabled, adjourned, suspended.

**posture** *n.* **1** [Stance] pose, carriage, demeanor, aspect, presence, condition. **2** [Attitude] way of thinking, feeling, sentiment.

**pot** *n.* **1** [Container] vessel, kettle, pan, jug, jar, mug, tankard, cup, can, crock, canister, receptacle, bucket, urn, pitcher, bowl, cauldron, melting pot. **2** [*Marijuana] *cannabis sativa* (Latin), grass*, weed*. —**go to pot** deteriorate, go to ruin, fall apart.

**pouch** *n.* sack, receptacle, poke*.

**pouring** *a.* streaming, gushing, spouting, rushing, raining, flooding, showering, discharging, emitting, issuing, escaping, emanating, welling out, spurting, spilling, draining, running down, running out, flowing.

**poverty** *n.* **1** [Want of earthly goods] destitution, pennilessness, indigence, pauperism, want, need, insufficiency, starvation, famine, privation, insolvency, broken fortune, straits, scantiness, deficiency, meagerness, aridity, sparingness, stint, depletion, reduction, emptiness, vacancy, deficit, debt, wolf at the door*, pinch*, bite*, tough going*.—*Ant.* wealth, prosperity, comfort. **2** [Want of any desirable thing] shortage, inadequacy, scarcity.

**power** *n.* **1** [Strength] vigor, energy, stamina. **2** [Controlling sway] authority, command, jurisdiction, dominion, ascendency, superiority, domination, dominance, mastery, control, sway, sovereignty, prerogative, prestige, omnipotence, supreme authority, the last word, rule, law, first-strike capability, warrant, supremacy, legal sanction, government, say-so*. **3** [Ability; *often plural*] skill, endowment, capability. **4** [Force] compulsion, coercion, duress. **5** [Energy] horsepower, potential, dynamism. —**in power** ruling, authoritative, commanding.

**powerful** *a.* **1** [Wielding power] mighty, all-powerful, almighty, superhuman, omnipotent, overpowering, great, invincible, dominant, influential, authoritative, overruling, potent, forceful, forcible, compelling, ruling, prevailing, preeminent, commanding, supreme, highest, important, authoritarian, ruthless, having the upper hand, in control.—*Ant.* weak, incompetent, impotent. **2** [Strong] robust, stalwart, sturdy. **3** [Effective] efficacious, effectual, convincing.

**practical** *a.* matter-of-fact, pragmatical, unimaginative, practicable, feasible, workable, functional, useful, sound, unromantic, sound-thinking, down-to-earth, realistic, sensible, sane, reasonable, rational, to one's advantage, operative, utilitarian, possible, usable, serviceable, efficient, effective, working, in action, in operation, with both feet on the ground.—*Ant.* unreal, imaginative, unserviceable.

**practice** *n.* **1** [A customary action] usage, wont, custom. **2** [A method] mode, manner, fashion. **3** [Educational repetition] exercise, drill, repetition, iteration, rehearsal, recitation, recounting, relating, tuneup*, prepping*. **4** [A practitioner's custom] work, patients, clients.

**practice** *v.* **1** [To seek improvement through repetition] drill, train, exercise, study, rehearse, repeat, recite, iterate, put in practice, make it one's business, work at, accustom oneself, act up to, polish up*, sharpen up*, build up. **2** [To employ one's professional skill] function, work at, employ oneself in.

**praise** *n.* **1** [The act of praising] applause, approval, appreciation. **2** [An expression of praise] laudation, eulogy, regard, applause, recommendation, hand-clapping, hurrahs, bravos, ovation, cheers, cries, whistling, tribute, compliment, acclaim, flattery, blessing, benediction, boost, rave.—*Ant.* blame, censure, condemnation.

**praise** *v.* **1** [To commend] recommend, applaud, cheer, acclaim, endorse, sanction, admire, eulogize, adulate, elevate, smile on, cajole, give an ovation to, clap, pay tribute to, do credit to, have a good word for, make much of, extend credit, advocate, compliment, appreciate, admire, celebrate, honor, congratulate, flatter, rave over, boost, give a big hand, raise the roof*. **2** [To speak or sing in worship] glorify, adore, reverence.

**prayer** *n.* **1** [An earnest request] entreaty, petition, appeal. **2** [An address to a deity] invocation, act of devotion, supplication, devotions, benediction, litany.

**preach** *v.* exhort, discourse, moralize, teach, lecture, talk, harangue, inform, address, evangelize, witness.

**precede** *v.* go before, come first, be ahead of, move ahead of, take precedence over, preface, introduce, usher in, ring in, herald, forerun, head, lead, go ahead, scout, light the way, go in advance, come before, come to the front, forge ahead, head up.—*Ant.* succeed, come after, come last.

**preceding** *a.* antecedent, precedent, previous, other, prior, aforesaid, ahead of, earlier, former, forerunning, past, foregoing, above-mentioned, above-named, above-cited, aforementioned, before-mentioned, above, before, prefatory, front, forward, anterior, preliminary, preparatory, introductory, aforeknown, already indicated, previously mentioned.

**precision** *n.* exactness, correctness, sureness.

**predicament** *n.* strait, quandary, plight, puzzle, perplexity, dilemma, scrape, corner, hole, impasse, tight situation, state, condition, position, lot, circumstance, mess, muddle, deadlock, pinch, crisis, bind*, fix*, pickle*, hot water*, jam*.

**predict** *v.* prophesy, prognosticate, foretell.

**prefer** *v.* single out, fancy, favor.

**preference** *n.* favorite, election, option, decision, selection, pick, choice.

**pregnant** *a.* gestating, gravid, fruitful, with child, big with child, hopeful, anticipating, in a family way*, expecting*, knocked up*.

**prejudice** *n.* partiality, unfairness, spleen, bias, detriment, enmity, prejudgment, dislike, disgust, aversion, antipathy, race prejudice, bigotry, apartheid, misjudgment, coolness, animosity, contemptuousness, bad opinion, displeasure, repugnance, revulsion, preconception, foregone conclusion, quirk, warp, twist.—*Ant.* admiration, appreciation, good opinion.

**prejudiced** *a.* preconceived, prepossessed, biased, directed against, influenced, inclined, leaning, conditioned, presupposing, predisposed, dogmatic, opinionated, partisan, extreme, hidebound, narrow, intolerant, canting, racist, sexist, chauvinistic, bigoted, blind, partial, narrow-minded, parochial, provincial, one-sided, not seeing an inch beyond one's nose*, squinteyed, intolerant of, disliking, having a predilection, closed against, judging on slight knowledge, smug.—*Ant.* generous, open-minded, receptive.

**prepare** *v.* **1** [To make oneself ready] get ready, foresee, arrange, make preparations, make arrangements, fit, adapt, qualify, put in order, adjust, set one's house in order, prime, fix, settle, fabricate, appoint, furnish, elaborate, perfect, develop, prepare the ground, lay the foundations, block out, smooth the way, man, arm, cut out, warm up, lay the groundwork, contrive, devise, make provision, put in readiness, build up, provide for, provide against, make snug, be prepared, be ready. **2** [To make other persons or things ready] outfit, equip, fit out. **3** [To cook and serve] concoct, dress, brew.

**prescribe** *v.* guide, order, give directions.

**present** *a.* **1** [Near in time] existing, being, in process, in duration, begun, started, commenced, going on, under consideration, at this time, contemporary, immediate, instant, prompt, at this moment, at present, today, nowadays, these days, already, even now, but now, just now, for the time being, for the occasion.—*Ant.* past, over, completed. **2** [Near in space] in view, at hand, within reach.

**present** *n.* **1** [The present time] instant, this time, present moment. **2** [A gift] grant, donation, offering.

**present** *v.* **1** [To introduce] make known, acquaint with, give an introduction. **2** [To submit] donate, proffer, put forth. **3** [To give] grant, bestow, confer. **4** [To give a play, etc.] put on, do, perform.

**preserve** *v.* **1** [To guard] protect, shield, save. **2** [To maintain] keep up, care for, conserve. **3** [To keep] can, conserve, process, save, put up, put down, store, cure, bottle, do up, season, salt, pickle, put in brine, put in vinegar, pot, tin, dry, smoke, corn, dry-cure, smoke-cure, freeze, quick-freeze, freeze-dry, keep up, cold-pack, refrigerate, dehydrate, seal up, kipper, marinate, evaporate, embalm, mummify, mothball, fill.—*Ant.* waste, allow to spoil, let spoil.

**preserved** *a.* **1** [Saved] rescued, guarded, secured. **2** [Prepared for preservation] canned, corned, dried, sun-dried, freeze-dried, dehydrated, evaporated, smoked, seasoned, pickled, salted, brined, put up, conserved, cured, marinated, tinned, potted, bottled, embalmed, mummified.

**press** *v.* **1** [To subject to pressure] thrust, crowd, bear upon, bear down on, squeeze, hold down, pin down, force down, crush, drive, weight, urge.—*Ant.* raise, release, relieve. **2** [To smooth, usually by heat and pressure] finish, mangle, iron.

**prestige** *n.* renown, influence, fame.

**presume** *v.* assume, suppose, take for granted.

**pretend** *v.* **1** [To feign] affect, simulate, claim falsely, imitate, counterfeit, sham, make as if, make as though, mislead, beguile, delude, pass off for, cheat, dupe, hoodwink, be deceitful, bluff, falsify, be hypocritical, fake, put on*, let on*, go through the motions, keep up appearances. **2** [To make believe] mimic, fill a role, take a part, represent, portray, put on a front, play, make believe, act the part of, put on an act*, act a part, put on airs*, playact.

**pretty** *a.* **1** [Attractive] comely, good-looking, beautiful. **2** [Pleasant] delightful, cheerful, pleasing. **3** [*Considerable] sizable, notable, large. **4** [Somewhat] rather, tolerably, a little.

**prevalent** *a.* widespread, accepted, common.

**prevent** *v.* preclude, obviate, forestall, anticipate, block, arrest, stop, thwart, repress, interrupt, halt, impede, check, avert, frustrate, balk, foil, retard, obstruct, counter, countercheck, counteract, inhibit, restrict, block off, limit, hold back, hold off, stop from, deter, intercept, override, circumvent, bar, ward off, keep from happening, nip in the bud, put a stop to, stave off, keep off, turn aside.—*Ant.* help, aid, encourage.

**previous** *a.* antecedent, prior, former.

**price** *n.* expenditure, outlay, expense, cost, value, worth, figure, dues, tariff, valuation, quotation, fare, hire, wages, return, disbursement, rate, appraisal, reckoning, equivalent, payment, demand, barter, consideration, amount, marked price, asking price, estimate, output, ransom, reward, pay, prize, par value, money's worth, price ceiling, ceiling. **—at any price** whatever the cost, money is no object, anyhow.

**pride** *n.* **1** [The quality of being vain] conceit, vainglory, egoism, egotism, self-esteem, self-love, self-exaltation, self-glorification, self-admiration, pretension.—*Ant.* humility, self-effacement, unpretentiousness. **2** [Conduct growing from pride or conceit] haughtiness, vanity, disdain, condescension, patronizing, patronage, superiority. **3** [Sense of personal satisfaction] self-respect, self-satisfaction, self-sufficiency. **4** [A source of satisfaction] enjoyment, repletion, sufficiency.

**primarily** *a.* mainly, fundamentally, in the first place.

**primitive** *a.* **1** [Simple] rudimentary, elementary, first. **2** [Ancient] primeval, archaic, primordial. **3** [Uncivilized] crude, rough, simple, rude, atavistic, uncivilized, savage, uncultured, natural, barbaric, barbarous, barbarian, fierce, untamed, uncouth, ignorant, undomesticated, wild, animal, brutish, raw, untaught, green, unlearned, untutored, underdeveloped.

**principal** *a.* leading, chief, first, head, prime, main, foremost, cardinal, essential, capital, important, preeminent, highest, supreme, prominent, dominant, predominant, controlling, superior, prevailing, paramount, greatest, incomparable, unapproachable, peerless, matchless, unequaled, unrivaled, maximum, crowning, unparalleled, sovereign, second to none.—*Ant.* unimportant, secondary, accessory.

**principle** *n.* **1** [A fundamental law] underlying truth, basic doctrine, postulate. **2** [A belief or set of beliefs; *often plural*] system, opinion, teaching.

**print** *n.* **1** [Printed matter] impression, reprint, issue. **2** [A printed picture] engraving, lithograph, photograph. **—in print** printed, available, obtainable. **—out of print** O.P., unavailable, remaindered.

**print** *v.* **1** [To make an impression] impress, imprint, indent. **2** [To reproduce by printing] run off, print up, issue, reissue, reprint, bring out, go to press, set type, compose, start the presses.—*Ant.* talk, write, inscribe. **3** [To simulate printing] letter, do lettering, hand-letter.

**prior** *a.* antecedent, above-mentioned, preceding.

**private** *a.* special, separate, retired, secluded, withdrawn, removed, not open, behind the scenes, off the record, privy, clandestine, single.—*Ant.* public, open, exposed. **—in private** privately, personally, not publicly.

**prize** *n.* reward, advantage, privilege, possession, honor, inducement, premium, bounty, bonus, spoil, booty, plunder, pillage, loot, award, accolade, recompense, requital, acquisitions, laurel, decoration, medal, trophy, palm, crown, citation, scholarship, fellowship, feather in one's cap, title, championship, first place, payoff*, cake*, plum.

**probably** *a.* presumably, seemingly, apparently, believably, reasonably, imaginably, feasibly, practicably, expediently, plausibly, most likely, everything being equal, as like as not, as the case may be, one can assume, like enough, no doubt, from all appearances, in all probability.—*Ant.* unlikely, doubtfully, questionably.

**problem** *n.* **1** [A difficulty] dilemma, quandary, obstacle. **2** [A question to be solved] query, intricacy, enigma.

**proceed** *v.* move, progress, continue.

**proceeding** *n.* [*Often plural*] process, transaction, deed, experiment, performance, measure, step, course, undertaking, venture, adventure, occurrence, incident, circumstance, happening, movement, operation, procedure, exercise, maneuver.

**process** *n.* means, rule, manner. **—in (the) process of** while, when, in the course of.

**produce** *v.* **1** [To bear] yield, bring forth, give birth to, propagate, bring out, come through, blossom, flower, deliver, generate, engender, breed, contribute, give, afford, furnish, return, render, show fruit, fetch, bring in, present, offer, provide, contribute, sell for, bear fruit, accrue, allow, admit, proliferate, be delivered of, bring to birth, reproduce, foal, lamb, drop, calve, fawn, whelp, kitten, litter, hatch, usher into the world, spawn. **2** [To create by mental effort] originate, author, procreate, bring forth, conceive, engender, write, design, fabricate, imagine, turn out, churn out, devise. **3** [To cause] effect, occasion, bring about. **4** [To show] exhibit, present, unfold. **5** [To make] assemble, build, construct. **6** [To present a performance] present, play, prepare for public presentation.

**profession** *n.* **1** [A skilled or learned occupation] calling, business, avocation, vocation, employment, occupation, engagement, office, situation, position, lifework, chosen work, role, service, pursuit, undertaking, concern, post, berth, craft, sphere, field, walk of life. **2** [A declaration] pretense, avowal, vow.

**profit** *n.* **1** [Advantage] avail, good, value. **2** [Excess of receipts over expenditures] gain, returns, proceeds, receipts, take*, gate, acquisition, rake-off*, accumulation, saving, interest, remuneration, earnings.—*Ant.* loss, debits, costs.

**profitable** *a.* lucrative, useful, sustaining, aiding, remunerative, beneficial, gainful, advantageous, paying, successful, favorable, assisting, productive, serviceable, valuable, instrumental, practical, pragmatic, effective, to advantage, effectual, sufficient, paying its way, bringing in returns, making money, paying well, paying out, in the black.—*Ant.* unprofitable, unsuccessful, unproductive.

**profound** *a.* **1** [Physically deep] fathomless, bottomless, subterranean. **2** [Intellectually deep] heavy, erudite, scholarly, mysterious, sage, serious, sagacious, penetrating, discerning, knowing, wise, knowledgeable, intellectual, enlightened, thorough, informed.—*Ant.* superficial, shallow, flighty. **3** [Emotionally deep] heartfelt, deep-felt, great.

**program** *n.* **1** [A list of subjects] schedule, memoranda, printed program. **2** [A sequence of events] happenings, schedule, agenda, order of business, calendar, plans, business, affairs, details, arrangements, catalogue, curriculum, order of the day, series of events, appointments, things to do, chores, preparations, meetings, getting and spending, all the thousand and one things. **3** [An entertainment] performance, show, presentation.

**progress** *n.* **1** [Movement forward] progression, advance, headway, impetus, forward course, development, velocity, pace, momentum, motion, rate, step, stride, current, flow, tour, circuit, transit, journey, voyage, march, expedition, locomotion, passage, course, procession, process, march of events, course of life, movement of the stars, motion through space.—*Ant.* stop, stay, stand. **2** [Improvement] advancement, development, growth. **—in progress** advancing, going on, continuing.

**progress** *v.* proceed, move onward, advance.

**project** *n.* outline, design, scheme.

**projection** *n.* **1** [Bulge] prominence, jut, protuberance, step, ridge, rim. **2** [Forecast] prognostication, prediction, guess.

**prominent** *a.* **1** [Physically prominent] protuberant, extended, jutting, conspicuous, protruding, projecting, noticeable, rugged, rough, obtrusive, standing out, sticking out, hilly, raised, relieved, rounded.—*Ant.* hollow, depressed, sunken. **2** [Socially prominent] notable, preeminent, leading. **3** [Conspicuous] remarkable, striking, noticeable.

**promise** *v.* **1** [To give one's word] engage, declare, agree, vow, swear, consent, affirm, profess, undertake, pledge, covenant, contract, bargain, espouse, betroth, assure, guarantee, warrant, give assurance, give warranty, insure, cross one's heart, plight one's troth, bind oneself, commit oneself, obligate oneself, make oneself answerable, give security, underwrite, subscribe, lead someone to expect, answer for, pledge one's honor.—*Ant.* deceive, deny, break faith. **2** [To appear promising] ensure, insure, assure.

**promote** *v.* **1** [To further] forward, urge, encourage, profit, patronize, help, aid, assist, develop, support, boom, back, uphold, champion, advertise, advocate, cultivate, improve, push, bolster, develop, speed, foster, nourish, nurture, subsidize, befriend, benefit, subscribe to, favor, expand, improve, better, cooperate, get behind, boost.—*Ant.* discourage, weaken, enfeeble. **2** [To advance in rank] raise, advance, elevate, graduate, move up, exalt, aggrandize, magnify, prefer, favor, increase, better, dignify.—*Ant.* humble, demote, reduce.

**prompt** *a.* timely, precise, punctual.

**prone** *a.* inclined, predisposed, disposed.

**proof** *n.* **1** [Evidence] demonstration, verification, case, reasons, exhibits, credentials, data, warrant, confirmation, substantiation, attestation, corroboration, affidavit, facts, witness, testimony, deposition, trace, record, criterion. **2** [Process of proving] test, attempt, assay.

**prop** *n.* aid, assistance, strengthener.

**proper** *a.* **1** [Suitable] just, decent, fitting. **2** [Conventional] customary, usual, decorous. **3** [Prudish] prim, precise, strait-laced.

**property** *n.* **1** [Possessions] belongings, lands, assets, holdings, inheritance, capital, equity, investments, goods and chattels, earthly possessions, real property, personal property, taxable property, resources, private property, public property, wealth. **2** [A piece of land] section, quarter section, estate, tract, part, farm, park, ranch, homestead, yard, grounds, frontage, acres, acreage, premises, campus, grant, landed property, field, claim, holding, plot.

**prophet** *n.* seer, oracle, soothsayer, prophetess, seeress, clairvoyant, wizard, augur, sibyl, sorcerer, predictor, forecaster, prognosticator, diviner, medium, witch, palmist, fortuneteller, weather forecaster, meteorologist, magus, astrologer, horoscopist.

**proportion** *n.* relationship, dimension, share.

**proposal** *n.* **1** [Offer] overture, recommendation, proposition. **2** [Plan] scheme, program, prospectus.

**propose** *v.* **1** [To make a suggestion] suggest, offer, put forward, move, set forth, come up with, state, proffer, advance, propound, introduce, put to, contend, assert, tender, recommend, advise, counsel, lay before, submit, affirm, volunteer, press, urge upon, hold out, make a motion, lay on the line.—*Ant.* oppose, dissent, protest. **2** [To mean] purpose, intend, aim. **3** [To propose marriage] offer marriage, ask in marriage, make a proposal, ask for the hand of, pop the question*.

**prosper** *v.* become rich, become wealthy, be enriched, thrive, turn out well, fare well, do well, be fortunate, have good fortune, flourish, get on, rise in the world, fatten, increase, bear fruit, bloom, blossom, flower, make money, make a fortune, benefit, advance, gain, make good, do well by oneself*, make one's mark, roll in the lap of luxury*, come along, do wonders.

**protrude** *v.* come through, stick out, project.

**proud** *a.* **1** [Having a creditable self-respect] self-respecting, self-sufficient, self-satisfied, ambitious, spirited, vigorous, high-spirited, honorable, great-hearted, fiery, dignified, stately, lordly, lofty-minded, high-minded, impressive, imposing, fine, splendid, looking one in the eye, on one's high horse*, high and mighty*, holding up one's head.—*Ant.* humble, unpretentious, unassuming. **2** [Egotistic] egotistical, vain, vainglorious. **—do oneself proud*** achieve, prosper, advance.

**prove** *v.* justify, substantiate, authenticate, corroborate, testify, explain, attest, show, warrant, uphold, determine, settle, fix, certify, back, sustain, validate, bear out, affirm, confirm, make evident, convince, evidence, be evidence of, witness, declare, have a case, manifest, demonstrate, document, establish, settle once and for all.

**proverb** *n.* maxim, adage, aphorism, precept, saw, saying, motto, dictum, text, witticism, repartee, axiom, truism, byword, epigram, moral, folk wisdom, platitude.

**provide** *v.* **1** [To supply] furnish, equip, grant, replenish, provide with, accommodate, care for, indulge with, favor with, contribute, give, outfit, stock, store, minister, administer, render, procure, afford, present, bestow, cater, rig up, fit out, fit up, provision, ration, implement.—*Ant.* refuse, take away, deny. **2** [To yield] render, afford, give.

**provision** *n.* **1** [Arrangement] preparation, outline, procurement. **2** [Supplies; *usually plural*] stock, store, emergency. **3** [A proviso] stipulation, prerequisite, terms.

**provocative** *a.* alluring, arousing, intriguing.

**provoke** *v.* **1** [To vex] irritate, aggravate, bother. **2** [To incite] stir, rouse, arouse. **3** [To cause] make, produce, bring about.

**prowl** *v.* slink, lurk, sneak.

**prudent** *a.* **1** [Cautious and careful] cautious, circumspect, wary. **2** [Sensible and wise] discerning, sound, reasonable.

**prudish** *a.* narrow-minded, illiberal, bigoted, prissy, priggish, overrefined, fastidious, stuffy, conventional, stiff, smug, straitlaced, demure, narrow, puritanical, affected, artificial, scrupulous, overexact, pedantic, pretentious, strict, rigid, rigorous, simpering, finical, finicking, finicky, squeamish, like a maiden aunt, like an old maid.—*Ant.* sociable, broad-minded, genial.

**pry** *v.* **1** [To move, with a lever] push, lift, raise, pull, move, tilt, hoist, heave, uplift, upraise, elevate, turn out, jimmy. **2** [To endeavor to discover; *often used with "into"*] search, ferret out, seek, ransack, reconnoiter, peep, peer, peek, snoop, gaze, look closely, spy, stare, gape, nose, be curious, inquire.

**psychiatry** *n.* psychopathology, psychotherapy, psychoanalysis.

**psychology** *n.* science of mind, study of personality, medicine, therapy.

**public** *a.* **1** [Available to the public] free to all, without charge, open, unrestricted, not private, known. **2** [Owned by the public] governmental, government, civil, civic, common, communal, publicly owned, municipal, metropolitan, state, federal, county, city, township.—*Ant.* private, personal, restricted.

**publicize** *v.* announce, broadcast, advertise.

**publish** *v.* **1** [To print and distribute] reprint, issue, reissue, distribute, bring out, write, do publishing, become a publisher, get out, put to press, put forth, be in the newspaper business, be in the book business, own a publishing house, send forth, give out. **2** [To make known] announce, promulgate, proclaim.

**puddle** *n.* plash, mud puddle, rut.

**puff** *n.* whiff, sudden gust, quick blast.

**puff** *v.* distend, enlarge, swell.

**pull** *n.* **1** [The act of pulling] tow, drag, haul, jerk, twitch, wrench, extraction, drawing, rending, tearing, uprooting, weeding, row, paddle. **2** [Exerted force] work, strain, tug. **3** [*Influence] inclination, inducement, weight.

**pull** *v.* **1** [To exert force] tug, pull at, draw in. **2** [To move by pulling] draw, ease, drag, lift, stretch, move, jerk, haul, tear, rend, gather. **3** [To incline] slope, tend, move toward.

**punctual** *a.* prompt, precise, particular, on time, on schedule, exact, timely, seasonable, regular, cyclic, dependable, recurrent, constant, steady, scrupulous, punctilious, meticulous, on the nose*.—*Ant.* careless, unreliable, desultory.

**puncture** *n.* punctured tire, flat tire, flat.

**punish** *v.* correct, discipline, chasten, chastise, sentence, train, reprove, lecture, penalize, fine, incarcerate, expel, execute, exile, behead, hang, electrocute, dismiss, debar, whip, spank, paddle, trounce, switch, cuff, inflict penalty, come down on*, attend to, crack down on, make it hot for*, pitch into*, lay into*, give a dressing-down*, lower the boom on*, ground*, throw the book at*, blacklist, blackball.

**pupil** *n.* schoolboy, schoolgirl, student.

**pure** *a.* **1** [Not mixed] unmixed, unadulterated, unalloyed, unmingled, simple, clear, genuine, undiluted, classic, real, true, fair, bright, unclouded, transparent, lucid, straight, neat.—*Ant.* mixed, mingled, blended. **2** [Clean] immaculate, spotless, stainless, unspotted, germfree, unstained, unadulterated, unblemished, untarnished, unsoiled, disinfected, sterilized, uncontaminated, sanitary, unpolluted, purified, refined.—*Ant.* dirty, sullied, contaminated. **3** [Chaste] virgin, continent, celibate. **4** [Absolute] sheer, utter, complete.

**purify** *v.* cleanse, clear, refine, wash, disinfect, fumigate, deodorize, clarify, sublimate, purge, filter.

**purity** *n.* **1** [The state of being pure] pureness, cleanness, cleanliness, immaculateness, stainlessness, whiteness, clearness. **2** [Innocence] artlessness, guilelessness, blamelessness. **3** [Chastity] abstemiousness, continence, virtue.

**purpose** *n.* **1** [Aim] intention, end, goal, mission, objective, object, idea, design, hope, resolve, meaning, view, scope, desire, dream, expectation, ambition, intent, destination, direction, scheme, prospective, proposal, target, aspiration. **2** [Resolution] tenacity, constancy, persistence. **—on purpose** purposefully, intentionally, deliberately. **—to the purpose** to the point, pertinent, apt.

**pursue** *v.* **1** [To chase] seek, hound, track down, dog, shadow, search for, search out, stalk, run after, go after, hunt down, trail, tag, follow close upon, move behind, scout out, nose around, poke around, keep on foot, follow up. **2** [To seek] strive for, aspire to, attempt. **3** [To continue] persevere, proceed, carry on.

**push** *n.* shove, force, bearing, propulsion, drive, exertion, weight, straining, shoving, thrusting, forcing, driving, inducement, mass, potential, reserve, impact, blow.

**push** *v.* **1** [To press against] thrust, shove, butt, crowd, gore, ram, crush against, jostle, push out of one's way, lie on, shoulder, elbow, struggle, strain, exert, set one's shoulder to, rest one's weight on, put forth one's strength. **2** [To move by pushing] impel, accelerate, drive onward, launch, start, set in motion, push forward, shift, start rolling, budge, stir, shove along. **3** [To promote] advance, expedite, urge. **4** [*To sell illegally] sell under the counter, bootleg, black-market, moonshine*.

**put** *v.* **1** [To place] set, locate, deposit, plant, lodge, store, situate, fix, put in a place, lay, pin down, seat, settle. **2** [To establish] install, quarter, fix. **3** [To deposit] invest in, insert, embed.

**puzzle** *n.* **1** [The state of being puzzled] uncertainty, vexation, confusion. **2** [A problem] tangle, bafflement, question, frustration, intricacy, maze, issue, enigma, proposition, mystification, bewilderment, query, mystery, dilemma, muddle, secret, riddle, ambiguity, difficulty, perplexity, confusion, entanglement, stickler, paradox.—*Ant.* answer, solution, development.

**puzzle** *v.* **1** [To perplex] obscure, bewilder, complicate. **2** [To wonder] marvel, be surprised, be astonished.

# Q

**quack** *a.* unprincipled, pretentious, dishonest.

**quack** *n.* rogue, charlatan, humbug.

**quaint** *a.* fanciful, cute, pleasing, captivating, curious, ancient, antique, whimsical, affected, enchanting, baroque, Victorian, French Provincial, Early American, Colonial.—*Ant.* modern, up-to-date, fashionable.

**qualifications** *pl.n.* endowments, attainments, experience.

**qualify** *v.* **1** [To limit] reduce, restrain, temper. **2** [To fulfill requirements] fit, suit, pass, be capacitated for, have the requisites, meet the demands, be endowed by nature for, measure up, meet the specifications.—*Ant.* fail, become unfit, be unsuited.

**quality** *n.* **1** [A characteristic] attribute, trait, endowment. **2** [Essential character] nature, essence, genius. **3** [Grade] class, kind, state, condition, merit, worth, excellence, stage, step, variety, standing, rank, group, place, position, repute.

**qualm** *n.* indecision, scruple, suspicion.

**quantity** *n.* amount, number, bulk, mass, measure, extent, abundance, volume, capacity, lot, deal, pile, multitude, portion, carload, sum, profusion, mountain, load, barrel, shipment, consignment, bushel, supply, ton, ocean, flood, sea, flock, the amount of, score, swarm, quite a few, army, host, pack, crowd, bunch*, heap*, mess*, gob*, batch, all kinds of*, all sorts of*.

**quarrel** *n.* **1** [An angry dispute] wrangle, squabble, dissension. **2** [Objection] complaint, disapproval, disagreement.

**quarrel** *v.* wrangle, dispute, contend, fight, squabble, row, clash, altercate, dissent, bicker, struggle, strive, contest, object, complain, disagree, argue, charge, feud, strike, engage in blows, mix it up with*, step on someone's toes, get tough with*, lock horns, have words with, have a brush with, have it out*, fall out with, break with*.—*Ant.* agree, accord, harmonize.

**queen** *n.* ruler, female ruler, female sovereign, woman monarch, queen mother, regent, wife of a king, consort, queen consort, queen dowager, queen regent, fairy queen, May Queen, matriarch.

**quest** *n.* journey, search, crusade.

**question** *n.* **1** [A query] inquiry, interrogatory, interrogation, inquisition, feeler, catechism, inquest, rhetorical question, burning question, crucial question, leading question, academic question.—*Ant.* answer, solution, reply. **2** [A puzzle] enigma, mystery, problem. **3** [A subject] proposal, topic, discussion. **—beside the question** not germane, beside the point, unnecessary. **—beyond question** beyond dispute, without any doubt, sure. **—in question** being considered, under discussion, controversial. **—out of the question** not to be considered, by no means, no.

**question** *v.* **1** [To ask] inquire, interrogate, query, quest, seek, search, sound out, petition, solicit, ask about, catechize, show curiosity, pry into, ask a leading question, challenge, raise a question, make inquiry, quiz, cross-examine, probe, investigate, put to the question, bring into question. **2** [To doubt] distrust, suspect, dispute.

**quick** *a.* **1** [Rapid] swift, expeditious, fleet. **2** [Almost immediate] posthaste, prompt, instantaneous. **3** [Hasty] impetuous, mercurial, quick-tempered. **4** [Alert] ready, sharp, vigorous.

**quickly** *a.* speedily, swiftly, fleetly, flying, wingedly, with dispatch, scurrying, hurrying, rushing, shooting, bolting, darting, flashing, dashing, suddenly, in haste, in a hurry, just now, this minute, in a moment, in an instant, right away, at a greater rate, without delay, against the clock, racing, galloping, loping, sweeping, light-footedly, briskly, at once, like a bat out of hell*, on the double*, in a flash*, in a jiffy*, to beat the band*, at full blast, hellbent for leather*, hand over fist*, like mad*, by leaps and bounds, like a house afire*.—*Ant.* slowly, sluggishly, creepingly.

**quiet** *a.* calm, peaceful, hushed, muffled, noiseless, still, stilled, mute, muted, soundless, dumb, quieted, speechless, unspeaking, quiescent, taciturn, reserved, reticent, not excited, not anxious, not disturbed, silent, unexpressed, closemouthed, close, tight-lipped, uncommunicative, secretive.

**quiet** *v.* **1** [To make calm] calm, cool, relax, compose, tranquilize, satisfy, please, pacify, mollify, console, subdue, reconcile, gratify, calm down, soften, moderate, smooth, ameliorate, lull, appease, restrain, sober, slacken, soothe.—*Ant.* excite, increase, agitate. **2** [To make silent] still, deaden, silence, lower the sound level, muffle, mute, stop, check, restrain, suppress, break in, confute, eliminate, repress, refute, confound, answer, quell, to stop the mouth*, put the lid on*, button up*, choke off*, put the stopper on*.—*Ant.* sound, ring, cause to sound.

**quit** *v.* **1** [Abandon] surrender, renounce, relinquish. **2** [To cease] discontinue, cease, halt, pause, stop, end, desist. **3** [To leave] go away from, depart, vacate. **4** [To resign] leave, resign, stop work, walk out, quit, change jobs, cease work, give notice.

**quite** *a.* **1** [Completely] entirely, wholly, totally. **2** [Really] truly, positively, actually. **3** [To a considerable degree] pretty, more or less, considerably.

**quiver** *v.* vibrate, shudder, shiver.

**quiz** *n.* test, questioning, examination.

**quota** *n.* portion, part, division.

**quotation** *n.* **1** [Quoted matter] excerpt, passage, citation, cite*, citing, extract, recitation, repetition, sentence, quote, plagiarism. **2** [A quoted price] market price, current price, published price.

# R

**rabble** *n.* mob, masses, riffraff.

**race** *n.* **1** [A major division of mankind] species, culture, variety, type, kind, strain, breed, family, cultural group, color. **2** [Roughly, people united by blood or custom] nationality, caste, variety, type, the people, mankind, tribe, group, ethnic stock, human race, class, kind, nation, folk, gene pool, pedigree, lineage, community, inhabitants, population, populace, public, clan, breeding population. **3** [A contest, usually in speed] competition, run, sprint, clash, meet, event, engagement, competitive trail of speed, competitive action, pursuit, rush, steeplechase, handicap, chase, match, derby, regatta, sweepstakes, marathon, heat, time trial.

**race** *v.* **1** [To move at great speed] speed, hurry, run, pursue, chase, tear, bustle, spurt, post, press on, run swiftly, hasten, trip, fly, hustle, dash, rush, sprint, swoop, scuttle, dart, scamper, haste, plunge ahead, whiz, bolt, scramble, whisk, shoot, run like mad, burn up the road*, gun the motor*, skedaddle*. **2** [To compete] run a race, compete in a race, contend in running, follow a course, engage in a contest of speed, try to beat in a contest of speed, contend, enter a competition.

**racial** *a.* lineal, hereditary, ancestral, genetic, ethnic, genealogical, ethnological, patriarchal, paternal, parental.

**racket** *n.* **1** [Disturbing noise] uproar, clatter, din. **2** [Confusion accompanied by noise] squabble, scuffle, fracas, clash, row, wrangle, agitation, babel, pandemonium, turbulence, clamor, outcry, hullabaloo, tumult, hubbub, commotion, blare, turmoil, stir, noisy fuss, uproar, clatter, charivari, babble, roar, shouting, rumpus, riot, squall, brawl, fight, pitched battle, free-for-all, to-do*, fuss. **3** [A means of extortion] illegitimate business, confidence game, con game*.

**radial** *a.* branched, outspread, radiated.

**radiant** *a.* shining, luminous, radiating.

**radical** *a.* **1** [Fundamental] original, primitive, native. **2** [Advocating violent change] extreme, thorough, complete, insurgent, revolutionary, iconoclastic, advanced, forward, progressive, abolitionist, militant, extremist, recalcitrant, mutinous, seditious, riotous, lawless, racist, insubordinate, anarchistic, unruly, nihilistic, communistic, liberal, leftist, immoderate, freethinking, ultra, red*.—*Ant.* conservative, reformist, gradualist. **3** [Believing in violent political and social change] leftist, communistic, heretical.

**radical** *n.* insurgent, objector, revolutionist, revolutionary, insurrectionist, leftist, Bolshevik, anarchist, socialist, communist, pacifist, nihilist, traitor, mutineer, firebrand, renegade, extremist, crusader, individualist, fascist, Nazi, misfit, iconoclast, eccentric, freethinker, rightist, hippie, fanatic, demonstrator, peace marcher, rioter, fifth columnist, nonconformist, left-winger, right-winger, peacenik*, pinko*, red*.

**rage** *n.* **1** [A fit of anger] frenzy, tantrum, uproar, hysterics, explosion, storm, outburst, spasm, convulsion, eruption, furor, excitement, extreme agitation, madness, vehemence, fury, rampage, huff, wrath, raving, violent anger, ire, resentment, bitterness, gall, irritation, animosity, exasperation, passion, indignation, apoplexy, heat, temper, blowup*, fireworks*. **2** [The object of enthusiasm and imitation] style, mode, fashion, vogue, craze, mania, the last word, the latest.

**rage** *v.* **1** [To give vent to anger] rant, fume, rave, foam, splutter, yell, scream, roar, rail at, boil over, shake, quiver, seethe, shout, scold, go into a tantrum, have a fit, run amok, run riot, fly apart, flare up, carry on, show violent anger, bluster, storm, be furious, fret, lose one's temper, work oneself into a sweat*, go berserk, go into a tailspin, go up in the air*, blow one's top*, gnash one's teeth, raise Cain*, raise the devil*, raise hell*, take on*, throw a fit*, fly off the handle*, explode, vent one's spleen, snap at, blow up*, blow a fuse*, make a fuss over, kick up a row*, have a nervous breakdown, let off steam*, get oneself into a lather*, lose one's head*.—*Ant.* cry, be calm, pout. **2** [To be out of control] explode, flare, roar.

**ragged** *a.* tattered, in shreds, patched, badly worn, rough, worn out, broken, worn to rags, frayed, frazzled, threadbare, shoddy, out at the seams, shredded, battered, the worse for wear, worn to a thread, down at the heel, moth-eaten, full of holes, torn, badly dressed.—*Ant.* whole, new, unworn.

**raid** *v.* storm, plunder, attack.

**rail** *n.* **1** [A polelike structure] post, railing, barrier, picket, rail fence, siding, banister, paling, rest, hand rail, guard rail, brass rail. **2** [A track; *often plural*] railway, monorail, railroad track.

**rain** *n.* **1** [Water falling in drops] drizzle, mist, sprinkle, sprinkling, damp day, spring rain, rainfall, shower, precipitation, wet weather. **2** [A rainstorm] thunderstorm, tempest, cloudburst.

**rain** *v.* pour, drizzle, drop, fall, shower, sprinkle, mist, mizzle*, spit, lay the dust, patter, rain cats and dogs*, come down in bucketfuls.

**raise** *v.* **1** [To lift] uplift, upraise, upheave, pull up, lift up, hold up, stand up, heave, set upright, put on its end, shove, boost, rear, mount, pry.—*Ant.* lower, bring down, take down. **2** [To nurture] bring up, rear, nurse, suckle, nourish, wean, breed, cultivate, train, foster. **3** [To collect or make available] gather, borrow, have ready. **4** [To erect] construct, put up, build. **5** [To ask] bring up, suggest, put. **6** [To advance in rank] exalt, dignify, promote.

**rally** *v.* unite against, renew, redouble.

**ramble** *v.* **1** [To saunter] stroll, promenade, roam. **2** [To speak or write aimlessly] drift, stray, diverge, meander, gossip, talk nonsense, chatter, babble, digress, maunder, get off the subject, go on and on, expatiate, protract, enlarge, be diffuse, dwell on, amplify, go astray, drivel, rant and rave, talk off the top of one's head, go off on a tangent, beat around the bush.

**ramp** *n.* incline, slope, grade.

**rampant** *a.* raging, uncontrolled, growing without check, violent, vehement, impetuous, rank, turbulent, wild, luxuriant, tumultuous, profuse, plentiful, unruly, wanton, rife, prevalent, dominant, predominant, excessive, impulsive, impassioned, intolerant, unrestrained, extravagant, overabundant, sweeping the country, like wildfire*.—*Ant.* modest, mild, meek.

**random** *a.* haphazard, chance, purposeless, thoughtless, careless, blind, casual, fickle, eccentric, unpredictable, accidental. **—at random** haphazardly, by chance, aimlessly.

**range** *n.* **1** [Distance] reach, span, horizontal projection. **2** [Extent] length, area, expanse. **3** [A series of mountains] highlands, alps, sierras. **4** [Land open to grazing] pasture, grazing land, field. **5** [A kitchen stove] gas range, electric range, stove.

**range** *v.* **1** [To vary] differ, fluctuate, diverge from. **2** [To traverse wide areas] encompass, reach, pass over, cover, stray, stroll, wander, ramble, explore, scour, search, traverse, roam, rove. **3** [To place in order] line up, classify, arrange.

**rank** *a.* **1** [Having luxurious growth] wild, dense, lush. **2** [Having a foul odor] smelly, fetid, putrid, stinking, rancid, disagreeable, smelling, offensive, sour, foul, noxious, stale, tainted, gamy, musty, strong, rotten, moldy, turned, high, ill-smelling, nauseating, obnoxious, disgusting, reeking, malodorous, nasty, strong-smelling.—*Ant.* sweet, fragrant, fresh.

**rank** *n.* **1** [A row] column, file, string. **2** [Degree] seniority, standing, station. **3** [Social eminence] station, position, distinction, note, nobility, caste, privilege, standing, reputation, quality, situation, esteem, condition, state, place in society, status, circumstance, footing, grade, blood, family, pedigree, ancestry, stock, parentage, birth. **—pull (one's) rank on*** take advantage of, exploit, abuse subordinates.

**rank** *v.* **1** [To arrange in a row or rows] put in line, line up, place in formation. **2** [To evaluate comparatively] place, put, regard, judge, assign, give precedence to, fix, establish, settle, estimate, value, valuate, include, list, rate. **3** [To possess relative evaluation] be worth, stand, be at the head, have a place, go ahead of, come first, forerun, antecede, have supremacy over, have the advantage of, precede, outrank, take the lead, take precedence over, belong, count among, be classed, stand in relationship.

**ransom** *v.* release, rescue, deliver.

**rapid** *a.* speedy, accelerated, fast.

**rare** *a.* **1** [Uncommon] exceptional, singular, extraordinary. **2** [Scarce] sparse, few, scanty, meager, limited, short, expensive, precious, out of circulation, off the market, in great demand, occasional, uncommon, isolated, scattered, infrequent, deficient, almost unobtainable, few and far between.—*Ant.* cheap, profuse, tawdry. **3** [Choice] select, matchless, superlative. **4** [Lightly cooked] not cooked, not done, seared, braised, not overdone, nearly raw, underdone, red, moderately done, not thoroughly cooked.

**rarely** *a.* unusually, occasionally, once in a great while.

**rash** *a.* impetuous, impulsive, foolish, hotheaded, thoughtless, reckless, headstrong, bold, careless, determined, audacious, heedless, madcap, unthinking, headlong, incautious, wild, precipitant, overhasty, unwary, injudicious, venturous, foolhardy, imprudent, venturesome, adventurous, daring, jumping to conclusions, insuppressible, breakneck, irrational, fiery, furious, frenzied, passionate, immature, hurried, aimless, excited, feverish, tenacious, frantic, indiscreet, quixotic, ill-advised, unconsidered, without thinking, imprudent, unadvised, irresponsible, brash, precipitous, premature, sudden, harebrained, harumscarum, devil-may-care, daredevil.—*Ant.* calm, cool, levelheaded.

**rate** *n.* **1** [Ratio] proportion, degree, standard, scale, fixed amount, quota, relation, relationship, comparison, relative, weight, percentage, numerical progression. **2** [Price] valuation, allowance, estimate. **3** [Speed] velocity, pace, time.

**rate** *v.* **1** [To rank] judge, estimate, evaluate, grade, relate to a standard, fix, tag, calculate, assess, class, determine, appraise, guess at. **2** [*To be well-thought-of] be a favorite, triumph, succeed.

**rather** *a.* **1** [To some degree] fairly, somewhat, a little. **2** [By preference] first, by choice, in preference, sooner, more readily, willingly, much sooner, just as soon, as a matter of choice.

**ratify** *v.* sanction, approve, endorse.

**ratio** *n.* proportion, quota, quotient.

**rational** *a.* **1** [Acting in accordance with reason] stable, calm, cool, deliberate, discerning, discriminating, levelheaded, collected, logical, thoughtful, knowing, sensible, of sound judgment, having good sense, impartial, exercising reason, intelligent, wise, reasoning, prudent, circumspect, intellectual, reflective, philosophic, objective, farsighted, enlightened, well-advised, judicious, analytical, deductive, synthetic, conscious, balanced, sober, systematic.—*Ant.* rash, reckless, wild. **2** [Of a nature that appeals to reason] intelligent, sensible, reasonable. **3** [Sane] normal, lucid, responsible.

**raucous** *a.* hoarse, loud, gruff.

**ravage** *v.* pillage, overrun, devastate, destroy, crush, desolate, despoil, overspread, wreck, waste, disrupt, disorganize, demolish, annihilate, overthrow, overwhelm, break up, pull down, smash, shatter, scatter, batter down, exterminate, extinguish, trample down, dismantle, stamp out, lay waste, lay in ruins, sweep away, raze, ruin, plunder, strip, impair, sack, consume, spoil, harry, ransack, maraud, prey, crush, rape, rob, raid, pirate, seize, capture, gut, loot.—*Ant.* build, improve, rehabilitate.

**raw** *a.* **1** [Uncooked] fresh, rare, hard, unprepared, undercooked, fibrous, coarse-grained, unpasteurized, unbaked, unfried.—*Ant.* baked, cooked, fried. **2** [Unfinished] natural, untreated, crude, rough, newly cut, unprocessed, unrefined, untanned, coarse, newly mined, uncut, virgin.—*Ant.* refined, manufactured, processed. **3** [Untrained] immature, new, fresh. **4** [Cold] biting, windy, bleak. **5** [Without skin] peeled, skinned, dressed, galled, scraped, blistered, cut, wounded, pared, uncovered, chafed, bruised.—*Ant.* covered, coated, healed. **6** [*Nasty] low, dirty, unscrupulous. **—in the raw** nude, bare, unclothed.

**reach** *n.* compass, range, scope, grasp, stretch, extension, orbit, horizon, gamut.

**reach** *v.* **1** [To extend to] touch, span, encompass, pass along, continue to, roll on, stretch, go as far as, attain, equal, approach, lead, stand, terminate, end, overtake, join, come up to, sweep. **2** [To extend a part of the body to] lunge, strain, move, reach out, feel for, come at, make contact with, shake hands, throw out a limb, make for, put out, touch, strike, seize, grasp. **3** [To arrive] get to, come to, enter.

**reaction** *n.* reply, rejoinder, reception, receptivity, response, return, feeling, opinion, reflection, backlash, attitude, retort, reciprocation, repercussion, reflex.

**read** *v.* **1** [To understand by reading] comprehend, go through, peruse, scan, glance over, go over, gather, see, know, skim, perceive, apprehend, grasp, learn, flip through the pages, dip into, scratch the surface, bury oneself in. **2** [To interpret] view, render, translate, decipher, make out, unravel, express, explain, expound, construe, paraphrase, restate, put.

**readily** *a.* quickly, promptly, immediately.

**ready** *a.* **1** [Prompt] quick, spontaneous, alert, wide-awake, swift, fleet, fast, sharp, immediate, instant, animated.—*Ant.* slow, dull, lazy. **2** [Prepared] fit, apt, skillful, ripe, handy, in readiness, waiting, on call, in line for, in position, on the brink of, equipped to do the job, open to, fixed for, on the mark, equal to, expectant, available, at hand, anticipating, in order, all systems go*, all squared away*, in a go condition*.—*Ant.* unprepared, unready, unavailable. **3** [Enthusiastic] eager, willing, ardent. **—make ready** get in order, prepare for something, equip.

**real** *a.* **1** [Genuine] true, authentic, original. **2** [Having physical existence] actual, solid, firm, substantive, material, live, substantial, existent, tangible, existing, present, palpable, factual, sound, concrete, corporal, corporeal, bodily, incarnate, embodied, physical, sensible, stable, in existence, perceptible, evident, undeniable, irrefutable, practical, true, true to life.—*Ant.* unreal, unsubstantial, hypothetical. **3** [*Very much] exceedingly, exceptionally, uncommonly. **—for real*** actually, in fact, certainly.

**realization** *n.* understanding, comprehension, consciousness.

**realize** *v.* **1** [To bring to fulfillment] perfect, make good, actualize. **2** [To understand] recognize, apprehend, discern. **3** [To receive] acquire, make a profit from, obtain.

**really** *a.* **1** [In fact] actually, indeed, genuinely, certainly, surely, absolutely, positively, veritably, in reality, authentically, upon my honor, legitimately, precisely, literally, indubitably, unmistakably, in effect, undoubtedly, categorically, in point of fact, I assure you, be assured, believe me, as a matter of fact, of course, honestly, truly, admittedly, nothing else but, beyond any doubt, in actuality, unquestionably, as sure as you're born*, no buts about it*, beyond a shadow of a doubt. **2** [To a remarkable degree] surprisingly, remarkably, extraordinarily.

**realm** *n.* domain, area, sphere.

**reason** *n.* **1** [The power of reasoning] intelligence, mind, sanity. **2** [A process of reasoning] logic, dialectics, speculation, generalization, rationalism, argumentation, inference, induction, deduction, analysis, rationalization. **3** [A basis for rational action] end, object, rationale, intention, motive, ulterior motive, basis, wherefore, aim, intent, cause, design, ground, impetus, idea, motivation, root, incentive, goal, purpose, the why and wherefore. **4** [The mind] brain, mentality, intellect. **—by reason of** because of, for, by way of. **—in** (or **within**) **reason** in accord with what is reasonable, rationally, understandably. **—stand to reason** be feasible, seem all right, appeal. **—with reason** understandably, soundly, plausibly.

**reasonable** *a.* **1** [Rational] sane, levelheaded, intelligent, clear-cut, tolerant, endowed with reason, conscious, cerebral, thoughtful, reflective, capable of reason, reasoning, cognitive, perceiving, consistent, broad-minded, liberal, generous, sensible, unprejudiced, unbiased, flexible, agreeable.—*Ant.* prejudiced, intolerant, biased. **2** [Characterized by justice] fair, right, just. **3** [Likely to appeal to the reason] feasible, sound, plausible. **4** [Moderate in price] inexpensive, reduced, fair.

**reassure** *v.* convince, console, encourage.

**rebel** *n.* insurrectionist, revolutionist, revolutionary, agitator, insurgent, traitor, seditionist, mutineer, subverter, anarchist, overthrower, nihilist, guerrilla, member of the uprising, rioter, demagogue, revolter, separatist, malcontent, schismatic, deserter, dissenter, apostate, turncoat, counterrevolutionary, renegade, secessionist, underground worker.

**rebel** *v.* rise up, resist, revolt, turn against, defy, resist lawful authority, fight in the streets, strike, boycott, break with, overturn, mutiny, riot, take up arms against, start a confrontation, secede, renounce, combat, oppose, be insubordinate, be treasonable, upset, overthrow, dethrone, disobey, raise hell*, run amok*.—*Ant.* obey, be contented, submit.

**rebellious** *a.* revolutionary, insurgent, counterrevolutionary, warring, stubborn, contemptuous, insolent, scornful, intractable, unyielding, recalcitrant, insurrectionary, attacking, rioting, mutinous, dissident, factious, fractious, seditious, disobedient, treasonable, refractory, defiant, resistant, riotous, insubordinate, sabotaging, disloyal, disaffected, alienated, ungovernable, restless, threatening, anarchistic, iconoclastic, individualistic, radical, independent-minded, quarrelsome.—*Ant.* calm, docile, peaceful.

**rebound** *v.* reflect, ricochet, spring back.

**rebuild** *v.* touch up, patch, build up.

**recede** *v.* **1** [To go backward] fall back, shrink from, withdraw. **2** [To sink] ebb, drift away, lower, turn down, abate, decline, go away, drop, fall off, lessen.—*Ant.* rise, flow, increase.

**receive** *v.* **1** [To take into one's charge] accept, be given, admit, get, gain, inherit, acquire, gather up, collect, obtain, reap, procure, derive, appropriate, seize, take possession, redeem, pocket, pick up, hold, come by, earn, take in, assume, draw, win, secure, come into, come in for, catch, get from.—*Ant.* discard, abandon, refuse. **2** [To endure] undergo, experience, suffer. **3** [To support] bear, sustain, prop. **4** [To make welcome] accommodate, initiate, induct, install, make welcome, shake hands with, admit, permit, welcome home, accept, entertain, invite in, show in, usher in, let through, make comfortable, bring as a guest into, introduce, give a party, give access to, allow entrance to, roll out the red carpet for*, give the red-carpet treatment to*, get out the welcome mat for*, greet.—*Ant.* visit, be a guest, call.

**recent** *a.* **1** [Lately brought into being] fresh, novel, newly born. **2** [Associated with modern times] contemporary, up-to-date, streamlined.

**recently** *a.* lately, in recent times, just now, just a while ago, not long ago, a short while ago, of late, newly, freshly, new, the other day, within the recent past.—*Ant.* once, long ago, formerly.

**reception** *n.* **1** [The act of receiving] acquisition, acceptance, accession. **2** [The manner of receiving] meeting, encounter, introduction, gathering, welcome, salutation, induction, admission, disposition. **3** [A social function] tea, party, dinner.

**recite** *v.* **1** [To repeat formally] declaim, address, read, render, discourse, hold forth, enact, dramatize, deliver from memory, interpret, soliloquize. **2** [To report on a lesson] answer, give a report, explain. **3** [To relate in detail] enumerate, enlarge, report, account for, give an account for, impart, chant, convey, quote, communicate, utter, describe, relate, state, tell, mention, narrate, recount, retell, picture, delineate, portray.

**reckless** *a.* thoughtless, foolish, wild.

**reckon** *v.* consider, evaluate, estimate.

**recognize** *v.* **1** [To know again] be familiar with, make out, distinguish, verify, recollect, sight, diagnose, place, espy, descry, recall, remember, see, perceive, admit knowledge of, notice. **2** [To acknowledge] admit, appreciate, realize. **3** [To acknowledge the legality of a government] exchange diplomatic representatives with, have diplomatic relations with, sanction, approve, extend formal recognition to.

**recommend** *v.* **1** [To lend support or approval] agree to, sanction, hold up, commend, extol, compliment, applaud, advocate, celebrate, praise, speak highly of, acclaim, eulogize, confirm, laud, second, favor, back, stand by, magnify, glorify, exalt, think highly of, think well of, be satisfied with, esteem, value, prize, uphold, justify, endorse, go on record for, be all for, front for, go to bat for*.— *Ant.* denounce, censure, renounce. **2** [To make a suggestion or prescription] prescribe, suggest, counsel.

**reconcile** *v.* **1** [To adjust] adapt, arrange, regulate. **2** [To bring into harmony] conciliate, assuage, pacify, propitiate, mitigate, make up, mediate, arbitrate, intercede, bring together, accustom oneself to, harmonize, accord, dictate peace, accommodate, appease, reunite, make peace between, bring to terms, bring into one's camp, win over, bury the hatchet, patch up, kiss and make up.—*Ant.* bother, irritate, alienate.

**reconsider** *v.* reevaluate, think over, rearrange, consider again, recheck, reexamine, correct, amend, revise, retrace, rework, replan, review, withdraw for consideration, reweigh, amend one's judgment regarding.

**reconstruct** *v.* rebuild, remodel, construct again, make over, revamp, recondition, reconstitute, reestablish, restore, reproduce, refashion, reorganize, replace, overhaul, renovate, modernize, rework, construct from the original, copy, remake, repair.

**record** *n.* **1** [Documentary evidence] manuscript, inscription, transcription, account, history, legend, story, writing, written material, document, register, catalog, list, inventory, memo, memorandum, registry, schedule, chronicle, docket, scroll, archive, notes, contract, statement, will, testament, calendar, log, letter, memoir, reminiscence, dictation, confession, deposition, official record, sworn document, evidence, license, bulletin, gazette, newspaper, magazine, annual report, journal, *Congressional Record*, transactions, debates, bill, annals, presidential order, state paper, white paper, blue book, budget, report, entry, book, publication, autograph, signature, vital statistics, deed, paper, diary, stenographic notes, ledger, daybook, almanac, proceedings, minutes, description, affidavit, certificate, transcript, dossier, roll, tape, disk, microfilm, microfiche. **2** [One's past] career, experience, work. **3** [A device for the reproduction of sound] recording, disk, phonograph record, LP, transcription, compact disc, CD, laserdisc, canned music*, cut, take, platter*. **—go on record** assert, attest, state. **—off the record** confidential, unofficial, secret. **—on the record** recorded, stated, official.

**record** *v.* **1** [To write down] register, write in, jot down, set down, take down, put on record, transcribe, list, note, file, mark, inscribe, log, catalog, tabulate, put in writing, put in black and white, chronicle, keep accounts, keep an account of, make a written account of, matriculate, enroll, journalize, put on paper, preserve, make an entry in, chalk up, write up, enter, report, book, post, copy, document, insert, enumerate. **2** [To indicate] point out, explain, show. **3** [To record electronically] tape, cut, photograph, make a record of, make a tape, tape-record, film, videotape, cut a record.

**recover** *v.* **1** [To obtain again] redeem, salvage, retrieve, rescue, reclaim, recoup, find again, recapture, repossess, bring back, win back, reacquire, obtain, regain, rediscover, resume, catch up.—*Ant.* lose, let slip, fall behind. **2** [To improve one's condition] gain, increase, collect.—*Ant.* fail, go bankrupt, give up. **3** [To regain health] rally, come around, come to, come out of it, get out of danger, improve, convalesce, heal, get the better of, overcome, start anew, be restored, mend, revive, be oneself again, perk up, gain strength, recuperate, get well, get over, get better, get through, return to form, make a comeback*, get back in shape*, snap out of*, pull through*, sober up.—*Ant.* die, fail, become worse.

**recovery** *n.* **1** [The act of returning to normal] reestablishment, resumption, restoration, reinstatement, return, rehabilitation, reconstruction, reformation, re-creation, replacement, readjustment, improving, getting back to normal. **2** [The process of regaining health] convalescence, recuperation, revival, rebirth, renaissance, resurgence, resurrection, regeneration, cure, improvement, reawakening, renewal, resuscitation, rejuvenation, rehabilitation, return of health, physical improvement, healing, betterment. **3** [The act of regaining possession] repossession, retrieval, reclamation, redemption, indemnification, reparation, compensation, recapture, recouping, return, restoration, remuneration, reimbursement, retaking, recall.

**recreation** *n.* amusement, relaxation, diversion, play, fun, entertainment, enjoyment, festivity, hobby, holiday, vacation, pastime, pleasure, game, avocation, refreshment, sport.

**recruit** *n.* new man, novice, beginner, selectee, draftee, trainee, volunteer, enlisted man, enlisted woman, serviceman, servicewoman, soldier, sailor, marine, rookie*.

**recruit** *v.* **1** [To raise troops] draft, call up, select, supply, muster, deliver, sign up, induct, take in, find manpower, call to arms, bring into service. **2** [To gather needed resources] restore, store up, replenish.

**rectangular** *a.* square, four-sided, right-angled.

**recur** *v.* return, reappear, crop up again.

**red** *n.* scarlet, carmine, vermilion, crimson, cerise, cherry red, ruby, garnet, maroon, brick red, claret, rust, red gold, magenta, pink, fuchsia, coral red, blood red, russet, terra cotta, Chinese red, Congo red, Turkey red, aniline red, chrome red, rose. —**in the red*** in debt, losing money, going broke*. —**see red*** become angry, lose one's temper, get mad.

**redecorate** *v.* refurbish, refresh, renew, paint, repaint, repaper, restore, recondition, remodel, renovate, revamp, reaarrange, touch up, patch up, plaster, refurnish, wallpaper, clean up, carpet, do over, fix up*.

**redeem** *v.* **1** [To recover through a payment] buy back, repay, purchase. **2** [To save] liberate, set free, deliver.

**reduce** *v.* **1** [To make less] lessen, diminish, cut down. **2** [To defeat] conquer, overcome, subdue. **3** [To humble] degrade, demote, abase.

**reduction** *n.* **1** [The process of making smaller] conversion, contraction, abatement, reducing, refinement, diminution, lowering, lessening, shortening, condensation, decrease, loss, compression, depression, subtraction, discount, shrinkage, constriction, modification, curtailment, abbreviation, miniaturization, abridgment, modulation, mitigation, remission, decline.—*Ant.* increase, increasing, enlargement. **2** [An amount that constitutes reduction] decrease, rebate, cut.

**refer** *v.* **1** [To concern] regard, relate, have relation, have to do with, apply, be about, answer to, involve, connect, be a matter of, have a bearing on, bear upon, comprise, include, belong, pertain, have reference, take in, cover, point, hold, encompass, incorporate, touch, deal with. **2** [To mention] allude to, bring up, direct a remark, make reference to, ascribe, direct attention, attribute, cite, quote, hint at, point to, notice, indicate, speak about, suggest, touch on, give as an example, associate, exemplify, instance, excerpt, extract. **3** [To direct] send to, put in touch with, relegate, commit, submit to, assign, give a recommendation to, introduce.

**refined** *a.* **1** [Purified] cleaned, cleansed, aerated, strained, washed, clean, rarefied, boiled down, distilled, clarified, tried, drained.—*Ant.* raw, crude, unrefined. **2** [Genteel] cultivated, civilized, polished, elegant, well-bred, gracious, enlightened, gentlemanly, ladylike, restrained, gentle, mannerly, high-minded, subtle, courteous, polite.

**reflect** *v.* **1** [To contemplate] speculate, concentrate, weigh. **2** [To throw back] echo, reecho, repeat, match, take after, return, resonate, reverberate, copy, resound, reproduce, reply, be resonant, emulate, imitate, follow, catch, rebound. **3** [To throw back an image] mirror, shine, reproduce, show up on, flash, cast back, return, give forth.

**reflection** *n.* **1** [Thought] consideration, absorption, imagination, observation, thinking, contemplation, rumination, speculation, musing, deliberation, study, pondering, meditation, concentration, cogitation. **2** [An image] impression, rays, light, shine, glitter, appearance, idea, reflected image, likeness, shadow, duplicate, picture, echo, representation, reproduction.

**reform** *v.* **1** [To change into a new form] reorganize, remodel, revise, repair, reconstruct, rearrange, transform, ameliorate, redeem, rectify, better, rehabilitate, improve, correct, cure, remedy, convert, mend, amend, restore, rebuild, reclaim, revolutionize, regenerate, refashion, renovate, renew, rework, reconstitute, make over, remake.—*Ant.* corrupt, degrade, botch. **2** [To correct evils] amend, clean out, give a new basis, abolish, repeal, uplift, ameliorate, rectify, regenerate, give new life to, remedy, stamp out, make better, standardize, bring up to code. **3** [To change one's conduct for the better] resolve, mend, regenerate, uplift, make amends, make a new start, make resolutions, turn over a new leaf, go straight*, swear off.

**refrain** *n.* undersong*, theme, strain.

**refresh** *v.* invigorate, animate, exhilarate.

**refrigerate** *v.* chill, make cold, freeze.

**refuge** *n.* **1** [A place of protection] shelter, asylum, sanctuary, covert, home, retreat, anchorage, nunnery, convent, monastery, poorhouse, safe place, hiding place, game preserve, safe, safe house, harbor, haven, fortress, stronghold. **2** [A means of resort] alternative, resource, last resort.

**refund** *n.* return, reimbursement, repayment, remuneration, compensation, allowance, payment for expenses, rebate, discount, settlement, discharge, retribution, satisfaction, consolation, money back.

**refund** *v.* pay back, reimburse, remit, repay, relinquish, make good, balance, recoup, adjust, reward, restore, redeem, make repayment to, compensate, recompense, make amends, redress, remunerate, give back, settle, honor a claim, kick back*, make good*, make up for.

**refusal** *n.* repudiation, renunciation, rebuff, snub, nonacceptance, denial, disavowal, noncompliance, opposition, rejection, forbidding, veto, interdiction, proscription, ban, writ, exclusion, negation, repulse, withholding, disclaimer, nonconsent, unwillingness, regrets, repulsion, reversal, dissent, prohibition, disfavor, disapproval, curb, restraint.

**refuse** *v.* dissent, desist, repel, rebuff, scorn, pass up, reject, disallow, have no plans to, not anticipate, demur, protest, withdraw, hold back, withhold, shun, turn thumbs down on, evade, dodge, ignore, spurn, regret, turn down, turn from, beg to be excused, send regrets, not budge, cut out of the budget, not budget, not care to, refuse to receive, dispense with, not be at home to, say no, make excuses, disapprove, set aside, turn away, beg off, brush off*, not buy, hold off, turn one's back on, turn a deaf ear to.—*Ant.* allow, admit, consent.

**refute** *v.* disprove, answer, prove false.

**regard** *n.* **1** [A look] gaze, glance, once-over*. **2** [A favorable opinion] esteem, respect, honor, favor, liking, interest, fondness, attachment, deference, opinion, sympathy, estimation, appreciation, reverence, consideration, love, affection, value, devotion, admiration.

**regard** *v.* **1** [To look at] observe, notice, mark. **2** [To have an attitude] surmise, look upon, view, consider, think. **3** [To hold in esteem] respect, esteem, value.

**regime** *n.* administration, management, political system.

**regimentation** *n.* massing, collectivization, organization, planned economy, standardization, methodization, regulation, uniformity, arrangement, mechanization, institutionalization, classification, division, lining up, adjustment, harmonization, grouping, ordering.

**region** *n.* **1** [An indefinite area] country, district, territory, section, sector, province, zone, realm, vicinity, quarter, locale, locality, environs, precinct, county, neighborhood, terrain, domain, range. **2** [A limited area] precinct, ward, block. **3** [Scope] sphere, realm, field.

**register** *v.* **1** [To record] check in, enroll, file. **2** [To indicate] point to, designate, record. **3** [To show] express, disclose, manifest. **4** [To enlist or enroll] go through registration, check into, make an entry, sign up for, check in, sign in, join.

**regress** *v.* backslide, relapse, revert.

**regret** *v.* **1** [To be sorry for] mourn, bewail, lament, cry over, rue, grieve, repent, have compunctions about, look back upon, feel conscience-stricken, moan, have a bad conscience, have qualms about, weep over, be disturbed over, feel uneasy about, laugh out of the other side of one's mouth*, kick oneself*, bite one's tongue*, cry over spilled milk*.—*Ant.* celebrate, be satisfied with, be happy. **2** [To disapprove of] deplore, be opposed to, deprecate.

**regular** *a.* **1** [In accordance with custom] customary, usual, routine. **2** [In accordance with law] normal, legitimate, lawful. **3** [In accordance with an observable pattern] orderly, methodical, routine, symmetrical, precise, exact, systematic, arranged, organized, patterned, constant, congruous, consonant, consistent, invariable, formal, regulated, rational, steady, rhythmic, periodic, measured, classified, in order, unconfused, harmonious, systematic, normal, natural, cyclic, successive, momentary, alternating, probable, recurrent, general, usual, expected, serial, automatic, mechanical, hourly, daily, monthly, weekly, annual, seasonal, yearly, diurnal, quotidian, anticipated, hoped for, counted on, generally occurring, in the natural course of events, punctual, steady, uniform.—*Ant.* irregular, sporadic, erratic.

**regulate** *v.* **1** [To control] rule, legislate, direct. **2** [To adjust] arrange, methodize, dispose, classify, systematize, put in order, fix, settle, adapt, standardize, coordinate, allocate, readjust, reconcile, rectify, correct, improve, temper, set.

**rehabilitation** *n.* rebuilding, reestablishment, remaking, improvement, repair.

**rehearse** *v.* **1** [To tell] describe, recount, relate. **2** [To repeat] tell again, retell, do over, recapitulate, reenact. **3** [To practice for a performance] drill, test, experiment, hold rehearsals, speak from a script, run through, hold a reading, learn one's part, practice.

**reign** *v.* hold power, sit on the throne, wear the crown.

**rejoice** *v.* exult, enjoy, revel.

**relapse** *v.* lapse, retrogress, fall, backslide, revert, regress, suffer a relapse, deteriorate, degenerate, fall from grace, fall off, weaken, sink back, fall into again, slip back, slide back, be overcome, give in to again.

**related** *a.* **1** [Told] narrated, described, recounted. **2** [Connected] associated, in touch with, linked, tied up, knit together, allied, affiliated, complementary, analogous, correspondent, akin, alike, like, parallel, correlated, intertwined, interrelated, similar, mutual, dependent, interdependent, interwoven, of that ilk, in the same category, reciprocal, interchangeable. **3** [Akin] kindred, of the same family, germane, fraternal, cognate, consanguine, of one blood.

**relaxation** *n.* repose, reclining, loosening.

**release** *v.* liberate, let go, acquit.

**relent** *v.* soften, comply, relax.

**relentless** *a.* unmerciful, vindictive, hard.

**relevant** *a.* suitable, appropriate, fit, proper, pertinent to, becoming, pertaining to, apt, applicable, important, fitting, congruous, cognate, related, conforming, concerning, suitable, compatible, accordant, referring, harmonious, correspondent, consonant, congruent, consistent, correlated, associated, allied, relative, connected, to the point, bearing on the question, having direct bearing, having to do with, related to, on the nose.—*Ant.* irrelevant, wrong, not pertinent.

**reliable** *a.* firm, unimpeachable, sterling, strong, positive, stable, dependable, sure, solid, staunch, decisive, unequivocal, steadfast, definite, conscientious, constant, steady, trustworthy, faithful, loyal, good, true, devoted, tried, trusty, honest, honorable, candid, true-hearted, responsible, high-principled, sincere, altruistic, determined, reputable, careful, proved, respectable, righteous, decent, incorrupt, truthful, upright, regular, all right, kosher*, OK*, on the up and up*, true-blue, safe, honest, sound, solid, guaranteed, certain, substantial, secure, unquestionable, conclusive, irrefutable, incontestable, unfailing, infallible, authentic, competent, assured, workable, foolproof, sure-fire.—*Ant.* dangerous, insecure, undependable.

**relic** *n.* **1** [Something left from an earlier time] vestige, trace, survival, heirloom, antique, keepsake, memento, curio, curiosity, token, souvenir, testimonial, evidence, monument, trophy, remains, artifact, remembrance, bric-a-brac. **2** [A ruin] remnant, residue, remains, broken stone.

**relieve** *v.* **1** [To replace] discharge, throw out, force to resign. **2** [To lessen; *said especially of pain*] assuage, alleviate, soothe, comfort, allay, divert, free, ease, lighten, soften, diminish, mitigate, console, cure, aid, assist.

**relieved** *a.* **1** [Eased in mind] comforted, solaced, consoled, reassured, satisfied, soothed, relaxed, put at ease, restored, reconciled, appeased, placated, alleviated, mollified, disarmed, pacified, adjusted, propitiated, breathing easy*.—*Ant.* sad, worried, distraught. **2** [Deprived of something, or freed from it] replaced, dismissed, separated from, disengaged, released, made free of, rescued, delivered, supplanted, superseded, succeeded, substituted, interchanged, exchanged. **3** [Lessened; *said especially of pain*] mitigated, palliated, softened, assuaged, eased, abated, diminished, salved, soothed, lightened, alleviated, drugged, anesthetized.

**religion** *n.* **1** [All that centers about man's belief in or relationship to a superior being or beings] belief, devotion, piety, spirituality, persuasion, godliness, sense of righteousness, morality, theology, faithfulness, devoutness, creed, myth, superstition, doctrine, cult, denomination, mythology, communion, religious conscience, fidelity, conscientiousness, religious bent, ethical standard, faith. **2** [Organized worship or service of a deity] veneration, adoration, consecration, sanctification, prayer, rites, ceremonials, holy sacrifice, incantation, holiday, observance, orthodoxy, reformism. —**get religion*** become converted, believe, change.

**reluctant** *a.* disinclined, loath, unwilling, averse, opposed, tardy, backward, adverse, laggard, remiss, slack, squeamish, demurring, grudging, involuntary, uncertain, hanging back, hesitant, hesitating, diffident, with bad grace, indisposed, disheartened, discouraged, queasy.—*Ant.* willing, eager, disposed.

**remainder** *n.* remaining portion, leftover, residue, remains, relic, remnant, dregs, surplus, leavings, balance, residuum, excess, overplus, scrap, fragment, small piece, carry-over, rest, residual portion, whatever is left, salvage.

**remark** *n.* statement, saying, utterance, annotation, note, mention, reflection, illustration, point, conclusion, consideration, talk, observation, expression, comment, assertion, witticism.

**remark** *v.* say, mention, observe.

**remedy** *n.* **1** [A medicine] antidote, pill, drug. **2** [Effective help] relief, cure, redress, support, improvement, solution, plan, panacea, cure-all, assistance, counteraction.

**remember** *v.* **1** [To recall] recollect, recognize, summon up, relive, dig into the past, refresh one's memory, be reminded of, think of, revive, bring to mind, call to mind, think over, think back, look back, brood over, conjure up, call up, carry one's thoughts back, look back upon, have memories of, commemorate, memorialize, reminisce, carry in one's thoughts, keep a memory alive, enshrine in the memory.—*Ant.* lose, forget, neglect. **2** [To bear in mind] keep in mind, memorize, know by heart, learn, master, get, impress upon one's mind, fix in the mind, retain, treasure, hold dear, dwell upon, brood over, keep forever.—*Ant.* neglect, ignore, disregard.

**remind** *v.* **1** [To bring into the memory] bring back, make one think of, intimate. **2** [To call the attention of another] caution, point out, refresh the memory, remind one of, mention to, call attention to, bring up, prompt, prod, stress, emphasize, note, stir up, put a bug in one's ear, give a cue.

**reminder** *n.* warning, notice, admonition, note, memorandum, memo, hint, suggestion, memento, token, keepsake, trinket, remembrance, souvenir.

**remnants** *pl.n.* scraps, odds and ends, leftovers, particles, surplus, end-pieces, remains, leavings.

**remodel** *v.* renovate, refurnish, refurbish, readjust, reconstruct, readapt, rearrange, redecorate, refashion, improve, reshape, recast, rebuild, repair, modernize, repaint.

**remote** *a.* **1** [Distant] far-off, faraway, out-of-the-way, removed, beyond, secluded, inaccessible, isolated, unknown, alien, foreign, undiscovered, off the beaten track, over the hills and far away, godforsaken.—*Ant.* near, close, accessible. **2** [Ancient] forgotten, past, aged. **3** [Separated] unrelated, irrelevant, unconnected.

**remove** *v.* **1** [To move physically] take away from, cart away, clear away, carry away, take away, tear away, brush away, transfer, transport, dislodge, uproot, excavate, displace, unload, discharge, lift up, doff, raise, evacuate, shift, switch, lift, push, draw away, draw in, withdraw, separate, extract, cut out, dig out, tear out, pull out, take out, smoke out, rip out, take down, tear off, draw off, take off, carry off, cart off, clear off, strike off, cut off, rub off, scrape off. **2** [To eliminate] get rid of, do away with, exclude. **3** [To dismiss] discharge, displace, discard.

**render** *v.* **1** [To give] present, hand over, distribute. **2** [To perform, especially a service] do, act, execute. **3** [To interpret; *said especially of music*] play, perform, depict.

**renew** *v.* **1** [To refresh] revive, reawaken, regenerate, reestablish, rehabilitate, reinvigorate, replace, revive, rebuild, reconstitute, remake, refinish, refurbish, redo, repeat, invigorate, exhilarate, restore, resuscitate, recondition, overhaul, replenish, go over, cool, brace, freshen, stimulate, recreate, remodel, revamp, redesign, modernize, rejuvenate, give new life to, recover, renovate, reintegrate, make a new beginning, bring up to date, do over, make like new. **2** [To repeat] resume, reiterate, recommence. **3** [To replace] replenish, supplant, take over.

**rent** *v.* **1** [To sell the use of property] lease, lend, let, make available, allow the use of, take in roomers, sublet, put on loan. **2** [To obtain use by payment] hire, pay rent for, charter, contract, sign a contract for, engage, borrow, pay for services.

**repair** *v.* fix, adjust, improve, correct, settle, put into shape, reform, patch, rejuvenate, refurbish, retread, touch up, put in order, revive, refresh, renew, mend, darn, sew, revamp, rectify, right, ameliorate, renovate, reshape, rebuild, work over*, fix up.—*Ant.* wreck, damage, smash.

**reparation** *n.* indemnity, retribution, amends.

**repeat** *v.* **1** [To do again] redo, remake, do over, recur, rehash, reciprocate, return, rework, reform, refashion, recast, reduplicate, renew, reconstruct, reerect, revert, hold over, go over again and again. **2** [To happen again] reoccur, recur, revolve, reappear, occur again, come again, return. **3** [To say again] reiterate, restate, reissue, republish, reutter, echo, recite, reecho, rehearse, retell, go over, play back, recapitulate, drum into, rehash, come again.

**repel** *v.* **1** [To throw back] rebuff, resist, stand up against, oppose, check, repulse, put to flight, keep at bay, knock down, drive away, drive back, beat back, hold back, force back, push back, ward off, chase off, stave off, fight off.—*Ant.* fall, fail, retreat. **2** [To cause aversion] nauseate, offend, revolt. **3** [To reject] disown, dismiss, cast aside.

**replace** *v.* **1** [To supply an equivalent] repay, compensate, mend. **2** [To take the place of] take over, supplant, displace. **3** [To put back in the same place] restore, reinstate, put back.

**replica** *n.* copy, likeness, model.

**reply** *v.* retort, rejoin, return.

**report** *n.* **1** [A transmitted account] tale, narrative, description. **2** [An official summary] proclamation, outline, release. **3** [A loud, explosive sound] detonation, bang, blast.

**represent** *v.* **1** [To act as a delegate] be an agent for, serve, hold office, be deputy for, be attorney for, steward, act as broker, sell for, buy for, do business for, be spokesman for, be ambassador for, exercise power of attorney for. **2** [To present as a true interpretation] render, depict, portray. **3** [To serve as an equivalent] copy, imitate, reproduce, symbolize, exemplify, typify, signify, substitute, stand for, impersonate, personify.

**repress** *v.* control, curb, check.

**reproduce** *v.* **1** [To make an exact copy] photograph, print, Xerox (trademark). **2** [To make a second time] repeat, duplicate, recreate, recount, revive, reenact, redo, reawaken, relive, remake, reflect, follow, mirror, echo, reecho, represent. **3** [To multiply] procreate, engender, breed, generate, propagate, fecundate, hatch, father, beget, impregnate, bear, sire, repopulate, multiply, give birth.

**repulsive** *a.* **1** [Capable of repelling] resistant, unyielding, stubborn, opposing, retaliating, insurgent, counteracting, attacking, counterattacking, defensive, combative, aggressive, pugnacious.—*Ant.* yielding, surrendering, capitulating. **2** [Disgusting] odious, forbidding, horrid.

**reputation** *n.* **1** [Supposed character] reliability, trustworthiness, respectability, dependability, credit, esteem, estimation. **2** [Good name] standing, prestige, regard, favor, account, respect, privilege, acceptability, social approval. **3** [Fame] prominence, eminence, notoriety.

**require** *v.* **1** [To need] want, feel the necessity for, have need for. **2** [To demand] exact, insist upon, expect.

**requirement** *n.* **1** [A prerequisite] preliminary condition, essential, imperative, element, requisite, provision, terms, necessity, stipulation, fundamental, first principle, precondition, reservation, specification, proviso, fulfillment, qualification, vital part, *sine qua non* (Latin). **2** [A need] necessity, necessary, lack, want, demand, claim, obsession, preoccupation, prepossession, engrossment, stress, extremity, exigency, pinch, obligation, pressing concern, urgency, compulsion, exaction.

**rescue** *n.* **1** [The act of rescuing] deliverance, saving, release, extrication, liberation, ransom, redemption, freeing, salvation, reclamation, reclaiming, emancipation, disentaglement, recovering, heroism. **2** [An instance of rescue] action, deed, feat, performance, exploit, accomplishment, heroics.

**rescue** *v.* **1** [To save] preserve, recover, redeem, recapture, salvage, retain, hold over, keep back, safeguard, ransom, protect, retrieve, withdraw, take to safety.—*Ant.* lose, let slip from one's hands, relinquish. **2** [To free] deliver, liberate, release.

**research** *n.* investigation, analysis, experimentation, examination, study.

**resemble** *v.* be like, look like, seem like, sound like, follow, take after, parallel, match, coincide, relate, mirror, approximate, give indication of, remind one of, bring to mind, catch a likeness, have all the signs of, be the very image of, be similar to, come close to, appear like, bear a resemblance to, come near, pass for, have all the earmarks of, echo, compare with, be comparable to, smack of*, be the spit and image of*, be a dead ringer for*.—*Ant.* differ, contradict, oppose.

**reserve** *n.* **1** [A portion kept against emergencies] savings, insurance, resources, reserved funds, store, provisions, assets, supply, hoard, backlog, nest egg, something in the sock*, something for a rainy day. **2** [Calmness] backwardness, restraint, reticence, modesty, unresponsiveness, uncommunicativeness, caution, inhibition, coyness, demureness, aloofness. **—in reserve** withheld, kept back, saved.

**reserved** *a.* **1** [Held on reservation] pre-empted, claimed, booked. **2** [Held in reserve] saved, withheld, kept aside, preserved, conserved, stored away, funded, put in a safe, on ice*.—*Ant.* used, spent, exhausted. **3** [Restrained] shy, modest, backward, reticent, secretive, quiet, composed, retiring, private, controlling oneself, mild, gentle, peaceful, soft-spoken, sedate, collected, serene, placid.—*Ant.* loud, ostentatious, boisterous.

**reside** *v.* dwell, stay, lodge.

**resign** *v.* **1** [To relinquish] surrender, capitulate, give up. **2** [To leave one's employment] quit, separate oneself from, retire, step down, drop out, stand down, sign off, end one's services, leave, hand in one's resignation, cease work, give notice, walk out of the job, walk off the job.

**resigned** *a.* quiet, peaceable, docile, tractable, submissive, yielding, relinquishing, gentle, obedient, manageable, willing, agreeable, ready, amenable, pliant, compliant, easily managed, genial, cordial, satisfied, well-disposed, patient, unresisting, tolerant, calm, reconciled, adjusted, adapted, accommodated, tame, nonresisting, passive, philosophical, renouncing, unassertive, subservient, deferential.—*Ant.* rebellious, recalcitrant, resistant.

**resistance** *n.* **1** [A defense] stand, holding, withstanding, warding off, rebuff, obstruction, defiance, striking back, coping, check, halting, protecting, protection, safeguard, shield, screen, cover, watch, support, fight, impeding, blocking, opposition.—*Ant.* withdrawal, withdrawing, retirement. **2** [The power of remaining impervious to an influence] unsusceptibility, immunity, immovability, hardness, imperviousness, endurance, fixedness, fastness, stability, stableness, permanence. **3** [The power of holding back another substance] friction, attrition, resistance.

**resolve** *v.* determine, settle on, conclude, fix, purpose, propose, choose, fix upon, make up one's mind, take a firm stand, take one's stand, take a decisive step, make a point of, pass upon, decree, elect, remain firm, take the bull by the horns.

**resort** *n.* **1** [A relief in the face of difficulty] expedient, shift, makeshift, stopgap, substitute, surrogate, resource, device, refuge, recourse, hope, relief, possibility, opportunity. **2** [A place for rest or amusement] seaside resort, mountain resort, ski resort, amusement park, nightclub, spa, health spa, restaurant, club. **—as a last resort** in desperation, lastly, in the end.

**resource** *n.* reserve, supply, support, source, stock, store, means, expedient, stratagem, relief, resort, recourse, artifice, device, refuge.

**resourceful** *a.* original, ingenious, capable.

**respect** *v.* **1** [To esteem] regard, value, look up to. **2** [To treat with consideration] appreciate, heed, notice, consider, note, recognize, defer to, do honor to, be kind to, show courtesy to, spare, take into account, attend, regard, uphold.—*Ant.* ridicule, mock, scorn.

**respite** *n.* reprieve, postponement, pause.

**response** *n.* statement, reply, acknowledgment.

**responsibility** *n.* **1** [State of being reliable] trustworthiness, reliability, trustiness, dependability, loyalty, faithfulness, capableness, capacity, efficiency, competency, uprightness, firmness, steadfastness, stability, ability. **2** [State of being accountable] answerability, accountability, liability, subjection, engagement, pledge, contract, constraint, restraint.—*Ant.* freedom, exemption, immunity. **3** [Anything for which one is accountable] obligation, trust, contract.

**responsible** *a.* **1** [Charged with responsibility] accountable, answerable, liable, subject, bound, under obligation, constrained, tied, fettered, bonded, censurable, chargeable, obligated, obliged, compelled, contracted, hampered, held, pledged, sworn to, bound to, beholden to, under contract, engaged.—*Ant.* free, unconstrained, unbound. **2** [Capable of assuming responsibility] trustworthy, trusty, reliable, capable, efficient, loyal, faithful, dutiful, dependable, tried, self-reliant, able, competent, qualified, effective, upright, firm, steadfast, steady, stable.—*Ant.* irresponsible, capricious, unstable.

**rest** *n.* **1** [Repose] quiet, quietness, quietude, ease, tranquillity, slumber, calm, calmness, peace, peacefulness, relaxation, recreation, coffee break, rest period, sleep, siesta, doze, nap, somnolence, dreaminess, comfort, breathing spell, lounging period, loafing period, vacation, lull, leisure, respite, composure. **2** [State of inactivity] intermission, cessation, stillness, stop, stay, standstill, lull, discontinuance, interval, hush, silence, dead calm, stagnation, fixity, immobility, inactivity, motionlessness, pause, full stop, deadlock, recess, noon hour.—*Ant.* activity, continuance, endurance. **3** [Anything upon which an object rests] support, prop, pillar. **4** [*The remainder] residue, surplus, remnant. **5** [Death] release, demise, mortality. **—at rest** in a state of rest, immobile, inactive. **—lay to rest** inter, assign to the grave, entomb.

**rest** *v.* **1** [To take one's rest] sleep, slumber, doze, repose, lie down, lounge, let down, ease off, recuperate, rest up, take a rest, take a break, break the monotony, lean, recline, relax, unbend, settle down, dream, drowse, take one's ease, be comfortable, stretch out, nap, nod, snooze*. **2** [To depend upon] be supported, be seated on, be based on.

**restaurant** *n.* cafe, eatery, cafeteria, diner, hamburger stand, hotel dining room, inn, coffee shop, coffeehouse, chophouse, tearoom, luncheonette, lunch wagon, fast-food place, pizzeria, lunch bar, soda fountain, milk bar, hot-dog stand, snack bar, automat, rotisserie, cabaret, nightclub, grill, oyster house, barbecue, spaghetti house, canteen, food court.

**restless** *a.* fidgety, skittish, feverish, sleepless, jumpy, nervous, unquiet, disturbed, uneasy, anxious, up in arms, discontented, vexed, excited, agitated, angry, disaffected, estranged, alienated, resentful, recalcitrant, fractious, insubordinate, flurried, roving, transient, wandering, discontented, unsettled, roaming, nomadic, moving, straying, ranging, footloose, itinerant, gallivanting, meandering, traipsing, restive, peeved, annoyed, impatient, flustered, twitching, trembling, tremulous, rattled*, jittery*.—*Ant.* quiet, sedate, calm.

**restrain** *v.* check, control, curb, bridle, rein in, hem in, keep in, handle, regulate, keep in line, guide, direct, keep down, repress, harness, muzzle, hold in leash, govern, inhibit, hold, bind, deter, hold back, hamper, constrain, restrict, stay, gag, limit, impound, bottle up, tie down, pin down, pull back, contain, sit on, come down on.

**restraint** *n.* **1** [Control over oneself] control, self-control, reserve, reticence, constraint, withholding, caution, coolness, forbearance, silence, secretiveness, stress, repression, self-government, self-restraint, stiffness, abstinence, self-denial, unnaturalness, self-repression, constrained manner, abstention, self-discipline, self-censorship.—*Ant.* laziness, slackness, laxity. **2** [An influence that checks or hinders] repression, deprivation, limitation, hindrance, reduction, abridgment, decrease, prohibition, confinement, check, barrier, obstacle, obstruction, restriction, bar, curb, blockade, order, command, instruction, coercion, impediment, compulsion, duress, force, violence, deterrence, determent, discipline, assignment, definition, moderation, tempering, qualifying.—*Ant.* freedom, liberty, license.

**restricted** *a.* limited, confined, restrained, circumscribed, curbed, bound, prescribed, checked, bounded, inhibited, hampered, marked, defined, delimited, encircled, surrounded, shut in, hitched, tethered, chained, fastened, secured, bridled, held back, held down, reined in, controlled, governed, deterred, impeded, stayed, stopped, suppressed, repressed, prevented, fettered, deprived, blocked, barred, obstructed, dammed, clogged, manacled, frustrated, embarrassed, baffled, foiled, shrunken, narrowed, shortened, decreased, diminished, reduced, moderated, tempered, modified, qualified, out of bounds.

**result** *n.* consequence, issue, event, execution, effect, outcome, end, finish, termination, consummation, completion, aftereffect, aftermath, upshot, sequel, sequence, fruit, fruition, eventuality, proceeds, emanation, outgrowth, outcropping, returns, backwash, backlash, repercussion, settlement, determination, decision, arrangement, payoff*.—*Ant.* origin, source, root.

**result** *v.* issue, grow from, spring from, rise from, proceed from, emanate from, germinate from, flow from, accrue from, arise from, derive from, come from, originate in, become of, spring, emerge, rise, ensue, emanate, effect, produce, follow, happen, occur, come about, come forth, come out, pan out, work out, end, finish, terminate, conclude.

**resume** *v.* take up again, reassume, begin again, recommence, reoccupy, go on with, renew, recapitulate, return, keep on, carry on, keep up, continue.—*Ant.* stop, cease, discontinue.

**retaliate** *v.* fight back, return, repay.

**retire** *v.* **1** [To draw away] withdraw, part, retreat. **2** [To go to bed] lie down, turn in, rest. **3** [To cease active life] resign, give up work, sever one's connections, leave active service, relinquish, make vacant, lay down, hand over, lead a quiet life, sequester oneself, reach retirement age.

**retort** *n.* counter, repartee, response.

**retort** *v.* reply, respond, snap back.

**retract** *v.* withdraw, draw away, take in.

**retreat** *v.* recede, retrograde, back out, retract, go, depart, recoil, shrink, quail, run, draw back, reel, start back, reverse, seclude oneself, keep aloof, hide, separate from, regress, resign, relinquish, lay down, hand over, withdraw, backtrack, leave, back off*, back down, chicken out*.—*Ant.* stay, remain, continue.

**retrieve** *v.* regain, bring back, reclaim.

**return** *n.* **1** [The act of coming again] homecoming, arrival, reappearance. **2** [The act of being returned] restoration, restitution, rejoinder, recompense, acknowledgment, answer, reaction, reversion, repetition, reverberation, reappearance, reentrance, rotating, reoccurrence, rebound, recoil, reconsideration. **3** [Proceeds] profit, income, results, gain, avail, revenue, advantage, yield, accrual, accruement, interest.—*Ant.* failure, loss, disadvantage. **—in return** in exchange, as payment, as an equivalent, for a reward.

**return** *v.* **1** [To go back] come again, come back, recur, reappear, reoccur, repeat, revert, reconsider, reenter, reexamine, reinspect, bounce back, retrace one's steps, turn, rotate, revolve, renew, revive, recover, regain, rebound, circle back, double back, move back, turn back, reverberate, recoil, retrace, revisit, retire, retreat.—*Ant.* move, advance, go forward. **2** [To put or send something back] bring back, toss back, roll back, hand back, give back, restore, replace, render, reseat, reestablish, reinstate, react, recompense, refund, repay, make restitution.—*Ant.* hold, keep, hold back. **3** [To answer] reply, respond, retort. **4** [To repay] reimburse, recompense, refund. **5** [To yield a profit] pay off, show profit, pay dividends. **6** [To reflect] echo, sound, mirror.

**reunion** *n.* reuniting, meeting again, rejoining, reconciliation, reconcilement, homecoming, restoration, harmonizing, bringing together, healing the breach, get-together.

**reveal** *v.* disclose, betray a confidence, divulge, make known, confess, impart, publish, lay bare, betray, avow, admit, bring to light, acknowledge, give utterance to, bring out, let out, give out, make public, unfold, communicate, announce, declare, inform, notify, utter, make plain, break the news, broadcast, concede, come out with, explain, bring into the open, affirm, report, let the cat out of the bag, blab*, talk, rat*, stool*, make a clean breast of, put one's cards on the table, bring to light, show one's colors, get something out of one's system, give the low-down*, let on*, squeal*, blow the whistle*.

**revenge** *n.* **1** [The act of returning an injury] vengeance, requital, reprisal, measure for measure, repayment, counterplay, retaliation, retribution, avenging, counterinsurgency, getting even.—*Ant.* pardon, forgiveness, excusing. **2** [The desire to obtain revenge] vindictiveness, rancor, malevolence.

**revenue** *n.* **1** [Income] return, earnings, result, yield, wealth, receipts, proceeds, resources, funds, stocks, credits, dividends, interest, salary, profits, means, fruits, rents.—*Ant.* expenses, outgo, obligations. **2** [Governmental income] wealth, revenue, taxation.

**revere** *v.* venerate, regard with deep respect, respect.

**reverse** *v.* **1** [To turn] go back, shift, invert. **2** [To alter] turn around, modify, convert. **3** [To annul] nullify, invalidate, repeal. **4** [To exchange] transpose, rearrange, shift.

**review** *n.* **1** [A reexamination] reconsideration, second thought, revision, retrospection, second view, reflection, study, survey, retrospect.

**2** [A critical study] survey, critique, criticism. **3** [A summary] synopsis, abstract, outline. **4** [A formal inspection] parade, inspection, dress parade, drill, march, procession, cavalcade, column, file, military display, march-past.

**revive** *v.* **1** [To give new life] enliven, enkindle, refresh, renew, vivify, animate, reanimate, resuscitate, recondition, rejuvenate, bring to, bring around, wake up, resurrect, make whole, exhilarate, energize, invigorate, breathe new life into, reproduce, regenerate, restore, touch up, repair.—*Ant.* decrease, wither, lessen. **2** [To take on new life] come around, come to, freshen, improve, recover, flourish, awake, reawake, rouse, arouse, strengthen, overcome, come to life, grow well, be cured.—*Ant.* die, faint, weaken.

**revolution** *n.* **1** [A complete motion about an axis] rotation, spin, turn, revolving, circuit, round, whirl, gyration, circumvolution, cycle, roll, reel, twirl, swirl, pirouette. **2** [An armed uprising] revolt, rebellion, mutiny, insurrection, riot, anarchy, outbreak, coup, coup d'état, destruction, overturn, upset, overthrow, reversal, rising, crime, violence, bloodshed, turbulence, insubordination, disturbance, reformation, plot, underground activity, guerrilla activity, public unrest, upheaval, tumult, disorder, foment, turmoil, uproar, uprising, row, strife, strike, putsch, subversion, breakup, secession.—*Ant.* law, order, control.

**revolve** *v.* spin, rotate, twirl.

**reward** *n.* **1** [Payment] compensation, remuneration, recompense. **2** [A prize] premium, bonus, award.

**reward** *v.* compensate, repay, remunerate.

**rich** *a.* **1** [Possessed of wealth] wealthy, moneyed, affluent, well-to-do, well provided for, worth a million, well-off, well-fixed, in clover, swimming in gravy*, in the money*.—*Ant.* poor, poverty-stricken, destitute. **2** [Sumptuous] luxurious, magnificent, resplendent, lavish, embellished, ornate, costly, expensive, splendid, superb, elegant, gorgeous, valuable, precious, extravagant, grand.—*Ant.* cheap, plain, simple. **3** [Fertile] exuberant, lush, copious, plentiful, generous, fruitful, profuse, luxuriant, teeming, abundant, prolific, productive, fruit-bearing, propagating, yielding, breeding, superabounding, prodigal.—*Ant.* sterile, unfruitful, barren. **4** [Having great food value] nourishing, luscious, sweet, fatty, oily, nutritious, sustaining, strengthening, satisfying.—*Ant.* inadequate, not nourishing, deficient.

**riddle** *n.* problem, question, knotty question, doubt, quandary, entanglement, dilemma, embarrassment, perplexity, enigma, confusion, complication, complexity, intricacy, strait, labyrinth, predicament, plight, distraction, bewilderment.—*Ant.* simplicity, clarity, disentanglement.

**ride** *v.* **1** [To be transported] be carried, travel in or on a vehicle, tour, journey, motor, drive, go for an airing; go by automobile, bicycle, etc. **2** [To control a beast of burden by riding] manage, guide, handle. **3** [To tease harshly] ridicule, bait, harass.

**ridicule** *n.* scorn, contempt, mockery, disdain, derision, jeer, leer, disparagement, sneer, flout, fleer, twit, taunt, burlesque, caricature, satire, parody, travesty, irony, sarcasm, persiflage, farce, buffoonery, horseplay, foolery, razz*, rib*, roast*, raspberry*, horse laugh.—*Ant.* praise, commendation, approval.

**ridicule** *v.* scoff at, sneer at, laugh at, rail at, mock, taunt, banter, mimic, jeer, twit, disparage, flout, deride, scorn, make sport of, make fun of, rally, burlesque, caricature, satirize, parody, cartoon, travesty, run down, make fun of, put down*, razz*, rib*, pull someone's leg*, roast*, pan*.—*Ant.* encourage, approve, applaud.

**right** *a.* **1** [Correct] true, precise, accurate, exact, sure, certain, determined, proven, factual, correct. **2** [Just] lawful, legitimate, honest. **3** [Suitable] apt, proper, appropriate. **4** [Sane] reasonable, rational, sound. **5** [Justly] fairly, evenly, equitably, honestly, decently, sincerely, legitimately, lawfully, conscientiously, squarely, impartially, objectively, reliably, dispassionately, without bias, without prejudice. **6** [Straight] directly, undeviatingly, immediately. **7** [Opposite to left] dextral, dexter, righthanded, clockwise, on the right.—*Ant.* left, sinistral, counterclockwise.

**right** *n.* **1** [A privilege] prerogative, immunity, exemption, license, benefit, advantage, favor, franchise, preference, priority. **2** [Justice] equity, freedom, liberty, independence, emancipation, enfranchisement, self-determination, natural expectation, fairness. **3** [The part opposite the left] right hand, right side, strong side, active side. **—by rights** properly, justly, suitably. **—in one's own right** individually, acting as one's own agent, by one's own authority. **—in the right** correct, true, accurate.

**right** *v.* **1** [To make upright] set up, make straight, balance. **2** [To repair an injustice] adjust, correct, repair, restore, vindicate, do justice, recompense, reward, remedy, rectify, mend, amend, set right.—*Ant.* wrong, hurt, harm.

**righteous** *a.* **1** [Virtuous] just, upright, good, honorable, honest, worthy, exemplary, noble, right-minded, goodhearted, dutiful, trustworthy, equitable, scrupulous, conscientious, ethical, fair, impartial, fairminded, commendable, praiseworthy, guiltless, blameless, sinless, peerless, sterling, matchless, deserving, laudable, creditable, charitable, philanthropic, having a clear conscience.—*Ant.* corrupt, sinful, profligate. **2** [Religiously inclined] devout, pious, saintly, godly, godlike, angelic, devoted, reverent, reverential, faithful, fervent, strict, rigid, devotional, zealous, spiritual, holy, religious.—*Ant.* bad, impious, irreligious. **3** [Conscious of one's own virtue] self-righteous, hypocritical, self-esteeming.

**rim** *n.* edge, border, verge, brim, lip, brink, top, margin, line, outline, band, ring, strip, brow, curb, ledge, skirt, fringe, hem, limit, confine, end, terminus.—*Ant.* center, middle, interior.

**rip** *v.* rend, split, cleave, rive, tear, shred.

**ripe** *a.* **1** [Ready to be harvested] fully grown, fully developed, ruddy, red, yellow, plump, filled out, matured, ready.—*Ant.* green, undeveloped, half-grown. **2** [Improved by time and experience] mellow, wise, perfected. **3** [Ready] prepared, seasoned, consummate, perfected, finished, usable, fit, conditioned, prime, available, on the mark, complete.—*Ant.* unfit, unready, unprepared.

**rise** *n.* **1** [The act of rising] ascent, lift, climb. **2** [An increase] augmentation, growth, enlargement, multiplication, heightening, intensifying, stacking up, piling up, distention, addition, accession, inflation, acceleration, doubling, advance.—*Ant.* reduction, decrease, lessening. **3** [Source] beginning, commencement, start. **—get a rise out of*** get a response from by teasing, provoke, annoy. **—give rise to** initiate, begin, start.

**rise** *v.* **1** [To move upward] ascend, mount, climb, scale, surmount, soar, tower, rocket, surge, sweep upward, lift, bob up, move up, push up, reach up, come up, go up, surge, sprout, grow, rear, uprise, blast off, curl upward.—*Ant.* fall, drop, come down. **2** [To get out of bed] get up, rise up, wake. **3** [To increase] grow, swell, intensify, mount, enlarge, spread, expand, extend, augment, heighten, enhance, distend, inflate, pile up, stack up, multiply, accelerate, speed up, add to, wax, advance, raise, double.—*Ant.* decrease, lessen, contract. **4** [To begin] spring, emanate, issue. **5** [To improve one's station] prosper, flourish, thrive. **6** [To stand] be erected, be built, be placed, be located, be put up, go up, be founded, have foundation, be situated.

**risk** *v.* gamble, hazard, venture, run the risk, do at one's own peril, hang by a thread, play with fire, go out of one's depth, go beyond one's depth, bell the cat*, make an investment, take the liberty, lay oneself open to, pour money into, go through fire and water, leave to luck, skate on thin ice, defy danger.

**risky** *a.* perilous, precarious, hazardous.

**ritual** *n.* observance, rite, ceremony.

**rival** *a.* competing, striving, combatant, combatting, emulating, vying, opposing, disputing, contesting, contending, conflicting, battling, equal.—*Ant.* helpful, aiding, assisting.

**rival** *n.* competitor, antagonist, opponent.

**road** *n.* **1** [A strip prepared for travel] path, way, highway, roadway, street, avenue, thoroughfare, boulevard, high road, drive, terrace, parkway, byway, lane, alley, alleyway, crossroad, viaduct, subway, paving, slab, turnpike, trail, post road, secondary road, market road, national highway, state highway, county road, military road, Roman road, freeway, the main drag*. **2** [A course] scheme, way, plan. **—on the road** on tour, traveling, on the way.

**roam** *v.* ramble, range, stroll, rove, walk, traverse, stray, straggle, meander, prowl, tramp, saunter, knock around*, bat around*, scour, straggle, gallivant, struggle along, traipse*, hike.

**roar** *v.* bellow, shout, boom, thunder, howl, bay, bawl, yell, rumble, drum, detonate, explode, reverberate, resound, reecho.

**rob** *v.* thieve, take, burglarize, strip, plunder, deprive of, withhold from, defraud, cheat, swindle, pilfer, break into, hold up, stick up*, purloin, filch, lift*, abscond with, embezzle, pillage, sack, loot, snitch*, pinch*, swipe*, cop*, steal.

**robber** *n.* thief, burglar, cheat, plunderer, pillager, bandit, pirate, raider, thug, desperado, forger, holdup man*, second-story man*, privateer, buccaneer, swindler, highwayman, bank robber, pilferer, shoplifter, cattle-thief, housebreaker, pickpocket, freebooter, marauder, brigand, pickpurse*, sharper, safecracker, fence, rustler*, crook*, con man*, clip artist*, chiseler*, paper hanger*, stick-up man*.

**robust** *a.* hale, hearty, sound.

**rocky** *a.* stony, flinty, hard, inflexible, solid, petrified, ragged, jagged, rugged.—*Ant.* soft, flexible, sandy.

**rogue** *n.* outlaw, miscreant, criminal.

**roll** *v.* **1** [To move by rotation, or in rotating numbers] rotate, come around, swing around, wheel, come in turn, circle, alternate, follow, succeed, be in sequence, follow in due course. **2** [To revolve] turn, pivot, spin. **3** [To make into a roll] bend, curve, arch. **4** [To smooth with a roller] press, level, flatten, spread, pulverize, grind.—*Ant.* cut, roughen, toss up. **5** [To flow] run, wave, surge. **6** [To produce a relatively deep, continuous sound] reverberate, resound, echo. **7** [To function] work, go, start production.

**romantic** *a.* **1** [Referring to love and adventure] adventurous, novel, daring, charming, enchanting, lyric, poetic, fanciful, chivalrous, courtly, knightly. **2** [Referring to languages descending from Latin; *often capital*] Romanic, Romance, Mediterranean, French, Italian, Spanish.

**romp** *v.* gambol, celebrate, frolic.

**rotate** *v.* twist, wheel, revolve.

**rotten** *a.* **1** [Having rotted] bad, rotting, putrefying, decaying, putrefied, spoiled, decomposed, decayed, offensive, disgusting, rancid, fecal, rank, foul, corrupt, polluted, infected, loathsome, overripe, bad-smelling, putrid, crumbled, disintegrated, stale, noisome, smelling, fetid, noxious.—*Ant.* fresh, unspoiled, good. **2** [Not sound] unsound, defective, impaired. **3** [Corrupt] contaminated, polluted, filthy, tainted, defiled, impure, sullied, unclean, soiled, debauched, blemished, morbid, infected, dirtied, depraved, tarnished.—*Ant.* pure, clean, healthy.

**rough** *a.* **1** [Not smooth] unequal, broken, coarse, choppy, ruffled, uneven, ridged, rugged, irregular, not sanded, not finished, unfinished, not completed, needing the finishing touches, bumpy, rocky, stony, jagged, grinding, knobby, sharpening, cutting, sharp, crinkled, crumpled, rumpled, scraggly, straggly, hairy, shaggy, hirsute, bushy, tufted, bearded, woolly, nappy, unshaven, unshorn, gnarled, knotty, bristly.—*Ant.* level, flat, even. **2** [Not gentle] harsh, strict, stern. **3** [Crude] boorish, uncivil, uncultivated. **4** [Not quiet] buffeting, stormy, tumultuous. **5** [Unfinished] incomplete, imperfect, uncompleted. **6** [Approximate] inexact, unprecise, uncertain.

**round** *a.* **1** [Shaped like a globe or disk] spherical, globular, orbicular, globe-shaped, ball-shaped, domical, circular, cylindrical, ringed, annular, oval, disk-shaped. **2** [Curved] arched, rounded, bowed, looped, recurved, incurved, coiled, curled. **3** [Approximate] rough, in tens, in hundreds.

**round** *n.* **1** [A round object] ring, orb, globe, circle. **2** [A period of action] bout, course, whirl, cycle, circuit, routine, performance. **3** [A unit of ammunition] cartridge, charge, load.

**round** *v.* **1** [To turn] whirl, wheel, spin. **2** [To make round] curve, convolute, bow, arch, bend, loop, whorl, shape, form, recurve, coil, fill out, curl, mold.—*Ant.* straighten, flatten, level.

**route** *n.* **1** [A course being followed] way, course, path, track, beat, tack, divergence, detour, digression, meandering, rambling, wandering, circuit, round, rounds, range. **2** [A projected course] map, plans, plot.

**routine** *a.* usual, customary, habitual.

**rove** *v.* walk, meander, wander.

**row** *n.* series, order, file. **—in a row** in succession, successively, in a line.

**royal** *a.* **1** [Pertaining to a king or his family] high, elevated, highborn, monarchic, reigning, regnant, regal, ruling, dominant, absolute, imperial, sovereign, supreme. **2** [Having qualities befitting royalty] great, grand, stately, lofty, illustrious, renowned, eminent, superior, worthy, honorable, dignified, chivalrous, courteous, kingly, great-hearted, large-hearted, princely, princelike, majestic, magnificent, splendid, courtly, impressive, commanding, aristocratic, lordly, august, imposing, superb, glorious, resplendent, gorgeous, sublime.

**rub** *v.* **1** [To subject to friction] scrape, smooth, abrade, scour, grate, grind, wear away, graze, rasp, knead, fret, massage, polish, shine, burnish, scrub, erase, rub out, rub down, file, chafe, clean. **2** [To apply by rubbing; *usually with "on"*] brush, cover, finish.

**rude** *a.* **1** [Boorish] rustic, ungainly, awkward, crude, coarse, gross, rough, harsh, blunt, rugged, common, barbarous, lumpish, ungraceful, hulking, loutish, antic, rowdy, disorderly, brutish, boorish, clownish, stupid, ill-proportioned, unpolished, uncultured, unrefined, untrained, indecorous, unknowing, untaught, uncouth, slovenly, ill-bred, inelegant, ignorant, inexpert, illiterate, clumsy, gawky, slouching, graceless, ungraceful, lumbering, green, unacquainted, unenlightened, uneducated, vulgar, indecent, ribald, homely, outlandish, disgraceful, inappropriate.—*Ant.* cultured, urbane, suave. **2** [Not polite] churlish, sullen, surly, sharp, harsh, gruff, snarling, ungracious, unkind, ungentle, obstreperous, overbearing, sour, disdainful, unmannerly, ill-mannered, improper, shabby, ill-chosen, discourteous, ungentlemanly, fresh*, abusive, forward, loud, loudmouthed, bold, brazen, audacious, brash, arrogant, supercilious, blustering, impudent, crass, raw, saucy, crusty, pert, unabashed, sharp-tongued, loose, mocking, barefaced, insolent, impertinent, offensive, naughty, impolite, hostile, insulting, disrespectful, scornful, flippant, presumptuous, sarcastic, defiant, outrageous, swaggering, disparaging, contemptuous, rebellious, disdainful, unfeeling, insensitive, scoffing, disagreeable, domineering, overbearing, highhanded, hypercritical, self-assertive, brutal, severe, hard, cocky, bullying, cheeky*, nervy*, assuming, dictatorial, magisterial, misbehaved, officious, meddling, intrusive, meddlesome, bitter, uncivilized, slandering, ill-tempered, bad-tempered, sassy*, snotty*, snooty*, uppity*.—*Ant.* polite, courteous, mannerly. **3** [Harsh] rough, violent, stormy. **4** [Approximate] guessed, surmised, imprecise. **5**

[Coarse] rough, unrefined, unpolished. **6** [Primitive] ignorant, uncivilized, barbarous.

**rug** *n.* carpet, carpeting, floor covering, linoleum, straw mat, floor mat, woven mat, drugget.

**ruin** *n.* **1** [The act of destruction] extinction, demolition, overthrow. **2** [A building fallen into decay; *often plural*] remains, traces, residue, foundations, vestiges, remnants, relics, wreck, walls, detritus, rubble. **3** [The state of destruction] dilapidation, waste, wreck.

**ruin** *v.* **1** [To destroy] injure, overthrow, demolish. **2** [To cause to become bankrupt] impoverish, bankrupt, beggar.

**ruined** *a.* **1** [Destroyed] demolished, overthrown, torn down, extinct, abolished, exterminated, annihilated, subverted, wrecked, desolated, ravaged, smashed, crushed, crashed, extinguished, extirpated, dissolved, totaled*.—*Ant.* protected, saved, preserved. **2** [Spoiled] pillaged, harried, robbed, plundered, injured, hurt, impaired, defaced, harmed, marred, past hope, mutilated, broken, gone to the dogs*, done for*.—*Ant.* repaired, restored, mended. **3** [Bankrupt] pauperized, poverty-stricken, beggared, reduced, left in penury, penniless, fleeced, brought to want, gone under*, sold up*, through the mill*.—*Ant.* rich, prosperous, well-off.

**rule** *n.* **1** [Government] control, dominion, jurisdiction. **2** [A regulation] edict, command, commandment. **3** [The custom] habit, course, practice. **—as a rule** ordinarily, generally, usually.

**ruler** *n.* governor, commander, chief, manager, adjudicator, monarch, regent, director.

**rumor** *n.* report, news, tidings, intelligence, dispatch, hearsay, gossip, scandal, tattle, notoriety, noise, cry, popular report, fame, repute, grapevine, buzz*, breeze*, hoax, fabrication, suggestion, supposition, story, tale, invention, fiction, falsehood.

**run** *n.* **1** [The act of running] sprint, pace, bound, flow, amble, jog, gallop, canter, lope, spring, trot, dart, rush, dash, flight, escape, break, charge, swoop, race, scamper, tear, whisk, flow, fall, drop. **2** [A series] continuity, succession, sequence. **3** [The average] par, norm, run of the mill. **—in the long run** in the final outcome, finally, eventually. **—on the run** **1** busy, in a hurry, running. **2** retreating, defeated, routed.

**run** *v.* **1** [To move, usually rapidly] flow in, flow over, chase along, fall, pour, tumble, drop, leap, spin, whirl, whiz, sail. **2** [To go swiftly by physical effort] rush, hurry, spring, bound, scurry, skitter, scramble, scoot, travel, run off, run away, dash ahead, dash on, put on a burst of speed, go on the double*, light out*, have a free play, make tracks*, dart, dart ahead, gallop, canter, lope, spring, trot, single-foot, amble, pace, flee, speed, spurt, swoop, bolt, race, shoot, tear, whisk, scamper, scuttle. **3** [To function] move, work, go. **4** [To cause to function] control, drive, govern. **5** [To extend] encompass, cover, spread. **6** [To continue] last, persevere, go on. **7** [To complete] oppose, contest, contend with.

**rundown** *n.* report, outline, review.

**run into** *v.* **1** [To collide with] bump into, crash, have a collision. **2** [To encounter] come across, see, meet. **3** [To blend with] mingle, combine with, osmose.

**runner** *n.* racer, entrant, contestant, sprinter, distance runner, middle distance runner, cross-country runner, jogger, trackman, hurdler, messenger, courier, express, dispatch bearer.

**run-of-the-mill** *a.* mediocre, ordinary, common.

**rural** *a.* rustic, farm, agricultural, ranch, pastoral, bucolic, backwoods, country, agrarian, agronomic, suburban.—*Ant.* urban, industrial, commercial.

**rush** *v.* hasten, speed, hurry up.

**rust** *v.* oxidize, become rusty, degenerate, decay, rot, corrode.

**rustic** *a.* agricultural, pastoral, agrarian.

**ruthless** *a.* cruel, fierce, savage, brutal, merciless, inhuman, hard, cold, fiendish, unmerciful, pitiless, grim, unpitying, tigerish, ferocious, stony-hearted, coldblooded, remorseless, vindictive, vengeful, revengeful, rancorous, implacable, unforgiving, malevolent, surly, hard-hearted, hard, cold, unsympathetic, unforbearing, vicious, sadistic, tyrannical, relentless, barbarous, inhuman, atrocious, flagrant, terrible, abominable, outrageous, oppressive, bloodthirsty, venomous, galling.—*Ant.* kind, helpful, civilized.

# S

**sabotage** *v.* subvert, siege, undermine.

**sack** *n.* sac, pouch, bag.

**sacred** *a.* **1** [Holy] pure, pious, saintly. **2** [Dedicated] consecrated, ordained, sanctioned.

**sad** *a.* **1** [Afflicted with sorrow] unhappy, sorry, sorrowful, downcast, dismal, gloomy, glum, pensive, heavy-hearted, dispirited, dejected, depressed, desolate, troubled, melancholy, morose, grieved, pessimistic, crushed, brokenhearted, heartbroken, heartsick, despondent, careworn, rueful, anguished, disheartened, lamenting, mourning, grieving, weeping, bitter, woebegone, doleful, spiritless, joyless, heavy, crestfallen, discouraged, moody, low-spirited, despairing, hopeless, worried, downhearted, cast down, in heavy spirits, morbid, oppressed, blighted, grief-stricken, foreboding, apprehensive, horrified, anxious, wretched, miserable, mournful, disconsolate, forlorn, jaundiced, out of sorts, distressed, afflicted, bereaved, repining, harassed, dreary, down in the dumps*, in bad humor, out of humor, cut up*, in the depths*, blue, stricken with grief, making a long face, in tears, down in the mouth*.—*Ant.* happy, joyous, cheerful. **2** [Suggestive of sorrow] pitiable, unhappy, dejecting, saddening, disheartening, discouraging, joyless, dreary, dark, dismal, gloomy, moving, touching, mournful, disquieting, disturbing, somber, doleful, oppressive, funereal, lugubrious, pathetic, tragic, pitiful, piteous, woeful, rueful, sorry, unfortunate, hapless, heart-rending, dire, distressing, depressing, grievous.

**sadden** *v.* oppress, dishearten, discourage, cast down, deject, depress, break one's heart.

**sadistic** *a.* cruel, brutal, vicious.

**safe** *a.* **1** [Not in danger] out of danger, secure, in safety, in security, free from harm, free from danger, unharmed, safe and sound, protected, guarded, housed, screened from danger, unmolested, unthreatened, entrenched, impregnable, invulnerable, under the protection of, saved, safeguarded, secured, defended, supported, sustained, maintained, upheld, preserved, vindicated, shielded, nourished, sheltered, fostered, cared for, cherished, watched, impervious to, patrolled, looked after, supervised, tended, attended, kept in order, surveyed, regulated, with one's head above water, undercover, out of harm's way, on the safe side, on ice*, at anchor, in harbor, snug as a bug in a rug*, under lock and key.—*Ant.* dangerous, unsafe, risky. **2** [Not dangerous] innocent, innocuous, harmless. **3** [Reliable] trustworthy, dependable, competent.

**safe** *n.* strongbox, coffer, chest, repository, vault, case, safe-deposit box.

**safety** *n.* **1** [Freedom from danger] security, protection, impregnability, surety, sanctuary, refuge, shelter, invulnerability. **2** [A lock] lock mechanism, safety catch, safety lock.

**sailor** *n.* seaman, mariner, seafarer, pirate, navigator, pilot, boatman, yachtsman, able-bodied seaman, Jack Tar*, tar*, sea dog*, limey*, salt*, bluejacket.

**saintly** *a.* angelic, pious, holy.

**sale** *n.* **1** [The act of selling] commerce, business, traffic, exchange, barter, commercial enterprise, marketing, vending, trade. **2** [An individual instance of selling] deal, transaction, negotiation, turnover, trade, purchase, auction, disposal. **3** [An organized effort to promote unusual selling] bargain sale, clearance, stock reduction, fire sale, unloading, dumping, remnant sale, going out of business sale, bankruptcy sale. **—for** (or **on** or **up for**) **sale** put on the market, to be sold, marketable, available, offered for purchase, not withheld. **—on sale** reduced, at a bargain, cut.

**salve** *n.* ointment, unguent, lubricant, balm, medicine, emollient, unction, remedy, help, cure, cream.

**same** *a.* **1** [Like another in state] equivalent, identical, corresponding. **2** [Like another in action] similarly, in the same manner, likewise.

**same** *pron.* the very same, identical object, substitute, equivalent, similar product, synthetic product.

**sameness** *n.* uniformity, unity, resemblance, analogy, similarity, alikeness, identity, standardization, equality, unison, no difference.

**sanction** *n.* consent, acquiescence, assent.

**sanction** *v.* confirm, authorize, countenance.

**sanctuary** *n.* **1** [A sacred place] shrine, church, temple. **2** [A place to which one may retire] asylum, resort, haven.

**sane** *a.* **1** [Sound in mind] rational, normal, lucid, right-minded, sober, sound-minded, sound, in one's right mind, with a healthy mind, mentally sound, balanced, healthy-minded, reasonable, in possession of one's faculties.—*Ant.* insane, irrational, delirious. **2** [Sensible] reasonable, open to reason, wise.

**sanitary** *a.* hygienic, wholesome, sterile.

**sarcasm** *n.* satire, irony, banter, derision, contempt, scoffing, flouting, ridicule, burlesque, disparagement, criticism, cynicism, invective, censure, lampooning, aspersion, sneering, mockery.—*Ant.* flattery, fawning, cajolery.

**sarcastic** *a.* scornful, mocking, ironical, satirical, taunting, severe, derisive, bitter, saucy, hostile, sneering, snickering, quizzical, arrogant, disrespectful, offensive, carping, cynical, disillusioned, snarling, unbelieving, corrosive, acid, cutting, scorching, captious, sharp, pert, brusque, caustic, biting, harsh, austere, grim.

**sardonic** *a.* sarcastic, cynical, ironic.

**satisfaction** *n.* **1** [The act of satisfying] gratification, fulfillment, achievement. **2** [The state or feeling of being satisfied] comfort, pleasure, well-being, content, contentment, gladness, delight, bliss, joy, happiness, relief, complacency, peace of mind, ease, heart's ease, serenity, contentedness, cheerfulness. **3** [Something that contributes to satisfaction] reward, prosperity, good fortune. **4** [Reparation] reimbursement, repayment, compensation.

**satisfactory** *a.* adequate, satisfying, pleasing.

**satisfy** *v.* **1** [To make content] comfort, cheer, elate, befriend, please, rejoice, delight, exhilarate, amuse, entertain, flatter, make merry, make cheerful, gladden, content, gratify, indulge, humor, conciliate, propitiate, capture, enthrall, enliven, animate, captivate, fascinate, fill, be of advantage, gorge. **2** [To pay] repay, clear up, disburse. **3** [To fulfill] do, fill, serve the purpose, be enough, observe, perform, comply with, conform to, meet requirements, keep a promise, accomplish, complete, be adequate, be sufficient, provide, furnish, qualify, answer, serve, equip, meet, avail, suffice, fill the want, come up to, content one, appease one, fill the bill*, pass muster*, get by.—*Ant.* neglect, leave open, fail to do.

**saturate** *v.* drench, steep, soak.

**savage** *a.* **1** [Primitive] crude, simple, original. **2** [Cruel] barbarous, inhuman, brutal. **3** [Wild] untamed, uncivilized, uncultured.

**save** *v.* **1** [To remove from danger] deliver, extricate, rescue, free, set free, liberate, release, emancipate, ransom, redeem, come to the rescue of, defend.—*Ant.* leave, desert, condemn. **2** [To assure an afterlife] rescue from sin, reclaim, regenerate. **3** [To hoard] collect, store, invest, have on deposit, amass, accumulate, gather, treasure up, store up, pile up, hide away, cache, stow away, sock away*.—*Ant.* waste, spend, invest. **4** [To preserve] conserve, keep, put up.

**say** *v.* tell, speak, relate, state, announce, declare, state positively, open one's mouth, have one's say, break silence, put forth, let out, assert, maintain, express oneself, answer, respond, suppose, assume. **—to say the least** at a minimum, at the very least, to put it mildly, minimally.

**saying** *a.* mentioning, making clear, revealing.

**saying** *n.* aphorism, adage, maxim, byword, motto, proverb, precept, dictum.

**scandal** *n.* shame, disgrace, infamy, discredit, slander, disrepute, detraction, defamation, opprobrium, reproach, aspersion, backbiting, gossip, eavesdropping, rumor, hearsay.—*Ant.* praise, adulation, flattery.

**scanty** *a.* scarce, few, pinched, meager, little, small, bare, ragged, insufficient, inadequate, slender, narrow, thin, scrimp, scrimpy, tiny, wee, sparse, diminutive, short, stingy.—*Ant.* much, large, many.

**scare** *v.* panic, terrify, alarm.

**scarf** *n.* throw, sash, muffler, shawl, comforter, ascot, stole, wrapper.

**scatter** *v.* **1** [To become separated] run apart, run away, go one's own way, diverge, disperse, disband, migrate, spread widely, go in different directions, blow off, go in many directions, be strewn to the four winds*.—*Ant.* assemble, convene, congregate. **2** [To cause to separate] dispel, dissipate, diffuse, strew, divide, disband, shed, distribute, disseminate, separate, disunite, sunder, scatter to the wind*, sever, set asunder.—*Ant.* unite, join, mix. **3** [To waste] expend, dissipate, fritter away.

**scent** *n.* odor, fragrance, redolence, perfume, smell.

**scheme** *v.* intrigue, contrive, devise.

**scientific** *a.* **1** [Objectively accurate] precise, exact, clear. **2** [Concerning science] experimental, deductive, methodically sound.

**scoff** *v.* mock, deride, jeer.

**scold** *v.* admonish, chide, chew out*, bawl out*, get after, lay down the law*, jump on*, jump all over*, rebuke, censure, reprove, upbraid, reprimand, taunt, cavil, criticize, denounce, disparage, recriminate, rate, revile, rail, abuse, vilify, find fault with, nag, lecture, have on the carpet*, rake over the coals*, give one a talking to, chasten, preach, tell off*, keep after, light into*, put down.—*Ant.* praise, commend, extol.

**scorch** *v.* roast, parch, shrivel.

**score** *n.* **1** [A tally] stock, reckoning, record, average, rate, account, count, number, summation, aggregate, sum, addition, summary, amount, final tally, final account. **2** [Written music] transcription, arrangement, orchestration. **—know the score*** grasp, be aware of, comprehend.

**scorn** *v.* hold in contempt, despise, disdain.

**scoundrel** *n.* rogue, scamp, villain.

**scout** *n.* explorer, pioneer, outpost, runner, advance guard, precursor, patrol, reconnoiterer.

**scowl** *v.* glower, grimace, frown.

**scrape** *v.* abrade, scour, rasp.

**scrawny** *a.* lanky, gaunt, lean.

**scream** *v.* shriek, screech, squeal, cry, yell.

**screen** *n.* **1** [A concealment] cloak, cover, covering, curtain, shield, envelope, veil, mask, shade. **2** [A protection] shelter, guard, cover.

**scrimp** *v.* limit, skimp, economize.

**scrupulous** *a.* exact, punctilious, strict.

**scrutinize** *v.* view, study, examine.

**seal off** *v.* quarantine, close, restrict.

**search** *v.* explore, examine, rummage, look up and down, track down, look for, go through, poke into, scrutinize, ransack.

**seasoned** *a.* **1** [Spicy] tangy, sharp, aromatic. **2** [Experienced] established, settled, mature.

**seated** *a.* situated, located, settled, installed, established, rooted, set, fitted in place, placed, arranged, accommodated with seats.

**secluded** *a.* screened, removed, sequestered.

**secondary** *a.* **1** [Derived] dependent, subsequent, subsidiary. **2** [Minor] inconsiderable, petty, small.

**second-rate** *a.* mediocre, inferior, common.

**secrecy** *n.* concealment, confidence, hiding, seclusion, privacy, retirement, solitude, mystery, dark, darkness, isolation, reticence, stealth.

**secret** *a.* **1** [Not generally known] mysterious, ambiguous, hidden, unknown, arcane, cryptic, inscrutable, esoteric, occult, mystic, mystical, classified, dark, veiled, enigmatic, strange, deep, buried in mystery, obscure, clouded, shrouded, unenlightened, unintelligible, cabalistic.—*Ant.* known, revealed, exposed. **2** [Hidden] latent, secluded, concealed. **3** [Operating secretly] clandestine, underhand, underhanded, stealthy, sly, surreptitious, close, furtive, disguised, undercover, backdoor, confidential, backstairs, incognito, camouflaged, enigmatic, under false pretenses, unrevealed, undisclosed, dissembled, dissimulated, under wraps.—*Ant.* open, aboveboard, overt.

**secret** *n.* mystery, deep mystery, something veiled, something hidden, confidence, private matter, code, telegram, personal matter, privileged information, top secret, enigma, puzzle, something forbidden, classified information, confidential information, inside information, an unknown, magic number, the unknown. **—in secret** slyly, surreptitiously, quietly.

**secretive** *a.* reticent, taciturn, undercover, with bated breath, in private, in the dark, in chambers, by a side door, under one's breath, in the background, between ourselves, in privacy, in a corner, under the cloak of, reserved.

**secure** *a.* **1** [Firm] fastened, adjusted, bound. **2** [Safe] guarded, unharmed, defended. **3** [Self-confident] assured, stable, determined.

**security** *n.* **1** [Safety] protection, shelter, safety, refuge, retreat, defense, safeguard, preservation, sanctuary, ward, guard, immunity, freedom from harm, freedom from danger, redemption, salvation.—*Ant.* danger, risk, hazard. **2** [A guarantee] earnest, forfeit, token, pawn, pledge, surety, bond, collateral, assurance, bail, certainty, promise, warranty, pact, compact, contract, covenant, agreement, sponsor, bondsman, hostage.—*Ant.* doubt, broken faith, unreliability.

**seduce** *v.* decoy, allure, inveigle, entice, abduct, attract, tempt, bait, bribe, lure, induce, stimulate, defile, deprave, lead astray, violate, prostitute, rape, deflower.—*Ant.* preserve, protect, guide.

**see** *v.* **1** [To perceive with the eye] observe, look at, behold, examine, inspect, regard, view, look out on, gaze, stare, eye, lay eyes on, mark, perceive, pay attention to, heed, mind, detect, take notice, discern, scrutinize, scan, spy, survey, contemplate, remark, clap eyes on*, make out, cast the eyes on, direct the eyes, catch sight of, cast the eyes over, get a load of*. **2** [To understand] perceive, comprehend, discern. **3** [To witness] look on, be present, pay attention, notice, observe, regard, heed. **4** [To accompany] escort, attend, bear company. **5** [To have an appointment (with)] speak to, get advice from, consult.

**seek** *v.* search for, dig for, fish for, look around for, look up, hunt up, sniff out, dig out, hunt out, root out, smell around, go after, run after, see after, prowl after, go in pursuit of, go in search of.

**seem** *v.* appear to be, have the appearance, give the impression, impress one, appear to one, look, look like, resemble, make a show of, show, have the features of, lead one to suppose, have all the evidence of being, be suggestive of, give the effect of, sound like, make out to be, give the idea, have all the earmarks of.

**segregate** *v.* isolate, split up, separate.

**seize** *v.* **1** [To grasp] take, take hold of, lay hold of, lay hands on, catch up, catch hold of, hang onto, catch, grip, clinch, clench, clasp, embrace, grab, clutch, grapple, snag, pluck, appropriate, snatch, swoop up, enfold, enclose, pinch, squeeze, hold fast, possess oneself of, envelop.—*Ant.* leave, pass by, let alone. **2** [To take by force] capture, rape, occupy, win, take captive, pounce, conquer, take by storm, subdue, overwhelm, overrun, overpower, ambush, snatch, incorporate, exact, retake, carry off, apprehend, arrest, secure, commandeer, force, gain, take, recapture, appropriate, take possession of, take over, pounce on, usurp, overcome, impound, intercept, steal, abduct, snap up*, nab*, trap, throttle, lay hold of, lift, hook, collar*, fasten upon, wrench, claw, snare, bag, catch up, wring, get one's hands on, kidnap, rustle*, hold up, swipe*, scramble for, help oneself to, jump a claim*. **3** [To comprehend] perceive, know, understand.

**seldom** *a.* rarely, unusually, in a few cases, a few times, at times, seldom seen, usually, sporadically, irregularly, whimsically, sometimes, from time to time, on a few occasions, on rare occasions, infrequently, not often, not very often, occasionally, uncommonly, scarcely, hardly, hardly ever, scarcely ever, when the spirit moves, on and off, once in a while, once in a blue moon, once in a lifetime, every now and then, not in a month of Sundays*.—*Ant.* frequently, often, frequent.

**select** *v.* decide, pick, elect.

**selective** *a.* discriminating, judicious, particular.

**self-assured** *a.* self-confident, assured, certain.

**self-control** *n.* poise, self-restraint, reserve, self-government, reticence, discretion, balance, stability, sobriety, dignity, repression, constraint, self-regulation.—*Ant.* nervousness, timidity, talkativeness.

**selfish** *a.* self-seeking, self-centered, self-indulgent, indulging oneself, wrapped up in oneself, narrow, narrow-minded, prejudiced, egotistical, egotistic, looking out for number one*.

**self-satisfied** *a.* smug, vain, conceited.

**sell** *v.* market, vend, auction, dispose of, put up for sale, put on the market, barter, exchange, transfer, liquidate, trade, bargain, peddle, retail, merchandise, sell over the counter, contract, wholesale, retail, dump, clear out, have a sale, give title to, put in escrow.—*Ant.* buy, obtain, get.

**send** *v.* **1** [To dispatch] transmit, forward, convey, advance, express, ship, mail, send forth, send out, send in, delegate, expedite, hasten, accelerate, post, address, rush, rush off, hurry off, get under way, give papers, provide with credentials, send out for, address to, commission, consign, drop, convey, transfer, pack off, give, bestow, grant, confer, entrust, assign, impart, give out. **2** [To broadcast, usually electronically] transmit, relay, wire, cable, broadcast, televise, conduct, communicate.

**senility** *n.* old age, dotage, feebleness, anility, infirmity, decline, senile dementia, Alzheimer's disease, senescence, second childhood.

**senior** *a.* elder, older, higher in rank.

**sensational** *a.* **1** [Fascinating] exciting, marvelous, incredible. **2** [Melodramatic] exaggerated, excessive, emotional.

**sense** *n.* **1** [One of the powers of physical perception] kinesthesia, function, sensation. **2** [Mental ability] intellect, understanding, reason, mind, spirit, soul, brains, judgment, wit, imagination, common sense, cleverness, reasoning, intellectual ability, mental capacity, savvy*, knowledge.—*Ant.* dullness, idiocy, feeble wit. **3** [Reasonable and agreeable conduct] reasonableness, fair-mindedness, discretion. **4** [Tact and understanding] insight, discernment, judgment. **—in a sense** in a way, to a degree, somewhat. **—make sense** seem reasonable, look all right, add up.

**sensible** *a.* **1** [Showing good sense] reasonable, prudent, perceptive, acute, shrewd, sharp, careful, aware, wise, cautious, capable, having a head on one's shoulders*, endowed with reason, sane, discerning, thoughtful. **2** [Perceptive] aware, informed, attentive.

**sensitive** *a.* **1** [Tender] delicate, sore, painful. **2** [Touchy] high-strung, tense, nervous.

**sensuous** *a.* passionate, physical, sensual.

**sentimental** *a.* emotional, romantic, silly, dreamy, idealistic, visionary, artificial, unrealistic, susceptible, overemotional, affected, mawkish, simpering, insincere, overacted, schoolgirlish, sappy*, soupy*, gushy.

**separate** *v.* **1** [To keep apart] isolate, insulate, single out, sequester, seclude, rope off, segregate, intervene, stand between, draw apart, split up, break up. **2** [To part company] take leave, go away, depart.

**separation** *n.* **1** [The act of dividing] disconnection, severance, division, cut, detachment. **2** [The act of parting] coming apart, drawing apart, parting company, breaking up.

**sequence** *n.* **1** [Succession] order, continuity, continuousness, continuance, successiveness, progression, graduation, consecutiveness, flow, consecution, unbrokenness, subsequence, course. **2** [Arrangement] placement, distribution, classification. **3** [A series] chain, string, array.

**serene** *a.* calm, clear, unruffled, translucent, undisturbed, undimmed, tranquil, composed, cool, coolheaded, sedate, levelheaded, content, satisfied, patient, reconciled, easygoing, placid, limpid, comfortable, cheerful.—*Ant.* confused, disturbed, ruffled.

**serenity** *n.* quietness, calmness, tranquility.

**series** *n.* rank, file, line, row, set, train, range, list, string, chain, order, sequence, succession, group, procession, continuity, column, progression, category, classification, scale, array, gradation.

**serious** *a.* **1** [Involving danger] grave, severe, pressing. **2** [Thoughtful] earnest, sober, reflective.

**servant** *n.* attendant, retainer, helper, hireling, dependent, menial, domestic, drudge, slave, butler, housekeeper, chef, cook, second maid, kitchenmaid, maid of all work, general maid, laundress, chambermaid, parlormaid, lady's maid, seamstress, nursemaid, nurse, valet, doorman, footman, squire, chauffeur, groom, gardener.

**serve** *v.* **1** [To fulfill an obligation] hear duty's call, obey the call of one's country, subserve, discharge one's duty, assume one's responsibilities. **2** [To work for] be employed by, labor for, be in the employ of. **3** [To help] give aid, assist, be of assistance. **4** [To serve at table] wait on, attend, provide guests with food, help.

**serviceable** *a.* practical, advantageous, beneficial.

**set** *n.* **1** [Inclination] attitude, position, bearing. **2** [A social group] clique, coterie, circle. **3** [A collection of (like) items] kit, assemblage, assortment.

**setting** *n.* environment, surroundings, mounting, backdrop, frame, framework, background, context, perspective, horizon, shadow, shade, distance.—*Ant.* front, foreground, focus.

**settle** *v.* **1** [To decide] reach a decision, form a judgment, come to a conclusion about. **2** [To prove] establish, verify, make certain. **3** [To finish] end, make an end of, complete. **4** [To sink] descend, decline, fall. **5** [To establish residence] locate, lodge, become a citizen, reside, fix one's residence, abide, set up housekeeping, make one's home, establish a home, keep house. **6** [To take up sedentary life; *often used with "down"*] follow regular habits, live an orderly life, become conventional, follow convention, buy a house, marry, marry and settle down, raise a family, get in a rut, hang up one's hat*. **7** [To satisfy a claim] pay, compensate, make an adjustment, reach a compromise, make payment, arrange a settlement, get squared away, pay damages, pay out, settle out of court, settle up, work out, settle the score*, even the score*, dispose of, account with.

**several** *a.* **1** [Few] some, any, a few, quite a few, not many, sundry, two or three, a small number of, scarce, sparse, hardly any, scarcely any, half a dozen, only a few, scant, scanty, rare, infrequent, in a minority, a handful, more or less, not too many.—*Ant.* many, large numbers of, none. **2** [Various] plural, a number of, numerous.

**severe** *a.* **1** [Stern] exacting, uncompromising, unbending, inflexible, unchanging, unalterable, harsh, cruel, oppressive, close, grinding, obdurate, resolute, austere, rigid, grim, earnest, stiff, forbidding, resolved, relentless, determined, unfeeling, with an iron will, strict, inconsiderate, firm, unsparing, immovable, unyielding. **2** [Difficult or rigorous] overbearing, tyrannical, sharp, exacting, drastic, domineering, rigid, oppressive, despotic, unmerciful, bullying, uncompromising, relentless, unrelenting, hard, rigorous, austere, grinding, grim, implacable, cruel, pitiless, critical, unjust, barbarous, crusty, gruff, stubborn, autocratic, hidebound.—*Ant.* easy, easygoing, indulgent.

**sew** *v.* stitch, seam, fasten, work with needle and thread, tailor, tack, embroider, bind, piece, baste.

**sexual** *a.* **1** [Reproductive] generative, reproductive, procreative. **2** [Intimate] carnal, wanton, passionate.

**shadow** *v.* **1** [To shade] dim, veil, screen. **2** [To follow secretly] trail, watch, keep in sight.

**shady** *a.* **1** [Shaded] dusky, shadowy, adumbral, in the shade, shaded, sheltered, out of the sun, dim, cloudy, under a cloud, cool, indistinct, vague. **2** [*Questionable] suspicious, disreputable, dubious, fishy*, underhanded.

**shake** *v.* **1** [To vibrate] tremble, quiver, quake, shiver, shudder, palpitate, wave, waver, fluctuate, reel, flap, flutter, totter, thrill, wobble, stagger, waggle. **2** [To cause to vibrate] agitate, rock, sway, swing, joggle, jolt, bounce, jar, move, set in motion, convulse.

**shallow** *a.* **1** [Lacking physical depth] slight, inconsiderable, superficial, with the bottom in plain sight, with no depth, with little depth, not deep.—*Ant.* deep, bottomless, unfathomable. **2** [Lacking intellectual depth] simple, silly, trifling, frivolous, superficial, petty, foolish, idle, unintelligent, piddling, wishy-washy*.

**sham** *a.* not genuine, counterfeit, misleading.

**shame** *n.* **1** [A disgrace] embarrassment, stigma, blot. **2** [A sense of wrongdoing] bad conscience, mortification, confusion, humiliation, compunction, regret, chagrin, discomposure, irritation, remorse, embarrassment, abashment, self-reproach, self-disgust. **3** [A condition of disgrace] humiliation, dishonor, degradation.

**shame** *v.* humiliate, mortify, dishonor, disgrace, humble.

**shape** *n.* **1** [Form] contour, aspect, configuration. **2** [An actual form] pattern, stamp, frame. **3** [Condition] fitness, physical state, health. —**out of shape** distorted, misshapen, battered. —**take shape** take on form, mature, fill out.

**share** *n.* division, apportionment, part, portion, helping, serving, piece, ration, slice, allotment, parcel, dose, fraction, fragment, allowance, dividend, percentage, commission, cut*.

**share** *v.* **1** [To divide] allot, distribute, apportion, part, deal, dispense, assign, administer.—*Ant.* unite, combine, withhold. **2** [To partake] participate, share in, experience, take part in, receive, have a portion of, have a share in, go in with, take a part of, take a share of.—*Ant.* avoid, have no share in, take no part in. **3** [To give] yield, bestow, accord.

**sharp** *a.* **1** [Having a keen edge] acute, edged, razor-edged, sharpened, ground fine, honed, razor-sharp, sharp-edged, fine, cutting, knifelike, knife-edged.—*Ant.* dull, unsharpened, blunt. **2** [Having a keen point] pointed, sharp-pointed, spiked, spiky, peaked, salient, needle-pointed, keen, fine, spiny, thorny, prickly, barbed, needlelike, stinging, sharp as a needle, pronged, tapered, tapering, horned. **3** [Having a keen mind] clever, astute, bright. **4** [Distinct] audible, visible, explicit. **5** [Intense] cutting, biting, piercing. **6** [*Stylish] chic, in style, fashionable.

**sharpen** *v.* **1** [To make keen] grind, file, hone, put an edge on, grind to a fine edge, make sharp, make acute, whet, give an edge to, put a point on, give a fine point to.—*Ant.* flatten, thicken, turn. **2** [To make more exact] focus, bring into focus, intensify, make clear, make clearer, clarify, outline distinctly, make more distinct.—*Ant.* confuse, cloud, obscure.

**shed** *v.* drop, let fall, give forth, shower down, cast, molt, slough, discard, exude, emit, scatter, sprinkle.

**sheer** *a.* **1** [Abrupt] perpendicular, very steep, precipitous. **2** [Thin] transparent, delicate, fine.

**shelter** *n.* refuge, harbor, haven, sanctuary, asylum, retreat, shield, screen, defense, security, safety, guardian, protector, house, roof, tent, shack, shed, hut, shade, shadow.

**shelter** *v.* screen, cover, hide, conceal, guard, take in, ward, harbor, defend, protect, shield, watch over, take care of, secure, preserve, safeguard, surround, enclose, lodge, house.—*Ant.* expose, turn out, evict.

**shift** *n.* **1** [A change] transfer, transformation, substitution, displacement, fault, alteration, variation. **2** [A working period] turn, spell, working time.

**shift** *v.* **1** [To change position] move, turn, stir. **2** [To cause to shift] displace, remove, substitute. **3** [To put in gear] change gears, downshift, put in drive.

**shine** *v.* **1** [To give forth light] radiate, beam, scintillate, glitter, sparkle, twinkle, glimmer, glare, glow, flash, blaze, shimmer, illuminate, blink, shoot out beams, irradiate, dazzle, bedazzle, flash, flicker. **2** [To reflect light] glisten, gleam, glow, look good, grow bright, give back, give light, deflect, mirror. **3** [To cause to shine, usually by polishing] scour, brush, polish, put a gloss on, put a finish on, finish, burnish, wax, buff, polish up, make brilliant, make glitter.

**shining** *a.* radiant, gleaming, luminous.

**shirk** *v.* elude, cheat, malinger.

**shock** *v.* **1** [To disturb one's self-control] startle, agitate, astound. **2** [To disturb one's sense of propriety] insult, outrage, horrify, revolt, offend, appall, abash, astound, anger, floor, shake up, disquiet, dismay. **3** [To jar] rock, agitate, jolt.

**shocked** *a.* startled, aghast, upset, astounded, offended, appalled, dismayed.

**shocking** *a.* repulsive, revolting, offensive.

**shore** *n.* beach, strand, seaside, sand, coast, seacoast, seashore, brink, bank, border, seaboard, margin, lakeside, lakeshore, riverbank, riverside.

**short** *a.* **1** [Not long in space] low, skimpy, slight, not tall, not long, undersized, little, abbreviated, dwarfish, stubby, stunted, stocky, diminutive, tiny, small, dwarf, dwarfed, close to the ground, dumpy, chunky, compact, squat, thickset, pint-size, stumpy, sawed-off*, runty. **2** [Not long in time] brief, curtailed, cut short, fleeting, not protracted, concise, unprolonged, unsustained, condensed, terse, succinct, pithy, summary, pointed, precise, bare, abridged, summarized, epigrammatic, compressed, short-term, short-lived. **3** [Inadequate] deficient, insufficient, meager. **—fall short** not reach, be inadequate, fall down.

—**for short** as a nickname, familiarly, commonly. —**in short** that is, in summary, to make a long story short.

**shorten** *v.* curtail, abridge, abbreviate.

**shout** *v.* roar, scream, yell.

**show** *n.* **1** [An exhibition] presentation, exhibit, showing, exposition, expo*, display, occurrence, sight, appearance, program, carnival, representation, burlesque, production, concert, act, pageant, spectacle, light show, entertainment. **2** [Pretense] sham, make-believe, semblance. —**for show** for sake of appearances, ostensibly, ostentatiously. —**get** (or **put**) **the show on the road*** start, open, get started.

**show** *v.* **1** [To display] exhibit, manifest, present. **2** [To explain] reveal, tell, explicate. **3** [To demonstrate] attest, determine, confirm. **4** [To convince] teach, prove to, persuade. **5** [To indicate] register, note, point.

**showdown** *n.* crisis, turning point, culmination.

**show off** *v.* brag, swagger, boast.

**shrewd** *a.* astute, ingenious, sharp.

**shudder** *v.* quiver, quake, shiver.

**shy** *a.* retiring, bashful, modest, diffident, submissive, timid, passive, reticent, fearful, tentative, subservient, docile, compliant, humble, coy, restrained, timorous, demure.

**sick** *a.* ill, ailing, unwell, disordered, diseased, feeble, frail, weak, impaired, suffering, feverish, imperfect, sickly, declining, unhealthy, rabid, indisposed, distempered, infected, invalid, delicate, infirm, rickety, peaked, broken down, physically run-down, confined, laid up, under medication, bedridden, in poor health, at death's door, hospitalized, quarantined, incurable, out of kilter*, feeling poorly, sick as a dog*, in a bad way, not so hot*, under the weather*.—*Ant.* healthy, hearty, well.

**sickly** *a.* ailing, weakly, feeble.

**sift** *v.* **1** [To evaluate] investigate, scrutinize, probe. **2** [To put through a sieve] bolt, screen, winnow, grade, sort, colander, size, strain, filter.

**sigh** *v.* groan, moan, lament.

**sign** *n.* **1** [A signal] indication, clue, omen, divination, premonition, handwriting on the wall, foreshadowing, manifestation, foreboding, foreknowledge, token, harbinger, herald, hint, symptom, assurance, prediction, portent, prophecy, mark, badge, symbol, caution, warning, beacon, flag, hand signal, wave of the arm, flash, whistle, warning bell, signal bell, signal light, high sign*. **2** [An emblem] insignia, badge, crest. **3** [A symbol] type, visible sign, token.

**sign** *v.* **1** [Authorize] endorse, confirm, acknowledge. **2** [Indicate] express, signify, signal. **3** [Hire] engage, contract, employ.

**signal** *v.* give a sign to, flag, wave, gesture, motion, nod, beckon, warn, indicate.

**signed** *a.* endorsed, marked, autographed, written, undersigned, countersigned, sealed, witnessed, subscripted, registered, enlisted, signed on the dotted line.

**silence** *n.* **1** [Absence of sound] quietness, stillness, hush, utter stillness, absolute quiet, calm, noiselessness, quiet, deep stillness, soundlessness, loss of signal, radio silence, security silence, security blackout, censorship.—*Ant.* noise, din, uproar. **2** [Absence of speech] muteness, secrecy, reserve, reticence, inarticulateness, golden silence, respectful silence, sullen silence.

**silence** *v.* hush, quell, still.

**silent** *a.* **1** [Without noise] still, hushed, soundless. **2** [Without speech] reserved, mute, speechless.

**silly** *a.* senseless, ridiculous, nonsensical, absurd, brainless, simpleminded, unreasonable, foolish, irrational, inconsistent, stupid, illogical, ludicrous, preposterous.

**similar** *a.* much the same, comparable, related.

**similarity** *n.* correspondence, likeness, resemblance, parallelism, semblance, agreement, affinity, kinship, analogy, closeness, approximation, conformity, concordance, concurrence, coincidence, congruity, parity, harmony, comparability, identity, community, relation, correlation, relationship, proportion, comparison, simile, interrelation, association, connection, similar form, like quality, point of likeness, similar appearance.—*Ant.* difference, variance, dissimilarity.

**simple** *a.* **1** [Not complicated] single, unmixed, unblended, mere, unadulterated, not complex, simplistic, not confusing, pure. **2** [Plain] unadorned, unaffected, modest. **3** [Easy] not difficult, mild, done with ease.

**simultaneous** *a.* coincident, at the same time, concurrent, in concert, in the same breath, in chorus, at the same instant.

**sin** *n.* error, wrongdoing, trespass, wickedness, evildoing, iniquity, immorality, crime, ungodliness, unrighteousness, veniality, vice, disobedience to the divine will, transgression of the divine law, violation of God's law, pride, covetousness, lust, anger, gluttony, envy, sloth.

**sin** *v.* err, do wrong, commit a crime, offend, break the moral law, break one of the Commandments, trespass, transgress, misbehave, go astray, fall, lapse, fall from grace, sow one's wild oats, wander from the straight and narrow*, backslide, live in sin*, sleep around*.

**sincerely** *a.* truthfully, truly, really, genuinely, earnestly, aboveboard, seriously, naturally, candidly, frankly, profoundly, deeply, to the bottom of one's heart.

**sincerity** *n.* openness, frankness, truthfulness, honesty, reliability.

**sing** *v.* chant, carol, warble, vocalize, hum, trill, croon, twitter, chirp, raise a song, lift up the voice in song, burst into song.

**single** *a.* **1** [Unique] sole, original, exceptional, singular, only, without equal, unequaled, peerless, unrivaled.—*Ant.* many, numerous, widespread. **2** [Individual] particular, separate, indivisible. **3** [Unmarried] unwed, celibate, eligible, virginal, living alone, companionless, unattached, free, available, footloose, on the loose*, in the market*.—*Ant.* married, united, wed.

**single-handed** *a.* without assistance, self-reliantly, alone.

**sinister** *a.* evil, bad, corrupt, perverse, dishonest, foreboding, disastrous, malignant, hurtful, harmful, injurious, dire, poisonous, adverse, unlucky, unfortunate, unfavorable.

**sit** *v.* be seated, seat oneself, take a seat, sit down, sit up, squat, perch, take a load off one's feet*, have a place, have a chair, sit in, take a chair, take a seat, take a place.—*Ant.* rise, stand up, get up.

**size** *n.* **1** [Measurement] extent, area, dimension. **2** [Magnitude] bulk, largeness, greatness, extent, vastness, scope, immensity, enormity, stature, hugeness, breadth, substance, volume, mass, extension, intensity, capacity, proportion.

**skeptical** *a.* cynical, dubious, unbelieving, doubtful, suspicious.

**skin** *n.* epidermis, derma, cuticle, bark, peel, husk, rind, hide, coat, covering, surface, parchment. **—be no skin off one's back** (or **nose**)* not hurt one, do no harm, not affect one. **—by the skin of one's teeth** barely, scarcely, narrowly. **—get under one's skin*** irritate, disturb, upset. **—save one's skin*** get away, evade, escape.

**skin** *v.* peel, pare, flay, scalp, shed, strip, strip off, pull off, remove the surface from, skin alive, husk, shuck, lay bare, bare.

**skip** *v.* hop, spring, leap.

**slaughter** *n.* butchery, killing, massacre.

**slaughter** *v.* slay, murder, massacre.

**slave** *n.* bondsman, bondservant, chattel, serf, toiler, menial, drudge, drone, laborer, captive, bondsmaid, bondwoman, victim of tyranny, one of a subject people.

**sleep** *v.* slumber, doze, drowse, rest, nap, snooze, hibernate, dream, snore, nod, yawn, relax, go to bed, fall asleep, take forty winks*, catnap, turn in, hit the hay*, saw logs*, sack out*.

**sleepy** *a.* somnolent, sluggish, tired.

**slight** *a.* **1** [Trifling] insignificant, petty, piddling. **2** [Inconsiderable] small, sparse, scanty. **3** [Delicate] frail, slender, flimsy.

**slippery** *a.* glassy, smooth, glazed, polished, oily, waxy, soapy, greasy, slimy, icy, sleek, glistening, wet, unsafe, insecure, uncertain, tricky, shifty, slithery, slippery as an eel*.

**sloppy** *a.* clumsy, messy, awkward.

**slow** *a.* **1** [Slow in motion] sluggish, laggard, deliberate, gradual, loitering, leaden, creeping, inactive, slow-moving, crawling, slow-paced, leisurely, as slow as molasses in January*.—*Ant.* fast, swift, rapid. **2** [Slow in starting] dilatory, procrastinating, delaying, postponing, idle, indolent, tardy, lazy, apathetic, phlegmatic, inactive, sluggish, heavy, quiet, drowsy, inert, sleepy, lethargic, stagnant, negligent, listless, dormant, potential, latent.—*Ant.* immediate, alert, instant. **3** [Slow in producing an effect] belated, behindhand, backward, overdue, delayed, long-delayed, behindtime, retarded, detained, hindered.—*Ant.* busy, diligent, industrious. **4** [Dull or stupid] stolid, tame, uninteresting.

**slow** *v.* **1** [To become slower] slacken, slow up, slow down, lag, loiter, relax, procrastinate, stall, let up, wind down, ease up. **2** [To cause to become slower] delay, postpone, moderate, reduce, retard, detain, decrease, diminish, hinder, hold back, keep waiting, brake, curtail, check, curb, cut down, rein in, cut back.

**sly** *a.* wily, tricky, foxy, shifty, crafty, shrewd, designing, deceitful, scheming, deceiving, intriguing, cunning, unscrupulous, deceptive, conniving, calculating, plotting, dishonest, treacherous, underhanded, sneaking, double-dealing, faithless, traitorous, sharp, smart, ingenious, cagey*, dishonorable, crooked, mean, dirty, double-crossing*, slick*, smooth*, slippery, shady*.

**small** *a.* **1** [Little in size] tiny, diminutive, miniature. **2** [Little in quantity] scanty, short, meager. **3** [Unimportant] trivial, insignificant, unessential.

**smallness** *n.* littleness, narrowness, diminutive size, shortness, brevity, slightness, scantiness, tininess.

**smash** *v.* crack, shatter, crush, burst, shiver, fracture, break, demolish, destroy, batter, crash, wreck, break up, overturn, overthrow, lay in ruins, raze, topple, tumble.

**smell** *n.* **1** [A pleasant smell] fragrance, odor, scent, perfume, essence, aroma, bouquet. **2** [An unpleasant smell] malodor, stench, stink, mustiness, foulness, uncleanness, fume. **3** [The sense of smell] smelling, detection, olfaction.

**smell** *v.* **1** [To give off odor] perfume, scent, exhale, emanate, stink, stench. **2** [To use the sense of smell] scent, sniff, inhale, snuff, nose out, get a whiff of.

**smog** *n.* high fog, smoke, haze, mist, air pollution.

**smooth** *a.* **1** [Without bumps] flat, plane, flush, horizontal, unwrinkled, level, monotonous, unrelieved, unruffled, mirrorlike, quiet, still, tranquil, glossy, glassy, lustrous, smooth as glass.—*Ant.* rough, steep, broken. **2** [Without jerks] uniform, regular, even, invariable, steady, stable, fluid, flowing, rhythmic, constant, continuous. **3** [Without hair] shaven, beardless, whiskerless, cleanshaven, smooth-faced, smooth-chinned.—*Ant.* hairy, bearded, unshaven.

**smooth** *v.* even, level, flatten, grade, iron, polish, varnish, gloss, clear the way, smooth the path.

**smug** *a.* self-satisfied, complacent, conceited, pleased with oneself, snobbish, egotistical, self-righteous, stuck up*, stuck on oneself*.

**snarl** *n.* **1** [Confusion] tangle, entanglement, complication. **2** [A snarling sound] grumble, gnarl, growl.

**snarl** *v.* growl, gnarl, grumble, mutter, threaten, bark, yelp, snap, gnash the teeth, bully, quarrel.

**sneer** *v.* mock, scoff, jeer, taunt, slight, scorn, decry, belittle, detract, lampoon, ridicule, deride, caricature, laugh at, look down, insult, disdain, satirize, condemn, give the raspberry*, give the Bronx cheer*.

**snobbish** *a.* ostentatious, pretentious, overbearing.

**soak** *v.* **1** [To drench] wet, immerse, dip, immerge*, water, percolate, permeate, drown, saturate, pour into, pour on, wash over, flood. **2** [To remain in liquid] steep, soften, be saturated, be pervaded, sink into, waterlog. **3** [To absorb] dry, sop, mop.

**sober** *a.* solemn, serious, sedate, clearheaded, not drunk, calm, grave, temperate, abstemious, abstinent, abstaining, teetotaling, steady.

**sociable** *a.* affable, genial, companionable.

**soft** *a.* **1** [Soft to the touch] smooth, satiny, velvety, silky, delicate, fine, thin, flimsy, limp, fluffy, feathery, downy, woolly, doughy, spongy, mushy.—*Ant.* harsh, rough, flinty. **2** [Soft to the eye] dull, dim, quiet, shaded, pale, light, pastel, faint, blond, misty, hazy, dusky, delicate, pallid, ashen, tinted.—*Ant.* bright, glaring, brilliant. **3** [Soft to the ear] low, melodious, faraway. —**be soft on** treat lightly, not condemn, fail to attack.

**soften** *v.* dissolve, lessen, diminish, disintegrate, become tender, become mellow, thaw, melt, moderate, bend, give, yield, relax, relent, mellow, modify, mollify, appease, mash, knead, temper, tone down, qualify, tenderize, weaken.—*Ant.* strengthen, increase, tone up.

**soldier** *n.* warrior, fighter, private, enlisted man, draftee, volunteer, conscript, commando, mercenary, cadet, ranks, selectee, commissioned officer, noncommissioned officer, recruit, veteran, militant, marine, infantryman, guerrilla, guardsman, scout, sharpshooter, artilleryman, gunner, engineer, airman, bomber pilot, fighter pilot, paratrooper, machine-gunner, G.I. Joe*, grunt*.

**solemn** *a.* grave, serious, sober, earnest, intense, deliberate, heavy, austere, somber, dignified, staid, sedate, moody, pensive, brooding, grim, stern, thoughtful, reflective.

**solitary** *a.* sole, only, alone, single, secluded, companionless, lonely, separate, individual, isolated, singular.—*Ant.* accompanied, thick, attended.

**solitude** *n.* isolation, seclusion, retirement.

**solve** *v.* figure out, work out, reason out, think out, find out, puzzle out, decipher, unravel, interpret, explain, resolve, answer, decode, get to the bottom of, get right, hit upon a solution, work, do, settle, clear up, untangle, elucidate, fathom, unlock, determine, hit the nail on the head*, put two and two together, have it.

**soon** *a.* before long, in a short time, presently, in due time, shortly, forthwith, quickly, in a minute, in a second, in short order, anon*.

**soothe** *v.* quiet, tranquilize, alleviate, calm, relax, mollify, help, pacify, lighten, unburden, console, cheer, comfort, ease, relieve.

**sophistication** *n.* elegance, refinement, finesse.

**sorrow** *n.* sadness, anguish, pain.

**sorrowful** *a.* grieved, afflicted, in mourning, depressed, dejected, sad.

**sorry** *a.* **1** [Penitent] contrite, repentant, conscience-stricken, touched, softened, remorseful, regretful, sorrowful, apologetic. **2** [Inadequate in quantity or quality] poor, paltry, trifling, cheap, mean, shabby, stunted, beggarly, scrubby, small, trivial, unimportant, insignificant, worthless, dismal, pitiful, despicable.—*Ant.* enough, plentiful, adequate.

**soul** *n.* **1** [Essential nature] spiritual being, heart, substance, individuality, disposition, cause, personality, force, essence, genius, principle, ego, psyche, life. **2** [The more lofty human qualities] courage, love, affection, honor, duty, idealism, philosophy, culture, heroism, art, poetry, reverence, sense of beauty. **3** [A person] human being, being, individual.

**sound** *a.* **1** [Healthy] hale, hearty, well. **2** [Firm] solid, stable, safe. **3** [Sensible] reasonable, rational, prudent. **4** [Free from defect] flawless, unimpaired, undecayed.

**sound** *n.* **1** [Something audible] vibration, din, racket. **2** [The quality of something audible] tonality, resonance, note, timbre, tone, pitch, intonation, accent, character, quality, softness, lightness, mournfulness, loudness, reverberation, ringing, vibration, modulation, discord, consonance, harmony. **3** [Water between an island and the mainland] strait, bay, canal.

**sour** *a.* acid, tart, vinegary, fermented, rancid, musty, turned, acrid, salty, bitter, caustic, cutting, stinging, harsh, irritating, unsavory, tangy, briny, brackish, sharp, keen, biting, pungent, curdled, unripe.

**sour** *v.* turn, ferment, spoil, make sour, curdle.

**souvenir** *n.* memento, keepsake, relic.

**spacious** *a.* capacious, roomy, vast.

**sparse** *a.* scattered, scanty, meager.

**speak** *v.* **1** [To utter] vocalize, pronounce, express. **2** [To communicate] converse, articulate, chat. **3** [To deliver a speech] lecture, declaim, deliver.

**speaker** *n.* speechmaker, orator, lecturer, public speaker, preacher, spokesman, spellbinder, talker.

**special** *a.* specific, particular, appropriate, peculiar, proper, individual, unique, restricted, exclusive, defined, limited, reserved, specialized, determinate, distinct, select, choice, definite, marked, designated, earmarked.

**specific** *a.* particular, distinct, precise.

**spectacular** *a.* striking, magnificent, dramatic.

**speech** *n.* **1** [Language] tongue, mother tongue, native tongue. **2** [The power of audible expression] talk, utterance, articulation, diction, pronunciation, expression, locution, discourse, vocalization, oral expression, parlance, enunciation, communication, prattle, conversation, chatter. **3** [An address] lecture, discourse, oration, pep talk*, harangue, sermon, dissertation, homily, exhortation, eulogy, recitation, talk, rhetoric, tirade, bombast, diatribe, commentary, appeal, invocation.

**speed** *n.* swiftness, briskness, activity, eagerness, haste, hurry, acceleration, dispatch, velocity, readiness, agility, liveliness, quickness, momentum, rate, pace, alacrity, promptness, expedition, rapidity, rush, urgency, headway, fleetness, good clip, lively clip, steam*.

**spend** *v.* consume, deplete, waste, dispense, contribute, donate, give, liquidate, exhaust, squander, disburse, allocate, misspend, pay, discharge, lay out, pay up, settle, use up, throw away, foot the bill*, fork out*, ante up*, open the purse, shell out*, blow*.—*Ant.* save, keep, conserve.

**spicy** *a.* pungent, piquant, keen, fresh, aromatic, fragrant, seasoned, tangy, savory, flavorful, tasty.

**spineless** *a.* timid, fearful, frightened.

**spiral** *a.* winding, circling, coiled, whorled, radial, curled, rolled, scrolled, helical, screw-shaped, wound.

**spirited** *a.* lively, vivacious, animated.

**spiritual** *a.* refined, pure, holy.

**splash** *n.* plash, plop, dash, spatter, sprinkle, spray, slosh, slop.

**splendid** *a.* premium, great, fine.

**split** *n.* **1** [A dividing] separating, breaking up, severing. **2** [An opening] crack, fissure, rent.

**spoil** *v.* **1** [To decay] rot, blight, fade, wither, molder, crumble, mold, mildew, corrode, decompose, putrefy, degenerate, weaken, become tainted. **2** [To ruin] destroy, defile, plunder.

**sponsor** *n.* advocate, patron, supporter, champion.

**spontaneous** *a.* involuntary, instinctive, casual, unintentional, impulsive, automatic, unforced, natural, unavoidable, unwilling, unconscious, uncontrollable.—*Ant.* deliberate, willful, intended.

**spotted** *a.* **1** [Dotted] marked, dappled, mottled, dotted, speckled, motley, blotchy. **2** [Blemished] soiled, smudged, smeared.

**spread** *a.* expanded, dispersed, extended, opened, unfurled, sown, scattered, diffused, strewn, spread thin.—*Ant.* restricted, narrowed, restrained.

**spread** *n.* **1** [Extent] scope, range, expanse. **2** [A spread cloth] blanket, coverlet, counterpane. **3** [A spread food] preserve, conserve, jelly.

**spread** *v.* **1** [To distribute] cast, diffuse, disseminate. **2** [To extend] open, unfurl, roll out, unroll, unfold, reach, circulate, lengthen, widen, expand, untwist, unwind, uncoil, enlarge, increase, develop, branch off, expand.—*Ant.* close, shorten, shrink. **3** [To apply over a surface] cover, coat, smear, daub, plate, gloss, enamel, paint, spray, plaster, pave, wax, varnish. **4** [To separate] part, sever, disperse.

**spy** *n.* secret agent, foreign agent, scout, detective, undercover man, mole, double agent, CIA operative, observer, watcher.

**square** *a.* **1** [Having right angles] right-angled, four-sided, equal-sided, squared, equilateral, rectangular, rectilinear. **2** [*Old-fashioned] dated, stuffy, out-of-date.

**squeamish** *a.* finicky, fussy, delicate, hard to please, fastidious, particular, exacting, prim, prudish, queasy.

**squeeze** *v.* clasp, pinch, clutch.

**stab** *v.* pierce, wound, stick, cut, hurt, run through, thrust, prick, drive, puncture, hit, bayonet, knife.

**stability** *n.* **1** [Firmness of position] steadiness, durability, solidity, endurance, immobility, suspense, establishment, balance, permanence. **2** [Steadfastness of character] stableness, aplomb, security, endurance, maturity, resoluteness, determination, perseverance, adherence, backbone, assurance, resistance.

**stack** *n.* pile, heap, mound.

**staff** *n.* **1** [A stick] wand, pole, stave. **2** [A corps of employees] personnel, assistants, men, women, force, help, workers, crew, organization, agents, operatives, deputies, servants.

**stagnant** *a.* inert, dead, inactive.

**stain** *n.* blot, blemish, spot, splotch, stained spot, smudge, stigma, brand, blotch, ink spot, spatter, drip, speck.

**stall** *v.* **1** [To break down] not start, conk out, go dead. **2** [To delay] postpone, hamper, hinder.

**stammer** *v.* falter, stop, stumble, hesitate, pause, stutter, repeat oneself, hem and haw.

**standard** *a.* regular, regulation, made to a standard.

**standard** *n.* pattern, type, example.

**standing** *n.* position, status, rank.

**standoff** *n.* stalemate, deadlock, tie.

**state** *n.* **1** [A sovereign unit] republic, land, kingdom. **2** [A condition] circumstance, situation, welfare, phase, case, station, nature, estate, footing, status, standing, occurrence, occasion, eventuality, element, requirement, category, reputation, environment, chances, outlook, position.

**statement** *n.* **1** [The act of stating] allegation, declaration, assertion, profession, acknowledgment, assurance, affirmation. **2** [A statement of account] bill, charge, reckoning, account, record, report, budget, audit, balance sheet, tab*, check.

**statesman** *n.* legislator, lawgiver, administrator, executive, minister, official, politician, diplomat, representative, elder statesman, veteran lawmaker.

**statue** *n.* statuette, cast, figure, bust, representation, likeness, image, sculpture, statuary, marble, bronze, ivory, icon.

**stay** *n.* **1** [A support] prop, hold, truss. **2** [A visit] stop, sojourn, halt.

**stay** *v.* tarry, linger, sojourn.

**steady** *a.* uniform, unvarying, patterned. **—go steady (with)*** date, court, go together.

**steal** *v.* take, filch, thieve, loot, rob, purloin, embezzle, defraud, keep, carry off, appropriate, take possession of, lift, remove, impress, abduct, shanghai, kidnap, run off with, hold up, strip, poach, swindle, plagiarize, misappropriate, burglarize, blackmail, fleece, plunder, pillage, ransack, burgle*, stick up*, rip off*, hijack, skyjack*, pinch*, mooch*, gyp*.

**steep** *a.* precipitous, sudden, sharp, angular, craggy, uneven, rough, rugged, irregular, jagged, vertical, uphill, downhill, abrupt, sheer, perpendicular.

**step by step** *a.* by degrees, cautiously, tentatively.

**sterile** *a.* **1** [Incapable of producing young] infertile, impotent, childless, barren.—*Ant.* fertile, productive, potent. **2** [Incapable of producing vegetation] desolate, fallow, waste, desert, arid, dry, barren, unproductive, fruitless, bleak. **3** [Scrupulously clean] antiseptic, disinfected, decontaminated, germ-free, sterilized, uninfected, sanitary, pasteurized.

**stick** *n.* shoot, twig, branch, stem, stalk, rod, wand, staff, stave, walking stick, cane, matchstick, club, baton, drumstick, pole, bludgeon, bat, ruler, stock, cue, mast. **—the sticks*** rural areas, the back country, outlying districts.

**stick** *v.* **1** [To remain fastened] adhere, cling, fasten, attach, unite, cohere, hold, stick together, hug, clasp, hold fast.—*Ant.* loosen, let go, fall, come away. **2** [To penetrate with a point] prick, impale, pierce.

**stiff** *a.* **1** [Not easily bent] solid, rigid, petrified, firm, tense, unyielding, inflexible, hard, hardened, starched, taut, thick, stubborn, obstinate, unbending, thickened, wooden, steely, frozen, solidified.—*Ant.* soft, flexible, softened. **2** [Formal] ungainly, ungraceful, unnatural. **3** [Severe] rigorous, exact, strict. **4** [Potent] hard, potent, powerful.

**stimulating** *a.* intriguing, enlivening, arousing, high-spirited, bracing, rousing, energetic, refreshing, exhilarating, enjoyable, health-building, sharp, evocative, exciting, inspiring, provoking, animating.—*Ant.* dull, dreary, humdrum.

**stingy** *a.* parsimonious, niggardly, miserly, close, closefisted, greedy, covetous, tightfisted, tight*, grasping, penny-pinching, cheap, selfish, mean, cheeseparing, skimpy.—*Ant.* generous, bountiful, liberal.

**stir** *v.* move, beat, agitate.

**stomach** *n.* paunch, belly, midsection, bowels, intestines, viscera, entrails, insides*, guts, gut*, tummy, pot*, middle, breadbasket*.

**stone** *n.* mass, crag, cobblestone, boulder, gravel, pebble, rock, sand, grain, granite, marble, flint, gem, jewel. **—cast the first stone** criticize, blame, reprimand. **—leave no stone unturned** take great pains, be scrupulous, try hard.

**stoop** *v.* bend forward, incline, crouch.

**stop** *interj.* cease, cut it out*, quit it.

**stop** *n.* **1** [A pause] halt, stay, standstill. **2** [A stopping place] station, bus stop, depot. **—put a stop to** halt, interrupt, intervene.

**stop** *v.* **1** [To halt] pause, stay, stand still, lay over, stay over, break the journey, shut down, rest, discontinue, pull up, reach a standstill, hold, stop dead in one's tracks*, stop short, freeze, call it a day*, cut short. **2** [To cease] terminate, finish, conclude, withdraw, leave off, let up, pull up, fetch up, wind up, relinquish, have done, desist, refrain, settle, discontinue, end, close, tie up, give up, call off, bring up, close down, break up, hold up, pull up, lapse, be at an end, cut out, die away, go out, defect, surrender, close, peter out*, call it a day*, knock off*, lay off*, throw in the towel*, melt away, drop it, run out, write off, run its course.—*Ant.* begin, start, commence. **3** [To prevent] hinder, obstruct, arrest.

**storm** *n.* tempest, downpour, cloudburst, rainstorm, thunderstorm, disturbance, waterspout, blizzard, snowstorm, squall, hurricane, cyclone, tornado, twister*, gust, blast, gale, blow, monsoon.

**story** *n.* imaginative writing, fable, narrative, tale, myth, fairy tale, anecdote, legend, account, satire, burlesque, memoir, parable, fiction, novel, romance, allegory, epic, saga, fantasy.

**strained** *a.* forced, constrained, tense.

**strange** *a.* foreign, rare, unusual, uncommon, external, outside, without, detached, apart, faraway, remote, alien, unexplored, isolated, unrelated, irrelevant.—*Ant.* familiar, present, close.

**strategy** *n.* approach, maneuvering, procedure.

**street** *n.* highway, way, lane, path, avenue, thoroughfare, boulevard, terrace, place, road, route, artery, parkway, court, cross street, alley, circle, dead end, passage.

**strength** *n.* vigor, brawn, energy, nerve, vitality, muscle, stoutness, health, toughness, sturdiness, hardiness, tenacity, soundness.—*Ant.* weakness, feebleness, loss of energy.

**strengthen** *v.* intensify, add, invigorate, fortify, reinforce, encourage, confirm, increase, multiply, empower, arm, harden, steel, brace, buttress, stimulate, sustain, nerve, animate, reanimate, restore, refresh, recover, hearten, establish, toughen, temper, rejuvenate, tone up, build up, make firm, stiffen, brace up, rally, sharpen, enliven, substantiate, uphold, back, augment, enlarge, extend, mount, rise, ascend, wax, grow, back up, beef up*.—*Ant.* weaken, cripple, tear down.

**stress** *n.* **1** [Importance] significance, weight, import. **2** [Pressure] strain, tension, force, burden, trial, fear, tenseness, stretch, tautness, pull, draw, extension, protraction, intensity, tightness, spring.

**stretch** *v.* **1** [To become longer] grow, expand, be extended, extend oneself, spread, unfold, increase, swell, spring up, shoot up, open.—*Ant.* contract, shrink, wane. **2** [To cause to become longer, spread out, etc.] tighten, strain, make tense, draw, draw out, elongate, extend, develop, distend, inflate, lengthen, magnify, amplify, widen, draw tight.—*Ant.* relax, let go, slacken.

**strict** *a.* stringent, stern, austere.

**strike** *n.* **1** [An organized refusal] walkout, deadlock, work stoppage, quitting, sit-down strike, tie-up, slowdown, confrontation, sit-in. **2** [A blow] hit, stroke, punch. —**(out) on strike** striking, protesting, on the picket line.

**strip** *n.* tape, slip, shred.

**strip** *v.* **1** [Undress] divest, disrobe, become naked. **2** [Remove] pull off, tear off, lift off.

**strong** *a.* **1** [Physically strong; *said especially of persons*] robust, sturdy, firm, muscular, sinewy, vigorous, stout, hardy, big, heavy, husky, lusty, active, energetic, tough, virile, mighty, athletic, able-bodied, powerful, manly, brawny, burly, wiry, strapping, made of iron*.—*Ant.* weak, emaciated, feeble. **2** [Physically strong; *said especially of things*] solid, firm, staunch, well-built, secure, tough, durable, able, unyielding, steady, stable, fixed, sound, powerful, mighty, rugged, substantial, reinforced.—*Ant.* unstable, insecure, tottering. **3** [Wielding power] great, mighty, influential. **4** [Potent in effect] powerful, potent, high-powered, stiff, effective, hard, high-potency, stimulating, inebriating, intoxicating, spiked*. **5** [Intense] sharp, acute, keen. **6** [Financially sound] stable, solid, safe.

**stubborn** *a.* unreasonable, obstinate, firm, dogged, opinionated, contradictory, contrary, determined, resolved, bullheaded, mulish, fixed, hard, willful, dogmatic, prejudiced, tenacious, unyielding, headstrong.

**student** *n.* learner, undergraduate, novice, high school student, college student, graduate student, pupil, docent, apprentice.

**studious** *a.* industrious, thoughtful, well-read, well-informed, scholarly, lettered, learned, bookish, earnest, diligent, attentive.

**stunning** *a.* striking, marvelous, remarkable.

**stupid** *a.* senseless, brainless, idiotic, simple, shallow, imprudent, witless, irrational, inane, ridiculous, mindless, ludicrous, muddled, absurd, half-witted, funny, comical, silly, laughable, nonsensical, illogical, indiscreet, unintelligent, irresponsible, scatterbrained, crackbrained, addled, foolish, unwary, incautious, misguided, wild, injudicious, imbecile, addlebrained, lunatic, insane, mad, crazy, moronic, touched, freakish, comic, narrow-minded, incoherent, childish, senile, far-fetched, preposterous, unreasonable, asinine, unwise, thoughtless, careless, fatuous, light, lightheaded, flighty, madcap, giddy, cuckoo*, boneheaded*, goofy*, cracked*, dumb*, half-baked, in a daze, wacky*, harebrained, screwy*, cockeyed*, loony*, batty*, dopey*, nutty*.—*Ant.* sane, wise, judicious.

**style** *n.* **1** [Distinctive manner] way, form, technique. **2** [Fashion] vogue, habit, custom.

**suave** *a.* sophisticated, ingratiating, urbane.

**subject** *a.* governed, ruled, controlled, directed, obedient, submissive, servile, slavish, subservient, subjected, at one's feet, at the mercy of.

**subject** *n.* substance, matter, theme, material, topic, question, problem, point, case, matter for discussion, matter in hand, item on the agenda, topic under consideration, field of inquiry, head, chapter, argument, thought, discussion.

**subject** *v.* cause to experience something, lay open, expose, submit.

**submit** *v.* **1** [To offer] tender, proffer, present. **2** [To surrender] capitulate, yield, give in.

**subordinate** *n.* assistant, helper, aide.

**substance** *n.* matter, material, being, object, item, person, animal, something, element.

**substantial** *a.* **1** [Real] material, actual, tangible. **2** [Considerable] ample, abundant, plentiful.

**substitute** *v.* act for, do the work of, replace, supplant, displace, take another's place, double for, answer for, pass for, go for, go as, fill in for, pinch-hit for, take the rap for*, go to bat for*, front for, be in someone's shoes.

**succeed** *v.* **1** [To attain success] achieve, accomplish, get, prosper, attain, reach, be successful, fulfill, earn, do well, secure, succeed in, score, obtain, thrive, profit, realize, acquire, flourish, be victorious, capture, reap, benefit, recover, retrieve, gain, receive, master, triumph, possess, overcome, win, win out, work out, carry out, surmount, prevail, conquer, vanquish, distance, outdistance, reduce, suppress, worst, work, outwit, outmaneuver, score a point, be accepted, be well-known, grow famous, carry off, pull off, come off, come through, make one's way, make one's fortune, satisfy one's ambition, make one's mark, hit it, hit the mark, live high, come through with flying colors, beat the game*, work well, overcome all obstacles, play one's cards well, crown, top, do oneself proud*, make it*, make good, do all right by oneself, be on top of the heap*, go places*, click*, set the world on fire*, cut the mustard*, make a killing, put across*.—*Ant.* fail, give up, go amiss. **2** [To follow in time] follow after, come after, take the place of, ensue, supervene, supplant, supersede, replace, postdate, displace, come next, become heir to, result, be subsequent to, follow in order, bring up the rear.

**successful** *a.* prosperous, fortunate, lucky, victorious, triumphant, auspicious, happy, unbeaten, favorable, strong, propitious, advantageous, encouraging, contented, satisfied, thriving, flourishing, wealthy, ahead of the game*, at the top of the ladder, out in front, on the track*, over the hump*.—*Ant.* unsuccessful, poor, failing.

**sudden** *a.* precipitate, impromptu, immediate. **—all of a sudden** unexpectedly, suddenly, precipitously.

**sue** *v.* prosecute, follow up, claim, demand, indict, litigate, contest, pray, entreat, plead, petition, appeal, accuse, file a plea, enter a plea, claim damages, go to law, go to court, file suit, prefer a claim, enter a lawsuit, take one to court, file a claim, have the law on one, haul into court.

**sufficient** *a.* adequate, ample, satisfactory.

**suggest** *v.* **1** [To make a suggestion] advise, recommend, propose. **2** [To bring to mind] imply, infer, intimate.

**suggestion** *n.* **1** [A suggested detail] hint, allusion, suspicion, intimation, implication, innuendo, insinuation, opinion, proposal, advice, recommendation, injunction, charge, instruction, submission, reminder, approach, advance, bid, idea, tentative statement, presentation, proposition. **2** [A suggested plan] scheme, idea, outline. **3** [A very small quantity] trace, touch, taste.

**sullen** *a.* unsociable, silent, morose, glum, sulky, sour, cross, ill-humored, petulant, moody, grouchy, fretful, ill-natured, peevish, gloomy, gruff, churlish.—*Ant.* friendly, sociable, jolly.

**sum** *n.* amount, value, worth.

**summary** *n.* outline, digest, synopsis, recap, analysis, abstract, abbreviation, resume, précis, skeleton, brief, case, reduction, version, core, report, survey, sketch, syllabus, condensation, sum and substance, wrap-up*.

**summit** *n.* apex, zenith, crown.

**summon** *v.* request, beckon, send for, invoke, bid, ask, draft, petition, signal, motion, sign, order, command, direct, enjoin, conjure up, ring, charge, recall, call in, call for, call out, call forth, call up, call away, call down, call together, volunteer.

**superficial** *a.* flimsy, cursory, hasty, shallow, shortsighted, ignorant, narrow-minded, prejudiced, partial, external, unenlightened.—*Ant.* learned, deep, profound.

**supernatural** *a.* superhuman, spectral, ghostly, occult, hidden, mysterious, secret, unknown, unrevealed, dark, mystic, mythical, mythological, fabulous, legendary, unintelligible, unfathomable, inscrutable, incomprehensible, undiscernible, transcendental, obscure, unknowable, impenetrable, invisible, concealed.—*Ant.* natural, plain, common.

**supervise** *v.* oversee, conduct, manage.

**supervisor** *n.* director, superintendent, administrator.

**supply** *v.* furnish, fulfill, outfit.

**support** *n.* **1** [Aid] care, assistance, comfort. **2** [A reinforcement] lining, coating, rib, stilt, stay, supporter, buttress, pole, post, prop, guide, backing, stiffener, rampart, stave, stake, rod, pillar, timber. **3** [Financial aid] maintenance, livelihood, sustenance.

**support** *v.* **1** [To hold up from beneath] prop, hold up, buoy up, keep up, shore up, bear up, bolster, buttress, brace, sustain, stay, keep from falling, shoulder carry, bear.—*Ant.* drop, let fall, break down. **2** [To uphold] maintain, sustain, back up, abet, aid, assist, help, bolster, comfort, carry, bear out, hold, foster, shoulder, corroborate, cheer, establish, promote, advance, champion, advocate, approve, stick by, stand by, stand behind, substantiate, verify, get back of, stick up for*, go to bat for*, confirm, further, encourage, hearten, strengthen, recommend, take care of, pull for, agree with, stand up for, keep up, stand back of, take the part of, rally round, give a lift to, boost. **3** [To provide for] take care of, keep an eye on, care for, attend to, look after, back, bring up, sponsor, put up the money for, finance, pay for, subsidize, nurse, pay the expenses of, grubstake*, stake*, raise.—*Ant.* abandon, ignore, fail.

**supposed** *a.* assumed, presumed, presupposed.

**sure** *a. & interj.* certainly, of course, by all means, positively, absolutely, definitely.

**sure** *a.* positive, assured, convinced. **—for sure** certainly, for certain, without doubt. **—make sure** make certain, determine, guarantee. **—to be sure** of course, certainly, obviously.

**surprise** *n.* **1** [A feeling] astonishment, wonder, shock. **2** [The cause of a feeling] something unexpected, blow, sudden attack, unexpected good fortune, sudden misfortune, unawaited event, unsuspected plot. **—take by surprise** startle, assault, sneak up on.

**surprise** *v.* astonish, astound, bewilder, confound, shock, overwhelm, dumbfound, unsettle, stun, electrify, petrify, startle, stupefy, stagger, take aback, cause wonder, awe, dazzle, daze, perplex, leave aghast, flabbergast, floor*, bowl over*, jar, take one's breath away, strike dumb, beggar belief, creep up on, catch unaware.

**surrender** *v.* **1** [To accept defeat] capitulate, yield, give in. **2** [To relinquish possession] give up, let go, resign.

**surround** *v.* **1** [To be on all sides] girdle, circle, environ, enclose, close in, close around, circle about, envelop, hem in, wall in. **2** [To take a position on all sides] encompass, encircle, inundate, flow around, close in, close around, hem in, go around, beleaguer, blockade.—*Ant.* abandon, flee from, desert.

**surroundings** *pl.n.* setting, environs, vicinity.

**survival** *n.* endurance, durability, continuance.

**survive** *v.* **1** [To live on] outlive, outlast, outwear, live down, live out, weather the storm, make out, persist, persevere, last, remain, pull through, come through, keep afloat, get on. **2** [To endure] suffer through, withstand, sustain.

**suspend** *v.* **1** [To exclude temporarily] reject, exclude, drop, remove. **2** [To cease temporarily] postpone, defer, put off, discontinue, adjourn, interrupt, delay, procrastinate, shelve, waive, retard, protract, lay on the table, file, lay aside, break up, restrain, desist, break off, halt, put a stop to, check, put an end to.—*Ant.* continue, carry on, proceed.

**suspicious** *a.* **1** [Entertaining suspicion] jealous, distrustful, suspecting, doubting, questioning, doubtful, dubious, in doubt, skeptical, unbelieving, wondering.—*Ant.* trusting, trustful, without any doubt of. **2** [Arousing suspicion] not quite trustworthy, questionable, queer*, suspect, irregular, unusual, peculiar, out of line, debatable, disputable.—*Ant.* regular, usual, common.

**sustain** *v.* **1** [To carry] bear, transport, pack. **2** [To nourish] maintain, provide for, nurse.

**sweet** *a.* **1** [Sweet in taste] toothsome, sugary, luscious, candied, honeyed, saccharine, cloying, like nectar, delicious.—*Ant.* sour, bitter, sharp. **2** [Sweet in disposition] agreeable, pleasing, engaging, winning, delightful, reasonable, gentle, kind, generous, unselfish, even-tempered, good-humored, considerate, thoughtful, companionable.—*Ant.* selfish, repulsive, inconsiderate. **3** [Sweet in smell] fragrant, sweet-smelling, fresh, delicate, delicious, spicy, rich, perfumed, clean.

**swindle** *v.* dupe, victimize, defraud.

**swing** *n.* sway, motion, fluctuation, stroke, vibration, oscillation, lilt, beat, rhythm. **—in full swing** lively, vigorous, animated.

**swing** *v.* sway, pivot, rotate, turn, turn about, revolve, fluctuate, waver, vibrate, turn on an axis.

**symbol** *n.* token, figure, sign.

**symbolic** *a.* representative, typical, indicative, suggestive, symptomatic, characteristic.

**symmetry** *n.* proportion, arrangement, order, equality, regularity, conformity, agreement, shapeliness, evenness, balance, equilibrium, similarity.

**sympathize** *v.* pity, show mercy, comfort, understand, be understanding, love, be kind to, commiserate, express sympathy.

**synopsis** *n.* outline, digest, brief.

**synthetic** *a.* artificial, counterfeit, plastic.

**system** *n.* orderliness, regularity, conformity, logical order, definite plan, arrangement, rule, systematic order, systematic arrangement, logical process.

# T

**taboo** *a.* forbidden, illegal, restricted.

**tact** *n.* perception, discrimination, judgment, acuteness, penetration, intelligence, acumen, common sense, subtlety, discernment, prudence, aptness, good taste, refinement, delicacy, the ability to get along with others, finesse, horse sense*.—*Ant.* rudeness, coarseness, misconduct.

**tactless** *a.* stupid, unperceptive, inconsiderate, rude, discourteous, unsympathetic, unthoughtful, insensitive, boorish, misunderstanding, impolite, rash, hasty, awkward, clumsy, imprudent, rough, crude, unpolished, gruff, uncivil, vulgar.

**tag** *n.* **1** [A remnant or scrap] rag, piece, patch. **2** [A mark of identification] ticket, badge, card tab, trademark, stamp, stub, voucher, slip, label, check, emblem, insignia, tally, motto, sticker, inscription, laundry mark, price tag, bar code, identification number, button, pin. **3** [A children's game] hide-and-seek, freeze tag, capture the flag.

**take** *n.* **1** [Something that is taken] part, cut, proceeds. **2** [Scene filmed or televised] film, shot, motion picture. **3** [*Something that is seized] holding, catching, haul*.

**take** *v.* **1** [To seize] appropriate, take hold of, catch, grip, grab, pluck, pocket, carry off. **2** [To collect] gather up, accept, reap. **3** [To catch] capture, grab, get hold of. **4** [To choose] select, settle on, opt for, make a selection, pick, decide on, prefer. **5** [To acquire] win, procure, gain, achieve, receive, attain, obtain, secure. **6** [To require] necessitate, demand, call for. **7** [To contract; *said of a disease*] get, come down with, catch. **8** [To record] note, register, take notes. **9** [To transport] move, drive, bear. **10** [To captivate] charm, delight, fascinate. **11** [To win] prevail, triumph, beat. **12** [To buy] pay for, select, procure. **13** [To rent] lease, hire, charter. **14** [To steal] misappropriate, loot, rob. **15** [To undergo] tolerate, bear, endure. **16** [To lead] guide, steer, pilot. **17** [To escort] attend, go with, accompany. **18** [To admit] let in, welcome, give access to. **19** [To adopt] utilize, assume, appropriate. **20** [To apply] put in practice, exert, exercise. **21** [To experience] sense, observe, be aware of. **22** [*To cheat] defraud, trick, swindle. **23** [To grow] germinate, develop into, grow to be.

**take back** *v.* **1** [To regain] retrieve, get back, reclaim. **2** [To restrict] draw in, retire, pull in. **3** [To disavow] retract, recant, recall.

**take care** *v.* beware, heed, mind, take heed.

**take in** *v.* **1** [To include] embrace, comprise, incorporate. **2** [To understand] comprehend, apprehend, perceive. **3** [To cheat] swindle, lie, defraud. **4** [To give hospitality] welcome, shelter, receive. **5** [To shorten] reduce, lessen, cut down.

**taken** *a.* **1** [Captured] arrested, seized, appropriated. **2** [Employed or rented] occupied, reserved, held.

**take off** *v.* **1** [To undress] strip, divest, expose. **2** [To deduct] lessen, subtract, take away. **3** [To leave the earth] blast off, ascend, soar. **4** [To leave] go away, depart, shove off*.

**take-off** *n.* ascent, upward flight, fly-off, climb, rise, hop, jump, vertical takeoff.

**take on** *v.* **1** [To hire] employ, engage, give work to. **2** [To acquire an appearance] emerge, develop, turn. **3** [To undertake] attempt, handle, endeavor. **4** [To meet in fight or sport] engage, battle, contest.

**take out** *v.* **1** [To extract] cut out, pull out, draw out. **2** [To escort] lead, attend, accompany.

**take over** *v.* **1** [To take control] take charge, take command, assume control. **2** [To seize control] take the reins of, take the helm of, overthrow. **3** [To convey] transport, bear, move.

**take part** *v.* associate, cooperate, participate.

**talent** *n.* aptitude, faculty, gift.

**talk** *v.* **1** [To converse] discuss, confer, chat, interview, speak, communicate, talk together, engage in a meaningful dialogue, have a meeting of the minds, chatter, gossip, yammer, remark, be on the phone with, be in contact with, talk over, reason with, visit with, parley, read, hold a discussion, confide in, argue, observe, notice, inform, rehearse, debate, have an exchange, exchange opinions, have a conference with, talk away, go on*, gab*, yak*, chew the fat*, compare notes with, talk a leg off of*, go over*, shoot off one's mouth*, spit it out*, shoot the breeze*, pass the time of day, engage in conversation. **2** [To lecture] speak, give a talk, deliver a speech. **3** [To inform] reveal, divulge, notify. **4** [To utter] pronounce, express, speak.

**talkative** *a.* wordy, verbal, long-winded.

**tame** *a.* **1** [Domesticated] subdued, submissive, housebroken, harmless, trained, overcome, mastered, civilized, broken in, harnessed, yoked, acclimatized, muzzled, bridled.—*Ant.* wild, undomesticated, untamed. **2** [Gentle] tractable, obedient, kindly. **3** [Uninteresting] monotonous, routine, conventional.

**tangible** *a.* perceptible, palpable, material, real, substantial, sensible, touchable, verifiable, physical, corporeal, solid, visible, stable, well-grounded, incarnated, embodied, manifest, factual, objective, tactile.—*Ant.* spiritual, ethereal, intangible.

**tangled** *a.* tied up, confused, knit together, disordered, chaotic, out of place, mixed up, snarled, trapped, entangled, twisted, raveled, muddled, messed up*, balled up*, screwy*.

**taper** *v.* narrow, lessen, thin out.

**target** *n.* **1** [A goal] objective, aim, purpose, end, destination, mark. **2** [Bull's-eye] point, spot, butt, mark, dummy. **3** [A prey] quarry, game, scapegoat.

**task** *n.* chore, responsibility, duty.

**taste** *n.* **1** [The sense that detects flavor] tongue, taste buds, palate, senses. **2** [The quality detected by taste] flavor, savor, savoriness, aftertaste, tang, suggestion, zip*, wallop*, kick*, smack, bang*, jolt, zing*, punch*. **3** [Judgment, especially esthetic judgment] discrimination, susceptibility, sensibility, appreciation, good taste, discernment, acumen, penetration, acuteness, feeling, refinement, appreciation. **4** [Preference] tendency, leaning, attachment. **—in bad taste** pretentious, rude, crass. **—in good taste** delicate, pleasing, refined. **—to one's taste** pleasing, satisfying, appealing.

**taste** *v.* **1** [To test by the tongue] sip, try, touch, sample, lick, suck, roll over in the mouth, partake of. **2** [To recognize by flavor] sense, savor, distinguish. **3** [To experience] feel, perceive, know.

**tasteless** *a.* **1** [Lacking flavor] unsavory, bland, dull, unseasoned, vapid, flat, watery, flavorless, without spice.—*Ant.* delicious, seasoned, spicy. **2** [Plain] homely, insipid, trite. **3** [Lacking good taste] pretentious, ornate, showy, trivial, artificial, florid, ostentatious, clumsy, makeshift, coarse, useless, rude, uncouth, ugly, unsightly, unlovely, hideous, foolish, stupid, crass.—*Ant.* refined, civilized, cultivated.

**tax** *n.* **1** [A pecuniary levy] fine, charge, rate, toll, levy, impost, duty, assessment, tariff, tribute, obligation, price, cost, contribution, expense. **2** [A burden] strain, task, demand.

**teach** *v.* instruct, tutor, coach, educate, profess, explain, expound, lecture, direct, give a briefing, edify, enlighten, guide, show, give lessons in, ground, rear, prepare, fit, interpret, bring up, instill, inculcate, indoctrinate, brainwash*, develop, form, address to, initiate, inform, nurture, illustrate, imbue, implant, break in, give the facts, give an idea of, improve one's mind, open one's eyes, knock into someone's head*, bring home to*, cram.—*Ant.* learn, gain, acquire.

**tear** *n.* rent, rip, hole, slit, laceration, split, break, gash, rupture, fissure, crack, cut, breach, damage, imperfection.—*Ant.* repair, patch, renovation.

**tear** *v.* rend, rip, shred, cut, mangle, split, lacerate.

**technical** *a.* specialized, special, scientific, professional, scholarly, mechanical, methodological, restricted, highly versed, technological, industrial.—*Ant.* artistic, nontechnical, simplified.

**technique** *n.* procedure, system, method.

**temper** *n.* **1** [State of mind] disposition, frame of mind, humor. **2** [An angry state of mind] furor, ire, passion. **3** [The quality of being easily angered] impatience, excitability, touchiness, sourness, sensitivity, fretfulness, peevishness, irritability, ill humor, petulance, irascibility, crossness, churlishness, pugnacity, sullenness, grouchiness, huffiness.—*Ant.* patience, calmness, equanimity. **4** [The quality of induced hardness or toughness in materials] tensile strength, sturdiness, hardness. **—lose one's temper** become angry, get mad, fly off the handle.

**temperament** *n.* character, disposition, constitution, nature, inner nature, quality, temper, spirit, mood, attitude, type, structure, makeup, humor, outlook, peculiarity, individuality, idiosyncrasy, distinctiveness, psychological habits, mentality, intellect, susceptibility, ego, inclination, tendency, turn of mind, frame of mind.

**temperate** *a.* **1** [Moderate] regulated, reasonable, fair. **2** [Neither hot nor cold] medium, warm, mild. **3** [Not given to drink] abstemious, abstinent, restrained.

**temperature** *n.* heat, warmth, cold, body heat, weather condition, climatic characteristic, thermal reading, degrees of temperature.

**temporal** *a.* **1** [Transitory] temporary, transient, ephemeral. **2** [Worldly] secular, earthly, mundane.

**temporary** *a.* transitory, transient, fleeting, short, brief, ephemeral, fugitive, volatile, shifting, passing, summary, momentary, stopgap, makeshift, substitute, for the time being, overnight, *ad hoc* (Latin), impermanent, irregular, changeable, unenduring, unfixed, unstable, perishable, provisional, short-lived, mortal, pro tem, on the go*, on the fly*, on the wing, here today and gone tomorrow*.—*Ant.* permanent, fixed, eternal.

**tempt** *v.* lure, fascinate, seduce, appeal to, induce, intrigue, incite, provoke, allure, charm, captivate, entice, draw out, bait, stimulate, move, motivate, rouse, instigate, wheedle, coax, inveigle, vamp, make a play for*, make one's mouth water.

**tenant** *n.* renter, lessee, householder, rent payer, dweller, inhabitant, occupant, resident, roomer, lodger, holder, possessor, leaseholder, tenant farmer.—*Ant.* owner, proprietor, landlord.

**tend** *v.* **1** [To watch over] care for, manage, direct, superintend, do, perform, accomplish, guard, administer, minister to, oversee, wait upon, attend, serve, nurse, mind. **2** [To have a tendency (toward)] lead, point, direct, make for, result in, serve to, be in the habit of, favor, be predisposed to, be prejudiced in favor of, be apt to, gravitate toward, incline to, verge on.

**tendency** *n.* **1** [Direction] aim, bent, trend. **2** [Inclination] leaning, bias, bent.

**tender** *a.* **1** [Soft] delicate, fragile, supple. **2** [Kind] loving, solicitous, compassionate. **3** [Touching] moving, pathetic, affecting. **4** [Sensitive] touchy, oversensitive, raw.

**tense** *a.* **1** [Nervous] agitated, anxious, high-strung, on edge, fluttery, jumpy, jittery.—*Ant.* calm, unconcerned, indifferent. **2** [Stretched tight] rigid, stiff, firm.

**tension** *n.* **1** [Stress] tautness, force, tightness. **2** [Mental stress] pressure, strain, anxiety.

**tentative** *a.* provisional, probationary, makeshift.

**term** *n.* **1** [A name] expression, terminology, phrase, word, locution, indication, denomination, article, appellation, designation, title, head, caption, nomenclature, moniker*. **2** [A period of time] span, interval, course, cycle, season, duration, phase, quarter, course of time, semester, school period, session, period of confinement. **—come to terms** compromise, arrive at an agreement, arbitrate. **—in terms of** in reference to, about, concerning.

**terminate** *v.* complete, end, perfect.

**terrible** *a.* **1** [Inspiring terror] terrifying, appalling, fearful, awesome, horrifying, ghastly, awe-inspiring, petrifying, revolting, gruesome, shocking, unnerving.—*Ant.* happy, joyful, pleasant. **2** [*Unpleasant] disastrous, inconvenient, disturbing, awful, horrible*, atrocious*, lousy*.—*Ant.* welcome, good, attractive.

**test** *n.* **1** [A check for adequacy] inspection, analysis, countdown, probing, inquiry, inquest, elimination, proving grounds, training stable, search, dry run*. **2** [A formal examination] quiz, questionnaire, essay.

**testify** *v.* **1** [To demonstrate] indicate, show, make evident. **2** [To bear witness] affirm, give evidence, swear, swear to, attest, witness, give witness, give one's word, certify, warrant, depose, vouch, give the facts, stand up for, say a good word for. **3** [To declare] assert, attest, claim.

**testimony** *n.* **1** [The act of stating] attestation, statement, assertion. **2** [Evidence] grounds, facts, data. **3** [Statement] deposition, affidavit, affirmation.

**texture** *n.* **1** [Quality] character, disposition, fineness, roughness, coarseness, feeling, feel, sense, flexibility, stiffness, smoothness, taste. **2** [Structure] composition, organization, arrangement.

**thankful** *a.* obliged, grateful, gratified, contented, satisfied, indebted to, pleased, kindly disposed, appreciative, giving thanks, overwhelmed.

**thankless** *a.* **1** [Not returning thanks] unappreciative, ungrateful, self-centered. **2** [Not eliciting thanks] poorly paid, unappreciated, unrewarded.

**thanks** *pl.n.* appreciation, thankfulness, acknowledgment, recognition, gratitude, gratefulness.—*Ant.* blame, censure, criticism.

**theater** *n.* **1** [A building intended for theatrical productions] playhouse, concert hall, coliseum. **2** [The legitimate stage] stage, drama, Broadway.

**theft** *n.* robbery, racket, thievery, larceny, stealing, swindling, swindle, cheating, defrauding, fraud, piracy, burglary, pillage, pilfering, plunder, vandalism, holdup, pocket-picking, safecracking, extortion, embezzlement, looting, appropriation, shoplifting, fleecing, mugging, stickup*.

**theme** *n.* **1** [A subject] topic, proposition, argument, thesis, text, subject matter, matter at hand, problem, question, point at issue, affair, business, point, case, thought, idea, line. **2** [A recurrent melody] melody, motif, strain. **3** [A short composition] essay, report, paper.

**theory** *n.* **1** [Principles] method, approach, philosophy. **2** [Something to be proved] assumption, conjecture, speculation.

**therefore** *a. & conj.* accordingly, consequently, hence, wherefore, for, since, inasmuch as, for this reason, on account of, to that end, in that event, in consequence, as a result.

**thick** *a.* **1** [Dense] compact, impervious, condensed, compressed, multitudinous, numerous, rank, crowded, close, solid, packed, populous, profuse, populated, swarming, heaped, abundant, impenetrable, concentrated, crammed, packed together, closely packed, like sardines in a can*, jampacked*.—*Ant.* scattered, spacious, wide-open. **2** [Deep] in depth, edgewise, third-dimensional. **3** [Of heavy consistency] compact, heavy, viscous, viscid, dense, syrupy, ropy, coagulated, curdled, turbid, gelatinous, glutinous, gummy, opaque, clotted.—*Ant.* light, porous, filmy. **4** [Not clear] cloudy, turbid, indistinct. **5** [Stupid] obtuse, ignorant, doltish. **6** [*Intimate] cordial, familiar, fraternal. —**through thick and thin** faithfully, devotedly, in good and bad times.

**thicken** *v.* coagulate, curdle, petrify, ossify, solidify, freeze, clot, set, congeal, jell, grow thick.

**thickheaded** *a.* stupid, ignorant, idiotic.

**thickness** *n.* density, compactness, solidity, closeness, heaviness, stiffness, condensation, concentration, clot.—*Ant.* frailty, thinness, slimness.

**thin** *a.* **1** [Of little thickness] flimsy, slim, slight, diaphanous, sheer, rare, sleazy, permeable, paper-thin, wafer-thin.—*Ant.* thick, heavy, coarse. **2** [Slender] slim, lean, skinny, scraggy, lank, spare, gaunt, bony, wan, rangy, skeletal, scrawny, lanky, delicate, wasted, haggard, emaciated, rawboned, shriveled, wizened, rickety, spindly, pinched, starved.—*Ant.* fat, obese, heavy. **3** [Sparse] scarce, insufficient, deficient. **4** [Having little content] sketchy, slight, insubstantial. **5** [Having little volume] faint, shrill, weak.

**thing** *n.* **1** [An object] article, object, item, lifeless object, commodity, device, gadget, material object, being, entity, body, person, something, anything, everything, element, substance, piece, shape, form, figure, configuration, creature, stuff, goods, matter, thingamajig*, doohickey*, thingamabob*. **2** [A circumstance] matter, condition, situation. **3** [An act] deed, feat, movement. **4** [A characteristic] quality, trait, attribute. **5** [An idea] notion, opinion, impression. **6** [A pitiable person] wretch, poor person, sufferer, urchin. **7** [Belongings; *usually pl.*] possessions, clothes, property. **8** [Something so vague as to be nameless] affair, matter, concern, business, occurrence, anything, everything, something, stuff, point, information, subject, idea, question, indication, intimation, contrivance, word, name, shape, form, entity. **9** [Something to be done] task, obligation, duty. —**do one's**

**own thing*** live according to one's own principles, do what one likes, live fully.

**think** *v.* **1** [To examine with the mind] cogitate, muse, ponder, consider, contemplate, deliberate, stop to consider, study, reflect, examine, think twice, estimate, evaluate, appraise, resolve, ruminate, scan, confer, consult, meditate, meditate upon, take under consideration, have on one's mind, brood over, speculate, weigh, have in mind, keep in mind, bear in mind, mull over, turn over, sweat over*, stew, bone up*, beat one's brains, rack one's brains, use the old bean*, figure out, put on one's thinking cap*, use one's head, hammer away at, hammer out, bury oneself in.—*Ant.* neglect, take for granted, accept. **2** [To believe] be convinced, deem, hold. **3** [To suppose] imagine, guess, presume. **4** [To form in the mind] conceive, invent, create. **5** [To remember] recollect, recall, reminisce.

**thirsty** *a.* dry, parched, arid, eager, hankering for, burning for, craving, longing for, partial to, hungry for, itching for, inclined to, bone-dry*, crazy for*, wild for.—*Ant.* satisfied, full, replete.

**thorough** *a.* **1** [Painstaking] exact, meticulous, precise. **2** [Complete] thoroughgoing, out-and-out, total.

**thoroughly** *a.* fully, wholly, completely.

**thoughtful** *a.* **1** [Notable for thought] thinking, meditative, engrossed, absorbed, rapt in, pensive, considered, seasoned, matured, studied, philosophic, contemplative, studious, cogitative, examined, pondered, speculative, deliberative, reflective, introspective, clearheaded, levelheaded, keen, wise, well-balanced, judged, farsighted, reasoning, rational, calculating, discerning, penetrating, politic, shrewd, careful, sensible, retrospective, intellectual, brainy*, deep.—*Ant.* thoughtless, unthinking, irrational. **2** [Considerate] heedful, polite, courteous, solicitous, friendly, kind, kindly, unselfish, concerned, anxious, neighborly, regardful, social, cooperative, responsive, aware, sensitive, benign, indulgent, obliging, careful, attentive, gallant, chivalrous, charitable.—*Ant.* selfish, boorish, inconsiderate.

**thoughtless** *a.* **1** [Destitute of thought] irrational, unreasoning, unreasonable, inane, incomprehensible, witless, undiscerning, foolish, doltish, babbling, bewildered, confused, puerile, senseless, driveling, inept, dull, heavy-handed, obtuse, feebleminded, flighty. **2** [Inconsiderate] heedless, negligent, inattentive, careless, neglectful, self-centered, egocentric, selfish, asocial, antisocial, unmindful, unheeding, deaf, blind, indifferent, unconcerned, listless, apathetic, boorish, discourteous, primitive, unrefined.—*Ant.* careful, thoughtful, unselfish.

**thread** *n.* yarn, string, strand.

**threaten** *v.* intimidate, caution, admonish, hold over, scare, torment, push around, forewarn, bully, abuse, bluster, endanger, be dangerous, be gathering, be in the offing, imperil, be brewing, approach, come on, advance.—*Ant.* help, mollify, placate.

**thrifty** *a.* careful, frugal, economical.

**thrive** *v.* flourish, increase, succeed.

**through** *a. & prep.* **1** [Finished] completed, over, ended. **2** [From one side to the other] straight through, through and through, clear through. **3** [During] throughout, for the period of, from beginning to end. **4** [By means of] by, by way of, by reason, in virtue of, in consequence of, for, by the agency of, at the hand of. **5** [Referring to continuous passage] nonstop, unbroken, one-way.

**throughout** *a. & prep.* all through, during, from beginning to end, from one end to the other, everywhere, all over, in everything, in every place, up and down, on all accounts, in all respects, inside and out, at full length, every bit, to the end, down to the ground, from the word "go", to the brim*.

**throw** *v.* **1** [To hurl] fling, butt, bunt, pitch, fire, let go, sling, toss, heave, lob, dash, launch, chuck, bowl, cast, hurl at, let fly, deliver, cast off*, lay across*.—*Ant.* catch, receive, grab. **2** [To connect or disconnect] flip a switch, connect, start. **3** [To force to the ground] pin, nail*, flatten. **4** [*To permit an opponent to win] submit, yield, surrender.

**throw out** *v.* discharge, throw away, reject.

**thrust** *n.* **1** [A jab] punch, stab, blow. **2** [An attack] onset, onslaught, advance. **3** [A strong push] drive, impetus, momentum.

**thrust** *v.* poke, push, shove.

**thwart** *v.* stop, impede, frustrate.

**tie** *n.* **1** [A fastening] band, strap, bandage, zipper. **2** [A necktie] cravat, ascot, neckerchief, bow, knot, scarf, neckcloth, choker. **3** [Affection] bond, relation, kinship. **4** [An equal score, or a contest having that score] deadlock, draw, even game, dead heat, drawn battle, neck-and-neck contest, even-steven*, stalemate, nose finish*, standoff, wash*.

**tie** *v.* **1** [To fasten] bind, make fast, attach. **2** [To tie a knot in] knot, make a bow, make a tie, make a knot, do up, fix a tie, make a hitch. **3** [To equal] match, keep up with, parallel.

**tight** *a.* **1** [Firm] taut, secure, fast, bound up, close, clasped, fixed, steady, stretched thin, established, compact, strong, stable, enduring, steadfast, unyielding, unbending, set, stuck hard, hidebound, invulnerable, snug, sturdy.—*Ant.* loose, tottery, shaky. **2** [Closed] sealed, airtight, impenetrable, impermeable, impervious, watertight, hermetically sealed, padlocked, bolted, locked, fastened, shut tight, clamped, fixed, tied, snapped, swung to, tied up, nailed, spiked, slammed, obstructed, blocked, blind, shut, stopped up, plugged.—*Ant.* open, penetrable, unprotected. **3** [Closefitting] pinching, shrunken, snug, uncomfortable, cramping, skintight, short, crushing, choking, smothering, cutting.—*Ant.* loose, ample, wide. **4** [*Stingy] miserly, parsimonious, close.

**tilt** *n.* slant, slope, slide.

**time** *n.* **1** [Duration] continuance, lastingness, extent, past, present, future, infinity, space-time. **2** [A point in time] incident, event, occurrence, occasion, time and tide, instant, term, season, tide, course, sequence, point, generation. **3** [A period of time] season, era, interval. **4** [Experience] background, living, participation. **5** [Leisure] opportunity, free moment, chance. **6** [Circumstances; *usually plural; used with "the"*] condition, the present, nowadays. **7** [A measure of speed] tempo, rate, meter. **—ahead of time** ahead of schedule, fast, earlier than expected. —**at one time** simultaneously, concurrently, at once. —**at the same time** simultaneously, concurrently, at once. —**at times** occasionally, sometimes, once in a while. —**behind the times** old-fashioned, archaic, antediluvian. —**behind time** tardy, delayed, coming later. —**between times** now and then, occasionally, sometimes. —**do time*** serve a prison term, go to jail, be imprisoned. —**for the time being** for the present, for now, under consideration. —**from time to time** occasionally, sometimes, once in a while. —**in no time** instantly, rapidly, without delay. —**in time** eventually, after the proper time, inevitably. —**lose time** go too slow, tarry, cause a delay. —**make time** gain time, act hastily, hasten. —**many a time** often, regularly, frequently. —**on time** **1** at the appointed time, punctually, punctual. **2** by credit, in installments, on account. —**out of time** out of pace, unreasonable, improper. —**pass the time of day** exchange greetings, chat, converse.

**timely** *a.* opportune, seasonable, in good time, fitting the times, suitable, appropriate, convenient, favorable, propitious, well-timed, modern, up-to-date, newsworthy.—*Ant.* untimely, ill-timed, inappropriate.

**tint** *n.* tinge, hue, shade, color, cast, flush, dye, tinct, taint, glow, pastel color, luminous color, pale hue, tone, tincture, dash, touch, color tone, coloration, pigmentation, ground color, complexion.

**tiny** *a.* small, miniature, diminutive.

**tired** *a.* fatigued, weary, run-down, exhausted, overworked, overtaxed, wearied, worn, spent, wasted, worn-out, drooping, distressed, unmanned, drowsy, droopy, sleepy, haggard, faint, prostrated, broken-down, drained, consumed, empty, collapsing, all in*, finished, stale, fagged, dog-tired*, dead on one's feet*, pooped*, done in*, done for*, worn to a frazzle*, played out*, tuckered out*, fed up*.—*Ant.* active, lively, energetic.

**title** *n.* **1** [A designation] indication, inscription, sign. **2** [Ownership or evidence of ownship] right, claim, license. **3** [Mark of rank or dignity] commission, decoration, medal, ribbon, coat of arms, crest, order, authority, privilege, degree.

**together** *a.* **1** [Jointly] collectively, unitedly, commonly. **2** [Simultaneously] at the same time, concurrently, coincidentally, contemporaneously, at once, in connection with, at a blow, in unison, at one jump.

**toil** *n.* labor, drudgery, work.

**toil** *v.* sweat, labor, slave.

**toilet** *n.* water closet, lavatory, washroom, rest room, men's room, women's room, powder room, gentlemen's room, ladies' room, latrine, privy, outhouse, comfort station, bathroom, bath, little boy's room*, little girl's room*, head*, potty*, can*, pot*, john*, wc*.

**told** *a.* recounted, recorded, set down, reported, known, chronicled, revealed, exposed, made known, said, published, printed, announced, released, described, stated, set forth, included in the official statement, made public property, made common knowledge, related, depicted, enunciated, pronounced, given out, handed down, telegraphed, broadcast, telecast, confessed, admitted, well-known, discovered.—*Ant.* secret, concealed, unknown.

**tolerant** *a.* understanding, liberal, patient.

**tone** *n.* **1** [A musical sound] pitch, timbre, resonance. **2** [Quality] nature, trend, temper. **3** [Manner] expression, condition, aspect. **4** [A degree of color] hue, tint, coloration.

**tool** *n.* **1** [An implement] utensil, machine, instrument, mechanism, weapon, apparatus, appliance, engine, means, contrivance, gadget. **2** [One who permits himself to be used] accomplice, hireling, dupe.

**too much** *n.* excess, waste, extravagance, overabundance, superfluity, preposterousness, overcharge, ever so much, more than can be used, vastness, prodigiousness, immensity.—*Ant.* lack, want, shortage.

**tooth** *n.* **1** [Structure for chewing] fang, tusk, saber-tooth, ivory, artificial tooth, false tooth, bony appendage, incisor, canine, cuspid, eyetooth, bicuspid, premolar, molar, grinder, wisdom tooth. **2** [A tooth-like or tooth-shaped object] point, stub, projection. **—get** (or **sink**) **one's teeth into*** become occupied with, involve oneself in, be busy at.

**top** *n.* **1** [The uppermost portion] peak, summit, crown, head, crest, tip, apex, acme, cap, crowning point, headpiece, capital, pinnacle, zenith, spire.—*Ant.* bottom, lower end, nadir. **2** [A cover] lid, roof, ceiling. **3** [A spinning toy] spinner, musical top, whistling top. **4** [The leader] head, captain, chief. **—blow one's top*** lose one's temper, become angry, be enraged. **—off the top of one's head*** speaking offhand, chatting casually, spontaneous. **—on top** prosperous, thriving, successful.

**topic** *n.* question, theme, subject.

**torch** *n.* beacon, light, flare.

**torn** *a.* ripped, slit, split, severed, lacerated, mutilated, broken, rent, fractured, cracked, slashed, gashed, ruptured, snapped, sliced, burst, cleaved, wrenched, divided, pulled out, impaired, damaged, spoiled.—*Ant.* whole, repaired, adjusted.

**total** *n.* sum, entirety, result.

**totally** *a.* entirely, wholly, exclusively.

**touch** *n.* **1** [The tactile sense] feeling, touching, feel, perception, tactility. **2** [Contact] rub, stroke, pat, fondling, rubbing, petting, stroking, licking, handling, graze, scratch, brush, taste, nudge, kiss, peck, embrace, hug, cuddling, caress. **3** [A sensation] sense, impression, pressure. **4** [Skill] knack, technique, talent. **5** [A trace] suggestion, scent, inkling.

**touch** *v.* **1** [To be in contact] stroke, graze, rub, nudge, thumb, finger, paw, pat, pet, caress, lick, taste, brush, kiss, glance, sweep, fondle, smooth, massage, sip, partake. **2** [To come into contact with] meet, encounter, reach. **3** [To relate to] refer to, regard, affect.

**tough** *a.* **1** [Strong] robust, wiry, mighty. **2** [Cohesive] solid, firm, sturdy, hard, hardened, adhesive, leathery, coherent, inseparable, molded, tight, cemented, unbreakable, in one piece, dense, closely packed.—*Ant.* weak, fragile, brittle. **3** [Difficult to chew] uncooked, half-cooked, sinewy, indigestible, inedible, fibrous, old, hard as nails, tough as shoeleather*. **4** [Difficult] hard, troublesome, laborious. **5** [Hardy] robust, sound, capable. **6** [Rough and cruel] savage, fierce, ferocious. **7** [*Unfavorable] bad, unfortunate, untimely.

**tower** *n.* spire, mast, steeple, bell tower, lookout tower, keep, belfry, campanile, monolith, radio tower, skyscraper, obelisk, pillar, column, minaret.

**trace** *n.* **1** [A very small quantity] indication, fragment, dash, dab, sprinkling, tinge, pinch, taste, crumb, trifle, shred, drop, speck, shade, hint, shadow, nuance, iota, particle, jot, suggestion, touch, suspicion, minimum, smell, spot. **2** [A track] evidence, trail, footprint.

**track** *n.* **1** [A prepared way] path, course, road. **2** [Evidence left in passage] footprint, step, trace, vestige, impression, tire track, mark, footmark, footstep, trail, imprint, remnant, record, indication, print, sign, remains, token, symbol, clue, scent, wake, monument. **—keep track of** keep an account of, stay informed about, maintain contact with. **—lose track of** lose sight of, lose contact with, abandon. **—make tracks*** run away, abandon, depart quickly. **—off the track** deviant, variant, deviating. **—the wrong side of the tracks*** ghetto, poor side of town, slum.

**track** *v.* **1** [To follow by evidence] hunt, pursue, smell out, add up, put together, trail, follow, trace, follow the scent, follow a clue, follow footprints, draw an inference, piece together, dog, be hot on the trail of, tail*, shadow. **2** [To dirty with tracks] leave footprints, leave mud, muddy, stain, soil, besmear, spatter, leave a trail of dirt.

**trade** *n.* **1** [Business] commerce, sales, enterprise. **2** [A craft] occupation, profession, position. **3** [An individual business transaction] deal, barter, contract.

**trade** *v.* **1** [To do business] patronize, shop, purchase. **2** [To give one thing for another] barter, swap, exchange. **—trade in** turn in, make part of a deal, get rid of.

**traditional** *a.* folkloric, legendary, mythical, epical, ancestral, unwritten, balladic, told, handed down, anecdotal, proverbial, inherited, folkloristic, old, acknowledged, customary, generally accepted, habitual, widespread, usual, widely used, popular, acceptable, established, fixed, sanctioned, universal, taken for granted, rooted, classical, prescribed, doctrinal, conventional.

**tragedy** *n.* **1** [Unhappy fate] lot, bad fortune, misfortune, doom, problem, error, mistake.—*Ant.* happiness, fortune, success. **2** [A series of tragic events] adversity, affliction, hardship.—*Ant.* success, prosperity, good fortune. **3** [An artistic creation climaxed by catastrophe] play, tragic drama, melodrama.

**tragic** *a.* catastrophic, fatal, disastrous.

**train** *v.* **1** [To drill] practice, exercise, discipline. **2** [To educate] instruct, tutor, teach. **3** [To toughen oneself] prepare, grow strong, get into practice, reduce, make ready, fit out, equip, qualify, bring up to standard, whip into shape*, get a workout.—*Ant.* weaken, break training, be unfit. **4** [To direct the growth of] rear, lead, discipline, mold, bend, implant, guide, shape, care for, encourage, infuse, imbue, order, bring up, nurture, nurse, prune, weed.—*Ant.* neglect, ignore, disdain. **5** [To aim] bring to bear, level, draw a bead.

**trait** *n.* habit, peculiarity, characteristic.

**traitor** *n.* betrayer, deserter, renegade, Judas, informer, spy, counterspy, agent, double agent, hypocrite, impostor, plotter, quisling, conspirator, turncoat, sneak, double-crosser*, fink*, rat*, stool pigeon*, two-timer*.—*Ant.* supporter, follower, partisan.

**transform** *v.* convert, mold, reconstruct.

**transient** *a.* provisional, ephemeral, transitory.

**translate** *v.* decode, transliterate, interpret, decipher, paraphrase, render, transpose, turn, gloss, put in equivalent terms.

**translation** *n.* transliteration, version, adaptation, rendition, rendering, interpretation, paraphrase, rewording, gloss, reading.

**transport** *v.* convey, move, bring.

**trap** *v.* ensnare, seduce, fool, ambush, deceive.

**trapped** *a.* ambushed, cornered, with one's back to the wall.

**trash** *n.* **1** [Rubbish] garbage, waste, refuse, dregs, filth, litter, debris, dross, sweepings, rubble, odds and ends, stuff, rags, scraps, scrap, excess, scourings, fragments, pieces, shavings, loppings, slash, rakings, slag, parings, rinsings, shoddy, residue, offal, junk, sediment, leavings, droppings.—*Ant.* money, goods, riches. **2** [Nonsense] drivel, rubbish, senselessness.

**travel** *n.* riding, roving, wandering, rambling, sailing, touring, biking, hiking, cruising, driving, wayfaring, going abroad, seeing the world, sightseeing, voyaging, journeying, trekking, flying, globe-trotting, space travel, rocketing.

**travel** *v.* tour, cruise, voyage, roam, explore, jet to, rocket to, orbit, go into orbit, take a jet, go by jet, migrate, trek, vacation, motor, visit, traverse, jaunt, wander, journey, adventure, quest, trip, rove, inspect, make an expedition, cross the continent, cross the ocean, encircle the globe, make the grand tour, sail, see the country, go camping, go abroad, take a trip, cover, go walking, go riding, go bicycling, make a train trip, drive, fly, set out, set forth, sightsee.

**traveler** *n.* voyager, adventurer, tourist, explorer, nomad, wanderer, truant, peddler, roamer, rambler, wayfarer, migrant, excursionist, sightseer, straggler, vagabond, vagrant, hobo, tramp, gypsy, gadabout, itinerant, pilgrim, rover, passenger, commuter, globe-trotter.

**treasure** *n.* treasure-trove, riches, wealth.

**treat** *v.* **1** [To deal with a person or thing] negotiate, manage, have to do with, have business with, behave toward, handle, make terms with, act toward, react toward, use, employ, have recourse to.—*Ant.* neglect, ignore, have nothing to do with. **2** [To assist toward a cure] attend, administer, prescribe, dose, operate, nurse, dress, minister to, apply therapy, care for, doctor*. **3** [To pay for another's entertainment] entertain, indulge, satisfy, amuse, divert, play host to, escort, set up, stake to*.

**treaty** *n.* agreement, pact, settlement, covenant, compact, convention, alliance, charter, sanction, bond, understanding, arrangement, bargain, negotiation, deal.

**trespass** *v.* encroach, invade, infringe.

**trial** *a.* tentative, test, preliminary.

**trial** *n.* **1** [An effort to learn the truth] analysis, test, examination. **2** [A case at law] suit, lawsuit, fair hearing, hearing, action, case, contest, indictment, legal proceedings, claim, cross-examination, litigation, counterclaim, arraignment, prosecution, citation, court action, judicial contest, seizure, bill of divorce, habeas corpus, court-martial, impeachment. **3** [An ordeal] suffering, misfortune, heavy blow.

**tribute** *n.* applause, recognition, eulogy.

**trick** *n.* **1** [A deceit] wile, fraud, deception, ruse, cheat, cover, feint, hoax, artifice, decoy, trap, stratagem, intrigue, fabrication, double-dealing, forgery, fake, illusion, invention, subterfuge, distortion, delusion, ambush, snare, blind, evasion, plot, equivocation, concealment, treachery, swindle, feigning, impersonation, duplicity, pretense, falsehood, falsification, perjury, disguise, conspiracy, circumvention, quibble, trickery, beguiling, chicanery, humbug, maneuver, sham, counterfeit, gyp*, touch*, come-on*, fast one*, dodge*, plant*, clip*, sucker deal*, con game*, bluff, shakedown*, sell-out*, con*, funny business*, dirty work*, crooked deal, front*, gimmick*.—*Ant.* honesty, truth, veracity. **2** [A prank] jest, sport, practical joke. **3** [A practical method or expedient] skill, facility, know-how*.

**trick** *v.* dupe, outwit, fool.

**trifle** *n.* **1** [A small quantity] particle, piece, speck. **2** [A small degree] jot, eyelash, fraction. **3** [Something of little importance] triviality, small matter, nothing.

**trip** *n.* voyage, excursion, tour.

**trip** *v.* **1** [To stumble] tumble, slip, lurch, slide, founder, fall, pitch, fall over, slip upon, plunge, sprawl, topple, go head over heels.—*Ant.* arise, ascend, get up. **2** [To cause to stumble] block, hinder, bind, tackle, overthrow, push, send headlong, kick, shove, mislead.—*Ant.* help, pick up, give a helping hand.

**trite** *a.* hackneyed, prosaic, stereotyped.

**triumph** *n.* conquest, success, victory.

**trivial** *a.* petty, trifling, small, superficial, piddling, wee, little, insignificant, frivolous, irrelevant, unimportant, nugatory, skin-deep, meaningless, mean, diminutive, slight, of no account, scanty, meager, inappreciable, microscopic, atomic, dribbling, nonessential, flimsy, inconsiderable, vanishing, momentary, immaterial, indifferent, beside the point, minute, inessential, paltry, inferior, minor, small-minded, beggarly, useless, inconsequential, worthless, mangy, trashy, pitiful, of little moment, dinky*, small-town*, cutting no ice*, cut and dried.—*Ant.* important, great, serious.

**trouble** *n.* **1** [A person or thing causing trouble] annoyance, difficult situation, bother, bind, hindrance, difficulty, task, puzzle, predicament, plight, problem, fear, worry, concern, inconvenience, nuisance, disturbance, calamity, catastrophe, crisis, delay, quarrel, dispute, bad news, affliction, intrusion, irritation, trial, pain, ordeal, discomfort, injury, adversity, hassle*, hang-up*, case, bore, gossip, problem child, meddler, pest, tease, tiresome person, inconsiderate person, intruder, troublemaker, fly in the ointment, headache*, brat, holy terror*, peck of trouble*.—*Ant.* help, aid, comfort. **2** [Illness] malady, ailment, affliction. **3** [A quarrel] argument, feud, bickering, dispute, fight. **—in trouble** unfortunate, having trouble, in difficulty.

**trouble** *v.* **1** [To disturb] disconcert, annoy, irritate. **2** [To take care] make an effort, take pains, bother.

**troubled** *a.* disturbed, agitated, grieved, apprehensive, pained, anxious, perplexed, afflicted, confused, puzzled, overwrought, aggravated*, uptight, bothered, harassed, vexed, plagued, teased, annoyed, concerned, uneasy, discomposed, harried, careworn, mortified, badgered, baited, inconvenienced, put out, upset, flurried, flustered, bored, tortured, goaded, irritated, displeased, tried, roused, disconcerted, pursued, chafed, ragged, galled, rubbed the wrong way, tired, molested, crossed, thwarted, fazed, distressed, wounded, sickened, griped, restless, irked, pestered, heckled, persecuted, frightened, alarmed, terrified, scared, anguished, harrowed, tormented, provoked, stung, ruffled, fretting, perturbed, afraid, shaky, fearful, unsettled, suspicious, in turmoil, full of misgivings, shaken, dreading, bugged*, in a quandary, in a stew, on pins and needles*, hassled*, all hot and bothered*, worried stiff*, in a tizzy*, burned up*, miffed*, peeved*, riled*, floored*, up a tree*, hung-up*, up the creek without a paddle*.—*Ant.* calm, at ease, settled.

**truce** *n.* armistice, peace agreement, lull.

**true** *a.* **1** [Accurate] precise, verified, proved, certain, certified, definite, checked, exact, correct. **2** [Loyal] sure, reliable, trustworthy, faithful, dependable, sincere. **3** [Genuine] authentic, virtual, substantial, tangible, genuine, actual, pure. **—come true** become a fact, come about, develop, happen.

**truly** *a.* honestly, exactly, definitely, reliably, factually, correctly, unequivocally, sincerely, scrupulously, fairly, justly, validly, rightfully, righteously, faithfully, worthily, scientifically, without bias, without prejudice, fairly and squarely*.—*Ant.* wrongly, dishonestly, deceptively.

**trust** *n.* **1** [Reliance] confidence, dependence, credence. **2** [Responsibility] guardianship, liability, duty. **3** [A large company] corporation, monopoly, institution. **—in trust** in another's care, held for, reserved.

**trust** *v.* **1** [To believe in] swear by, place confidence in, confide in, esteem, depend upon, expect help from, presume upon, lean on, have no doubt, rest assured, be sure about, have no reservations, rely on, put faith in, look to, count on, assume that, presume that, be persuaded by, be convinced, put great stock in, set great store by, bank on*, take at one's word.—*Ant.* doubt, mistrust, disbelieve. **2** [To hope] presume, take, imagine. **3** [To place in the protection of another] lend, put in safekeeping, entrust. **4** [To give credit to] advance, lend, loan, let out, grant, confer, let, patronize, aid, give financial aid to.—*Ant.* borrow, raise money, pawn.

**trusted** *a.* trustworthy, dependable, reliable, trusty, tried, proved, intimate, close, faithful, loyal, true, constant, staunch, devoted, incorruptible, safe, honorable, honored, inviolable, on the level*, regular*, right, sure-fire*.—*Ant.* dishonest, questionable, unreliable.

**trusting** *a.* trustful, credulous, confiding, gullible, unsuspecting, easygoing, open, candid, indulgent, obliging, well-meaning, good-natured, tenderhearted, green.—*Ant.* suspicious, skeptical, critical.

**truth** *n.* **1** [Conformity to reality] truthfulness, correctness, sincerity, verity, candor, openness, honesty, fidelity, frankness, revelation, authenticity, exactness, infallibility, precision, perfection, certainty, genuineness, accuracy, fact, the gospel truth*, straight dope*, inside track*, the nitty-gritty*, the facts, the case.—*Ant.* lie, deception, falsehood. **2** [Integrity] trustworthiness, honor, probity. —**in truth** in fact, indeed, really.

**try** *v.* **1** [To endeavor] attempt, undertake, exert oneself, contend, strive, make an effort, risk, have a try at, contest, wrangle, labor, work, aspire, propose, try to reach, do what one can, tackle, venture, struggle for, compete for, speculate, make every effort, put oneself out, vie for, aspire to, attack, make a bid for, beat one's brains*, bear down, shoot at*, shoot for*, drive for, chip away at*, do one's best, make a pass at, go after, go out of the way, give a workout*, do all in one's power, buckle down, lift a finger, break an arm*, lay out, do oneself justice, have a go at*, make a go of it*, go all out, leave no stone unturned, move heaven and earth, knock oneself out*, break one's neck*, bust a gut*, take a crack at*, give it a whirl*. **2** [To test] assay, investigate, put to the proof. **3** [To conduct a trial] hear a case, examine, decide.

**tug** *v.* pull, haul, tow.

**tumble** *v.* drop, plunge, descend.

**tunnel** *n.* hole, burrow, underground passage, subway, tube, crawl space, crawlway, shaft, mine, pit.

**turn** *n.* **1** [A revolution] rotation, cycle, circle, round, circulation, pirouette, gyre, gyration, spin, round-about-face, roll, turning, circumrotation, spiral. **2** [A bend] curve, winding, twist, wind, hook, shift, angle, corner, fork, branch. **3** [A turning point] climax, crisis, juncture, emergency, critical period, crossing, change, new development, shift, twist. **4** [A change in course] curve, detour, deviation. —**at every turn** in every instance, constantly, consistently. —**by turns** taking turns, in succession, alternately. —**take turns** do by turns, do in succession, share.

**turn** *v.* **1** [To pivot] revolve, rotate, roll, spin, wheel, whirl, circulate, go around, swivel, round, twist, twirl, gyrate, loop. **2** [To reverse] go back, recoil, change, upset, retrace, face about, turn around, capsize, shift, alter, vary, convert, transform, invert, subvert, return, alternate. **3** [To divert] deflect, veer, turn aside, turn away, sidetrack, swerve, put off, call off, turn off, deviate, dodge, twist, avoid, shift, switch, avert, zigzag, shy away, redirect, draw aside. **4** [To become] grow into, change into, pass into. **5** [To sour] curdle, acidify, become rancid. **6** [To change direction] swerve, swing, bend, veer, tack, round to, incline, deviate, detour, loop, curve. **7** [To sprain] strain, bruise, dislocate. **8** [To bend] curve, twist, fold. **9** [To transform] transmute, remake, transpose. **10** [To repel] repulse, push back, throw back.

**turning** *a.* twisting, shifting, whirling, rotating, revolving, bending, curving, shunting.—*Ant.* permanent, static, fixed.

**turning point** *n.* peak, juncture, culmination.

**turn off** *v.* stop, shut off, douse, turn out, log off, halt, close, shut, extinguish, shut down, kill the light, turn off the juice*, cut the motor*, hit the switch.

**turn on** *v.* **1** [To start the operation of] set going, switch on, set in motion, log on, put in gear. **2** [To attack] strike, assail, assault. **3** [*To arouse] titillate, stimulate, excite. **4** [To depend on or upon] hinge on, be dependent on, be based on.

**turn over** *v.* **1** [To invert] overturn, reverse, subvert. **2** [To transfer] hand over, give over, deliver.

**tutoring** *n.* coaching, training, instruction.

**twig** *n.* offshoot, limb, sprig.

**twilight** *n.* dusk, nightfall, late afternoon, early evening, sunset, dawn, break of day.

**twirl** *v.* spin, rotate, twist.

**twist** *v.* wring, wrap, twine, twirl, spin, turn around, wrap around.

**twitch** *v.* **1** [To pluck] pull, tug, snatch. **2** [To jerk] shiver, shudder, kick, work, palpitate, beat, twinge.

**type** *n.* **1** [Kind] sort, nature, variety. **2** [Representive] representation, sample, example. **3** [Letter] symbol, emblem, figure, character, sign.

**type** *v.* **1** [To use a typewriter] typewrite, keyboard, key, copy, transcribe, teletype, input, touchtype, hunt and peck*. **2** [To classify] categorize, normalize, standardize.

**typical** *a.* characteristic, habitual, usual, representative, symbolic, normal, illustrative, conventional, archetypical, ideal, expected, suggestive, standardized, standard, patterned, ordinary, average, common, everyday, regular.—*Ant.* superior, exceptional, extraordinary.

**tyranny** *n.* oppression, cruelty, severity, reign of terror, despotism, absolutism.

**tyrant** *n.* despot, absolute ruler, dictator.

# U

**ugly** *a.* **1** [Ill-favored] unsightly, loathsome, hideous, homely, repulsive, unseemly, uncomely, deformed, bad-looking, plain, disfigured, monstrous, foul, horrid, frightful, revolting, repellent, unlovely, appalling, haglike, misshapen, misbegotten, grisly, looking a mess*, looking like the devil*, not fit to be seen*.—*Ant.* beautiful, handsome, graceful. **2** [Dangerous] pugnacious, quarrelsome, bellicose, rough, cantankerous, violent, vicious, evil, sinister, treacherous, wicked, formidable.—*Ant.* reasonable, mild, complaisant.

**ultimate** *a.* final, terminal, latest.

**unable** *a.* incapable, powerless, weak, incompetent, unskilled, impotent, not able, inept, incapacitated, inefficacious, helpless, unfitted, inefficient, unqualified, inadequate, ineffectual, inoperative.—*Ant.* able, capable, effective.

**unanimous** *a.* united, single, collective, combined, unified, concerted, harmonious, concordant, concurrent, public, popular, undivided, of one accord, agreed, common, communal, shared, universal, accepted, unquestioned, undisputed, uncontested, consonant, consistent, with one voice, homogeneous, accordant, assenting.—*Ant.* different, dissenting, irreconcilable.

**unauthorized** *a.* unofficial, unapproved, unlawful.

**unavoidable** *a.* inescapable, impending, sure.

**unaware** *a.* uninformed, oblivious, ignorant, not cognizant, unmindful, unknowing, heedless, negligent, careless, insensible, forgetful, unconcerned, blind, deaf, inattentive, without notice, deaf to, caught napping, in a daze, not seeing the forest for the trees*.—*Ant.* conscious, aware, cognizant.

**unbelievable** *a.* beyond belief, incredible, inconceivable, staggering, unimaginable, not to be credited, dubious, doubtful, improbable, questionable, implausible, open to doubt.—*Ant.* likely, believable, probable.

**uncertain** *a.* undecided, undetermined, unsettled, doubtful, changeable, unpredictable, improbable, unlikely, unfixed, unsure, indeterminate, haphazard, random, chance, casual, provisional, contingent, alterable, subject to change, possible, vague, conjectural, questionable, problematic, suppositional, hypothetical, theoretical, open to question, equivocal, perplexing, debatable, dubious, indefinite, unascertained, ambiguous, unresolved, debated, conjecturable, unknown, unannounced, imprecise, in abeyance, up in the air, in doubt.

**uncertainty** *n.* **1** [The mental state of being uncertain] perplexity, doubt, puzzlement, quandary, mystification, guesswork, conjecture, indecision, ambivalence, dilemma.—*Ant.* belief, certainty, decision. **2** [The state of being undetermined or unknown] questionableness, contingency, obscurity, vagueness, ambiguity, difficulty, incoherence, intricacy, involvement, darkness, inconclusiveness, indeterminateness, improbability, unlikelihood, low probability, conjecturability.—*Ant.* determination, sureness, necessity. **3** [That which is not determined or not known] chance, mutability, change, unpredictability, possibility, emergence, contingency, blind spot, puzzle, enigma, question, blank, vacancy, maze, theory, risk, leap in the dark.—*Ant.* truth, fact, matter of record.

**unchanged** *a.* unaltered, the same, unmoved, constant, fixed, continuing, stable, permanent, durable, unvarying, eternal, invariable, consistent, persistent, firm, unvaried, resolute, perpetual, continuous, maintained, uninterrupted, fast.—*Ant.* changed, altered, modified.

**uncivilized** *a.* barbarous, uncontrolled, barbarian.

**unclean** *a.* soiled, sullied, stained, spotted, filthy, bedraggled, smeared, befouled, nasty, grimy, polluted, rank, unhealthful, defiled, muddy, stinking, fetid, rotten, vile, decayed, contaminated, tainted, rancid, putrid, putrescent, moldy, musty, mildewed, besmirched, smirched, filmed over, bleary, dusty, sooty, smudgy, scurvy, scurfy, clogged, slimy, mucky, tarnished, murky, smudged, daubed, blurred, spattered.—*Ant.* clean, pure, white.

**uncomfortable** *a.* **1** [Troubled in body or mind] distressed, ill at ease, uneasy, nervous, disturbed, pained, miserable, wretched, restless, annoyed, angry, in pain, smarting, suffering, upset, vexed, on pins and needles, weary, tired, fatigued, exhausted, strained, worn, aching, sore, galled, stiff, chafed, cramped, agonized, hurt, anguished.—*Ant.* quiet, rested, happy. **2** [Causing discomfort] ill-fitting, awkward, annoying, irritating, distressful, galling, wearisome, difficult, hard, thorny, troublesome, harsh, grievous, dolorous, bitter, excruciating, afflictive, distressing, torturing, painful, agonizing, disagreeable.—*Ant.* easy, pleasant, grateful.

**uncommon** *a.* unusual, out of the ordinary, different, extraordinary, unheard of, unique, rare, exceptional, out-of-the-way, strange, exotic, arcane, remarkable, startling, surprising, fantastic, unaccustomed, unfamiliar, freakish, irregular, uncustomary, unconventional, unorthodox, abnormal, aberrant, peculiar, odd, bizarre, eccentric, original, nondescript, prodigious, fabulous, monstrous, curious, wonderful, unaccountable, noteworthy, queer, unparalleled, outlandish.—*Ant.* common, usual, ordinary.

**unconditional** *a.* positive, definite, absolute, unconstrained, without reserve, outright, final, certain, complete, entire, whole, unrestricted, unqualified, unlimited, actual, thorough, thoroughgoing, genuine, indubitable, assured, determinate, unequivocal, full, categorical, decisive, unmistakable, clear, unquestionable.

**unconscious** *a.* insensible, swooning, in a state of suspended animation, torpid, lethargic, inanimate, senseless, drowsy, motionless, benumbed, stupefied, numb, inert, paralyzed, palsied, tranced, entranced, in a stupor, in a coma, in a trance, raving, out of one's head, out like a light*, knocked out.—*Ant.* conscious, vivacious, awake.

**unconsciously** *a.* abstractedly, mechanically, carelessly, automatically, habitually, by rote, unintentionally, inattentively, heedlessly, without reflection, negligently, disregardfully, thoughtlessly, neglectfully, hurriedly, unthinkingly, without calculation, unguardedly.—*Ant.* deliberately, intentionally, willfully.

**unconventional** *a.* novel, individual, different.

**undecided** *a.* undetermined, in the balance, unsettled.

**undependable** *a.* careless, irresponsible, unreliable.

**under** *a. & prep.* **1** [Referring to physical position] on the bottom of, below, covered by, concealed by, held down by, supporting, pinned beneath, on the underside of, pressed down by, beneath.—*Ant.* above, over, on top of. **2** [Subject to authority] governed by, in the power of, subordinate. **3** [Included within] belonging to, subsequent to, following.

**underestimate** *v.* miscalculate, come short of, undervalue, depreciate, underrate, disparage, slight, minimize, think too little of, hold too lightly, make light of, deprecate.

**undergo** *v.* sustain, submit to, support, experience, feel, know, be subject to, bear, meet with, endure, go through, encounter, bear up under, put up with, share, withstand.—*Ant.* avoid, escape, resist.

**underground** *a.* **1** [Subterranean] buried, covered, earthed over, under the sod, in the recesses of the earth, hidden from the light of day, gone to earth. **2** [Secret] hidden, undercover, clandestine. **3** [Unconventional] experimental, radical, avant-garde.

**undermine** *v.* impair, ruin, threaten.

**understand** *v.* **1** [To comprehend] apprehend, fathom, take in, grasp, figure out, seize, identify with, know, perceive, appreciate, follow, master, conceive, be aware of, sense, recognize, grow aware, explain, interpret, see through, learn, find out, see into, catch, note, be conscious of, have cognizance of, realize, discern, read, distinguish, infer, deduce, induce, make out, become alive to, have been around*, experience, have knowledge of, be instructed in, get to the bottom of, get at the root of, penetrate, possess, be informed of, come to one's senses, see the light, make out, register*, savvy*, get the gist of, catch on, get the point of, dig*, read between the lines, be with it*, get the idea. **2** [To suppose] guess, conjecture, surmise. **3** [To accept] concede, take for granted, count on.

**understanding** *n.* **1** [The power to understand] intelligence, comprehension, judgment. **2** [The act of comprehending] recognition, knowing, perception. **3** [That which comes from understanding] conclusion, knowledge, perception.

**undertake** *v.* endeavor, engage, set out, promise, try out, try, begin, offer, set in motion, volunteer, initiate, commit oneself to, embark upon, venture, take upon oneself, answer for, hazard, stake, move, devote oneself to, take up for, take on, set about, go in for, put one's hand to, have one's hands in, have in hand, launch into, address oneself to, enter upon, busy oneself with, tackle, pitch into*, fall into, buckle down, take on, take the plunge, fall to, have a try at.

**underwear** *n.* undergarments, underclothing, unmentionables*, lingerie, intimate things, underlinen, underclothes, shorts, briefs, drawers, flannels, union suit, jockey shorts, T-shirt, boxer shorts, long underwear, underskirt, slip, petticoat, girdle, brassiere, garter belt, bra-slip, bra, camisole, halfslip, corset, corselet, bodice, vest, foundation garment, panty girdle, panties, pantyhose, knickers (British).

**undesirable** *a.* objectionable, shunned, disliked, to be avoided, unwanted, outcast, rejected, defective, disadvantageous, inexpedient, inconvenient, troublesome, unwished for, repellent, loathed, unsought, dreaded, annoying, insufferable, unacceptable, scorned, displeasing, distasteful, loathsome, abominable, obnoxious, unpopular, bothersome, unlikable, unwelcome, unapprovable, useless, inadmissible, unsatisfactory, disagreeable, awkward, embarrassing, unfit.—*Ant.* welcome, proper, suitable.

**undress** *v.* strip, take off one's clothes, disrobe, dismantle, divest, become naked, peel*.—*Ant.* dress, put on one's clothes, attire oneself.

**uneasy** *a.* unquiet, anxious, fearful, irascible, troubled, harassed, vexed, perturbed, alarmed, upset, afraid, apprehensive, nervous, frightened, shaky, perplexed, agitated, unsettled, suspicious, peevish, irritable, fretful, worried, anguished, in turmoil, disquieted, shaken, full of misgivings, fidgety, jittery, on edge, all nerves, jumpy, snappish, uncomfortable, molested, tormented, in distress.—*Ant.* quiet, placid, soothed.

**unemployed** *a.* out of work, jobless, idle, inactive, laid off, without gainful employment, on the dole, on welfare, cooling one's heels*.—*Ant.* busy, employed, at work.

**unending** *a.* everlasting, infinite, neverending.

**unethical** *a.* sneaky, immoral, unfair.

**uneven** *a.* **1** [Rough] bumpy, rugged, jagged. **2** [Irregular] notched, jagged, serrate. **3** [Variable] intermittent, spasmodic, fitful.

**unexpected** *a.* unforeseen, surprising, unlooked for, sudden, startling, unpredicted, coming unaware, astonishing, staggering, stunning, electrifying, amazing, not in the cards, not on the books, unanticipated, not bargained for, left out of calculation, wonderful, unprepared for, instantaneous, eye-opening, like a bolt from the blue.—*Ant.* expected, predicted, foreseen.

**unfair** *a.* **1** [Unjust] wrongful, wrong, low, base, injurious, unethical, bad, wicked, culpable, blamable, blameworthy, foul, illegal, inequitable, improper, unsporting, shameful, cruel, shameless, dishonorable, unreasonable, grievous, vicious, vile, undue, unlawful, petty, mean, inexcusable, unjustifiable, immoral, criminal, forbidden, irregular.—*Ant.* fair, proper, sporting. **2** [Not in accord with approved trade practices] unethical, criminal, discriminatory.

**unfamiliar** *a.* **1** [Unacquainted] not introduced, not associated, unknown, not on speaking terms, not versed in, not in the habit of, out of contact with.—*Ant.* friendly, intimate, acquainted. **2** [Strange] alien, outlandish, exotic, remote, novel, original, different, unusual, extraordinary, unaccustomed, unexplored, uncommon.—*Ant.* common, ordinary, usual.

**unfasten** *v.* unsnap, untie, unlock.

**unfavorable** *a.* inopportune, untimely, unseasonable, adverse, calamitous, unpropitious, inexpedient, bad, ill-chosen, ill-fated, ill-suited, ill-timed, unsuitable, improper, wrong, abortive, untoward, inauspicious, unlucky, ill, unfortunate, regrettable, premature, tardy, late, unfit, inadvisable, objectionable, inconvenient, disadvantageous, damaging, destructive, unseemly, ill-advised, obstructive, troublesome, embarrassing, unpromising, awkward.

**unfinished** *a.* **1** [Not completed] uncompleted, undone, half done, incomplete, under construction, unperformed, imperfect, unconcluded, deficient, unexecuted, unaccomplished, in preparation, in the making, not done, in the rough, sketchy, tentative, shapeless, formless, unperfected, unfulfilled, undeveloped, unassembled, defective, found wanting, cut short, immature, faulty, crude, rough.—*Ant.* done, completed, perfected. **2** [Without a finish] unpainted, unvarnished, bare, raw, rough, crude, unprotected, uncovered, plain, undecorated, unadorned.

**unfit** *a.* **1** [Incompetent] unqualified, feeble, unpracticed, inexperienced, weak, impotent, inept, clumsy, debilitated, incapacitated, badly qualified, incompetent, unable, unprepared, ineffective, unapt.—*Ant.* able, fit, effective. **2** [Unsuitable] improper, ill-adapted, wrong, ill-advised, unlikely, unpromising, inexpedient, inappropriate, inapplicable, useless, valueless, mistaken, incorrect, inadequate, flimsy.—*Ant.* fit, suitable, correct.

**unforeseen** *a.* surprising, sudden, unexpected.

**unforgettable** *a.* notable, exceptional, extraordinary.

**unforgivable** *a.* inexcusable, unpardonable, unjustifiable, indefensible, inexpiable.

**unfortunate** *a.* unlucky, luckless, unhappy, afflicted, troubled, stricken, unsuccessful, without success, burdened, pained, not prosperous, in adverse circumstances, broken, shattered, ill-fated, on the road to ruin, in a desperate plight, ruined, out of luck, in a bad way, jinxed*, behind the eight ball*, gone to the dogs*, down on one's luck.—*Ant.* happy, lucky, prosperous.

**unfriendly** *a.* **1** [Hostile] opposed, alienated, ill-disposed, against, opposite, contrary, warlike, competitive, conflicting, antagonistic, estranged, at variance, irreconcilable, not on speaking terms, turned against, with a chip on one's shoulder*.—*Ant.* friendly, intimate, approving. **2** [Lacking friendly qualities] grouchy, bearish, surly, misanthropic, gruff, ill-disposed, envious, uncharitable, faultfinding, combative, quarrelsome, grudging, malignant, spiteful, malicious, vengeful, resentful, hateful, peevish, aloof, unsociable, suspicious, sour.—*Ant.* generous, frank, open.

**ungainly** *a.* clumsy, gawky, awkward.

**ungrateful** *a.* thankless, selfish, lacking in appreciation, grasping, demanding, forgetful, self-centered, unmindful, heedless, careless, insensible, dissatisfied, grumbling, unnatural, faultfinding, oblivious.—*Ant.* thankful, grateful, obliged.

**unhappy** *a.* **1** [Sad] miserable, sorrowful, wretched. **2** [Unfortunate] afflicted, troubled, in a desperate plight.

**unhealthy** *a.* sickly, sick, in a decline, in ill health, infirm, delicate, feeble, shaky, undernourished, rickety, spindling, ailing, weak, in a run-down condition.—*Ant.* healthy, robust, hale.

**unhurt** *a.* uninjured, all right, whole.

**unified** *a.* made one, united, joined, combined, concerted, synthesized, amalgamated, conjoined, incorporated, blended, identified, coalesced, federated, centralized, intertwined, consolidated, associated, cemented, coupled, allied, wedded, married, confederated.—*Ant.* separated, distinct, disjoined.

**unimaginable** *a.* inconceivable, incomprehensible, incredible, unbelievable, unheard-of, indescribable, unthinkable, improbable.

**unimportant** *a.* trifling, inconsiderable, slight, worthless, inconsequential, insignificant, unnecessary, immaterial, indifferent, beside the point, frivolous, useless, of no account, worthless, trivial, paltry.—*Ant.* important, weighty, great.

**unintentional** *a.* unthinking, involuntary, erratic.

**union** *n.* **1** [The act of joining] unification, junction, meeting, uniting, joining, coupling, embracing, coming together, merging, fusion, mingling, concurrence, symbiosis, amalgamation, confluence, congregation, reconciliation, conciliation, correlation, combination, connection, linking, attachment, coalition, conjunction, consolidation, incorporation, centralization, affiliation, confederation, copulation, coition.—*Ant.* divorce, separation, severance. **2** [A closely knit group] association, federation, society. **3** [A marriage] wedlock, conjugal ties, matrimony, cohabitation, nuptial connection, match, matrimonial affiliation. **4** [A labor union] laborers, workingmen, employees.

**unique** *a.* single, peerless, matchless, unprecedented, unparalleled, novel, individual, sole, unexampled, lone, different, unequaled, sui generis.—*Ant.* common, frequent, many.

**unite** *v.* join, meet, ally, combine, solidify, harden, strengthen, condense, confederate, couple, affiliate, merge, band together, blend, mix, become one, concentrate, consolidate, entwine, intertwine, grapple, amalgamate, league, band, embody, embrace, copulate, associate, assemble, gather together, conjoin, keep together, tie in, pull together, hang together, join forces, coalesce, fuse, wed, marry, mingle, stick together, stay together.—*Ant.* divide, separate, part.

**united** *a.* unified, leagued, combined, affiliated, federal, confederated, integrated, amalgamated, cooperative, consolidated, concerted, congruent, associated, assembled, linked, banded, in partnership.—*Ant.* separated, distinct, individual.

**unity** *n.* **1** [The quality of oneness] homogeneity, homogeneousness, sameness, indivisibility, identity, inseparability, singleness, similarity, uniqueness, integration, universality, all-togetherness, ensemble, uniformity, wholeness.—*Ant.* difference, diversity, divorce. **2** [Union] federation, confederation, compact, combination, correspondence, alliance, agreement, concord, identity of purpose, unification, aggregation. **3** [Harmony] concord, agreement, accord.

**universal** *a.* **1** [Concerning the universe] cosmic, stellar, celestial, sidereal, astronomical, cosmogonic. **2** [Worldwide] mundane, earthly, terrestrial, sublunary, terrene, human, worldly.—*Ant.* local, restricted, district. **3** [General] entire, all-embracing, prevalent, customary, usual, whole, sweeping, extensive, comprehensive, total, unlimited, limitless, endless, vast, widespread, catholic, common, regular, undisputed, accepted, unrestricted.—*Ant.* special, limited, peculiar.

**universe** *n.* cosmos, creation, the visible world, astral system, universal frame, all created things, everything, nature, the natural world.

**unjust** *a.* wrong, inequitable, wrongful.

**unkind** *a.* malignant, spiteful, mean, malicious, inhuman, inhumane, sadistic, cruel, hateful, malevolent, savage, barbarous.—*Ant.* kind, benevolent, helpful.

**unknown** *a.* **1** [Not known; *said of information*] uncomprehended, unapprehended, undiscovered, untold, unexplained, uninvestigated, unexplored, unheard-of, unperceived, concealed, hidden, unrevealed.—*Ant.* known, established, understood. **2** [Not known; *said of people*] alien, unfamiliar, not introduced, unheard-of, obscure, foreign, strange, unacknowledged, ostracized, outcast, friendless, private, retired, aloof, forgotten. **3** [Not known; *said of terrain*] unexplored, far-off, remote, far, distant, foreign, undiscovered, exotic, transoceanic, transmarine, at the far corners of the earth, faraway, outlandish, unheard-of, unfrequented, untraveled, desolate, desert, unvisited, legendary, strange.

**unlike** *a.* dissimilar, different, incongruous, contradictory, hostile, opposed, inconsistent, heterogeneous, diverse, contrasted, conflicting, contrary, disparate, dissonant, discordant, clashing, separate, opposite, divergent, various, variant.—*Ant.* like, similar, correspondent.

**unlikely** *a.* improbable, unheard-of, incredible, implausible, not to be thought of, unbelievable, absurd, unconvincing, not likely, scarcely possible, apparently false, contrary to expectation, inconceivable, doubtful, dubious, questionable, extraordinary, marvelous, out of the ordinary, strange.—*Ant.* likely, probable, credible.

**unlimited** *a.* infinite, limitless, boundless, unending, extensive, universal, unrestricted, unconditional, unfathomable, inexhaustible, unconfined, immense, illimitable, measureless, incalculable, interminable, without number, unfathomed, unsounded, untold, countless, numberless, incomprehensible, immeasurable, endless.

**unload** *v.* disburden, discharge, dump, slough, lighten, cast, unpack, relieve, remove cargo, disgorge, empty, deplane, unburden, break bulk.—*Ant.* fill, load, pack.

**unlock** *v.* unbar, unfasten, open the lock.

**unmistakable** *a.* conspicuous, distinct, evident.

**unnecessary** *a.* needless, fortuitous, casual, chance, haphazard, wanton, accidental, unessential, nonessential, beside the point, irrelevant, futile, extraneous, additional, redundant, useless, exorbitant, superfluous, worthless, undesirable, optional, avoidable, objectionable, disadvantageous, random, noncompulsory, dispensable, adventitious, without compulsion, uncalled-for, gratuitous.—*Ant.* necessary, essential, required.

**unofficial** *a.* unconstrained, personal, casual.

**unprecedented** *a.* unparalleled, novel, original.

**unqualified** *a.* **1** [Absolute] downright, utter, outright. **2** [Incompetent] inexperienced, unprepared, incapable.

**unreal** *a.* visionary, delusive, deceptive, illusory, imagined, hallucinatory, ideal, dreamlike, unsubstantial, nonexistent, fanciful, misleading, fictitious, theoretical, hypothetical, fabulous, notional, whimsical, fantastic.—*Ant.* real, substantial, genuine.

**unreasonable** *a.* **1** [Illogical] irrational, biased, fatuous. **2** [Immoderate] exorbitant, extravagant, inordinate. **3** [Senseless] foolish, silly, thoughtless.

**unreliable** *a.* undependable, unstable, wavering, deceitful, tricky, shifty, furtive, underhanded, untrue, fickle, giddy, untrustworthy, vacillating, fallible, weak, unpredictable.

**unrest** *n.* **1** [Lack of mental calm] malaise, distress, discomfort, perturbation, agitation, worry, sorrow, anxiety, grief, trouble, annoyance, tension, ennui, disquiet, soul-searching, irritation, harassment, upset, vexation, chagrin, mortification, perplexity, unease, disease, moodiness, disturbance, bother, dither, tizzy*. **2** [Social or political restlessness] disquiet, agitation, turmoil, strife, disturbance, uproar, debate, contention, bickering, change, altercation, crisis, confusion, disputation, contest, controversy, quarrel, sparring, uncertainty, insurrection, suspicion, dissatisfaction.

**unripe** *a.* green, tart, immature.

**unsafe** *a.* hazardous, perilous, risky, threatening, treacherous, fearsome, unreliable, insecure, venturesome, unstable, alarming, precarious, ticklish, giddy, dizzy, slippery, uncertain, unpromising, shaky, explosive.—*Ant.* safe, harmless, proof.

**unsatisfactory** *a.* disappointing, below expectation, displeasing, undesirable, regrettable, disconcerting, disquieting, vexing, distressing, upsetting, disturbing, offensive, unacceptable, disagreeable, unwelcome, shocking, deficient.—*Ant.* excellent, satisfactory, gratifying.

**unscrupulous** *a.* unprincipled, wicked, dishonest.

**unseen** *a.* imagined, imaginary, hidden, obscure, unobserved, veiled, occult, sensed, unperceived, unnoticed, unsuspected, curtained, unobtrusive, viewless, invisible, sightless, dark, shrouded, impalpable, imperceptible, inconspicuous, undiscovered, impenetrable, dense.

**unsettled** *a.* **1** [Undetermined] undecided, unfixed, unresolved. **2** [Unstable] confused, agitated, troubled, changing, explosive, shifting, precarious, ticklish, unpredictable, uneasy, unbalanced, perilous, complex, complicated, fluid, kinetic, active, busy, critical.—*Ant.* simple, stable, solid.

**unstable** *a.* **1** [Having a high center of gravity] unsteady, wavering, unbalanced, giddy, wobbly, wiggly, weaving, shifty, precarious, top-heavy, teetering, shifting, uncertain, rattletrap, beetling, jutting, lightly balanced.—*Ant.* firm, steady, solid. **2** [Easily disturbed] variable, changeable, giddy, capricious, fluctuating, shifty, volatile, rootless, dizzy, unpredictable, uncertain, sensitive, oversensitive, thin-skinned, timid, delicate.

**unsteady** *a.* **1** [Wobbly] wiggly, wavering, shaky, treacherous, unbalanced, top-heavy, leaning, ramshackle, giddy, weaving, heaving, precarious, teetering, uncertain. **2** [Inconstant] changeable, fluctuating, vacillating, variable, uncertain, unfixed, capricious, volatile, unreliable, tricky, shifty, shaky, jerky, fluttering.

**unsuccessful** *a.* defeated, disappointed, frustrated, aborted, disastrous, unprosperous, unfortunate, unlucky, futile, failing, fruitless, worthless, sterile, bootless, unavailing, ineffectual, ineffective, immature, useless, foiled, shipwrecked, overwhelmed, overpowered, broken, ruined, destroyed, thwarted, crossed, disconcerted, dashed, circumvented, premature, inoperative, of no effect, balked, left holding the sack*, skunked*, stymied, jinxed*, out of luck, stuck*.—*Ant.* successful, fortunate, lucky.

**unsuitable** *a.* inadequate, improper, malapropos, disagreeable, discordant, incongruous, inharmonious, incompatible, clashing, out of place, jarring, dissonant, discrepant, irrelevant, uncalled-for, dissident, inappropriate, ill-suited, unseemly, conflicting, opposite, contrary, unbecoming, unfitting, unfit, disparate, disturbing, mismatched, disproportionate, divergent, mismated, inapplicable, unassimilable, inconsistent, intrusive, amiss, interfering, disagreeing, inept, unbefitting, inadmissible, absurd, senseless, unseasonable, unfortunate, ill-timed, unsympathetic, not in keeping, out of joint, at odds, at variance, repugnant, out of kilter*, cockeyed*.—*Ant.* fit, suitable, proper.

**unsure** *a.* unreliable, hesitant, doubtful.

**unthinkable** *a.* inconceivable, unimaginable, improbable.
**unthinking** *a.* heedless, rude, inconsiderate.
**untidy** *a.* slovenly, unkempt, disorderly.
**untimely** *a.* unseasonable, awkward, ill-timed, inauspicious, badly timed, too early, abortive, too late, unpromising, ill-chosen, improper, unseemly, inappropriate, wrong, unfit, disagreeable, mistimed, intrusive, badly calculated, inopportune, out-of-date, malapropos, premature, unlucky, unfavorable, unfortunate, inexpedient, anachronistic.—*Ant.* early, timely, seasonable.
**untouched** *a.* **1** [Not harmed] intact, whole, secure, unbroken, in good order, unharmed, in good condition, in a good state of preservation, safe and sound, out of danger, shipshape. **2** [Not contaminated] virgin, clear, pure.
**untrue** *a.* false, misleading, specious, lying, hollow, deceptive, delusive, untrustworthy, deceitful, sham, spurious, incorrect, prevaricating, wrong.
**unusual** *a.* **1** [Remarkable] rare, extraordinary, strange, outstanding, great, uncommon, special, distinguished, prominent, important, noteworthy, awe-inspiring, awesome, unique, fine, unheard-of, unexpected, seldom met with, surprising, superior, astonishing, amazing, prodigious, incredible, inconceivable, atypical, conspicuous, exceptional, eminent, significant, memorable, renowned, refreshing, singular, fabulous, unprecedented, unparalleled, unexampled, unaccountable, stupendous, unaccustomed, wonderful, notable, superior, marvelous, striking, overpowering, electrifying, dazing, fantastic, startling, astounding, indescribable, appalling, stupefying, ineffable, out of sight*.—*Ant.* common, familiar, customary. **2** [Different] unique, extreme, uncommon, particular, exaggerated, distinctive, choice, little-known, out of the ordinary, marked, forward, unconventional, radical, exceptional, peculiar, strange, foreign, unnatural, puzzling, perplexing, confounding, disturbing, novel, advanced, startling, shocking, staggering, uncustomary, breaking with tradition, infrequent, mysterious, mystifying, surprising, extraordinary, unparalleled, deep, profound, aberrant, singular, unorthodox, unconformable, not to be expected, eccentric, unbalanced, unprecedented, inconsistent, individual, original, refreshing, newfangled, new, modern, recent, late, fresh, curious, unfamiliar, irregular, odd, unaccountable, alien, queer, quaint, freakish, bizarre, far-fetched, neurotic, exotic, outlandish, old-fashioned, out-of-the-way, abnormal, irrational, monstrous, anomalous, fearful.—*Ant.* common, ordinary, normal.
**unveil** *v.* uncover, reveal, make known.
**unwelcome** *a.* uninvited, unwished for, repellent.
**unwilling** *a.* backward, resistant, reluctant, recalcitrant, unenthusiastic, doubtful, wayward, unready, indisposed, disinclined, averse, opposed, against, contrary, indifferent, indocile, intractable, demurring, shrinking, flinching, hesitating, shy, slack, evasive, loath, shy of, malcontent, slow, remiss, grudging, uncooperative, contrary, against the grain.—*Ant.* ready, willing, eager.
**up** *a. & prep.* **1** [Situated above] at the top of, at the crest of, at the

summit of, at the apex of, nearer the top of, nearer the head of, nearer the source of.—*Ant.* down, nearer the bottom of, farther from the head of. **2** [Moving from the earth] upward, uphill, skyward, heavenward, away from the center of gravity, perpendicularly, into the air, higher, away from the earth. **3** [Expired] lapsed, elapsed, run out, terminated, invalid, ended, come to a term, outdated, exhausted, finished, done. **4** [Happening] under consideration, being scrutinized, moot, live, current, pertinent, timely, relevant, pressing, urgent. **5** [Next] after, in order, prospective.

**update** *v.* modernize, bring up to date, refresh.

**upright** *a.* **1** [Vertical] erect, perpendicular, on end. **2** [Honorable] straightforward, honest, fair.

**uproar** *n.* babble, confusion, turmoil, ado, hassle, commotion, clamor, disturbance, tumult, din, racket, clatter, hubbub, fracas, clangor, jangle, bustle, bickering, discord, row.

**upset** *a.* disconcerted, amazed, shocked.

**upset** *n.* overthrow, destruction, subversion.

**upset** *v.* **1** [To turn over] overturn, upturn, subvert, turn bottom-side up, turn inside out, upend, reverse, keel over, overset, topple, tip over, turn topsy-turvy, overbalance, invert, capsize, tilt, pitch over, overthrow.—*Ant.* stand, erect, elevate. **2** [To disturb] agitate, fluster, perturb. **3** [To beat] conquer, outplay, overpower.

**upstanding** *a.* honorable, upright, straightforward.

**up-to-date** *a.* in vogue, in fashion, fashionable, conventional, stylish, modern, modernistic, streamlined, popular, faddish, brand-new, current, up-to-the-minute, according to the prevailing taste, modish, the latest, all the rage, trendy*, in*, with-it*.

**urban** *a.* **1** [Concerning city government] city, municipal, civil. **2** [Concerning city living] big-city, civic, municipal, metropolitan, within the city limits, inner-city, central-city, downtown, zoned, planned, business-district, civil, nonrural, ghetto, shopping, residential, apartment-dwelling.

**urge** *v.* **1** [To present favorably] favor, further, support. **2** [To induce] charge, beg, plead, adjure, influence, beseech, implore, ask, command, entreat, desire, request, press, inveigle, talk into, incite, move, allure, tempt, attract, influence, prompt, instigate, exhort, advise, solicit, inspire, stimulate, conjure, coax, wheedle, maneuver, draw, put up to*, prevail upon.—*Ant.* restrain, deter, discourage. **3** [To drive] compel, drive, propel, impel, force, coerce, constrain, press, push, make, oblige, goad, prod, spur.—*Ant.* deny, block, withhold.

**urgent** *a.* **1** [Of immediate importance] pressing, critical, necessary, compelling, imperative, important, indispensable, momentous, wanted, required, called for, demanded, salient, chief, paramount, essential, primary, vital, principal, absorbing, all-absorbing, not to be delayed, crucial, instant, leading, capital, overruling, foremost, exigent, crying. **2** [Insistent] compelling, persuasive, imperious, solemn, grave, weighty, impressive, earnest, importunate, clamorous, hasty, breathless, precipitate, frantic, impetuous, imperative, convincing, beseeching, seductive, commanding, imploring, eager, zealous, anxious, moving, excited, impulsive, vigorous, enthusiastic, overpowering, masterful.

**usable** *a.* available, at hand, useful, employable, unused, good, serviceable, applicable, ready, subservient, helpful, valuable, beneficial, profitable, advantageous, fit, desirable, efficacious, instrumental, fitting, conformable, suitable, proper, practical, convenient.—*Ant.* useless, worthless, no good.

**use** *n.* **1** [The act of using] practice, employment, application, usage, appliance, effecting, manner, adoption, utilization, manipulation, bringing to bear, management, handling, performance, conduct, recourse, resort, exercise, treatment, method, technique, control, resolution, realization, association.—*Ant.* neglect, disuse, dismissal. **2** [The state of being useful] utility, usefulness, usability, employment, application, value, advantage, excellence, helpfulness, convenience, suitability, expedience, aid, serviceability, merit, profit, practicability, practicality, fitness, subservience, effectiveness, applicability.

**use** *v.* **1** [To make use of] avail oneself of, employ, put to use, exercise, exert, put forth, utilize, apply, bring to bear, practice, play on, do with, draw on, adopt, take advantage of, make do, accept, work, put in practice, relate, make with, put to work, make shift with.—*Ant.* discard, reject, refuse. **2** [To make a practice of; *now used principally in the past tense*] be accustomed to, practice, adapt, conform, habituate, regulate, suit, familiarize, attune. **3** [To behave toward] deal with, handle, bear oneself toward.

**used** *a.* **1** [Employed] put to use, utilized, applied, adopted, adapted, accepted, put in service, practiced, turned to account.—*Ant.* discarded, rejected, unused. **2** [Accustomed] practiced, customary, suited. **3** [Secondhand] castoff, depreciated, reconditioned.

**useless** *a.* **1** [Unserviceable] worthless, unusable, ineffectual, expendable, incompetent, of no use, ineffective, inoperate, dysfunctional, counterproductive, inefficient, unprofitable, no damn good*.—*Ant.* efficient, usable, operative. **2** [Futile] vain, pointless, fruitless.

**usual** *a.* **1** [Ordinary] general, frequent, normal. **2** [Habitual] prevailing, accustomed, customary.

**utilize** *v.* employ, appropriate, turn to account.

**utter** *a.* complete, total, thorough.

**utter** *v.* pronounce, talk, express, articulate, voice, whisper, mutter, shout, exclaim, enunciate, air, speak, tell, disclose, declare, say, assert, affirm, ejaculate, vocalize, proclaim, give tongue to, recite, blurt out, let fall, announce, come out with.

# V

**vacant** *a.* **1** [Without contents] devoid, void, unfilled. **2** [Without an occupant] unoccupied, untenanted, tenantless, uninhabited, idle, free, deserted, abandoned, without a resident, not lived in.—*Ant.* inhabited, occupied, tenanted.

**vagrant** *a.* **1** [Having no home] roaming, itinerant, nomadic. **2** [Having no occupation] begging, mendicant, profligate, idling, prodigal, loafing, beachcombing, panhandling*, bumming*, mooching*. **3** [Having no fixed course] wayward, capricious, erratic.

**vagrant** *n.* beggar, idler, loafer.

**vague** *a.* **1** [Not clearly expressed] indefinite, unintelligible, superficial. **2** [Not clearly understood] uncertain, undetermined, unsure, doubtful, dubious, questionable, misunderstood, enigmatic, puzzling, nebulous, inexplicable, unsettled, bewildering, perplexing, problematic.—*Ant.* certain, sure, positive. **3** [Not clearly visible] dim, nebulous, dark.

**vain** *a.* **1** [Possessing unwarranted self-esteem] proud, arrogant, haughty. **2** [Useless] worthless, hopeless, profitless.

**valid** *a.* **1** [Capable of proof] sound, cogent, logical, conclusive, solid, well-grounded, well-founded, tested, accurate, convincing, telling, correct, determinative, compelling, persuasive, potent, stringent, strong, ultimate, unanswerable, irrefutable.—*Ant.* wrong, erring, misleading. **2** [Genuine] true, original, factual, real, actual, pure, uncorrupted, authentic, confirmed, authoritative, trustworthy, credible, attested, efficient, legitimate, adequate, substantial, proven, unadulterated.—*Ant.* false, fictitious, counterfeit.

**validate** *v.* confirm, sanction, legalize.

**valley** *n.* vale, glen, canyon, depression, trough, notch, channel, lowland, river valley, stream valley, hollow, plain, dell, valley floor, coulee, dale, river bottom.—*Ant.* mountain, ridge, hilltop.

**value** *n.* **1** [Monetary value] price, expense, cost, profit, value in exhange, equivalent, rate, amount, market price, charge, face value, assessment, appraisal. **2** [The quality of being desirable] use, benefit, advantage. **3** [Quality] worth, merit, significance, consequence, goodness, condition, state, excellence, distinction, desirability, grade, finish, perfection, eminence, superiority, advantage, power, regard, importance, mark, caliber, repute. **4** [Precise signification] significance, force, sense.

**vanish** *v.* fade out, go away, dissolve.

**vanity** *n.* ostentation, display, conceit, show, self-love, narcissism, self-glorification, self-applause, pretension, vainglory, conceitedness, affection, complacency, smugness.

**vapor** *n.* mist, steam, condensation, smog, exhalation, breath, fog, gas, haze, smoke.

**variety** *n.* **1** [Quality or state of being diverse] diversity, change, diversification, difference, variance, medley, mixture, miscellany, disparateness, divergency, variation, incongruity, fluctuation, shift, change, modification, departure, many-sidedness. **2** [Sort] kind, class, division, species, genus, race, tribe, family, assortment, type, stripe, nature, ilk, character, description, rank, grade, category, classification, quality.—*Ant.* equality, equalness, similarity.

**various** *a.* different, disparate, dissimilar, diverse, diversified, variegated, varicolored, many-sided, several, manifold, numerous, unlike, many, sundry, variable, changeable, inconstant, uncertain, of any kind, all manner of, of every description, distinct.—*Ant.* alike, undiversified, identical.

**vary** *v.* dissent, diverge, differ, deviate, digress, swerve, depart, fluctuate, alternate, diverge from, be distinguished from, range, be inconstant, mutate, be uncertain.—*Ant.* remain, be steady, hold.

**vast** *a.* **1** [Large] huge, enormous, immense. **2** [Extensive] broad, far-flung, wide, spacious, expansive, spread-out, ample, far-reaching, widespread, comprehensive, detailed, all-inclusive, astronomical, prolonged, stretched out, expanded.—*Ant.* narrow, limited, confined.

**vegetation** *n.* plants, plant growth, trees, shrubs, saplings, flowers, wildflowers, grasses, herbage, herbs, pasturage, weeds, vegetables, crops.

**vein** *n.* **1** [A fissure] cleft, aperture, opening, channel, cavity, crack, cranny, rift, chink, break, breach, slit, crevice, flaw, rupture. **2** [A persistent quality] strain, humor, mood, temper, tang, spice, dash. **3** [A blood duct leading to the heart]

**venerate** *v.* revere, reverence, adore.

**vengeance** *n.* retribution, return, retaliation.

**venom** *n.* poison, virus, toxin, bane, microbe, contagion, infection.

**venture** *n.* adventure, risk, hazard, peril, stake, chance, speculation, dare, experiment, trial, attempt, test, gamble, undertaking, enterprise, investment, leap in the dark, plunge*, flyer*, crack*, fling*.

**verbal** *a.* told, unwritten, lingual, oral, spoken.

**verdict** *n.* judgment, finding, decision, answer, opinion, sentence, determination, decree, conclusion, deduction, adjudication, arbitrament.

**verify** *v.* establish, substantiate, authenticate, prove, check, test, validate, settle, corroborate, confirm.

**versatile** *a.* many-sided, adaptable, dexterous, varied, ready, clever, handy, talented, gifted, adroit, resourceful, ingenious, accomplished.

**verse** *n.* **1** [Composition in poetic form] poetry, metrical composition, versification, stanza, rhyme, lyric, sonnet, ode, heroic verse, dramatic poetry, blank verse, free verse. **2** [A unit of verse] line, verse, stanza, stave, strophe, antistrophe, hemistich, distich, quatrain.

**very** *a.* extremely, exceedingly, greatly, acutely, indispensably, just so, surprisingly, astonishingly, incredibly, wonderfully, particularly, certainly, positively, emphatically, really, truly, pretty, decidedly, pressingly, notably, uncommonly, extraordinarily, prodigiously, hightly, substantially, dearly, amply, vastly, extensively, noticeably, conspicuously, largely, considerably, hugely, excessively, imperatively, markedly, enormously, sizably, materially, immensely, tremendously, superlatively, remarkably, unusually, immoderately, quite, indeed, somewhat, rather, simply, intensely, urgently, exceptionally, severely, seriously, in a great measure, to a great degree, beyond compare, on a large scale, ever so, beyond measure, by far, in the extreme, in a marked degree, to a great extent, without restraint, more or less, in part, infinitely, very much, real*, right, pretty, awfully*, good and*, powerful*, powerfully*, hell of a*, precious*, so*, to a fault, a bit of, no end*.

**vestige** *n.* trace, remains, scrap.

**vibrant** *a.* energetic, vigorous, lively.

**vibration** *n.* quake, wavering, vacillation, fluctuation, oscillation, quiver, shake.

**vice versa** *a.* conversely, in reverse, the other way round, turn about, about-face, in opposite manner, on the contrary, in reverse.

**vicious** *a.* bad, debased, base, impious, profligate, demoralized, faulty, vile, foul, impure, lewd, indecent, licentious, libidinous.—*Ant.* pure, noble, virtuous.

**victory** *n.* conquest, mastery, subjugation, overcoming, overthrow, master stroke, lucky stroke, winning, gaining, defeating, subduing, destruction, killing, knockout, pushover.

**view** *n.* glimpse, look, panorama, aspect, show, appearance, prospect, distance, opening, stretch, outlook, way, extended view, long view, avenue, contour, outline, scene, spectacle. **—in view** visible, in sight, not out of sight, perceptible, perceivable. **—on view** displayed, on display, exposed. **—with a view to** in order to, so that, anticipating.

**vigorous** *a.* **1** [Done with vigor] energetic, lively, brisk. **2** [Forceful] powerful, strong, potent.

**vile** *a.* sordid, corrupt, debased.

**vindication** *n.* defense, acquittal, clearance.

**vindictive** *a.* revengeful, resentful, spiteful.

**vine** *n.* creeper, climbing plant, creeping plant, trailing plant, stem climber, leaf climber, tendril climber.

**violate** *v.* **1** [To transgress] outrage, disrupt, infringe, break, tamper with. **2** [To rape] dishonor, profane, defile, ravish.

**violent** *a.* strong, powerful, forceful, forcible, rough, mighty, great, potent, coercive, furious, mad, savage, fierce, passionate, splitting, vehement, frenzied, demoniac, frantic, fuming, enraged, disturbed, agitated, impassioned, impetuous, urgent, maddened, aroused, inflamed, distraught, infatuated, hysterical, great, vehement, extreme, unusual, destructible, murderous, homicidal, rampageous.—*Ant.* calm, gentle, quiet.

**virile** *a.* masculine, potent, manly.

**virtue** *n.* **1** [Moral excellence] ideal, ethic, morality, goodness, righteousness, uprightness, ethical conduct, good thing, respectability, rectitude, honor, honesty, candor, merit, fineness, character, excellence, value, chastity, quality, worth, kindness, innocence, generosity, trustworthiness, faithfulness, consideration, justice, prudence, temperance, fortitude, faith, hope, charity, love.—*Ant.* evil, immorality, depravity. **2** [An individual excellence] quality, characteristic, attribute, temper, way, trait, feature, accomplishment, achievement, property, distinction, capacity, power.—*Ant.* lack, inability, incapacity. **3** [Probity in sexual conduct] virginity, purity, decency. **—by virtue of** on the grounds of, because of, looking toward.

**vision** *n.* **1** [The faculty of sight] sight, perception, perceiving, range of view, optics, eyesight. **2** [Understanding] foresight, discernment, breadth of view, insight, penetration, intuition, divination, astuteness, keenness, foreknowledge, prescience, farsightedness. **3** [Something seen through powers of the mind] imagination, poetic insight, fancy, fantasy, image, concept, conception, ideality, idea. **4** [Something seen because of an abnormality] revelation, trance, ecstasy, phantom, apparition, ghost, wraith, specter, apocalypse, nightmare, spirit, warlock.

**visionary** *a.* **1** [Impractical] ideal, romantic, utopian. **2** [Imaginary] chimerical, delusory, dreamy.

**visit** *n.* social call, call, appointment, interview, formal call, talk, evening, stay, weekend, holiday, visitation.

**visit** *v.* stay with, stop by, call on, call upon, come around, be the guest of, make a visit, sojourn awhile, revisit, make one's compliments to, look in on, visit with, call for, stop off, stop in, stop over, have an appointment with, pay a visit to, tour, take in, drop in on, hit, look around*, look up, go over to, look in, drop over, pop in, have a date.

**visitor** *n.* caller, visitant, guest.

**visualize** *v.* see in the mind's eye, picture mentally, conceive, imagine.

**vitality** *n.* life, liveliness, animation, vim, vigor, intensity, continuity, endurance, energy, spirit, ardor, audacity, spunk, fervor, verve, venturesomeness.

**vivid** *a.* **1** [Brilliant] shining, rich, glowing. **2** [Distinct] strong, vigorous, lucid.

**vocal** *a.* **1** [Verbal] expressed, uttered, voiced. **2** [Produced by the voice: *said especially of music*] sung, scored for voice, vocalized.

**voice** *n.* **1** [A vocal sound] speech, sound, call, cry, utterance, tongue, whistle, moan, groan, song, yell, hail, howl, yowl, bark, whine, whimper, mutter, murmur, shout, bleat, bray, neigh, whinny, roar, trumpet, cluck, honk, meow, hiss, quack.—*Ant.* silence, dumbness, deaf-mutism. **2** [Approval or opinion] decision, conclusion, assent, negation, approval, recommendation, wish, view. **—with one voice** all together, by unanimous vote, without dissent.

**void** *a.* barren, sterile, fruitless, meaningless, useless, invalid, vain, voided, unconfirmed, unratified, null and void, worthless, unsanctioned, set aside, avoided, forceless, voted out, ineffectual, ineffective, voidable.—*Ant.* valid, in force, used.

**volume** *n.* **1** [Quantity] bulk, mass, amount. **2** [Contents] cubical, size, dimensions. **3** [A book] printed document, tome, pamphlet. **4** [Degree of sound] loudness, amplification, strength.

**voluntary** *a.* willing, freely, spontaneous.

**volunteer** *v.* come forward, enlist, sign up, submit oneself, take the initiative, offer oneself, do on one's own accord, do of one's own free will, take the initiative, take upon oneself, speak up, stand up and be counted, go in*, chip in*, do on one's own hook*, take the bull by the horns, stand on one's own feet, take the bit between one's teeth, paddle one's own canoe, take the plunge.

**vomit** *v.* throw up, eject, bring up, spit up, dry heave, be seasick, retch, ruminate, regurgitate, give forth, discharge, belch forth, spew, puke*, barf*, toss one's cookies*, hurl*.

**vote** *n.* **1** [A ballot] tally, ticket, slip of paper, ball, yes or no, rising vote, Australian ballot, secret ballot. **2** [A decision] referendum, choice, majority. **3** [The right to vote] suffrage, the franchise, manhood suffrage, universal suffrage, woman suffrage.

**vote** *v.* ballot, cast a vote, cast a ballot, give a vote, enact, establish, determine, bring about, effect, grant, confer, declare, suggest, propose.

**vulgar** *a.* sordid, ignoble, mean, base, obscene, indecent, gross, filthy, villainous, dishonorable, unworthy, fractious, inferior, disgusting, base-minded, mean-spirited, malicious, ill-tempered, sneaking, deceitful, slippery, loathsome, odious, foul-mouthed, brutish, debased, contemptible, abhorrent, profane, nasty.—*Ant.* noble, high-minded, lofty.

# W

**wage** *v.* conduct, make, carry on.

**wages** *pl.n.* salary, earnings, payment.

**wail** *v.* moan, weep, lament.

**wait** *v.* **1** [To await] expect, anticipate, tarry, pause, wait for, look for, watch for, abide, dally, remain, idle, bide one's time, mark time, stay up for, lie in wait for, ambush, lie low, hole up*, hang around*, stick around, cool one's heels*.—*Ant.* leave, hurry, act. **2** [To serve food at a table] serve, deliver, tend, act as waiter, act as waitress, arrange, set, ready, place on the table, bus, help, portion.

**wake up** *v.* rise and shine, arise, get up, awake, awaken, get going*, get cracking*.

**walk** *n.* **1** [Manner of walking] gait, tread, stride. **2** [Course over which one walks] pavement, sidewalk, pathway, footpath, track, trail, sheepwalk, boardwalk, pier, promenade, avenue, street, road, alley, dock, platform, gangway. **3** [A short walking expedition] stroll, ramble, turn, hike, promenade, airing, saunter, tramp, trek, march, circuit, jaunt, tour.

**walk** *v.* **1** [To move on foot] step, pace, march, tread, amble, stroll, hike, saunter, wander, ramble, go out for an airing, take a walk, promenade, trudge, tramp, trek, tour, take a turn, roam, rove, meander, traipse about, patrol, file off, knock about*, knock around*, hoof it*, toddle along, shuffle, wend one's way, cruise. **2** [To cause to move on foot] lead, drive, exercise, train, order a march, escort, accompany, take for a walk.

**wall** *n.* **1** [A physical barrier] dam, embankment, dike, ditch, bank, levee, stockade, fence, parapet, retainer, rampart, bulwark, palisade, fort, cliff, barricade, floodgate, sluice. **2** [An obstacle; *figurative*] barrier, obstruction, bar, cordon, entanglement, hurdle, resistance, defense, snag, hindrance, impediment, difficulty, limitation, restriction, retardation, knot, hitch, drawback, stumbling block, check, stop, curb, red tape, fly in the ointment, bottleneck, red herring, detour.

**wallop** *v.* thump, thrash, strike.

**wandering** *a.* **1** [Wandering in space] roving, roaming, nomadic, meandering, restless, traveling, drifting, straying, going off, strolling, ranging, prowling, ambulatory, straggling, on the road, peripatetic, itinerant, roundabout, circuitous.—*Ant.* idle, home-loving, sedentary. **2** [Wandering in thought] incongruous, digressive, disconnected.

**wane** *v.* decline, subside, fade away.

**want** *v.* **1** [To desire] require, aspire, fancy, hanker after, have an urge for, incline toward, covet, crave, long for, lust for, have a fondness for, have a passion for, have ambition, thirst after, hunger after, be greedy for, ache*, have a yen for*, have an itch for. **2** [To lack] be deficient in, be deprived of, require.

**wanting** *a.* **1** [Deficient] destitute, poor, in default of, deprived of, bereft of, devoid of, empty of, bankrupt in, cut o ff, lacking, short, inadequate, defective, remiss, incomplete, missing, substandard, insufficient, absent, needed, unfulfilled, on the short end. **2** [Desiring] desirous of, covetous, longing for.

**wanton** *a.* **1** [Unrestrained] extravagant, capricious, reckless, unreserved, unfettered, free, wayward, fluctuating, changeable, whimsical, fitful, variable, fanciful, inconstant, fickle, frivolous, volatile. **2** [Lewd] wayward, lustful, licentious.

**warm** *a.* **1** [Moderately heated] heated, sunny, melting, hot, mild, tepid, lukewarm, summery, temperate, clement, glowing, perspiring, sweaty, sweating, flushed, warmish, snug as a bug in a rug*.—*Ant.* cool, chilly, chilling. **2** [Sympathetic] gracious, cordial, compassionate.

**warm** *v.* heat up, warm up, put on the fire.

**warn** *v.* forewarn, give notice, put on guard, give fair warning, signal, advise, prepare, alert, inform, remind, enjoin, hint, prepare for the worst, offer a word of caution, admonish, counsel, exhort, dissuade, reprove, threaten, forbid, predict, remonstrate, deprecate, prescribe, urge, recommend, prompt, suggest, advocate, cry wolf, tip off*, give the high sign, put a bug in one's ear*.

**warning** *n.* caution, admonition, notice, advice, forewarning, alert, intimation, premonition, notification, sign, omen, alarm, indication, token, hint, lesson, information, example, distress signal, prediction, signal, injunction, exhortation, high sign, word to the wise, tip-off, SOS*, handwriting on the wall.

**warrant** *v.* **1** [To guarantee] assure, insure, vouch for. **2** [To justify] bear out, call for, give grounds for.

**wary** *a.* circumspect, cautious, alert.

**wash** *n.* **1** [Laundry] wet wash, washing, linen, family wash, soiled clothing, clean clothes, washed clothing, rough-dry wash, flat pieces, finished laundry. **2** [The movement of water] swishing, lapping, roll, swirl, rush, surging, eddy, wave, undulation, surge, heave, flow, murmur, gush, spurt. **3** [A stream bed that is usually dry] arroyo, gulch, canyon. **4** [A prepared liquid] rinse, swab, coating.

**wash** *v.* **1** [To bathe] clean, cleanse, shine, immerse, douse, soak, take a bath, take a shower, soap, rub the dirt off, scour, scrub, rinse, wipe, sponge, dip, freshen up, wash up, clean up, brush up. **2** [To launder] clean, starch, scrub, put in a washing machine, boil, soap, send to the laundry, scour, rinse out, soak, drench.—*Ant.* dirty, stain, spoil. **3** [To brush with a liquid] swab, whitewash, color. **4** [*To be convincing] be plausible, stand up, endure examination.

**waste** *a.* futile, discarded, worthless, valueless, useless, empty, barren, dreary, uninhabited, desolate, profitless, superfluous, unnecessary, functionless, purposeless, pointless, unserviceable.

**waste** *n.* **1** [The state of being wasted] disuse, misuse, dissipation, consumption, uselessness, devastation, ruin, decay, loss, exhaustion, extravagance, squandering, wear and tear, wrack and ruin.—*Ant.* use, profit, value. **2** [Refuse] rubbish, garbage, scrap. **3** [Unused land] desert, wilds, wilderness, wasteland, fen, tundra, marsh, marshland, bog, moor, quagmire, dustbowl, badlands, swamp, wash.

**waste** *v.* **1** [To use without result] dissipate, spend, consume, lose, be of no avail, come to nothing, go to waste, misuse, throw away, use up, misapply, misemploy, labor in vain, cast pearls before swine.—*Ant.* profit, use well, get results. **2** [To squander] burn up, lavish, scatter, splurge, spend, be prodigal, indulge, abuse, empty, drain, fatigue, spill, impoverish, misspend, exhaust, fritter away, ruin, be spendthrift, divert, go through, gamble away, throw money away*, run through, blow*.—*Ant.* save, be thrifty, manage wisely. **3** [To be consumed gradually] decay, thin out, become thin, wither, dwindle, lose weight, be diseased, run dry, wilt, droop, decrease, disappear, drain, empty, wear.—*Ant.* grow, develop, enrich.

**watch** *n.* **1** [A portable timepiece] wristwatch, pocket watch, stopwatch, digital watch, analog watch, sportsman's watch, fashion watch, ladies' watch, men's watch, children's watch, chronometer. **2** [Strict attention] lookout, observation, observance, awareness, attention, vigilance, guard, heed, watchfulness.—*Ant.* neglect, sleepiness, apathy. **3** [A period of duty or vigilance] patrol, guard duty, nightwatch. **4** [Persons or a person standing guard] guard, sentry, sentinel.

**watch** *v.* **1** [To be attentive] observe, see, scrutinize, follow, attend, mark, regard, listen, wait, attend, take notice, contemplate, mind, view, pay attention, concentrate, look closely. **2** [To guard] keep an eye on, patrol, police.

**watchful** *a.* on guard, vigilant, prepared.

**watch over** *v.* protect, look after, attend to.

**water** *v.* sprinkle, spray, irrigate.

**water down** *v.* dilute, restrict, weaken.

**watery** *a.* moist, damp, humid, soggy, sodden, wet, thin, colorless, washed, waterlike.—*Ant.* dry, parched, baked.

**wave** *n.* **1** [A wall of water] comber, swell, roller, heave, tidal wave, billow, tide, surge, crest, bore, breaker, whitecap. **2** [A movement suggestive of a wave] surge, gush, swell, uprising, onslaught, influx, tide, flow, stream, come and go, swarm, drift, rush, crush, fluctuation. **3** [Undulating movement] rocking, bending, winding.

**wave** *v.* **1** [To flutter] stream, pulse, flow, shake, fly, dance, flap, swish, swing, tremble, whirl.—*Ant.* fall, droop, hang listless. **2** [To give an alternating movement] motion, beckon, call, raise the arm, signal, greet, return a greeting, hail. **3** [To move back and forth] falter, waver, oscillate, vacillate, fluctuate, pulsate, vibrate, wag, waggle, sway, lurch, bend, swing, dangle, seesaw, wobble, reel, quaver, quiver, swing from side to side, palpitate, move to and fro.

**waver** *v.* fluctuate, vacillate, hesitate, dillydally, seesaw, deliberate, reel, teeter, totter, hem and haw, pause, stagger.

**way** *n.* **1** [Road] trail, walk, byway. **2** [Course] alternative, direction, progression, trend, tendency, distance, space, extent, bearing, orbit, approach, passage, gateway, entrance, access, door, gate, channel. **3** [Means] method, mode, means, plan, technique, design, system, procedure, process, measure, contrivance, stroke, step, move, action, idea, outline, plot, policy, instrument. **4** [Manner] form, fashion, gait, tone, guise, habit, custom, usage, behavior, style. **—by the way** casually, by the by, as a matter of fact. **—by way of** routed through, detoured through, utilizing. **—get out of the** (or **one's**) **way** go, remove oneself, retire. **—make one's way** progress, succeed, do well. **—make way** draw back, give way, withdraw. **—on the way out** declining, no longer fashionable, going out. **—out of the way** disposed of, terminated, taken out. **—parting of the ways** breakup, agreement to separate, difference of opinion. **—under way** going, prospering, making headway.

**wayward** *a.* unruly, disobedient, perverse, headstrong, capricious, delinquent, refractory, willful, unruly, unmanageable, insubordinate, incorrigible, recalcitrant, self-indulgent, changeable, stubborn.—*Ant.* obedient, stable, resolute.

**weak** *a.* **1** [Lacking physical strength; *said of persons*] delicate, puny, flabby, flaccid, effeminate, frail, sickly, debilitated, senile.— *Ant.* strong, healthy, robust. **2** [Lacking physical strength; *said of things*] flimsy, makeshift, brittle, unsubstantial, jerry-built, rickety, tumbledown, sleazy, shaky, unsteady, ramshackle, rotten, wobbly, tottery.— *Ant.* strong, shatter-proof, sturdy. **3** [Lacking mental firmness or character] weak-minded, nerveless, fainthearted, irresolute, nervous, spineless, unstrung, palsied, wishy-washy, hesitant, vacillating, frightened.—*Ant.* brave, courageous, adventurous. **4** [Lacking in volume] thin, low, soft, indistinct, feeble, faint, dim, muffled, whispered, bated, inaudible, light, stifled, dull, pale.—*Ant.* loud, strong, forceful. **5** [Lacking in military power] small, paltry, ineffectual, ineffective, inadequate, impotent, ill-equipped, insufficiently armed, limited, unorganized, undisciplined, untrained, vulnerable, exposed, assailable, unprepared. **6** [Lacking in capacity or experience] unsure, untrained, young.

**weaken** *v.* **1** [To become weaker] lessen, lose, decrease, relapse, soften, relax, droop, fail, crumble, halt, wane, abate, limp, languish, fade, decline, totter, tremble, flag, faint, wilt, lose spirit, become disheartened, fail in courage, slow down, break up, crack up*, wash out*.— *Ant.* strengthen, revive, straighten. **2** [To make weaker] reduce, minimize, enervate, debilitate, exhaust, cripple, unman, emasculate, castrate, devitalize, undermine, impair, sap, enfeeble, unnerve, incapacitate, impoverish, thin, dilute, take the wind out of, wash up*.—*Ant.* revive, quicken, animate.

**wealth** *n.* capital, capital stock, economic resources, stock, stocks and bonds, securities, vested interests, land, property, labor power, commodities, cash, money in the bank, money, natural resources, assets, means, riches, substance, affluence, belongings, life savings, property, fortune, hoard, treasure, resources, revenue, cache, cash, competence, luxury, opulence, prosperity, abundance, money to burn*.—*Ant.* poverty, pauperism, unemployment.

**wealthy** *a.* opulent, moneyed, affluent.

**weapon** *n.* armament, protection, weaponry, deadly weapon, military hardware, sophisticated hardware, lethal weapon, defense.

**wear** *n.* depreciation, damage, loss, erosion, wear and tear, loss by friction, diminution, waste, corrosion, impairment, wearing away, disappearance, result of friction.—*Ant.* growth, accretion, building up.

**wear** *v.* **1** [To use as clothing or personal ornament] bear, carry, effect, put on, don, be clothed, slip on, have on, dress in, attire, cover, wrap, harness, get into*.—*Ant.* undress, take off, disrobe. **2** [To consume by wearing] use up, use, consume, wear thin, wear out, waste, diminish, cut down, scrape off, exhaust, fatigue, weather down, impair. **3** [To be consumed by wearing] fade, go to seed, decay, crumble, dwindle, shrink, decline, deteriorate, decrease, waste, become threadbare.

**weary** *a.* exhausted, fatigued, overworked.

**weave** *n.* pattern, design, texture.

**weave** *v.* **1** [To construct by interlacing] knit, sew, interlace, spin, twine, intertwine, crisscross, interlink, wreathe, mesh, net, knot, twill, fold, interfold, ply, reticulate, loop, splice, braid, plait, twist. **2** [To move in and out] sidle through, make one's way, twist and turn, snake, zigzag, beat one's way, insinuate oneself through, wedge through.

**weep** *v.* wail, lament, cry.

**weigh** *v.* **1** [To take the weight of] measure, scale, put on the scales, hold the scales, put in the balance, counterbalance, heft*. **2** [To have weight] be heavy, carry weight, be important, tell, count, show, register, press, pull, be a load, burden, tip the scales*. **3** [To consider] ponder, contemplate, balance.

**weight** *n.* **1** [Heaviness] pressure, load, gross weight, net weight, dead weight, molecular weight, gravity, burden, mass, density, ponderability, tonnage, ballast, substance, G-factor*.—*Ant.* lightness, buoyancy, airiness. **2** [An object used for its weight] counterbalance, counterweight, counterpoise, ballast, paperweight, stone, rock, lead weight, sinker, anchor, plumb, sandbag. **3** [Importance] influence, authority, sway.

**weird** *a.* uncanny, ominous, eerie.

**welcome** *n.* greetings, salute, salutation, a hero's welcome, handshake, warm reception, free entrance, entree, hospitality, friendliness, the glad hand*.—*Ant.* rebuke, snub, cool reception.

**welfare** *n.* **1** [Personal condition] health, happiness, well-being, prosperity, good, good fortune, progress, state of being. **2** [Social service] poverty program, social insurance, health service.

**well** *a.* **1** [In good health] fine, sound, fit, trim, healthy, robust, strong, hearty, high-spirited, vigorous, hardy, hale, blooming, fresh, flourishing, rosy-cheeked, whole, in fine fettle, hunky-dory*, great*, fit as a fiddle, chipper*.—*Ant.* sick, ill, infirm. **2** [Satisfactorily] up to the mark, suitably, adequately, commendably, excellently, thoroughly, admirably, splendidly, favorably, rightly, properly, expertly, strongly, irreproachably, capably, soundly, competently, ably.—*Ant.* badly, poorly, unsatisfactorily. **3** [Sufficiently] abundantly, adequately, completely, fully, quite, entirely, considerably, wholly, plentifully, luxuriantly, extremely.—*Ant.* hardly, insufficiently, barely. **—as well** in addition, additionally, along with. **—as well as** similarly, alike, as much as.

**well** *n.* **1** [A source of water] spring, fountain, font, spout, geyser, wellspring, mouth, artesian well, reservoir. **2** [A shaft sunk into the earth] pit, hole, depression, chasm, abyss, oil well, gas well, water well. **3** [Any source] beginning, derivation, fountainhead.

**well-being** *n.* prosperity, happiness, fortune.

**wet** *a.* **1** [Covered or soaked with liquid] moist, damp, soaking, soaked, drenched, soggy, muggy, dewy, watery, dank, slimy, dripping, saturated, sodden.—*Ant.* dry, dried, clean. **2** [Rainy] drizzly, slushy, snowy, slippery, muddy, humid, foggy, damp, clammy, showery, drizzling, cloudy, misty.—*Ant.* clear, sunny, cloudless.

**wet** *v.* sprinkle, dampen, moisten.

**wheel** *n.* **1** [A thin circular body that turns on an axis] disk, ratchet, ring, hoop, roller, caster, drum, ferris wheel, wheel trolley, flywheel, cogwheel, steering wheel, sprocket wheel, chain wheel, water wheel. **2** [*An important person] personage, VIP, big shot*. **—at** (or **behind**) **the wheel** driving, in control, running things.

**wheeze** *v.* breathe heavily, puff, pant.

**whenever** *conj.* at any time, at any moment, on any occasion, at the first opportunity, if, when, should.

**wherever** *a. & conj.* where, in whatever place, anywhere, in any place that, wheresoever, regardless of where, in any direction.

**while** *conj.* **1** [As long as] during, at the same time that, during the time that, whilst*, throughout the time that, in the time that. **2** [Although] whereas, though, even though.

**whim** *n.* notion, vagary, caprice.

**whirl** *n.* **1** [Rapid rotating motion] swirl, turn, flurry, spin, gyration, reel, surge, whir. **2** [Confusion] hurry, flutter, fluster, ferment, agitation, tempest, storm, rush, tumult, turbulence, commotion, hurly-burly, bustle.

**whirl** *v.* turn around, rotate, spin.

**whisper** *n.* **1** [A low, sibilant sound] rustle, noise, murmur, hum, buzz, drone, undertone, hissing. **2** [A guarded utterance] disclosure, divulgence, rumor.

**whisper** *v.* speak softly, speak in a whisper, speak under one's breath, speak in an undertone, tell, talk low, speak confidentially, mutter, murmur, speak into someone's ear.—*Ant.* yell, speak aloud, shout.

**whistle** *v.* **1** [To produce a shrill blast] fife, pipe, flute, trill, hiss, whiz, wheeze, shriek, howl, blare, toot, tootle. **2** [To call with a whistle] signal, summon, warn.

**white** *a.* **1** [The color of fresh snow] ivory, silvery, snow-white, snowy, frosted, milky, milky-white, chalky, pearly, blanched, ashen, pale, wan, albescent.—*Ant.* dark, black, dirty. **2** [Colorless] clear, transparent, clean, blank, spotless, pure, unalloyed, neutral, achromatic, achromic. **3** [Concerning the white race] fair-skinned, light-complexioned, Caucasian. **4** [Pale] ashen, wan, pallid.

**whole** *a.* **1** [Entire] all, every, inclusive, full, undivided, integral, complete, total, aggregate, indivisible, organismic, inseparable, indissoluble, gross, undiminished, utter.—*Ant.* unfinished, partial, incomplete. **2** [Not broken or damaged] thorough, mature, developed, unimpaired, unmarred, full, unbroken, undamaged, entire, in one piece, sound, solid, untouched, without a scratch, intact, uninjured, undecayed, completed, preserved, perfect, complete, safe, in A-1 condition*, shipshape, in good order, together, unified, exhaustive, conclusive, unqualified, fulfilled, accomplished, consummate.—*Ant.* broken, mutilated, defective. **3** [Not ill or injured] hale, hearty, sound.

**whole** *n.* unity, totality, everything, oneness, entity, entirety, collectivity, sum, assemblage, aggregate, aggregation, body, lump, gross, entire stock, length and breadth, generality, mass, amount, bulk, quantity, universality, combination, complex, assembly, gross amount.—*Ant.* part, portion, fraction.

**wholesome** *a.* nutritive, nourishing, beneficial.

**wholly** *a.* totally, entirely, fully, completely.

**wicked** *a.* sinful, immoral, corrupt, evil, base, foul, gross, dissolute, wayward, irreligious, blasphemous, profane, evil-minded, vile, bad, naughty, degenerate, depraved, incorrigible, unruly, heartless, shameless, degraded, debauched, hard, toughened, disreputable, infamous, indecent, mean, remorseless, scandalous, atrocious, contemptible, nasty, vicious, fiendish, hellish, villainous, rascally, devilish, malevolent, plotting, conspiratorial, flagrant, criminal, heinous, murderous, tricky, sinister, ignoble, monstrous, rotten*, lowdown*, good-for-nothing, dirty, felonious, dangerous, cut-throat, ratty*, slippery, crooked.—*Ant.* honest, just, kind.

**wide** *a.* **1** [Broad] extended, spacious, deep. **2** [Loose] broad, roomy, full. **3** [Extensive] large-scale, all-inclusive, universal.

**widen** *v.* **1** [To make wider] add to, broaden, stretch, extend, increase, enlarge, distend, spread out, give more space, augment. **2** [To become wider] unfold, grow, open, stretch, grow larger, increase, swell, multiply.

**width** *n.* breadth, wideness, girth, diameter, distance across, amplitude, cross dimension, cross measurement, expanse.—*Ant.* length, height, altitude.

**wield** *v.* handle, manipulate, exercise.

**wild** *a.* **1** [Not controlled] unrestrained, unmanageable, boisterous. **2** [Uncivilized] barbarous, savage, undomesticated. **3** [Not cultivated] luxuriant, lush, exuberant, dense, excessive, desolate, waste, desert, weedy, untrimmed, impenetrable, uninhabited, native, natural, untouched, virgin, overgrown, uncultivated, untilled, uncared for, neglected, overrun, free, rampant. **4** [Inaccurate] erratic, off, unsound. **5** [Stormy] disturbed, raging, storming. **6** [Excited] hot, eager, avid. **7** [Dissolute] loose, licentious, profligate. **8** [Imprudent] reckless, foolish, incautious.

**will** *n.* **1** [Desire] inclination, wish, disposition, pleasure, yearning, craving, longing, hankering. **2** [Conscious power] resolution, volition, intention, preference, will power, mind, determination, self-determination, decisiveness, moral strength, discretion, conviction, willfulness.—*Ant.* doubt, vacillation, indecision. **3** [Testament for the disposition of property] bequest, disposition, instructions, last wishes, bestowal, dispensation, last will and testament. **—at will** whenever one wishes, at any time, at any moment.

**will** *v.* **1** [To exert one's will] decree, order, command, demand, authorize, request, make oneself felt, decide upon, insist, direct, enjoin. **2** [To wish] want, incline to, prefer. **3** [An indication of futurity] shall, would, should, expect to, anticipate, look forward to, hope to, await, foresee, propose.

**willing** *a.* energetic, prompt, reliable, active, obedient, enthusiastic, zealous, responsible, agreeable, prepared, voluntary, ready, compliant, amenable, tractable, feeling, like, in accord with.—*Ant.* Opposed, averse, unwilling.

**win** *n.* triumph, conquest, victory.

**wind** *n.* draft, air current, breeze, gust, gale, blast, flurry, whisk, whiff, puff, whirlwind, flutter, wafting, zephyr, trade wind, sirocco, northeaster, nor'easter, southwester, sou'wester, tempest, blow, cyclone, typhoon, twister, hurricane, sandstorm, prevailing westerlies, stiff breeze, chinook, Santa Ana. **—get** (or **have**) **wind of*** hear about, have news of, hear. **—take the wind out of someone's sails** best, get the better of, overcome.

**wind** *v.* **1** [To wrap about] coil, reel in, entwine, wreathe, shroud, fold, cover, bind, tape, bandage. **2** [To twist] convolute, screw, wind up. **3** [To meander] zigzag, weave, snake, twist, loop, turn, twine, ramble, swerve, deviate.

**wind up** *v.* conclude, be through with, come to the end of.

**windy** *a.* breezy, blustery, raw, stormy, wind-swept, airy, gusty, blowing, fresh, drafty, wind-shaken, tempestuous, boisterous.—*Ant.* calm, quiet, still.

**wink** *v.* squint, blink, flirt, make eyes at, bat the eyes.

**winner** *n.* victor, conqueror, prizewinner, champion, winning competitor, hero, successful contestant, leading entrant, Olympic champion, titleholder, champ*, front-runner.

**wipe out** *v.* slay, annihilate, eradicate.

**wiry** *a.* agile, sinewy, tough.

**wisdom** *n.* prudence, astuteness, sense, reason, clear thinking, good judgment, brains, sagacity, understanding, sanity, shrewdness, experience, practical knowledge, carefulness, vigilance, tact, balance, poise, stability, caution, solidity, hardheadedness, common sense, horse sense*, savvy*.—*Ant.* stupidity, irrationality, rashness.

**wise** *a.* **1** [Judicious] clever, sagacious, thoughtful. **2** [Shrewd] calculating, cunning, crafty. **3** [Prudent] tactful, sensible, wary. **4** [Erudite] scholarly, smart, learned. **5** [Informed] wise to*, acquainted with, aware of.

**wish** *n.* longing, yearning, hankering, desire, thirst, disposition, request, hope, intention, preference, choice, want, prayer, invocation, liking, pleasure, injunction, command, order.

**wish** *v.* **1** [To desire] covet, crave, envy. **2** [To express a desire] hope, request, entreat, prefer, want, pray for, invoke, command, order, solicit, beg, look forward to, require.

**wishy-washy*** *a.* cowardly, feeble, weak.

**wit** *n.* wittiness, smartness, whimsicality, pleasantry, drollery, banter, burlesque, satire, jocularity, witticism, sally, whimsy, repartee, joke, aphorism, jest, quip, epigram, pun, wisecrack*, gag. **—at one's wits' end** downhearted, desperate, helpless. **—have** (or **keep**) **one's wits about one** be ready, take precautions, be on one's guard. **—live by one's wits** use sharp practices, live dangerously, take advantage of all opportunities.

**witch** *n.* sorcerer, warlock, magician, enchantress, charmer, hag, crone.

**withdraw** *v.* **1** [To retire] depart, draw back, take leave. **2** [To remove from use or circulation] revoke, rescind, abolish, repeal, annul, abrogate, veto, suppress, repress, retire, stamp out, declare illegal, ban, bar, nullify, repudiate, reverse, retract, throw overboard, invalidate, quash, dissolve.

**withered** *a.* shriveled, wilted, decayed, deteriorated, shrunken, dead, browned, faded, parched, dried up, drooping, wrinkled.—*Ant.* fresh, blooming, alive.

**witness** *n.* observer, onlooker, eyewitness, bystander, spectator, testifier, beholder, signatory.

**witty** *a.* quick-witted, clever, amusing.

**woman** *n.* **1** [An adult female] lady, dame, matron, gentlewoman, maid, spinster, debutante, nymph, virgin, girl, old woman, chick*, doll*, babe*, broad*. **2** [A wife or mistress] love, lover, wife. **3** [Womankind] femininity, fair sex, womanhood, the world of women, the female of the species*.

**wonder** *n.* **1** [Amazement] surprise, awe, stupefaction, admiration, wonderment, astonishment, puzzlement, wondering, stupor, bewilderment, perplexity, fascination, consternation, perturbation, confusion, shock, start, jar, jolt, incredulity. **2** [A marvel] miracle, curiosity, oddity, rarity, freak, phenomenon, sensation, prodigy, act of God, portent, wonderwork, spectacle, perversion, prodigious event, something unnatural, the unbelievable.

**wonder** *v.* **1** [To marvel] be surprised, be startled, be fascinated, be amazed, be dumbfounded, be dumbstruck, be confounded, be dazed, be awestruck, be astonished, be agape, be dazzled, stand aghast, be struck by, be unable to take one's eyes off, admire, gape, be taken aback, stare, be flabbergasted. **2** [To question] be curious, query, hold in doubt.

**wonderful** *a.* fine, enjoyable, pleasant.

**wood** *n.* **1** [A forest; *often plural*] grove, woodland, timber. **2** [The portion of trees within the bark] log, timber, lumber, sapwood, heartwood.

**word** *n.* **1** [A unit of expression] term, name, expression, designation, concept, vocable, utterance, sound, a voicing, form of speech, speech, locution, free morpheme, lexeme. **2** [Promise] pledge, commitment, word of honor. **3** [Tidings] report, message, information. **—a good word** favorable comment, recommendation, support. **—by word of mouth** orally, verbally, spoken. **—have words with** argue with, differ with, bicker. **—in so many words** succinctly, cursorily, briefly. **—take someone at his** (or **her**) **word** trust in, have confidence in, put one's trust in. **—the word** information, the facts, the lowdown*.

**wordiness** *n.* redundance, redundancy, diffuseness, circumlocution, repetition, verbiage, verbosity, bombast, tautology, indirectness, vicious circle, flow of words, rhetoric, copiousness, tediousness.—*Ant.* silence, conciseness, succinctness.

**wordy** *a.* tedious, bombastic, long-winded.

**work** *n.* **1** [Something to be done] commitment, task, obligation. **2** [The doing of work] performance, endeavor, employment, production, occupation, practice, activity, manufacture, industry, operation, transaction, toil, labor, exertion, drudgery, functioning, stress, struggle, slavery, trial, push, attempt, effort, pains, elbow grease*, muscle*. **3** [The result of labor; *often plural*] feat, accomplishment, output. **4** [Occupation] profession, business, job. **—at work** working, on the job, engaged. **—in the works*** prepared for, budgeted, approved. **—make short** (or **quick**) **work of** finish off, deal with, dispose of. **—out of work** dismissed, looking for a job, unemployed.

**work** *v.* **1** [To labor] toil, slave, sweat, do a day's work, do the chores, exert oneself, apply oneself, do one's best, overexert, overwork, overstrain, get to work, work overtime, work day and night, work one's way up, tax one's energies, pull, plod, tug, struggle, strive, carry on, do the job, punch a time clock*, put in time, pour it on*, work one's fingers to the bone*, buckle down, bear down, work like a horse*, work like a dog, work like a slave, keep at it, stay with it, put one's shoulder to the wheel, burn the candle at both ends, burn the midnight oil. **2** [To be employed] earn a living, have a job, hold a post, occupy a position, report for work, be off the welfare rolls, be among the employed, be on the job. **3** [To function] go, run, serve. **4** [To handle successfully] control, accomplish, manage. **5** [To fashion] give form to, sculpture, mold.

**worker** *n.* laborer, toiler, workman.

**working** *a.* **1** [Functioning] toiling, laboring, moving, in process, in good condition, in force, in gear, in collar, in exercise, going, twitching, effective, practical, on the job, never idle, on the fire. **2** [Employed] with a job, engaged, on the staff.

**world** *n.* **1** [The earth] globe, wide world, planet. **2** [The universe] cosmos, nature, creation. **3** [A specific group] realm, division, system. **4** [All one's surroundings] environment, atmosphere, childhood, adolescence, adulthood, experience, life, inner life, memory, idealization. **—bring into the world** give birth to, bear, have a baby. **—on top of**

**the world** feeling fine, exuberant, successful. **—out of this world** extraordinary, strange, remarkable.

**worldly** *a.* mundane, earthly, ungodly, practical, matter-of-fact, secular, strategic, grubbing, moneymaking, unprincipled, power-loving, self-centered, opportunistic, sophisticated, cosmopolitan, terrestrial, profane, human, natural, temporal.

**worldwide** *a.* global, universal, extensive.

**worn** *a.* **1** [Used as clothing] carried, put on, donned, displayed, exhibited, used, sported*. **2** [Showing signs of wear] frayed, threadbare, old, secondhand, ragged, shabby, impaired, used, consumed, deteriorated, torn, patched, the worse for wear.—*Ant.* fresh, new, whole.

**worry** *n.* **1** [The state of anxiety] concern, anxiety, misery. **2** [A cause of worry] problem, upset, disturbance.

**worry** *v.* **1** [To cause worry] annoy, trouble, bother. **2** [To indulge in worry] fret, chafe, grieve, take to heart, break one's heart, despair, stew, be anxious, worry oneself, have qualms, wince, agonize, writhe, suffer, turn gray with worry, become sick with worry, sweat out*.

**worship** *v.* sanctify, pray to, invoke, venerate, glorify, praise, exalt, offer one's prayers to, pay homage to, recite the rosary, say grace, give thanks, offer thanks to, sing praises to, reverence, celebrate, adore, revere, laud, extol, chant, sing, bow down.

**worth** *a.* deserving, meriting, equal in value to, priced at, exchangeable for, valued at, worth in the open market, pegged at, cashable for, good for, appraised at, having a face value of, reasonably estimated at, bid at, held at. **—for all one is worth** greatly, mightily, hard.

**worthless** *a.* profitless, counterproductive, barren, unprofitable, unproductive, unimportant, insignificant, counterfeit, bogus, cheap, sterile, waste, wasted, no good, trashy, inconsequential, petty, piddling, paltry, trivial, trifling, unessential, beneath notice, empty, good-for-nothing, no-account*, not worth a damn*, not worth the trouble*, not worth speaking of*, not able to say much for*.

**worthwhile** *a.* good, serviceable, useful, important, profitable, valuable, remunerative, estimable, worthy, helpful, beneficial, meritorious, excellent, rewarding, praiseworthy.

**worthy** *a.* good, true, honest, honorable, reliable, trustworthy, dependable, noble, charitable, dutiful, philanthropic, virtuous, moral, pure, upright, righteous, decent, incorruptible, meritorious, creditable, deserving, right-minded, worthy of, model, exemplary, sterling, sinless, stainless, blameless.—*Ant.* worthless, bad, evil.

**would-be** *a.* anticipated, assuming, supposed.

**wound** *a.* twisted, coiled, wrapped.

**wound** *n.* bruise, hurt, scar.

**wounded** *a.* injured, hurt, disabled, stabbed, cut, shot, scratched, bitten, gashed, hit, beaten, attacked, winged, nicked.

**wrap** *v.* roll up, swathe, muffle, bind, fold about, encircle, coil, enclose, swaddle, bandage, envelop, enwrap, protect, encase, sheathe, cover up, shelter, clothe, cover with paper, enclose in a box.—*Ant.* unwrap, unsheathe, open up.

**wrath** *n.* fury, vengeance, madness.

**wreck** *n.* **1** [Anything wrecked] junk, ruins, skeleton, hulk, stubble, collapse, bones, scattered parts, rattletrap, relic, litter, pieces, shreds, waste, wreckage, debris. **2** [A person in poor physical condition] incurable, invalid, consumptive, nervous case, overworked person, goner*, washout*, shadow, skin-and-bones*, walking nightmare*.

**wreck** *v.* spoil, ruin, destroy, disfigure, mangle, smash, tear down, break, split, efface, batter, torpedo, tear to pieces, put out of order, impair, injure, bash in, mess up, play hell with*, put out of commission.—*Ant.* repair, restore, rebuild.

**wretched** *a.* **1** [Afflicted] distressed, woeful, sorrowful. **2** [Poor in quality] weak, faulty, cheap.

**wring** *v.* squeeze out, compress, twist.

**wrinkle** *v.* rumple, crease, furrow, screw up, pucker, twist, crumple, compress, crinkle.—*Ant.* straighten, smooth out, iron.

**write** *v.* **1** [To compose in words] set forth, record, formulate, draft, turn out, give a report, note down, transcribe, pen, put in writing, comment upon, go into, typewrite, communicate, rewrite, produce fiction, do imaginative writings, correspond, scribble. **2** [To set down in writing] inscribe, sign, scrawl, address, print, letter, autograph, reproduce, dash off, put in black and white. **—write off** charge off, take a loss on, recognize as a bad debt. **—write up** expand, work up, deal at length with.

**writer** *n.* author, journalist, reporter, newspaperman, magazine writer, contributor, poet, novelist, essayist, biographer, dramatist, playwright, literary critic, foreign correspondent, feature writer, sports writer, fashion writer, shorthand writer, stenographer, anecdotist, amanuensis, ghostwriter, songwriter, copyist, scribe, editor, contributing editor, war correspondent, special writer, freelance writer, representative, member of the Fourth Estate, scribbler, pen pusher*, hack, newshound*.

**writhe** *v.* contort, move painfully, squirm, distort, suffer, twist and turn, undergo agony, turn with pain, throw a fit*.—*Ant.* rest, be at ease, move easily.

**writing** *n.* **1** [The practice of writing] transcribing, inscribing, reporting, corresponding, letter-writing, copying, typewriting, penmanship, lettering, printing, graphology, signing, autographing, stenography. **2** [Anything written] literature, written matter, document, composition, article, poem, prose, paper, theme, editorial, discourse, essay, thesis, dissertation, book, manuscript, novel, play, literary production, scenario, drama, piece, work, signature, letter, pamphlet, tract, treatise, disquisition, comment, commentary, review, recitation, certificate, record, bill, bit*, item, piece. **3** [The occupation of a writer] journalism, reporting, literature, authorship, freelance writing, professional writing, auctorial pursuits, the pen, the Fourth Estate, creative writing; novel-writing, verse-writing, feature-writing, etc.; newspaper work, the writers' craft, pencil-pushing*, hack writing, writing for the slicks*, ghostwriting.

**written** *a.* **1** [Composed] set forth, authored, penned, drawn up, reported, signed, turned out, fictionalized, arranged, rearranged, adapted, ghostwritten, recorded, dictated. **2** [Inscribed] copied, scriptural, transcribed, printed, lettered, autographed, signed, put in writing, in black and white, under one's hand.

**wrong** *a.* **1** [Immoral] evil, sinful, wicked, naughty, salacious, base, indecent, risqué, blasphemous, ungodly, amoral, dissolute, dissipated, wanton, profane, sacrilegious, depraved, corrupt, profligate, shady*, low-down*, smutty.—*Ant.* good, righteous, virtuous. **2** [Inaccurate] inexact, erroneous, mistaken, in error, incorrect, fallacious, untrue, erring, astray, amiss, ungrounded, spurious, unsubstantial, unsound, erratic, deceiving oneself, in the wrong, under an error, beside the mark, laboring under a false impression, out of line, at fault, to no purpose, not right, awry, faulty, mishandled, miscalculated, misfigured, misconstructed, misconstrued, mismade, altered, not precise, perverse, wide of the mark, not according to the facts, badly estimated, a mile off*, all off, crazy*. **3** [Inappropriate] unfitted, disproportionate, ill-fitting.

**wrong** *n.* vice, sin, misdemeanor, crime, immorality, indecency, transgression, unfairness, imposition, oppression, foul play, prejudice, bias, favor, unlawful practice, villainy, delinquency, error, miscarriage, mistake, blunder, offense, wrongdoing, violation, tort, hurt, persecution, malevolence, cruelty, libel, abuse, harm, damage, spite, slander, false report, slight, misusage, outrage, inhumanity, over-presumption, insult, discourtesy, raw deal*, bum steer*, dirt.—*Ant.* kindness, good deed, consideration.

**wrong** *v.* hurt, oppress, defame.

**wrongly** *a.* unfairly, prejudicially, wrongfully, partially, badly, unjustifiably, illegally, disgracefully, sinfully, unreasonably, unlawfully, criminally, inexcusably, unsuitably, improperly, awkwardly, incongruously, incorrectly, unbecomingly, indecorously, out of the question, imprudently, rashly, unnaturally, illogically.—*Ant.* appropriately, tastefully, prudently.

# Y

**yard** *n.* **1** [An enclosure, usually about a building] court, courtyard, barnyard, backyard, corral, fold, patch, patio, terrace, play area, lawn, grass, garden, clearing, quadrangle, lot. **2** [An enclosure for work] brickyard, coalyard, junkyard, navy yard, dockyard, railroad yard, stockyard, lumberyard. **3** [Tracks for making up trains; *often plural*] railroad yard, switchyard, railway yard, marshalling yard, terminal. **4** [A unit of measurement] three feet, pace, step, arm-span, thirty-six inches.

**yardstick** *n.* **1** [A rule three feet long] thirty-six-inch ruler, measuring stick, molding rule, yard, yard measure. **2** [A unit for comparison] criterion, basis for judgment, standard.

**yarn** *n.* **1** [Spun fiber] spun wool, twist, flaxen thread, cotton fiber, rug yarn, crochet thread, knitting yarn, alpaca yarn. **2** [A tale] anecdote, sea story, adventure story, fictional account. **3** [A lie] fabrication, tall tale*, alibi, fish story*, cock-and-bull story*.

**yawn** *v.* **1** [To open wide] gape, split open, spread out. **2** [To give evidence of drowsiness] gape, be sleepy, make a yawning sound, show weariness.

**yearn** *v.* want, crave, long for, fret, chafe, grieve, mourn, droop, pine, languish, be eager for, be desirous of, be ardent, be fervent, be passionate, wish for, thirst for, hunger for, aspire to, set one's heart upon, hanker for, have a yen for*.—*Ant.* avoid, be content, be indifferent.

**yell** *n.* **1** [A shout] bellow, cry, yelp, roar, whoop, howl, screech, shriek, squeal, holler*, hoot, yawp, hubbub, hullabaloo, hue and cry, protest. **2** [Organized cheering] hip-hip-hurray, rooting, cheer.

**yell** *v.* bellow, cry out, scream, shout, yelp, yap, bawl, roar, halloo, vociferate, whoop, howl, screech, shriek, shrill, squeal, squall, yammer, hoot, cheer, call, yip, give encouragement, call down, raise one's voice, holler, whoop it up.

**yelp** *v.* howl, screech, hoot.

**yen*** *n.* longing, craving, desire.

**yet** *a.* **1** [Nevertheless] notwithstanding, however, in spite of, despite, still, but, though, although, at any rate, on the other hand. **2** [Thus far] until now, till, hitherto, prior to, still. **3** [In addition] besides, additionally, further.

**yield** *v.* **1** [To surrender] give up, capitulate, succumb, resign, abdicate, relinquish, quit, cede, bow, lay down arms, cease from, let go, submit, give oneself over, relent, admit defeat, suffer defeat, forgo, humble oneself, waive, throw in the towel*, call it quits*, back down*, holler uncle*, eat crow*.—*Ant.* resist, withstand, repulse. **2** [To produce] bear, bring forth, blossom. **3** [To grant] accede, concur, acquiesce.

**yokel** *n.* rustic, bumpkin, hayseed*.

**yonder** *a.* farther, away, faraway.

**young** *a.* **1** [In the early portion of life] puerile, boyish, girlish, adolescent, juvenile, budding, in one's teens, childlike, youthful, pubescent, boylike, girllike, new-fledged, blooming, burgeoning, childish, half-grown, growing, blossoming, at the breast, babe in arms, knee high to a grasshopper*.—*Ant.* old, aged, senile. **2** [Inexperienced] callow, green, immature, tender, raw, untutored, unlearned, junior, subordinate, inferior, unfledged, ignorant, undisciplined, tenderfoot, wet behind the ears*.—*Ant.* experienced, veteran, expert. **3** [New] fresh, modern, recent.

**youth** *n.* **1** [The state or quality of being young] boyhood, adolescence, girlhood, childhood, early manhood, early adulthood, puberty, tender age, minority, youthfulness, virginity, bloom, teens, age of ignorance, age of indiscretion, awkward age, salad days.—*Ant.* maturity, old age, senility. **2** [Young people] the younger generation, the rising generation, the next generation, children, the young, college youth, working youth. **3** [A young person] boy, junior, teenager, lad, youngster, stripling, minor, young man, miss, girl, maiden, fledgling, juvenile, urchin, adolescent, student, kid*, teen, preteen, gosling, pup*, calf*.

**yowl** *n.* howl, yelp, wail.

# Z

**zeal** *n.* **1** [Enthusiasm] ardor, eagerness, fervor, enthusiasm. **2** [Industry] earnestness, hustle, hustling, bustle, bustling, intensity, industry, willingness, inclination, application, determination, promptitude, dispatch, diligence, perseverance, intentness, readiness, aptitude, enterprise, initiative, push*, what it takes*, stick-to-itiveness*.—*Ant.* idleness, slackness, indolence.

**zealot** *n.* partisan, fan, bigot, fanatic, lobbyist, devotee, enthusiast, dogmatist, opinionist, missionary, fighter, cultist, follower, disciple, propagandist, bitter-ender*, crank*, addict, bug*, faddist, fiend*.

**zero** *n.* **1** [A cipher] naught, nothing, nadir, love, below freezing, the lowest point, goose egg*. **2** [Nothing] nullity, oblivion, void, nix*, zip*, zilch*, *nada* (Spanish), bupkes*.

**zigzag** *a.* oblique, inclined, sloping, awry, crooked, sinuous, twisted, askew, transverse, diagonal, curved, bent, crinkled, serrated, jagged, straggling, meandering, devious, erratic, rambling, oscillating, fluctuating, waggling, undulatory, vibratory, indirect, spiral, tortuous.—*Ant.* straight, parallel, undeviating.

**zip*** *n.* energy, vigor, vim.

**zip*** *v.* run, dash, rush.

**zone** *n.* **1** [A band] circuit, meridian, latitude. **2** [An area] region, district, territory.

**zoology** *n.* life science, biological science, natural history.

**zoom** *v.* speed, rush, hurry.